A DIPLOMAT'S HANDBOOK

A DIPLOMAT'S HANDBOOK

for Democracy Development Support

Third Edition

Jeremy Kinsman and Kurt Bassuener

Published by The Centre for International Governance Innovation in partnership with the Council for a Community of Democracies.

ISBN 978-0-9867077-8-0 (paper)
ISBN 978-0-9867077-9-7 (ebook)

The opinions expressed in this publication are those of the authors and do not necessarily reflect the views of The Centre for International Governance Innovation or its Operating Board of Directors or International Board of Governors.

Care has been taken to trace the ownership of copyright material contained in this book. The publisher will gladly receive any information that will enable them to rectify any reference or credit line in subsequent editions.

The Centre for International Governance Innovation thanks and acknowledges the Council for a Community of Democracies for its partnership in publishing the third edition of *A Diplomat's Handbook for Democracy Development Support*.

Published by The Centre for International Governance Innovation.

Printed and bound in Canada.

The Centre for International Governance Innovation
57 Erb Street West
Waterloo, ON Canada N2L 6C2

Council for a Community of Democracies
1801 F Street NW, Suite 308
Washington, DC 20006

www.cigionline.org

www.ccd21.org

CONTENTS

CONTENTS

ACRONYMS

AK	Justice and Development Party (Turkey)
AMG	Advisory and Monitoring Group (OSCE)
ANC	African National Congress
ASEAN	Association of Southeast Asian Nations
BOP	Brigade of Public Order (Tunisia)
CCD	Council for a Community of Democracies
CCP	Chinese Communist Party
CEC	Central Election Commission (Ukraine)
CFSP	Common Foreign and Security Policy (EU)
CIDA	Canadian International Development Agency
CIGI	The Centre for International Governance Innovation
CIO	Central Intelligence Organization (Zimbabwe)
CIS	Commonwealth of Independent States
CPR	Congress for the Republic (Tunisia)
CSCE	Commission on Security and Cooperation in Europe
CSO	Conflict and Stabilization Operations (US Department of State Bureau)
DFLL	Democratic Forum for Labour and Liberties (Tunisia)
EHU	European Humanities University
FAO	UN Food and Agriculture Organization
FAR	Revolutionary Armed Forces (Cuba)
FSB	Federal Security Service of the Russian Federation
GDR	German Democratic Republic
GFW	Great Firewall
GONGO	government-organized NGOs
ICCPR	International Covenant of Civil and Political Rights
IDEA	International Institute for Democracy and Electoral Assistance
IMF	International Monetary Fund
IFI	international financial institution
IFIT	Institute for Integrated Transitions
IOM	International Organization for Migration
IRI	International Republican Institute
IWP	Institute of World Policy
JOC	Joint Operations Centre (Zimbabwe)
MAP	Membership Action Plan (NATO)
MDC	Movement for Democratic Change (Zimbabwe)

MENA	Middle East and North Africa
MP	Member of Parliament
NDI	National Democratic Institute
NDP	National Democratic Party (Egypt)
NGO	non-governmental organization
NLD	National League for Democracy (Burma/Myanmar)
NPC	National People's Congress (China)
NYU	New York University
OAS	Organization of American States
ODIHR	Office for Democratic Institutions and Human Rights (OSCE)
OECD	Organisation for Economic Co-operation and Development
OIF	Organization of Francophone Countries
OSCE	Organization for Security and Co-operation in Europe
PACE	Parliamentary Assembly of the Council of Europe
PDP	Progressive Democratic Party (Tunisia)
PLO	Palestine Liberation Organization
PPP	Popular Petition Party (Tunisia)
RCD	Democratic Constitutional Rally Party (Tunisia)
RMB	renminbi
SABC	South African Broadcasting Corporation
SADC	Southern African Development Community
SADF	South African Defence Force
SIDA	Swedish International Development Agency
SLORC	State Law and Order Restoration Council (Burma/Myanmar)
SPDC	State Peace and Development Council (Burma/Myanmar)
SSR	Soviet Socialist Republic (Belarus)
TNC	Transitional National Council (Libya)
UDF	United Democratic Front (South Africa)
UGTT	Union Générale Tunisienne du Travail
UN	United Nations
UNHCR	UN High Commissioner for Refugees
UNICEF	United Nations Children's Fund
UPB	Union of Poles of Belarus
USAID	United States Agency for International Development
USDP	Union Solidarity and Development Party (Burma/Myanmar)
USSR	Union of Soviet Socialist Republics
WMD	weapons of mass destruction
WTO	World Trade Organization
ZANU	Zimbabwe African National Union
ZANU-PF	Zimbabwe African National Union-Patriotic Front
ZAPU	Zimbabwe African People's Union
ZBC	Zimbabwe Broadcasting Corporation
ZMC	Zimbabwe Media Commission

ABOUT THE DIPLOMAT'S HANDBOOK

The *Diplomat's Handbook* is a project conceived by Ambassador Mark Palmer and commissioned by the Community of Democracies, produced through the Council for a Community of Democracies (CCD) and published by The Centre for International Governance Innovation (CIGI) in Waterloo, Ontario. Earlier editions were produced with the financial support of the International Center on Nonviolent Conflict, Freedom House, the Princeton Project on National Security, the Smith Richardson Foundation, the governments of Chile, India, Italy, Lithuania, Morocco and Poland, and the US Department of State. The Government of Canada's Department of Foreign Affairs and International Trade repeated as a supporter.

The original project emerged from the active partnership between Project Director Jeremy Kinsman and Director of Research Kurt Bassuener, and support that Princeton University's Woodrow Wilson School of Public and International Affairs extended during Kinsman's tenure there as Ambassador in Residence in 2007-2008. In the partnership, Ambassador Kinsman was principally responsible for writing the *Handbook*'s introduction, chapters 1–4 and specific case studies. Kurt Bassuener supervised, edited and wrote several country case studies.

The *Handbook* text which follows and its case studies benefit from the generous contributions and advice of many former and current diplomatic practitioners, scholars, members of policy centres and non-governmental organizations (NGOs), and development experts. As detailed in earlier editions, graduate students of the Wilson School of Princeton University made a special contribution to case studies in 2007-2008.

In the third edition, the new case study on Tunisia was drafted by Dr. Larry Michalak and the case study on democracy in Russia was drafted by Jeremy Kinsman.

Originally designed and produced by the Office of External Affairs at the Woodrow Wilson School of Public and International Affairs in collaboration with the CCD, this third edition is published by CIGI in Waterloo, Ontario, in 2013.

For further details about the project, please consult www.cigionline.org and www.diplomatshandbook.org. Jeremy Kinsman can be reached via email to jeremykinsman@diplomatshandbook.org and Kurt Bassuener can be reached at kurtbassuener@diplomatshandbook.org.

IN MEMORIAM

Ambassador Mark Palmer 1941–2013

Mark Palmer was a dedicated US foreign service officer. His creative talent and clarity of principle made him a "go-to" speech writer for three presidents and six secretaries of state. After he left the foreign service following his tenure as Ambassador to Hungary, he became one of the first venture entrepreneurs in the redevelopment of free central and Eastern Europe. But his professional heart and soul were invested in the opportunities and obligations faced by a foreign service officer from a democratic society. His life and actions defied the false notion that diplomats are irrelevant or disconnected to real people and events. He believed passionately in public diplomacy.

Wherever he was, on overseas posts and otherwise, Mark Palmer had an intense interest in other peoples and empathy for them as individuals. However disparate our respective circumstances, he remained convinced that all of us on this planet share the same goals and have the same immutable human rights.

He was a model of the brave diplomat. The Honourable Frank R. Wolf's speech on May 8, 2013 in the US House of Representatives recounts that, "But for Mark's controversial determination while US Ambassador to Hungary that the barbed wire fences between Hungary and Austria should be severed in order to allow East Germans to leave the Communist orbit, the Berlin Wall might still be standing. But for his brave willingness to openly challenge Hungary's Communist government when conventional thinkers at the State Department and elsewhere were worried about the 'destabilizing' effects of a Communist collapse, the Soviet Empire might still be in power."

Mark Palmer conceived the idea of this *Handbook* and lent his wisdom and strength of character to the project.

PREFACE

President Václav Havel,
Leader of the Velvet Revolution in Czechoslovakia
Prague, April 2008

I was thrust into top-level politics by the revolutionary events at the turn of the year 1989-1990 without any diplomatic training — "from the prison cell straight into the presidential palace," so to speak. At the same time, hundreds of my similarly unprepared fellow citizens found themselves, like me, in high office or posts of influence. I often envied all those graduates of diplomatic schools, with their command of several languages and international law, and their wealth of personal experience. During those first months, we were obliged to overcome any shortcomings in the introduction of democratic standards in our country by means of improvisation, dramatic invention and concepts based more on common sense than on hundreds of analyses and expert documents. I am still amazed that in those years it was possible to push through things in a single week that in conditions of stability would take several years to prepare and have approved. I also recall how many governments were taken unawares — as often before in history — by the lightning course events in countries, whose evolution and situations have been monitored for years by hundreds of diplomats and international observers, who had provided thousands of detailed reports. I cited those two examples simply to demonstrate that diplomacy cannot function properly without personal commitment and a strong determination to find solutions and attain objectives; it cannot simply rely on the recommendations or decisions of central machinery. I hope that this book will inspire all its readers to take a creative part in the propagation of civic freedoms and democratic standards throughout the world.

Václav Havel

MINISTERS' FOREWORD

Responding to requests from civil society and governments, diplomats make important contributions to democratic development. Their work is largely unknown. Outdated stereotypes of our profession persist. This *Diplomat's Handbook* begins to tell our story through case studies of practical measures that diplomats from many democratic countries have taken across the globe.

The *Handbook* recognizes that democracy cannot be exported or imported. It must be developed by the citizens of the country concerned. There is no one formula for success. But outside assistance is often requested, and there is a dearth of professional material for training and guiding our diplomats in deciding how they can appropriately respond. Civil society as well as governments can benefit from the *Handbook*, gaining a better understanding of what they can request from diplomats, who in today's public diplomacy represent their own civil society as well.

Therefore, the *Handbook* offers a menu of choice, a tool box of steps which have worked, beginning with listening and understanding and proceeding through many forms of cooperation.

We urge the 125 diplomatic services represented in the Community of Democracies to use and to contribute to this new tool for our profession. The *Handbook* is a "living" document. The Community's Convening Group and Secretariat, the nongovernmental International Steering Committee, the Council for a Community of Democracies and Canadian Ambassador Jeremy Kinsman, the *Handbook*'s primary author, and its Research Director Kurt Bassuener will regularly update it and welcome your comments and contributions online at: www.diplomatshandbook. org. We wish to recognize the work of our democratic diplomats by featuring them in further case studies and through practical examples.

Signed by:

Luís Amado
Minister of State and Foreign Affairs, Portugal 2007-2009
Chair, Community of Democracies

Audronius Ažubalis
Minister of Foreign Affairs, Lithuania
2009-2011 Chair, Community of Democracies

Radosław Sikorski
Foreign Minister of Poland
Host to the Permanent Secretariat, Community of Democracies

INTRODUCTION TO THE THIRD EDITION

In the three years since publication of the revised second edition of the *Handbook* in June 2010, trends and developments continue to reshape the environment for democracy development. The learning experience of democracies in their varied approaches to democracy development support also continues to evolve.

There are some encouraging global trends. Most visibly, Tunisians launched what has become known as "The Arab Spring." The Middle East and North African (MENA) region had long been depicted as being mired in immunity to desire for political change. But the reverberations in the MENA region to the national revolution in Tunisia have shown that no region is immune to the aspiration for inclusive democratic governance.

Moreover, there was no outside "hidden hand" in what occurred in Tunisia. Tunisian, Egyptian and Libyan citizens were not acting in favour of "Western values," but on behalf of their own right to inclusiveness and dignity, and their desire to reconcile religion and civics in their respective societies.

Across the globe, the relationships of people to their governments are changing. Individuals are asserting their own agency over decisions that affect them. The expansion of economic opportunities in many emerging economies is accompanied by a growing impatience with old authoritarian ways.

The reaction of some authoritarian regimes to developments in North Africa has been a less encouraging development over the past three years, as we witness their greater intransigence at home, curtailing modest political rights and attempting to smother civil society's connections with potential supporters from civil society outside. The mouthpiece of the ruling Communist Party of China, the *People's Daily*, described perceived Western efforts to export democracy and human rights to China as "a new form of colonialism," a defensive epithet which would suit the views of several other non-democratic states.

The expansion of Internet interconnectivity had strengthened the role and importance of international civil society in cohering aspirations to common norms of inclusive governance. For example, it radiated to youth in the Middle East a sense of participation in a global political debate from which they had long felt excluded. The Internet and social media permitted activists everywhere to uplink images, news and ideas to a wider audience.

In 1982, the massacre of thousands in Hama, Syria by security forces passed unnoticed in the world for several weeks. In 2012, the evidence of reprisal killings by security forces in that same town was uplinked to media within a few days, prompting swift condemnation of the massacre by UN Secretary-General Ban Ki-moon and the international community.

Meanwhile, unmediated Internet sites preached forms of extremism and organized hostility, often on religious or ethnic grounds.

The issue of Internet freedom has become a major topic internationally, as authoritarian governments attempt to block access to outside influence, as well as inside discussion about governance within their own societies. As Carne Ross (2012), founder of the Independent Diplomat diplomatic advisory group and a proponent of an alternative democratic diplomacy, has noted, "power adapts to new technology, and swiftly."

The issues of repression of civil society, freedom of the press, and connections with solidarity partners outside are therefore as topical and challenging as ever.

While the revolutions in Tunisia, Egypt and Libya succeeded in bringing authoritarian regimes to an end, the variably vexed post-revolutionary experience in these three countries confirms the *Handbook*'s sober advice that getting rid of a dictator is the easier part of the struggle for democratic governance. It is the long, hard slog that follows — building inclusive institutions and a viable civil society, particularly in a religious environment — that constitutes the more complex and daunting challenge, one which insists on solidarity, patience and direct support from international civil society and democratic governments abroad. For the most part, the protest movements that brought the dictators down were without hierarchy or even visible leaders. They did not generate a natural class of administrators.

Without outside support during the difficult transitional phase that follows the heady experience of expelling a dictator, the process of widening inclusive democracy may encounter too many organizational and other obstacles to deliver the public order and economic security that citizens expect.

Established democracies, however, faced an uncertain landscape and urgent priorities. Struggling to cope with a stubborn economic recession and daunting budgetary challenges, several were also fatigued by the long and costly conflicts in Iraq and Afghanistan, which themselves underlined intractable difficulties of attempts to "export" democratic reform without the necessary absorptive capacity for its adaptation. Pew polls showed that US public support for democracy promotion and support for human rights abroad plunged by 2009 to 10 percent and 24 percent, respectively. For the first time since World War II, as many as half of Americans polled judged the United States should "mind [its] own business."

Moreover, in 2012, the Latinobarometer poll revealed low satisfaction with the working of their democracies by Mexicans (20 percent), Brazilians (45 percent) and Chileans (32 percent).

Yet, there were positive learning experiences for democracies as they approached the challenges of democracy development support. A need for consistency became clear after belated recognition that for decades, democracies had tended to over-invest in the status quo in some authoritarian states where continuity of leadership had been seen as a contributor to regional stability and to certain overarching interests, such as the "war on terrorism." False choices had been presented, such as dictatorship or militant jihadism.

Democratic governments were reminded that dictatorships are inherently unstable in the long run. In the aftermath of lessons learned from the fall of dictatorial regimes in Tunisia and Egypt that Westerners partnered for too long, "dual-track" approaches that integrate both interests and values are now more apt to underpin international relationships, which are no longer monopolized by relations between states. Governance is not just about governments. For decades, non-state actors have been growing in importance as agents of change and international challenge. Case-specific interests, which can often be handled in private, should not alter the constant of public messaging that emphasizes enduring democratic values.

Democratic governments know they need to invest for the long term in their relationships with peoples. This is markedly true for the global experience of democracy development. The primary role of civil society in this landscape is vital and multiple, and needs thoughtful consideration.

It is axiomatic that civil society forms the building blocks of democratic development within a country. Supporting the enlargement of its capacity is the most helpful tool outside of which democracies can wield in their contribution to democracy development, which will, of course, always be in the hands of democrats in the country itself.

But the best vehicles for such outside support are rarely governments and their own programs, however well-intentioned. They are not good at it. Outside support for democratic capacity-building potential comes best from international civil society partnerships, with the lead partner being the one inside the country. Recognition of this reality is increasingly the trend in international democracy development support, especially as states that sought to promote democracy directly have met with pushback on the classic grounds of non-interference in the internal affairs of other states. The lesson that democracy promotion is best done when it's not called "democracy promotion" has become a truism of policy and outreach.

For these purposes, how democratic governments and their representatives abroad relate to civil society both at home and abroad, and how civil society relates back to them, is the overarching challenge that is a focus of the *Handbook* and particularly, of this third edition. The new case study on Russian democracy identifies misguided claims by Russian authorities that international civil society's solidarity with Russian civil society is a surrogate for Western democracies' alleged ambitions to co-opt the nation's political development in order to weaken the Russian state. Democratic governments no longer fund political activity of any kind in Russia. But they must, and do, support the principle that citizens of every country have certain fundamental and human rights permitting political activity. Outside democracies also judge that a key and legitimate role of their diplomatic representatives is today to engage directly with civil society in the host country.

In consequence, the trend to public diplomacy and dual virtual accreditation to and from civil society for ambassadors became an increasingly prominent feature of "expeditionary public diplomacy," described by US Secretary of State Hillary Clinton as "21st-century diplomacy that demands the US be more attuned to the grassroots of the world and relies on development and civilian power as much as military might."

Ambassador Pierre Vimont, head of the European Union's External Action Service, posed as the first obligation of democracies the protection of human rights defenders, but also the question, "How far can you go?"

Democracies are not engaged in an "us against them" divided world. Democrats share a community of values but are not a bloc. Their citizens do take encouragement, though, that the percentage of the world's population that is "free" has increased from 25 percent in 1992 to 43 percent today.

The global democratic North has much to learn from the democratic South. The stature of such democracies as Brazil, India, Indonesia and South Africa can be of great support to global democracy development. Cooperation of the kind initiated by Brazil and the United States in the Open Government Partnership can make a persuasive contribution.

While some autocratic countries seem to get some of the "hardware" of governance — such as infrastructure, health and technical education — right, they tend to get critical "software" — such as basic freedoms, leadership, the mitigation of inequalities and inclusiveness of the aspirations of youth — wrong.

Democracy may not necessarily be synonymous with modernization, nor should it be seen as an inevitable end stage of development. But it represents the best vehicle for the fulfillment of individual lives and for social progress. The long arc of history is on its side.

The primary tasks of democratic governments are to pay attention to change, and in a spirit of solidarity of free peoples, support legitimate aspirations of people everywhere to widen their democratic space.

WORK CITED

Ross, Carne (2012). *The Leaderless Revolution: How Ordinary People Will Take Power and Change Politics in the 21st Century*. New York: Blue Rider Press.

1 THE RATIONALE FOR DEMOCRATIC SOLIDARITY

When the Community of Democracies was convened for the first time in Warsaw in 2000, it was to find ways "to work together and strengthen democracy" in the spirit of solidarity with peoples aspiring to basic human rights everywhere.

For the first time in 300 years, as Professor Robert Legvold observed, there was no strategic rivalry among the world's leading powers. The Community of Democracies member states made it clear that while they welcomed and actively encouraged further peaceful progress toward democratic governance in the world, the organization had no ambition to be a bloc defined by or formed in antagonism to non-democratic states. Democracies did not seek, in creating a like-minded "community," to erect new walls between states.

Democracies see their vocation for the strengthening of democracy everywhere as flowing from the "venerable practice of international solidarity," so well described in 1989 by Václav Havel in a letter he wrote to the PEN International Congress in Montreal, which he was not permitted by Czechoslovak authorities to attend in person: "In today's world, more and more people are aware of the indivisibility of human fate on this planet, that the problems of anyone of us, or whatever country we come from — be it the smallest and most forgotten — are the problems of us all; that our freedom is indivisible as well, and that we all believe in the same basic values, while sharing common fears about the threats that are hanging over humanity today."

Globalization has since strengthened the context for democratic indivisibility by multiplying awareness through greater ease of communication, even within formerly closed or remote societies.

Democracy is not an end in itself. As a form of governance relying on the consent of the governed, it is a means of fulfilling individual lives and pursuing common purposes. No single model of inclusive democracy has pride of place. Nonetheless, its most essential positive components are straightforward: elected, accountable government; the positive adjacency of a pluralist civil society; transparent and equitably applied rule of law; independent media; protection of human rights and freedom of speech, assembly and worship; and equal participation by all in selecting inclusive political representation.

While each country experiences, in its own way, the passage toward the democratic form its citizens choose as most suitable, there is one cardinal point in common to all such passages: democracy cannot be imported from outside, much less imposed.

While reform movements can only emerge from within societies, democrats from outside can, in the spirit of solidarity, support aspiring democrats by defending their entitlement to non-violent defence and the pursuit of human rights, long-judged to be universal. Democratic governments and civil society can, and should, help to prepare those aspiring to democracy and their efforts to consolidate inclusive democracy once their passage begins.

How such support has been extended, or not, as the case may be, by democracies and democrats, in government and in civil society, is the substance of this *Handbook*.

THE LIVES OF OTHERS:
THE COUNTER-RATIONALE

As Cambridge scholar John Dunn has observed, while democracy has come to "dominate the world's imagination," it has also aroused fear and suspicion in some quarters. In recent years, rivalry has deepened between authoritarian governments and democracies, though not in any existential sense of military confrontation.

A counter-community of non-democratic states has, to some extent, emerged as an informal coalition, termed by some "the authoritarian internationale."[1] Modernization specialist Seymour Martin Lipset pointed out the "irresistible charm of authoritarian growth," persuading coalition members to go so far as to claim that pseudo-liberal authoritarianism delivers superior performance to its societies than that of what they characterize as increasingly illiberal democracies. The Russian Federation presents a revisionist doctrine of "managed democracy" which democratic critics prefer to describe as "imitation democracy."

The Chinese model presents itself as a systemic alternative to liberal democracy, able to mobilize economic growth and distribute prosperity without the gridlocks of political competition. Deng Xioping had vaunted "modernization with Chinese characteristics."

The late Chinese physicist and dissident Fang Lizhi famously asked his university students if they believed in physics with Chinese characteristics.

Fang recalled five scientific axioms that inevitably lead to democracy:

- Science begins with doubt, not Mao-ordained fixed beliefs.

- Science stresses independence of judgment, not conformity.

- Science is egalitarian — no one's subjective "truth" starts ahead of any other.

- Science needs a free flow of information.

---

1   The term itself was coined by the late Belarusian analyst Vitali Silitski, in a publication of the German Marshall Fund.

- Scientific truths are like human rights principles — they are universal and do not change when they cross a border. (cited in Link, 2012)

In a *Foreign Affairs* essay in response to the perception that the "euphoria" of the great third wave of democratization has "crested and may be receding," Daniel Deudney and G. John Ikenberry (2009) called for a new "liberal internationalism," which could strengthen the sense of community among democracies, moderate great power rivalry and strengthen resistance to resurgent nationalist, populist and xenophobic movements.

Surveys show the record is mixed. There have been over 60 democratic revolutions since 1974. The number of countries judged to be "free" today approaches 100. But in 2012, overall, for the seventh year in a row, Freedom House recorded more democratic declines than gains. While Egypt, Libya, Côte d'Ivoire, Burma/Myanmar and Senegal moved toward the democratic column, more regimes — notably in the Middle East — showed evidence of illiberal backlash: Iraq, Jordan, Kuwait, Oman and, of course, Syria, which was plunged into a cruel civil war.

It is especially noteworthy that mixtures of democratic progress and recession are present on every continent, reinforcing the reality that democracy is not a "Western" phenomenon.

As Chilean novelist Isabel Allende (2006) declared, "Latin America has opted for democracy." At the same time, in some countries in the hemisphere, still-shallow democratic roots are struggling against militant and divisive populism. In Africa, there will be 23 competitive national elections in 2013, but the continent is also home to the world's largest number of corrupt dictatorships. The Middle East is a cauldron of emerging democratic aspiration pressing against authoritarian regimes that are reluctant to concede their monopoly on power. Asia, too, is a mixture of notable progress, such as in Burma/Myanmar and the abject repression of North Korea. The experience of North Americans and Europeans is also mixed: even if their democracies are established, their own democratic and pluralistic practices are being critically scrutinized by citizens reeling from recent economic challenges.

The mixed record shows that no region or culture is exempt from democracy and, moreover, democracy is a garden that needs constant tending. To cite Allende (2006) again, democracies are "like husbands. There is always room for improvement." At the onset of democratic transitions, institutional fragility and initial efforts at consolidation are almost inevitably ragged and contradictory. But the process is never-ending: Poland's Foreign Minister Radosław Sikorski spoke at the Lisbon 2009 Ministerial of the Community of Democracies of the continuing need of a democracy "to re-design itself consensually, without violence."

While it is hardly plausible that humans anywhere would prefer governments that ignore the principle of consent of the governed in favour of coercion, authoritarian repression can keep the lid on for a time. Public fear of violence and disorder is the authoritarian's friend. Often, as in Syria, repressive regimes claim they are defending against repressive takeover by an ethnic or sectarian majority on behalf of fearful minorities.

But repressive government will fail in the longer run: as Gandhi observed, "Even the most powerful cannot rule without the cooperation of the ruled" — an axiom truer now than ever, when democratic norms are much more widely apparent because of migration patterns and the information revolution.

THE DEMOCRATIC PROCESS AND NON-VIOLENT CHANGE

Democratic Transition

Democracy theorist Thomas Carothers (1999) has famously described democratic transition as consisting of two "chapters." Chapter one is the preparation and completion of a revolution to throw off a dictator or repressive regime; chapter two represents the transition to democracy, which commences the morning after. There is no shortage of those with direct experience who ruefully recognize the first chapter as the relatively "easy" part.

Among authoritarian regimes, there are both "hard" cases and "softer" ones. The hard cases are seldom only one-man rule. As Morgan Tsvangirai pointed out when he was opposition leader in Zimbabwe, a political culture of abuse and corruption can outlive any specific authoritarian leader, as beneficiaries seek to consolidate and perpetuate their dominance. The security apparatus and other elites that repressive leaders install to maintain order and their own power acquire vested interests against change, often becoming the real powers behind authoritarian government.

It is why "pacting" between old and incoming orders — at least in "softer" cases of transition such as Chile, Spain and to some extent Egypt — enabled a relatively peaceful transition. The pacts consisted of compromises and guarantees from both sides, preserving property rights and limiting the agenda for change, but committing the retainers of power from the old order to the democratic project.

Harder cases, however, resist pacting. Syrian President Bashar al-Assad has confided that he wouldn't be "allowed" to pursue an exit strategy by the myriad of those whose sectarian privilege or even security and material stakes under the current regime would be at risk if "his" regime fell.

Hard cases include those where the regime's control over the society has been developed and implanted over many years. But a critical feature would include the willingness to use deadly force against the people if dissent emerges.

Democracy activists and members of civil society struggling to create democratic conditions under undemocratic regimes face the harsh dilemma of finding the most effective methods for wresting change from unbending authoritarians. Impatient partisans of change are sometimes tempted by the option of violent, direct action. But repressive state security machinery can wield a cruel upper hand against violent insurrection, which can, in any case, alienate the majority of citizens concerned about safety.

> Non-violence is the greatest force at the disposal of mankind. It is
> the supreme law. By it alone can mankind be saved.

— Mohandas K. Gandhi

The most effective approach to authoritarian repression has been that of peaceful assembly and demonstration, including organized civil resistance, often when a specific issue or grievance fires public discontent and protest. Gandhi defined the model for non-violent civil disobedience against unjust laws in the first human rights campaigns he launched in South Africa, which he then applied in the campaign for the self-determination of India.

Non-violent civil resistance has played an important and beneficial role in democratic transition because in contrast to violent insurgency, it teaches democratic values en route to change. Non-violent movements provide autonomous space for learning decentralized and deliberative methods of policy choice and coalition building. Because non-violent movements are participatory and decentralized, they can constitute "incubators of democracy" that assist the transition to democratic governance after a repressive regime collapses. Non-governmental organizations (NGOs) constitute a factor of continuity as a country transitions from top-down control to an institutionally accountable pluralist society.

It is sometimes argued that resorting to violent means to overturn a repressive regime is faster. It usually is not. Violent repression of non-violent protest can discourage reform movements for a time, as was the case in Burma/Myanmar in 2007 or Iran in 2009. It can also lead to civil war, as happened in Libya and is now the case in Syria.

"Sniper, sniper, what do you see? Here are our necks; here are our heads" was the chant of the incredibly brave non-violent demonstrators in Dara'a in 2011. The Syrian security forces shot to kill. By the spring of 2013, 70,000 had died in the ensuing civil war. Its outcome cannot conceivably be happy for the regime. The question is whether the effects of the traumatic conflict can ever be repaired.

When Regimes Collapse: Democratic Transition's Chapter One

When Do Democratic Revolutions Occur?

US scholar Clay Shirky (2011) has outlined a thesis that the buildup of "shared awareness" of the unacceptability of control by a non-democratic regime over peoples' lives reaches a tipping point when "open secrets become public truths" about abusive entitlement and privilege, corruption, cronyism and systemic police abuse in the repression of rights. Glaring social inequity, the lack of opportunities for poor and professional citizens alike, and often-abrupt adverse changes, such as the rise of food prices, all fuel discontent to a point where the people feel the need to act in support of change.

There can be flashpoints — such as a flagrantly fixed false election, the self-immolation of alienated vegetable vendor Mohammed Bouzizi in Tunisia or the Facebook dissemination of photos of Khaled Said's fatal beating at the hands of police in Egypt — but in reality, combustible resentment builds over years.

Outside democracies are usually caught by surprise. There is a long history of over-investment in dictators who promise support for wider interests, such as the Shah of Iran and the Cold War rivalry; Egyptian President Hosni Mubarak and his convenience as a working ally in the "war" against Muslim extremists and Egypt's pivotal role in Mid-East relationships regarding Israel; or the Uzbek dictator Islam Karimov and the NATO countries' need to facilitate supply to their troops in Afghanistan.

There is an inherent conservatism in diplomatic reporting when such interests are at stake. Even when the extent of regime abuse and growing public resentment are detailed in reporting, officials in capitals have often turned a blind eye in deference to national "interests" and personal relationships with despots, as the *Handbook* will illustrate.

The *Handbook* details the ways that outside democracies have helped prepare for successful transitions through capacity building, human rights defence, direct negotiation with repressive governments, international networking and, when necessary, the organization of concerted sanctions.

Pasting it Together:
The Hard Slog of Chapter Two's "Morning After"

Once launched, democracy's concrete rewards must be evident to citizens. There is a certain urgency to this task: showing that democracy works for the benefit of citizens is essential before a would-be Napoleon occupies the vacuum of public confidence.

Democracy relies on the realization of certain basic human needs and must aim for their improvement. The test of the democratic process is at the intersection of the citizens' participation in their own governance and the effectiveness of governance in confronting the practical challenges that individuals face. Freedom from extreme poverty, for example, has been termed the first of the essential freedoms. As Amartya Sen (2001) succinctly put it, "Freedom and development are inextricable."

John Dunn records the history of democracy's triumphs as a "history of political choice." To succeed, the choice must be a demonstrably effective one, not just for the majority reaping the spoils of electoral victory, but across society as a whole.

Elections

As noted earlier, holding elections represents only one of many starting points for democracy. In some cases, election winners are tempted to limit democracy or slide back toward outright autocracy once they are in power. "One person, one vote, one time" was a slogan skeptical of democracy in South Africa and has been used to deny office to the Muslim Brotherhood in more than one Arab country.

Sadly, the slogan has described a real tendency elsewhere. Elections are abandoned or become rigged in order to preserve power, with a deeply corrosive effect on public morale that can endure for many years. Publics whose protests led to the introduction of democratic reform can reignite when the outcomes slide back into authoritarianism, as in Kyrgyzstan, or are overturned by the military, as in Thailand.

When elections take place in thoroughly non-transparent and repressive conditions, as in Iran's presidential election in June 2009; where there is neither independent electoral commission, nor foreign observers, and where opposition representatives were pushed away from scrutinizing the transport and opening of ballot boxes and the counting of ballots, a regime pays an enormous price in international credibility. But the internal costs run even deeper. Ultimately, regimes without demonstrable, verifiable public support through a legitimate and transparent electoral process will be contested and will fall.

Unfortunately, the attention of too many democratic donor countries tends to flag once sufficiently free and fair elections have been held. There is a "legitimacy moment" when a new democracy needs immediate international support. Yet, it is only at this point that the really hard chore of transparent and accountable self-government begins. The Kenyan experience shows the importance of helping emerging democracies to do more than mimic election management techniques: human rights need to be embedded in practice and in law so that winning partisan or ethnic majorities do not suppress minority losers. Effective mechanisms for the mediation of conflicts are needed to ensure post-election stability. Office holders need to habituate themselves to the competition of those who legitimately oppose them, which runs against the grain of custom in many societies.

Inclusive Pluralism

The management of inclusive pluralism is an imperative for successful development. Ethnic, tribal, sectarian and confessional pluralisms capture much of the attention — but there are also cultural and social factors that must be addressed for democracy to succeed. In Yemen, the displacement of the Saleh regime has been followed by an organized national dialogue prior to the elaboration of a new constitution and the forthcoming presidential elections in February 2014. The exercise has brought together representatives of all the pluralities — northerners, southerners, easterners, Islamists, women, youth, political activists and stalwarts of the old regime are enmeshed in a pacting framework where concessions are expected from all involved and no one side needs to accept "defeat." Eastern tribesmens' comments to the BBC — that it is the first time they have ever been consulted on their place and future — are typical.

Opportunities for Women

Achieving both rightful opportunities for, and the end to the abuse of, women are fundamental tasks in this context, which if well managed, have vast developmental benefits. "The world is awakening to a powerful truth," Nicholas Kristof and Sheryl WuDunn have written in *The New York Times* (2009). Recalling the Chinese saying that "women hold up half the sky," they stress the growing recognition on the parts of organizations as different as CARE and the US Joint Chiefs of Staff that "focusing on women and girls is the most effective way to fight global poverty and extremism." Education, the availability of daycare, microloans for women and even such mundane but essential things as the generalized provision of sanitary pads for girls are essential areas for democracies to support.

Succession

The orderly succession of democratically elected political leadership is also a universal need. The Mo Ibrahim Prize for Achievement in African Leadership recognizes and rewards a voluntary, democratic and peaceful succession of power. While it has not been bestowed every year because of a dearth of qualified candidates, its citations illuminate considerable progress.

In announcing the winner of the prize in October 2007, Kofi Annan cited ex-President of Mozambique Joaquim Chissano's efforts to build democracy on conciliation among ex-opponents. The following year, the prize was given to Festus Gontebanye Mogae of Botswana for "careful stewardship of the economy and management of Botswana's mineral resources, a tough stance on corruption, and success in combatting HIV/AIDS" (Mo Ibrahim Foundation, 2013). In 2011, Pedro de Verona Rodrigues Pires was honoured for "transforming Cape Verde into an African success story, recognized for good governance, human rights, prosperity and social development" (ibid.).

Economic Conditions and Models

It is debated whether specific economic conditions and models favour democracy taking roots in a given society. Some argue that democracy works most effectively only above a certain income threshold — generally a per capita income of about US$2,000 per year, which is the applicable level in Egypt and Indonesia — to accommodate an aspiring middle class and social network capacity. Zambian economist Dambisa Moyo is one who maintains that democratic transition first needs an established middle class to succeed. The author of *Dead Aid: Why Aid Is Not Working and How There Is a Better Way for Africa* charges that the West's "obsession with democracy" has been harmful to countries unequipped for it. While it is true that an emerging middle class fuelled democratic reform in Mexico, Korea and Taiwan, there are also notable examples of poorer developing countries choosing and sustaining democracy, such as Botswana or Mongolia, both of which have been lifted economically. Supporting the development of the capacity for civil society to habitualize the demands of democracy to increase the absorptive capacity of the new democratic government are the essential preparatory duties of outsiders responding to the impulses of solidarity.

As to models, China's one-party rule system, combined with pragmatic reliance on free markets and state enterprise in the economy seems at first a seductive model for some poor countries, with special appeal among autocrats who welcome China's economic cooperation that comes without lectures on corruption and human rights. The model, however, fails to provide a context for creativity, invention and innovation.

Rule of Law

A central focus of democracy development support needs to be helping to build the capacity of transitional countries to support the rule of law at the core of free societies and market economies. But as Thomas Carothers (1999) has written, statutes and courts are not enough if the sense of law does not reside "within the heads" of citizens. Moreover, as Gary Haugen and Victor Boutros (2010) point out, in many countries laws are rarely enforced. They note that in a June 2008 report, the United Nations estimated that four billion people live outside the rule of law because "without functioning public justice systems to deliver the protections of the law to the poor, the legal reforms of the modern human rights movement rarely improve the lives of those who need them most" (ibid.).

Religion and Democracy

Building democracy and human rights are secular political issues for many, but the reconciliation of religion and democracy is a central theme of the search for change in MENA, where the Muslim Brotherhood in its various forms has effectively challenged authoritarian rule, as the case studies on Egypt and Tunisia document.

There is a long history of faith-based groups assuming active roles in democracy development support. The Roman Catholic Church played a central ethical and practical role in comforting opponents of the dictatorships in Poland, Chile and the Philippines, though it has deferred to authoritarian regimes in Argentina and Spain. The martyrdoms of Archbishop Oscar Romero in El Salvador and of the Maryknoll sisters have inspired countless Salvadorans and democrats everywhere. Buddhist monks have been at the forefront of opposition to dictatorial rule in Burma/Myanmar and in support of human rights in Tibet today. In Cuba, religious communities draw social partnership and development support from related congregations outside.

It is not surprising that the sense of values at the core of democracy support in foreign policy has also helped enlist the support of faith-based groups in promoting human rights abroad. Particularly noteworthy was the expulsion of the South African Dutch Reformed Church from the World Alliance of Reformed Churches, which deepened the sense of isolation felt by those parts of the public on whose support the apartheid regime relied.

Church groups are at the forefront of advocacy for development assistance as well, and many support faith-based NGOs such as World Vision, Caritas or Catholic Relief Services. The Sant'Egedio Foundation is an example of a faith-based group dedicated to the mediation and peaceful settlement of disputes.

Private Investment

Socially responsible outside private investment can undoubtedly support democratic transformation if an ethical corporation can transfer habits of transparency and meritocracy, and valorize the local population in the upgrades, promotions and responsibilities it extends to local associates. International companies are learning that it is more important to generate goodwill with the public in the long term than to curry favour with powerful individuals. But the rewards of outside investment need to be felt generally by the population as a whole. What is clear is that to sustain public confidence, governments must be able to point to positive economic achievement with public benefit from outside investors whose projects they have welcomed.

The US government vaunted "start-up diplomacy" to support employment-generating entrepreneurship, but it has been slow to engage in Egypt and, in this sense, risks making the same mistake as it did in Russia in the 1990s, by providing too little economic assistance too late. Thomas R. Nides, former deputy Secretary of State told *The New York Times* that the "US Government has done a terrible job focusing on economic issues in the Middle East. You have huge public unemployment and no hope" (cited in Rohde, 2013). US Secretary of State John Kerry has requested that Congress approve US$580 million for an "incentive fund" for Middle Eastern countries that, in the spirit of the EU's guideline of "more for more," would reward democratic norms, independent courts, civil society and market-based economic initiatives.

National Defence

Even though the record of free peoples in self-defence is eloquent, it has been charged that democracy can impede the firm conduct of foreign relations or the organization of national defence, especially at a time of peril. Authoritarian regimes such as Cuba and Iran invoke threats from outside to justify the arbitrary imprisonment of democratic opponents and the general curtailing of civil liberties. In recent years, democratic societies have debated the need to constrain some measure of their established civil liberties in the interests of national security and counterterrorism. The process of narrowing freedoms is often vexed and the outcome one of unsatisfactory compromises. It is clear that transparency of purpose and full democratic debate are essential to public support.

Subject to civilian controls, military leadership in democracies can have a significant mentoring benefit for military colleagues in countries on the verge of transition to democracy, by supporting the principle of defending the people, rather than defending the entrenched regime. (For further details, see the military handbook *Military Engagement: Influencing Armed Forces Worldwide to Support Democratic Transitions,* also published in cooperation with the CCD.)

This *Handbook* cites numerous examples where the military refused orders to repress nonviolent protests — often decisively and in communication with military colleagues from democracies urging restraint. In democratic transitions, the training of competent civilian defence officials that uniformed personnel report to is another key function.

Ten Features of Successful Democratic Transition

Each democratic culture emerges from civil society in a singular way, but many of the challenges in achieving and consolidating democracy are shared, especially the always-challenging transition from a non-democratic society toward democracy.

Drawing from the *Handbook's* ongoing consultative process and workshops on how diplomats can best support democracy development, some basic, if somewhat self-evident, conclusions can be drawn about the process of democratic transition.

- What happens in a country emerges from its own citizens, not from outside. As Freedom House has put it, "The men and women of each country are really the authors of their own democratic development." Change cannot be imported or exported.

- There is no single model or template for democratic development. Each trajectory is different, depending on traditions and states of readiness.

- Violence is rarely effective as a force for change, as repressive governments have a near-monopoly on instruments of violence and the risk of violence alienates many citizens from campaigns in favour of change. But non-violent civil disobedience has historically been an important determinant of the course of events, as well as an essential preparation for post-transition responsibilities.

- The refusal of military and security units to use deadly force against protestors — as in Moscow in 1991, Kiev in 2005 or present-day Egypt and Tunisia — can be decisive. Contrary examples, such as in Tiananmen Square in 1989, Rangoon in 2007 or Iran in 2009, can have the opposite effect — but for how long? Much depends on whether the armed forces have a system of civilian control.

- The building blocks of change are in civil society. Supporting the building of capacity capable of underpinning a successful transition to democracy is an essential preparatory contribution from outside. Civil society necessarily forms a broad tent that includes citizens organized for any peaceful civil purpose. As nineteenth-century political philosopher Alexis de Tocqueville so famously put it, "civil society makes citizens" and also places a limit on the scope and power of government itself.

- Organic and durable change is rarely elite-driven; rather, it is usually bottom-up and is often generated by functional causes and socially or culturally oriented groups with practical and non-political aims.

- Successful transition relies on civic behaviour. It is not a process to be downloaded or transferred; thus, democracy has to be learned and implemented over time. It is essential for established democracies to keep a chronological perspective and humility about comparisons. As Egyptian democracy pioneer Saad Eddin Ibrahim has said, "You gave Mubarak thirty years. Give the Egyptian people some time as well."

- New governments should make — preferably in partnership with civil society — a determined effort to instill democratic values through education, as well as through the power of example.

- Free and fair elections constitute only one of many starting points. Equally decisive for representative electoral democracy is the acceptance of the transfer of power after elections and the inclusion of women, youth and minorities of all kinds.

- Democracy needs a viable state able to ensure security, which predominates in the hierarchy of needs. To sustain popular acceptance, democracy must deliver beneficial outcomes, such as transparency, fairness, justice and adequately shared economic progress.

What is clear, as Fareed Zakaria (2003) has warned, is that the "long, hard slog" of democratic consolidation means that donor and partner democracies must accept "constant engagement, aid, multilateral efforts and a world not of black and white, but of grey."

The citizens of the new democracies are the ones who will bring clarity and definition to their own society. External support should play a secondary role in helping to provide them with the greater capacity and means their development process requires; its design is to support their self-empowerment to choose their own government representatives and policy goals. As President Salvador Allende predicted for Chile, it is the people who make history. It is then up to the people to perform what Sikorski calls the "audit function" of elected government: through vibrant participatory and representative democracy, buttressed by free and responsible media. But all this requires mentoring and support.

If this general policy of outreach and support is contradicted by selective and uncritical support for non-democrats as a function of energy, economic or security interests, there are costs to credibility. As former British Foreign Secretary David Miliband (2008) said in Oxford, "We must resist the arguments on both the left and the right to retreat into a world of *realpolitik*."

This is not to dismiss lightly either the merits of foreign policies grounded in the realities of national interests or aspirations. But the tendency to concentrate funding for democracy support in a relatively small number of countries where interests are particularly evident, such as Mexico, Ukraine, Indonesia, Georgia, Mali, Afghanistan or Iraq, should not come at the expense of other countries whose democratic transitions are at a vulnerable stage.

The Hippocratic oath's admonition to "do no harm" also has merit in this context. There is indeed a harmful *realpolitik* history, especially during the Cold War, of democracies intervening to influence, and even to counter, democratic outcomes elsewhere. The subversion of democratically elected governments for perceived reasons of international competition — Iran comes to mind — leaves a bitter legacy that haunts some relationships for generations. When non-democracies band together, there can also be consequences once a democratic shift occurs. Fidel

Castro's support of the Soviet-backed coup against the Czechoslovak government in 1968 and invasion to stifle political reform haunts Czech-Cuban relations to this day.

More recently, there have been efforts to force democracy on others, most notably the invasion of Iraq, which was justified by some using a misappropriation of the tenets of the "responsibility to protect" doctrine. Ill-prepared attempts to democratize unstable states by force without the support of the people invite ethnic and sectarian conflict. This *Handbook* favours outside democracies' arm's length commitments to the long-term development of civil rights and civil society, with an emphasis on responsive support for citizens, democracy activists or human rights defenders already engaged in peaceful efforts toward democratic empowerment.

There is, of course, something of a paradox involved. On the one hand, there is a long international history of democrats aiding each other, from the intermingling of the American and French revolutions, to the waves of change that swept over Europe in 1848 or in 1989. On the other hand, democracy is about people developing popular self-government for themselves. Diplomats from democracies need to carry on the tradition of supporting democrats and sharing practical know-how, while deferring to the truth that ultimately, democracy is a form of self-rule requiring that things be done by a domestic civil society itself.

It is in this spirit that the Community of Democracies' participating countries, on behalf of democrats everywhere, value the opportunity to respond to requests for support from reform-minded groups and individuals struggling to introduce and improve democratic governance and human rights in their own societies, and to work with governments and non-governmental groups to improve democratic governance.

Attempts to block such responsive support for international civil society are a matter of great concern, especially, as the *Handbook* will set out, the rights to help and be helped are consistent with the aims and obligations of the UN Covenant on Civil and Political Rights, the Universal Declaration of Human Rights and the Declaration on Human Rights Defenders, as well as the Warsaw Declaration. These documents, as well as others committing signatories to best practices are catalogued in the Annex, available on the project website.

WORKS CITED

Allende, Isabel (2006). "Chile Under the Gun." *The Independent*, December 12.

Carothers, Thomas (1999). *Aiding Democracy Abroad: The Learning Curve*. Washington, DC: Carnegie Endowment for International Peace.

Deudney, Daniel and G. John Ikenberry (2009). "The Myth of the Autocratic Revival." *Foreign Affairs*, January/February.

Haugen, Gary and Victor Boutros (2010). "And Justice for All." *Foreign Affairs*, May/June.

Kristof, Nicholas and Sharon WuDunn (2009). "The Women's Crusade." *The New York Times*, August 17.

Link, Perry (2012). "On Fang Lizhi (1936–2012)." *New York Review of Books*, May 10.

Miliband, David (2008). "The Democratic Imperative." Aung San Suu Kyi Lecture at St. Hugh's College, Oxford.

Mo Ibrahim Foundation (2013). "Prize Laureates." Available at: www.moibrahimfoundation.org/prize-laureates/.

Rohde, David. (2013). "Start-Up Diplomacy." *The New York Times*, May 7.

Sen, Amartya (2001). *Development as Freedom*. New York: Alfred A. Knopf.

Shirky, Clay (2011). "The Political Power of Social Media." *Foreign Affairs*, January/February.

Zakaria, Fareed (2003). "Iraq Is Not Ready for Democracy." *The Guardian*, November 12.

2 THE INTERNATIONAL CONTEXT

THE SOLIDARITY OF INTERNATIONAL CIVIL SOCIETY

The importance of civil society in forming the basic building blocks of democratic governance cannot be overstated. The encouragement and assistance of links forged with civil society outside have been vital in the formation of broad-based coalitions of activists and reformers in such struggles, as the case studies on Chile and South Africa demonstrate, as do the experiences today in all the countries where aspirants to reform are seeking inclusive democratic change.

The "inside" story is essential. Within countries in transition, success will, to a large extent, be determined by the availability of human capital that the country can deploy to confront the very difficult tasks ahead. Difficulties in democratic transitions in Libya were exacerbated by its long history of civil society suppression. As a result of the suppression, there was no civil society to speak of. People had not had any opportunity to gain adequate experience in self-governance of their own affairs through local groups for activities such as issues of women's and youth rights, ecological protection, free press, culture and performance, home or landowners' rights or professions such as law or architecture.

Such groups need not have explicit political goals to qualify as incubators of the human capital that is essential for self-governance. In South Africa, for example, many African National Congress (ANC) organizers had gained earlier experience by setting up football clubs. A more recent example might be the network of daycare centres for single mothers established under the Catholic Church in Cuba, tolerated by the authorities because of public perception that the state's daycare facilities were overloaded and under-resourced. Most of the young women using the alternate facility and directing its activities in each local chapter were taking decisions over a key aspect of their own lives for the first time, rather than just accommodating themselves to a top-down state apparatus. It is through such experiences that members of civil society learn the necessity and practice of compromise in working with others, listening to others, self-starting and personal accountability, and transparency.

In most democracies, programs to support the development of these skills in emerging leaders and eventual administrators of newly transited democracies are offered through educational facilities, leadership programs and the targeted training of professional cadres. For example, the supporters of the Syrian National Coalition are being trained in municipal administration in sites in the region. They benefit from the support of the extensive international networks of foundations, agencies and organizations in democratic countries with a mandate to promote contact and democracy development across borders. Helping them make the connections is an essential task of the new democratic diplomacy.

In response, authoritarian regimes are increasingly limiting space for civil society to operate. They often ban outside financial and other assistance for civil society from foreign governments, or make an example of reformers. For instance, Cuba has made it a criminal act to accept financial support from foreign governments. Rulers such as Russian President Vladimir Putin attempt to portray reformers as anti-patriotic, in the pay of foreign embassies. In an extreme example of the confusion of perceptions of the authoritarians, Iranian prosecutors in the Tehran "show trials" charged the accused with being "arms of the velvet revolution…the women's movement, the human rights movement, the labor-syndicate movement, non-governmental organizations and civil-ethnic movements." In effect, the prosecution was indicting the Iranian people themselves as being anti-patriotic. The sobering reality, though, is that such paranoid circumstances have made direct embassy and other external financial support for local civil society, however modest, risky in some locales, especially for the recipients.

International civil society is increasingly put in the position of picking up the slack, not because they are "agents" of governments, but because of the solidarity of their core missions. Their credibility and effectiveness establish them as adversaries for authoritarian governments ill at ease with having to compete, which is why Russian and other authorities are now turning to harassing international humanitarian and human rights agencies such as Amnesty, Médecins sans Frontières or Human Rights Watch.

International NGOs such as these receive the vast majority of their funding from private contributions and only receive democratic government financing for very specific programs. They ensure that their in-the-field democracy support programs are at a demonstrable arm's length from any government. Nonetheless, their activity is under stress in several locales where repressive governments operate seemingly under the delusion that their publics can be closed off from the world around them.

A NEW PARADIGM FOR DIPLOMACY

As both a profession and practice, diplomacy is undergoing radical change as it opens to public diplomacy, even though, as the signatory foreign ministers point out in the Foreword, "Outdated stereotypes of our profession persist."

The conduct of diplomatic relations was once strictly on a state-to-state basis, pursued through private exchanges between diplomats and government officials. In recent years, however, the practice of diplomacy has "gone public" in many democratic nations and has taken on more of a human face. For most democracies, the days when their embassies were concerned only with maintaining "good relations" with the host government, irrespective of its character, are long past, as a former diplomat recalled of his mandate in Burma/Myanmar in the 1980s, when human rights were not high on the hierarchy of embassy priorities. Indeed, bilateral relationships and strategic engagement, even with authoritarian regimes, can be put to use to support the rights of civil society and democracy advocates in the host country.

Today, ambassadors and diplomats are much more likely to emphasize broader and direct engagement with the people of the host countries, not just government officials. The *Handbook* documents the many ways that embassies and ambassadors give public communication pride of place.

Diplomatic communications platforms are only one international channel, however, and by no means the most important. International "relations" are today composed of a myriad of non-governmental contacts. Everywhere, international networks of NGOs, scholars, researchers, business people and citizens are forming around issues, interests and tasks, all facilitated by communications technologies. The working landscape for internationalists and democratic activists is multifaceted.

Contemporary diplomacy needs to adapt to respond — to be, in the words of Ambassador Jií Gruša at the Maputo meeting of the International Forum on Diplomatic Training, "a tree with many roots." Embassies and consulates are going beyond public diplomacy and outreach, becoming brokers promoting contact and communication between the peoples and NGOs and groups of both sending and host countries. Democratic embassies, therefore, need to promote and defend the rights of people to so communicate.

IMPLICATIONS OF AN ERA OF GLOBAL COMMUNICATIONS

Article 19 of the UN Declaration of Human Rights guarantees that all people can "seek, receive, and impart information and ideas through any media and regardless of frontiers." In deepening the truth that all democrats are potential partners, the revolution in information technologies and techniques has dramatically altered international reality by providing, at least for those with the necessary means, virtually free access to information from outside — unless local authorities block it.

The demonstrable power of popular interconnectivity beyond the control of the state has had the inevitable result that attempts to block it are on the rise. The globalization of information makes the erection of barriers and firewalls ultimately futile, though authoritarian regimes keep trying to stifle both connections to, and awareness of, norms elsewhere, as well as the comparing of notes on best policies and practices. The young, who are increasingly new-technology literate, are connected to each other at home and abroad through their computers and mobile communications devices.

The cascade of new communications technologies has had a profound impact on events, not all of which are positive. Terrorist and xenophobic groups also use these technologies to mobilize and recruit supporters, and even convey lethal information on the fabrication of weapons of mass murder, without mediation or moderating influence. Films and hate texts that demonize Islam continue to burst like firestorms on volatile youth in the Middle East and South Asia. In Kenya, organized racist messages circulated to millions through cellphone texts prior to the January 2008 elections that broke down along tribal lines. In the struggle between the government and military against "Red Shirt" opposition in Thailand in May 2010, both sides used Twitter to attack the other. Authoritarian governments have learned to mimic social networking sites with their own propaganda.

But one does not have to be a "techno-utopian" to recognize the immense benefits of new communications technologies to democracy overall. It is not a new phenomenon. Western radio and TV broadcasts hastened change in Eastern Europe. Fax machines connected Chinese students to the outside world in 1989. The Internet then became pivotal in rallying widespread participation in civil resistance. In Serbia, Ukraine, Southeast Asia, Lebanon and Venezuela, text messaging mobilized popular demonstrations. In Iran, Twitter and Facebook became key connectors, though the regime tried intermittently to shut the networks down. In April 2008, Egypt's "Facebook Revolution" mobilized a general strike, and street actions over economic and political issues anticipated the events of the Arab Spring three years later.

Non-governmental international networks as disparate as the Genocide Intervention Network, the Sunlight Foundation (whose aim is making US governance "accountable and transparent"), the Gaza Reporting International Network or the International Center for Journalists all share the vocation of trying to get at the perceived truth. The disconsolate fact is that international news coverage has been in steep decline for years as print and electronic media close bureaus abroad. Writer Claire Berlinsky (2012) has documented an 80 percent drop in foreign coverage in US print and TV since the end of the Cold War. Non-traditional networks attempt to close the gaps.

Though access to outside reporting and other information is invaluable, the most vital contributions of Internet connections are to the internal discussions in countries without free media.

Moreover, new technologies radiate outward the witnessing function of a new internationalist culture of "netizens." Hand-held communications devices enable activists to witness and communicate real images of atrocity to the world as they unfold, via Internet uplinks in real time. Such netizens and bloggers made the whole world witness to the harshly violent repression of peaceful demonstrations in

Burma/Myanmar in 2007. The combination of netizens' digital cameras and global websites such as YouTube showed the world the tragic killing of Iranian student Neda Agha Soltan on a street in Tehran. The battered face of Khaled Said held a whole regime responsible for murder in Egypt. Such episodes demonstrate that it is becoming harder and harder for repressive regimes to use brutal force without being exposed.

There is, regrettably, every indication they will continue to try. There have been obvious recent high-profile examples of constrained societies adopting defensive moves, especially during periods of agitation or protest through targeted efforts to restrict Internet access and close off sites, and shutting down wireless networks.

In China, many foreign news outlet sites or specific news reports are periodically blocked or selectively filtered by "The Great Firewall" created by the Chinese government to keep Internet users from communicating freely with the outside world in an enduring effort to impose a considerable degree of censorship, especially when public protests occur such as in Tibet and Xinjiang.

Such walls have been circumvented with the assistance of supporters of access to outside information, including the US State Department, which has spent US$70 million in 2013 alone to support the development and deployment of anti-censorship software. The Global Internet Freedom Consortium, a private international NGO, developed FreeGate, software that bypasses the blockage of sites within a country by accessing rapidly changing servers outside of it. FreeGate can be downloaded by Internet users everywhere and was widely used during the shutdown of servers and sites in Iran in 2009.

Enabling "mesh networks" for cellphone communications has been critical for activists inside repressive countries when state-controlled networks are slowed during times of public protest and agitation to hinder the uplinking of Facebook postings and videos. The Chinese Internet Project at the University of California, Berkeley, the international Tor Project, and scholars at the Munk School of Global Affairs at the University of Toronto also provide programs that enable Internet users in closed societies to maintain access to outside news outlets, contacts with the outside world, and above all, continued communication inside the country among like-minded reform activists.

But as Professor Xiao Qiang, who heads the Berkeley Chinese Internet Project has said about the authoritarian regimes, "They're getting more sophisticated. They learn from past mistakes." The Chinese authorities studied episodes of protest in Eastern Europe and Iran to devise defensive technological intervention techniques, in an attempt to control communications, monitor email and define public opinion.

Sadly, Western-based technology companies have exported monitoring software and hardware that enable repressive regimes to take such measures to counter a free Internet. As John Seabrook (2013) reported in *The New Yorker,*

> Oppressive regimes from Syria to Bahrain use the latest cyber-surveillance tools, many of them made by western companies

to spy on dissidents. Finfisher spyware, for example, made by Gamma International, a UK-based firm, can be used to monitor Wi-Fi networks from a hotel lobby, hack cell phones and P.C.s, intercept Skype conversations, capture passwords, and activate cameras and microphones. Egyptian dissidents who raided the office of Hosni Mubarak's secret police after his overthrow found a proposal from Gamma offering the state Finfisher hardware, software, and training for about four hundred thousand dollars.

These are commercial activities whose lawfulness is subject to whether or not international sanctions apply, but it should be clear that democratic embassies should not in any way be facilitating the commercial representation of companies seeking such opportunities.

While targeted attacks to limit connectivity are attractive defences to authoritarian regimes, they are also costly for the country's development. Competitiveness in a digital world, particularly in societies such as China or Iran where Internet users are multiplying daily, will be greatly hampered by limiting Internet access. A workforce without Internet access risks isolation. Cuban authorities seem to recognize belatedly that by continuing to block Internet access for young people, the regime will greatly handicap Cuba's future.

As technology continues to evolve, the tension between the formidable momentum toward open communication and repressive governments' wishes to control events will continue. Embassies do have a role to play, sometimes *in extremis* opening mission communications systems to local citizens.

A DIPLOMACY OF COMMITMENT

Committed diplomacy — going beyond formal duty and applying a humanist perspective — not a legalist or a "realist one — to international relations is nested in the oldest tradition of that discipline…The diplomatic field can obtain concrete results, which enable the recognition, assistance, and even the freedom of victims of dictatorial persecution. No diplomat should feel out of bounds when doing so. Quite the opposite.

— Pablo Brum and Mariana Dambolena, On Diplomatic Commitment to Human Rights Documentos, May 14, 2009

There is, in practice, a "right to be helped" as well as a "right to help." The role of outsiders is never primary, but their catalytic support can be pivotal.

In certain circumstances, where the legitimacy of direct support of civil society, especially advocacy groups, is challenged, NGOs, to which embassies should defer, often take up the slack. NGOs are not cats' paws of embassies or of national interests per se, but they share developmental ideals and have a common interest in civil society's aspirations to democratic governance.

Diplomats cannot leave it to international civil society to support democracy development and human rights. On instruction, and even on personal initiative, diplomats increasingly intervene when necessary to defend and support threatened human rights defenders and democratic activists. To answer how this is best done varies with circumstances, either demonstrably in public view, or, as the case merits, privately, below the radar. Examples of both approaches — such as European diplomats accompanying Las Damas de Blanco on their peaceful marches in Havana, US Ambassador Mark Palmer marching with demonstrators in Budapest in 1989, or the ambassadors of several democracies attending the vigil of a Syrian activist murdered in custody — occur throughout the *Handbook*.

Consistent Messaging

Consistent messaging on human rights and governance is a central necessity. Commitment on human rights and governance issues is part of the country missions of many democracies, as agreed with authorities at home. A democracy has to be able to demonstrate democratic leadership by solidarity.

Sadly, there have been many examples when democratic values in the representation of a democracy's interests in diplomatic relations with an authoritarian state are contradicted by the obvious priorities placed on the pursuit of privileged economic relations or political support on security issues. There is no question that the Gadhafi regime in Libya gamed the attraction of economic contracts for Italian or Canadian business against what Libyan authorities evaluated as strictly pro forma representation on human rights by these countries' representations. In reality, security and economic interests can build a strategic relationship, which can then enhance the opportunity to communicate basic messages on human rights with greater effectiveness.

Of course, there can be pushback when diplomats take public positions of solidarity within the countries of accreditation to repressive regimes. The *Handbook* will illustrate the many ways this has happened in the past, including occasions when authoritarian governments attempted to intimidate or expel diplomats for legal activity in support of human rights. Iran provided another extreme example in 2009, where locally engaged employees of the UK Embassy not enjoying immunity were arrested and put on trial for subversion. In circumstances where local authorities are seeking to blame outsiders for internal protests whose legitimacy they do not wish to acknowledge, different outreach methods are required.

A MULTILATERAL PROJECT FOR DEMOCRACY SUPPORT AND THE COMMUNITY OF DEMOCRACIES

There is, of course, considerable activity in multilateral fora on human rights and democratic development; the *Handbook* project is itself an undertaking of a multilateral organization, the Community of Democracies.

> When the United Nations can truly call itself a community of democracies, the Charter's noble ideals of protecting human rights and promoting social progress in larger freedoms' will have been brought much closer.
>
> — UN Secretary-General Kofi Annan, at the founding conference of the Community of Democracies, Warsaw, 2000

It is self-evident that the effectiveness of democratic development support is enhanced when democratic partners work together. There is no formal common strategy or work plan, however, although progress has been made in identifying desirable common approaches, such as in democracy education, the theme of the Mongolian presidency of the Community of Democracies 2012-2013.

There are variances in the extent to which democratic governments are comfortable pursuing democracy support agendas for other countries. In a seeming paradox, in their bilateral relationships, democracies such as India, Brazil and even South Africa tend to not wish to introduce issues that touch upon the internal affairs of partner states, possibly because of their own histories as colonies, even though the path to independence of many benefitted precisely from international solidarity.

The mixed record of multilateral organizations reflects the mixed governance of the nations of the world. Older democracies are more apt to charge their representatives with proactive mandates to connect directly to civil society and to support the efforts of democracy development, especially since the costs of inconsistency through the unquestioning support of regimes in Tunisia, Libya and Egypt became clear.

Some newer democracies prefer classic *realpolitik* diplomacy, demonstrating their solidarity with developing countries regardless of their governance. They place their priority on narrowly defined national interests in bilateral relationships over the notion that democracy proponents have a right to be helped and that democratic societies are inferentially engaged. But, as the *Handbook* illustrates, there are multiple examples of all democracies falling short of ideals as far as that is concerned.

The Role of the United Nations

Despite such variations in approach, democratic development is now a major theme at the United Nations, particularly through the UN Democracy Fund.

Moreover, UN agencies and programs place prominent emphasis on consulting with civil society in the field, including in peacekeeping operations, such as in Timor Leste, the Democratic Republic of the Congo and Côte d'Ivoire.

The UN provides extensive commitment to free and fair elections through its electoral support unit and to democracy development through its development program. The UN Human Rights Council is meant to be a central instrument in the search for the advancement of human rights, although its effectiveness remains stymied by the manoeuvring of some non-democracies determined to block scrutiny of their human rights abuses. The doctrine of non-interference in internal affairs continues to be invoked as a principle protecting such states for not safeguarding the human rights of their citizens.

Intergovernmental Organizations and Agencies

Other intergovernmental organizations, such as the Organization for Security and Co-operation in Europe (OSCE) and its Office for Democratic Institutions and Human Rights, the Organization of American States (OAS) or the Commonwealth of Nations, consider democracy to be interdependent with the imperatives of economic development and human security, and commit programs to democracy development support.

International agencies help and advise in the technical organization and administration of elections, as well as the elaboration of electoral laws. Several development assistance programs support projects that are designed to assist and engage greater public understanding of how citizens benefit from and participate in the electoral process.

Regional and Inter-regional Organizations

Regional or inter-regional organizations, such as the European Union, the Council of Europe, the OSCE, the OAS, the Organisation internationale de la Francophonie or the Commonwealth of Nations, formally prescribe democratic practice as a precondition of membership and monitor and verify elections.

These organizations, however, vary widely in the extent to which they apply democracy criteria to membership. La Francophonie, for example, is more cultural than political in emphasis. It has suspended memberships to nations such as Mauritania, Madagascar, Mali and Guinea-Bissau, but includes several long-standing non-democracies such as Equatorial Guinea and Vietnam. Initiatives to agree to a charter that binds members to democracy have been dismissed.

The Community of Democracies reviews its membership and accredited observer countries regularly to verify they are indeed democratic. There have been multiple demotions, promotions and suspensions.

The Commonwealth of Nations has a history of democratic integrity that was forged over its exclusion of apartheid-era South Africa. The modern Commonwealth suspends membership of countries that depart from democratic norms. In recent years, Pakistan, Zimbabwe and Fiji have been targeted by the membership for their abuses of democratic practice, and Zimbabwe, in fact, left the organization. While some members made efforts to embed a more strenuous commitment to a rule of law, democracy and human rights agenda in a new charter, it was turned aside by other members more committed to non-interference in internal affairs. A watered-down charter was adopted in 2013, committing members to "good governance," human rights and gender equality.

The OSCE, successor to the Commission on Security and Cooperation in Europe (CSCE), which had a key role in hastening the end of the Cold War, has generally been a disappointment since the founding members' conference and the adoption of the Charter of Paris in November 1990, in large part because several member states, most notably Uzbekistan and Azerbaijan, are clear violators of democratic principles and human rights. The Russian Federation has become an alienated participant as a result of what it believes is excessive criticism of its conduct regarding the situation in Chechnya and because of adverse OSCE monitoring of Russian elections.

When elections are at risk of being manipulated, a full range of international contacts and experience in mobilizing civil society can come into play. Ongoing NGO contacts had a key role in electoral crisis management, such as in Ukraine in 2004, or earlier in Slovakia, Croatia, Serbia and Georgia, and later in Kyrgyzstan. The success in redeeming the 2004 Ukraine election's integrity was due to the democratic and reform movements' mass protests and pressures, but over time, sustained international support from governments, embassies and people-to-people NGOs played an important background role, as the *Handbook* case study on Ukraine will demonstrate.

There is an important regional dimension. Evidence shows that mentoring emerging democracies from regional partners is particularly effective because of the shared perspectives of regional (and often social) adjacency. Members are taking the strengthening of capacity for democracy assistance within regional organizations more seriously, as the creation of an Asian democracy network at the 2013 Ministerial Meeting of the Community of Democracies illustrates.

The *Handbook*'s focus is on "in-country" mandates and activity associated with bilateral accreditations. But it is important to note that most countries, including non-democracies, have systematically signed on to the intentions and principles that the above multilateral organizations supposedly confer. These commitments are useful reminders in the practice of bilateral democratic diplomacy.

Bilateral Relations and the Value of Example in International Solidarity

The nation-state remains the most relevant context, however. States sign and hopefully ratify international conventions and organizations affirming the acceptance of human rights. But ultimately, these are subject to circumstances, laws and justice systems within states. Moral philosopher Tzvetan Todorov (2001) pointed out in his Oxford Amnesty Lecture that the inhabitants of most countries derive their legal rights much more as citizens of states than as citizens of the world. The Community of Democracies therefore counts the strengthening of the capacity of states to assure the rights of its citizens as an important objective.

The *Handbook* and its case studies examine, in particular, what embassies and diplomats can do on their assignments in the field in dealings with civil society and local authorities to respond helpfully to requests to support democracy's development.

Of course, the odds against them can often seem uneven. As US author Robin Wright (2008) observes, the contests between "inexperienced democratic activists with limited resources" and regimes "who have no intention of ceding control" can seem an "unfair battle." While external support and mentoring skills can help the diplomats to succeed, outside allies and helpers must always follow the lead of domestic reformers and agents of change. We have seen in both Burma/Myanmar and Iran that security force crackdowns that are willing to use deadly force to support the status quo can obtain more time for an authoritarian regime, but its time will inevitably run out in favour of justice for the people.

Influence is often wielded through the power of example. Activists and reformers seek inspiration from models that other societies provide and take counsel from the comparable prior experiences of other reformers, most of which are relatively recent. After all, the consolidation of effective democratic systems is mostly a phenomenon of the latter half of the twentieth century, spurred by the aftermath of World War II, decolonization, the end of dictatorships in Greece, Portugal and Spain in the mid-1970s and, more recently, the end of Cold War competition.

The examples of non-violent conflict that were developed in the Indian independence movement and the US civil rights movement have provided strategic and tactical inspiration to hundreds of millions of aspiring democrats. More recently, the experience of the Solidarnosc ("solidarity") movement in Poland had immense influence beyond its region. Institutional example can be passed on, such as the Chilean effort to construct a Truth and Reconciliation Commission, whose model lent itself to later adaptations in Peru, South Africa, Rwanda and Morocco, as well as in other post-authoritarian and post-conflict locales. Civil society's response to threats to the integrity of election processes also takes instructive cues from those who experienced similar attempts elsewhere — an example being the learning process of Ukrainian democrats with transition veterans from other European countries such as Serbia and Slovakia.

Internal, domestic actions that were decisive in these and other struggles for democracy — the demonstrations, boycotts and other forms of non-violent civil resistance — drew from a supportive external framework of psychological, political and practical measures circumscribing the options of non-democratic governments.

Positions taken internationally by outside democratic governments and prestigious individuals can be crucial. In Chile, external support to civil society began with humanitarian action offering asylum to thousands of refugees after the coup d'état of September 11, 1973. For the next 15 years, the resulting diaspora of Chilean exiles kept the repressive political condition of Chile high in the consciousness of democrats everywhere.

In consequence, trade union movements in Europe and North America, political parties, such as European social and Christian democrats, and individual political leaders, such as German Chancellor Helmut Kohl or US Senator Edward Kennedy, provided Chilean citizens with the confidence that they were not alone in the struggle that was beginning to build up against the Pinochet dictatorship's repression. Activists in South Africa recall the inspiration provided by US Senator Robert Kennedy's speech in South Africa in 1968, which was preciously preserved on forbidden long-playing records.

Not taking a position in support of democratic activists or reformers can also be negatively crucial. As President of Venezuela Carlos Andrés Pérez once said, non-response can be a form of intervention.

Repressive regimes also study prior examples.

Authoritarian regimes do try to claim legitimacy by pointing to support from countries reliant on them for security or other interests. As noted above, it is usual for democratic governments and their representatives to condition state-to-state cooperation (except humanitarian aid) on the modification of behaviour, but it is vital for democratic governments to do more than episode-by-episode protests of human rights violations. They need to maintain sustained programs of democratic development support, including insisting on ongoing dialogues with the host countries in order to deal with basic conditions, especially those affecting civil society. Even many authoritarian regimes feel obliged to feign some reformist intentions. These can provide democratic activists and reformers with potentially valuable openings and opportunities. Once it is clear, however, that engagement with host country authorities will be unproductive, or when a regime resorts to deadly force to try to preserve its authoritarian status quo, human rights dialogues can be counterproductive.

It is important, then, that democracies make their positions clear, to offset claims of international support by repressive regimes abusing their populations. A powerful method is coordinated international action for targeted sanctions, such as the embargo on petroleum products and arms on the South African apartheid regime. Coordinated sanctions also made South Africa's finances unsustainable, especially its expenses of equipping for war with front-line states. In this case, the crucial factor was that external sanctions were demanded by the ANC and the United Democratic Front (UDF), two South African anti-apartheid movements. A vital question today is the extent to which international solidarity is available: if rich petro-states or others unsympathetic to democracy counter sanctions with their own economic aid, the effect is weakened.

Sanctions can also be controversial because they can hurt the innocent in an oppressed society, unless they carefully target the accounts, assets and international mobility of the oppressors themselves. The US sanctions and embargo on Cuba have long been held up as being more punitive than remedial. Sanctions on Iraq during the

1990s were also judged by many as being both ineffective and destabilizing to the population as a whole. On the other hand, targeted sanctions by the European Union, the United States and others against members of the Burmese judiciary responsible for the legal persecution of opposition leader Aung San Suu Kyi, and against state-run enterprises and the key personnel of the ruling junta had a definite impact on the improvement of the political landscape.

Of course, sanctions are a coercive tool that can only be deployed once (though they can be adjusted). Once used, the value of the threat of sanctions is spent. When a regime such as Zimbabwe's or Syria's decides that the sanctions are tolerable or can be evaded, their remedial effect is reduced.

The most counterproductive management of sanctions imposed for human rights abuse is their removal without visible improvement. Hugh Williamson and Steve Swerdlow (2013) of Human Rights Watch describes the lifting of the EU sanctions on Uzbekistan as a "litmus test of the challenge of dealing with an authoritarian government with which countries need to do 'business.'" It was an offence against consistency undermining the credibility of the EU's positions on human rights across the board.

The EU imposed sanctions on the Karimov dictatorship in Uzbekistan after security forces gunned down hundreds of peaceful protestors in Andijan in May 2005. Human Rights Watch reports that the EU then lifted the sanctions in 2009, "though Uzbekistan met none of the human rights conditions the EU had set." The EU's relaxed views stood in sharp contrast to the actions of international civil society, best exemplified by the International Committee of the Red Cross, which judged that Uzbekistan's intractable behaviour regarding political dissent and prisoners made it impossible to fulfill the its humanitarian mandate in the country.

A HANDBOOK TO SUPPORT DIPLOMATIC DEMOCRATIC COMMITMENT

Case Studies

All Situations Are Different

The Community of Democracies members' diplomatic missions can aspire to achieve representation on human rights, or activity in support of democratic development on the ground, through individual and sometimes concerted action. Chapter 3, on tool box applications, is meant to spell out the ways that such individual and coordinated efforts have succeeded, or not, in the past.

Chapter 3 sets out the sorts of opportunities and constraints that diplomats encounter in democracy development support from three perspectives: the resources and assets at a diplomat's disposal; the ways in which diplomats have deployed these assets in support of civil society, democratic development and human rights in a multitude of situations over the last decades; and their applications in favour of local partners, policy goals and programs. Clearly, the local context is paramount, including the attitude, sometimes hostile, of local authorities.

It is emphasized that these are tools of "soft power," as opposed to sanctions from outside or armed revolt from the inside. A review of the many narratives of democratic transition of the last decades shows that just as democracy cannot be imposed on a people from outside, nor are democratic activists likely to succeed by using violent means from inside.

In reaching out, civil society groups have often turned to embassies or consulates of Community of Democracies' participating states for advice and assistance. There is no codified set of procedures for diplomats to follow in order to respond effectively. Each situation is different, presenting its own unstructured problems and opportunities, which diplomats need to interpret according to local as well as general merits, including the bilateral relationship itself. The actions of authorities in Iran — emulated in Russia — show that, faced with popular protest, repressive regimes can construct a false narrative of foreign interference and contest the legitimacy of any contacts between diplomatic representatives and local civil society. This can be potent when popular memory recalls a history of foreign interference.

Over the last decades, the activity of diplomats from democratic countries constitutes a considerable record of experience with almost every eventuality. On the basis that the record of such activity could provide helpful guidance to practitioners in the field, the *Handbook* attempts to record it. Increasingly, the Handbook also describes the work of international civil society and NGOs in support of democracy development, which is assuming an ever-larger responsibility for engaging civil society in transitional countries.

This *Handbook* identifies a tool box of creative, human and material resources available to missions. It records the ways in which missions and diplomats, and to some extent NGOs, have drawn from these tools in the past in the interest of democracy development support. The *Handbook* means to cover a full range of conditions and situations, from regimes that are flatly undemocratic and repressive, to phases of post-conflict recovery, to democratic transition and consolidation.

The *Handbook* includes a representative variety of case studies, documenting and explaining specific country experiences. While it is important that each case study be seen for its specific contextual properties, there are characteristics that obviously recur. Moreover, it should always be borne in mind that activities and outcomes in one locale might have ripple effects in the region and on wider or other specific relationships. Each country and situation is different, but there are common patterns in how international solidarity benefits extended struggles for human rights and self-determination.

We also hope to catalogue the growing number of examples of "older" democracies adapting democratic techniques from "younger" ones. The democratic learning experience is not all one-way, and capacity building continues for all. For example, innovative Brazilian methods for enabling citizens to participate in budget-setting exercises in local government have been adapted for use in local government from Brooklyn, New York, to the United Kingdom.

A review of all these experiences bears out the validity of our belief in our interdependence, and hopefully provides practitioners with encouragement, counsel and a greater capacity to support democrats everywhere.

This *Handbook*, with its tool box and wide portfolio of case studies, is meant to be applicable to a wide variety of conditions. Diplomats of democratic governments have different challenges, depending on whether they are assisting democrats living under repressive regimes that actively abuse the population, supporting fragile emerging democracies in the process of transition, including in stabilizing post-conflict recovery conditions, or working with recently transformed democracies to consolidate democratic gains.

The country case studies reflect a wide distribution of experience, both geographically and chronologically: democratic societies flourish on every continent. The case studies are also selected to present an apt variety of transition types, but the country case studies focus principally on diplomatic activity to support in-country civil society prior to the end of authoritarian rule. In such countries, where democratic activists worked to end authoritarian conditions, transitions to democracy were greatly aided by their access to internationally administered programs over the years to develop their competence in law, economics and other key areas of governance in order to prepare for democracy. The importance of organized civil resistance as an "incubator" of democracy is stated in the introduction.

The first edition of the *Handbook* documented peaceful transitions in self-governance, such as in Tanzania. The obligation of democratic solidarity, however, must support a wide array of countries and civil societies in the difficult process of democratic development and consolidation, not just countries self-nominated by their strategic or other interests. The first edition also presented case studies of successful transitions from repressive societies to democracy, such as South Africa and Chile, and case studies of ongoing situations, such as in Burma/Myanmar and Zimbabwe, where repressive regimes were seemingly indifferent to outside counsel (at least from democracies), and where diplomats operate in difficult circumstances of minimal productive communication with host authorities, but continue to be seen as sources of encouragement and support by democratic activists in those countries. These latter two studies, as well as those on Belarus and Ukraine, are updated in this third edition, while the others are available online on the project website.

The second edition included case studies on China, Cuba and Egypt, important undemocratic countries facing challenging circumstances, where civil society and democracy activists were narrowly constrained, and where outside influence was officially contested. This third edition now includes new case studies on Tunisia, which sparked "the Arab Spring," and democracy in Russia, 1987–2013, which is as much an examination of the complexity of the policy process and lessons learned from the standpoints of both the country in transition and the engaged democracies from outside, as it is of the activity of diplomats on the ground.

The third edition also includes updates of all the "live" cases where democracy is still in the balance. These run the gamut from revolution and uncertain aftermath in Egypt, through hopeful, but far from certain or complete reform in Burma/Myanmar, to questionable progress in Zimbabwe, and outright retreat from democracy in Ukraine and intensified repression in Belarus. The third edition includes unamended, but historically significant and evocative cases from Chile and South Africa, as well.

WORKS CITED

Berlinsky, Claire (2012). "How to Read Today's Unbelievably Bad News." Available at: www.berlinski.com/node/180.

Brum, Pablo and Mariana Dambolena (2009). "On Diplomatic Commitment to Human Rights." *Documentos*, Centro Para la Apertura y es Desarrollo de América Latina, May 14.

Seabrook, John (2013). "Network Insecurity: Are We Losing the Battle Against Cyber Crime?" *The New Yorker*, May 20.

Todorov, Tzvetan (2001). "Right to Intervene or Duty to Assist?" Oxford Amnesty Lecture, February.

Williamson, Hugh and Steve Swerdlow (2013). "Uzbekistan: A Massacre that Should Not Fade into History." *European Voice*, May 12.

Wright, Robin (2008). *Dreams and Shadows: The Future of the Middle East.* New York: The Penguin Press.

3 THE DIPLOMAT'S TOOL BOX

INTRODUCTION

Scholars in the social sciences that were consulted in the preparation of this *Handbook* have recommended a ranking of "best practices" in an evidence-based analysis from the growing catalogue of examples of democracy development support. Clearly, some support practices will be more effective than others, depending on the circumstances and the mix of contextual issues. There are several ongoing analytical exercises that attempt to provide evidence-based guidance, such as the various conferences and workshops organized under the aegis of the Oslo Governance Centre of the UN Development Programme, working, for example, with the Norwegian Peacebuilding Resource Centre and the Jordan-based Foundation for the Future. But there is reluctance within the Community of Democracies to either generalize or theorize with prescriptive recommendations. In this chapter, the *Handbook* follows methodology that is fact-based and descriptive rather than prescriptive, but attempts to identify some general principles and approaches by citing specific cases of diplomatic engagement.

FIVE CAVEATS

The *Handbook* assumes that most foreign ministries of democratic countries accept a need to adapt their bilateral diplomatic representation to the new paradigms of public diplomacy, even though, as noted, differences persist in national practices of providing visible support to civil society's efforts to advance democracy development. But there are five noteworthy caveats:

- At any time, a country usually has a range of public and discrete interests engaged in a bilateral relationship. Diplomats in the field need to manage the range of interests simultaneously and effectively. Support for human rights and democracy development is a value-based interest. Yet, there are many examples of human rights concerns and democracy support being soft-pedalled so that security or economic goals in play in a relationship with an authoritarian country are not undermined. (The example of the European

Union lifting sanctions on Uzbekistan without human rights improvement is especially egregious.) The truth is that democracies do not have to pursue interests in the belief that it must be at the expense of their values, or vice-versa. The notion that there is a conflict between interests and values is false; rather, they are interdependent. The support of democratic values is generally in the national interests of a democracy's diplomacy. Successfully managing interests in a bilateral relationship can usually build influence necessary for the support of the rights of local civil society. Apart from consistency with declared values of solidarity, the spread of democracy and rule of law buttress international security as well as protection for investment and trade. Democratically elected partners interrelate in ways that favour predictability and assurance in international relations.

- The capitals' empowerment of local diplomatic initiative can be crucial, within a clear understanding of the interests and aims of the overall mission that diplomats must represent. Diplomats in the field have to be able to react to swiftly evolving events. As Canadian diplomat Pierre Guimond described democracy support activity in Prague in the 1980s:

> Diplomats have to know where the governments want to go in terms of foreign policy and then the ambassador is responsible for delivering the policy. But it's impossible for people in the capital city to decide "you should do this and you should do that." The foreign ministry knows what we do because we report. It is result-based, not event-based. It's not because we've been to 36 demonstrations that anything will happen. We were there because something is happening. (cited in Velinger, 2007)

The "happening" determines the outcome, and its fate is in the hands of local reformers and activists with the legitimate support of democratic embassies, representing their citizens at home. Members of the diplomatic staff need to feel confidence in their abilities to decide on the ground how to proceed and to know they won't be contradicted by parallel messaging by another agency or by a lack of support back home.

- When complications ensue in bilateral relations, it is essential that diplomatic initiative in support of human rights defenders and democratic activists be welcomed and even rewarded by the career culture of foreign ministries. Even in the most difficult and circumscribed circumstances, there is much that a creative and committed diplomat can do, as the following pages will illustrate. This is the purpose of the Community of Democracies Palmer Prize, awarded to diplomats who "display valor under difficult circumstances and take risks or are especially inventive in their sustained efforts to assist civil society to advance democracy in their countries of assignment." Awards have been given to Czech, Dutch, American, Polish, Peruvian, Canadian, Swedish and other diplomats from the field in recent years.

- Time frames are unpredictable. On one hand, the impact of activity or demarches may not be apparent for some time. It takes consistent and sustained effort to contribute to building the self-confidence of civil society and to restraining repressive behaviour on the part of non-democratic authorities. Yet, in authoritarian societies, the gains of democracy can also come swiftly. Repressive regimes tend to implode from within. As Shari Villarosa, former US chargé d'affaires for Burma/Myanmar has said, "Living in any authoritarian country, while you're in the midst of it, it's hard to see that they'll ever cede power or go away. But actually, they cause their own destruction. And their foundations are rotting. It's a question of time" (cited in Watson, 2008).

- Lastly, as our case studies make clear, local conditions vary. Some authoritarian regimes are neuralgic about embassies connecting with civil society and a few are positively hostile about direct financial assistance, especially to advocacy groups, even from international civil society. Such host country authorities may try to confine the activity of diplomats to interaction only with designated official channels. They often aim to restrict interaction with local civil society by withholding official access for diplomats they consider straying from these narrow confines. In the longer run, these practices lead to international isolation for the authorities in question. There are international norms for ensuring diplomatic practice does not directly interfere with internal affairs, but there are also overriding obligations for governments to respect international norms with respect to human rights, and for democratic governments to persist in representation of these obligations, even though they may calibrate their practices differently to suit different locales.

TOOL BOX RESOURCES AND ASSETS

Diplomats can underestimate the potential impact that the inherent resources and assets at their disposal may contribute to the validation of the activities of civil society. The following are some of the resources and assets that diplomats can usually draw from. In the chapter and case studies that follow, the *Handbook* shows how these resources have been applied in practice.

Immunity

The unique asset of diplomatic immunity can be employed and virtually shared in ways that benefit individuals and groups pursuing democratic development goals and reform.

Nota bene: While host countries cannot withdraw immunity, several have expelled diplomats for alleged interference in internal affairs. The excuse is often that they had supported specific political or partisan outcomes rather than democracy development in general. In lieu of expulsion, intimidation is also a recourse of authoritarian regimes, including against the families of diplomats.

Examples: There is an extensive record of democratic governments' diplomats preventing punitive state violence by their mere presence at the scene. In Kiev, in 2004, representatives of the French Embassy, the European Commission and the OSCE's Office for Democratic Institutions and Human Rights (ODIHR) arrived at the home of a youth leader as security forces were about to arrest him and other democratic activists present. Unaccustomed to witnesses they couldn't intimidate, the state security agents retreated. In Nepal in 2005, threatened dissidents were granted visas by resident embassies; diplomats of asylum countries accompanied them to the airport and to departure gates to block their seizure by authorities. In Cuba, diplomats from several EU countries and the United States have been appearing in person to support Las Damas de Blanco (Ladies in White), the wives of jailed prisoners of conscience who have been harassed and intimidated by groups mobilized by the regime.

There is also a record of harsh state counter-reaction to diplomats' on-the-ground intervention against repression. In Chile in 1973, diplomats from several democracies made their ways to the stadium and other locales where the military putschists had assembled arrested activists, many of whom were subsequently imprisoned, tortured or killed. The regime expelled the most prominent of the diplomats, Swedish Ambassador Harald Edelstam.

Expulsions of foreign representatives have since occurred under many repressive regimes, most recently in Sudan, Burma/Myanmar and Belarus, but the number of times that diplomats have deployed physical presence to discourage arbitrary repression of legitimate activity has increased to a larger degree, to considerable effect. Missions also have a record of using their immunity to provide asylum to democrats under threat, providing them shelter, as the US Embassy did for Chinese scientist and dissident Fang Lizhi, who spent almost a year there after the Tiananmen protests in 1989.

It often serves the purposes of repressive regimes to attribute peaceful civic protest to outside agitation from foreign countries, including their embassies, as the case studies on Egypt and Russia illustrate. Further, there is a long history of repressive governments warning individual diplomats that their activities threaten to compromise their immunity, and that expulsion could follow. Such warnings are often accompanied by the presentation of police photos of diplomats attending demonstrations or meeting activists, a technique apartheid-era South Africa copied from police states in Eastern Europe and the Union of Soviet Socialist Republics (USSR). To underscore the warning to diplomats that that their immunity is tenuous, pressure sometimes extends to intimidation and even violence against family members. A more pernicious technique is the use of gangs of toughs to harass and intimidate diplomats by proxies, such as the disturbances created by Nashi, the

Kremlin-sponsored youth group against the UK ambassador in Moscow. Old habits of intimidation die hard, even if they seldom succeed.

More complex are cases of authoritarian regimes such as Cuba that withdraw diplomats' normal access to local authorities when they are alleged to be supporting local opposition or reform activists and movements. But here, too, there are costs, as reciprocal access will be curtailed against the country's own diplomats abroad. Most democratic embassies in Cuba have managed to sustain a supportive relationship with representatives of civil society, despite the state's attitude.

Such efforts to intimidate and discourage outreach to civil society have usually been in vain over the long term and only serve to deepen diplomatic isolation. The consequences of reciprocal action curtailing the access and mobility of their own diplomats abroad, together with the costs in terms of the relationship's benefits, are often enough for authorities to accept reasonable ground rules for diplomats' access to civil society.

That being said, there is an emerging genre of isolated and internationally shunned dictatorial regimes indifferent to or disdainful of the benefits of diplomatic interchange altogether, to the costs of local society. Diplomats in Belarus and Zimbabwe, for example, have been working in such an atmosphere of withdrawal from international reality, as our case studies on those countries demonstrate. The actions of the government of Iran against diplomatic missions have been similarly harsh, from the time that the revolutionary regime authorized the occupation of the US Embassy and the holding hostage of diplomatic personnel in 1979. These actions show that there is a side to the government that is indifferent to costs to Iran internationally of such conduct. As our case studies on Cuba, Russia, Belarus and Zimbabwe illustrate, circles in the political and security apparatus show indifference to foreign public opinion, international norms or even to benefits that their people could derive from greater outside contact.

The practice of greater reliance on locally engaged employees extends to responsibility for contact with civil society and liaison work on the ground to support democracy development. The authorities in Iran actually placed local employees of the British Embassy on trial as surrogates for embassy officials who have immunity, in an attempt to discredit the 2009-2010 protests in the public mind. In such circumstances, diplomats are mindful of the need not to expose locally engaged colleagues or others to the risk of arbitrary retribution. Embassies have developed internal protocols and training to reduce the vulnerability of local non-diplomatic status personnel.

The Support of Home Authorities

Unambiguous support from their own authorities in sending capitals provides diplomats with effective leverage, the ability to link benefits to behaviour, and in extremis, the opportunity to recommend the imposition of sanctions.

Nota bene: Diplomatic relations are reciprocal. As benefits are a two-way street, linkage provides diplomats with leverage to work in favour of greater freedom of action for diplomats in support of civil society. Diplomats can urge their own capitals to facilitate or discourage access for visiting host country officials seeking potentially advantageous business or other partners, and home-state cooperation programs and connections. Diplomats also generate crucial support from home authorities when their own nationals come under attack abroad.

Once on an assignment, multi-tasked diplomats are often stressed under the burden of a variety of reporting and representational requirements. Reports indicate a tendency of senior managers to discourage ongoing democracy development activity in favour of more apparently immediate bureaucratic functions. This argues for clear and explicit corporate support from headquarters for human rights and democracy defence as core priorities of the country programs. The ultimate human rights officer should be the ambassador, even if specifically confrontational personal situations are avoided.

Coup and Crisis Management

In his recollections of a working life spent in the British diplomatic service, Ambassador Sherard Cowper-Coles (2012) emphasizes a "truth about diplomacy: just as soldiers love a good fight (but can't say so), so diplomats love a good crisis (but won't admit it). In each case, it is what the profession is about."

Many episodes requiring the support and even intervention of diplomats develop rapidly. Events in Egypt from 2011 through to the re-seizure of power by the military in July 2013 illustrate the complexity of communications and advice from the US and other embassies which become the local symbol of an outside country's support or non-support in a volatile situation. It is essential that officers in the field be able to respond to the requirements without worrying that their actions will be second-guessed at headquarters, and their careers affected negatively. Otherwise, hesitant embassies may fail to oppose arbitrary uses of force by the government in time, or may fail to take action early enough to precipitate a coup against a legitimate government. Some democratic embassies in Moscow in September 1991 hesitated in this way to condemn the coup. This is a powerful argument for training foreign service officers in democracy support and human rights beforehand. Case study simulation is an increasingly frequent preparatory tool for diplomats.

The leaders of authoritarian states generally want international prestige and positive reception on international travel, not to mention business partnerships sought by industry and economic interests at home. This enables democratic embassies to condition their support for helping to arrange such media, political and business contacts on moderation of anti-democratic behaviour.

In cases when authorities try to intimidate diplomatic representatives, the support of home authorities is crucial. Canadian diplomats reacted to the South African foreign ministry's warnings of expulsion in the 1980s by pointing out that the South African Embassy in Ottawa would suffer swift retaliation with a corresponding negative impact on South African economic and other interests.

It is now apparent that in 2004, the warning by senior US diplomats that their government would freeze Ukrainian officials' personal offshore assets in the event of the Ukraine government's repression had considerably affected decision makers who might otherwise have ordered the use of force against demonstrators.

Sanctions can be a powerful weapon to moderate repressive behaviour, provided they have sufficiently widespread international support. If they are invoked out of general enmity, however, they can be counterproductive, enabling an authoritarian regime to claim a role of patriotic defence against outside interference. Even when regimes feign indifference, as Pinochet did when the United States cut off all but humanitarian aid to Chile in 1976, the international opprobrium of sanctions stings, as does the economic impact.

Selective targeting of responsible top officials' personal offshore financial and other transactions, as well as those of their families, is increasingly used against anti-democratic regimes, such as in Zimbabwe, Burma/Myanmar and, in 2012, Russia. US Congress passed the Magnitsky Act as a measure against the Russian officials implicated in the death of auditor Sergei Magnitsky, who died in prison after presenting evidence of massive fraud by Russian tax officials. Diplomats on the ground advise home authorities on timing, targeting and potential impact of sanctions being considered. For example, the EU targeted sanctions of travel bans and asset freezes on 31 individuals in Belarus and 126 in Zimbabwe were developed in consultation with EU missions.

As pointed out earlier, though, it should be borne in mind that the threatened use of sanctions can sometimes be more influential in promoting behaviour modification than the finality of sanctions themselves. Sanctioning an unpopular regime can have the effect of punishing the most vulnerable in civil society, or curtailing exposure to international visitors and other beneficial contacts with the outside.

A cautionary note about "megaphone" diplomacy: Taking a public stand to denounce the clear abuse of rights of individuals, or suppression, is important. But if the motivation is more to cater to a domestic audience by publicly "bashing" an adversary, the effect on the ground can be negative, for embassies and democratic civil society allies alike. Private demarches to an authoritarian government and low-key media references can have more concrete outcomes. Diplomats may find they need to discourage home authorities from seeking to reap tempting domestic political dividends from threatening statements against unpopular regimes.

International solidarity is very pertinent, particularly since the impact of sanctions can be neutralized when there are offsetting flows of material support from non-democracies or opponents of sanctions, as in Zimbabwe, Burma/Myanmar or Belarus today. Iran receives reinforcement for repressive behaviour from its beneficial validation from, for example, Venezuela, which professes to be like-minded. In return, Iran has continued to support the beleaguered and internationally sanctioned Assad regime in Syria with weapons and financing.

When nationals who are human rights activists are threatened or arrested, the declaration of support for their situation can be crucial. As James Mawdsley, who was imprisoned in Burma/Myanmar for his human rights work, put it, there are "ways in which consular duties were more than consular." He commented "If the FCO [Foreign & Commonwealth Office] had not said the same thing on the outside, I would have been beaten up. But the regime was too afraid to beat me up over issues where the FCO gave me backing."

Influence

In the new paradigm of public diplomacy, diplomats more consciously represent their whole society to the host society, beyond traditional government-to-government communication. The reputation of the society they represent and project locally, its experience, values and capacities to help are deployable assets. Democracies that have only recently emerged from repressive conditions themselves may have experience that has special relevance. The effect of public diplomacy is obviously reinforced where the sending country's institutions, achievements, governance and lifestyles have appeal locally, adding credibility through the force of example in dialogue with local authorities on democratic development — but not all democracies have comparable influence to bring to bear. The threat of suspending membership in multilateral organizations can also be invoked when necessary. Indeed, regional and transnational bodies follow a variety of plans and practices to encourage members in the effort to build democratic and transparent governance.

Examples: Countries in transition tend to identify with the examples of those to which they can readily relate. On some mentoring issues, the best mentors can often be those of countries with recent comparable experience in democratization. As a Czech ambassador expressed his country's interest in democracy support, "We were grateful for the help we received from the West in the 1980s. So it should be a priority in our foreign policy to help."

Polish Foreign Minister Radek Sikorski described how:

> there is very little that we as outsiders can do to affect events, except to set a good example. We sponsored a multipart documentary in Arabic on the Polish democratic transition on Al Jazeera. We sent Lech Walesa to Tunisia to tell them how we did it. I was the first foreign minister in Benghazi, when Qaddafi was still fighting. And meeting with the then Provisional National Council made me realize that the challenges that these societies face are identical to what we in central Europe faced two decades ago. (*Foreign Affairs*, 2013)

Influence is also a function of international stature and impact. At least until popular unrest in the spring of 2013 tarnished its image, Turkey had become a prominent role model for many Arab reformers because of its apparent success in bridging religion and democracy and because of its economic performance. Much is made of the purported rivalry for influence of China and the United States. China's indifference to human rights standards in authoritarian countries may earn favour from such leaders, but the central fact of influence is more likely to be determined by the impact a major power can have on conditions in the country concerned.

It is no doubt true that economic or political difficulties at home can reduce the amount of influence a democracy can deploy abroad because its example is less appealing and because its attention to foreign opportunities is reduced. But great powers have multiple points of direct and indirect leverage.

The military handbook, *Military Engagement: Influencing Armed Forces Worldwide to Support Democratic Transitions* (Blair, 2013), outlines the ways in which close relations between uniformed personnel — that are built, among other reasons, as a result of training together — can build significant influence in times of crisis, when the military's role can be crucial. A similar effect can be seen in relations of confidence between partners within the intelligence community.

The European Union's requirement that applicants for membership fulfill the acquis communautaire of democratic and effective governance has had a profound influence on building what is an enlarging arc of stability and democracy across Europe.

Outside inducements to undertake a rigorous program of democratization and institution-building also emerge from conditionalities that are increasingly prominent features of multilateral and bilateral relationships. These exist on every continent, including standards of regional organizations, though there is often a yawning gap between theory and practice.

African peer pressure, the efforts of the African Union, and the best practices approach of the New Partnership for Africa's Development, as well as positive governance conditions from international economic institutions, have had mixed effects on governance in Africa. To date, only a few African countries have followed up with the complete self-assessments of governance and action programs intended by the African Peer Review Mechanism. The role of civil society in governance remains unrecognized by African summits.

Progress toward greater democracy in Africa should, in principle, be reinforced by the obligations of membership in the Commonwealth of Nations and l'Organisation Internationale de la Francophonie, both of which state that the encouragement of democracy and human rights is at the core of their activity and purpose, as stated by the relevant Harare, Millbrook, and Bamako Declarations. However, enforcement can be soft and la Francophonie, in particular, tolerates dictatorships in its membership, such as the petro-dictatorship of Equatorial Guinea, ranked regularly by Freedom House as one of "the worst of the worst" for systematic human rights abuse.

The OAS supports democratic development in Latin America building deeper roots, although populist nationalism is evident in several countries. The OAS took a strong stand against what was labelled a military coup d'état in Honduras in 2009-2010.

Although some of its members, such as Vietnam, retain one-party non-democratic governance, the Association of Southeast Asian Nations (ASEAN) is at last making governance increasingly part of its mandate, as can be seen by its criticism of the regime in Burma/Myanmar before recent changes. Both Singapore and Malaysia have held multiparty elections. Australia's enhanced regional cooperation programs, via the Pacific Islands Forum, place governance development assistance at the centre of their mandate; both Australia and New Zealand have been strong players in efforts to encourage democratic outcomes in East Timor, the Solomon Islands and Fiji.

The central point here is that external support bolsters civil society in its efforts to construct democratic and effective governance in a suitable and organic fashion. This outward-looking aspiration provides diplomats geared to the merits of public diplomacy multiple opportunities. By choosing to showcase those aspects and features of their own democratic society which are most admired — for example, the way US diplomats can bond with the high esteem that the Lebanese hold for the quality of American post-secondary education — diplomats can at least help to compensate for any perception of policy differences between governments, or public resentment for foreign policy stands. The US Fulbright program and the EU's Erasmus Mundi constitute people-to-people tools, which have many counterparts elsewhere, and which can greatly improve the context within which US and European diplomatic representatives operate. But diplomats whose countries have themselves recently experienced winning and consolidating democratic reform may be able to bring special credibility to bear.

Funds

Small amounts of post funding can be precious to start-up reform groups and NGOs. While most democracy development financial support is provided through NGOs and institutions, small-grant seed money for grassroots organizations from discretely administered and easily disbursed post funds can have swift direct positive effect. However, authoritarian governments have taken issue with the practice of direct embassy financial support to local civil society and have made it illegal. This calls for selective alternative strategies.

Examples: In 2002, the Czech Ministry of Foreign Affairs established its Transformation Policy Unit and Fund to enable Czech embassies to support democratization, human rights and transition-related projects in countries with repressive regimes. Most of these projects were deliberately small to enable disbursement directly to local civil society actors without the local government's scrutiny and involvement.

There are numerous examples of embassies being empowered in this way. Sweden provides its embassies funding specifically for democracy development support. In South Africa in the 1980s, the Canadian government created a large embassy-administered fund with a mandate for direct assistance to civil society, especially assistance to victims of apartheid. The advantage of having the embassy administer the fund directly drew from the perception that diplomatic representatives on the ground are, in liaison with international NGOs, best placed to identify suitable partners and beneficiaries. The funds helped groups to sustain essential activity and often enabled small but identity-building successes, such as the distribution of T-shirts or publicity for civil society rallies, and funds were also dispersed in aid of legal support for human rights defenders.

Many embassies from democratic countries in Russia in the early 1990s also found that such small amounts they could disburse rapidly from post funds directly to soup kitchens, orphanages and women's groups, among others, were clearly having a helpful humanitarian effect and contributing to the rudimentary beginnings of civil society at an especially disruptive time in the society. Diplomats report that such programs earned a degree of public credit often not available from the heavily funded, large-scale infrastructure programs that characterized transitional assistance in those years. In Ukraine in 2004, embassy funding requiring little, if any, paperwork was critical to the survival of youth groups such as Pora! that, despite a lack of much administrative capacity, were able to stand up for the integrity of Ukraine's elections and for democracy itself at a decisive time.

There is, however, a downside in several countries where direct financing of advocacy groups is problematic. Obviously, diplomats have to be careful not to expose local members of civil society to the risk of political or even legal retribution. Some governments have made outside material support for advocacy or opposition groups a major issue. Most notoriously, Cuba has used embassy financial support as evidence to prosecute and convict activists. It is essential that foreign funding not be available to support specific political outcomes.

Russian authorities took exception to the role they allege that foreign foundation and embassy funds played in helping to finance the "colour" revolutions in Europe, which the Russians perceived as being against "their" candidates and interests. They charged that the funding overstepped the line by supporting specific partisan political outcomes, when, in fact, outside financing for political parties was at the margin. Its purpose was to support civil society's right to free and fair elections, not to back specific contestants for power. Nonetheless, as the Russian case study describes, the "orange shock" caused deepened adversarial attitudes from Russian authorities toward Russian NGOs. Severe constraints placed on the operational mobility of international NGOs have been aggravated in 2012-2013, despite efforts by ex-President Medvedev to seek a positive modus vivendi.

Non-political organizations that constitute the foundations of civil society are often able still to benefit from well-intended embassy support. Even most repressive regimes still make a differentiation between development NGOs and advocacy groups. International NGOs often can fill the role of providing small amounts of funding, but they do not act as surrogates for embassies.

Solidarity

Solidarity is a valued asset at all phases of democratic development. In democratic assistance programs among like-minded missions and international NGOs, solidarity multiplies impact and minimizes duplication. It also enhances political messaging through witnessing trials, joint demarches on human rights and other issues, and reduces the ability of authoritarian regimes to play the commercial interests of partners off against each other. Within civil society, NGOs and democratic reformers and activists value the solidarity of mentors with prior experience in democratic reform. Diplomats can assist in making the connections.

Examples: Solidarity among diplomats has been especially important in support of human rights defenders and democratic activists on trial for their activities. This expression of solidarity conveys to the authorities that the conduct of such proceedings is indeed being monitored by democratic partners, and not only by the country which may be more specifically concerned if there is an issue of dual nationality or some other national tie to defendants. Prominent early examples include the trial of Nelson Mandela in 1963 and the trials of Václav Havel and other human rights activists in Prague in the 1980s, followed by many in recent years, such as Daw Aung San Suu Kyi in Rangoon or Ayman Nour in Cairo.

Demonstrable gestures of solidarity are multiple and also include the appearance of working solidarity between democracies in the demonstration effort. French and US ambassadors attended vigils for murdered activists in Syria together and coordinated joint regional visits to cities where atrocities had taken place. Solidarity can also extend to the monitoring of prosecution of violence against human rights defenders, when its perpetrators are brought to trial because of international or other pressures — for example, the methodical attendance of resident EU diplomats at the trial of security personnel who had beaten Canadian-Iranian photojournalist Zahra Kazemi-Ahmadabadi to death in Tehran.

Solidarity in diplomatic representations through joint demarches can also multiply effectiveness. The virtually unprecedented prosecution and trial of locally engaged employees of the British Embassy in Tehran in 2009 has been met with a joint response from all EU missions. Forceful joint demarches have been called for when human rights come under stress in an allied country, such as the case in 2005 when the United States, the United Kingdom and Canada made a joint demarche to Afghan authorities against curbs on freedom of speech. Such representations have, however, been notoriously unsuccessful on several laws circumscribing the status of Afghan women.

Solidarity among donor democracies and with international NGOs has also been instrumental in avoiding duplication or errors of omission in democratic support programs. In Serbia in 2000, democracies and NGOs cooperated via a "donors' forum," which greatly increased the effectiveness and coverage of such assistance, a technique now in good use among democratic country embassies and NGOs in many locales.

The most effective form of solidarity among donors and democracy-supportive embassies is that which avoids competition and benefits from comparative advantage. As a Czech ambassador stated, "We learned how to plug in from the Dutch, the Norwegians and the US. We tried to find where we would have the most value added, and learned quickly that our democratic transition experience was that. So we concentrated on transfer of know-how. Not everything is transferable, of course. But we still had a lot to offer. If they want, they can even learn from our mistakes."

Civil Society Solidarity Is the Most Effective Form of Outside Democracy Development Support

In the transitional countries of Europe, building up to and following the great changes of 1989, the mentoring of successive reformers contributed to the self-confidence and effectiveness of catalytic groups in civil society — Solidarnosc had close ties to Czechoslovak and Hungarian dissidents in the late 1980s; Slovakian reformers helped Croatians, Serbians and Ukrainians in 2000–2004; and the Serbian youth movement Otpor! aided Pora! in Ukraine in 2004. Many of these efforts were facilitated or channelled by diplomats from countries that had undergone the earlier reforms, a pattern which has been apparent in Latin America and now characterizes the foreign policies of many newer democracies in their relationships throughout the world. The very effective Indian civil society protest initiative "I paid a bribe," with its astute use of social networks to expose petty corruption, has now locally generated initiatives in Kenya and Ukraine.

Legitimacy

Many democratic activists would agree with Francis Fukuyama (2004) that "in today's world, the only serious form of legitimacy is democracy." Diplomats themselves are personifications of the principle advanced by "Independent Diplomat" Carne Ross (2012) that "diplomacy's prerequisite is not sovereignty but authority." They bring to bear the authority of the state they represent, its influence and the legitimacy of its concern for those seeking to exercise rights considered to be universal.

Diplomats can draw for support from a variety of basic international agreements. Prominent examples include the UN Covenant on Civil and Political Rights, the Universal Declaration of Human Rights and the UN Declaration on Human Rights Defenders. These put forward the international norms that diplomats of democratic countries can legitimately claim to represent. Repressive jurisdictions may well maintain that such texts are not internationally binding on non-signatories and that outside support for democracy development and civil society amounts to interference in internal sovereign matters by foreign representatives, but international norms on human rights are increasingly conditioning behaviour and limiting the number of countries that insist on the primacy of national sovereignty, in part because specially mandated regional and other transnational authorities monitor performance.

Examples: Even authoritarian non-democracies go to elaborate lengths to buttress their claim to legitimacy through recourse to superficial facets of democratic practice: rigged elections and the shameless and profligate use of the word "democratic" to describe republics that are anything *but* democratic. On one hand, the affirmation of democratic belief provides considerable leverage to democratic governments to try to persuade such governments to open up more to their own civil society in reality; on the other hand, repressive governments' protestations that the support of democratic embassies and NGOs to civil society is illegitimate runs counter to such an affirmation. But these objections themselves counter a wide body of international and regional agreements calling for open democratic governance. The UN Secretary-General's Special Representatives on Human Rights, and on Torture, the Special Rapporteur on Human Rights Defenders in Africa, the African Union itself, the Inter-American Commission on Human Rights, the Charter of Paris for the OSCE, or Commonwealth of Nations, and la Francophonie charters can all be pointed to by democratic diplomatic representatives for validation of the legitimacy of their own efforts at democracy development support.

Regional agreements have been effective in conditioning the behaviour of some countries, although regimes that remain resistant to outside opinion, such as Uzbekistan, Zimbabwe, Syria or North Korea, are unlikely to be influenced. The most prominent example of an effective regional agreement is the CSCE Helsinki Accords, which provided the benchmark textual references in the 1980s for Charter 77 in Czechoslovakia, for the Sakharov-Bonner campaign in the USSR, and for freeing up information and expression generally. These agreements were effective because they had been signed by the states in question and provided a platform for citizens to confront them about the contradiction between word and deed.

A potentially similar example is Cuba's signature, in 2008, of the UN Covenant on Civil and Political Rights, which guarantees the rights to self-determination of citizens, their peaceful assembly, freedom of worship and freedom to leave the country. The signature alone provides diplomats with a commitment to point to in discussion of human rights with Cuban authorities.

FIFTEEN WAYS THAT DIPLOMATS HAVE MADE A DIFFERENCE

In putting their assets to work on behalf of supporting civil society's democrats and human rights defenders, diplomats draw from a tool box of activities and techniques. The tools described below are potentially powerful, especially when deployed using the proactive and public outreach approach that is the hallmark of modern democratic diplomacy.

Arranged in escalating sequence from more conventional diplomatic activities to more interventionist action, these tools offer diplomats the potential to develop and refine specific professional skill sets in democracy development support. These skills are also integrally related to skills needed for work in support of economic and social development, as well as human security. Democracy, after all, does not sit astride a hierarchy of needs: economic development, human security and human rights are interdependent and equally important to the human condition.

Nor do diplomats themselves sit astride the international community. Just as a vibrant civil society represents the essential foundation of democratic development, so international civil society accounts for much of the content of public-to-public relations today. In this respect, diplomacy is a complement and conduit for broader currents of international democracy development assistance that are occurring continuously.

The Golden Rules

Listening, Respecting and Understanding

All diplomats make it their task to try to grasp the culture, psychology and situation of their countries of accreditation. Sir Sherard Cowper-Coles (2012), who had successive assignments as Ambassador to Israel and Saudi-Arabia, "underlined the importance for a diplomat of showing both understanding and affection for the country to which he is accredited. Only then does the diplomat have a chance of making a difference. If he doesn't see the good — however limited — in his host country, he has little to work with." When diplomats include local NGOs and groups on their initial rounds of calls on taking up their postings, it gives a boost to civil society. This is especially true for the introductory calls by incoming heads of missions. It should be mandatory at the outset to seek advice from local civil society on how best to support their efforts. Respecting and understanding the different roles and interests of all partners in the democratic development process is a basic requirement for productive relationships and successful support. Outsiders also have to understand and respect the ways in which the local reform process needs to take account of traditional values: social and political practices common in one country can be abrasive in another.

Nota bene: Overall, the first maxim of "respecting" is to listen — ideally, in the language of the country. Deference to local culture is essential whenever possible. This includes the need for diplomats to recognize the risks and sacrifices incurred by democratic activists that protest authoritarian regimes, as well as the challenges reformers face in actually running for political office in semi-authoritarian settings. Dissidents need to make and offer the judgment whether contact with diplomats is protective and helpful, or whether it is untimely and risky. But their judgment should prevail.

Such as: Diplomats should also defer to the different and often primary roles played by international NGOs in local activity. Local NGOs should be respected. There were demonstrable lifts to civil society groups when newly arrived US Ambassador Harry Barnes made introductory calls to them at the same time as calling on officials of the Pinochet regime in Chile. Since then, connecting ambassadors and high-level visitors to civil society in countries where human rights are under stress has become almost routine. The high-level meetings of the EU and US in Russia, for example, now always include consultations with Russian NGOs. Norway's foreign service has been a leader in reaching out to NGOs. Vidar Helgeson, who was Norwegian Secretary of State before becoming Secretary-General of the International Institute for Democracy and Electoral Assistance (IDEA), has described Norway's approach as being "intensely interested in everything below the radar."

International NGOs are frequently closer to the ground than diplomats and often better able to pursue productive working partnerships with civil society. Diplomats need to know when to seek partnerships with them and when to recognize that the integrity of NGO work also needs distance from government connections, even when government programs in capitals provide project funding.

It should always be recognized that in repressive situations, democratic activists need space and often discretion. A Czech ambassador confides that countries which have themselves "experienced life under a repressive regime are often best placed to understand the situation of dissidents having to face their families and friends' vulnerability to reprisal — loss of job, imprisonment, worse — for their anti-regime activity." In Iran, a recent campaign by women's groups to obtain a million signatures from Iranian women on a petition to improve the status of women would have had its credibility undermined if opponents could show evidence of support from outside. On occasion, democratic activists, human rights defenders and reformers in Iran, Cuba or elsewhere have sent the message that they needed for a time to pursue their work without outside support.

Whatever the country, its preoccupations and identity issues are functions of its unique history and current conditions for ordinary people, and diplomats need to show sensitivity to them. In many traditional societies, local values can collide with the practices or aspirations of outsiders.

As political activities in most Western democracies are generally secular, Western analysts misunderstood the extent to which religious conviction needed to find reflection in democratic institutions in Egypt and Tunisia. In the most traditional Islamic societies, it has been necessary to respect the strength of tradition in supporting democratic transition on essential but challenging issues such as gender equality. A decade ago in Yemen, US Ambassador Barbara Bodine was able to support expanded women's rights without creating local traditionalist backlash by deferring to the need of local groups to build their bridges to others. By 2013, women were an important force in the post-Saleh constitutional convention discussions.

In Afghanistan, donor democracies have been keen to emphasize to publics back home the priorities of publicly valued issues such as girls' schooling, immunization and fighting corruption and drugs, while most Afghans were more concerned with jobs and the local availability of electricity. In 2009, the signing into law of provisions reducing the status of women in accordance with sharia law (in order to obtain electoral support from certain tribal areas) presented a real dilemma for countries attempting to build support at home for the costly efforts to help achieve democratic Afghan governance. The essence of "democratic diplomacy," then, has to be to find a middle ground respecting traditional values while enabling public support back home for the overall democratic and inclusive direction.

Chief EU diplomat Pierre Vimont acknowledges the problems that have arisen from the tendencies diplomats have had from being an inherently "conservative profession," leading to an over-investment in the status quo and failure to see the warning signs of a popular drive for change. Carne Ross (2012) writes that this "inherited tradition" assigns a "hierarchy of priorities where security...ranks at the top, followed by economic interests....In recent years, it has become fashionable for the exponents of foreign policy to talk about 'values' as important in diplomacy — things like democracy and human rights. But in truth the underlying calculus remains little changed, as does the diplomatic mindset."

Writing of the failure of the UK Foreign Office to foresee the Iranian revolution of 1979, Sir Sherard Cowper-Boles (2012: 52) cites an internal Foreign and Commonwealth Office inquiry which "concluded that the Embassy in Iran had been too preoccupied with selling tanks and tractors to the shah to notice what was happening in the bazaars of South Tehran." But Cowper-Boles adds that the comment, made by the UK Ambassador in Tehran at the time, Sir Anthony Parsons (later Ambassador to the United Nations), "was probably closer to the mark: 'our failure to foresee the fall of the Shah was [Parsons wrote], due not to a failure of intelligence or information, but to a failure of imagination. We simply could not conceive of Iran without the Shah.' Just as later we found it difficult to imagine Egypt without Mubarak, or Libya without Quadafi" (ibid.).

The errors of the diplomatic mindset also became vividly apparent when the Arab Spring came as such a surprise to Western analysts and authorities. It is equally important now that they display the patience that is consonant with the need for time to build effective democratic governance.

Sharing

Solidarity among democracies multiplies effectiveness. Like-minded embassies and engaged international NGOs need to share information and practice project coordination and team play in order to optimize beneficial impacts. Cooperation on democracy development support between democracies of the global "North" and "South" is still at an early stage, but can be especially effective. Monitoring elections is frequently done as a shared diplomatic project. All these efforts are most effective when local partners are also a prominent part of the sharing process and are able to assume responsible local "buy-in." Diplomats in the field can become "cohering agents" of support programs combining democracy and development.

Nota bene: It is generally easier to organize informal cooperation in the field than among capitals, especially among representatives of like-minded countries. Informal cooperation often also includes international NGOs, which are well placed to provide a wider and more authentic picture of grassroots and technical activity to promote democracy development. An emphasis on "sharing," however, must respect the differences in role between embassies and NGOs. As embassies diversify activity in democracy assistance, diplomats need to defer to the prior, primary and often locally preferred engagements of NGOs in the field.

Such as: Missions regularly compare analyses of country situations, specifically regarding human rights in countries such as China, where the issues are complicated and evolving, making assessments difficult. In repressive situations such as in Burma/Myanmar until recent developments, some democratic embassies worked closely together to exchange information and coordinate strategies, and then regularly met with a broader group of democratic embassies from the region.

The central point is that there should not be a competition among like-minded democratic missions, resident and non-resident, as described by a Czech ambassador in the earlier section on solidarity. The best outcomes are when missions work within informal "affinity groups," permitting some to defer to work already ongoing or to specifically advantageous roles of others, or even to compensate for the handicaps of others due to difficulties in their bilateral relations.

Diplomatic representatives share duties to monitor and verify functions, such as court dates and trials of democracy activists or scholars, or when possible, to cover such events in force, highlighting the international political stakes for repressive regimes. The practice has been extensive, from South Africa in the 1960s to selective use as appropriate in Burma/Myanmar, Iran, Russia and Venezuela, though in recent trials of prisoners of conscience in China and Iran, diplomats have been excluded from witnessing the legal proceedings.

Joint demarches are also de rigueur on human rights and democratic transparency. Sometimes, because of specific and long-standing issues in bilateral relations, particular embassies and governments are more "radioactive" than others. This may leave more room for the less controversial to sustain contact and protection. A differentiation of roles that best enables particular countries to play to comparative strengths, credibility and experience is very useful, without suggesting that such activity is a surrogate for the interests of others.

In Burma/Myanmar, some European democratic representatives plugged into other countries' programs that were already running, such as the Netherlands' "foreign policy training" seminars in the region for young refugees from Burmese ethnic groups. Some missions enjoy or have connections to cultural facilities, which they share with other embassies, or make available to non-resident diplomats on a visit, as the French cultural organization the Alliance Française has done in Burma/Myanmar.

Sharing information locally on development issues, including on governance support activity, is becoming recognized as essential to avoid duplication or omissions, and increasingly includes international NGOs and multilateral agencies active in the country. In rapidly developing crises, democratic embassies and international NGOs have often set up informal coordinating and clearing house groups for fast disbursal of aid to local civil society and the electoral process, such as the "Donors Group" in Belgrade in 2000.

It is most productive when democratic host governments are themselves dynamic partners in the process — though not when more authoritarian regimes insist on controlling all development funding, as in Nepal when NGO funds had to be channelled through the Queen.

Bangladesh's Local Consultative Group plenary brought together 32 Bangladesh-based representatives of donor missions and multilateral agencies with key local officials. Supplementary groupings such as the Like-minded Donor Group comprised local representatives of Canada, Denmark, the Netherlands, Norway and Sweden. These groups work in turn with groups of NGOs, such as the Bangladesh Rural Advancement Committee or the Association for Development Agencies, which have track records of enhancing the democratic input by civil society into the development process. The process can go beyond coordination into joint programming: in Ghana, with the support of a government and civil society seeking governance development assistance, like-minded donor countries (Canada, Denmark, the Netherlands and the United Kingdom) have created a collaborative US$8 million program, the Ghana Research and Advocacy Program.

There has been, of course, a contrary narrative of inadequate donor coordination, particularly in circumstances of post-conflict reconstruction where the aid flows are very substantial and usually urgent. In Bosnia-Herzegovina, the international tendency was initially toward too much humanitarian assistance, not always strategically coordinated, but insufficient development assistance. There was also inadequate coordination of planning and operations for development and security. Later, in Afghanistan, the aid effort began in 2001 with an unprecedented degree of donor coordination that enabled an overall development strategy. But in subsequent years, it fell much more to diplomats, aid officials and the military of individual missions to try to ensure coordination and effectiveness on the ground. "Coordinating groups" proliferated with only mixed results as far as international coordination is concerned, though UN and NATO representatives are working now to encourage the integration of democracy support, development and defence in a coordinated way. The US Agency for International Development (USAID), for example, launched Making All Voices Count, a cooperative program with British and Swedish development assistance authorities and the Omidyan Network to support inclusive governance and development, especially in new democracies in Sub-Saharan Africa and South Asia.

An extremely important potential development is an exercise in South-North sharing of experience and cooperation which also bridges government and civil society: The Open Government Partnership is an extension of bilateral cooperation between Brazil and the United States to work together to support inclusive development in new democracies. Founding members of the intergovernmental organization are Brazil, Indonesia, Mexico, Norway, the Philippines, South Africa, the United Kingdom and the United States. They are joined by leading civil society representatives from Brazil (Instituto de Estudos Socioeconomicos), India (Mazdoor Kisan Shakti Sangathan), Kenya (African Centre for Open Governance), Mexico (Instituto Mexicano para la Competetividad), and Tanzania (Twaweza). There are now almost 50 participating countries from the South and North. The commitments and goals include fiscal transparency, training of officials, access to information and citizen participation.

Truth in Communications

Reporting

Confidential assessment to home authorities is at the centre of the diplomat's traditional role. Missions' regular assessments — of the local situation, capacity, and psychological, political or even cultural constraints — on the likelihood of a democratic process emerging or being successfully sustained can help develop a template approach to benchmarks and norms that will assist in comparisons and common evaluations by NGOs and centres of excellence. Accurate reporting of human rights situations forms the basis for international scrutiny and helps to determine whether to initiate official intervention.

Nota bene: Reporting must be demonstrably comprehensive and balanced in its sourcing. Diplomatic professionals always heed the caution that their confidential and value-added reporting of circumstances and conditions in the host country should draw from a wide range of contacts in the society and avoids excessive deference to official sources or to overarching security or other bilateral interests.

Such as: The "township attachés" at the British Embassy in early-1990s South Africa are an early example of the need to get out of the capital. There are multiple examples of regular human rights reporting, since this is a core vocation of diplomatic representation, made virtually mandatory by the various national and international human rights monitoring requirements.

In high profile and relatively open crisis situations, mission reporting competes with international media, but because of the extensive reductions in foreign coverage, media correspondents today are often "fly-in/fly-out" non-experts who have to rely on diplomats, NGOs and "fixers" to obtain context or important background. There are frequently situations, such as in Zimbabwe or Iran, where international media have been basically expelled.

The responsibility of missions to report the conditions and prospects for change is enhanced, though rendered more difficult by a regime very suspicious of contacts between citizens and foreign representatives. In Zimbabwe, diplomats, including ambassadors, have undertaken fact-finding missions in the countryside to document the beatings and intimidation of Movement for Democratic Change (MDC) supporters, which Zimbabwe security personnel have tried ineffectively to block. We know from Wikileaks of the excruciatingly accurate portrayals of personal excess and offensive official entitlement that have been reported by US diplomats on post in authoritarian situations such as Tunisia and Uzbekistan.

Many examples of misleading diplomatic reporting exist. Some situations are potentially so unprecedented in the experience of observers that there is a tendency of diplomatic representatives empathetic toward the country to "look away from the dark signs," as occurred in the build-up to unimaginable atrocity in Rwanda in 1994.

A failure to do people-level reporting has led to persistent and damaging misreadings of the public mood, assumptions of assured continuity in power, and missing the signs of impending ethnic or communal conflict. Some authoritarian regimes have objected to having a strategic ally contact their domestic opposition, or even reporting confidential adversary political analysis back home, a condition that constrained US official reporting on Iran in the 1970s, leading to an underestimation of the public groundswell for reform. A form of over-deference to the need for restraint has caused some countries to speak about the "participation" of Saudi Arabians in a political process, rather than speaking about democracy itself.

Conversely, home country headquarters can themselves become overly reliant on their leaders' relationships with specific authoritarian leaders, and may discourage or ignore diplomatic reporting that is critical of a given regime, as happened in the past in Pakistan, Egypt and Indonesia, among many examples. EU representatives in Ethiopia in 2005 repeatedly warned authorities in Brussels that "basic human rights abuses are being committed by the government on a daily basis," and that "the EU must respond firmly and resolutely" — but nothing happened (Barr, 2011).

Informing

In circumstances where the host state attempts to interrupt or circumscribe access to information, providing the public with pertinent objective information is a public service of open diplomacy. Supporting the emergence of local independent media, which is an essential companion of democratic governance, is a valued contribution by democracies, as is assisting the development of objective public broadcasting in transitional and emerging democracies. From outside, several international support programs exist to enable Internet users in countries shutting down local networks and sites to access alternative servers beyond the regime's control.

Nota bene: The existence of a healthy independent local media sector is an essential component of democratic governance. Independent media support has, in consequence, become a basic tool of public diplomacy. The value of independent media outlets is commonly associated with enabling a plurality of voices, including responsible political opposition. From both developmental and governance points of view, the existence of sustainable, independent media able to monitor and advocate the quality of governance is an under-recognized but essential audit asset, in both developing and developed democracies.

Such as: In the absence of free information, the regular communication of news bulletins and information by missions have been used to help fill gaps and correct the record on international or other matters, especially as authoritarian regimes are apt to expel foreign correspondents who criticize them. Today's embassies use websites to communicate to a much larger audience than printed communication had permitted in the past, and manage to prompt an interactive conversation with the local readership.

Preserving access to the Internet is now a central interest of democracies. International cooperative software programs can now be downloaded by Internet users to enable access to international news outlets such as BBC World Service, Radio Free Europe/Radio Liberty, Radio-France and Al-Jazeera in societies where broadcast or online transmissions are jammed in crisis situations. In such circumstances, diplomats can also serve as witnesses of events and developments otherwise hidden from international view through interviews with international outlets. These reports frequently find their way back to the closed society itself by being picked up by local language border services, as exist among the Burmese refugee communities clustered over the border with Thailand.

Defending journalists in support of such organizations as Reporters Without Borders, PEN International and various national NGOs is an important part of human rights defence. Iran and China lead the world for imprisonment of journalists reporting factual stories of journalistic merit, a practice that stands in the way of normal relations with societies that enjoy freedom of the press. Canada's leading media development organization, Journalists for Human Rights, has mentoring programs in techniques of reporting local issues in the interest of transparency specifically for journalists "covering city hall."

The merits of adversarial broadcasting from outside vary. Essentially, adversarial broadcasts, such as those sponsored and funded by the US government in Cuba in past years tend to be discounted as propaganda. When they emphasize, instead, objectively presented news and non-political magazine content, such as the Farsi language reporting of BBC World Service (that is feared by authorities because of its credibility), they can be very effective in enabling a fact-based counter-story to regime propaganda.

A very noteworthy initiative is the satellite TV service Belsat, founded by Agnieszka Romaszewska-Guzy, and supported financially by the Polish Ministry of Foreign Affairs. Since December 2007, Belsat, in collaboration with Polish public TV Telewizja Polska, and drawing from a large network of news contributors in Belarus, has transmitted programming and objective news from transmitters in Poland.

In Africa, radio is a more widespread information medium than the Internet. In 2012, the US Information Agency produced a dedicated radio information service for Northern Mali when it was under occupation by rebels. Increasingly, information platforms are being re-profiled to reach hand-held communications devices, which are becoming the dominant technology in Africa.

The US Department of State's Bureau of Conflict and Stabilization Operations (CSO) has supported the efforts of the Syrian Opposition Coalition to provide Syrians with real-time broadcasting, not from outside the country, but from inside. Broadcasting professionals mentor Syrian personnel in broadcasting techniques, and the support program provides equipment such as small hand-held transmitters. Residents of Syria's major population centres can tune into programming that covers topics such as the role of women in leadership and the psychological impact of war on Syrian children. The reporters associated with the Free Syria broadcast services are accredited alongside national and international media at all opposition news events. The program will help to assure a reliable public information network during a political transition.

The mentality of repressive regimes emerges clearly from the indictments presented by the public prosecutor of Tehran against Iranian citizens in a 2009 show trial. Those indicted were variously accused of having colluded with Western governments, foundations and individuals in "exposing cases of violations of human rights," training reporters in "gathering information" and "presenting full information on the 2009 electoral candidates." The charges suggest that Iranian citizens are meant to believe that abusing human rights and repressing information, including on candidates for public office, are all in the national interest.

Helping start-up independent media outlets has been an increasing activity in democratic development support and there are many examples of such support, especially in transitional situations, such as *Ukrainska Pravda*, Croatia's 1990s *Feral Tribune*, or *Sud* in Senegal. In Senegal in 1985, a journalist-editor sought start-up funding for a desktop-published newspaper. The US Embassy put him in contact with the Ford Foundation and within months, the daily newspaper *Sud* was on its way to its current position as a preeminent daily newspaper at the centre of a conglomerate, Sud Communication. As a diplomat there at the time observed, "Through its reporting, it has made government more transparent and opened new channels for political dialogue, thereby bolstering Senegal's political system." The successful transition from the regime of President Abdoulaye Wade relied on relatively free reporting in Senegalese media.

The Portuguese Embassy in Moscow gave seed funding to a fledgling private radio station that became, the flagship of a communications "empire." In Algeria, democratic governments contributed to such start-ups, but at the same time supported the improvement and expansion of standards and coverage on the part of state press and broadcasting.

In recent years, missions have supported bloggers and websites such as StopTheBribes.net in Nigeria (built with help from the Canadian High Commission), which enables mobile phone users to immediately report police misbehaviour, among other things.

In Honduras, an effort to combat corruption and improve accountability relies on improvements in transparency. The US CSO has helped the Honduras Security Tax Commission to build a website enabling the public to track spending of tax revenues as a pilot project to lay the foundation for broader transparency effort and create the habit of greater governmental accountability.

Multiple international programs exist to support the upgrade of journalistic norms, through workshop and mentoring programs that emphasize the need to report all sides to a story, and to counter hostile and inflammatory rhetoric. Diplomatic officers scout for candidates for individual journalist support programs that are particularly suited to the circumstances of the country. The US Department of State's Hubert

H. Humphrey Fellowship Program includes journalists in its fellowships for future African leaders, picked by US diplomatic personnel on the ground. In Colombia, the UK Embassy proposed safety training for journalists and a training program to help them report more effectively on specific issues there, such as child abuse. In some societies with severe limitations on the press, Czech embassies have provided non-political courses in basic film and media training, including how to write an article, work with a camera and edit. These skills were vital in covering 2007's abortive "Saffron Revolution" in Burma/Myanmar.

In post-authoritarian circumstances, state broadcasters, in particular, benefit from outside journalistic training. In South Africa, a consortium of public broadcasters from Australia, the United Kingdom and Canada aided the conversion of radio and television from being instruments of state propaganda into responsible news and information agencies. In all these transitional circumstances, diplomatic missions have useful contributions to make by providing access to content, as well as to training.

Helping to use the visits of foreign democratic leaders and their in-country press events is also useful. For example, in Algiers, the robust exchanges between visiting political leaders and their accompanying press corps had an exemplary effect on the normally passive local journalists witnessing the journalistic give-and-take of the visitors.

In circumstances where communications are blocked or where services are prohibitively expensive, embassy and consular information offices, libraries and cultural centres provide precious connections to the outside world. The American Cultural Center in Rangoon was a survivor of the sorts of information outlets the United States maintained decades ago and, during the harsh periods of the regime's crackdown, played a vital role in making books, DVDs, Internet connections, seminars and English lessons available to an avidly interested population. Other embassies in Rangoon were also able to provide Internet access to those who are willing to expose themselves to security scrutiny from Burmese police. In the absence of journalists, certain democratic missions — Australia, the United States, the United Kingdom and others — were able to report publicly to international news outlets what they were able to witness, and these reports were then played back to the Burmese, especially via exile news organizations, often in frontier areas, where the state was not able to block incoming transmissions entirely. When all foreign news correspondents were expelled from Burma/Myanmar in 2007-2008, UK Ambassador Mark Canning objectively described to outside journalists the "fearful and angry" mood of the population, and provided analysis of the regime's probable intentions. His words found their way back to the Burmese public.

Working with the Government

Advising

In transitional situations, working with local authorities and civil society in support of their capacity for effective and transparent democratic governance is a core vocation of most diplomatic missions and diplomats from Community of Democracies member states. Clearly, it is easier for democracies to work as partners with governments already in the process of transition, but engaging with still-authoritarian regimes on joint interests can often build confidence that permits advice and representation on governance and human rights issues a better hearing.

Nota bene: Considerable experience has now been accumulated concerning advice to governments managing democratic transitions, especially in Europe post-1989 and in Africa. Initially, strong emphasis was placed on economic governance. Advice was, as the Russian case study underlines, often inappropriate to the circumstances and capacities at the time, leading to the oversimplification and underestimation of the problems of lack of capacity. Increasing attention has since been paid to reforms aimed at improving the machinery of governance and public oversight, and deepening democratic accountability, as well as advising how to encode human rights, legislative and electoral practices, and the role of civil society. Diplomatic representatives have even been able to advise on areas believed to be culturally sensitive by situating the advice carefully, such as the work of many diplomats in counselling on the expansion of the rights of women, and on inclusive pluralism, the rights of refugees or indigenous peoples.

Such as: The body of best practices over the years comprises a substantial record of different techniques. Often, regional programs to improve democratic governance have a special resonance as they draw more directly from the experiences of nearby countries that have recently passed through roughly similar phases of democratic development. Diplomatic representatives who were part of that experience have a special credibility and role to play. Whatever the democracy providing advice, it must be made clear to government authorities that outsiders are not taking political sides.

Blair's (2013) military handbook outlines the experience of uniformed personnel from democracies advising counterparts in the "deep state" of military and security departments of government on issues of democratic governance, emphasizing the obligations military officers usually share to defend the people. Enhancing civilian control of the military is a function of supporting the enhancement of civilian capacity and advising the military.

Some advice is transferable from direct analogous experience, such as the role of Mauritius in advising neighbouring countries such as Tunisia in the organization of elections. Chile counselled South African authorities on the establishment of a Truth and Reconciliation Commission, a technique central to closure to the trauma of conflict that has been used in adapted forms elsewhere, such as Rwanda. As

Gillian Slovo, South African writer and human rights activist has noted, there will be some more interested in truth than in reconciliation, but the interplay of justice and coming to terms with the past to permit going forward follows similar patterns in different post-authoritarian and post-conflict societies. A model question on preparation material for the 2013 French baccalaureate exam in philosophy asked responders to weigh whether "peace" is more important to assure than "truth." Truth and reconciliation experience can be usefully interdependent but benefit from taking others' experience into account.

There is also a long record of ineffective or counterproductive advice, often stemming from an overreliance on outside consultants with little experience with working conditions in the consumer country. The founder of a Russian bank recalls asking outside financial consultants sent by an international financial institution to leave his premises on the grounds their advice was hewn entirely from optimum conditions available in Western financial centres, but not in Moscow. He agreed to invite them back only if they first observed how local employees needed to relate to local conditions and capacities, and then tried themselves to function in the local circumstances before attempting to work together to upgrade the operation. It is up to donor missions to make the point that there may be an overreliance on expensive outside consultants with little familiarity with local culture and practice, and to propose experts with more relevant expertise. Patrice McMahon and Jon Western (2009) cite another example, through the words of a Bosnian NGO officer: "Bosnians have come to understand the bargain well. Westerners came with money and ideas, wanting to do good. In the end, we waste their money and they waste our time."

As this *Handbook* stresses, strategic partnerships with some authoritarian regimes are essential to international peace and security, and to national interests of the democracy concerned. As the current US administration points out, engagement can enhance the prospects for communicating key points about governance and transparency, and for legitimizing the space occupied by civil society. The key to credibility is consistency.

Dialoguing

Diplomats on the ground take part in, and supplement, regularly scheduled government-to-government human rights and democracy discussion. The aim is to ensure that democracy development and respect for human rights are maintained in balance near the centre of the relationship, and that host authorities accept that cooperation programs are conditional on positive trends of governance. Such regular discussion can also aim to legitimize democracy development support work undertaken by missions in collaboration with local civil society. The promotion of dialogue processes to promote common ground in divided societies is a strong emphasis of international organizations such as the International IDEA, which has undertaken several participatory dialogue exercises in support of positive change in countries such as Guatemala, Mauritania and Nepal.

Nota bene: It is important that such government-to-government discussions be held regularly. They need to cover the "end-state" aims in democracy development and not be confined to specific and sporadic human rights violations or outrages. In order to avoid the "fig leaf" effect of going through the motions for the sake of appearances, discussants should, ideally, not be limited to host country diplomatic authorities, but also include authoritative representatives of "power ministries," as well as having the in-country support of security agencies of both sides. It is essential that the dialogue not be degraded into just a process at the expense of substance.

Such as: Many Community of Democracies members undertake human rights dialogues with partners under bilateral agreements such as the EU "structural dialogues" or its monitoring obligations under the "essential human rights clause" of the Cotonou Agreement with African, Caribbean and Pacific area partners.

Several of China's partners maintain human rights dialogues with Chinese authorities. The European Union and the United Kingdom have urged China to ratify the International Covenant on Civil and Political Rights and have discussed how China might meet the requirements of articles 6 (death penalty), 9 (arbitrary arrest and punishment), and 14 (right to a fair trial). There is interest among NGOs to see China being held to fulfill Article 19 on freedom of information.

While any dialogue is better than none, the dialogues should always aim for some results on the broader picture of democratic governance; the risk is that reluctant regimes will only go through the motions and maintain the status quo in practical terms, and even pretend the dialogue confers a seal of approval. Or self-confident countries feeling the pressure may simply refuse to hold human rights dialogues, as was the case of Iran with the European Union. Russia holds dialogues on human rights, but only outside of Russia.

Dialogues should not skirt issues embarrassing to the partner, such as corruption. Critical comment by international NGOs such as Transparency International or the International League for Human Rights deserves validation in human rights dialogues by democratic governments.

It is normal that degrees of disunity of purpose may emerge within the governments of transforming countries, between hardline authoritarians and more outward-looking officials. Hardliners who resist change are reinforced and emboldened if a parallel competition of purpose is discernible by representatives of democratic countries who are protecting special interests, such as occurred in the conduct of relations with Gadhafi's Libya.

Human rights dialogues are without practical effect if the intelligence and security agencies of a repressive regime are absent from discussion of human rights, or worse, can claim the authority of ongoing privileged relationships with the security agencies of the sending democracy. Such a human rights and justice dialogue, undertaken by US Ambassador Marilyn McAfee in Guatemala in 1994, was undermined by a parallel relationship of privilege and confidence between intelligence agencies. In general, the principle of "do no harm" has to be overriding in bilateral relationships across the board. Dictators rely on the decisive support of their security services for their continued rule and very survival. Getting these to the point where they will not open fire on peaceful demonstrations for human rights is often the key moment in a transition. Military attachés and intelligence officers within embassies can be central assets in the diplomacy of democracy.

Dialogues on human rights and democratic governance reinforce subsequent bilateral demarches by diplomatic representatives on specific cases, as discussed below. They can also serve as the place to establish the legitimacy both of diplomatic contacts with civil society and indirectly to validate certain activities of civil society without implying that the civil society groups are acting on anything other than their own domestic behalf.

Ultimately, of course, repressive regimes prefer to present decisions to moderate behaviour as being taken in their own interest and not as a result of outside pressure, though outside benefits resulting from positive change can be useful to cite publicly as supportive validation of the regime's decision. Dialoguing democracies should always publicly defer to that preference, while privately keeping up the pressure.

Civic dialogue is also an increasingly used technique for promoting common ground solutions in divided societies or situations with challenging problems, where debate can often lead to divisive position-taking. In 2004, for example, International IDEA commissioned wide-ranging and broadly inclusive citizens' surveys in Nepal to determine their conceptions of good governance, democracy and human security at a time of constitutional stress. The survey results were presented by key stakeholders in civil society at "People's Forums," with the delegation of the European Commission in Nepal taking responsibility for hosting the poll and survey presentation to the international community. The findings were ultimately included into the constitutional processes, which benefitted from the participation of experts with comparative experiences of constitutional processes in India, Cambodia, Afghanistan, Thailand, South Africa and Kenya.

Demarching

Using official channels to identify emerging or actual problems involving local authorities in order to protest human rights violations and to seek the removal of restrictions and obstacles to reformers and NGOs remains a classic tool of diplomats and missions, best exercised as part of the above sustained dialogue on the status of human rights.

Nota bene: Privileged diplomatic contact has also been very important in conveying messages to the host country about future conduct or further developments and rewards or costs involved in different courses of action. Usually, such demarches are private, if public stands are judged apt to harden the authorities' positions, or otherwise be counterproductive. High-profile quarrels between an embassy and the host government should not be allowed to undermine the efforts of local democratic reformers, which always merit pride of place.

Such as: Diplomats reminding host governments of international obligations have had positive effects in many circumstances, most notably with regard to the joint undertakings under the CSCE's Helsinki Final Act in Prague and other capitals in the late 1980s. Privately emphasizing to host authorities that they risk offending international public opinion at considerable national cost can also be effective, as was the case when religious authorities sentenced women to corporal or capital punishment in Nigeria and Saudi Arabia. Sometimes, of course, such advice is both ignored and resented. In Zimbabwe in the early 1990s, democratic embassies conveyed their deep misgivings over the withdrawal of legal redress for farmers whose property was summarily nationalized, which was a precursor of the deterioration to come in relations between the Zimbabwean government and accredited diplomats.

Currently, European governments are demarching Russian authorities at the highest level over restrictions in Russia on the activities of outside NGOs and on civil society. The US had similar messages for the Egyptian authorities in 2012. The EU's policy of "more for more" (or conversely "less for less") is central to the linkage between human rights observance and the strength of the relationship.

As a peak form of intervention, direct warnings by accredited ambassadors not to proceed with certain courses of repressive action are vital, such as the US Ambassador's cautioning of Chilean authorities in the late 1980s, or warnings in 2004 to Ukrainian authorities that they would be held accountable for use of force, and to desist from jamming mobile phone networks. Marc S. Ellenbogen (2009), who writes "The Atlantic Eye" column from Prague, recalls Boris Pankin, who he describes as "the last Soviet Ambassador to Prague [and]…the highest-ranking Soviet diplomat to stand against the putsch against Gorbachev in the early '90s…[he] stood down Czech troops who were preparing to put down the Velvet Revolution in 1989. He not only stood down the troops, he stood down the Czechoslovak [Communist] government as well."

During Kenya's presidential elections in 2008, missions communicated similar warnings about inciting ethnic violence, when there was evidence of organized text message transmissions denigrating and dehumanizing threats about people considered tribal and partisan rivals. The Kenyan telecommunications authorities and mobile phone companies then launched their own campaign of text messaging urging, instead, national peaceful reconciliation.

In Côte d'Ivoire in 2010-2011, diplomatic messaging insisted on an orderly transfer of power from losing President Laurent Gbagbo to President-elect Olussane Ouatarra, an issue that eventually had to be settled by French-led military intervention.

There are multiple examples of diplomatic demarches on the conduct of trials, arbitrary imprisonment and the treatment of prisoners. International and domestic public opinions often argue for making the fact of such demarches public, but the record shows that with a variety of countries, especially China, diplomats have counselled keeping some initial demarches as private as possible, and have been rewarded on several occasions by positive results. In Cuba, too, some visiting democratic ministers have made public announcements of demands to release prisoners of conscience for domestic political purposes. The public approach has not been productive with Cuban authorities; however, private negotiations prior to some high-level visits, as outlined in the Cuba case study, have had concrete results.

Reaching Out

Connecting

Connecting is related to the "informing" tool discussed earlier, but more in the sense of putting people — such as academic institutions, researchers, activists and experts — in contact with each other. Civil society provides democracy's building blocks, and increasingly, civil society within a given country is finding support from international civil society. Much of the content of international relations is now carried through informal transnational networks of working contacts. Bringing local reform groups and individuals into contact with outsiders is at the heart of people-to-people diplomacy, through activities such as visits, conferences, exchanges and safe public access to the Internet or satellite communications from mission libraries. Embassies also enable civil society to access international assistance programs. Connecting senior levels of government and members of the democratic opposition and society to contacts in the sending state are important tools. In more closed societies, the message from civil society outside that non-violent change is possible builds confidence and hope among civil society groups inside and even among authorities more inclined to reform.

Nota bene: Civil society is formed by networks of groups that are, by definition, beyond the direct control of the state. Such groups, which take time to develop, are often mobilized around specific purposes, such as women's and youth issues, human rights, ecological protection, HIV/AIDS, culture, science, professional norms or even sports. Often, their purpose is non-political, such as the movements in Cuba to create a network of lending libraries. Such interest and action groups value contacts with NGOs and others able to help them on questions of material progress. Taken together, they form the continuity of social capital, which can form the foundation for democratic development. The experience of citizens' participation in seeking to advance issues of specific concern can promote a jump from narrow functional objectives to wider ones, especially as their experience and demonstrable achievements earn such groups legitimacy and influence.

Such as: Widespread transitional assistance programs for democracy development and consolidation are monitored and often calibrated by diplomatic personnel. They scout for opportunities, make contacts and identify programs that are not working, as well as helping to ensure that assistance takes account of local conditions, capacities and needs. Diplomats in the field can also advise how to support groups in civil society most capable of encouraging bottom-up and "middle-out" change essential to the process of democratic transformation.

There are eloquent histories of groups of democratic activists and others inside who have connected to supportive groups outside, but none more effective than the connections arranged for the ANC in South Africa and then for the UDF after its formation in 1983. Diplomatic representatives in South Africa maintained constant liaison with activists. Their ability to connect activists to supportive groups outside contributed to the preparation of personnel for the eventual responsibilities of government office. Diplomats also assisted with initial informal connections between the ANC and South African authorities or interest groups close to the authorities such as the Afrikaner Broederbund.

Embassies have traditionally been more easily connected to the elites in a society, but experience in many different situations shows that the impulses for political transformation and reform will not succeed if propelled from this top-down approach. Support for change is needed across society, from grassroots groups and, increasingly, from the growing numbers of citizens who are fluent with modern communications and are able to compare their situations with others outside. As one ambassador who is familiar with the incremental changes in governance occurring in several countries in the Middle East put it (prior to the Arab Spring), "It is not top-down, nor bottom-up, but led in the main by a sort of middle-out." Experience has also shown, however, that care must be taken not to ignore the economically and socially marginalized, including victims of destabilizing forces of crime and extremism and, specifically, indigenous peoples.

Connecting to democratic opposition activists and leaders is important to help provide skills that enable them to pursue their democratization goals and to help prepare a new generation of leaders to assume office in a democratic transformation. Most of the Community of Democracies' participating states are conscious of the need to be consistent in coverage, and note that civil society activity in several authoritarian states in the Middle East is undertaken by the Muslim Brotherhood and its affiliates, with which diplomatic representatives maintain contact. In Algiers in the 1990s, it became the practice for democratic embassies to ensure that visiting dignitaries called on opposition leaders, which both connected these leaders to important outside contacts, and enhanced their legitimacy at home. This policy is pretty much *de rigueur* today in authoritarian regimes such as Cuba, as the case study illustrates. Community of Democracies members will undertake sought-after political-level visits and engage cooperative programs, but will insist on meeting civil society and democratic opposition figures. In 2003-2004, embassies in Ukraine developed travel programs to capitals for opposition leaders for similar reasons. It is also useful to connect to democratic opposition leaders in exile, sometimes through diplomats and programs in third countries. Such programs have been instrumental in democracy preparation, from the South African experience to that of Burma/Myanmar today.

In repressive societies, diplomats can use modern communications technologies to circumvent travel restrictions against local human rights defenders or other activists seeking outside connections. In this fashion, late Cuban human rights advocate Oswaldo Payá, animator of the Varela Project, a citizens' petition aimed at promoting greater freedoms, was able to communicate by video link to an EU NGO forum on freedom of expression after he was denied an exit visa. EU diplomats also facilitated his telephone connections to EU ministers, journalists and NGOs as well.

Canada has adopted a "direct diplomacy" policy, a fusion of the new paradigm of reaching out to civil society and an innovative application of social media reflexes. It aims to engage and support non-state political actors contributing to the democratization process in their respective countries. Since each country must pursue its own path to democracy, the strategy that Canada adopts for each direct diplomacy campaign varies. Activities include building and sustaining relationships both in person and online; small-scale programming to strengthen political mobilization skills to improve strategic communications or ensure internet security; and a cycle of listening, messaging and measuring impacts. The technique is even used in Syria and Iran, where Canada has had to close its diplomatic missions.

The China case study outlines Canada's e-diplomacy there, which uses Sina Weibo — the largest social media website in China — to post 140-character messages on dedicated webpages, providing relevant information on current affairs and earning the embassy a very wide following of hundreds of thousands who can interact with the embassy via the site. Canadian Ambassador Mark McDowell underscores the importance of having a "young" voice and sharing interesting information with users, which "doesn't come naturally to diplomats." The messaging also has to come across as a completely transparent exercise in communications — without hidden agendas — to both establish and retain credibility.

What distinguishes direct diplomacy and e-diplomacy from other diplomatic forms of democracy support is the priority they place on engaging non-state actors and the way they use social media and other technology to engage a much more dispersed set of political actors, in parallel to working with governmental authorities.

Convening

Providing a safe and discreet locale for discussion, including among adversaries, has enabled contacts and exchanges aimed at political conciliation and the resolution of conflicts. Diplomats can also offer a venue for democratic activists to meet safely among themselves, helping them promote a legitimate status.

Nota bene: As mentioned previously, diplomats posted to third countries can also play a convening role vis-à-vis locally resident political exiles, as well as supporting visiting oppositionists from inside the country, or organizing confidential third country contacts between adversaries.

Such as: The first mediated and authoritative contacts between the ANC and South African authorities took place outside the country and were sometimes arranged based on diplomatic liaison with the ANC offices in Lusaka. But embassy locales inside South Africa were often where South Africans of influence, such as the judiciary, first met ANC members informally. The Syrian opposition has been convening under the auspices of a pool of democracies in Turkey.

Inside repressive states, diplomatic officers can provide neutral ground for round table discussion on sensitive topics that would not be allowed in public, or for participants to speak off the record. US and Canadian officers frequently hosted such events in South Africa. It is essential, of course, that embassies not be seen as playing political favourites among the various participants; political choice must be left in the hands of the citizens concerned. The EU delegation in Moscow is playing such a role, hosting civil society discussion and involving state authorities as well as NGOs, as the case study on Russia shows. The US makes space available at its missions for civil society groups struggling against local bias to hold discussion, such as the lesbian, gay, bisexual and transgender community, and also invites local officials when this could be helpful.

Publicly visible receptions to honour civil society, cultural groups and political dissidents, which were frequent at democratic embassies in Prague and Budapest in the 1980s, help elevate the influence of protest and reform movements. Receptions can also have the merit of putting democracy activists and authorities together, although practice varies. Some embassies, such as the Czech Embassy in Havana insist on such mingling. Others hold separate national day receptions for civil society and authorities. The local authorities attend or not, depending on the company.

In transitional countries, embassies can also play a convening role to bring disparate parties and leaders together prior to democratic elections, as the US Embassy did in Liberia and Ghana, facilitating the parties' ability to work with one another after elections in a politically pluralist landscape. This counters a post-election tendency in several countries for majority winners to feel entitled to "take all" and to penalize losing opponents, especially if they represent ethnic minorities.

Facilitating

Using the good offices of missions and diplomats can facilitate positive cooperation among democrats, the reconciliation of different ethnic or other groups in pluralist societies, or encourage democrats and local authorities to advance democratic outcomes. Diplomats can legitimately help peace activists with the transmission of messages to others both within and outside the country. Missions can also play a role in facilitating third-country peaceful abdication or exit strategies for discredited authoritarian figures.

Such as: At times of crisis, diplomats, especially from neighbouring countries, can play an important role in encouraging the mediation of disputes, including in the aftermath of contested elections. Sometimes, however, governments that are protecting their monopoly of power can shy away from mediation efforts, as was the case initially in Kenya after the integrity of its January 2008 election results were challenged. In this case, international mediation was ultimately effective, especially through the efforts of fellow African, ex-UN Secretary-General Kofi Annan to help establish a power-sharing deal. Satisfactory mediated outcomes were also obtained in Côte d'Ivoire and Kyrgyzstan. Conversely, Robert Mugabe has consistently frustrated diplomatic attempts by South Africa and Nigeria to facilitate reconciliation in Zimbabwe.

The support of democracies from outside helped Kenya to avoid repeating the post-electoral violence in 2008 by undertaking a program of electoral reform, civil society strengthening, civic education, and youth leadership and empowerment. Through its embassy in Nairobi, the US CSO supported the creation of Champions of Peace, a coalition of Kenyan civil society groups composed of women's, professional and religious groups, and district peace committees in the Rift Valley and Nyanza provinces. The umbrella coalition worked to counter political manipulation, strengthen constructive engagement with police and other security actors, and build a system to coordinate consultation and intervention on early warning and early response.

Opposition movements often begin as rival factions, or splinter into them. Diplomats in South Africa, Chile and Serbia helped opposition movements in these countries overcome their factional disarray and build united alliances for democratic reform. The case study on Chile records the role of the Mitterrand socialists in France in convening diverse exile groups together to encourage a united front against Pinochet. A similar dynamic has played out in relations between democratic governments and diplomats and the Syrian opposition, especially in Turkey.

A dedicated US program to support democratic transitions under Ambassador Bill Taylor, special coordinator for Middle East transitions, was created in September 2011. Following the formation of the Syrian Opposition Coalition in November 2012, a series of workshops was organized in coordination with Ambassador Robert Ford and the US Embassy, mostly in Turkey. The workshops facilitate planning for civil administration and transition by supporting the training of activists, organizations and professionals to prepare them for transition. Workshops were devoted to consensus building, women's issues, youth and grassroots activism, media, civil resistance and local administration, placing special emphasis on countering sectarian violence and convening participants from different religious and ethnic communities. As one participant commented, "Even though we all know of each other, we never would have come together if we hadn't attended this course."

The case studies on Tunisia and Egypt relate the difficulties democrats had in uniting with parties, particularly religious ones. Religious parties garnered half the vote, but dominated because they had a common representation. While religious parties and the democratic movement share the search for dignity and affirmation of identity, they can sometimes be at odds. As one active player has put it, "if they collide — disaster; but if the effort succeeds to keep them compatible, there is a chance for an overall success." Embassies in Tunis, Cairo and elsewhere in the Arab world are using their convening power to help the efforts of, for example, Radwan Masmoudi of the Centre for the Study of Islam and Democracy to convene the disparate players in the unfolding political narratives.

Many of the divisive forces in societies devolve from irredentist ethnic, sectarian or tribal differences, which can surface with sudden violence and force, and can be amplified by waves of migration — even in working democracies. Inclusive pluralism is a fundamental prerequisite to successful democratic governance; indeed, as Daron Acemoglu and James Robinson (2012) argue, inclusive institutional structures are critical to economic achievement.

Studies by the RAND Corporation show that since 1900, 80 percent of conflicts within states have been resolved by political processes rather than by force prevailing in favour of one side. Some democracies have pursued a special vocation in public and private diplomacy by attempting to mentor and support the reconciliation of ethnic, social, cultural or other divisions in, for example, the Western Balkans, Northern Ireland, across the Middle East and in Sri Lanka where (despite the initiatives of Norway, in particular) there is still a vivid community problem adversely affecting the Tamil population. The Norwegian Foreign Ministry annually hosts conflict mediators and key peace process actors from conflict states such as Somalia, Mali and Syria at the Oslo Forum at the Losby Gods Hotel in partnership with the Centre for Humanitarian Dialogue.

Settlement immigration countries such as Canada and Australia have gained specific expertise regarding the integration and accommodation of diverse communities. But where ethnic or other irredentist antagonisms surface and break into violence, the democratic international community, mindful of the horrors of the Rwandan genocide, must attempt to intervene. In fact, several democracies have established a "genocide prevention" capacity in their governments, which relies heavily on diplomats on the ground to identify warning signs. Prevention becomes paramount: in Kenya, prevention activities were accompanied by clear diplomatic warnings that those responsible for inciting ethnic violence would pay a price in prosecution and would be barred from travel to the democratic countries concerned.

Another technique of facilitation is an "endgame" strategy, offering "safe exits" to resolve acute crises. Such an exit was made for President Marcos of the Philippines, for Mobutu Sese Seko of Zaire and President Fujimori of Peru, defusing potential threats of violent resistance to democratic transition. The endgame to the crisis in Kyrgyzstan in 2010 depended on an exile arrangement that was brokered by the US, Russia, Kazakhstan and the help of Belarus.

A reverse example would be the strong leadership role of Japan's diplomats and government in brokering a solution enabling Cambodian political leaders in exile to return to Phnom Penh to contest the first democratic multi-party elections in 1998 without fear of reprisal. Indeed, several diplomats personally visited one such leader, Prince Ranariddh, in exile in Bangkok to provide the assurances.

Lastly, in societies where outside contacts are restricted, diplomats can pass messages and legitimately facilitate communications between democratic activists and outside supporters, or contact between ordinary citizens and family members and civil society elsewhere, using embassy communications channels and Internet access.

Financing

Arm's length resources can be especially valuable to start-up NGOs, independent media or anti-poverty action groups. Often, small projects avoid the sorts of government controls and bureaucratization associated with large-scale aid activity. Embassies have the critical role of "spotting" for more substantial financing for larger worthwhile projects.

Nota bene: This is a notoriously sensitive area. Protests by authorities of "outside financing" are common and lead, in many cases, to curbs and restrictions. Precious financial assistance will be marred if it can be made to appear motivated by ulterior political considerations.

Such as: There are examples of diplomatic missions fast-disbursing funds to grassroots local initiatives wherever there has been a democratic transition. Mission funds should, however, avoid competition with the programs of international NGOs, which have the longer-term development of civil society as a central purpose. Embassy-directed donations often go toward very specific and modest cash flow requirements of youth movements, start-up independent media operations, the organization of public events or serve a humanitarian need in emergencies. Czech, Slovak, Danish, Norwegian and Swedish funding today operates in such a manner in repressive societies. In countries in the midst of difficult democratic transitions, such as the Democratic Republic of the Congo, the funds can be rapidly directed to pockets of need, but this is best carried out in consultation with other donors to avoid duplication and oversight. In the 1980s, Canadian Embassy funds in South Africa could be deployed immediately to victims of apartheid to cover legal or other court costs. In all cases, even though such funds are often modest, for shoestring beneficiaries, the merits of fast-disbursement and being unencumbered by paperwork obligations in emergency situations are significant.

There is a record of repressive governments alleging that such disbursements engage embassies and diplomats improperly in internal matters of state. Authorities in apartheid South Africa and Pinochet's Chile threatened expulsions over the practice. In Russia, beginning in 2005, local reform groups and NGOs that accepted such funds were penalized through the denial of accreditation and, thus, their ability to operate. Both Cuba and Iran have prosecuted opposition groups and human rights activists, alleging that their acceptance of foreign funds constituted treasonable activity. Embassies adjust their practices to ensure that there is no liability to recipients from such small-scale funding, and in some countries refrain from financial support of opposition figures, concentrating on development NGOs. It is important that any embassy funding be demonstrably at arm's length to specific electoral or partisan political purposes so that embassies can vigorously contest any constraining action by authorities. In short, the purpose can legitimately support efforts to obtain a transparent democratic process without supporting one political candidate or outcome over others.

Showcasing

At the heart of public diplomacy, democratic development showcasing is less a matter of national self-promotion than an effort to present examples, models or solutions suitable for local application. There is, of course, no more powerful example than the election of an African-American US president, or a female president of Brazil who had been tortured as a prisoner of conscience. Through their outreach, missions are in a position to highlight norms accepted elsewhere, best practices and successful achievements through seminars, training, conferences and even cultural narratives. These can be of instructive or motivational benefit to the public, local authorities, NGOs and reform groups. As mentioned earlier, representatives of democracies that have themselves emerged from repressive regimes have enhanced credibility as mentors for human rights defenders and democratic activists today. Most societies have had to confront the need to correct the abuse of civil liberties in their own histories, and these narratives can be presentational assets in emerging democracies facing the challenges of change and reconciliation.

Nota bene: Sometimes "best practices" in civil behaviour are evident in host countries in non-political spheres such as sports, or economic and cultural activities that cross ethnic or confessional lines in otherwise divided societies. They merit support for showcasing these values from within the host country itself. Civic consciousness is especially important for security forces and personnel. Exposing security forces to best practices in human rights and democracy through international training can help to prevent harsh reactions to non-violent protests. Discipline training in non-violent techniques is also valuable for civil society to reduce the risk of counterproductive provocation.

Such as: Democratic societies have had experience in many aspects of governance whose features can be immensely instructive to societies looking for guidance as they undergo transition, with the caveat that most applications are not directly transferable, needing considerable adaptation to local social and cultural conditions. Some of the demonstration and assistance can be very specific and technical: Canada, for example, promotes guidance to multilingual societies on the practices of simultaneous legislative drafting to enable legal linguistic equivalencies. Especially compelling is training conducted by countries that have themselves emerged from repressive regimes, since the representatives of such newer democracies can more readily relate to the challenges and conditions of dissidents and civil society operating under the strains of repression.

Much public diplomacy is more general, however, in support of the merits of pluralistic accommodation, the peaceful settlement of disputes or moderation in the pursuit of political objectives. Such showcasing efforts exposed Chilean opposition groups of the left, for example, which were somewhat doctrinaire, to the advantages of dialogue and pragmatic adaptation evident among successfully elected European social-democrats in the 1980s. Showcasing exemplary efforts in non-sectarian hiring practices can help lead the way: examples include the coffee growing industry in Rwanda, or Northern Ireland, where major Canadian employers hired across traditional sectarian lines, and where the Belfast professional ice hockey team, composed of foreigners, refused to reveal members' religious affiliations.

A growing series of workshops for activists and civil society together with officials and experts from democracies aim at building capacity and preparedness for inclusive pluralism, such as the conference on pluralism in MENA in December 2012 at the Centre Culturel Canadien in Paris, co-organized by the *Handbook* team with the European Council for Foreign Relations, The Ligue Internationale des Droits de l'Homme and the Institut de Recherche et Débat sur la Gouvernance.

More general still are events presenting the cultural or other achievements of a democratic society to enhance its capacity to serve as a democratic role model. Again, the American Cultural Center in Rangoon deserves recognition as an example of a facility providing a public precious exposure to international culture otherwise denied by the repressive and inward Burmese military regime.

The showcasing of ethics for military and security personnel has only been accorded importance relatively recently, but with demonstrable beneficial effect. The training of Ukraine military officers in democratic governance responsibilities in NATO partnership programs contributed in some measure to their restraint in dealing with demonstrations during the electoral crisis of the Orange Revolution. NGO-to-NGO training workshops showcasing the techniques of disciplined non-violent protest contributed to a counterpart restraint on the part of dissident and protest groups in those and other demonstrations.

Such training has been ongoing for representatives of the Syrian opposition, though sadly, repressive force has regrettably turned the conflict in Syria into a violent one. Training is provided for the defensive use of communications technologies, human rights monitoring and evidence-gathering and leadership training, including training for Imams in democracy provided by the International Federation for Human Rights, with its unique assets of national representations on the ground, and Human Rights Watch. In cooperation with the Centre for Civil Society and Democracy in Syria, the US State Department has been helping Syrian activists build in workshops and programs in Turkey capacity for local administration and providing secure communications training.

The training of police, customs officials and prosecutors to provide an understanding of civic responsibility has been a staple of many democracy support programs of Community of Democracies donor countries. By way of contrast, during the Cold War, counter-insurgency training in inter-American programs that did not emphasize human rights indirectly contributed to subsequent massive abuses by Latin American militaries against democratic activists and others.

The issue of consistency is paramount. There is little benefit in showcasing positive narratives of civil behaviour if there are contrary examples of illegal or abusive treatment of people in the custody of the showcasing state, or if the state coddles relationships with abusive partners for strategic reasons.

"Older" democracies have, of course, experienced large-scale abuses of civil rights in their own pasts, in respect of racial or religious minorities, indigenous people, women or labour movements, and have also suspended normal civil liberties at times of exceptional stress such as during war or at other times of fear. The process of democratic self-correction is endless. But the transparent presentation of the lessons of such corrections can also be a showcase feature for the benefit of emerging democracies struggling with ethnic and other tensions and inequalities — not in the manner of preaching, but in that of empathy for the challenges involved in pursuing change.

The instructional exhibit of better practices can be indirect. The Canadian Embassy's Weibo site in China caused a major stir when Ambassador David Mulroney's official car, a modest Toyota, was highlighted for its fuel efficiencies; Chinese readers took from the illustration the contrast with the myriad of Chinese officials flaunting late-model luxury limos. The rather utilitarian wristwatch of Polish Foreign Minister Sikorski drew favourable and ironic comment in Ukrainian media when contrasted to the ostentatiously worn luxury watches of some of his Ukrainian counterparts.

The economic downturns in Western economies have raised the question of reverse showcasing. "What do you have to teach us?" is a rhetorical question posed since the financial crisis of 2007. Commentary from China has been trenchant. Alex Lo (2013) asks why the world refers still to the "Asian" financial crisis of 1997-1998, or to "Mexican," "Russian" or "Brazilian" crises, and yet calls the current crisis a "global" one and not "Western"? "For decades," Lo continues, "everyone assumed western policymakers and central bankers knew all about economics and finance, so such crises happened only to little brown people. But hubris is the moment before you fall flat on your face." Nobody wants to have to showcase systemic difficulties, but in discussing them, democracies and their diplomats can showcase transparency and objectivity, and self-corrective remedial behaviour.

Defending Democrats

Demonstrating

By using the prestige and offices of the head of mission and other diplomats to show public respect and even solidarity for human rights defenders, democratic activists and reformers sends the message that such citizens and groups have legitimacy and importance in the eyes of outside partners. Diplomats understand that such demonstration needs to stop short of seeming to embrace particular individuals or parties with respect to democratic political outcomes. Care should always be taken to ensure that diplomats are seen to be supporting a democratic process rather than specific results. Encouraging international humanitarian awards and recognition for human rights defenders also helps legitimize their positions in their own countries.

Nota bene: Public demonstrations or protests in authoritarian societies require courage and the willingness of citizens to entertain risks in the exercise of freedom of speech. Such courage merits the public support of democratic representatives. The public representation of sympathy by diplomats on specific issues or events can be used in tandem with private demarches to authorities. All diplomats need access to grassroots activity and opinion, and some embassies in non-democratic countries assign primary responsibility for contact with dissidents to specific embassy officers, but in presentation, it is important to demonstrate that the head of mission remains visibly engaged as the chief human rights officer, without making him or her a lightning rod for the hostility of host country authorities.

Such as: Historically, changes in repressive regimes occur because the people support change as their democratic right. In the absence of elections, this is habitually expressed by public protests or demonstrations, though "street action" alone is often less effective than the buildup of a civil society capacity to support democratic transition in the longer term. It is standard practice for repressive regimes to ban such gatherings, but the people often find a way to peacefully circumvent the states of emergency or special laws that authorities decree and erect to protect the undemocratic status quo. In apartheid South Africa, marches to the public funerals of fallen activists became a vehicle for protest and the presence of the representatives of democratic diplomatic missions among the people sent a message of support, as well as offering a shield of sorts against violent repression. The role of diplomats in showing support for the rights to protest by appearing personally at such demonstrations or symbolic marches has been established in such locales as Budapest, Santiago, Manila, Belgrade, Kyiv, Havana and Kathmandu. Gay rights demonstration in the Balkans in recent years have drawn violence tolerated officially, but visible diplomatic solidarity at parades and marches has contributed to improvement.

The role of the late Mark Palmer, US Ambassador to Hungary between 1986 and 1990, was groundbreaking in the profession. In 1988-1989, Ambassador Palmer made a point of being visibly and personally engaged with opposition and activist groups, marching with demonstrators for change. It was, at the time, a controversial role for a foreign diplomat, including in circles in Washington, DC, but in a state visit to Budapest in 1989, US President George H. W. Bush declared that the Hungarian authorities had to face up to such change as inevitable, thereby validating Ambassador Palmer's role. Mark Palmer is remembered in Hungary as one of the 10 most influential "Hungarians" of the twentieth century, an extraordinary accolade for a diplomat, and one anticipating the changes that are central to this *Handbook*'s themes of change and transformation.

In other locales, such as Zimbabwe, ambassadors were especially targeted by security forces, and it fell more often to embassy political officers to be present at witness protests, although some ambassadors, such as James McGee of the US, took a proactive personal role in going out to show support for intimidated and even abused opposition supporters.

Whatever the level of representation, it has been reinforcing for democrats to see the support of the kind that US Ambassador to Syria Robert S. Ford and French Ambassador to Syria Eric Chevallier extended when they visited Hama during peaceful protests and stayed an extra day. "Residents feel a kind of protection with the presence of the ambassador," said Omar al-Habbal, an activist. "The authorities wouldn't dare react with violence" (cited in Shadid, 2011). The same two ambassadors together with colleagues from the United Kingdom, Germany, Canada, Japan, the Netherlands and the European Union, aimed to show the same kind of support when they attended the vigil for reform activist Giyath Matar, who was killed under torture by security forces. "It is important to show Giyath's family and Syrians that the world has noticed what is going on," said UK Ambassador Simon Collis (cited in Ali, 2011). That troops opened fire on mourning demonstrators once the ambassadors were out of the way does not diminish the value of their message of support.

Australian diplomat Roland Rich recalls that Indonesian pro-democracy demonstrators said at the time that "having foreigners alongside was like borrowing a little piece of their democracies." But the demonstration of privately communicated support for the rights of activists can also be very effective in sending a message to authorities monitoring communications. Maintaining regular phone contact with democratic opposition leaders has been a protective recourse in many crisis situations, and especially when it is assumed that local security is listening in.

More publicly visible are diplomats' home visits to threatened or confined democracy activists, or, as in Havana in 2009, to the wives of prisoners of conscience and the monitoring of political trials. Some embassies of democracies in repressive societies make a habit of inviting the families of political prisoners to embassy events with a family theme, such as parties at Christmas or other festivals. Ambassadors in such societies also accompany released political prisoners home from prison at the time of their release. Such gestures, as well as receptions and other hospitality events that make a point of including both dissidents and officials, can reinforce the self-confidence of civil society in the legitimacy of their peaceful work, and help to create productive initial contacts between authorities and civil society leadership. The most important value to demonstrate is consistency.

Validating suspicions that what really counted for Western countries were security and economic advantages can be costly and devastatingly demoralizing to civil society while emboldening dictators and their henchmen. When a new Canadian prime minister chose Libya as his first destination on behalf of an engineering company (subsequently disgraced for the systemic bribery of officials to win contracts), he undercut Ottawa's moral credibility and leverage. In Bahrain, the United States sent a counterproductive message when it felt obliged to defer to Saudi support for the fellow Sunni Khalifa regime in its crackdown on the Shia majority, including the prosecution of dozens of doctors and nurses for having treated peaceful demonstrators injured by security forces.

Egyptian activists make the point that, after the US invaded Iraq in 2003 — an action which was opposed by 90 percent of Arabs — the Bush administration placed its priority in relations with Egypt to acquire Mubarak's support. This unpopular position made the regime repress the population even more, and conveyed the message to beleaguered democrats that their democratic cause didn't matter.

Verifying and Witnessing

The verifying of election processes and results is an important and widespread international practice in which diplomatic missions have an ongoing responsibility. The witnessing of trials and hearings by diplomats is also widespread and is now generally accepted internationally as a means of providing or supporting an independent verification of disputes or the health of detainees. There are, of course, terrible histories of the fearful and depraved repression of opponents and activists without any concession to pretense of legal authority, such as the tens of thousands of murders carried out by the Argentine military between 1976 and 1983. But today, even autocratic regimes prefer to display the trappings of a legal process, however sham. In the Internet age, summary trials of dissidents and activists can rarely be completely hidden from view. "Show trials," meant to distort the truth for public consumption, are similarly exposed for what they are. In taking public and private issue with the distortion of the process of justice for repressive political purposes, diplomats are representing the norms and standards of universally applicable human rights and the rule of law, and the arguments by repressive authorities that these matters are strictly internal concerns are without merit.

Nota bene: In addition to the conditions and circumstances of prisoners, enquiries and demarches about detainees and political prisoners need to focus on the illegitimacy of their incarceration. International and diplomatic scrutiny of elections themselves is also by now widespread, but inadequate attention is paid to prior and ongoing support for the selection, formation and training of preparatory and supervisory national election commissions able to adjudicate fairness in pre-election publicity, as well as the election process itself.

Such as: Diplomatic representatives have been prominent whenever possible at the prosecution trials of democratic activists, journalists and representatives of civil society, for example in Prague, Cairo and Tashkent. As British diplomat Philip Barclay (2010) reports, "Part of the role of a British diplomat in a repressive country is to attend political trials. This is ostensibly to monitor the quality of justice being dispensed, but often — when the charges are blatantly groundless — it's also a statement of protest." Of course, there are still repressive jurisdictions where such trials are secret and closed, including mass sentencing of demonstrators and monks in Burma/Myanmar and of dissidents in Iran. The fates of such prisoners remain an enduring prima facie concern of missions. The very fact of incarceration is the forefront issue; the presentation of "prisoners' lists" to authorities in China and Cuba has been a mainstay of diplomatic representation for years.

An iconic case concerned Azerbaijani blogger and human rights activist Emin Milli, who was director of the Friedrich Ebert Foundation in Azerbaijan, and who had assisted the Council of Europe with over 40 cases of prisoners of conscience in Azeribaijani jails. Milli was himself attacked by police in 2009 and eventually tried along with a colleague in a selective prosecution for the sake of example: "When two bloggers are punished in this way, there will not be a third," said Vafa Guluzade, an ex-adviser on security to President Heydar Aliyev whose son Ilham has succeeded him as dictator (cited in Barry, 2011). Reporters Without Borders, the EU, the Council of Europe and several embassies made strenuous representations about Emin Milli and ultimately, US President Barack Obama intervened in September 2010 when meeting Azerbaijani President Heydar Aliyev at the United Nations in New York. Milli was eventually released and, amazingly, continued his campaign of agitation for human rights.

The conduct of authorities toward those in custody also matters greatly. Diplomatic representatives in various jurisdictions insist, when possible, on verifying the health of such prisoners, such as after arbitrary arrests of Zimbabwe opposition leader Morgan Tsvangirai and colleagues in the opposition MDC.

The Magnitsky case in Russia has received wide attention. As mentioned previously, Magnitsky was a forensic lawyer who became a whistle-blower and brought to public notice a massive tax fraud. He was then himself arrested and died in prison of medical neglect. In 2012, US Congress passed a law imposing targeted sanctions on Russian prosecution, prison and tax officials implicated in the case.

When violent prisoner abuse becomes public knowledge to the point that authorities are pressured to conduct official inquiries or even trials of security personnel, such as with respect to the killing of Canadian-Iranian photojournalist Zahra Kazemi-Ahmadabadi at Iranian hands, diplomats have sought to witness these legal proceedings as well, with admirable solidarity.

International observation and assessment of elections, especially by regional organizations, is now an almost universal practice. Some democratic groupings have been able to provide such authoritative monitoring that they attract wide international participation, such as EU-led election monitoring in Lebanon, and the Democratic Republic of the Congo, which included many non-EU observers among the team, or Commonwealth monitoring of elections in member countries.

The ODIHR election observation missions have become integral to the OSCE's raison d'être. Though its bestowal of "failing grades" for elections in Kazakhstan, Uzbekistan or Azerbaijan that it deemed not to be "fair and free" was often ignored by authorities at the time, the accumulated challenge to their legitimacy is an important asset for diplomatic representatives in those countries. The observation exercise does more than legitimize the election returns: as demonstrated in the case of South Africa, the presence of international observers provides encouragement and reassurance to democracy advocates and to the general public. It also bestows a measure of security by showing that the eyes of the world are watching. This helps promote restraint on the part of all parties to the process. However, more attention needs to be paid to the training of local election commissions whose credibility is essential to sustaining belief in the integrity of results and avoidance of post-electoral violence.

For years, embassies and their personnel have taken an active and significant role in the observation process, including observing local elections, as the Japanese mission did in Ukraine in 2004, observing violations in a by-election in Mukacheve that anticipated abuses practiced in the general election shortly after. In Senegal's 1988 presidential elections, several democratic embassies agreed to pool their efforts. "Embassy officers who attended rallies shared their impressions with counterparts, and a coordinated election-day schedule was drawn up to avoid overlapping visits to polling stations. The candidates and party campaign leaders knew of and appreciated this careful, coordinated attention to their campaign efforts." Ultimately, "the diplomats agreed that the results reflected the will of the people: the majority of Senegalese voters wanted Abdou Diouf to remain in office. This joint position proved useful in maintaining a common diplomatic position in response to civil disturbances which broke out in poorer sections of Dakar as dissatisfied voters felt their preferred candidate should have been chosen."

Such efforts are sometimes not appreciated by the host country. In Zimbabwe's 2002 presidential elections, the EU observation team's leader, Swedish politician Pierre Schori, was declared unwelcome and the observation team pulled out on the grounds that it could not do its job without him. But resident EU and other democratic embassies coordinated coverage of the polling booths on their own which, while less than adequate, was extremely helpful in reaching the conclusion the election had not been fair and free.

Protecting

> We were very active in attending political trials, so that defendants knew that if anything would happen to them, there would be protests.
>
> — a diplomat in Prague, 1980s

Visible support for individuals and groups under threat, as well as their families, provides some reassurance for democratic activists and human rights defenders and NGOs. Ultimately, in the event of breakdown and crisis, missions have performed an essential humanitarian function by giving refuge to asylum seekers.

Such as: In periods of tension, diplomats can often defuse a crisis. Their presence may persuade security authorities to back off a violent confrontation with peaceful groups.

Protection can be implicit, communicated by signs of support, telephone calls to check on the security of targeted activists and by declarations. The authorities may seek to label such declarations as outside interference; it suits the political narratives of repressive regime to paint protests as being foreign-inspired. But as the Burmese confrontations in 2007, or those of Iran in 2009 illustrated, the people know when their protests and appeals for change are popular and authentically and wholly indigenous. They welcome supportive declarations as statements of solidarity endorsing the legitimacy of their popular cause.

Diplomats can cast a wide protective net. People who are arbitrarily jailed fear for their families. In Turkmenistan, the British Embassy made a point of being in visible contact with the families of persons arrested for political reasons. In more dire circumstances, when the force of repression is without brakes or beyond persuasion, the episodes of diplomats extending protection have been many, going back to the legendary work of Swedish diplomat Raoul Wallenberg during World War II, or US Consul in Marseilles Varian Fry, who, without much support from superiors, saved many artists, Jews and leftists on Nazi arrest lists. Latin American diplomats in Europe also saved thousands of lives, notably Mexican Consul in Marseilles Gilberto Bosques, Salvadoran Consul in Geneva José Arturo Castellanos and Luis Martins de Souza Dantas of Brazil. It was Australian diplomat Bruce Haig who drove South African democrat and editor Donald Woods to safety out of South Africa. It was New Zealand's Ambassador John McArthur who spirited a trade union official dressed as a woman to the Swedish Embassy and asylum.

Sadly, however, the list of embassies that did not intervene or provide refuge because it was seen to be outside the scope of classically sanctioned diplomatic conduct was, for many years, a much longer one. More recent practice, however, has increasingly been to help wherever possible. Numerous examples include the humanitarian acceptance of thousands of asylum seekers in Santiago, Chile, after September 1973 and at the Embassy of Peru in Havana in 1980; the events of 1989 in Prague when embassies opened their grounds to East German refugees; the granting of safe shelter for a year to Chinese dissident Fang Lizhi by the US Embassy in Beijing in the aftermath of Tiananmen; the assistance from the embassies of Poland, Czech Republic, Hungary and Slovakia in gaining safe exit for threatened democratic opposition members in Ukraine prior to 2004; and Australia's acceptance of West Papua self-determination activists in 2006.

The asylum-seeking episode of Chinese dissident Chen Guangcheng in April 2012 is exemplary. When Chen sought asylum, the US Embassy in Beijing had to weigh the fallout with Chinese authorities, particularly on the eve of key Strategic and Economic Dialogue meetings. With "clear eyes for what we were getting into," US Secretary of State Hillary Clinton made this an opportunity to build a more solid China-US relationship. But Chinese "choices" had to be reconciled with "our values." There could not be a better metaphor for the themes of the *Diplomat's Handbook.*

THE PARTNERS AND APPLICATIONS

In becoming "coherence agents" with specific skill sets, diplomats are usually more likely to be effective in their support of democratic development by focussing on practical applications rather than the articulation of lofty aspirations of political theory. The partnerships that matter the most are those with a human face.

People-to-People, Democrat-to-Democrat

Local Groups and Coalitions: Students, Youth, Ecologists and Trade Unions

Coalitions of groups and bodies such as the UDF in South Africa are often the foundations of an emerging democratic society. In retrospect, they even constituted a form of government-in-waiting, though often, because of the closed circumstances of their society, they have little opportunity to gain the relevant and necessary experience. Nearly every country has informal local groupings of NGOs — although until recently, they were sparser in number in the Middle East. Their activities and primary interests are often not even political: groups that are trying to fill social services gaps, such as childcare or centres for the elderly are basic components of emerging civil society and merit support on humanitarian and developmental levels. Beyond their specific interests, through informal publications, performances and public outreach, together, they can also spawn a new civic sense of national identity and purpose. In the process, civil society acquires a growing stature of legitimacy and builds capacity for continuity in transition and eventual self-government. The process is reinforced by the efforts of democratic embassies and NGOs to engage them as partners and provide them support and, as appropriate, training.

Women's Groups

As underlined in the *Handbook's* introduction, the issue of women's rights is crucial to successful economic and democratic development. Countries that do not accept gender equality as a universal human right condemn themselves dually: they deny the rights of half their citizens, and in so doing they hobble their prospects.

In many societies and situations, groups formed to defend and advocate on behalf of women are often the first experience that women may have of personal involvement in public and social issues. Representing home and family perspectives, as well as specific workplace or professional interests, women's groups have a central role in the emergence of civil society. The mothers and widows of those missing or killed under repressive regimes, such as the Mothers of the Disappeared in Argentina, the Women in Black in Serbia or the wives of prisoners of conscience, such as Las Damas de Blanco in Cuba, earn a special place in national consciences.

Cultural Groups

When he was Vice President of the International Crisis Group, Alain Délétroz wrote, in homage to a murdered theatre director in Tashkent in 2009, "art is one of the finest forms of resistance to dictators."

The role of cultural groups in expanding the habit of freedom of expression was essential in many experiences in democratic transformation. One long-time NGO observer of Nigeria reflected, "The cause of Nigerian democracy, human rights and dignity has been infinitely better served by its artists and writers such as Chinua Achebe, Wole Soyinka, Ken Saro-Wiwa, and his son Ken Wiwa, and the great musician Fela Kuti, than by its compromised political class."

Cultural groups and artists have catalytic roles going beyond performance or art, and diplomats have a convening capacity that can showcase such artists and creators. As far back as 1975, Australian diplomat Diane Johnstone invited black artist Michael Muapola to her Pretoria apartment to exhibit his paintings, incurring the wrath of the apartheid regime, but contributing mightily to African self-respect. From Minsk to Rangoon, diplomats have hosted performances by artists banned from presenting in public.

Writing of Prague in the late 1980s, Canadian diplomat Rob McRae (1997) recounts his introduction to Karl Srp, "the head of the so-called Jazz Section.... of the musician's union [which] under Srp...had become a hotbed of underground music and video production, as well as samizdat (clandestine) publishing." McRae subsequently observed that through culture, "a new civic society had begun to emerge outside the control of the state, with a whole network of underground publications, performances, exhibitions, videos, newspapers, artistic and literary 'salons.' These had started to reach beyond the opposition to the grey zone of individuals who were at least inwardly, if not openly, opposed to the regime" (ibid.: 31).

Human Rights Defenders

The work of human rights defenders in repressive societies is completely central. It is lonely and is always courageous. Their cause is immensely assisted by the solidarity shown by the representatives of democracies and the international acknowledgement of their efforts, such as the Nobel Peace Prize bestowed on Iranian human rights defender Shirin Ebadi and on Yemeni women's advocate Tawakkol Karman. Chilean human rights lawyer Ignacio Walker (later Chile's foreign minister) recalls that, over four years under the Pinochet regime spent defending hundreds of unjustly accused and jailed democracy activists, he won few cases in the biased courts, but the demonstrable support he received from embassies and especially the Roman Catholic Church and the international recognition they bestowed, saved many lives.

Scholars, Researchers, Academic Institutes, Think Tanks and Centres of Excellence

Conferences on the challenges facing democrats in authoritarian settings are constantly taking place in democracies with the participation of dissidents and scholars in exile, and embassies often facilitate attendance from civil society from within the countries in question.

Connecting scholars with scholars and think tanks with think tanks is a multiple enrichment. For embassies, partnerships and projects undertaken with the scholarly and research community often engage the future leaders of the country, however unlikely it may seem in repressive societies at the time. They also engage a country's construction of objective collective memory, which is important in building a process of reconciliation. One of the most ambitious projects in preparation for the assumption of the responsibilities of government occurred as the result of a request made by Nelson Mandela shortly after his release from prison, to Canadian Prime Minister Brian Mulroney, to help the ANC boost its competence in economic matters. The initiative spawned the Macro-Economic Research Group, involving over 100 economic specialists from several developed democracies.

Institutional Partnerships and Processes

Independent Media

The role of independent media goes beyond the healthy practice of speaking truth to power. Media, including the rapidly growing phenomenon of blogs, have a monitoring role on governance, and catalyze public discussion. Supporting the emergence of independent media outlets has been one of the consistently successful partnership activities of embassies, often conducted in partnership with NGOs and news gatherers from Community of Democracies member countries. Programs that help to train reporters in "covering city hall" to promote transparency at local levels is a less politically sensitive approach to building capacity. Through support for networks of alternative outside servers, democracies can encourage access to international information and websites for Internet users inside repressive and closed societies.

On occasion, missions also directly help local news agencies and outlets with project funding. Examples include start-up funding for a radio station in Moscow and a desktop newspaper in Dakar, which became hubs of successful diversified independent communications enterprises. The first principle, of course, has been to separate such assistance from any intention of influencing the news or views reported by the outlet in question.

Support can be threefold. In Algiers, over the last several years, embassies have encouraged the emergence of independent newspapers and outlets without seeking to influence the news or editorial content of their publications. At the same time, they have encouraged the state-operated newspaper *El Moudjahid* in its efforts to present balanced reporting of events. Lastly, embassies have encouraged training for local journalists, who also benefit from the examples of travelling press corps accompanying visiting dignitaries, and their direct and candid questioning in pursuit of transparency and newsworthy information.

The transition to democracy from authoritarian regimes can be particularly challenging for public broadcasters as they transit from a propaganda role to one of objective newsgathering and reporting, as well as analysis. Such democratic arm's length public broadcasters such as the Australian, Canadian and British broadcasting corporations have mentored transitions, as with the South African Broadcasting Corporation (with its 15 million daily radio listeners) at the behest, originally, of their resident embassies, and after an initial grant by Apheda, the Australian labour organization.

Legal Proceedings

The rule of law and the building of national justice and judicial systems are essential to democracy building, providing the basis for "horizontal accountability," which democracy theorist Larry Diamond describes as the essential counterpart to the "vertical accountability" represented by the electoral process. As former Premier of China Zhao Ziyang, who spent the last 16 years of his life under house arrest, confided to visiting Soviet leader Mikhail Gorbachev in 1989, the rule of law has to replace rule by men. But as democracy scholar Thomas Carothers (2003) has written, "Law is not just the sum of courts, legislatures, police, prosecutors, and other formal institutions with some direct connection to law. Law is also a normative system that resides in the minds of the citizens of a society." It is behavioural, and takes time to evolve in this way.

Some countries, such as China, hold to the "rule by law," but in a somewhat rigid way. They lack transparency, accountability and the appeal systems that in democratic legal cultures invest parliamentary bodies with law-making prerogatives and the independent judiciary with an ongoing capacity for review and reversal.

In many countries, the legal and judicial communities play important roles in civil society. There are several recent examples of bar associations and even groups of judges taking public stands on issues of governance or corruption, such as in Burma/Myanmar, Lebanon, Pakistan and the Philippines. It can be rewarding, therefore, to develop embassy partnerships and soundings with local bar associations, law faculties and NGOs, such as the Moscow Helsinki Group, in order to support their efforts to improve the functioning of the court system and its capacities for legal aid. Embassies can also help to connect such groups to international norms and to experienced partner institutions in member states of the Community of Democracies.

Corruption issues merit a separate and very important emphasis. The 2010 US National Security Strategy identifies pervasive corruption as a violation of basic human rights. Working with the United Nations, the Organisation for Economic Co-operation and Development (OECD) and other international agencies, members of the Community of Democracies are committed to working through their embassies to promote greater transparency in all financial transactions, including those concerning their nationals working for foreign corporations, and especially concerning all flows of development assistance. The rigorous OECD Code of Conduct obliges member states to prosecute nationals who engage in corrupt practices abroad but not all developed countries have done so with consistency and seriousness. Foreign direct investors can play a very important role in contributing capacity building in transparency, accountability, meritocracy and responsible stewardship of the environment and social responsibility by example and by training.

Security Agencies and Policing

It is commonplace that security is essential to the building of support for democracy and to development, and international agencies such as the Geneva Centre for Democratic Control of Armed Forces play an important developmental and counselling role.

Embassies increasingly pay attention to opportunities to strengthen police training in transitional democracies via closer relations with local authorities. As Gary Haugen and Victor Boutros (2010) have written, "the human rights community must focus on building up the political will and capacity of local law enforcement institutions to bring justice to the world's poor."

Even in repressive regimes, it has often been important to maintain productive contacts with security and police agencies. Indeed, elements of military and intelligence services have, on occasion, shown themselves to be among the more moderate components of hardline governments. Embassies that partner with the police agencies for essential matters of cooperation against transnational criminal activity, including anti-terrorism, have found these professional contacts could be engaged to lower the temperature at times of internal political confrontation.

Political Parties

Obviously, paying attention to political parties and groupings or democratic oppositionists, where they are able to function, is a long-standing core activity of embassies. Repressive regimes resent the cultivation of their political opponents. Even some close authoritarian allies of democracies, such as Singapore and Iran in the 1970s, actively discouraged such contacts. But diplomats who support the right of beleaguered opposition parties to exist and travel outside the country can hardly do objective reporting without contact with political actors.

Most definitions of democracy insist on the existence of a multi-party competitive and open electoral system. Embassies cannot legitimately attempt to influence the electoral success of specific parties. Some of the party-to-party mentoring is technical, and most is developmental without regard to specific policy choices or programs. Some political experiences of democratic parties in donor states have had a profound effect on the development of democratic options elsewhere. It has been usual for embassies to connect parties or groupings of one democratic tendency or another to similar groupings in their home countries, where parties have frequently formed foundations for the purposes of such outreach. Examples include the German Stiftungen, the Swedish Olof Palme Foundation, the US National Democratic Institute (NDI) or International Republican Institute (IRI), or la Fondation Robert Schumann and la Fondation Jean-Jaures in France. Democracies also have multi-party foundations for outreach, such as the Westminster Foundation in the UK, the Netherlands' Institute for Multiparty Democracy, the National Endowment for Democracy in the US, or the Norwegian Centre for Democracy Support.

Parliaments and Government Agencies

Whether democracies are heavily presidential or primarily parliamentary as far as the exercise of power is concerned, their democratic bona fides depend on there being competitive and fair elections to office.

The Handbook of National Legislatures by M. Steven Fish and Matthew Kroenig (2011) presents a global survey of parliaments. Direct parliament-to-parliament mentoring between democracies and emerging or transitional democracies has been a feature of democracy support for decades. Agencies such as the Netherlands Institute for Multiparty Democracy, the Westminster Foundation, or the Canadian Parliamentary Centre or various other inter-parliamentary assemblies have provided programs for such functions as committee organization, presiding officer responsibilities or independent fiscal and other oversight. Capacity-building support activity continues for such functions as an ombudsman's office, freedom of information, privacy and various watchdog and regulatory offices and agencies that have been brought into being over the years in the public interest in democracies, even if their independence is sometimes challenged by democratic governments more open in theory than in practice.

Even in circumstances where there are not obvious democratic bona fides, support programs for parliamentary transparency, the audit capacity and technical issues can have an impact on developing the beginnings of democratic capacities and reflexes.

International NGOs and Organizations

Of all local partnerships for diplomats and embassies, international NGOs are among the most valuable in the complementarity they represent to diplomatic activity and their role and purposes merit great deference. Organizations such as Human Rights Watch, the International Crisis Group, members of the World Movement for Democracy, Amnesty International, the San Egedio Foundation, and developmental NGOs of all kinds such as Oxfam, Médecins Sans Frontières, CARE, Action Contre la Faim, World Vision and, of course, intergovernmental organizations such as United Nations High Commissioner for Refugees (UNHCR), United Nations Children's Fund (UNICEF), the UN World Food Programme, or the International Organization for Migration (IOM) reach segments of society in their work and issues close to the ground, which are often out of accredited diplomats' reach. If diplomats and NGOs share values, they do not share roles; sensitivity to this fact is paramount. For the purposes of information exchange and avoidance of duplication, there are, in several capitals, useful mixed donors' groups composed of embassies, NGOs and international organizations.

Capacity Building

Democracies are easily distinguishable from tyrannies, but their governmental goal is not the pursuit of identity-based objectives of the majority; rather, it should be effective action to the benefit of all citizens, inclusively defined. Successful action relies on hard work over time and on achieving a mix of the right capacities for building achievement and public confidence. The most obvious characteristic of failed and failing states is their "negative capacity," which almost always negates the chances of democracy until stability and progress are restored.

Building democratic capacity requires sound, transparent, accountable and inclusive governmental institutions, as well as properly functioning infrastructure and orderly processes. Assistance and support for democratic governance is pointless without support for economic development and capacities to deliver education, health care and other essential aspects of infrastructure. But many assistance programs over the last decades, in Eastern Europe as well as in developing countries, invested excessively in process and institutions and not enough in civil society, which must form the building blocks of democratic transformation, particularly via the emergence of action groups which for environmental, economic or other specific interests challenge the status quo. Microfinance facilities have particular importance because of the contribution they can make to the capacity for acquiring self-reliance. Connecting such groups to international NGO partners is a major part of democratic capacity-building.

Methods are not self-evident. There is no transferable template for democratic transformation, no one size or style of economic or political model that fits all. The necessity of adaptation to local conditions and deference to local civil society relies on the existence of effective civil society partners and consultation with them. Ultimately, the chances of success will be in their hands and in their collective abilities to encourage a national governance culture that does assume transparency and accountability and responsiveness to the public. These capacity-building issues represent the substance of the work of a myriad of partners — governmental, intergovernmental and non-governmental, in all phases of international cooperation.

An annex is available online, indicating how missions might identify and contact NGOs and development organizations pertinent to capacity-building activities. The list of partners is far from complete; diplomats in the field will know how to identify local NGOs and potential partners from their own NGO community.

The capacity-building activities and issue areas, all interrelated, include several main emphases:

Anti-poverty and Humanitarian Relief

> Microfinance recognizes that the poor people are remarkable reservoirs of energy and knowledge. And while the lack of financial resources is a sign of poverty, today it is also understood as an untapped opportunity to create markets, bring people in from the margins and give them the tools with which to help themselves.

> — Kofi Annan, Remarks to Geneva Symposium, 2005

Intergovernmental bodies, such as the Council of Europe, the OAS, international agencies, NGOs and research institutes are working constantly on applications and long-term solutions. Development economics increasingly uses "randomization" to determine the validity of courses of action in different circumstances and locales. The impact of small-scale assistance projects and microcredit initiatives on setting the foundation for start-up economic activity has been promising; but it also benefits the building and spreading of civil society roots and capacity for autonomous self-administration and governance.

The work of organizations such as the World Food Programme and the FAO, and NGOs such as Action Contre la Faim on food security is very germane to democratic capacity, as is work on refugees and migration undertaken by the UNHCR, IOM and many NGOs. Especially important is building the democracy and human rights issues into the development agenda.

Elections, Electoral Machinery and Public Education

The International Fund for Election Systems, the ODIHR, International IDEA, the United Nations, the Commonwealth of Nations, the European Union and others team up to provide, in many cases, one-stop shopping on election preparation and administration issues. Electoral capacity is more than the technical administration of elections that are free and fair. It requires apt electoral laws, governing all aspects of the electoral and political cycles from expenditure through news presentation. Especially important are workable and accepted provisions for adjudicating disputes and ensuring that post-election outcomes are not winner-take-all, but rather, inclusive.

Governance and Institution Building

Member country and multilateral programs, activity of the trades union and labour movements, and activity of various coalitions of educational and professional coalitions work in the preparation of inclusive institutional reforms. These can often have an emphasis on functions vital for public confidence building and legitimacy, such as data collection (as in Liberia's 2008 census, conducted in partnership with the UN Development Programme), residential taxation systems that are fair and functional actuarial services. As mentioned under the section on partnerships, the development of offices of ombudsmen, privacy oversight bodies, freedom of information adjudicators, reliable statistical agencies, auditor-generals and a host of regulatory agencies that inform and protect the public interest are increasingly the object of government-to-government assistance programs or administered through international NGOs.

Environmental

Issues such as deforestation, desertification, drought, extractive industries and hydro dams become political causes with rapidity. The tens of thousands of environmental action groups that have been formed to mobilize opinion against action inimical to local and specific interests have been responsible for the politicization of millions. International partner NGOs have been part and parcel of the progress toward a more sustainable approach to developmental capacity building. As mentioned above, the international private sector also has a role to play.

Gender Equality

Generations of rural and urban women have been introduced to democratization through groups formed to address the situations and specific interests of women, whose capacity to contribute to development is obviously critical to success, but often underdeveloped. The practical goals of many such groups — material concerns, such as the cost of living — combine with preoccupations about violence to women, a phenomenon on the increase in many countries.

Judiciary

International NGOs on the rule of law and judicial reform, international bar sections and associations on the role of defenders and legal aid, holding offenders accountable, combatting corruption, are essential for developing capacity for public confidence.

Health, Education and Essential Infrastructure

International NGOs, international financial institutions (IFIs) such as the World Bank, humanitarian agencies, think tanks, research centres and authoritative policy analysts address the fundamental capacity issues of infrastructure, including sanitation and air quality. The Community of Democracies has placed a special emphasis on democracy education. It is testimony to the power of democratic principle that a resolution of the UN General Assembly, supporting democracy education for all, was adopted in 2012 by a consensus which included, obviously, non-democratic regimes. While democracy education has a classroom and public education function, it also includes the dynamic of education by example and experience as a society transits toward inclusive democracy institutionally and via civil society.

Local, Sub-federal, Ethnic and Tribal Groups

Federal member states of the Community of Democracies, the Forum of Federations and many other organizations and NGOs assist transforming democracies to extend democratic benefits to include more marginal members of society and indigenous peoples, who are often overlooked by elites, as well as addressing the issues of ethnic, tribal and sectarian conflict which sadly still ravage the population in much of the world.

Human Security, Including Conflict Prevention

Human security networks, the United Nations, international NGOs and foreign policy and security research centres address the fundamentally necessary capacities for security and public safety, without which neither democracy nor development can survive. Early warning systems for mass atrocity activity are increasingly relied upon, requiring diplomats on the ground to do much of the monitoring and reporting.

THE POWER OF INDIVIDUALS

The history of the struggle to realize human rights and to consolidate inclusive and effective democratic governance is a narrative replete with heroes and with countless anonymous individuals. Leaders, martyrs, activists and citizens working below the radar are the ones who own this human story of immutable ideals and the great risks taken in their pursuit.

The Activists

Wherever humans live, there will be notable protagonists for human rights. These include giants such as Mahatma Gandhi, Martin Luther King, Jr., Nelson Mandela and Miss Suu Kyi, but also many devoted and anonymous activists. In his tribute to Ambassador Mark Palmer in a speech to US Congress, US Congressman Frank Wolf stressed that the "world's destinies are shaped...by the courage and determination of individual men and women," rather by "impersonal forces." The following individuals represent just a sample for the sake of illustration.

Communicators and Journalists

- Agnieszka Romaszewska-Guzy founded Belsat TV, which has been broadcasting from Poland into Belarus since December 2007 as the only alternative to state-run television. Her parents, Zbigniew (the founder of the

Warsaw Helsinki Committee) and Zofia were both prisoners of conscience under 1981 martial law in Poland.

- Anna Politkovskaya, Russian journalist and human rights activist, was assassinated by a contract murderer in October 2006, following decades as an investigative reporter, most recently with Novaya Gazeta (1999–2006), in which she repeatedly challenged the Putin regime and the virtual Ramzan Kadyrov dictatorship of Chechnya. Threatened with death many times and treated brutally by Russian security forces in Chechnya, Anna represents the hundreds of journalists in the world killed in the line of reporting duty in recent years.

- Bloggers, such as Azerbaijani human rights activists Emin Milli and Rashad Agaadin Ramazanov, who have both been tortured while in police custody and yet continue to oppose the klepto-dictatorship of the Aliyev clan.

- Mona Eltahawy, Egyptian feminist and journalist, who wrote of physical and sexual assaults on her in 2011 post-revolution protests in Tahrir Square.

- Tawakkol Karman, a militant for press freedom who founded Women Journalists Without Chains in Yemen in 2005, and was awarded the Nobel Peace Prize in 2011.

- Samuel Kofi Woods, journalist and human rights activist in Liberia who has documented human rights abuses.

- Yoani Sanchez posted her "Generation Y" blog from Cuba, intrepidly providing an accurate account of the Cuban people.

Human Rights Defenders

- Nigerian artists have demonstrated a fierce sense of injustice over the years. Playwright (and Nobel Laureate for Literature, 1986) Wole Soyinka was a declared opponent of the dictator General Sami Abacha (1993–1998), as was Highlife and Afrobeat musician Fela Kuti, who died in 1997. Playwright Ken Saro-Wiwa led the Movement for the Survival of the Ogoni People, an environmental rights group contesting the destruction of fishing beds and wetlands principally by Shell Oil and the Abacha regime. He was hanged by the regime in November 1997, a "man of peace, ideas," as he wrote in his final statement from the dock of his rigged tribunal. His eldest son, Ken Wiwa, is President Goodluck Jonathan's senior special assistant on civil society and international media.

- Rami Nakhle, a Syrian dissident, who has created an impromptu network of cyberactivists inside Syria, smuggling in satellites, mobile phones, modems, laptops and cameras to encourage the witnessing of crimes by state security which are uplinked, especially to the Facebook page "Syria Revolution."

- Ales Bialiatski, Belarusian political activist, laureate of the 2012 Lech Walesa Award and vice president of the International Federation for Human Rights, founded the Viasna Human Rights Centre in Belarus in 1996, having been for many years an anti-Soviet dissident. The Centre provided financial and legal assistance to political prisoners and their families. He was arrested in 2011 for "tax evasion" and sentenced to four-and-a-half years in prison, and the Centre was closed.

- Ogtay Gulaliyev, a human rights and environmental activist in Azerbaijan, and founder of the Kur Civic Society, was tortured by the regime for defending those affected by oil-industry environmental damage. He was released in June 2012.

- Chen Guangcheng is internationally known for the prominence of his flight from house arrest to the protection of the US Embassy in Beijing and the subsequent negotiation with Chinese authorities permitting him to leave China. For many years prior to that event, he had been a human rights activist especially on behalf of the rights of rural Chinese women and environmental rights. In 2005, he contested the one-child policy in China and was subsequently tried on trumped-up charges and jailed for five years. Chen is representative of many rights-defending activists in China. There were 350 Chinese intellectuals and human rights activists who signed the Charter 2008 document, along with 2010 Nobel prize laureate Liu Xiaobo, who called for political reforms and the end of single-party rule.

- There are also many Chinese human rights defenders in exile — the most prominent of whom is Wei Jingsheng, who was deported to the US in 1997, after spending 18 years in prison. An early contributor to the Freedom Wall in Beijing, Wei is a laureate of the Sakharov and Olof Palme Prizes and many others.

- Born in 1927, Lyudmila Alexeyeva remains an iconic figure among Russian activists, having been a leader in the defence of human rights ever since inaugural demonstrations in Pushkin Square in 1965. A founding member of the Moscow Helsinki Group, she was forced to emigrate in 1977 and returned in 1993. Since 1996, she has been Chairperson of the revived Moscow Helsinki Group and an animator of "Strategy 31," devoted to defending by action Article 31 of the Russian Constitution, guaranteeing freedom of assembly.

- Natalya Estemirova was a human rights monitor in Chechnya for Memorial, the human rights organization. Her criticism of human rights abuse by Chechen militias prompted her abduction and murder in July 2009, illustrating the risks to which dedicated human rights defenders expose themselves everywhere.

- Laura Pollán was a prominent Cuban opposition leader, and with Berta Soler Fernandez founded Las Damas in Blanco, a group made up of the wives and partners of prisoners of conscience, who demand their release. The group was founded after the Group of 75 (among them, Pollán's husband) was jailed in 2003, following a peaceful protest march after Sunday Mass (with the attendant support of European diplomats).

- Tek Nath Rizal is a political and human rights activist in Bhutan, who defended the rights of ethnic Nepalese and Nepalese refugees. He was imprisoned in Bhutan from 1989–1999 and has written *Torture, Killing Me Softly*, a memoir about having been in prison a victim of mind control strategy.

- Fathi Terbil represented the families of the 12,000 political prisoners Gadhafi security forces slaughtered in 1996 in Abu Salim prison. He was at the centre of the Benghazi protests that launched the Libyan revolution in 2011 and became the interim government's minister of youth and sports.

- Jenni Williams founded Women of Zimbabwe Arise (Woza) and has been arrested more than 40 times for her work as a human rights defender, and opponent of Mugabe's one-man rule. She received Amnesty International's Ginetta Sagan Fund prize awarded to women working to protect the lives and rights of women and children.

- Oswaldo Payá, another Sakharov laureate, founded the Christian Liberation Movement in Cuba in 1987 and then the Varela Project, which gathered more than 25,000 signatures to claim the rights of freedom of speech and assembly and to oppose one-party rule. He died in controversial circumstances in 2012.

- Min Ko Naing has been a key democracy activist in Burma/Myanmar. He has spent most of the years since 1988 in prison.

- Sakeena Yacoobi is the Director of the Afghan Institute of Learning that, for 20 years, has advocated and provided for girls' schooling, including in underground schools in areas of Taliban occupation.

Officials and Professionals

- Maria Lourdes Afiuni, a Venezuelan judge defending independence of the judiciary, was arrested in 2009 on charges of corruption after ordering conditional release on bail of a businessman held three years without trial. Her continued incarceration has galvanized support from such as the Episcopal Conference of Venezuela, Human Rights Watch and the European Parliament.

- Abdul Tejan-Cole, human rights lawyer and trial attorney for human rights defenders, is Sierra Leone's former anti-corruption commissioner, a model for other African countries. He now serves as the executive director of the Open Society Initiative for West Africa.

- John Githongo is a former investigative journalist in Kenya who was appointed permanent secretary for governance and ethics in 2003. He uncovered a large-scale fraud involving senior ministers and after death threats, had to go into exile. He returned to Kenya in 2008 and founded anti-corruption NGO Kenya Ni Yetu (Kenya Is Ours).

- Muhammad Yunus, a Bangladeshi banker, won the Nobel Prize in 2006 for his commitment as an economist to developing facilities for microfinance and microcredit.

- Ela Ramesh Bhatt founded the Self Employed Women's Association of India, which did landmark work extending microfinance to poorer women entrepreneurs.

- The toll of killings of politically neutral humanitarian workers by jihadists and other extremists has grown. A particularly egregious atrocity was the Badakhshan Massacre in 2010, of a team of professionals from the Nuristan eye camp team.

The Diplomats

Since 2011, the Palmer Prize has been awarded to diplomats exhibiting risk-taking initiative on behalf of human rights and democracy development while on assignment, often in stressful conditions. They are exemplary of the many diplomats working to support democracy development and human rights defence anonymously around the world. Recent laureates include:

- Jaroslav Olša, Jr., who served as Czech Ambassador to Zimbabwe from 2000–2006. As an advocate for free and fair elections during the 2002 presidential and 2005 parliamentary elections, he did his best to ensure that a true record of what he observed reached local and other observer missions and the international community. In his exploration of ways to support the Zimbabwean people's struggle for democracy, he stood behind the rights of the opposition party, MDC, while retaining open communications with the then ruling party, headed by Robert Mugabe, to underline their need to respect democracy and human rights.

- Ernesto Pinto-Bazurco Rittler was, in 1980, chargé d'affaires of the Peruvian Embassy in Havana and argued for democracy, non-violence and human rights in Cuba. When thousands of asylum seekers sought refuge in the Peruvian Embassy, Pinto-Bazurco Rittler met with Fidel Castro and refused to hand the asylum seekers over to Cuban authorities. The standoff eventually gained international attention and resulted in the Mariel boatlift, a chaotic five-month period in which more than 125,000 Cubans defected to the United States. He is also lauded for his efforts in promoting human rights in Eastern Europe by the Journalists League Sibiu, Romania. He is a respected legal academic and has been a major contributor to international law in Latin America on the issue of the right to asylum.

- James McGee, former US Ambassador to Zimbabwe, played a leading role in calling for free and fair elections and speaking out against human rights abuses committed by the Zimbabwean government. McGee worked to draw attention to political violence in Zimbabwe and has led various delegations of diplomats through the country to assess the electoral and post-election environment. Additionally, McGee provided unwavering support for various programs, to foster civic participation, defend human rights and strengthen the electoral process in the highly volatile and challenging environment of Zimbabwe in 2008.

- Ben Rowswell founded the Canadian foreign ministry's democracy unit, in his devotion "to enhancing the legitimacy and effectiveness of democracy support as an essential tool for diplomacy." Rowswell worked for democracy support in Iraq and Afghanistan, and successfully lobbied for the creation of Kabul's Electoral Complaints Commission (the body that adjudicated allegations of fraud during the Afghanistan's 2009 presidential election).

- Caecilia Wijgers is a Dutch diplomat who took multiple initiatives to aid emerging civil society opposition groups in Cuba. Most notably, she helped distribute its publications — many of which are considered "subversive material and enemy propaganda" by the Cuban government — to opposition groups. Wijgers has been repeatedly lauded by numerous Cuban dissidents for her strong commitment to human rights, Internet and media freedom, and democratic reform.

- A special posthumous award was made to Mariusz Handzlik, a Polish diplomat who was a tireless advocate of democratic reform in Central Europe and the Baltic States during his years of diplomatic service. He heavily contributed to the development of civil society whose central role as a principal actor in international relations he worked to valorize.

- US Ambassador J. Christopher Stevens was killed in the US Consulate in Benghazi, Libya in September 2012. He was a determined advocate of human rights and a champion of getting diplomats out onto "the street," where they could connect directly with the people — a gesture which was ultimately his undoing. He began his appointment as Ambassador to Libya in May 2012 after two previous appointments as Special Representative to the Libyan Transitional National Council (TNC) from March to November 2011, and US Deputy Chief of Mission from 2007 to 2009. While serving as Special Representative to the TNC, Stevens acted as the top US envoy to the opposition during the rebel movement. Ambassador Stevens worked tirelessly to assist those working to liberate the people of Libya from Gadhafi's regime. In his address to the UN General Assembly, President Obama commended Stevens for supporting "the birth of a new democracy, as Libyans held elections, and built new institutions, and began to move forward after decades of dictatorship."

- Stefan Eriksson served as Swedish Ambassador to Belarus from 2008 to 2012. While in Belarus, Ambassador Eriksson worked with civil society and NGOs to bring the repression of the Belarusian government against democracy activists to light. He made it his mission to engage with marginalized communities fighting for access to civil and political rights and used the knowledge to coordinate assistance projects. He attended trials held against intellectuals, such as the president of the Belarusian author's union and encouraged the community to form networks with activists outside the country. Ambassador Eriksson also showed solidarity with democracy activists protesting the 2010 presidential election and attended the trials of several of the seven presidential candidates arrested after the government's brutal crackdown on opposition protestors. In 2012, as a result of his work with civil society and democracy activists, Ambassador Eriksson's credentials were not renewed by the Belarusian authorities, and he was forced to leave his post.

WORKS CITED

Acemoglu, Daron and James Robinson (2012). *Why Nations Fail: The Origins of Power, Prosperity, and Poverty*. New York: Crown Publishers.

Ali, Nour (2011). "Ambassadors to Syria Unite in Public Solidarity at Vigil for Murdered Activist." *The Guardian*, September 14.

Barclay, Philip (2010). *Zimbabwe: Years of Hope and Despair*. New York: Bloomsbury Publishing.

Barr, Caelainn (2011). "Leaked Reports Expose Abuses." *The Bureau of Investigative Journalism*, August 4.

Barry, Ellen (2011). "A Dissident is Free from Jail, but His Punishment Is Not Over." *The New York Times*, June 24.

Blair, Dennis C. (2013). *Military Engagement: Influencing Armed Forces Worldwide to Support Democratic Transitions*. Washington, DC: Council for a Community of Democracies and Brookings.

Carothers, Thomas (2003). *Promoting the Rule of Law Abroad: The Problem of Knowledge*. Democracy and Rule of Law Project Working Paper No. 34. Carnegie Endowment for International Peace.

Cowper-Coles, Sherard (2012). *Ever the Diplomat: Confessions of a Foreign Office Mandarin*. London: HarperPress.

Ellenbogen, Marc S. (2009). "Atlantic Eye: Linked by the Cold War's End." UPI. com, August 24. Available at: www.upi.com/Top_News/Special/2009/08/24/Atlantic-Eye-Linked-by-the-Cold-Wars-end/UPI-50851251132550/.

Fish, M. Steven and Matthew Kroenig (2011). *The Handbook of National Legislatures: A Global Survey*. Cambridge: Cambridge University Press.

Foreign Affairs (2013). "The Polish Model: A Conversation with Radek Sikorski." *Foreign Affairs*, May/June.

Fukuyama, Francis (2004). *State-Building: Governance and World Order in the Twenty-First Century*. Ithaca: Cornell University Press.

Haugen, Gary and Victor Boutros (2010). "And Justice for All." *Foreign Affairs*, May/June.

Lo, Alex (2013). "Admit it's a 'Western Financial Crisis.'" *South China Morning Post*, January 31.

McMahon, Patrice C. and Jon Western (2009). "The Death of Dayton: How to Stop Bosnia from Falling Apart." *Foreign Affairs*, September/October. Available at: www.foreignaffairs.com/articles/65352/patrice-c-mcmahon-and-jon-western/the-death-of-dayton.

McRae, Rob (1997). *Resistance and Revolution: Václav Havel's Czechoslovakia*. Ottawa: Carleton University Press.

Ross, Carne (2012). *The Leaderless Revolution: How Ordinary People Will Take Power and Change Politics in the 21st Century*. New York: Blue Rider Press.

Shadid, Anthony (2011). "Envoys Stay in Syrian City Where Protests Continue." *The New York Times*, July 8.

Velinger, Jan (2007). "The Role of the Canadian Embassy in Prague in the 'Age of Normalisation.'" Radio Praha, October 16. Available at: www.radio.cz/en/section/talking/the-role-of-the-canadian-embassy-in-prague-in-the-age-of-normalisation.

Watson, Paul (2008). "A Digitally Enhanced Myanmar Opposition." *Los Angeles Times*, January 7.

4 CONCLUSIONS

The Community of Democracies is not a political alliance, but its member states are joined by a shared hope for further progress toward democracy in the world. They support the efforts of civil society to create a virtual international community of democrats.

The working ground rules for the *Handbook's* construction held that there are no hard and fast prescriptions for democracy transformation, apart from the fact that the process and its outcomes best emerge peacefully from civil society itself. But active democrats and human rights defenders expect, and benefit from, the encouragement and support of democrats everywhere.

Democracy development is a function of process and sound institutions, but also very much one of behaviour, which cannot just be transferred as technique. It requires time, patience and hard application. Outside support needs to be sustained over time. The most critical resources are those of human capital in the countries concerned. Civil society forms the building blocks of democratization.

The *Handbook* aims to explain how democratic governments have used their embassies, consulates and diplomatic officers to provide such encouragement and support in the past. Each situation is different, and there is a varying mix of factors involved for each of the members of the Community of Democracies in policy emphasis and deployment of personnel.

International relations today form a complex of networks, contacts, transactions and activity that is mostly outside the scope of governments. The importance of international civil society in this process is primordial, amplified by the ongoing revolution in global communications.

The *Handbook* underlines the extent to which diplomatic representation has itself been undergoing transformation, from being an enterprise consisting of private government-to-government transactions to one in which people-to-people and public diplomacy are central features of the professional skill sets required today.

Of course, the skills involved are used in differing mixtures, depending on whether the host country is a failed, failing or post-conflict state, a military or theocratic dictatorship, a regime of populist authoritarianism, a fledgling and fragile democracy, or a complex democracy trying to consolidate democratic institutions and purposes. In citing examples from the last decades, we avoid slotting host countries into one category or another. The Community of Democracies' member states wish to avoid attempts to judge member countries according to snapshots of their governance. Independent NGOs already analyze relative governance very effectively.

Instead, a number of country case studies are presented, attempting to show a wide variety of situations and challenges. Some of the narratives, such as Chile, South Africa, Poland or Ukraine, are in the past tense — which is obviously not to suggest that history is over for the countries concerned. Other narratives are very much in the here and now. Those case studies that were in the *Handbook's* first edition, such as Belarus, Burma/Myanmar and Zimbabwe, and those presented for the second edition on China, Cuba and Egypt have all been updated in this third edition. The new edition also includes new case studies on the Tunisian Revolution and on Russian democracy, 1987–2013.

The next phases of all these studies remain to be written by the people themselves.

In these case studies, and in such instructive episodes of transition as Sierra Leone and Tanzania, which are available online, we expect that practitioners in the field — whether diplomats, NGOs or other personnel — will recognize elements familiar to the situation they are closest to at present, and will be assisted in developing their own approaches and programs for democracy development support on the ground.

In the years to come, we shall continue to update the existing case studies, and add new ones as they arise. We constantly modify and expand the *Handbook* itself to take account of comments from readers and users and hope that the *Handbook* serves the helpful concrete purposes intended — the higher interest of promoting both greater satisfaction for the aspirations of many millions of individuals, and a more secure and open international environment for all.

CASE STUDIES

1 TUNISIA: IGNITING ARAB DEMOCRACY

By Dr. Laurence Michalak, 2013

*N**ota Bene: At the time of publication, Tunis is experiencing large protests calling for the resignation of the current moderate Islamist Ennahdha government. The demonstrations follow on the six-month anniversary of the still-unsolved assassination of Chokry Belaid, and in the wake of the killing in late July 2013 of a second secular leftist politician, Mohamed Brahmi. The national labour union, Union Générale Tunisienne du Travail (UGTT), has called on its hundreds of thousands of members to join the rally. Work on a new constitution and election law have been suspended. The constituent assembly has been suspended pending negotiations between the government and opposition, after 70 members withdrew in protest over Brahmi's murder. The demonstrations are the largest of their kind since the ouster of Zine El Abine Ben Ali in January 2011. Elections are scheduled for December 2013.*

Tunisia is an instructive case study in democracy development because the uprising that began there in December 2010 has ignited an ongoing movement in the Arab world. Tunisia's movement is still evolving, but a summary of events to date is as follows:

- The Tunisian uprising was essentially homegrown, illustrating that democracy cannot be imported but must, in each country, emerge from the people themselves.

- France, the most powerful diplomatic presence in Tunisia, gave almost unqualified support to the autocratic President Ben Ali for nearly a quarter century, although the French Socialist government elected in May 2012 supports Tunisia's democratic development.

- The US supported President Ben Ali until the George W. Bush administration, but changed its approach to encourage democracy, a policy continued by the Obama administration.

- The Western democracies supported autocratic leaders in the MENA region because they incorrectly thought they had to choose between a secular dictator and violent Islamists.

- In a broad-based social uprising beginning in December 2010, Tunisians expelled an autocrat, dissolved a ruling party and chose representatives to draft a new constitution.

- Tunisia's main Islamist party, Ennahdha, won a 41 percent plurality of seats in the October 2011 election, allying with two secularist parties to form a coalition government.

- The Tunisian economy has worsened between 2011 and 2013, with increased unemployment, frequent strikes and high inflation. Tourism has been slow to recover, investment from abroad remains low and many foreign businesses have left.

- The delay in producing a new constitution (now approaching two years) and the continuing weakness of the economy have led to a steady decline in approval of the elected government.

- Tunisian public discourse has been marked by low-level violence and at least two serious incidents — the attack on the US Embassy and American School in September 2012 and the assassination of secularist leader Chokri Belaid in February 2013 and Mohamed Brahmi in July 2013.

- The misdeeds of the jihadist wing of Tunisia's Salafist minority are a problem for the moderate Ennahdha and its allies, who have been slow to condemn them.

- The most important assistance that diplomats and NGOs can provide is facilitating economic programs that create jobs to alleviate unemployment and regional inequality.

- Despite current difficulties, long-term prospects for democracy are good for Tunisians, who are unlikely to give up their hard-won rights to fair elections and free speech.

- Though many consider democracy to be a universal value that is European in origin, Tunisians are developing a style of democracy that has its own local characteristics.

INTRODUCTION: A MOVEMENT BEGINS

On December 17, 2010, in a rural city in the interior of Tunisia, a poor fruit and vegetable vendor named Mohamed Bouazizi doused himself with paint thinner and set himself on fire in front of the provincial government headquarters. He was reportedly protesting because a municipal official had slapped him and confiscated his wares for peddling without a licence. The incident ignited a series of demonstrations that spread throughout the country, finally reaching the capital city of Tunis, whose streets filled with thousands of protesters shouting "Dégage!" ("Get out!" in French). On January 14, 2011, Tunisia's autocratic and corrupt President Ben Ali fled with his family to Saudi Arabia.

Since then, the uprising has developed into a true revolution which has spread throughout the Arab world, inspiring hope for democracy — especially among Arab youth, who have become more politically active through engagement with the Internet, social networks and media such as Al-Jazeera.

This political explosion caught almost everyone by surprise. The MENA region had been the least democratic and least politically engaged part of the world. Dictatorships had crumbled in other regions, such as Latin America and Sub-Saharan Africa, but the MENA region — and especially the Arab world — seemed to be the last bastion of autocracy. Some scholars spoke of a regional democracy deficit and speculated that features of Arab culture and/or Islam might be causal factors for this condition.

Recent events have decisively undermined such ideas, but they were once current and may have hindered scholars and diplomats from detecting signs of growing popular resentment in the region. Whatever the reason, Western democracies had, for decades, tended to soft-pedal issues of democratic governance and human rights when dealing with Arab dictators. The motivations for this policy were access to oil, geostrategic concerns and, in the case of the United States, support for Israel. In recent years, a new purpose was added: securing cooperation in the struggle against Islamism, which many viewed as synonymous with violence and terrorism.

In pursuing closer relations with the Mediterranean countries under the Barcelona Process, the European Union found that authoritarian regimes in the MENA region reacted unfavourably to suggestions of democratic reform. The conflict was especially acute with the Tunisian regime. Of the 10 subcommittees created to implement the European Neighbourhood Policy under the Barcelona Process, the committee on human rights languished.

Journalists and scholars still struggle to find appropriate terms to describe the movement that began in Tunisia. At first some called it the "Jasmine Revolution," perhaps implying a parallel to the "Velvet" and "Orange" revolutions of Eastern Europe. The term that seems to have stuck, at least in the West, is "Arab Spring" — like the "Prague Spring" in Czechoslovakia and the "Berber Spring" in Algeria. The analogy is weak, however, because both of these movements were crushed — one by the Soviets in 1968 and the other by the Algerian regime in 1980 — and neither historical context resembles that of the MENA region today. "Arab Spring" may be a problematic name for the movement but — like other imprecise terms, such as Islamic "fundamentalism" (a term borrowed from Protestantism), "Islamism" (which lacks the parallel constructions of "Judism" and "Christianism") and "Middle East" (a Eurocentric term) — it has persevered.

Examining the case of Tunisia, we address a number of questions. Why did a movement against autocracy begin there, and why in a rural area? Is it a true revolution? Is it democratic? How has the movement evolved? What is likely to happen? And to what extent can we generalize from Tunisia to other countries of the region?

Especially relevant to the purposes of this *Handbook*, the last and most important question is: What lessons does Tunisia teach about how diplomats and NGOs from democratic countries can effectively support transitions to democracy? We ask this while bearing in mind that democracy and civil society cannot be simply imported, but must emerge in each country in culturally appropriate ways.

HISTORICAL BACKGROUND

Precursory Conditions

Although its awakening surprised many, Tunisia has long been the Arab country most suited for democracy. As a semi-autonomous Ottoman province, Tunisia was the first country in the MENA region to adopt a constitution (in 1861) and the first to start a modern secondary school (College Sadiki in Tunis in 1875). Under the French protectorate that began in 1881, the Tunisian elite were quick to imbibe the principles of the Enlightenment and, soon after World War I, were calling on their colonial rulers to practice their own principles by granting independence.

Independence

In contrast to the brutal war of independence in neighbouring Algeria, where France had a large and long-established population of colonists and had annexed the country, Tunisia was able to negotiate a relatively peaceful independence beginning in 1956. In 1957, Tunisia abolished the Beylical monarchy, which had been in power since 1705. Independent Tunisia became a republic with a strong presidency, a weak Parliament and a progressive, Western-inspired code of law. The pre- and post-independence history of Tunisia has been characterized by several conditions that are propitious for the development of democracy. These include:

- A high level of education. In the 1950s and 1960s, independent Tunisia spent a third of its national budget on education, achieving high rates of school enrollment and literacy and fostering the emergence of a university-educated technical and professional elite. As a result, the population, despite decades of state-controlled media, has a sophisticated level of political discourse, avid recourse to the Internet and aspirations to democracy.

- A large middle class. Despite regional inequality, Tunisia is relatively well endowed with manufacturing, mining, agriculture and tourism resources. Although the Ben Ali regime inflated statistics on prosperity and underestimated poverty, Tunisia tripled per capita GNP between 1986 and 2008 and built an abundant consumer economy. A substantial middle and professional class supports property and individual rights and transparency in governance, the ingredients of a stable democracy.

- An active civil society. Tunisia had the beginnings of civil society — trade unions and professional and cultural associations — although the government closely controlled these groups. Prior to the uprising, only a handful of organizations were truly independent. Many groups were denied permits to organize and chafed under authoritarian rule, especially in the later years of the Ben Ali regime. The revolution in Tunisia has removed most of these obstacles and eased a transition to democratic and pluralistic governance.

- Respect for women's rights. At independence, Tunisia abolished polygamy, gave women the vote, introduced free and effective birth control, and has gradually reduced the fertility to replacement rate. A concern with gender issues in Tunisia goes back to at least 1930, with modernist Tahar Haddad, and even to the eighth-century Contract of Kairouan, an interpretation of Islamic law that facilitated monogamy. Women make up more than half of university students and Tunisia has promoted the active participation of women at all levels of society. There is a higher percentage of women in Tunisia's Parliament than in those of France, the United Kingdom and the United States.

- A relatively homogenous society. Tunisia is by no means homogenous, and class and regional inequalities contributed to the uprising. However, Tunisia lacks the deep ethnic and religious cleavages — Sunni/Shia, Muslim/ Christian, Arab/Berber — that characterize most other Arab countries. Tunisia is 99 percent Sunni Arab Muslim and has a history of religious tolerance and minimal social conflict.

Lost Opportunities

On at least two occasions, independent Tunisia almost took the path of democracy. Because of his far-sighted policies and because he had been imprisoned for a decade by the French, Tunisia's charismatic first president, Habib Bourguiba benefitted from prestige and legitimacy at the outset of independence. Like many popular first presidents, from George Washington to Nelson Mandela, Bourguiba could have left office after one or two terms. Instead, he monopolized power through a single hegemonic party and made himself "President for Life."

Another opportunity for democracy came in 1987, when Prime Minister Ben Ali deposed the by-then frail and senile Bourguiba. In his first speech, Ben Ali said that Tunisia was ready for democracy. He instituted both a two-term limit and an age limit for presidents. After this opening flourish and other early liberal gestures, however, he succumbed to the temptation of power, changing the constitution and clinging to control for 23 years. He "privatized" Tunisia by transferring ownership of many state companies to his family and their cronies, especially the numerous relatives of his second wife, Leila Trabelsi. The resentment engendered by Ben

Ali's corruption and nepotism, combined with economic hard times and the severe regional inequality that had existed since Bourguiba, fuelled Tunisia's broadly based popular uprising.

PROTEST

A Spark in Rural Tunisia

Mohamed Bouazizi, the vendor who sold fruits and vegetables from a wooden pushcart in Sidi Bouzid, was in many ways typical of the poor of the Global South who are unable to find real jobs. Many of them enter the inflated commercial sector and eke out a bare subsistence living as petty vendors. At least a produce peddler can eat what he doesn't sell.

However, because Bouazizi lacked proper permits, paid no taxes and had an unlicenced scale, local authorities confiscated his cart, his scale and his wares. Some sources say he attempted to obtain permits but was denied, and that the scale was borrowed from a friend. When the authorities would neither hear his appeal nor return his means of livelihood, Bouazizi, who was the sole support of his family, despaired and burned himself in protest.

Bouazizi became not only a national but an international hero. Even President Ben Ali felt obliged to be photographed at Bouazizi's bedside — although it was later reported that Ben Ali had actually been photographed with a different burn victim whose face was swathed in bandages. It was widely rumoured that Bouazizi had already died but that the announcement of his death was delayed to provide a photo opportunity for Ben Ali.

Overnight, Bouazizi's face appeared on placards and his name on walls throughout the country. After having ignored quiescent Tunisia for decades, the international press corps flocked to Sidi Bouzid to report the gruesome story. Only three months after his death, a biography glorifying Bouazizi was published in Tunis. In July 2011, the well-known Moroccan writer Tahar Ben Jelloun published another hagiographic biography of Bouazizi in the form of a novel, *Par le Feu* (By Fire). The mayor of Paris named a square in Bouazizi's honour. The European Parliament posthumously bestowed its Sakharov Prize for Freedom of Thought on Bouazizi. A mural dedicated to Bouazizi was painted on a wall in the Mission District of San Francisco. He had become an international martyr.

Upon closer scrutiny, however, it became apparent that these initial reports were riddled with contradictions. At first Bouazizi was reported to be a college graduate who couldn't find a job, but it turned out that he hadn't finished high school. It was reported that he had been slapped and publicly humiliated by Faida Hamdy, a 45-year-old policewoman who was hastily jailed as a symbol of arbitrary authority and corruption; however, an investigation and trial found her innocent. There was even testimony that, on the contrary, it was Bouazizi who had insulted and harassed

Hamdy, and it seemed that President Ben Ali had tried to make this unfortunate woman into a scapegoat. Many began to question how Bouazizi could be considered a martyr, since suicide is strictly forbidden in Islam.

Other Tunisian protesters had burnt themselves to death, both before and after Bouazizi, including another peddler under similar circumstances in the Tunisian coastal city of Monastir in March 2010 — so why was Bouazizi's suicide the spark that set off the uprising? The answer is testimony to the power of social networking to create a mobilizing narrative and attract popular support.

A small group of astute activists in Sidi Bouzid organized quickly on the day of the suicide. Within an hour and a half, they had disseminated a shocking story and a horrible photograph of a burning man. Bouazizi's self-immolation was invested with the powerful message that Tunisians could no longer live without social and economic dignity — a message that resonated deeply throughout the country. A number of Sidi Bouzid activists later admitted that they had coordinated their version of the facts in order to arouse public opinion, exaggerating Bouazizi into a flawless hero and casting Hamdy as the villainess.

Underlying Factors

We will probably never know exactly how the incident transpired. Certainly, Bouazizi's suicide was not the cause of the uprising, but rather the incident that triggered it. Tunisia's revolt had been building for many years and was the outcome of a mix of deeper causes. In 2008, workers in the phosphate mines of the Gafsa region had gone on strike for six months; the regime brutally repressed the strike but it remained an open wound. Labour unrest spread throughout the country. The gap of regional inequality between the poor interior and the relatively wealthy coast and capital city widened. Since 2008, especially, the price of food had increased sharply, and the country's economic problems were compounded by world recession. Corruption and nepotism were rampant, led by the families of Ben Ali and his wife Leila, who controlled much of the economy. This was the fuel, and Bouazizi's suicide was the spark that ignited it.

The Geography of Protest

From the Interior to the Capital

Starting in Sidi Bouzid, the uprising spread rapidly throughout the interior and the south. Protesters attacked police stations and burned public buildings. Under Ben Ali's orders, the police reacted brutally, shooting to kill, arresting and torturing, but to no avail. After a successful general strike in Sfax, Tunisia's second-largest city, the demonstrations spread northward up the coast toward the capital.

On January 11, 2011, the revolt finally reached the capital city of Tunis. As it had begun in the poorest region of Tunisia, so also in Tunis, the uprising began in the poorest neighbourhoods, collections of grim high-rise housing projects on the outskirts of the city. The people who lived there were part of a rural exodus from places in the interior like Sidi Bouzid. The protest attracted ever-broader segments of Tunisian society, including many with no prior experience of political activism.

Inside the Capital

In Tunis, the demonstrators congregated on either side of the medina, or old Arab city. At first, the main locus of protest was the Avenue Habib Bourguiba, which, under a series of changing names, has always been the main thoroughfare of the European city. The protesters gathered there, in front of the Ministry of Interior. The second locus for demonstrations was on the west side of the medina in the casbah, also called "Government Square," around which several ministries, including the prime minister's office and the Ministry of Defence, are located.

Several kinds of forces maintained order in Tunisia. These included the Presidential Guard, composed of 2,500 men under the command of Ben Ali intimate Ali Seriati. The national police and security forces numbered between 100,000 and 130,000, including the elite Brigade of Public Order (BOP), but they were unable to cope with the thousands of demonstrators who filled downtown Tunis, so the government called in the army.

Tunisia's army is relatively small (about 35,000) and well-disciplined, having earned international plaudits as a professionally competent UN contingent. The members of the officer corps, largely US-trained, are not allowed to join political parties and, unlike their Egyptian counterparts, they have no economic advantages. The officer corps had reason to resent the regime, since Ben Ali is widely thought to have engineered a helicopter crash that killed much of the army high command in 2002.

The decisive moment came when Ben Ali ordered General Rachid Ammar, the Tunisian Armed Forces chief of staff, to fire on the protesters. General Ammar refused, thereby aligning himself with other military professionals whose ethical principles had undermined autocrats in other settings, such as Kyiv, Moscow and Belgrade.

In a series of public speeches, Ben Ali tried to quell the protest. His first two speeches were stern proclamations in classical Arabic condemning "outside agitators." His third and last speech, however, delivered the day before he fled, was contrite. He spoke on television in Tunisian dialect, and the nation of spectators could see that his hands were shaking. "Ghaltooni!" pleaded the president — "They misinformed me!" Like Bourguiba and the Ottoman beys before him, Ben Ali tried to blame his lieutenants for the crisis. He dismissed several ministers and three regional governors, promising to address people's grievances, to create hundreds of thousands of new jobs, and not to stand for re-election. But it was too late.

The President Flees

On January 14, 2011, with the streets of Tunis packed with protesters, President Ben Ali, his wife and a planeload of family members fled the country, after which the army closed the airport. A second plane with more of the president's wife's relatives was detained and its passengers arrested. Apparently, Ben Ali had not intended to leave, only to send his wife and family away temporarily. He accompanied them to the airport to see them off, but at the last minute, at the urging of his wife and of his close adviser, Ali Seriati, he decided to leave with them. Ben Ali planned to return to Tunis the next day and instructed the pilot to wait for him, but the pilot disobeyed his orders and flew back to Tunis without him.

At long last, a movement for democracy had begun in the Arab world. The impact was felt next in Egypt, followed by major uprisings in Yemen, Bahrain, Libya and Syria, as well as demonstrations in other Arab states. Aspirations to remove their dictators spread throughout the region, particularly among the young. Many were transfixed by the reporting of Al-Jazeera and Al-Arabiya and by blogs from Tunisian activists, while others used more traditional venues of organization, such as the mosque. Friday, the traditional day of Muslim communal prayer, became the favorite day of protest throughout the region.

From Uprising to Revolution

The term "revolution" is often used loosely, in cases when "uprising" would be more appropriate. Strictly defined, a revolution means a basic change — not just transplanted leadership, but the wiping away of an old order and its replacement by a new order that is fundamentally different.

For example, Egypt from the 1950s onward was run by a series of three generals — Nasser, Sadat and Mubarak. Even after the uprising of January 2011, the real ruler of Egypt remained the army, which oversaw elections but reserved most of the power, especially economic control, for itself. At one point, it even appeared that a military figure might be elected president. A good case can be made that until a civilian president took office and, in August 2012, dismissed the top generals and disestablished the military, Egypt had not yet had a "revolution." The coup of July 2013 underscored where the real power lay all along.

Tunisian democracy, on the other hand, was facilitated by the military, which refused to obey Ben Ali. From early on, it became clear that Tunisia was experiencing not just a short-lived uprising, but a movement with promise of systematic long-term change — a revolution.

Dismantling Autocracy

Since the flight of Ben Ali, Tunisia has been marked by contradictions — exhilaration and unease, order and chaos, optimism and pessimism. At first, there were violent attempts to reverse the uprising. Black-clad snipers fired into crowds from the roofs of buildings in Tunis — but the protesters stood their ground, and within a few days these last remnants of repression had disappeared.

Prime Minister Mohamed Ghannouchi, Ben Ali's right-hand man since the late 1980s, announced that the president was "temporarily unable to exercise his duties" and that he himself had become acting president. During the brief time that he was president, Ghannouchi tried to placate the protesters by appointing a new cabinet. The Parliament, however, decided that Ben Ali had vacated the presidency and that, under the Tunisian Constitution, the position of acting president should devolve onto the elderly and sickly Speaker of the Parliament, Fouad Mbazaa. Mbazaa reluctantly accepted the presidency, and then disappeared almost completely from sight for the next nine months.

Continuing demonstrations forced Ghannouchi and every other minister to resign. The Parliament was dismissed, the ruling Democratic Constitutional Rally Party (RCD) was disbanded, and an interim government was formed with non-RCD ministers, many of whom had been vocal critics of Ben Ali.

THE MORNING AFTER

Tunisia enjoyed a period of celebration with cheering crowds who waved signs and chanted slogans, but it was brief. A major problem was that about 11,000 felons had escaped or been released from Tunisia's prisons. Some were political prisoners, but others were violent criminals. A crime wave spread across the country. In an encouraging sign of initiative at the grassroots level, Tunisian towns and neighbourhoods formed watch groups with checkpoints to protect themselves and their communities. The same thing later happened during the uprising in Cairo, where the police similarly disappeared from sight.

The Tunisian police, especially the BOP, had discredited themselves. In the interior, they had beaten, gassed, shot, tortured and killed demonstrators. The snipers were generally thought to be BOP sharpshooters or foreign mercenaries. People saw the police as villains and the army as heroes. Perhaps out of shame, the police were seldom seen in public in early 2011 and have been slow to reappear.

The immediate effects of the Tunisian Revolution were politically positive but economically negative. Between May 2010 and May 2011, the unemployment rate in Tunisia increased from 13 percent to 18.3 percent, leaving over 800,000 jobless in a country of only a little over 10 million. Those who did have jobs demanded salary increases to catch up with the cost of living. There were more strikes than before. Tourism, which had employed 400,000 people directly and another 300,000 indirectly, declined in 2011 by over 50 percent from 2010 levels. Tourism recovered slightly in 2012, but has flattened in the first third of 2013 due to foreign perceptions of insecurity.

Much of Tunisia's post-revolutionary economic decline was due to the uprising and civil war in neighbouring Libya, where hundreds of thousands fled across the border. These refugees from Libya included Libyans, Sub-Saharan African expatriates and an estimated 60,000 Tunisians who had been working in Libya and fled home, swelling the ranks of the unemployed. Events in Libya also contributed to Tunisia's rising cost of living — especially rents and food prices — due to exports to Libya and an increase in the number of resident Libyans.

Tunisians were worried, especially about security. With the breakdown of law and order and the retreat of the police, young women were afraid to go out at night. Parents feared that their children would be kidnapped. People protected their houses and apartments with extra locks and reinforced metal doors and plastered the tops of their courtyard walls with broken bottle glass. Taxi drivers cursed the revolution as bad for business. Many quoted Al-Ghazali, an eleventh-century Islamic philosopher who taught that dictatorship is better than anarchy. As sometimes happens, satisfaction at getting rid of a dictator had given way to fear of the unknown and preoccupation with safety and security.

Interim to an Election

Tunisia's first task was to replace the old constitution, which had given nearly unlimited power to the presidency. The interim government appointed an electoral commission under Kamal Jendoubi, a widely respected human rights leader who had opposed Ben Ali, to organize an election for a constituent assembly that would then draft a new constitution. The commission scheduled the election for October 23, 2011, to choose 217 representatives through a proportional list voting system. They divided the country into 33 districts, including six for Tunisians living abroad. Each district would elect up to 10 representatives, based on population. Candidates had to be from the districts in which they were running. Parties would present lists in each district, with the progressive stipulation that each electoral list had to alternate men and women candidates.

Would members of the RCD be allowed to run for office? Anti-RCD sentiment was still strong and there was little spirit of reconciliation. The commission decided that members from the last decade would not be allowed to run, but that old Bourguibists and RCD members from before 10 years ago would be permitted. Those who had signed a notorious public letter encouraging Ben Ali to be a candidate again for president would not be allowed to run, although some claimed that their names had been used without their consent.

The Interim Government

Until the election for the constituent assembly, Tunisia had a caretaker government led by Prime Minister Beji Caid Essebsi, an 84-year-old politician who had served in the government in the 1960s, pressed Bourguiba for democratic reforms in the 1970s and then resigned. Under Ben Ali, he had served briefly as head of the Chamber of Deputies, but had not joined the RCD and had retired from politics with a relatively untainted reputation in 1994. Thus, Caid Essebsi had a reputation for honesty, although some raised questions about events during his tenure as Interior Minister from 1965 to 1969.

In the new climate of free speech, Tunisians were critical of everything, beginning with the election plan. Some said that the constituent assembly was too large. Some criticized the voting system as complicated and confusing. Some argued that the election should be held earlier. Some deplored that people would be voting for parties rather than candidates. By the time of the election, 112 parties had been approved — a confusing alphabet soup of acronyms. People had trouble telling them apart. Some parties had only a handful of members.

There were criticisms of the interim government. Caid Essebsi had been appointed rather than elected, so he lacked legitimacy. When he took initiative, he was criticized for exceeding his mandate, and when he did not take initiative, he was criticized for inaction. For example, Tunisia needed to purge the judiciary of corrupt judges from the Ben Ali era, but the prime minister resisted because he knew that sorting honest from corrupt judges would be a controversial task. When criticized for inaction, he responded by delegating the task to a commission.

Many asserted that those running for office were opportunists interested only in drawing a salary. The most serious problem was that many Tunisians did not plan to vote, stating openly that they considered politics and politicians inherently evil. After decades of corruption and nepotism, they were skeptical that change was possible. As one lawyer said, "There used to be one Ben Ali but now there are 10 million of them."

A voter registration drive began July 11 but elicited little response. Polls indicated that more than half of Tunisians either were undecided or planned not to vote. The electoral commission extended the registration period and announced that Tunisians would be able to vote without having registered if they did so in the district listed on their identity cards. In the end, a little over half of the eligible electorate voted.

Due to distrust of the government-controlled press, Tunisia had always been rich in rumours and conspiracy theories. One rumour was that the ministers of the interim government had all been appointed by Kamal Letaief, a relative of Ben Ali who headed a small group of pro-French Tunisians who spent most of their time in Paris. A contradictory rumour was that Ben Ali's overthrow was a CIA plot, and that US Assistant Secretary of State Jeffrey Feltman had chosen the interim government during a visit to Tunis.

Tunisia's Main Islamist Returns

A pivotal event of the election campaign was the return from exile of moderate Islamist leader Rached Ghannouchi — not to be confused with Mohamed Ghannouchi, Ben Ali's long-standing prime minister. In the early 1970s, he helped found Tunisia's Islamist movement, which at that time, had been harshly repressed. Ghannouchi had been imprisoned under Bourguiba, but was later released by Ben Ali. Since overtly Islamic parties were illegal, Ghannouchi changed the name of his party from the Islamic Tendency Movement to Ennahdha ("Renaissance"). The party was again refused approval. Ghannouchi fled to France and then to England, where he lived in London until the uprising. He credited Britain with values of tolerance and pluralism, which he said would be the hallmarks of Ennahdha's approach. Thousands of supporters turned out at the Tunis airport for Ghannouchi's triumphant return on January 30, 2011.

Ennahdha was approved as an official party in March 2011 and immediately became the front-runner in the polls by a small margin. The Progressive Democratic Party (PDP), a secularist party, was said to be a close second. Besides Ennahdha, four other major political parties emerged:

- The PDP, a secular and social-democratic party, was led by Nejib Chebbi and Maya Jribi. It had been legal but was repressed under Ben Ali and had boycotted the past two presidential elections. Generally considered the major party of the left, it hovered in second place to Ennahdha in pre-election polls but then began to decline. The PDP ran a high-profile campaign on a strongly secularist platform and was highly critical of Ennahdha.

- The Congress for the Republic (CPR), a nationalist and slightly leftist party, was led by Moncef Marzouki, a doctor with origins in the Tunisian south (although he was born in the Cap Bon peninsula). Marzouki had been active in Tunisia's much-beleaguered human rights movement. He had run for president against Ben Ali in 1994, but had been disqualified and imprisoned. After his release, he went into exile in France. A respected figure, Marzouki refrained from criticizing Ennahdha.

- The Democratic Forum for Labour and Liberties (DFLL), a secular, centre-left party led by Mustapha Ben Jafar, was another opposition party approved under Ben Ali; however, the party had never been allowed any seats and Ben Jafar had been disqualified from running for president. DFLL steadily gained in popularity over the course of the campaign and, like the CPR, did not criticize Ennahdha.

- The Popular Petition Party (PPP) was a populist conservative party led by Mohamed Hechmi Hamdi, a controversial Tunisian expatriate millionaire from Sidi Bouzid. Based in London, Hamdi had at one time been a member of Ennahdha. He founded a news magazine and two satellite television stations. Hamdi was suspect because he had run positive television stories about Ben Ali and was reputed to have accepted bribes from him.

No public opinion surveys were allowed in the last month of the campaign, in order to prevent the results of polls from affecting the election. It was predicted that Ennahdha would win about a quarter to a third of the vote, with PDP a close second. Half the electorate was undecided, however, and the polls were out of date, so the results of the election were highly unpredictable.

A Democratic Election

The Tunisian election had both international and Tunisian observers, including Tunisian NGOs that had organized for this purpose. According to the monitors, the October 23, 2011 election was peaceful, orderly and fair, with only minor irregularities. Many Tunisians had said they might not vote, but most of the eligible voters did. Optimists pointed out that 86 percent of those registered went to the polls. Skeptics retorted that, since only a little over half the eligible voters had registered, the real turnout was considerably lower; however, the turnout exceeded 50 percent of eligible voters. In the end, there was general satisfaction with both the turnout and the fairness of the election, especially considering that it had been organized from scratch in only a few months.

The Moderate Islamist Party Wins a Plurality

Ennahdha won a larger plurality than expected, with 41 percent of the seats. The secular-left PDP had been expected to finish second, but surprisingly won only seven percent of the seats. Clearly, many analysts had overestimated the appeal of Western-style secular parties against a well-organized moderate Islamic alternative. The two parties that had not demonized Ennahdha — CPR and DFLL — won 13 percent and nine percent of the seats, respectively, and joined Ennahdha in forming a three-party majority coalition.

After a low-profile campaign, the PPP finished a surprising third, but they were charged by the election commission with violating campaign regulations for illegal contributions, campaigning during the blackout period and one ineligible candidate. Nine of their elected assembly members were disqualified, but eight were restored on appeal, giving them 12 percent of the assembly seats. Because of the controversies surrounding the PPP, the leaders of Ennahdha did not invite any of its members to join the ruling coalition.

Women and Democracy

Women's participation is a benchmark of democracy and, as mentioned earlier, Tunisia has a history of support for women's rights. Women won 49 of the 217 seats in the Tunisian Constituent Assembly. By law, the party lists were required to alternate the names of men and women candidates, but since most of the electoral lists were headed by men and from most of these lists only one person was elected, men won most of the seats.

The exception was Ennahdha, the moderate Islamist party. In many districts, more than one Ennahdha candidate was elected, and many of the Ennahdha lists were headed by women. Out of the 49 assemblywomen elected, 42 were from Ennahdha; nearly half of Ennahdha's assembly members were women. By June 2012, some male assembly members had resigned to become ministers and were replaced by women, so the number of women in the assembly increased from 47 to 52, thus, women made up 24 percent of the assembly — a greater percentage than in the United Kingdom, France or the United States.

Some might be surprised that women are so prominent in an Islamist party. Monica Marks, who has interviewed 51 Ennahdha women, notes that they tend to be assertive and well-educated. Many of them have endured arrests and prison terms, and often, they are the wives of Ennahdha men who spent years in prison, during which time these women became wage-earners and small-scale entrepreneurs, working to hold their families together. Now that their husbands have returned from prison, the women continue to play active decision-making roles in both the family and in Ennahdha.

Marks notes the sharp contrast between Ennahdha and Egypt's Muslim Brotherhood, which separates men and women. Ennahdha reaffirmed the Personal Status code of 1956-1957, which abolished polygamy and gave women broadly equal rights. In Ennahdha, men and women mix freely in offices, rallies and committees. Twenty of the 50 members of Ennahdha's policy-setting body are women. Egypt's Muslim Brotherhood is against the idea of a Coptic Christian or woman president, but Ennahdha has declared that it favours the full participation of women and minorities at all levels of government. In the case of Tunisia, Islamist does not mean anti-feminist. The contrast with Egypt shows that not all Islamist parties are the same.

A Government Is Established

After the election, the ruling "troika" (Ennahdha, CPR and DFLL) allotted the most important post in the government, that of prime minister, to Ghannouchi's second-in-command, Hamadi Jebali, and Moustapha Ben Jafar of DFLL became Speaker of the Assembly. Rounding out the troika, Moncef Marzouki of CPR became president of Tunisia. After two presidents in 55 years (Bourguiba and Ben Ali), Tunisia had now had three "acting" presidents, two of them unelected, in only nine months — Mohamed Ghannouchi (for one day), Fouad Mbazaa (for nine months) and now Moncef Marzouki. The task of writing different sections of the new constitution was assigned to different committees consisting of members from all parties. The assembly was given a year to complete its work, although they could (and did) vote to extend their mandate, drafting and debating the constitution well into summer 2013. A new election is not expected until late 2013 or perhaps even early 2014.

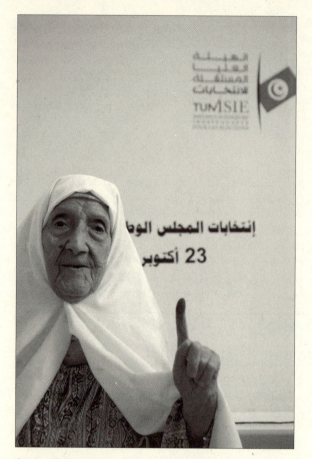

October 23, 2011, Tunis, Tunisia: Mannana Jarraya shows her ink-stained finger after casting her ballot during an election in Tunis. Jarraya is a 101-year-old Tunisian woman and has 11 children, who is voting for her first time in Tunisia's historic election. She says she has never voted before, because Ben Ali won no matter what, but today she is proud to be Tunisian. Ten months since the uprising forced the resignation of President Ben Ali, 81 political parties, as well as hundreds of independent candidates, competed in the countries first free election. 217 candidates will serve in the constituent assembly, which will rewrite the country's constitution and appoint a new government. The election could set the template for other Arab countries emerging from the Arab Spring uprisings. Photo credit: Benedicte Desrus / Sipa Press/ bdtunisia.046/1110241832 (Sipa via AP Images)

Economic Woes Deepen

The economic problems that were among the causes of the uprising have continued and, in fact, worsened. Tunisia's GNP declined by two percent in 2011, the first year of the revolution. In 2012, the GNP increased by 3.6 percent and is projected to increase to four percent in 2013. There are 820,000 unemployed, more than before. Strikes persist, many of them ill-considered. For example, in a factory with inflammable products, workers went on strike, demanding the right to smoke. In Jendouba, workers at Tunisia's only yeast factory announced a strike that would have deprived the entire country of bread (the army intervened to restore yeast production). Mining strikes have reduced the production of phosphate, one of Tunisia's major exports, by 80 percent, preventing the country from taking advantage of a large increase in the world price of phosphate. Faced with undependable supplies of manufactured goods from Tunisia, some foreign clients have begun to buy their products from other countries. Many French firms have left Tunisia, and because of continuing insecurity, foreign investment and tourism remain low.

Labour Relations

In February 2012, the municipal garbage collectors of Tunis went on strike and stinking refuse began to pile up in the streets. UGTT supported the garbage strike, leading some frustrated citizens (allegedly from Ennahdha) to pile garbage outside the doors of the UGTT office in Tunis. Near Bizerte, jobless locals organized a sit-in at an oil refinery and refused to move unless they were given jobs, which forced the refinery to shut down and suspend production.

Part of the problem is that ever since independence, Tunisian labour has lacked a strong voice in government, yet the labour union movement is almost as old as political parties in Tunisia. Mohamed Ali El Hammi founded the Tunisian labour movement in 1924, only four years after the founding of first Tunisian political party, the Destour (which later split and was succeeded in 1934 by the Neo-Destour, under Bourguiba). The trade union movement was resuscitated when UGTT was founded in 1946. UGTT leader Farhat Hached and Bourguiba were the two main political leaders of Tunisia until Hached was assassinated by French terrorists in 1952.

During the 1960s and 1970s, Bourguiba kept the UGTT under the control of the Neo-Destour (which changed its name in 1964 to the Destour Socialist Party). Bourguiba co-opted UGTT leader Ahmed Ben Salah into the government in the 1960s, then turned against him and had him imprisoned in 1969. When the union leadership called for higher wages in the 1970s, they were crushed in a bloodbath in January 1978, in which scores of Tunisians died.

The union continued to play a subservient role under Ben Ali. The union leadership was complaisant, but trade unionists in the interior and the south played an important role in the 2010-2011 uprising. Since the revolution, two new unions have sprung up and the UGTT has had to compete with them. Labour will undoubtedly play an important role in wage and price policies in post-revolutionary Tunisia.

Secularism versus Islamism

This continues to be a main issue of political debate in Tunisia. Tunisia has fervent secularists in the tradition of Bourguiba who question whether Ghannouchi is a sincere democrat. Ghannouchi replies with reassurances that Ennahdha will not legalize polygamy, require women to veil or ban alcohol. Many secularists accuse Ghannouchi and the Islamists of "double discourse" — telling different things to different audiences. At the same time, the mixed legacy of Bourguiba is being challenged and reinterpreted.

A few Salafists (conservative Muslims) have disrupted university campuses, insisting that women be allowed to attend classes and take examinations wearing the niqab (full covering including the face). They also demand that women teachers be required to wear headscarves and that the universities provide prayer rooms on campus. Salafists have demonstrated against alcohol sales and legalized prostitution. They have also objected to the screening of two movies they considered insulting to Islam — *Laïcité Inch'Allah* by Nadia El Fani, a documentary advocating the freedom to profess atheism and agnosticism, and *Persepolis*, an animated film based on the work of Iranian director Marjane Satrapi, which includes an image of God and was shown on Tunisian television.

There is diversity among Tunisian Salafists. Some are associated with Ettahrir Party, the local branch of an international movement. Because they reject democracy, Ettahrir was not allowed to present candidates in the October 2011 election. Salafists insist that the Tunisian constitution be amended to acknowledge Islamic law as the main source of legal legitimacy, a position that Ennahdha rejects. Ghannouchi, the leader of Ennahdha, has suggested that Ettahrir can be legalized if only they disavow violence. Others, such as Radwan Masmoudi of the Centre for the Study of Islam and Democracy, would require that Ettahrir accept democracy before being legalized as a party. The more extreme Salafists support Al-Qaeda, condemn Ghannouchi as an apostate and boycotted the election, while more moderate Salafists form a conservative wing of Ennahdha.

Tunisia's secularists insist that there is no such thing as a "moderate Islamist." Despite Ghannouchi's protestations to the contrary, his critics warn that Ennahdha might enlarge the domain of Islamic law, which currently applies only to inheritance. In the October 2011 election, most Tunisians either supported or took a benign view of Ennahdha; however, as the main party in power, Ennahdha is held responsible for the country's doldrums. The popularity of Ennahdha and of the Constituent Assembly in general has steadily decreased. Former interim Prime Minister Beji Caid Essebsi has formed a new party, Nida Tounes ("Call of Tunis"), which, in spring 2013, pulled ahead of Ennahdha in the polls. The secular left has also reorganized and is attempting to form a unified party.

High Expectations and Impatience

Many Tunisians are demanding and impatient. When reminded that they are doing well relative to the rest of the Maghreb, they reply that they do not compare themselves with Morocco, Algeria or Libya, but rather with France, Italy or Germany. They expect improvement in their standard of living, despite the climate of world recession. The new Constituent Assembly had barely taken office when crowds began protesting outside the Parliament, calling for more jobs, higher wages, lower prices and development of the interior and the south.

TOOLS FOR SUPPORTING DEMOCRACY

Preliminary Observations

Against this background, we now address the question, "What have diplomats and NGOs done to support democracy in Tunisia?" Our answer is organized according to the template of tools described in chapter three of the *Handbook*. How have these diplomatic tools been used (and not used) in the case of Tunisia? Before answering this question, however, two preliminary contextualizing observations are necessary:

A Change in Historical Context

The question of how to promote democracy has changed after the Tunisian Revolution. Under Bourguiba, and especially under Ben Ali, the question was: "How does one promote democracy under conditions of autocracy?" The old regime has now been swept away, but the question of what diplomats and NGOs might have done differently is relevant because many autocracies remain in the world. Conditions have changed in Tunisia, and the form of the question is now: "How can the major world democracies best support a former autocracy struggling to consolidate its democratic beginnings?"

The Key Role of France

France has abiding historic, cultural, political and economic ties with Tunisia, which was a French protectorate for 75 years, from 1881 to 1956. Tunisia's second official language is French. There are 1,200 French companies in Tunisia, and France is by far Tunisia's main trade partner for both imports and exports. Nearly half a million Tunisians live in France, including 10 members of the Tunisian Constituent Assembly. France is consistently the European country that provides the largest number of tourists to Tunisia.

In the Tunisian narrative, therefore, French policy merits disproportionate attention, much as British policy once stood out with regard to South Africa, or US policy with regard to Cuba. No other country has comparable impact on the behaviour of Tunisia. Under Ben Ali, the primacy of France meant that, in the absence of significant French initiatives, other diplomats were reluctant to support democracy and human rights in Tunisia. Why France turned a blind eye to autocracy in Tunisia is an important question to which we will return.

USING THE DIPLOMAT'S TOOL BOX IN TUNISIA

The Golden Rules

Listening, Respecting and Understanding

Clearly, in the years leading to the revolution, France did not do a very good job of listening to, respecting or understanding Tunisians. French Ambassador to Tunisia between 1995 and 1999, Admiral Jacques Lanxade retrospectively regrets France's lack of objectivity in Ben Ali's later years. As he told the *International Herald Tribune* after the Tunisian Revolution, "Since 2000, people saw the Tunisian regime closing itself into a semi-dictatorship, but we did not react. We continued public support of this regime because of economic interests, because we thought Ben Ali had a role in fighting Islamists" (Erlanger, 2011).

There were differences in Tunisian policy among France's three presidents during the Ben Ali years; however, it was during Ben Ali's last five years in power, while Nicolas Sarkozy was president of France, that public disaffection in Tunisia reached the boiling point. French foreign policy makers badly underestimated the strength of anti-regime sentiment. Mitterrand's and Chirac's public statements about Ben Ali had been positive, but Sarkozy's were even more supportive, despite the deteriorating human rights climate in Tunisia. The 2010-2011 uprising took the Sarkozy government completely by surprise. Even as the protests grew and spread, the Sarkozy government still mistakenly thought that Ben Ali would be able to maintain control.

Some of the most emphatic critics of French policy in Tunisia were journalists within France. For years, there had been critics of the successive French governments that had done nothing to promote democracy and human rights in Tunisia. One such critic was Nicolas Beau, who co-authored two bestselling books — *Notre Ami Ben Ali* in 1999 and *La Régente de Carthage* in 2009 — deploring French complicity in the misdeeds of Ben Ali and his wife Leila. Once Ben Ali was out of power, Sarkozy tried to make amends in his four remaining months in office, beginning with a forthright admission that he had "misjudged Tunisian popular sentiment."

Did other diplomatic missions understand Tunisia any better? Some countries — such as the United States (under President George W. Bush), Germany and some of the states of Northern Europe — took a more proactive human rights position in Tunisia, but they had less to lose than France. Wikileaks has documented that, well before Tunisia's uprising, Canadian Ambassador Bruno Picard told fellow ambassadors from the United States, the United Kingdom, France, Germany and Italy that the Tunisian authorities' claims that they did not torture accused terrorists were "bullshit" — an admirably candid assertion for a diplomat.

The European Union was heavily invested in the Tunisian regime, both politically and economically; yet, Ambassador Marc Pierini, a French national who was at the head of the European Union's representation in Tunis between 2002 and 2006, criticized the Tunisian government's authoritarian practices, even on local Tunisian TV. Unfortunately, there was no consensus among EU member states to press Tunisia on human rights. Pierini's successor as EU Ambassador, Adrianus Koetsenruijter, was instructed by officials in Brussels to be as "non-committal as possible," leading to criticism in the European press that he was "too cautious and consensual."

Since the revolution, French President François Hollande and his European counterparts have improved communications with Tunisia. Ambassador Koetsenruijter, with special responsibilities for Tunisia and Libya, has interacted extensively with the public and civil society to identify ways in which the EU can better listen, respect and understand Tunisians and address their expectations.

Sharing

Could diplomats have worked together more effectively during the Ben Ali era to coordinate support for democratic values? In Tunisia, as elsewhere, diplomatic affinity groups share information. The EU ambassadors and junior officials in Tunisia met periodically, but democracy and human rights were not major topics of discussion. Instead, EU efforts were centred on consolidating Tunisian government support for various Mediterranean partnership exercises. The aid provided by the EU went to the Tunisian government rather than to the people and civil society.

At least one European ambassador suggested privately that the topic of human rights was absent from the agenda in part because of the suspicion that there were Ben Ali informers among the EU ambassadors. Whatever the reason, EU authorities did not significantly support a human rights agenda. According to one critic, "The EU was a lot worse than neutral. Having been on the wrong side of history, they have a credibility problem to fix." The basic problem was that internal EU differences over how hard to press Tunisia on human rights meant that the EU was an unresponsive partner for related topics. For example, the EU could not manage to assemble common support for a joint protest of Tunisian Internet blockage. The Wikileaks cables noted that EU representatives acknowledged to US embassy officials that, because of resistance within the EU, joint protests of Tunisian behaviour would not be possible.

Admittedly, under Ben Ali there was little oppositional Tunisian civil society for the diplomatic community to support — only a handful of groups such as the Tunisian League of Human Rights, the Tunisian Association of Democratic Women and the lawyer's guild, plus a few brave figures, such as journalist Sihem Bensedrine, human rights lawyer Bouchra Ben Hamida and PDP leaders Maya Jribi and Ahmed Nejib Chebbi. Since the revolution, these have been joined by many more democracy and human rights groups and have received extensive foreign aid, a situation making coordination essential.

Truth in Communications

Reporting

Diplomats prepare reports and analyses that help shape the foreign policies of their home governments. They often offered critical assessments of Tunisia but these were kept private, with the exception that the US Embassy posted human rights reports critical of the Ben Ali regime on its website. Another exception, albeit inadvertent, came in 2010 when Wikileaks made public confidential reports, especially those between 2006 and 2009 from US Ambassador Robert Godec.

One of Godec's leaked reports described the lavish lifestyle of Ben Ali's son-in-law, Sakher El-Materi, who was considered at that time to be Ben Ali's most likely successor. Godec noted that El-Materi kept a pet tiger and flew in desserts from Saint-Tropez. Other Wikileaks cables reported widespread corruption by Ben Ali's extended family. Wikileaks confirmed what Tunisians already knew, and added memorable images of decadence and excess.

Diplomatic missions in Tunis were small, with the exception of a few countries with major interests. The few available officers had to cover a wide range of topics, resulting in a lack of reporting about human rights in Tunisia. The Canadian mission actually cut the position of political officer, partly for budgetary reasons and partly because of an increasing emphasis on economic topics; however, the training and assignment of diplomats who monitor and support human rights is essential for all diplomatic missions. Wider acceptance of the axiom that strategic and economic partnerships can co-exist with frank communications about democracy and human rights is needed.

Informing

Supporting independent media is an important way to help promote democracy. The Ben Ali regime kept the media under close control. Tunisia's newspapers ran flattering pictures of Ben Ali on their front pages until the very day that he fled. The press agency Tunis Afrique Presse, staffed by RCD members, provided the government line that the local press dutifully parroted. Typically, 40 percent of television news broadcasts was devoted to reviewing the president's day. Democratic NGOs organized a few training programs to acquaint journalists and the emerging community of bloggers with free media standards, but these sessions had to be held outside Tunisia.

Occasionally, the authorities would seize a publication or jail a journalist, but most press control was exercised through self-censorship. As one of the post-revolution ministers accurately and succinctly described the behaviour of the Tunisian press, "For 50 years the only time they ever opened their mouths was to go to the dentist."

The first crack in the propaganda wall came with satellite television. Increasingly, Tunisians were turning to satellite news, beginning with Al-Jazeera, founded in Qatar in 1996, which was followed by other outspoken Arabic stations in Lebanon and the Gulf, such as Al-Arabiya. The regime tried to suppress parabolic antennas in 1994, but this proved both unpopular and unenforceable, so they turned instead to harassing foreign reporters, seizing objectionable publications and concentrating on controlling the media within Tunisia. When there was a foreign television program critical of Ben Ali, occasionally the authorities would even shut off electricity throughout the country until the program was over.

Tunisia's post-revolution landscape has exploded with new media. A dozen new newspapers have sprung up and applications for new radio and television licences flow at a rapid pace. Bloggers are ubiquitous. "Tunisia Girl" Lina Ben Mhenni, who began blogging and tweeting while Ben Ali was in power, has continued her blog and published a popular book. Blogger Slim Amamou, jailed and tortured under Ben Ali, was appointed Secretary of State for Youth and Sports in January 2011 (although he later resigned). New faces are entering journalism and new voices are being heard.

Tunisians have been exercising press freedom with a vengeance, and much of the media have been hypercritical of the interim and constituent assembly governments. They criticize the assembly members' monthly stipend of 2,300 dinars (US$1,432) as excessive. The media inaccurately reported that the assembly voted in April 2013 to increase their basic monthly pay to over 4,000 dinars, following which a crowd gathered to shout "Shame on you!" and pelted assembly members with tin five-millime pieces.

The stipend of the assembly members is indeed high relative to the incomes of most Tunisians; however, all but the few members from Tunis have to maintain two residences and they have heavy travel expenses for commuting to their home constituencies. Mabrouka Mbarak, for example, a CPR representative of Tunisians in the US, has to contribute 15 percent of her stipend to the party (for Ennahdha the figure is 25 percent). She shares a small apartment in a suburb of Tunis with two other women, has childcare and research assistant expenses, has been away from her husband and son in the US for all but six weeks of the past year and has to pay US taxes on her Tunisian stipend. Radwan Masmoudi, an unsuccessful assembly candidate from the US, told me that he was relieved, frankly, that he lost the election, because if he had won, he would have had to leave his job and family and move to Tunisia — only to be denounced as an opportunist, one might add.

Tunisian journalists try to outdo each other in the ferocity of their muckraking. One newspaper ran a daring cartoon insulting the Ministry of Interior, portraying the building in the form of a naked man with his anus as the entrance to the building. This hardly seems fair to the new Minister of the Interior, a man who had been tortured in that very building under the old regime. It is true that there were honest journalists who suffered in the past, yet there are other journalists who have gone from fulsome praise of Ben Ali to ferocious criticism of the new government. Perhaps this is a way of trying to restore their credibility.

In the post-revolution era, diplomats and NGOs have increased their support for Tunisian journalism and independent media through travel scholarships and seminars and have helped new media start-ups, such as the English language website TunisiaLive. Canada and the EU have put support for freedom of expression and information as one of their top priorities.

There have been a few protests about police brutality toward reporters and a few instances of censorship for religious reasons. The head of Nesma Television, the station that showed the movie *Persepolis*, was arrested for blasphemy, found guilty in May 2012 and fined US$2,870, but at least he did not have to serve jail time. In February 2012, an editor whose newspaper ran a photo of a Tunisian soccer star in Germany with his hand over a naked woman's breast was arrested but freed after eight days and had to pay a US$665 fine.

A serious instance of censorship arose in April 2012, when two Tunisian atheists were sentenced to prison terms of seven-and-a-half years each for posting caricatures of the Prophet Mohamed and documents critical of Islam on the Internet. The draft Tunisian constitution currently includes an article that will criminalize such religious offences. As Monica Marks has reported, this measure has elicited little debate, since Tunisians (and Muslims generally) tend to feel strongly that free speech does not include the right to insult Islam. They point out that all societies place limits on free speech (such as laws against "hate speech" in the US) and that laws against blasphemy currently exist in European countries such as Greece, Poland and Ireland (and until recently in England, although only blasphemy against the Church of England was considered illegal).

Working with the Government

Advising

After an uprising, the leaders of clandestine movements are not uniformly successful in consolidating democracy. New ministers, chosen for being untainted, often have no experience running a large government office. Having spent years in prison may enhance their moral standing, but it does nothing for their administrative and planning skills.

Since the revolution, each ministry has had a succession of two or three (or even more) ministers, with the prospect of yet another set of new ministers, once the new constitution is completed and new elections are held. Understandably, the civil servants who have worked in these ministries for years tend not to take the new ministers seriously because they know they will be gone soon. As in all bureaucracies, the safest course is to avoid taking any initiatives at all.

Friendly governments and NGOs can help build capacity for democratic governance through training programs which increase capacity of newly democratically controlled government institutions and promote civil society alike. Prior to 2011, such programs — information technology training, for example — had to be held outside Tunisia. The Tunisian government blocked conferences on sensitive topics, such as a European-sponsored (Friedrich Ebert Stiftung) conference on labour issues. Officials of the IRI and the NDI describe how, before their flights back to Tunis, Tunisians at overseas programs would throw their training materials into the trash for fear that customs agents back in Tunisia would consider them subversive and arrest them.

Beginning in 2011, capacity-building programs could finally be openly conducted in Tunisia. Tunis now abounds with uncensored conferences, debates, round tables and training programs. An example was a major conference in March 2012, organized by the Paris-based Institut de Recherche et Débat sur la Gouvernance.

Since the ouster of Ben Ali, several democracies have provided support for the electoral process, voter registration, campaign management and election observation. Before the election, various groups (including IRI, NDI and the foundations of five different German parties) held seminars open to all political parties about how to conduct effective election campaigns and win votes. Not all the advice was good. For example, the PDP was criticized by the Tunisian press for conducting a campaign featuring large posters of Nejib Chebbi, which some viewed as a throwback to the cult of the leader.

Dialoguing and Demarching

There was little opportunity to engage in dialogue about democracy with Ben Ali, a secretive man who kept his contacts with the diplomatic community to a minimum. British Ambassador Alan Goulty, who served in Tunisia from 2004 to 2008, reports that he met Ben Ali in a collective presentation of credentials by new ambassadors. After that, apart from rare visits by high British government officials, he had no opportunity for substantive conversation with Ben Ali, although there were meetings about democracy and civil society at lower levels between British and Tunisian officials. The regime tried to keep the British on the defensive about human rights by demanding that they suppress Tunisian "terrorists" such as Rached Ghannouchi, who lived in exile in London at the time. UK Ambassador Christopher O'Conner, one of the more experienced European diplomats in Tunisia, having served there since 2008, has ensured that human rights are at the top of his mission's agenda. Cooperation with Tunisian security agencies for counterterrorism continues, though security priorities no longer trump human rights.

The French had exceptional access to the highest levels of Tunisian government but apart from rare interventions to assist high-profile political prisoners such as journalist Taoufik Ben Brik, they avoided raising issues of democracy and human rights. The EU, as discussed above, was hamstrung by resistance from the French.

The US was reluctant to deal with Tunisia's human rights record until an unproductive dialogue with Ben Ali in Washington finally led to a change in policy. NGOs fared no better. The Ben Ali regime harassed the Arab Institute for Human Rights for over a decade, at one point freezing their assets and even arranging for their president to be denied a chequing account in Tunis. Since the revolution, Tunisia's long-delayed dialogue on democracy has finally begun.

Today, it is possible for governments to work through official channels to address human rights problems, but under Ben Ali, such efforts were futile. The regime legalized a few opposition parties, but severely restricted their operations. Like Egypt, Tunisia was theoretically a multi-party state but, in fact, a one-party regime with window dressing. Under both Bourguiba and especially under Ben Ali, those in opposition were ferreted out, tried for sedition and sentenced to death, life at hard labour or long prison terms. A few Islamists were freed after Ben Ali deposed Bourguiba in 1987, but the most active opposition leaders soon had to flee the country.

After January 2011, opposition parties and human rights groups that had previously been hobbled were revitalized. More than a hundred new political parties and hundreds more civil society groups have been granted permits. Tunisians can now dialogue with authorities about human rights without being arrested. However, questions remain, especially regarding the law that disallows religious or ethnic parties. Ennahdha was legalized after the revolution, while Hizb Ettahrir, the main Salafist party, has been allowed to organize but was not permitted to participate in 2011 election.

Reaching Out

Connecting

Despite deterrence, there was nevertheless a certain level of civic dialogue among Tunisians under Ben Ali. Tunisian bookstores such as Ars Libris held events at which Tunisian political and cultural leaders lectured and presented their books. The most daring of NGOs during this time was the Temimi Foundation that, despite government threats, held public symposia on controversial topics such as censorship, Bourguiba's legacy, the Black Thursday riots of 1978 and the 1961 assassination of Bourguiba's rival Salah Ben Youssef.

Under Ben Ali, diplomatic missions and foreign NGOs were able to sponsor events where Tunisians could connect about cultural and quasi-political topics. The Embassy of the Netherlands in Tunisia, the Konrad Adenauer Foundation, the French Institut de Recherches sur le Maghreb Contemporain, and the American Center for Maghreb Studies in Tunis all held lectures and conferences about cultural and political topics that pushed the boundaries of censorship.

At one time, the Ben Ali regime tried to restrict contacts between foreign representatives and Tunisian civil society organizations. Norwegian Vice Consul in Tunis, Reidun Breivik Andersen, reported that embassies could have contacts with NGOs without informing the Ministry of Foreign Affairs, but if they gave funds to an NGO, it had to be reported. Finnish Ambassador Laura Reinilä ignored this regulation, with the ludicrous consequence that there were "no flowers on the Finnish independence day" and no medal from Ben Ali when she departed Tunisia at the end of her ambassadorship.

An example of the change in connecting since the revolution is El Taller, an international NGO headquartered in Tunis since 1992. Among other activities, El Taller has organized international "Courts of Women" for connecting about women's issues. Previously, none of these events could be held in Tunis. Tunisia's Minister of Women's Affairs explained to Corinne Kumar, the head of El Taller, that "women had achieved equality in Tunisia and had no need of such programs." In 2008, El Taller applied more than a year in advance to hold a conference in Tunis, even providing the names of all the participants, but the Ministry of Foreign Affairs never responded. The event had to be moved to India, where it took only two weeks to receive approval and organize the conference. El Taller now holds events in Tunisia for Tunisians and others to connect on social issues.

Convening

Before the revolution, Tunisia had some diplomatic successes at bringing together adversaries to try to resolve their differences. Having achieved independence with minimal bloodshed, Tunisia cultivated a reputation as a moderate Arab state, able to convene disputing parties for bridging differences. In a famous speech in Jericho in March 1965, Bourguiba counselled the Palestinians to recognize and negotiate with the Israelis, though he was severely criticized by the Arab League and others for doing so. In 1970, Tunisia attempted mediation between the Jordanian monarchy and the Palestine Liberation Organization (PLO). In 1982, Tunisia provided an exit for the PLO leadership from Lebanon, hosting them in Tunisia for a decade. Throughout its history, Tunisia has made efforts to convene leaders from Arab countries for mediation.

Tunisia has been less successful at resolving its own internal societal conflicts, especially the conflict between UGTT and the national party (the Destour Socialist Party, later the RCD). Social and political divisions have occasionally erupted into violence — for example, the Black Thursday riots of January 1978, when the UGTT and the Party clashed in the streets of Tunis, and the bread riots of January 1984, sparked by increases in the price of food. Tunisia is a relatively peaceful country, but the Tunisian Revolution has not been without violence, especially in Kasserine and Sidi Bouzid provinces, where Tunisians used firearms and burned police stations.

By contrast, the electoral campaign leading to the election of October 2011 was relatively civil. The Center for the Study of Islam and Democracy was among the groups active in convening the competing parties at public forums to discuss their party platforms, debate issues and air their differences. Since the election, there is promise of a new order for conflict resolution and national reconciliation — a process which outside diplomats support.

Since the revolution, Tunisia's vocation for convening countries has resumed: in March 2012, Tunisia hosted a major international conference of the "Friends of Syria" to seek ways to attenuate the conflict and promote democracy there.

Facilitating

It is important for governments to promote cooperation to advance democratic outcomes, including exit strategies. For example, in accepting Ben Ali, Saudi Arabia performed a useful service. Tunisia has judged and condemned Ben Ali to decades in prison and appropriately huge fines, and has asked that Ben Ali be extradited. If he had remained in Tunisia and fought to keep power, there would undoubtedly have been far more bloodshed, thus Ben Ali's departure helped Tunisia to avoid the same problems that Egypt (where they had to decide what to do with Mubarak), Yemen (where the exit of Ali Abdullah Saleh took a year), Libya (where Gadhafi fought an eight-month civil war) and Syria (where a popular revolt against the Assad regime is now well into its third year) had done. There were 338 deaths in Tunisia's uprising, compared with 846 in Egypt (although this represents a higher casualty rate in Tunisia because Egypt has eight times Tunisia's population). The uprisings in Tunisia and Egypt have been far less costly in lives than the uprisings in Libya (15,000 dead) and especially Syria (estimated as being more than 100,000 by the UN in late July 2013, with more than four million internally displaced and 1.9 million driven outside Syria). Over the long run, none of the Arab countries has matched Tunisia's slow but steady institutional progress.

Problems of corruption were not limited to Ben Ali's family. To varying extents, the police, the banks, the judiciary, the media and especially the RCD collaborated in the regime's corruption. A commission was set up to review 5,000 dossiers of alleged corruption, to bring charges against those who misused public office and to seize ill-gotten gains in Tunisia and abroad. The many Tunisian companies that belonged to Ben Ali and his family have been placed in government receivership and caretakers have been appointed to run them.

Not all RCD members were corrupt, so the electoral commission had to devise rules to determine who would be allowed to run as candidates for the new Constituent Assembly. Not only RCD members, but also many others had been tainted by complicity with the regime to different degrees. The leadership of the national labour union in Tunis (but not the rural union officials) had collaborated with Ben Ali. Among judges and lawyers, some were complicit and others not. As in South Africa and Chile, Tunisia has recently decided to create a truth and reconciliation commission to heal wounds and promote national unity, although the scope and time range of its activities have not yet been defined. Unfortunately, the wounds of the Ben Ali era are still fresh, making it difficult to reintegrate and reconcile with those who are perceived as having benefitted from Ben Ali's regime.

Financing

Tunisia has a rule against political funding from outside the country, but no effective financial disclosure procedures. During the election campaign, questions were raised about possible outside funding by several groups: Ennahdha was accused of receiving financing from Qatar; there was speculation about how the PDP was able to afford an expensive campaign (for their 260 offices alone, they reportedly spent 900,000 dinars, or US$560,000); and the PPP was rumoured to have received funding from former RCD members. Of course, all swore that their funding came exclusively from legitimate contributions within Tunisia.

After the election, a minor controversy erupted that focussed not on Tunisians, but on foreign NGOs. It followed an incident in Egypt in December 2011, when police arrested 43 people (15 of them Americans) from 10 NGOs, accusing them of working for illegal organizations, fomenting unrest and spying. Following this, the Tunisian newspaper *Le Temps* published an article suggesting that "international NGOs and their affiliates operating on Tunisian soil" might be "antennas of espionage."

Unlike Egypt, the authorities in Tunisia have never bothered foreign NGOs, although they require them to register. The controversy is, however, a healthy reminder that foreign NGOs should be alert to local sensitivities and transparent about their funding sources and activities. Foreign NGOs have generally eschewed involvement in domestic partisan politics, limiting their activities to technical support that is not overtly political.

Showcasing

Showcasing means presenting examples, models or solutions for democratic development suitable for local application. An indication that Tunisians are eager to learn from the experiences of other countries has been their attention to the post-authoritarian experiences of countries such as Spain and Portugal. Tunisians identify with countries where dictatorships were followed by the formation of many new political parties. Tunisians are alert to best practices. Post-uprising, the EU showcased best practices by bringing speakers and organizing seminars about the post-authoritarian democratic experiences of other countries.

In an interview in early 2012, Assemblywoman Mabrouka Mbarak noted an example of showcasing. The EU brought a panel of members from different European parliaments to Tunisia to offer advice to the newly elected members of the Constituent Assembly on how to be effective legislators. Mbarak recalls that a member of the British House of Commons advised them to make friends with the members of other parties "so that later you can get them to support your legislation." After that, Mbarak says that she noticed her colleagues becoming friendlier with members of opposition parties.

Defending Democrats

Demonstrating

Maya Jribi of the PDP recalls that in September 2007, the authorities tried to evict her and her colleagues from their party headquarters building in Tunis. She and Nejib Chebbi protested by going on a 30-day hunger strike. They appreciated that US Ambassador Robert Godec demonstrated support for their rights by paying them a public visit, and they also appreciated that some embassies invited them to official dinners and receptions, despite the displeasure of the Ben Ali regime. Jribi said that while to some these embassy invitations might seem a small thing, to her they conveyed the message, "You are not alone."

French journalist Nicolas Beau reported that Admiral Jacques Lanxade, the French Ambassador to Tunisia from 1995 to 1999, avoided opponents of the Ben Ali regime. The explanation probably lies in the more traditional diplomacy practiced by some European foreign ministries, which see the ambassador as a link with the local authorities, as opposed to the dual-purpose missions of countries like the US, Holland, the Czech Republic or Norway, whose ambassadors practice a diplomacy of simultaneous outreach to civil society.

Another example cited by Beau is that US Ambassador Robert Godec had "multiple contacts with dissidents" and invited Tunisian opposition educator Mohamed Bouebdelli to the US Embassy, complimenting him on his courage and assuring him of US support. France, on the other hand, has preferred private diplomacy. Beau quotes a letter that Bouebdelli received from a French official explaining, "I think that it is better not to make public my evaluation of the situation in Tunisia, which would render much less effective the aid that I can provide to activities such as yours."

To what extent do US, French and other diplomats simply follow their home offices' directives about promoting human rights? Robert Godec reports that, while the State Department sets the parameters within which ambassadors operate, in Tunisia he was given the discretion to promote democracy and human rights as the embassy's highest priority. This range of discretion varies, however. Because Egypt looms larger than Tunisia in US foreign policy, it is likely that the US Ambassador in Cairo had less discretion in setting priorities.

Verifying and Witnessing

Sending diplomatic observers to political trials shows support for the rights of dissent and due process. Under Ben Ali, the US, UK and Germany sent observers to trials, but the French did not. As Tunisian dissident lawyer Radhia Nasraoui reported, "The day of my last trial, several Western embassies sent representatives to the Palace of Justice. It was a clear signal addressed to the regime to tell it that not everything was permitted. There was nobody from the French Embassy."

Observing elections is another form of witness. After years of rubber-stamp elections, Tunisia held its first truly democratic national election on October 23, 2011, observed by over 7,000 Tunisian volunteers and 533 international monitors from the EU, the OSCE, the Council of Europe and the non-governmental Carter Center. They reported instances of inefficiency, long voting lines and the potential for abuse (for example, when illiterate voters were assisted at the polls). Ennahdha was criticized for providing social services that bordered on vote-buying. The consensus was that there was room for improvement in future elections, but that overall, Tunisia's election had been free and fair.

Protecting

In the modern history of Tunisia, the most significant instance of protection of a political prisoner by a diplomat probably came when US Consul Hooker Doolittle intervened with the French Resident General at the end of World War II on behalf of independence leader Habib Bourguiba. Bourguiba credited Doolittle with saving his life.

During the Bourguiba years, Tunisia sheltered Arab political refugees. In 1982, Tunisia took in both the PLO leadership and its fighting forces from Lebanon. This was a risky gesture, since the PLO presence had previously destabilized first Jordan, then Lebanon. As a consequence, Tunisia suffered in 1985 when Israel bombed the PLO headquarters in Bordj Cedria, just outside the capital city of Tunis. Tunisia suffered again in 1988 when a squad of Israeli commandos infiltrated Tunisia and assassinated PLO leader Khalil Al-Wazir. The PLO was headquartered in Tunis until the early 1990s when they were permitted to return to the Occupied Territories, under the Oslo Accords.

As mentioned earlier, during the Ben Ali years, the French occasionally intervened discreetly to protect dissidents. France also gave asylum to political figures such as Ahmed Ben Salah, a labour leader and economic planner whom Bourguiba scapegoated for problems in the cooperative movement of the 1960s. Ben Salah escaped from a Tunisian prison and fled to Algeria and from there to Europe. France was not so hospitable in 1989 when they gave in to pressure from Ben Ali and refused to renew Islamist Rached Ghannouchi's visa. To their credit, the British provided asylum to Ghannouchi for two decades, rejecting Ben Ali's argument that that Ghannouchi was an Islamic terrorist.

The US record of protecting dissidents is mixed. The State Department gave Rached Ghannouchi a visa for one lecture tour in the US, but turned down a subsequent application. Beginning in 2004, the US refused a visa to Islamist moderate Tariq Ramadan, a Swiss citizen of Egyptian origin, to teach and lecture, finally relenting and allowing him into the US in 2010.

How Have Different Countries Used Diplomatic Tools in Tunisia?

Turning from the tools of diplomacy to the countries that have used them, how have the tools in the *Handbook* been used by the diplomats of various countries? We attempt a historicized comparative account of the approaches of various national, regional and international entities to Tunisian autocracy and nascent democracy, beginning with the most important case, France, and proceeding to other selected other countries' policies toward Tunisia, and then to regional and international organizations.

French Policy toward Tunisia

Ben Ali's sudden accession to power in 1987 took the French by surprise. At first, the French government was cool toward Ben Ali. They had come to like Bourguiba, who had been a moderate independence leader and an unabashed francophile. While Bourguiba had lived in France and studied law there, and his first wife was French, Ben Ali had no such ties. The French distrusted Ben Ali because he had received security training in the US (although he had also received military training at St. Cyr in France) and they suspected that Ben Ali might be under the influence of the Americans.

The French quickly warmed to Ben Ali, however, especially after he entrusted to them the sensitive task of training and equipping Tunisia's extensive security forces, while he delegated the training and equipping of the smaller and less strategically important Tunisian Army to the United States. For the next two decades, first Mitterrand and then Chirac maintained close ties and positive relations with Ben Ali, and there were periodic visits exchanged by heads of state and top ministers between Paris and Tunis.

Taking office in 2007, Sarkozy was even more effusive than Mitterrand or Chirac in his support of Ben Ali, but the Tunisian uprising spelled disaster for this policy. Sarkozy's Foreign Minister, Michèle Alliot-Marie, paid a badly timed holiday visit to Tunisia in late December 2010, at the very moment that the uprising was spreading. As the guest of a wealthy Tunisian business associate of Ben Ali, she flew in a private plane that passed over the very region of Sidi Bouzid and Kasserine while the uprising was at its most violent point. Back in Paris after the holidays, she compounded her gaffe by offering France's "savoir faire" for putting down the uprising. Sarkozy reversed policy only when Ben Ali had already fled Tunisia. After having been Sarkozy's good friend, Ben Ali had suddenly become *persona non grata*.

In defence of French policy, one should note that times changed during Ben Ali's reign. The events of the 1990s seemed to vindicate Ben Ali's hard line against Islamists. Algeria fell into the throes of a civil war between the Islamic Army Group and the Algerian government and Muslim extremists committed terrorist bombings in Europe. Early in the new millennium, there was the 9/11 attack in New York City, bringing Islamic terrorism to the forefront of international attention. The French had no desire to see the Eiffel Tower, which had already been the target of one terrorist attempt, go the way of New York's Twin Towers. Thus, French diplomacy saw the autocracy of Ben Ali as the alternative to Islamic extremism. Denis Jeambar, director of the French newspaper *L'Express*, accurately captured the main idea behind 25 years of French policy with the phrase, "Better Ben Ali than Bin Laden." With the benefit of hindsight, it is clear that the French were wrong, but they were not alone.

Immediately after the Tunisian Revolution, an anonymous Quai d'Orsay official retrospectively rejected criticism of French policy during Ben Ali's reign as "inaccurate and unfair," arguing that "if France had criticized Tunisian policy, the same press which today is expressing its outrage would have accused us of interference and neo-colonialism." This assumes that a country can represent only one interest at a time, and such a view still characterizes many ex-colonial powers toward their former colonies.

The French Ambassador to Tunisia between 2001 and 2005, Yves Aubin de la Messuzière, reported after the revolution that he and other diplomats in Tunis had warned their home countries about "the decay of the Ben Ali regime and the discontent among Tunisian youth long before the Revolution started." He stated, "I and my ambassadorial colleagues of the United States and European capitals personally shared information and sent reports to our governments about corruption and bribery, nepotism and illicit enrichment of Ben Ali's close associates at a time while the exasperation and discontent of the Tunisian youth [were] spreading," although he adds that "no one expected Ben Ali's regime to end the way it did." This suggests that the failure was not so much on the part of the diplomatic corps to report accurately from Tunis but rather on the part of the home governments to respond appropriately to the reports they received from the field.

After Ben Ali's fall, Sarkozy tried to correct his foreign policy and make a fresh start in Tunisia. In late February 2012, he appointed Alain Juppé as his new foreign minister. Earlier in the month, he had chosen a new Ambassador to Tunisia, Boris Boillon, a young diplomat fluent in Arabic and with experience in Algeria, Libya and Iraq. But Boillon got off to a terrible start, inviting the Tunisian press to the French Embassy, challenging their objectivity with intemperate language and then apologizing on Tunisian television that same evening. Tunisians demonstrated in front of the French Embassy with signs demanding that, like Ben Ali, Boillon should "get out!" French-Tunisian relations soon calmed, but popular distrust toward France remains.

Elected in in May 2012, French President Hollande has committed France to assisting Tunisian democracy. To a Tunisian interviewer who brought up France's record of lenience toward Ben Ali, Hollande pointed out that, as a Socialist opponent of both Chirac and Sarkozy, he had long criticized French policy toward the Tunisian regime. Hollande noted that under his leadership, the French Socialist Party had participated in the expulsion of Ben Ali's party, the RCD, from the Socialist International. Nonetheless, Tunisians have been slow to forgive past French support for Ben Ali and many feel that Hollande's strong reaction to the assassination of Chokry Belaid, a fellow socialist, has slowed French tourism. They also note that Hollande's reciprocation of Marzouki's visit to France has been slow to come. Hollande did replace the erratic Boris Boillon with a more solid diplomat, François Gouyette, as ambassador. France and Tunisia now both have new leadership and are working to mend their relations. They have too long and deep a history of close interaction and too much of a mutual investment to quarrel for long.

US Policy toward Tunisia

US presidents Ronald Reagan, George H. W. Bush and Bill Clinton all kept cordial relations with Ben Ali's Tunisia and offered low levels of military aid combined with periodic expressions of public approval. At first, George W. Bush continued this policy, but Ben Ali persisted in resisting democratic reforms and the Bush administration gradually became more critical. The US had little leverage on Tunisia, however, since they had already sharply reduced American economic aid and closed down the USAID and Peace Corps offices in Tunis. All that remained was a sacrosanct military and intelligence cooperation program for suppressing terrorism.

A telling moment came at a joint press conference with the younger Bush and Ben Ali in Washington, DC on January 12, 2008. Bush administered a public rebuff to Ben Ali, suggesting that he should consider granting greater press and political freedoms. Bush's criticism at the press conference became a popular Internet clip among Ben Ali's Tunisian critics.

As mentioned earlier, Robert Godec, US Ambassador to Tunisia from 2006 to 2009, made human rights the top priority of the US Embassy. He posted Tunisia's negative human rights record on the Embassy website in Tunis, which is standard State Department policy, but went beyond this, in privately raising democracy and human rights issues with Ben Ali. Godec also publicly met with Tunisian dissidents and invited opposition leaders to the embassy. His visit to Maya Jribi and Nejib Chebbi during their hunger protest was perhaps his boldest gesture. The response of the Ben Ali regime was to restrict the movements of the ambassador and his staff, harass the American-run International School, curtail the Fulbright program and refuse permits for American scholars to do research in Tunisia.

In contrast to the French government, when the Tunisian uprising broke out and deaths were reported, the US State Department criticized Tunisia's violent treatment of protesters, affirming the importance of respecting freedom of expression. Authorities in Tunis responded by summoning US Ambassador Gordon Gray, Robert Godec's successor, lodging a formal complaint about Washington "meddling in Tunisia's domestic affairs." In July 2012, Jacob Walles, an experienced career foreign service officer, took over as US Ambassador to Tunisia and has continued the pro-democracy policies of his predecessors.

Public opinion polls suggest that, for Tunisians, the recent positive aspects of US policy have been overshadowed by its support for Israel and its military interventions in Iraq and Afghanistan. Periodic incidents of US Islamophobia are widely reported in Tunisia and have taken their toll. In September 2012, an amateurish video produced in the United States went viral on the Internet. The video, which contained images denigrating the Prophet Muhammad, led to an attack on the US Embassy and the burning and looting of the American School in Tunis. Although the demonstration was expected, the embassy was only lightly guarded by the Tunisians. President Marzouki responded quickly to a call from Hillary Clinton, sending the Presidential Guard. Two of the violent demonstrators were shot and killed, 29 were wounded and 60 people, mostly Salafists, were arrested and imprisoned (one of them has died after going on an extended hunger strike). Following closely on the assassination of the US Ambassador to Libya, the State Department responded by evacuating American diplomatic families, reducing the embassy to a skeleton staff, cancelling a project to bring back the Peace Corps to Tunisia and issuing a travel warning.

From the pre- to the post-revolution, US support for democracy and civil society in Tunisia exhibits continuity. During the revolution, US President Obama was quick to deplore Ben Ali's use of violence and he applauded the "courage and dignity" of Tunisian protesters. Since the revolution, the United States has joined Europe in supporting the new government and shoring up the beleaguered Tunisian economy. American aid includes a short-term US$100 million cash transfer through USAID and long-term plans for US$300 million in loan guarantees, as well as expanded Middle East Partnership Initiative funding and several private sector funding initiatives.

Italian Policy toward Tunisia

Italy, Tunisia's closest European neighbour, has loomed large in Tunisian history, and has been second in importance only to France in modern times. From France's seizure of Tunisia as a protectorate in 1881 until World War II, the largest foreign population in Tunisia was Italian. In 1987, Bettino Craxi and the Italian military secret service played a key role in Ben Ali's deposing of Bourguiba, after which Italy was unequivocally supportive of Ben Ali. Prime ministers Craxi and Berlusconi were especially close to Ben Ali, rewarding him for his efforts to curb illegal migration. With Ben Ali's help, Craxi fled to Tunisia in 1994 after an Italian court sentenced him to 27 years in prison for corruption. Berlusconi had important financial investments in Tunisia and continued to defend Ben Ali even after he had fled to Saudi Arabia. Since the mid-1980s, illegal migration has been a sore point in Tunisian-Italian relations. In the year after the revolution, an estimated 25,000 Tunisians attempted to flee to Italy on small boats, many of them drowning. Those that were intercepted were interned on the island of Lampedusa under terrible conditions. Tunisians continue to criticize the Italian government for this, contrasting it with the extensive hospitality of Tunisians toward refugees from Libya.

EU Policy toward Tunisia

Because of Europe's geographical closeness to Tunisia and the magnitude and coordination of European aid resources, the EU constitutes a formidable bloc; however, this diplomatic potential was not effectively realized in Tunisia. The Euro-Mediterranean Partnership, or Barcelona Process, created in 1995, was generally acknowledged to be a disappointment by the time of its failed summit meeting in 2005. The much-publicized Union for the Mediterranean, an idea of Sarkozy's in 2008, was similarly inconsequential, reaching a low point when the organization failed to hold summits in 2009 and 2010.

Europeans have dealt with Tunisia primarily through bilateral relations with individual countries, rather than as a unified bloc. As noted elsewhere, the United Kingdom, Germany and other Northern European countries made some modest attempts to encourage democracy in Tunisia. This was true on occasion for the EU representation in Tunisia, despite internal disagreement on the subject of Tunisian human rights.

Illegal immigration from Tunisia and other North African countries has long been a sensitive issue for the EU. Right-wing parties in France, Italy, Germany, Austria, Switzerland, Spain and Holland have made the growing European presence of Arabs and Muslims into a major political issue. Some leaders tolerated Ben Ali, in part because he kept his pledge to work hard at curtailing illegal migration. The economic downturn that followed the uprising, accompanied by the suspension of Tunisia's maritime controls, has led to a huge increase in attempts at illegal migration. In March 2011 alone, Italy intercepted 78 boatloads of would-be migrants fleeing Tunisia.

Since the Tunisian Revolution, the EU has been supportive of the Constituent Assembly and of Tunisian civil society through multiple technical, economic and governance aid programs. For the period 2011–2013, the EU earmarked €400 million in donations and €3 billion in loans through the European Investment Bank and other EU organizations.

Turkish Policy toward Tunisia

Turkey has long been, and still remains, a powerful model for Tunisia. Bourguiba borrowed many of his ideas from Mustafa Kemal Ataturk — including, unfortunately, Ataturk's undemocratic reluctance to cede power to a successor. Unlike Bourguiba, Ataturk stopped short of having himself declared president for life, although in practice he ended up being just that. Ennahdha leaders have cited Turkey's Adalet ve Kalkinma Partisi ([AK], the Justice and Development Party) as an exemplar of moderate Islamist policies. Ennahdha would no doubt love to emulate the AK's economic record. Between 2003 (the year after the AK was elected) and 2012, Turkey has averaged a 5.1 percent growth rate. Although the rate slipped to 2.2 percent in 2012, this is a remarkable achievement. Yet Turkey differs from Tunisia in important respects. The Turkish Army, for example, plays a much stronger political role than the Tunisian Army. Turkey also officially separates Islam and the state, while Tunisia's constitution proclaims Islam as the religion of the Tunisian people.

Regional Organizations

Tunisia is a member of the Arab League, which was headquartered in Tunis from 1979 to 1990, during the time that Egypt was ostracized for Sadat's separate peace with Israel at Camp David. The Arab League, however, has not been a force for democracy. Other Arab states have been even more autocratic than Tunisia and the Arab League has, for the most part, been little more than a forum. Tunisia is also a member of the Maghreb Arab Union (along with Mauritania, Morocco, Algeria and Libya), but Moroccan-Algerian animosity has rendered the Union ineffective and, like the Arab League, it offers scant lessons for democracy.

Tunisia is a member of the Organization of African Unity, however, unlike Libya, Algeria and Morocco, Tunisia has neither borders nor important relations with sub-Saharan states. This is unfortunate, since Burkina Faso and especially Senegal — a country which is 94 percent Muslim, but whose first president was a Christian — offer models of Muslim majority countries that have separated religion and the state. Finally, Tunisia has been a member of the International Organization of Francophone Countries (OIF) since its inception in 1970, but the OIF's commitment to democracy is only nominal; its members have no review mechanisms for governance nor do they have sanctions for violations of human rights, permitting regimes like Ben Ali's (and some with worse records) to coast along in confidence.

Policies of the IMF and the World Bank

IFIs, such as the International Monetary Fund (IMF) and the World Bank, constitute a special category of organizations that contributed to Tunisia's human rights predicament by awarding high levels of aid without criticizing the regime. During the years leading to the uprising, the annual reports of IMF and World Bank underestimated Tunisia's problems, focussing narrowly on economic factors and ignoring or downplaying autocracy, corruption and human rights violations.

The aid awarded by the IMF and the Bank, which in turn instilled confidence in other international donors, was based on distorted metrics. For example, according to IMF and World Bank statistics, in 2010, Tunisians below the poverty line accounted for less than four percent of the population. However, this is true only if one defines "the poor" as those whose annual income is below 400 dinars (US$250) per person per year — a very low standard. If the poverty level income is increased to 600 dinars, this yields a more realistic estimate of about 12 percent of Tunisians being poor.

Another example is that, again according to the IMF and World Bank, the percentage of non-performing loans was only moderately high; however, this masked the fact that a disproportionate share of bad loans were to the president's family. What the IMF and World Bank viewed as "privatization" was, in reality, the purchase of state companies at bargain prices by members of Ben Ali's entourage with money borrowed from banks that could not refuse to loan to them. Ben Ali's allies then did not even bother to make payments.

In fairness, one should note that the Tunisian economy performed well in Ben Ali's early years and that the downturn after 2008 was due in part to the world recession and record increases in the prices of food and fuel; moreover, IMF and World Bank officials in Tunisia, as elsewhere, are more vulnerable than other diplomats, since local appointments are subject to host country approval and receive a high degree of continuing review.

Everyone knew there was corruption in Tunisia, but many reasoned that all countries have corruption in different forms and to different degrees. Some suspected that stories of corruption were exaggerated or attributable to misogyny toward the president's wife. Unfortunately, it turned out that the magnitude of corruption of the Ben Ali-Trabelsi clan was far greater than anyone had thought.

After the flight of the president and his family, a national commission began tallying their ill-gotten gains and placing companies in receivership. Transparency International estimates that the president and his family controlled about a third of the Tunisian economy, including whole sectors of activity. This avarice was enabled in part by the IMF and the World Bank — a complicity that was no doubt unintentional, but nevertheless misguided and disastrous.

Comparing Policies

Events since the beginning of the Tunisian uprising might, at first glance, seem to reflect better on US than on French diplomacy, with other European states at various points in between. However, the United States did not begin criticizing Ben Ali until he had been in power for over a decade and a half. Not a single country in the world consistently pressed Tunisia for democratic reforms. The few entities that can claim this distinction include Amnesty International, Human Rights Watch and the International Federation for Human Rights, whose President Souhayr Belhassen is a distinguished Tunisian dissident.

Comparing policies toward Tunisia is difficult, in part because of the variation in countries' political systems and the latitude permitted each one's representatives. The French president, for example, has more foreign policy leeway and less legislative scrutiny than his US counterpart. France's ambassadors tend to see themselves as representing the French government to the Tunisian government and dealing through discreet contacts, rather than also representing of the French people to the Tunisian people.

Another historic difference is that, to a certain degree, France tends to follow the European diplomatic tradition of open and unapologetic pursuit of its own national interest. This contrasts with the US practice of engaging in policies that promote US national interest while clothing them in the garments of high principle (such as "democracy").

As the former colonial master, France had a complex relationship with Tunisia that led the French to be less critical. The United States, on the other hand, had both less leverage on Tunisia and less at stake. There is an analogy here with Egypt, where the United States had a major continuing commitment and a lot at stake, and was therefore reluctant to criticize Mubarak. By comparison, France had less involvement and less at stake in Egypt — although President Mubarak was co-chair of a much-vaunted Europe-Mediterranean partnership. US policy fared poorly for democracy in Egypt, in comparable ways and for comparable reasons that French policy fared poorly in Tunisia.

When Many People Stir the Pot

Turning to the post-revolutionary period and looking at the overall ensemble of embassies and NGOs, one notes the sudden flood of advice and assistance into Tunisia. This was a positive development, but one which paradoxically created a new set of problems. Soon after the dictator fled, embassies and NGOs began organizing scores of training programs and conferences on diverse topics for the newly liberated Tunisians. In an April 2013 report evaluating this expert assistance, the Institute for Integrated Transitions (IFIT) described the result as "event overload." Indeed, much useful help was provided, but there were too many one-size-fits-all events. Some trainers knew little about Tunisia and lacked language skills.

The IFIT report (2013) suggests that the diplomats and NGOs discussed in this Tunisian case study constitute more than the sum of their parts. That is, diplomats and NGOs offer important and useful services, especially for the promotion of democracy and civil society. They work best, however, when they work together (and, in post-autocracy situations, with the host country government) to avoid scheduling conflicts and duplication, to tailor assistance to local needs and to provide coordinated and sustained services with follow-up.

CONCLUSION: DEMOCRACY WITH A DASH OF HARISSA

Tunisia's political landscape is taking on greater definition as events unfold. The major political parties, whose platforms in the October 2011 election tended to be vague, have been forced to take specific positions on issues in the Constituent Assembly. It has been especially interesting to see what positions Ennahdha adopts, because Islam provides no real guidance on issues such as unemployment, worker-management conflicts, job creation and debt management. Some parties have disappeared or split while others have merged, and new parties continue to emerge.

Some aspects of Tunisia's future are fairly predictable. The new constitution will no doubt delegate more power than before to the legislature and less to the president. It will resemble France's constitution in some respects but it will mention Islam. Debate on the first draft of the constitution began in mid-September 2012 and three drafts were completed by spring 2013. The Tunisian public is understandably impatient. Completion and approval of the constitution was not completed at the time of publication (August 2013), with new elections in late 2013 or early 2014. These will be preceded by a campaign that will no doubt be strident, but hopefully non-violent. Given the popular unrest and suspension of the process at the time of writing, this has been thrown into doubt. Tunisia's political future is unclear.

Tunisia's democratic achievements are not likely to be reversed in the near future. Tunisians will not easily give up their hard-won freedoms of speech, press, assembly and open elections. Tunisians of all political stripes remain vigilant for any signs of backsliding to autocracy. The Tunisian experience has already shattered myths, the most insidious of which is that Arabs are somehow culturally incapable of democracy.

Both inside and outside Tunisia, some have become pessimistic about the future. They warn that public impatience and frustration over the economy may erupt into yet another uprising. Outsiders who once spoke of the authoritarian tendencies of Arabs dismiss Tunisia's accomplishments and speak of the Arab Spring as devolving into an Arab Winter.

There is cause, however, for guarded optimism in the long term. Although there are still security concerns in Tunisia, the crime rate is falling. With greater security, tourism will recover, which will help reduce unemployment. The corrupt ex-president — who, in 23 years is estimated to have looted the equivalent of half a year's GNP — is gone, so more money will remain in the economy to be reinvested. Banks will no longer be forced to give bad loans to the parasitical entourage of the president.

The brakes on Tunisian entrepreneurship are lifting. The Constituent Assembly has been working on programs to address poverty and regional inequality. The next Parliament, freed of the burden of writing a constitution while governing at the same time, will have an easier task. They will appoint ministers who will stay for more than a year and who will be taken more seriously. The international community is providing aid to promote democracy and to help the economy. Thus there are good reasons to believe that in the long term, the economy will improve, although much will depend on the European and world economies to which Tunisia is tied.

But the short term has been difficult. Tunisian civil society has become increasingly uncivil — characterized by intemperate discourse, increasing crime, school riots, juvenile delinquency, a high suicide rate, soccer hooliganism, market conflicts and even bank robberies. Debate is shrill — and becoming more contentious with the demonstrations beginning in early August 2013. But apart from the US Embassy riot and the assassinations of Chokry Belaid and Mohamed Brahmi, the level of violence has remained low to date.

Tunisia is not only drafting a new constitution, but also working out its national identity, resuming a debate on Islam that was interrupted for half a century. Until 2011, a dominant secularist ideology of national identity had been imposed by a succession of regimes — the Ottoman beys, the French protectorate, and presidents Bourguiba and Ben Ali. Much will depend on how successful Tunisia is in integrating an Islamic component into its national identity, rising above sterile binary oppositions of secularism and Islamism.

Tunisia's moderate Islamist party, Ennahdha, has shown its willingness to compromise and seek consensus. Ennahdha was, for many months, tolerant toward the Salafists, who smashed the windows of theatres that showed films to which they objected, attacked bars and brothels, blocked access to the university and, in some rural areas, attempted to set up local "mini-caliphates," where they enforced dress codes and other "Islamic" rules. Ennahdha has finally begun to crack down on these Salafist extremists and have even received a public warning from Al-Qaeda of the Islamic Maghreb for this. Some Tunisian Salafists profess to support Al-Qaeda, but as yet they have not embraced its methods. In general, the Tunisians have managed to avoid the kinds of deadly violence that are all too common elsewhere in the MENA region.

Labour relations continue to be a serious problem for Tunisia. Strikers and militant job seekers have shut down factories. The Tunisian economy keeps shooting itself in the foot. As of summer 2012, 170 foreign companies had closed. The UGTT has been engaged in what the press calls an "arm-wrestling match" with Ennahdha over strikes. Some describe the UGTT as "the Salafists of the left."

Tunisia must find a way to make peace between workers who want higher wages and the unemployed who want work, to stimulate the entrepreneurs who have long been kept down by nepotism, and to help the poor, especially those in the rebellious interior and the south, who all too often see no way out except through suicide or attempts to flee across the Mediterranean to an unwelcoming Europe.

Much of Tunisia's current incivility is linked to its struggling economy. Ultimately, the success of democracy in Tunisia will be closely tied to economic performance. The poor economic conditions that were a major factor in causing the revolution worsened at first, and the long-awaited recovery has been slow in coming. A basic problem is the continuing weakness of the world economy, and especially the economy of Tunisia's Mediterranean neighbourhood. Self-inflicted wounds, such as strikes, have disrupted mining and manufacturing. Self-immolations continue, but have become so common that they receive only brief press comment.

The fragility of the economy and the slowness of recovery are the main difficulties that Tunisia's nascent democracy faces. As Radwan Masmoudi of the Center for the Study of Islam and Democracy points out, much is at stake. Masmoudi worries that if the seeds of democracy do not take root in Tunisia, the country where the "social soil" is most propitious, then democracy will be set back indefinitely throughout the Arab world. The Egyptian corollary to "If the Tunisians can do it, so can we," is "If the Tunisians can't do it, then maybe we can't either."

The help of democratic governments and international NGOs is crucial. Perhaps the most important form of assistance is promoting programs that generate jobs — such as marketable skills training, improved job placement, investment in new enterprises and providing microcredit loans to small- and medium-scale businesses.

Tunisians are well-known for their entrepreneurship, but they lack capital. Tunisia is filled with people who have gone abroad, worked, saved, returned with hard-earned capital and started small businesses, but the low levels of capital that come from temporary migration and self-exploitation are not sufficient.

Western democracies, despite their own hard times, must work together to help Tunisia's economy. Priority should go to helping Tunisians create their own wealth, without depending on their government for everything. One way to do this is through attracting more investment from the large Tunisian expatriate community. Another way is to attract funding for new company start-ups by insuring investors against losses (the Overseas Private Investment Corporation and Eximbank offer models for this). Microcredit organizations such as Enda Inter-Arabe have proven very successful. Tunisia's success is very much in the interest of the West. The alternative — standing by and watching Tunisian democracy founder because it has come onto the scene at an economically difficult time — will be far more costly in the long term.

Tunisia represents an example and a model — albeit a turbulent one — for democratic evolution in the Arab world. It is to be hoped that Tunisia's relative inclusiveness and tolerance will offer solutions especially to those Arab countries that are religiously and ethnically pluralistic.

Many take it as axiomatic that democracy is a universal value, though some contest Europe's paternity claim — that democracy emerged during the Enlightenment and continues spread from the West to the rest of the world. Whatever its origins, Tunisians are adapting democracy to their own cultural setting. In important respects, each democratic system must grow from within. The homegrown political system that Tunisians are cooking up, like the national cuisine, will no doubt have its own special flavour. So far, the local spice in Tunisian democracy appears to be harissa, the national hot sauce made from red peppers.

WORKS CITED

Erlanger, Steven (2011). "France Cautions in Stance on Tunisian Crisis." *International Herald Tribune*, January 18.

IFIT (2013). *Inside the Transition Bubble: International Expert Assistance in Tunisia*. Barcelona: IFIT.

2 RUSSIA AND DEMOCRACY

By Jeremy Kinsman, 2013

INTRODUCTION: UNDERSTANDING THE RUSSIAN EXPERIENCE

The Russian struggle to transform from a totalitarian system to a homegrown democracy has been fraught with challenges. Today, steps backward succeed and compete with those going forward. Democratic voices mingle with the boorish claims of presidential spokesmen that the democratic phase in Russia is done with, in favour of a patriotic authoritarian hybrid regime under the strong thumb of a charismatic egotist. Meanwhile, excluded by Russian government fiat from further direct engagement in support of democratic development, Western democracies back away, though they are unwilling to abandon solidarity with Russia's democrats and members of civil society seeking to widen democratic space in their country.

Russia's halting democratic transition has now spanned more than a quarter of a century. The Russian experience can teach much about the difficulties of transition to democratic governance, illuminating the perils of overconfidence surrounding the way developed democracies operated with regard to other countries' experiences 20 years ago. This Russian case study is more about the policies of democratic governments than about the field practice of diplomats. It is a study whose amendment in coming years and decades will be constant.

RUSSIAN EXCEPTIONALISM

As the *Handbook* insists, each national trajectory is unique. Russia's towering exceptionalism is not, as US scholar Daniel Treisman (2012) reminds us, because the country has a particularly "dark side," nor because the famous Russian "soul" makes the country an "enigma" to outsiders. The Russian experience is highly complex, but objectively understandable.

The Russian journey is unique in dimension, but also in significance: the bumpy transformation of the Soviet Union and then Russia from a totalitarian state, a command economy and a harsh empire to what followed — a partly democratic extractive market economy whose world view is one of non-aligned post-imperial nationalism — certainly matches any other democratic transition experience in scale, political distance to be travelled and global significance.

Russia's October 1917 revolution had itself been a massive global game-changer, dubbed, in 1919, the "Ten Days that Shook the World" by American journalist John Reed. Seven decades later, the envisioned counter-passage has moved, in just a few years, from one extreme to another, and would have represented a reversal without human precedent. The vision, from the rigid and cruel Communist Party dictatorship, which over several generations consolidated the Bolshevik capture of the revolution, to an imagined virtual opposite: a pluralistic political and economic system whose rough, if elusive, lines were on the minds of hundreds of thousands of marchers in Moscow in 1989, and millions who discovered free debate in those first glasnost years. It should be no surprise that Russia's transformation faltered. Transformative political journeys in institutional development and behaviour modification that were less extreme in the United Kingdom, the United States and France each took a century and a half at least.

At the time of Russian transformation, German Chancellor Helmut Kohl termed it a defining handicap that "70 years of dictatorship have left the Russians in total ignorance of the world around them. Two generations couldn't get out into the world." Any notion that a short-cut remedy for Russia was simply to copy the ways of the democratic and market societies of "the world," however, woefully underestimated the extent of change Russia would face.

In 1998, Václav Havel predicted that it would take Russia 50 or 100 years to develop a democratic vocation. Indeed, as we know, in the first years of the twenty-first century, Russia's new leadership subtracted an increasing amount of the democratic space carved out by Mikhail Gorbachev and then Boris Yeltsin. In 2013, the compression of basic individual rights continues. Havel's literary associate Paul Wilson (2012) recently pointed out the importance of understanding such backward steps as a key part of the "teachable experience" for outside democracies when he proposed that "In today's world, knowledge of how democracies can be lost may be as valuable an instrument of democracy as an understanding of how they are won."

Western democracies were motivated to support Russia's efforts because there was a generalized acknowledgement that in ending the Cold War, Mikhail Gorbachev had changed our world almost as profoundly as their own. The case study sets out the ways that, despite best intentions (most of the time), Western democracies failed to address the complexities inherent in Russian transformation challenges after 1989. Even if they had got Russian politics right and understood how Russia could pull off a transformation whose complexity and extremity were unprecedented, and had the support at home to help more amply in concrete terms, the challenge of Russian reformers would still have been incredibly difficult.

Regardless of the strong solidarity felt by democrats everywhere with the Russian people, it is emphatically a Russian struggle, not that of Western democracies. Today,

Russian democrats insist theirs is not a lost cause. Though the word "democracy" itself had become tainted for many in Russia because of their ragged experience over the first transitional 20 years, the evidence collected by polling and research organizations such as Levada and the Center for Strategic Research shows that an increasing number of Russian citizens again hold the objective of a more democratic Russia as a devoutly cherished purpose.

This case study is in two parts, which are closely linked. The first part begins with a historical overview, then weighs Russia's experiences in the 1990s and assesses the effectiveness of Western democracies' efforts to support Russian democratic transitions in that crucial period. The second, shorter part of the case study documents the individual actions of diplomats and international civil society in response to events in Russia since 2000.

PART I: RUSSIAN DEMOCRATIC TRANSITIONS BEFORE 2000

A historical perspective on democratic transformation is essential. As Sheri Berman (2013) recently wrote:

> Every surge of democratization over the last century — after World War I, after World War II, during the so-called third wave in recent decades — has been followed by an undertow, accompanied by widespread questioning of the viability and even desirability of democratic governance in the areas in question. As soon as political progress stalls, a conservative reaction sets in as critics lament the turbulence of the new era….One would have hoped that by now people would….understand that this is what political development actually looks like, what it has always looked like….and that the only way ahead is to plunge forward rather than turn back.

Beginnings: Glasnost and Perestroika

When Mikhail Gorbachev launched a campaign for greater openness and decontrol in Soviet society after he became Soviet leader in 1985, it was already known that centrifugal forces were pulling the state apart at the seams. Many Soviet industrial, educational and scientific achievements in the first 60 years had been monumental, though obtained through massive human cost at the time. By the 1970s, however, the USSR had been trumped in the space race and pushed beyond its capacity in the arms race. While official statistics continued to show modest growth in wages, the Soviet economy was, in competitive terms, stagnating at almost every level, and always to the detriment of citizens/consumers who were the least understood and satisfied component of the top-down command and control central planning equation.

Moreover, as Leon Aron (2012) reminds us, Gorbachev had become persuaded by adviser Alexander Yakovlev that perestroika "was first and foremost a moral and spiritual transformation," an "attempt to...end the amorality of the regime." The two men were convinced that the moral legacy of the Soviet police state imposed an insupportable burden on society and needed to be confronted and exposed, though doing so discomfited many in the *nomenklatura*. Gorbachev took pains to valorize the party's socialist vocation in his speech to the party's celebration of the seventieth anniversary of the October Revolution in November 1987. But in an unaccustomed spirit of making open secrets public truths, he also spoke of its history of "real crimes based on the abuse of power" and "mass repressions" that were "immense and unforgiveable."

BUT HOW TO REFORM? A QUESTION UNANSWERED

If circumstances argued there was no real alternative to political and economic liberalization, how to do it and how far to go were both untested questions. Intense debate and differing views still colour recollection and analysis of that turbulent period, especially whether Gorbachev's decentralizing reforms — without first building the backstop of a market-based supply function to fill the gaps — didn't have the inevitable effect of turning economic stagnation into a chaotic downward spiral for many Russians. Reformist critics credit Gorbachev with launching a historic process, but judge him harshly for temerity when faced with key decisions.

Of course, Gorbachev was engaged in a massive and complex balancing act, weighing heavy, internal political and economic challenges while simultaneously struggling with gravely aggravating adverse external economic conditions. Forced by its own production inefficiencies to import massive amounts of grain, the Soviet state found itself unable to finance these essential food imports, as the world price of oil — the main earner of hard currency — plunged by 50 percent between 1980 and 1989.

Meanwhile, state supply functions in the centrally planned economic system broke down. Producers used newly awarded autonomy to drop inefficient suppliers and insolvent customers. Stark inequalities widened as wages in the relatively few enterprises that were succeeding climbed without top-down controls, while unemployment elsewhere soared, particularly in production locations chosen over the years of centrally planned nation building for political rather than economic rationales. During the 1980s, shortages spread beyond food supplies to the whole range of consumer goods, deepening the state's need to borrow more money to finance hard-currency purchases from abroad. Foreign debt climbed from US$29 billion in 1985 to US$97 billion by 1991.

Ecological degradation was widespread. Traumatic disaster struck — at Chernobyl on April 12, 1986, and then in Armenia in 1988, when an earthquake crumpled buildings constructed illegally with substandard materials. Post-disaster dissembling by the authorities added to the public shame, further agitating restiveness over systemic incompetence and corruption.

The "Undertow" that Succeeded the Euphoric First Wave of Reform

Glasnost released widespread and swift public antipathy to the Soviet political and economic order. It seemed increasingly apparent the majority of citizens had lost faith in the system and the religious and cultural repressions that the Communist party had, as a matter of course, imposed for so long.

By 1988, citizens' expectations underwent a seismic transformation. Free debate exploded as society began getting used to telling the truth about itself. The circulation of the journal *Argumentiifakty* ("arguments and facts"), which had been a dreary Communist Party propaganda sheet, soared into tens of millions when it became a purveyor of hitherto secret information and essays calling for liberating reforms of the state and society. *Komsomol'skaya Pravda, Literaturnaya gazeta,* and the satiric weekly *Ogonyok* also reached tens of millions avid readers, creating "the first national forum of open political and social debate open to Soviet citizens" who eagerly debated opinions which a decade earlier would have earned lengthy prison terms (Aron, 2012).

The intoxicating experience of freedom of thought and expression captivated society. Soon, however, it had to examine evidence of a deteriorating economic reality. As the state's fiscal disarray deepened, budget deficits reached 30 percent of GDP with immediate inflationary effect. The state expropriated savings. Living standards fell sharply.

Once the genie was out of the bottle and all controls were open to question, the long-repressed people, while ready to embrace deep changes, were faced with unexpected consequences for which they were unprepared. There was no template for their experience. As the system came apart and inflation eroded the value of pensions and savings, backlash set in. Having lost faith in the communist system and having seen their heightened expectations of change deflated, citizens began to lose confidence in the tentative and uncoordinated replacement reforms undertaken by leaders who could not communicate end goals with clarity or conviction.

Though he ended the Cold War and envisaged a Europe which, in President George H. W. Bush's phrase, was to be "whole and free," Gorbachev still lacked a clear plan for the democratic transformation of the Soviet Union itself, or of a role for the Communist Party in a political landscape where it no longer held a monopoly of power.

Gorbachev's indecision was in large part existential: as Alexander Yakovlev much later regretted, Gorbachev was intrinsically wired to judge that turning away from the "socialist choice" would be "inconceivable." Always playing catch-up to public opinion and trying to react to economic pressures, and unaware himself of where the process was heading or how to shape it, Gorbachev, according to Yakovlev, "could never take the next step toward democratization" during his six-and-a-half years in power (cited in Remnick, 1994).

Yakovlev had privately broached with Gorbachev the idea of splitting the Communist Party into reform and conservative wings and allowing their electoral competition, but Gorbachev still seemed to believe the "humanization" of communism could extend the life of the Party's singular and privileged status. By 1989, Gorbachev's faith that the Communist Party might become humanized and inclusive had waned. He ended the Party's monopoly on political power and permitted the formation of rival political parties to compete in direct legislative elections scheduled for later that year. Though electoral rules reserved two-thirds of the seats in the Congress of Peoples' Deputies for Party loyalists, a minority of newly elected reformers, including Andrei Sakharov, whose banishment to internal exile in Gorky had recently been ended by Gorbachev personally, were able to challenge authority at every turn during sessions televised for the first time. The commotion of 85 hours of free debate galvanized a massive public audience that reacted sharply to Gorbachev's authoritarian hostility to Sakharov (whose microphone he turned off). When Sakharov suddenly died on December 14, 1989, a cortège of 50,000 followed his coffin through the streets.

As evident from the history of democratic evolution elsewhere, inclusive political and economic conditions in society emerge most enduringly when they are the product of extensive political and social conflict and bargaining over time between the elites who held power and those seeking its wider dispersal. In Russia, a combination of external and internal factors was accelerating a process that pre-empted such bargaining. Polarization widened between rejectionists of the old system and those in authority who lagged behind the curve and felt threatened.

Meanwhile, the foundering economy was aggravated by unprecedented strikes by Siberian miners. Growing numbers of older citizens and life-long Party members who felt undermined and destabilized by the monumental changes taking place turned out in the streets in counter-protests against reform. Doctrinaire hardliners began to conspire against the Politburo's domination by a handful of reformist members (basically, Yakovlev, Shevardnadze, and until his dismissal in 1987, Yeltsin) who were then pressing Gorbachev to step up the tempo and scale of change, especially Boris Yeltsin, who challenged Gorbachev to more radical reform — though he was also vague on specifics.

Public questioning of the regime's legitimacy as well as its competence deepened. Support for Gorbachev and his non-specific outline of a softer form of communism collapsed after 1990. In January 1991, 52 percent of the population had approved of Gorbachev's actions, but by February, only 15 percent did. By this time, Yeltsin's popularity was overcoming that of Gorbachev by a considerable margin. Gorbachev tried to manoeuvre through the shoals of declining public support and growing opposition in Party ranks, tacking backward and forward. In a brutal concession to KGB hardliners, he authorized the use of force against pro-independence demonstrators in Vilnius, Lithuania in January 1990, which killed 13.

Anatoly Sobchak, the ostensibly liberal political leader in Leningrad, observed in 1991 that the forces of "dictatorship and democracy were living side by side." Gorbachev's hardline adversaries in the Politburo were becoming emboldened to attempt to reverse the trends and return the country to dictatorship.

On August 19, 1991, at 4:00 a.m., a throwback dictatorship cabal absorbing the leadership of the power ministries (including the vice president of the USSR, the prime minister, the ministers of defence and the interior, and the head of the KGB) tried to seize control of the USSR while Gorbachev vacationed in Crimea. But their amateurish attempted coup collapsed within days in the face of public non-support for these wooden figures who hearkened to a darker past. A protective crowd of 100,000 surrounded the headquarters of Russian Republic President Boris Yeltsin, who called on the people to reject the coup. Several things contributed to the coup's collapse:

- The coup leaders, as incompetent as they were unappealing, were no match for the buoyant Boris Yeltsin, who enjoyed the status of being the first (and until then, only) elected leader in the Soviet Union.

- USSR security forces refused the orders of putsch leaders to fire on protesting Soviet citizens.

- Western democracies regarded the seizure of power as unacceptable, even though in some foreign ministries the pragmatic argument was initially that this was Soviet "business as usual" and that democratic governments should "wait and see."

For democratic embassies in Moscow, the coup experience was a wake-up call about the fragility of the democratic experiment. They doubled down on programs to support democrats in civil society, institutional transformation and national programs of humanitarian relief. But they hardly anticipated the extent to which the coup's aftermath would undermine Gorbachev and ultimately the Soviet Union itself.

Yeltsin Ascendant

Boris Yeltsin, a renegade communist establishment figure, was the great beneficiary of September's dramatic events. For several years, he had been anything but deferential to Gorbachev's authority. After Yeltsin criticized Gorbachev's policies and even his personal example at a Communist Party plenum in 1987, Gorbachev sought to crush and humiliate Yeltsin. Expelled from the central command of the USSR, Yeltsin succeeded, in May 1990, in wresting election as Chairman of the Supreme Soviet of the Russian Republic. He then proceeded to win a historic popular election in June 1991 to the newly created post of President of the Russian Soviet Federative Socialist Republic.

Gorbachev, who had declined the option of an open election for his own post of President of the USSR, failed to grasp that, as the first genuinely elected leader in the Soviet Union, Boris Yeltsin had benefitted from the more open environment and had become, for Russians, the symbol of their hopes for democracy.

By November, Yeltsin had begun to create distinct parallel institutions in Russia and pressed his ambitions outward. Taking advantage of a CSCE ministerial conference in Moscow, he and his newly minted "Foreign Minister" Andrei Kozyrev (who had been a rising star in the USSR Foreign Ministry), summoned its delegates and ministers to an essentially competitive showcase encounter. Most delegates viewed the command performance as a theatrical exercise in *amour-propre*. Few grasped the extent to which political force had leaked away from the once-galvanizing international figure of Gorbachev toward Yeltsin who, in a matter of weeks, would eclipse the President of the USSR and end the USSR itself.

Boris Yeltsin, president of the Russian Federation, makes a speech from atop a tank in front of the Russian Parliament building in Moscow on August 19, 1991. Yeltsin called on the Russian people to resist the Communist hardliners in the Soviet coup. (AP Photo)

The USSR Breakup

Was the ensuing breakup of the USSR inevitable? As early as 1978, French historian Hélène Carrère d'Encausse had predicted the intensification of the USSR's "nationalities problem." She pointed out that Soviet citizens in republics as different as Christian European Estonia and Muslim Asian Turkmenistan had virtually nothing in common beyond the shared afflictions of chronic economic inefficiency and the straitjacket of a top-down and partly alien and atheistic police state. Polls a decade later showed that even ethnic Russians in the constituent republics in Central Asia, the Baltics and Ukraine favoured independence from Moscow, which became increasingly the outcome pursued by state legislatures and local leaders.

The economic crisis driving public opinion in 1990-1991 had undermined the regime's authority and opened the door further for the constituent republics to seize more of the economic reins and shed Moscow's leadership. The 1991 coup attempt only accelerated their eagerness to institutionalize change. The leaders of the constituent republics — often opportunistic ex-USSR *apparatchiks* — recognized that without formal changes, newly loosened federation controls could always be tightened again if conservatives succeeded in retaking power in Moscow.

Gorbachev began to attempt different formulas for a looser USSR "Union Treaty" to accommodate the mood, but without success. On December 1, 1991, Ukrainians voted by majority of 92.3 percent to secede from the USSR, electing Leonid Kravchuk as president of independent Ukraine the same day. Yeltsin was only too willing to join Western countries in forcing the issue by recognizing Ukraine as an independent state the next day.

In concert with the leaders of Belarus and Ukraine, on Sunday, December 8, 1991 at the Belvezha Forest hunting lodge in Belarus, Yeltsin declared the simultaneous independence of the three republics, which would in effect write the Soviet Union out of existence.

Two weeks later, in Brussels, at a ministerial meeting of the NATO-Warsaw North Atlantic Cooperation Council (an innovation launched to support East-West reconciliation and transition), Soviet Ambassador Nikolai Afanassievsky was called away to speak to Moscow by phone. He returned to inform the meeting that he had been instructed to remove the USSR nameplate from the conference table. On December 25, 1991, Gorbachev resigned. The flag of the USSR was lowered from the Kremlin tower over Red Square and a pre-revolutionary flag was raised in the historic name of Russia.

The End of the Cold War

Soviet and then Russian transformation unilaterally altered the entire global military equation. For East-West relations, the effect on the international political and strategic landscape was profound, even existential.

There is no specific moment when the Cold War ended. Hardliners on either side gave it up grudgingly, and vestiges of Cold War habits resurface even today. Together, President Reagan and Secretary Gorbachev (who assumed the title of President of the USSR only in 1990) relaxed the overarching nuclear rivalry, especially at their summit meeting in Reykjavik in October 1986, when they agreed to ban potentially destabilizing intermediate range nuclear missiles via the Intermediate-range Nuclear Forces Treaty.

Once socialist regimes collapsed across Central and Eastern Europe in late 1989, the rationale for perpetuating the institutional confrontation between NATO and the

Warsaw Pact was invalidated. Even so, profound uncertainties remained, notably what Soviet Foreign Minister Eduard Shevardnadze then cast as "the mother of all questions," that is, the future military status of a united Germany.

Diplomatic activity over the next two years was intense. At the suddenly redundant confidence-building conference on "Open Skies" between Warsaw Pact and NATO alliances in Ottawa in January and February 1990 (the first East-West gathering since the fall of the Berlin Wall two months before), the formula of "two plus four" was launched by the US, the USSR, France and Germany to find agreement on the German unification process, at least within the exclusive circle of these key countries. UK Prime Minister Margaret Thatcher and French President François Mitterrand initially had mixed feelings about German unification, but Washington seemed committed to drive a process as rapid and conclusive as possible and Germany was prepared to offer the USSR massive compensation. The parties came quite swiftly to agreement and a treaty on Final Settlement on Germany was signed in Moscow on September 12, 1990.

As negotiations over the German endgame issues proceeded, the rival alliances began to put the Cold War behind them. In June 1990, the semi-annual NATO Foreign Ministers' meeting at the Turnberry Golf Club in Scotland extended to the Warsaw Pact "the hand of friendship and cooperation."

Meanwhile, presidents Bush and Gorbachev conducted their own historic parallel diplomacy at summits in Malta, Washington and Helsinki, the last of which secured a non-objection from the USSR to a UN Security Council resolution to expel Iraq from just-invaded Kuwait. Soviet acquiescence briefly transformed the Council into the cooperative body the UN's postwar founders had intended.

By November 1990, at a Paris summit meeting, the CSCE cemented the notion of a common security framework stretching from "Vancouver to Vladivostok." In July 1991, Russian President Gorbachev was invited as a special guest to the G7 summit in London. As he appeared on the balcony of Lancaster House, hundreds of G7 aides on a lunch break in the garden below broke into spontaneous applause.

An Enemy Transformed? The USSR's Peaceful Withdrawal

It is exceptionally rare for a military-supported empire to evacuate its lands voluntarily without suffering military defeat. In 1985, the Soviet military still ranked as the world's largest, numbering almost six million in uniform. But by 1990, it had been reduced to 3.4 million, which the dissolution of the USSR further reduced. By 1996, troops under Moscow's command were down to 1.3 million.

Though lives and assumptions were certainly disrupted, the Soviet empire's dissolution was as peaceful as any in history, if one considers the scale of change involved. The costs of withdrawing personnel from Eastern and Central Europe were massive. Moscow brought home about 1.7 million personnel (800,000 troops, 400,000 civilians and 500,000 family members). Germany contributed significantly to resettlement. The US announced the intention to do so as well, but found itself frustrated by a lack of congressional support at home.

Central and Eastern European Warsaw Pact members abruptly found themselves independent actors. Ex-USSR frontline republics Ukraine and Belarus proceeded to de-nuclearize the USSR strategic military assets left behind. Obviously, Western democracies welcomed the drastic revision of USSR military doctrine, which suspended military planning for a major confrontation versus NATO or China, leading to a suspension of mutual targeting.

In consequence, barriers to cooperation crumpled. In an example unthinkable a few years before, in 1993, Canadian military transport aircraft were landing at what had been secret air bases around Moscow, making humanitarian deliveries of obstetric and other maternal health supplies from the Canadian Red Cross to adjacent rural communities devastated by change. Local councils that had never seen a foreigner greeted each delivery with civic receptions. At Vladivostok on the Pacific, a Canadian Navy frigate became the first NATO vessel to call on the till-then closed strategic port. The sailors' first duty was to tend to the graves of a few dozen Canadian policemen who had died there from the flu epidemic in 1919.

Russia's withdrawal from empire and reversal of history had unique challenges. Unlike European colonial empires that wound down gradually or by force of military defeat in far-away foreign lands, Russia's stunning changes occurred on Russia's borders, and in lands where citizens were literally at home in what had been their own country.

Moreover, as Dmitry Trenin (2011), director of the Moscow Carnegie Centre has pointed out, the effects and costs were not buffered for Russia in the ways that softened comparable loss of overseas territories for Western Europeans following World War II. The European recovery was supported by the Marshall Plan, contributing to the *Wirtschftswunder*, the postwar German economic miracle. Recovery also found a new defining framework in the emergence of the historic European cooperation project, which would lead to the European Union. Russia, too, embarked on changes, which were inherently voluntary and faced huge costs which, except for German military resettlement funds, had to be borne mostly by Russia.

The Western Democratic Response to the Breakup of the USSR and to Russia's Internal Drama

By November 9, 1989, when the Berlin Wall fell, Gorbachev had already made clear to communist leaders in Prague and Berlin that they were essentially on their own. The next day, the communist regime in Prague resigned en masse. Electoral democracy seemed imminent throughout the former Warsaw Pact area. The Soviet Empire itself was already shaking at its roots.

Western leaders grasped the significance of what was happening, but moved hesitantly to adapt to change. Initially, NATO Secretary-General Manfred Wörner told a group of Western ambassadors that it might be important to maintain the

Warsaw Pact to ensure an orderly transition in the East. There were widespread fears that the end of the Cold War and the lifting of barriers between East and West would lead to a flood of refugees, especially from the Soviet Union; however, by the end of 1989, having been largely supportive of liberalizing or dissident movements in Poland, Hungary and Czechoslovakia, and Mikhail Gorbachev's reforms, Western leaders began to realize they had a responsibility to help the democratization process.

NATO Secretary-General Wörner travelled to Western capitals to drum up support for the creation of aid programs aimed at facilitating political and economic transitions. Party foundations and NGOs in the West initiated programs to help fledgling and inexperienced liberal political forces who were reaching for outside democratic support for a multi-party electoral system for which they had virtually no preparation. Each country and case would be specific, but Russia's unique power and role and the scale of transformation envisaged made the Russian experience uniquely significant.

Western democracies did not intend to undercut Soviet authorities. Their wish was to contribute indirectly to a more level playing field on their understanding that local authorities had chosen pluralistic political competition. The purpose of Western encouragement was not to pick winners, but to support political competition in newly opening political landscapes seemingly tilted in favour of well-established communist parties (whose popular strength the West overestimated). But in the USSR, the pluralistic choice had opposition. Apparent conversion at the top did not convince conservative elements in the *nomenklatura* which feared open political competition as a profound threat both to their own power and positions and to the overall influence of the Soviet state.

Once the USSR broke up, Western leaders knew it was politically essential to characterize the territorial retreat as something other than a national reversal. President George H. W. Bush and US Secretary of State James Baker bent over backwards to avoid triumphalism — though as candidate for re-election in 1992, Bush did once brag on the campaign trail that he had "won the Cold War," that stylistic and political breach was unusual. Later, the claim that Ronald Reagan had "won" the Cold War, primarily by forcing the USSR into defence spending it could not afford, gained some partisan traction in the US, but it ignored evidence that Gorbachev was actually responding to a myriad of adverse internal and external circumstances.

In any event, despite statesmanlike efforts to avoid the notion of "winners" and "losers," it soon became evident that many Russians felt like losers. They became truculent in the belief the West had taken advantage of them. This was the psychological and experiential challenge that Bill Clinton was assessing when, in 1993, he judged that what was happening in Russia was "the biggest and toughest thing out there. It's not just the end of communism, the end of the Cold War. That's what's over and done with. There's also stuff starting — stuff that's new. Figuring out what it is, how we work with it, how we keep it moving in the right direction: that's what we've got to do" (cited in Talbott, 2003).

But it was overreaching to believe "we" could so nimbly adapt to the challenge involved, as President Clinton later acknowledged when he came inevitably to recognize "the shortcoming of our policy and of Russian reform itself. We, like the reformers, had a far clearer notion of where we wanted to see Russia go than how it could get there, how long it would take, and what we could do to help" (ibid.). The lessons learned are very much worth retaining.

THE NATO "EXPANSION" ISSUE

Yeltsin reached out to the West early in his tenure as president of Russia, writing to NATO in December 1991 about "the question of Russia's membership." He received no reply. When Yeltsin described the two powers as being on the way to becoming "allies," President George H. W. Bush balked at accepting the term, under the pressure of advice and Republican habit.

The issue of NATO expansion eastward became especially vexed. The Soviet side, most prominently Mikhail Gorbachev himself, claimed that early discussions in "two plus four" and bilaterally with US Secretary of State Baker and other Western statesmen assumed NATO would not expand to absorb former Warsaw Pact members. That had been an initial assumption on the part of several, notably British Prime Minister John Major and Václav Havel. But there was nothing in writing on the point.

The truth probably resides in the confusion of real intentions being lost in translation. Baker acknowledges he did tell Gorbachev that "NATO will not expand one inch to the East" if the USSR acquiesced to a reunified Germany being in NATO, but that he had been referring to foreign NATO forces replacing Soviet troops in East Germany. In his recollection, NATO expansion to other countries eastward simply never came up at that time.

Havel, in any case, soon changed his mind in office as President of Czechoslovakia, joining Hungarian and Polish leaders in claiming their proper place in European institutions, which the Iron Curtain had excluded them from for so long. As Timothy Garton Ash (2012) wrote, "For the half of Europe stuck behind the Iron Curtain — what the Czech writer Milan Kundera called 'the kidnapped West' — the will to "return to Europe went hand in hand with the struggle for national and individual freedom."

NATO members took these leaders' point that Russia should not be awarded a veto on this defining aspiration of countries that had been held "captive" for two generations. Later, of course, the rationale was extended to other Warsaw Pact ex-members Bulgaria and Romania, and even to the ex-USSR Baltic republics, which had been forcibly drawn into the USSR by the Hitler-Stalin alliance in 1939. However, the possible induction of Ukraine and Georgia into NATO became a political "bridge too far" for many NATO members, especially after the risky

Georgia-Russia conflict in 2008, when an eastward line for NATO was implicitly clarified for the foreseeable future.

The Russians were progressively unsettled by the ambivalence of the expansion process. By 1989, many Russians had presumed that, having themselves thrown off Communist dictatorship, they were pursuing common causes with fellow victims. Their neighbours' inability to accept the notion of a common political cause implied to Russians that enduring hostility was directed at Russians per se. This impression was reinforced by repeated warnings over hidden Russian intentions by some more or less Russophobic political personalities in Eastern Europe. Russians' ability to understand the depth of East European sentiments was no doubt clouded by the effects of decades of propaganda at home, which had blocked them from grasping the extent of the resentment felt by the people of Eastern and Central Europe over their capture through local Communist parties, manipulation and brute Soviet force, as in Hungary in 1956 and Prague in 1968.

The overall experience persuaded Russians that their efforts to embrace the West were being denigrated. This could — and should — have been handled much better by all concerned, but time sped by. In the normal press of events, Western political leaders had their own urgencies and priorities to deal with, while the whole complex Russian file seemed to insist on heavy maintenance.

Nonetheless, an ongoing program of building cooperation with Russia was always high on policy agendas. It is worth noting that during his two terms, US President Clinton met Russian President Yeltsin at 18 summit meetings in efforts to establish effective ways to support Russia's democratic transition, as well as international cooperation. Additionally, the Gore-Chernomyrdin Commission met 10 times to try to steer intensified bilateral cooperation in space, energy and technology.

The West was sufficiently well disposed, but the relaxation of tensions induced complacency, which was reinforced when policy goals became heavily invested in personal relations with Boris Yeltsin, who bonded with key leaders and whose instinctive affection for freedoms reassured them.

Governments were inadequately aware of the unprecedented depth of change convulsing Russian society. Foreign Minister Andrei Kozyrev tried to communicate an unusual wake-up call at the CSCE ministerial conference in Stockholm in December 1992, when he delivered a shockingly "mock" hardline speech which, he explained to the media an hour later, was an attempt to convey what Russia's policies would be like if the anti-democratic hardliners got power in Moscow. But Kozyrev's theatrical device was largely lost on Western officials unaccustomed to theatrical irony in the rituals of multilateral diplomacy at this high level.

A harsher wake-up call for Russia's partners rang during the attempted coup against Yeltsin from the parliamentary "White House" during the political and constitutional crisis in October 1993. Foreign Minister Kozyrev prophetically urged the G7 ambassadors summoned to an urgent meeting in the Foreign Ministry to: "Tell your leaders to support Yeltsin in this because we are as pro-Western a government as you are ever likely to see in Moscow."

G7 leaders did, in consequence, make more of an effort to generate demonstrable political rewards, extending Russia partial G8 membership by 1995, and proposing other formulas for integrating it more effectively into multilateral institutions, such as accession to the World Trade Organization (WTO). But unfortunately, as Russian democratic governance began visibly to stumble, questions arose about Russia's qualifications, commitments and overall preparedness.

It was a chicken and egg scenario. The issue of wounded Russian psychology and its belief that the West was seeking to consolidate its gains over a "defeated" Russia would colour for a decade or more the whole process of democracy development in Russia. The charge that outside support for democracy had a geo-strategic agenda directed against Russian interests challenged the legitimacy of Western activity in support of Russian civil society.

Restrictive laws and the harassment of NGOs and international human rights organizations through unnecessary tax audits and building code inspections began in 2006. The trend has culminated in drastically restrictive laws against freedoms of association, assembly and speech being adopted against NGOs in Russia in the summer of 2012, a course of action that has drawn open criticism and approbation from Western leaders, including directly at President Vladimir Putin.

NORM-GIVERS AND NORM-TAKERS

The misunderstanding between the West and Russia about original expectations was in part due to assumptions of Western democracies about the transition process. Finnish political scientist Sinikukka Saari (2009) of the Finnish Institute of International Affairs recalls how 1990s democratization theory assumed the goal was to assist transiting states and integrate them into multilateral institutions based on common (i.e., Western) values. Political theorists were tempted to proclaim that the process of development everywhere had "natural phases," the ultimate of which would be full-fledged democracy. In this context, Westerners instinctively saw themselves as the norm-givers and transiting states as the norm-takers. Others have described this mindset as "putting our labels on things."

It was a time when progress toward democracy was being euphorically depicted in Western commentary as "irreversible," in that it was expected citizens would take to effective democratic behaviour naturally. While democratic institutions and a market-based economy were seen by IFIs as being interchangeably linked in a complementary package of reform objectives, the emphasis, and indeed the priority of Western governments seemed, in practice, to be on the "cure-all" effect of market forces. The point made strongly 20 years later — that market forces alone are not enough for success; they must be inclusive, including in benefits — was hardly gleaned by IFIs and most Western treasury departments (Aceomglu and Robinson, 2012). They held to the "Washington consensus" that policies devoted to economic growth and open markets mattered the most. This mantra presupposed the reach of markets into every aspect of life, as recounted by Michael J. Sandel (2012) much later. Journalist Thomas L. Friedman (2012) saw this as "partly a result of the end of the Cold War when America's victory was interpreted as a victory for unfettered markets, thus propelling the notion that markets are the primary instruments for achieving the public good," which seemingly was indifferent to social purposes and costs.

Overconfidence that the correct path of forward direction was so self-evident contrasted the evidence on the ground that reality was not turning out so well at all. The expectation of optimists in the West and of some reformers in Russia that the country could naturally accede to Western norms "took no account of a ruined economy, depleted and exhausted human capital and the mental and moral dent made by 70 years of Soviet rule" (*The Economist*, 2011). The inevitable shortfalls in economic reform had a devastating effect on the appetite for political reform. Russian realities provided a severe learning experience.

MORE SHOCK THAN THERAPY?

Soviet and then Russian citizens debated fairly existential choices in the first momentous years of change launched by Mikhail Gorbachev. An initial "500 Days Plan" headed by Grigory Yavlinsky foresaw conversion to a market economy, but as revealed earlier, Gorbachev dithered over concrete decisions. Others in the Politburo were openly opposed.

At this time in China, profound economic reforms initiated by Deng Xiaoping in 1978 were visibly taking effect without concomitant relaxation of political controls. But unlike China, the Soviet Union and then Russia, loosened political controls right off, with Western encouragement. As Leon Aron (2012) details, the effects of glasnost had created a clamour for freedoms across the board, but there was a vacuum of replacement institutions.

After Yeltsin dissolved the Soviet Union and replaced Gorbachev in the Kremlin, he appointed a new team of economic reformers who aimed to adopt more radical approaches for Russia, including "shock therapy" to replace Gorbachev's more gradualist approach to economic reform.

There were many reasons the experience floundered, but all wrapped up in the unprecedented extent and scale of the transformation enterprise, whose nature is by definition as behavioural as it is systemic. As former US Deputy Secretary of State Strobe Talbott (2003) put it, "Russian reformers never figured out the right formula for mixing shock and therapy, but neither did the well-wishers, creditors, advisors, and would-be partners in the West." Nor did practitioners have adequate experience or instinct for the practice of inclusive democratic governance.

Some Western economists, notably Jeffrey Sachs, had hoped to repeat the relatively successful reform experience of post-communist Poland, which had a much smaller economy and built-in civil society capacities supporting the less complex "shock therapy" reform process in Poland. Russian reformist Prime Minister Yegor Gaidar never had the extent of public support for his radical reforms as Polish Deputy Prime

Minister Leszek Balcerowicz who had managed the reform process there. Overall, Russians felt more shock in these early years of reform than therapy and the political costs were high.

There has been a polemical debate as to whether the application of shock therapy in Russia failed because it was too drastic or, as free Lithuania's first Head of State Vytautas Landsbergis argued in 1994, because it was not drastic enough. The inarguable facts are that Russian society felt deeply and suddenly the cumulative impact of the elimination of price controls and state subsidies fuelling hyperinflation, which in turn destroyed savings. At the same time, essential social services such as health care were devastated by the radical loss of state financing. The disastrous result was what David Remnick (1994) termed "the wreckage of everyday life."

DIRE TIMES AND DRASTIC MEASURES

The public began to believe that the transformation of Russia was a project of unprecedented magnitude with uncertain outcomes. In the absence of positive results — indeed, faced with deteriorating social conditions — public support began to waver and then bleed away, declining sharply during 1992 with a majority coming to favour a more gradual approach. Dismay at deteriorated conditions was reinforced by the perception of brutally uneven application.

Most enterprises proved unprofitable. Enterprises that could turn a profit became controlled increasingly by single shareholders, some of whom conspired with regional governments to evade Moscow's tax and regulatory authority. Revenues of the state treasury were far less than expected or needed.

By 1995, reformers were faced with an eroding national financial situation. Politically, they also feared that because of the backlash, the Communist Party would win the 1996 presidential election and rescind much of the privatization accomplished. A hastily concocted loans-for-shares process — termed by Tony Judt as a "fire sale" without precedent — aimed to lock as much of industry as possible into private ownership before the 1996 election rescinded the privatization process. An additional rationale, as confided to US Ambassador Tom Pickering by a top Russian political strategist, was to obtain the financing necessary for an effective re-election campaign for the cash-strapped regime.

This headlong rush to privatize state assets without what is now acknowledged as the requisite institutional framework in law, regulation, financial institutions and infrastructure, as well as established behavioural capacity, resulted in massive gains for well-placed insiders who were the early winners, positioned to exploit the absence of controls and able to muscle positions of privilege and power out of the chaos.

Russian banks were offered shares in the most attractive dozen state enterprises in return for loans of US$800 million to the Treasury. The banks then auctioned off the shares to insiders in a process that was anything but transparent. A relatively small number of insiders accumulated sudden and sizable personal wealth and power through ownership of companies that produced or acquired natural resources at artificially low domestic cost which they could then market abroad at vastly higher world prices.

Today, the perspective of time has favoured the emergence of an argument validating the reformers' long game on privatization, based on the evidence that the companies that then emerged, such as oil giants Yukos and Sibneft, and Norilsk Nickel gradually became much more efficient, despite the impropriety of their passage from the state to controlling shareholders.

This was not apparent at the time, as national economic trends deteriorated. Between 1990 and 1998, Russian GDP per capita dropped 42 percent. The 1990 level was not again reached until 2007. The overall impact of the early 1990s cataclysmic economic changes on Russia is estimated to have had double the effect that the 1930s Great Depression had on US society.

Defenders of the long game argue that these apparent national trends reflected, primarily, the discarding of hopelessly inefficient enterprises rather than the deterioration in the standard of living. It is true that for many Russians, despite negative GDP growth, quality of life improved in some significant respects, at least in major cities, as supply chains, freed from price controls, began to fill by-now privatized grocery shelves with a variety of goods actually unprecedented in Russia and as citizens were able to capitalize newly awarded personal residential property.

But politically, the exercise was a disaster, as far as public opinion was concerned. It solidified the impression of built-in unfairness. That impression eroded confidence in a democratic state, already sapped by social hardships. Indeed, a principal casualty of the whole process was the strength and integrity of the Russian state itself. As Aron (2012) described it, citizens felt that "the state had failed not only them, their village, or their town; it had let down an entire great country." Restoring the state would become the central purpose of the post-Yeltsin era under Vladimir Putin.

Revisiting the Reform Experience in Russia

What explains a formula mix now seen as having underestimated social costs and damage to the state's integrity with a corresponding devastating political downside? Russian reformers were not oblivious to their lack of practical experience with reform. But urgency was on their minds. The reformers under Yeltsin knew their window of political opportunity would soon begin to close because of the buildup of opposition. Gradualism was not a formula which would meet their target of locking in defining policy changes as early as possible: "We decided to put all our eggs in one basket," reformist Prime Minister Yegor Gaidar later recalled.

Privatization Chief (and later, First Deputy Prime Minister) Anatoly Chubais described the process as doing it "Canadian-style," a reference that drove the puzzled Canadian ambassador to seek personal clarification. It was an ice hockey metaphor, the minister explained privately, drawing from the iconic and well-remembered 1972 USSR/Canada hockey championship, when the Soviet team's style of play aimed to control the puck, passing it back and forth until a perfect scoring opportunity emerged, contrasting the Canadians' style of shooting the puck to the Soviet end right away and chasing it pell-mell in the hope that unforeseen opportunities would emerge from the ensuing melee. "And", Chubais added, "Canada won." The Minister asked rhetorically, "How do you decontrol a society and economy in a controlled way?" It was a valid philosophical question, especially given that the full process had never been done before. As US Ambassador Jack Matlock allowed later, "There were no sure bets. Nobody had a road map."

The high point in reformers' expectations had occurred in 1992 under Gaidar, Chubais and Minister of Finance Boris Fyodorov. But once growing public dismay and political agitation (including the need to reach some accommodation with legislators) made Yeltsin sack Gaidar at the end of 1992 and replace him by former Party boss Viktor Chernomyrdin, any coherence shock therapy may have claimed was lost from that point on.

Obviously, the speed and scope of privatization in the hands of early winners playing only for themselves ran away from the reformers' intentions. Anatoly Chubais had hoped to encourage the emergence of Russian modern-day equivalents of US nineteenth-century "robber barons" like Carnegie, Ford, Leland Stanford or the Rockefellers who would leave behind a legacy of foundations, educational institutions and good works. Instead, Russia got their oligarchs.

The removal of controls also fostered a permissive culture of corruption that, for two decades, has affected virtually every aspect of Russian economic and also judicial life. The effect was to identify "democracy" for much of the public with disruption, crime and arbitrary unfairness, especially for powerless ordinary citizens and even honest business competitors.

EVENTS, EVENTS, EVENTS

Much has been written about (and by) Boris Yeltsin and his beliefs. Westerners who knew him well were convinced he had come to detest communism and had an instinctive and overriding conviction that citizens deserved fundamental rights: to vote out governments (though arguably not his), to free speech and to their own property. But beyond these broad principles, he did not embrace reform fully, proceeding in a staggered and often contradictory path while he confronted a cascade of momentous political events and developments.

By autumn 1993, political institutions of Russia were in collision. The Russian Congress of Deputies had been inherited from rules that applied in 1989 USSR. Reform-resistant deputies who had been "elected" according to those rules cited ample grounds in the still-applicable Soviet-era Constitution to deny President Yeltsin authorization for most reform projects.

One of Yeltsin's overriding objectives was, therefore, the replacement of the inappropriate Soviet Constitution by one representing Russia as a federal democratic state committed to the rule of law. Russian scholars and legal experts incorporated many of the best democratic principles into a document but old-line Duma members were vehemently opposed on this fundamental issue. Yeltsin moved to dissolve the Congress. The Head of the Constitutional Court, Valery Zorkin, sided with the Parliamentary leadership, which pushed through a vote ousting Yeltsin as president and declared Vice President Alexander Rutskoi in his place. Yeltsin, of course, rejected the Parliament's self-proclaimed authority.

President of the Parliament Ruslan Khasbulatov saw himself as Yeltsin's constitutional and political rival. With parliamentary approval, he mobilized the 5,000 strong parliamentary military guard armed guard that had been a legacy of the Supreme Soviet. Along with one of the 1991 coup organizers, General Vladislav Achalov, Vice President Aleksandr Rutskoi and various hardline agitators, he launched an insurrection.

Traumatized and disappointed citizens watched in trepidation on TV as flatbed trucks carrying heavily armed insurgents headed for the Ostankino television tower. On live TV, bodies fell to the ground as the tower's security guards put up a vigorous defence. Then, the shot-up TV station went off the air, leaving the public in the dark as to the outcome and desperately unsure how much of their democratic beginnings would survive the weekend.

After some apparent uncertainty, the Russian military, under General Pavel Grachev, moved decisively to support the government. By the time worried Russians awoke Monday morning, TV was back on the air and showed four T-80 tanks outside the "White House" as Parliament was then called. Khasbulatov and the heavily armed insurgents held out inside, refusing to give up their private arsenal of arms. The four tanks fired 12 shells, all but two dummies, but it was enough to end the crisis.

For hours, TV panels of traumatized citizens then struggled with the question of why Russians seemed cursed by an inability to behave like *normalniye lyudi* ("normal people") — generally understood as the citizens of Western Europe.

Chechnya

Crises have unintended consequences. In legislative elections in December 1993, the democrats were trounced by a combination of communists and extreme nationalists, a reflection of post-traumatic dismay with the dangers of reform processes that weren't understood. The outcome was also spurred by nationalists' denunciation of NATO's willingness to proceed with expansion to include former members of the Warsaw Pact.

Meanwhile, Russia's breakaway South Caucasus Republic of Chechnya revolted. The Kremlin's harsh but ineffective military response further conditioned events inside and outside the Russian Federation. The Chechen rebellion itself remains hard to characterize. For some, this was an act of self-affirmation by a proud and ancient Muslim people who had historically suffered greatly from tsarist and then Soviet domination, and were forced into mass exile. But the various rebel leaders and factions included many with criminal histories. The rebellion eventually attracted ex-jihadists who were veterans of the fight against the forsaken Soviet occupation of Afghanistan.

At this point, the Russian public, trying still to digest the breakup of the USSR, supported Yeltsin's refusal to tolerate a unilateral reduction of the territorial integrity of the newly minted Russian Federation, especially by force. The performance of the Russian military, however, in what is known as the First Chechen War, came as a rude shock both inside and outside of Russia. To minimize military personnel losses, the Russian Army relied extensively on heavy artillery and air power, destroying Grozny and displacing its entire surviving population. Loss of life was colossal. Both sides resorted to torture and arbitrary seizure.

Ultimately, a ceasefire was obtained. But heavy costs deepened. Inside Russia, Chechen militants performed acts of mass terrorism, leading to calls for a crackdown. Outside Russia, opprobrium over Russian methods began to colour relations with Western democracies. It weakened the Western aid effort in Russia. By 1999, recurring dismay over conduct in the Chechnya conflict caused the EU to limit new projects under the Technical Assistance to Commonwealth of Independent States program to those promoting human rights, rule of law and support for civil society. This essentially marked the end of general concrete support for Russian transitions, which had begun in earnest in 1991. By 2000, Western aid, such as it was, was winding down before an effective civil society in Russia able to anchor democratic structures had been built.

WESTERN AID: HOW MUCH AND HOW EFFECTIVE?

How much aid had been disbursed? The short answer is much less than believed. In April 1992, US President Bush announced that the United States would contribute US$24 billion to support the reform process in Russia. US expenditure fell far short of that. Bilateral aid to Russia in the form of grants over the 10-year period from 1990 to 2000 was less than US$5 billion, or less than one year's aid to Israel and Egypt at that time. Of this, only US$130 million, or 2.3 percent, was devoted to programs directly supporting democratic reform (Stoner and McFaul, 2013).

The US Congress stayed generally opposed, reading US public opinion as being against cash grants to Russia. US President Clinton announced an effort to increase effective real aid, but ran into opposition in Congress and also fell way short. Yeltsin returned to Moscow in 1993 from his first summit meeting with Clinton with promises of just US$1.6 billion, again much of it in the form of credits and food aid.

At the same time, Western countries insisted that the Russian Republic assume responsibility for Soviet foreign debt, which, at its peak stood at US$97 billion, a sum far exceeding all disbursements in aid to Russia. Treisman (2012) asserts that "Russia was bullied into taking responsibility for the entire Soviet debt," though Russia itself saw merit in succeeding to the Soviet Union's status in other respects, such as permanent membership of the UN Security Council. In any event, that debt has now also been repaid in full.

On the size of the global support effort, a November 2000 report of the US General Accounting Office to the House of Representatives Committee on Banking and Financial Services cites a US government estimate of US$66 billion through September 1998. G7 background papers indicate that, between 1991 and 1997, 30 countries and IFIs spent US$50 billion in aid. Much of the aid was multilateral and in the form of loans, not grants. From 1990 to 2000, IMF aid of about US$20 billion was directed to the central government of Russia, intended to support reforms aimed at controlling inflation and accelerating macroeconomic stability. By March 2005, rising oil revenue had permitted Russia to repay the IMF in full. For its part, the World Bank contributed about US$12 billion, almost all of which has been repaid.

Whether multilateral or bilateral, the effectiveness of the aid was at best very mixed, largely because of what the Government Accounting Office report terms "no comprehensive strategy regarding the level, timing and priorities of assistance and how assistance would be coordinated" (Government of the United States, 2000).

The report (ibid.) itemizes the following items as "lessons" learned:

- An essential degree of consensus and political commitment within Russia was lacking.

- Donors underestimated the scale and complexity of the challenges.

- Russia had "almost no exposure to the western market culture and principles it set out to adopt, and with a vacuum in terms of internal institutions."

- "The lack of a social safety net to cushion the impact of transition on workers and vulnerable groups....increased the social costs of transition [and] decreased public support for reform."

- Programs were "sometimes poorly designed or implemented"

- "Russia's transition path has been made harder by the concentration of power and income in the hands of a few....accelerated through the privatization [process]."

Janine R. Wedel's (1999) earlier analysis had also described the "massive aid.... for market reforms [as] largely ineffective....plagued by a number of problems.... whether provided in the form of technical assistance, grants to political groups or NGOs, loans and guarantees to the private sector, or direct financial aid to post-communist governments." Moreover, "because providing official funds to countries in transition is an inherently political process," Wedel argues, "reform efforts often backfire when they are perceived to follow an agenda set by Western governments." Wedel also suggests that "aid has become an end in itself, and, in prominent instances, has resulted in conflicts of interest or self-enrichment of aid-financed advisors." This referred particularly to Harvard's Institute for International Development, which won several non-competitive grants worth US$40.4 million in fees to coordinate USAID's US$300 million economic development program, subsequently cited for "personal gain" and as support for "tycoon capitalism." The argument is made that "Western consultancies probably profited more from Western aid packages than the Russians did" (Roxburgh, 2013).

For Peter Darby, a Russian/American banker who had returned to start up Dialog Bank, the aid amounted to a "slush fund" for consultants. Darby caused a stir among donor multilateral institutions when he refused their highly paid consultants further access to his premises until they demonstrated they understood conditions and realities of working in Russia, rather than parroting how they did things in the totally different business culture of New York or Frankfurt.

This goes to the vexing issue of "style." As Roxburgh (2013) put it, "The West's handling of post-Soviet Russia….has been just about as insensitive as it could have been….the overbearing and ultimately counterproductive tone that Washington and its allies took toward Moscow in the 1990s reinforced Russian insecurity and would later help to justify the reactionary and standoffish strain in Russia's Putin-era foreign policy."

Today, Clinton believes the US should have done much more to underwrite the transition. On multilateral aid, Talbott (2003) reports the president termed the IMF effort a "40-watt bulb in a damned big darkness." Of course, it was a two-way street.

Russia needed to enact critical reforms for the aid to work. If Clinton is right that the IMF and the US "neglected the politics of it," and "never really figured out how to insure that its money had an impact on 'real people' in Russia," Russian reformers failed politically as well.

Because of expediency in the face of hostile opposition, the Yeltsin administration began to adopt what reforms they could by presidential decree, bypassing the Duma and other political stakeholders, and thereby reinforcing the political polarization that persisted throughout the 1990s. To succeed, Russian economic transformation needed the Duma from the outset to pass laws establishing clear legal regimes for property, contracts and taxation. Western democracies spent a lot of effort mentoring Russian officials on these topics. But in the divisive early years of the Yeltsin administration, opposition legislators were too preoccupied with their political goal of blocking the executive to pass the laws that would have made a significant economic difference.

Some significant Russian "reforms" were probably wrong-headed to begin with. Decentralization makes sense in a country as vast as Russia. But a strong case can be made that the decentralization of power away from the central state went too far, too fast, in favour of the regional governments, which were often co-opted by new business interests seeking to block the application regionally of Moscow-led reforms and necessary efforts to regulate industry. The combination of high speed privatization and decentralization enabled a pocket of insider and private interests to game the federal system by consorting with regional governors to avoid the authority of Moscow.

Based on interviews with 824 regional officials, Kathryn Stoner-Weiss (2004) concluded that the Russian state became gravely penalized by the loss of its ability to maintain a single economic expanse during this time of rampant change. And yet, some Western democracies, notably federal states such as Canada, tended to view Russian decentralization as a good in and of itself, and pursued extensive programs in support for federalism which took little if any account of the need of the central state to regulate economic activity on the periphery.

The notorious "loans for shares" policy initiative had been opposed by Larry Summers, Clinton's deputy secretary of the treasury as "bad economics, bad civics, and bad politics." Talbott later judged that "we, as the reformers' constant backers and occasional advisers, should have debated it more with them." But Talbott and others deferred to the argument that enabling a small class of oligarchs to amass fabulous wealth was part of the political struggle to prevent the return to power of the communists: "The importance of a victory outweighed our disagreement with them over some of the methods they were using to ensure that victory" (ibid.). In retrospect, he conceded it was a "debatable" thesis, even though a win for Gennady Zyuganov and the Communists would have been a grim outcome for the US and the democracy experiment in Russia.

Looking Away from Election Fraud

The Constitution of the Russian Federation, which Yeltsin wished to see the Duma adopt in 1993, (and which sparked the White House revolt) was adopted in a national referendum on December 12, 1993. It is emphatically democratic in its stipulation that Russia is a federal democratic state committed to the rule of law.

By 1996, Western democracies feared that the monumental "acquis" of this achievement was in jeopardy, because they feared the Communists would win the 1996 presidential election and repeal it. In the 1995 Duma elections, the Communists had won in 70 of Russia's 89 regions with 25 percent overall. Vladimir Zhirinovsky's right-wing nationalists (the inaptly named Liberal Democratic Party) came in second with 11 percent. Liberals and democrats had been pushed to the margins.

There began a slippery slope. Post-Soviet scholars like Valerie Bunce, Steve Fish and others charge that preserving the democratic Constitution from repeal came at the expense of democratic behaviour. Russia would soon be on its way to becoming an "imitation democracy."

Ultimately, Yeltsin did win the second round of the June 1996 presidential election with 54 percent. Western observers called the election free and fair, even though many irregularities were documented.

By the time of parliamentary elections in 1999, the administration had strengthened its unfair media control advantage. The Communists still led the vote count with a narrow plurality of 24 percent over Unity, the intended new "party of power" under Sergei Shoigu. The Council of Europe judged the election to have been "not fair, not clean" because of the "not honest" advantage in the media, but on the whole, "satisfactory."

Successive parliamentary and presidential elections built on increasingly unfair advantage as a matter of routine, until the egregiously rigged ballot for parliamentary elections in December 2011 reached a tipping point. By then, Russia's democratic partners had to take a more principled and consistent stand. But this only deepened the strain in relations.

Disenchantment Turns Russians Against Western Democracy

A growing number of Russians believed charges that Westerners were promoting democracy in order to weaken Russia. 1996 presidential candidate Alexander Lebed (14.5 percent in the first round) had termed democracy "alien" to Russia. He easily outdistanced democrat Grigory Yavlinsky's vote count of only 7.3 percent. By the 1999 parliamentary elections, democratic Yabloko's support at the polls had dropped to only six percent.

Russian disillusion with the democratic experiment was largely due to the collapse in the Russian economic and social landscape, and the sense of improvisation that governed politics. As Trenin (2011) writes, "Most Russians did not so much want democracy with its rights balanced by responsibilities; its principles of accountability and participation; or freedom married to self-discipline. Rather, most people wanted to get rid of the oppressive and corrupt Soviet communism and step — as soon as possible — into a free world of material abundance. What they got instead was formal democracy, but also instant inequality, and, for some, real impoverishment. The fittest, who survived and succeeded, were not always the best. No wonder democracy soon lost its attractiveness to many ordinary people."

Russia's disappointment with the West was reflected by Yeltsin's withdrawal of his initial embrace and wish (initially renewed briefly by successor Vladimir Putin) to be "part of Europe" and the West. From Trenin's perspective, there followed an intermediate period of seeking balance with the West, then one of "non-alignment," which under Putin included efforts to create a Russian sphere of influence which in several ways aimed to parry Western policy objectives as a matter of perceived rivalry.

The international issues vexing to Russians are well-known — NATO's bombing of Serbia, the enlargement of NATO eastward, the anti-missile defence network to be set up in Poland and the Czech Republic, the invasion of Iraq, the recognition of Kosovo, the cultivation of what Russians viewed as anti-Russian personalities in Ukraine, Georgia and Poland — are among the most prominent grievances. Underlying them at the official level was resentment that Russia wasn't taken seriously by successive US administrations, especially when, after 2000, the Bush administration turned its back on joint exercises and a shared centre on missile defence. Nuclear issues had given the Soviet Union and its officials their exclusive superpower relationship to the US. The unilateral withdrawal of the relationship by the US seemed like a breach of faith. Complicating the picture was Russia's continuing difficulty in connecting darker realities inside Russia to its deteriorating image abroad.

The leitmotiv of Russian politics after 2000, that the West sought to weaken Russia as a systematic policy aim, was reinforced by reaction to the growing Western criticism of Russia for human rights abuse (especially in Chechnya), rollbacks of democracy and chronic corruption. These failings were real enough but even if they were recognized as such by Russians, it didn't strike them they were so relevant to the conduct of bilateral relations.

Russians, disillusioned with democracy as they had experienced it so far, and resentful of Western support for democrats, launched the pushback against outside support on patriotic grounds of sovereignty defence which persists today.

The Positive Record for Operational Democracy Development Support, 1991–2000

If, at a policy level, the IFIs and national governments had been insensitive in their assumptions and prescriptions for Russian economic development, their efforts were overall more helpful than hurtful. Plus, on a practical level, there were multiple individual programs and projects that Russia's democratic partners had established over the decade to support Russian transitions, often at a local and even street level. Stopgap relief for unemployed factory workers, physicists, soup kitchens, women's shelters, orphanages, church restoration and a myriad of civil society projects issued from informal embassy programs. Whatever the criticism of their overall policy coherence and effectiveness, countless Russians were helped by such ad hoc efforts to bridge the enormous changes in their circumstances and build adaptive capacities for the future.

In many ways, they had a more marked public impact than the much larger-scale structured capacity-building programs for officials and professionals that began to proliferate in cooperation with state institutions and which suffered from the usual waste and inefficiencies of the kind we have seen in large-scale aid elsewhere, such as recently in Afghanistan. The early challenges of meeting short-term disbursement needs for transition support meant that Western aid operations had to seriously alter existing practices.

Aid projects for the Commonwealth of Independent States (CIS) were organized according to different principles and processes from development assistance projects normally. Donor governments did not have time to initiate projects in consultation with host authorities and send out tenders to potential project administrators and then to engage in lengthy analysis. Instead, most donor government programs were in response mode: they sought fast-disbursing proposals from "donor" civil society to partner a comparable activity or institution in the CIS. Universities, municipal councils and organizations, trade and professional associations, political parties, social policy advocates, policing experts, courts, all sorts of humanitarian assistance groups, and, inevitably, firms with financial, legal and organizational expertise bombarded the custodians of national programs, such as Britain's very successful "Know-How Fund," with ideas for partnering and mentoring.

That these partnerships were often a profit centre for donor partners whose financing at home was under pressure from government austerity policies is indisputable, but the motivation to assist a historic and inspiring transformation was the driving factor.

One Western embassy recalls how small businesses with no foreign experience — a dry cleaner and a bagel bakery — set themselves up in St. Petersburg out of a simple desire to be of service. They succeeded — at least until local mafias were drawn to corral a piece of the cash flow. At this point, out of their depth, they sought the support of their embassy, which intervened with Mayor Sobchak, who in turn assigned the files to his new deputy, Vladimir Putin. These small businesses left Russia before long, but in their way, their hope of transmitting technique and process was fulfilled. That process was repeated throughout the service industry, with respect to standards of food safety, reliability of products and the cleanliness of locales. McDonald's may be taken to task for its menu's impact on nutritional health standards, but in Russia, where the Canadian subsidiary had to source all products from local producers because of currency exchange prohibitions, the company created a whole supply chain of small agricultural suppliers and a distribution network that transformed local communities.

The role that multinational extractive companies in the energy and mineral sectors can play in upgrading technical skills of the local labour and professional cadres is especially important. The boardroom clashes between outside investors and Russian joint venture partners have captured the headlines, but over time, joint ventures did enable many Russian operations to adapt to the requirements of economic efficiency, while already technically fluent workers adopted more advanced technical and governance standards which enabled their industries a faster acceleration to a competitive position internationally. The newly privatized oil and gas companies succeeded in modernizing. As Treisman (2012) says,

> After consolidating control, the tycoons set out to restructure their companies and attract foreign investors. They introduced international accounting standards, appointed independent board members, hired experienced foreign executives. Yukos and Sibneft engaged the oil service firms Schlumberger and Halliburton to improve efficiency. The results were dramatic. Between 1996 and 2001, pretax profits of Yukos, Sibneft and Norilsk Nickel rose by 36, 10, and 5 times respectively (this despite only a modest increase in the oil price from $21 to $24 a barrel). Productivity rose much faster in oligarch-owned oil companies than in similar state-owned enterprises or firms led by "red directors."

More Shock in 1998 and 1999

In 1998, after several years of declining growth had levelled off, Russia was whacked by the Asian financial crisis, which caused a sharp drop in the price of oil — from US$23 at the end of 1996 to only US$9 in 1998 — gravely affecting Russian finances. Russia's deficits also deepened because of the state's inability to collect taxes — the tax debts of enterprises amounted to six percent of GDP. Many foreign holders of short-term treasury bills (GKOs) decided to cash them in, which accelerated the deficit spiral as the government jacked up interest rates to over 80 percent.

Again, IMF support was inadequate. Though US$22.6 billion was promised, less than US$5 billion was made available in time to try to avert the crisis.

On August 17, Russia devalued the ruble and placed a 90-day moratorium on payment of foreign debts. Remaining GKOs were converted by fiat to long-term bonds at the expense of their holders. The social costs soared along with inflation. The political impact was vivid.

As Treisman (2012) reports it, "The financial crisis resulted in the final discrediting of the economic reformers still in government — Boris Nemtsov, Anatoly Chubais, and Sergei Kirienko. Nemtsov's prospects as a potential presidential candidate in 2000 dimmed, and the Yeltsin team's search for a successor focused even more than before on officials with a martial background. Absent the August default, the odds would have been much higher of a regime emerging that would have reconciled the creation of a more effective state with liberal democracy."

Kosovo

In 1999, Serbia tried to expel from Kosovo its predominantly Muslim Kosovar residents toward Albania and Macedonia. Western democracies had ineffectively stood by over earlier Serbian atrocities at Srebrenica, failing to keep their promise to protect those who had fled to this designated "safe area." But the Kosovar expulsions were judged intolerable across the European political spectrum because of the psychological connection the images of people forced from their home onto trains had to collective memory of the Holocaust.

Russia, however, vowed to veto a UN Security Council Resolution aimed at authorizing intervention by the international community. The bombing campaign went ahead under NATO without UN authority, but with a sense of moral legitimacy — at least in Western capitals. It lasted almost three months until June 1999, when former Prime Minister of Russia Viktor Chernomyrdin helped to broker the withdrawal of Serbian forces from Kosovo, permitting the return of the refugees. The next year, a democratic uprising in Serbia pushed its President Slobodan Milosevic from power.

Overall, the Russian experience with the aftermath of the breakup of the Yugoslav Republic contributed to a sense of being marginalized. The sentiment was deepened by NATO's eastward expansion in 1999 to the Czech Republic, Hungary and Poland, formally adopted at the 1999 NATO Summit held during the unexpectedly prolonged bombing campaign of Serbia. Bristling at Western "regime change" would become a hallmark of Russian foreign policy, particularly after the invasion of Iraq and then the "colour" revolutions that Russian leaders ascribed to Western interference.

Putin Ascendant

Vladimir Putin joined the KGB in 1975. Posted to Dresden in 1985, he returned to his hometown of St. Petersburg in 1990 after the fall of the Berlin Wall. In Dresden, he had witnessed the collapse of the German Democratic Republic (GDR) first-hand. But within the GDR's information bubble, he missed out on observing the heady years of glasnost in his home country (Hill and Gaddy, 2013).

By the time he returned to St. Petersburg, the local economy had broken down. Putin's initial intention was to resume work on his doctoral dissertation on international trade at the Faculty of Law, and he soon also resumed his close relationship with his former mentor and law professor, Anatoly Sobchak.

As the mayor of renamed St. Petersburg, Sobchak boosted his city relentlessly, especially with foreign representatives. Sobchak recruited Putin to the city council. Before long, despite his KGB past, Putin won election as one of three deputy mayors, with particular responsibilities for external relations. Sobchak delegated to him contacts with Western diplomatic and business representatives. He impressed several by what appeared as candour and an ironic attitude toward his past. He seemed to have turned the page toward reform. When small foreign investors found themselves suddenly being squeezed by criminal extorters, Putin intervened effectively.

Putin's attempts to manage a complex barter process to obtain food resources from abroad to replenish empty city stores were by all accounts less effective as unscrupulous dealers siphoned off funds and the food itself. Burned by the experience, the ex-KGB officer found himself reinforced in his former professional training to trust only closest associates. It encouraged him to develop a tough aptitude for keeping control in the rough-and-tumble environment of deals and intimidation characteristic of the new Russia in St. Petersburg as elsewhere. This reputation would stand him in good stead before long in Moscow.

After Sobchak lost his bid for re-election in 1996, Putin was recommended to some worried top reformers in the federal administration by Alexei Kudrin, a former colleague on Sobchak's team and an economist of great competence who had joined Yeltsin's immediate office.

Putin's rise in Moscow was swift: by 1998, after a period on Yeltsin's staff, the ex-KGB mid-level officer was appointed head of the (successor) security service, the FSB. In March 1999, he was awarded the chairmanship of the Russian Security Council, which coordinated national security activity, including national defence.

During 1999, the situation in Chechnya again darkened Russia's political atmosphere. After the first Chechen War, Chechnya's chronic lawlessness and serial terrorism had sufficiently abated to permit an election that was won, more or less fairly, by Aslan Maskhadov, a military commander of moderate views. But by the end of the year, an upsurge in kidnappings and a murderous incursion by warlord Shamil Basayev into the adjacent republic of Dagestan prompted Putin in his new position at the top of security to send Russian troops back into Chechnya.

In a tragic, dramatic and psychologically defining moment, bombs exploded in apartment buildings in Rostov, Moscow and Dagestan, killing over 300 people. A terrorized Russian public turned to the newly prominent Putin. Vowing to chase the terrorists down, to "kill them in their outhouses" (using a cruder term in Russian), Putin's words and actions seemed chosen to position him in as just the man "with a martial background" the Yeltsin team had been looking for as a possible successor to the failing president. (There has been much speculation about whether FSB operatives, acting as rogue provocateurs or as part of a concerted plan even with the knowledge of Putin himself, carried out the bombings to create a sense of crisis and need: several journalists have attempted to document this thesis. The evidence adduced is unconvincing.)

Putin to the Kremlin

Vladimir Putin's propulsion upward was fuelled by the sense of vulnerability felt by the Yeltsin family. It had the support of several key liberals in addition to Aleksey Kudrin, notably Andrey Illiaronov and Mikhail Leontyev. They had every reason to fear that Yeltsin and his family and allies might face a successor regime's prosecution, unless the successor was himself an ally.

By first naming him Prime Minister, Yeltsin positioned Putin to become acting president, should the failing president voluntarily give up power. Yeltsin did so on the last day of the twentieth century, asserting in his TV address to the nation that Russia in the new millennium needed a younger leader. Meanwhile, Putin himself had released a lengthy essay in which he affirmed above all the need to resolve "the crisis of the destroyed state."

Putin's pole position made him the instant favourite to win the presidential elections on March 26, 2000. Though he had demurred initially, confiding prophetically that he "did not like elections," he indeed emerged a clear winner, with 53 percent in the first round against communist Gennady Zyuganov. Russians welcomed the ascendance (and novelty) of a vigorous, abstemious, fit and obviously competent and articulate leader.

The Best Intentions...

President Putin promised in his acceptance speech that "the state will stand firm to protect freedom of speech, freedom of conscience, freedom of the mass media and property rights, those fundamental elements of a civilized society." What happened to these categorical intentions? For Putin, the restoration of the state's viability was the overwhelming priority. To him, this was a common cause for all Russians. Competition and dissidence were signs of disloyalty.

Some argue that Vladimir Putin just didn't have the DNA for democratic behaviour, especially when it came with political competition. He was wired behaviourally in an earlier authoritarian time, was vocationally trained to distrust appearances and had no first-hand exposure to the heady days of 1987–1991, when Russians were questioning everything in an explosion of unaccustomed freedom of speech. His repeated lapses into authoritarian mode became an influence on, but also something of a metaphor for, his country's staggered efforts to transit to inclusive democratic behaviour. For Putin, the illiberal course he grew to follow may not have been his intention going in, but events convinced him.

A "Decade Lost for Politics"?

As Putin took charge, Russians felt relieved that they had at last earned some time free from crisis, drastic changes and existential questions — a "time of calming down" as Andrey Illianarov put it. The unfamiliar pleasures of private lives and personal freedoms combined with rising incomes to win a lot of support for the new president. He used it to gain a free hand in reshaping the political landscape.

Early in the new millennium, the Russian administration and the judiciary began to subtract from the democratic space opened earlier by Boris Yeltsin. Insiders within the system of non-inclusive "vertical power" worked to vest all significant authority in the Kremlin once again. Corruption also became generalized. An aura of impunity surrounded those holding the levers of power, supported by a politicized judiciary.

The poor reputation of the justice system was reinforced by the limpid investigation and prosecution of murders of investigative journalists. Human rights organizations in the West radiated outrage at the killing of high-profile victims such as Anna Politkovskaya, Nataliya Estemirova, Paul Klebnikov and Yuri Shchekochikhin; indeed, over 500 Russian journalists died violently in the course of work in the two decades after the end of the USSR, many in Chechnya. In fact, the Putin and Medvedev administrations improved the rate of prosecution and conviction as time went on, but the impression persisted that authorities did not welcome journalists shining a light on criminal and corrupt behaviour. An official mindset devoted to information control masked an underlying inability to contemplate the real sharing of power.

Terrorism continued to shake citizens psychologically: 129 hostages and all 41 Chechen hostage takers died when the Dubrovka Theatre was seized in October 2002. In September 2004, 334 hostages, many of them children, died in another Basayev atrocity in the North Ossetian town of Beslan. A heavy-handed and botched use of force by security services contributed to the number of fatalities in both incidents, but also reinforced Putin's hard hand of control in the eyes of a terrorized public. The implicit contract that the Kremlin offered Russians seemed increasingly accepted: "Your lives will be good but leave politics to us." Those who strayed would receive a blast of intimidation.

TV AND OIL

Of course, it mattered greatly where they strayed. Founding oligarchs tried to get involved in broadcasting. Boris Berezovsky had bought the main TV channel, ORT, and Vladimir Gusinsky the principal independent network, NTV. Earlier, both had been instrumental in helping Yeltsin to win a second term in 1996, but shortly after Putin's inauguration in 2000, tax police raided NTV and its parent company Media Most, in what seemed to be political retaliation for critical reporting on the administration's handling of (and even involvement in) the Ryazan apartment bombing, as well as having supported the opposition in December 1999 Duma elections. Gusinsky was arrested and forced to sell his media empire to state energy giant Gazprom (to which NTV was considerably indebted). This placed Russia's biggest media group under the Kremlin's direct control.

Berezovsky soon followed Gusinsky into exile after retaliation against him after his TV network ORT attacked Putin for what it termed callous incompetence and initial presidential nonchalance over the ghastly sinking of the submarine Kursk in August 2000, which cost 188 sailors' lives. Berezovsky was forced to concede ORT to the state.

This completed the state's near-monopoly of control of Russian TV. While print media continued to contain pockets of independent reporting, notably *Novaya Gazeta*, where Politkovskaya had done her investigative work before being murdered, newspapers had ceased to be a major source of news for Russians who overwhelmingly relied on TV. The radio station Ekho Moskvy won great credibility among democrats but was little heard outside the capital, though it was streamed on the Internet to a wider audience avid for objective reporting.

The case of Yukos CEO and billionaire "oligarch" Mikhail Khodorkovsky has received vast coverage. He had been one of the principal beneficiaries of the "loans for shares" scheme which enabled him to control first a bank, Menatep, and then what was to become the world's fourth-largest energy company. Khodorkovsky began to get involved in "politics," first as a benefactor of various civil society causes and then as a financial backer of political opponents of the Putin regime, from the Communist Party to democratic Yabloko. Indeed, the Communist bloc in the Duma on one occasion voted against bills to increase the tax take on energy companies for that reason. At the same time, Khodorkovsky dared to criticize the regime for high-level corruption. He was careless in allowing it to be known he was contemplating entering politics himself and even a run at the presidency. Once he began to explore with Exxon Mobil and Chevron Texaco willingness to take a major stake in Yukos, Khodorkovsky was arrested. Putin was demonstrating to other oligarchs that the political game was off limits.

Putin also rearranged political institutions in Russia to centralize control in the Kremlin's "vertical of power." Putin appointed "super governors" to oversee the country's 89 regions. The Federation Council, the Parliament's upper chamber, would henceforth be appointed by Putin rather than by the regions. To some extent, these changes, complemented by an increase in the central government's share of taxes, corrected what had been seen as an excessive swing toward the regions at the expense of effective management of the country, but they were also at the expense of democracy.

President Putin and the Outside

President Putin initially sought better relations with the West, telling his first visitor, NATO Secretary-General George Robertson, that he wanted Russia to be a "part of Europe." Washington's non-committal response to Russian overtures had the effect of reinforcing Putin's intuitive distrust of US sincerity and indirectly of inclusive and competitive democracy which Washington seemed always keen to promote.

Later, Putin entertained inflated expectations that his immediate support offered US President George W. Bush after the attacks of 9/11 would make a lasting and rewarding impression, consolidating a special relationship, including on the threat of Sunni jihadism, which had, in Putin's mind, been the principal force behind Chechen separatism. Instead, the US proceeded with the invasion of Afghanistan without seeking much advice from Russia (or anyone else). Washington then severed a number of US-Russia nuclear weapons agreements, most prominently the Anti-Ballistic Missile Treaty, while continuing to lecture Russia about its behaviour in its own region.

The impact was cumulative. As Treisman (2012) puts it, "By his second term, Putin clearly felt he had been played for a fool, shown up as naïve in hoping for a real partnership with the United States. This doubtless left him vulnerable to the arguments of the conservative generals who had warned against trusting the Americans all along." On the other hand, Moscow had been grudging in meeting US requests for ease of transport access into Afghanistan. There was vexing behaviour on both sides.

Did nothing remain from the investment and efforts to build trust by US presidents George H. W. Bush and Bill Clinton, chancellors Kohl and Schroeder, prime ministers Major and Blair, presidents Mitterrand and Chirac, Prime Minister Prodi, prime ministers Mulroney and Chrétien, NATO Secretary-General Solana, IMF Chief Camdessus and initially George W. Bush, as well as many other leaders beyond the G7, to consolidate a positive partnership with Russian leaders?

The personal and political investment made by these various partners didn't naturally translate into working political capital with Yeltsin's successor, who hadn't himself been part of the narrative. Coming in, Putin's politics drew from the palpable public mood of growing nationalism prompted by a bristling national psychology that appealed to his own instincts and training. As it became increasingly evident he didn't, in any case, have in his bones the sort of natural instinct for democracy that Western partners had grown used to with Boris Yeltsin, Russia's backward steps on democracy aggravated already testy relationships with Western partners. These became more vexed when Russia made it apparent it was turning away from the West, having abandoned any ambition to be part of the European family.

Initially, NATO's 1999 enlargement to include the Czechs, Hungarians and Poles had been jarring to Russian psychology, but in a few years, even the Kremlin had come around. At the 2003 NATO Summit in Prague, however, the decision to admit the three breakaway Baltic republics from the USSR itself (in addition to Bulgaria, Romania, Slovenia and Slovakia) cut Russian psychology more deeply, especially as Lithuania, Latvia and Estonia were engaged in disputes with Russia. Long-standing Baltic bitterness over the forced annexation of the three countries into the Soviet Union had never receded, and Baltic voices added something of a specialized anti-Russian chorus to NATO's ranks, which Russian media amplified out of all proportion.

In 2003, the joint US-UK invasion of Iraq drew support and troops from all recent entrants to NATO ("New Europe") and from aspirants such as Ukraine and Georgia. Their zeal was rewarded, at least implicitly, by US alignment with their declarations of concern over Russia's threat in their own region.

Saddam Hussein had been a Soviet ally, but Gorbachev had been able to agree in 1991 he should be thrown out of Kuwait by a very broad UN-mandated international coalition. In 2003, however, Russia and most other UN members, including half of NATO — "Old Europe" plus Canada — were not able to agree whether Hussein's regime should be toppled by force in Iraq without evidence of a clear and present danger to neighbours and evidence of weapons of mass destruction (WMD). That the invasion became mired in an incompetent occupation and a tragic civil war may have given some satisfaction to Russian policy makers, but the principal effect was to erode even more any remaining trust in US intentions, especially when it came to rhetoric about democracy promotion. The "coalition's" massaging of disinformation about Iraqi WMD and the whole mismanaged venture blew wind into Russian nationalist sails. Russia's choice to be essentially unaligned with the West was confirmed from this point on.

Ukrainian elections in 2004 drained Russian trust further. The episode also exposed chronic blind spots in Russia's ability to analyze events objectively. As the *Handbook* case study on the Ukraine and the "Orange Revolution" shows, Western interest and activity was not to promote regime change, but rather to support the right of Ukrainian citizens to avert and then to protest a flagrant electoral fraud. However, Putin seemed unable to credit the protests as sincerely meant, though he had to know the extent of the fraud in question. Indeed, the technique of vote rigging used by Kuchma/Yanukovych resembled what OSCE observers judged had been done in Russian parliamentary elections in 2003, which they had termed "not free, not fair." In March 2004, Putin had himself been re-elected president with a tally over 70 percent, but in a way the OSCE declared "overall did not adequately reflect principles necessary for a healthy democratic election process." Putin's sole focus was on the possibility that protests could deny the Russian-supported candidate

Yanukovych the prize that his Russian neighbours had so dearly sought and assumed would be his. Putin had heavily invested his own prestige in a Yanukovych victory.

After exit polls showed Yuschenko had won, rigged official results that had awarded the victory to Yanukovych were nullified. In the mind of the president of the Russian Federation, Yuschenko's victory in the re-run December 26, 2004, by 52 to 44 percent, was another example of Western pursuit of regime change.

Putin's inability to view events without the lens of imagined Western agitation blinded him to genuine public indignation at cheating and signalled a pattern that would repeatedly colour his view of protest in Russia itself several years later. He has frequently shown reluctance to accept motivations at face value, ascribing intentions to deeper and darker agendas.

The Ukraine experience especially alerted the Kremlin at home to prepare defences against the mobilization of younger citizens by foreign-funded NGOs via the "Orange threat" which was allegedly stimulated and financed by government-backed Western advocacy NGOs. The pro-Kremlin Russian nationalist youth movement Nashi ("Ours") was created by the presidential *apparat* as a counterforce. It was used as a weapon against Russian activists, NGOs enjoying Western support, and even Western diplomats, such as UK Ambassador Tony Brenton in 2007, whose embassy was accused of financing Russia's political opposition.

Other disagreements between Western democracies and Russia followed. The harsh interruption of Ukrainian gas supplies from Russia on January 1, 2006, was a function of Russia's wish to lift CIS-subsidized prices for gas to market rates. Russian suppliers who cut off the vital shipments cost Russia its reputation for reliability of supply. The heavy-handed tactics made it easier for adversaries to label Russia a "threat," which in turn made Russia feel unfairly maligned. The crisis over the recognition of Kosovo following the Kosovar unilateral declaration of independence on February 18, 2008 roiled the waters further and ultimately had an impact on the "frozen conflicts" over Russian enclaves that were seeking their own independence from adversarial Georgia. But that crisis would take place in the tenure of a new Russian president. Vladimir Putin stepped down from the presidency because of term limits. He ceded the presidency to his former chief of staff, whom he replaced as prime minister.

Tandem Politics: The Medvedev Presidency

Dmitry Medvedev was elected March 2, 2008, with 70 percent of the popular vote. The Medvedev years represented the appearance of dilution of top-down insider "vertical power" control associated with Putin, but, particularly in retrospect, it was more a matter of appearances than one of a changed reality. Each of the two principals seemed to tailor messaging to different respective constituencies: Medvedev to the upwardly mobile urbanites, and Putin to his own numerically larger and more conservative rural and small-town base in the regions.

President Medvedev's messaging sought to convey a reformist theme. He was a more contemporary figure whose taste for Western rock music reflected the experience of a younger man who had lived the explosion in the 1980s of euphoric glasnost that Putin had missed. Shortly after the election, he declared (notably at the Fifth Krasnoyarsk Economic Forum, 2008) his commitment to supporting "freedom in all its manifestations, personal freedom, economic freedom, and finally, freedom of expression." In practical consequence, though, the commitments did not extend to freedom of open competition for political power.

In the same speech, he condemned Russia's culture of "legal nihilism." A former professor of law, he tried to make the creation of an effective independent and professional judiciary a hallmark of his term. He spoke out openly against corruption, which he judged "characterizes the life of Russian society." But by 2011, he had to admit his government had failed in its anti-corruption policies. He also attempted reform of Russia's political institutions, reinstituting direct election of regional governors. But his tone was more conciliatory than that of his predecessor — now prime minister — who spoke of NGOs and civil society with open derision. Medvedev tried to open a sincere dialogue with them.

NGOs AND CIVIL SOCIETY IN RUSSIA

A non-governmental advocacy sector had emerged from the reforms of the 1980s and early 1990s. Its first urgent civil preoccupation was to extract truth about the Soviet Union's repression and to move toward some sort of closure in justice. The NGO Memorial became the conscience of Russia's past and its archivist, earning the hostility of increasingly reactionary state security authorities.

As reforms proceeded, the ambit of civil society began to widen considerably, taking up advocacy for human, economic and other rights going forward, as well as the need for transparency and fairness in the exercise of Russia's institutions. The Moscow Helsinki group, for example, focussed on the need of an independent and professional judiciary. Informal protest movements, such as the movement of mothers of conscripts against the Chechnya war and later movements opposing environmental damage, spontaneously sprang up.

However, the NGO sector never constituted a united front. After several generations of forced regimentation, there was always a preference among Russian social activists for informality and individual protest as opposed to hierarchy. Nor were the NGO sector's roots deep. Chronic fragmentation made civil society easier to marginalize in the inevitable confrontation between the administration and activists and advocates associated with the very disparate NGO movement. Despite Medvedev's surface moderation, authorities seemed to relish the adversarial relationship in which the state cast itself as the "patriotic" party, while increasingly assigning advocacy NGOs the role of handmaidens to "foreign" democratic interests, a tendency that ramped up considerably after Putin's humiliation over the Orange Revolution in Ukraine in 2004.

Ultimately, there were over 2,000 loosely connected NGOs dealing with democracy and human rights issues. The government largely ignored their substantive concerns, increasingly preferring to denounce them as "foreign agents." After the Orange Revolution, Nashi conducted a counter-campaign in the streets to intimidate foreign-funded NGOs and even, as mentioned earlier, in 2006 directly harassing UK Ambassador Brenton for "interference in Russian politics."

The Kremlin sought to keep Russians under its boot and foreign democracies on notice that they were to mind their own business. As another gesture to make the point, the offices of the British Council were closed on phony pretexts of "non-payment of taxes."

In 2006, the Duma adopted a law obliging NGOs to disclose all sources of funding and to ensure their activities complied with Russian "national interests." The law was enforced with great energy; over 13,000 NGO inspections and audits for taxes and violations of building or fire safety codes were conducted in the first year alone. International NGOs such as Amnesty International, Human Rights Watch, Médecins sans Frontières, and various humanitarian and refugee groups had to halt their work temporarily.

Objectionable "political activities" of Russian NGOs were defined as almost any attempt to influence government policy or public opinion. In 2008, Memorial's headquarters and archive in St. Petersburg were raided and invaluable records destroyed.

The non-state European University in St. Petersburg, which had received grants from the Ford and MacArthur foundations, was cited for 52 fire safety violations and forced to close immediately. The university's offence had been to accept a €700,000 grant from the EU to support research on election monitoring. The university could open its doors after two months, only after renouncing the grant and activity in question (and after the March 2008 election of President Medvedev). Despite the official harassment, which continued even as President Medvedev was himself meeting with NGO leaders, civil society in Russia began to strengthen in numbers, competence and self-confidence.

In interviews with the *Handbook* project in Moscow in the winter of 2011-2012, NGO representatives emphasized their much greater self-reliance. As one activist put it, the previous decade may have been "lost for politics," but not for the development of "civic skills." Analysts captured the extent to which Russian civil society had "grown up" over the period. Joshua Yaffa (2012) underlined that "apathy and individualism…[were] finally giving way to civic consciousness."

At the same time, however, NGO activists, in conversation with the *Handbook* authors, asked if there had been sufficient soil for civil society's roots to take hold. Government pressure, restrictions, name-calling, and punitive tax and other campaigns against NGOs meant that supportive foreign financing from Western governments fell away, though in some cases private outside support was tolerated. Some groups, such as the Moscow School, a reform-oriented think tank and training centre with prominent Western support, and the Eurasia Foundation, found their activities constrained by lack of funds. For others, small-donation private charity from Russian citizens began to take up the slack, facilitated by the Internet, but it was hard to gain traction. NGO advocacy spread from Moscow and St. Petersburg and became increasingly visible in Russia's regions, constituting today a local force to be reckoned with in provincial capitals such as Kazan, Perm, Nihzny Novgorod and Novosibirsk.

"A National Mood Can Change"

Despite the economic and social turmoil of the 1990s, and evidence of wide disappointment in the way the democratic experiment was handled, joint polling by the Centre for the Study of Public Policy at the University of Strathclyde and the Levada Centre of Moscow show that two-thirds of the public has nonetheless maintained the belief that "Russia needs democracy" at more or less constant levels over 20 years. A survey by Henry Hale of the Elliott School at George Washington University found that 87 percent of Russians wanted their president chosen by free and fair elections. On the other hand, as Treisman (2012), citing Levada polling, puts it, "Russians are unhappy about the actual practice of democracy in Russia."

In interviews in February 2012, Levada polling experts told the *Handbook* project that, contrary to assumptions, this unhappiness had become prevalent in rural as well as in urban sectors. The difference is that outside the major cities (where demonstrators in 2011-2012 carried signs urging "Russia Without Putin"), rural and regional publics wary of agitation wanted to rely on the ability and willingness of the Putin regime itself to improve democratic practice. This was consistent with Pew Center polls in the spring of 2011, which showed deep dissatisfaction with the "way things were going," but a simultaneous belief that "a strong leader" represented the best way forward for the country.

Events over the winter of 2011-2012 cast a new light on these assumptions, at least for a time. On September 24, 2011, Prime Minister Putin casually broke the news that he and President Medvedev had conferred and agreed that Putin would once again be the candidate for the presidency in spring 2012 elections, on the grounds that he had the higher public approval rating of the two. Moreover, the prime minister continued, their decision had been taken a year earlier.

The public impact of this decision was wholly unanticipated by the Kremlin. While Putin's return to the top position was not a great surprise, multiple interviews revealed the extent to which people felt "duped" by the way this was done, the sense of entitlement it conveyed, as well as the apparent assumptions at the top about the electorate's "political infancy." A deceived public looked to parliamentary elections on December 4, 2011 as the opportunity to voice protest.

In those elections, the party of power, United Russia, lost 77 seats in official tallies. Its popular vote dropped from 64 percent to under 50 percent (despite an officially recorded score of 99.5 percent in Chechnya), sinking to below 40 percent of the popular vote in Moscow and Leningrad regions. It became increasingly obvious that even these official results had been falsified to inflate United Russia's score. Exit polls seemed to suggest that the accurate overall score for United Russia would have been about 35 percent (Shevtsova, 2012).

The authorities had never intended a fair contest. Pre-election arrangements had, as usual, worked to the distinct disadvantage of opposition parties: their publicity was seized by authorities, rallies were forbidden or interrupted, candidate registrations refused and access to TV barred for their competitive political messages. The openly biased electoral commission distributed 2.6 million absentee ballots, enabling holders to vote anywhere, directly to United Russia, which bussed convenience voters in to wavering districts from outside. The OSCE delivered a scathing report of the entire electoral process. Until its website was blocked, Russian election watchdog, the GOLOS Association documented violations, reinforced by YouTube videos showing blatant ballot stuffing.

Repression of dissent deepened. Independent radio station Ekho Moskvy was shut down. "Denial-of-service" website attacks were launched against independent media such as the magazine *New Times,* whose Editor-in-Chief Evgenya Albats had launched an analysis of fraudulent vote-counting patterns. Western democracies expressed "serious concerns" (US Secretary of State Clinton), to which the Russian administration responded with hostility, accusing the countries in question of having spent "hundreds of millions" to try to influence Russian politics.

The day after the election saw the beginning of a popular eruption which, over the course of the next three months, brought between 70,000 and 120,000 protestors out on several occasions (December 10, 24; February 4; March 5, 10). While these demonstrations did not match the crowds of half a million or more attained in 1990-1991, they signalled that the decade "of sleep" was over. Lilia Shevtsova (2012) has termed it "the end to the postcommunist status quo." Russian writer and activist Viktor Shenderovich captured the mood, declaring that a "point of no return has been passed."

The effect was to break the regime's sheen of popularity and invincibility for many citizens. The childish election mismanagement exposed Putin's "managed democracy" as inherently fraudulent and insulting in its confidence that voters would settle for the illusion of choice. The Kremlin's reaction to the protest movement was counterproductive. Instead of acknowledging voters' dissatisfaction (even on the basis of official results) and addressing it, Prime Minister Putin indicated that public opinion was of little concern to him. He excoriated NGOs, framing them as "Judases" who took money from the West (prompting a variety of protestors' signs asking "Hillary! Where's My Money?").

THE PUBLIC HAS ITS OPINIONS

Who were the demonstrators? Surveys revealed them to be, in the main, from an educated and professional class for whom the bargain of private prosperity in exchange for surrendering real political choice was no longer acceptable. Putin depicted the protestors as selfish urban elitists, setting them up against the Russian non-urban "narod." In doing so, he applied the accusation of non-patriotic behaviour to a vastly wider swath of society, which he had earlier used only to try to marginalize NGOs.

The prior gulf in attitude between urban and non-urban and poorer populations had narrowed. Levada polling in February 2012 showed that discontent was generalized. Only 14 percent of Russians expressed belief that Putin had the "best solutions" for Russia. By March 2012, only 23 percent expressed a positive view of those in power. Only five percent had confidence that those in government "are concerned with the well-being of ordinary people."

Mikhail Dmitriev and Daniel Treisman (2012) published results from a survey of 62 focus groups drawn from the residents of 16 Russian regions. These, too, confirmed that the shift in public opinion in favour of freedom and democracy has especially animated a professional urban class that had most benefitted from consciousness-raising via the technological revolution in communications (60 percent of all Russian households have personal computers), widespread foreign travel and generalized economic empowerment. But the results also underlined that a wish for change is felt across the country. Dmitriev and Treisman (2012) write:

> The answers were surprising. Yes, Russians outside Moscow and St. Petersburg have no appetite for the noisy street politics and abstract slogans of their big-city counterparts. (The March survey by Levada showed 52% of Russians opposed the demonstrations, compared with 32% who supported them.) But they are far from content with the current political system, which they see as hopelessly corrupt and inept at providing basic services.... Like the liberal activists, Russians from other parts of the social spectrum exhibit a powerful desire for change. But their focus is quite different. Whereas the Moscow crowds have rallied behind abstract concepts, such as fairness and democracy, much of the rest of the country is fiercely non-ideological and cares far more about concrete, local issues. Across different regions and social classes, Russians are most concerned with the state's dwindling ability to provide essential services, such as health care, education, housing, personal security and effective courts.

But it is also worth noting that in the survey they reported that "Suspicion of the West was one area in which Putin's rhetoric struck a chord with the focus groups" (ibid.). That psychological theme which had played such a role over the previous 20 years — not to mention during Soviet times — promised to be a bell which the Russian leadership could continue to ring for popular support.

This may account for the restrained Western reaction to Vladimir Putin's re-election in March 2012, with an official tally of 63.8 percent — thereby avoiding the necessity of a second round. Once again, watchdogs such as GOLOS and Citizen Observer dissented, estimating from exit polls that voter support was 51 percent and 45 percent, respectively. They each concluded that billionaire Mikhail Prokhurov, who was parachuted in as an opposition candidate to give the illusion of choice (after such well-known democratic figures as Grigory Yavlinsky and Boris Nemtsov were disqualified by authorities), had his vote reduced to seven percent from 16 to 22 percent. Russian analysts close to the regime contest these revisionist figures, claiming that GOLOS and Citizen Observer overemphasize the Moscow and St. Petersburg results in their numbers. In any event, Vladimir Putin would have won the election by the second round, if not outright in the first.

THE RETURN

The post-election question was whether President Putin would attempt to reconcile with the alienated urban middle classes, or whether the dislike of political competition he had demonstrated since 2000 would persuade him to be more confrontational.

Whereas the police had been surprisingly restrained in handling earlier demonstrations, the repression of protests on May 6, 2012 against the returned President's inauguration was brutal. More generally, a pattern developed of arrests of opposition leaders and personalities, such as Alexei Navalny, Boris Nemtsov, Kseniya Sobchak and Gennady Gudkov, as well as the intimidation of NGOs and civil society.

Politically, Putin appeared to have abandoned the pretense he was the leader of all Russians, dividing Russia between his supporters and the "bad Russians" who aligned against him, and whom he accused of acting on behalf of foreign powers to weaken Russia.

A new law on NGOs was adopted by the Duma in July 2012, forcing NGOs accepting financial support from abroad to register as "foreign agents," and to accept a heavy burden of financial reporting and constant audits and inspections. Failure to comply exposes managers to prison sentences. In fact, NGOs were hardly a factor in the public protests of the winter, but it suited the Kremlin's narrative to attempt to demonize them. Dozens of NGOs — including major advocates such as GOLOS, Memorial, and Agora (legal assistance for protestors), but also environmental defence groups and even the Kostroma Soldiers' Mothers Committee — were warned they faced sanctions.

In May 2013, Levada was informed by prosecutors that it could not continue to publish its polling results without identifying itself as "a foreign agent." The prosecutors ruled the centre "influences public opinion and therefore does not constitute research but political activity." According to Levada, however, foreign sources constitute no more than three percent of its funding, mainly via the Open Society Institute Foundation and the Ford and McArthur foundations. Losing the independent source of public opinion surveys would be, according to Levada Director Lev D. Gudkov, the "end of an epoch that began with Gorbachev's perestroika.... Russians would be restricted to a one-sided picture....like the Soviet time, when there was one newspaper, *Pravda,* and one TV channel" (cited in Barry, 2013b).

Russian officials also shut down foreign-financed humanitarian aid operations, including UNICEF and USAID. Under the umbrella of the new legislation and new official mood, Russian agencies began to freelance in intimidation tactics in strange ways. The Federal Security Service of the Russian Federation (FSB) announced in October 2012 that 20 non-governmental humanitarian aid organizations operating in Ingushetia would be shut down. In 2013, a pattern emerged of hostile forensic visits from the state prosecutor's office, the FSB and tax officials to foreign NGOs like Human Rights Watch, Amnesty and the Konrad Adenauer Foundation.

Yuri Sheryshev, local spokesman of the FSB, explained to the Interfax news agency that "it would be naïve to think that foreign organizations allot large sums of money to non-governmental organizations for democracy development. By declaring some high goals of their work, they in fact collect intelligence for foreign states." This is precisely President Putin's mindset.

All governments are liable to occasional misstatement of intention from individuals but the underlying assumption of this declaration — paranoid as it appears — unfortunately fits into a pattern of fostering suspicion and "spy mania" that is a frontal challenge to the whole premise of the legitimacy of support for democracy development from outside.

GOING FORWARD

The activities of foreign democracies in support of democracy development are now severely circumscribed by Russian authorities. Russian authorities have made it illegal for any "politically engaged" NGO to receive foreign funds. More than 2,000 Russian NGOs are engaged in one form or another in political advocacy.

But NGOs in Russia have repeatedly told the *Handbook* that the last two decades have in fact enabled them to attain a degree of empowerment that will favour human rights defence and the expansion of democracy in the country. Building the capacity for self-sufficiency is ultimately the shared goal of all concerned.

Western democracies assert a need to continue being vigilant in support of civic and NGO rights and of the general human rights climate in Russia. The regime has tolerated some egregious crimes, such as the non-prosecution of those responsible for the arrest and death of Sergei Magnitsky.

The US Congress should have repealed the Soviet-era Jackson-Vanik Act, which made economic ties with Russia conditional on the right of dissidents to emigrate, 20 years ago. Emigration from Russia is free and frequent. But Cold War mentalities in the Congress blocked repeal. Today, the Act is being replaced by the Magnitsky Act, tying bilateral economic benefits to transparency in human rights and imposing sanctions for offence. It specifically targets Russian officials presumed to be involved in the acts of corruption that Magnitsky sought to expose.

It is assumed that much of Russia's pressure on NGOs is in retaliation. Russia objects to a foreign parliament passing laws against Russian nationals who have not been convicted of crime in a court. That prosecution of the crimes in Russia has been negligible seems irrelevant to Russian official reasoning. The Russian Duma has since adopted a law preventing Russian orphans from being adopted by US nationals as some kind of symmetrical response.

The Duma, under the control of the party in power in the Kremlin, has adopted other reactionary and xenophobic legislation, anti-gay and specifically anti-American: anyone with a US passport, for example, cannot participate in a Russian organization that is politically engaged. Moreover, foreign passport holders are prevented from public commentary on Russian events on television.

The appeal of such reactionary and defensive measures seems to be rooted in an official drive at the top to tap into support for traditional Russian values, and especially Orthodox Christianity. The severe prosecution of the punk rock group Pussy Riot for desecrating a holy site by a provocative anti-Putin improv stunt can be seen in this light.

Much comes down to the personal role of the Russian Federation's president. Vladimir Putin's popularity with the Russian electorate, which was in the 80-percent approval range at one time, had been earned. Between 1998 and 2008, real household incomes rose 140 percent. Poverty fell dramatically. Oil-rich nations have typically been "extractive" in regard to the benefits, but Russia re-channelled oil revenue (which represents 40 percent of government spending) to public services. In the last decade, pensions have been significantly increased six times. Today, the president's approval rating has declined, though it is no doubt still at a respectable 50 percent or more.

The issue for democracies is not to pretend otherwise or to suggest that voter discontent with their governance (which is every bit as high in Western democracies) is of itself a legitimate reason for outside concern. The issue for the international democratic community is that democracy and democratic values are still being rolled back in Russia. Russian self-correction will be up to Russians themselves. As Dmitri V. Trenin (2013) wrote in an op-ed, "Russia is for Russians to fix. Outsiders can influence Russian development only on the margins and not always positively."

Russia retains respect as a great country, and effective relationships with it are vital to international security. Strategic partnerships are called for, but democracies have learned from experience in supporting dictatorships for the sake of wider strategic interests, that such political investment cannot be at the expense of democratic values. The question is how democrats everywhere can legitimately show their solidarity and support of civil society in Russia.

PART II: DIPLOMACY ON THE GROUND

THE DIPLOMAT'S TOOL BOX: RESOURCES AND ASSETS

Today, diplomats from democracies stationed in Russia are operating in a "twilight zone" of what is locally permissible, in terms of public outreach and direct connection to Russian civil society. They report that their determination to sustain solidarity with those in Russia arguing for the right to pursue democratic principles is more than ever pertinent to their diplomatic presence. However, pushback from Russian authorities is a direct challenge to the very premises of public diplomacy. In practice, the diplomats balance their refusal to operate in secrecy on issues of basic values ("We're not out to hide anything," in a Canadian's words) with the need for discretion.

The Support of Home Authorities

In terms of effective policy support for initiative in the field, the support of home authorities is more than ever a vital asset for diplomats in the field.

Though the EU discontinued its already truncated bilateral government-to-government cooperation program in 2010, after Russian authorities declared they no longer welcomed it, the EU relationship with Russia retains high policy interest for both partners. But it is not at the expense of principles, even if Russian authorities contest the enduring priority for EU diplomats "to defend human rights defenders." However, methods have become more circumspect.

Daniel Treisman (2012) captured a similar mood and rationale in Washington:

> More and more people seemed to recognize that, when it came to encouraging the deepening of democracy, patience was in order. Most now accepted that lectures did not work. Although not specifically focused on democracy at all, the kind of regularized, multidimensional contacts between states and societies that Obama seemed keen to develop were the best hope for gradually changing the culture within bureaucracies and spreading knowledge about democratic procedures and methods. Broad, non-ideological business and ideological exchanges were the most effective way of transmitting western values. Of course, such contacts worked slowly and would not necessarily prompt convergence. But they had a better chance than isolation. The promotion of democracy in a country like Russia worked best when it was not called the promotion of democracy.

But how well has it worked at all?

At the outset of his administration in 2009, US President Obama reviewed the constriction of bilateral relations that had taken place in recent years and called for a "reset" of the US-Russia relationship, which he judged to be crucial for each country, but also for the conduct of international peace and security.

Shortly after his arrival in Moscow in 2012, US Ambassador Michael McFaul told the *Handbook* that US dual-track engagement is a theme that had been channelled by the *Handbook* itself. The US would not link country-to-country relations with Russian behaviour on human rights and democracy, holding diplomatic and military cooperation hostage. However, the US would continue to engage directly with Russian civil society, including Russian political opposition figures, on issues that "we consider important as well."

Some critics have interpreted this balanced approach as a step backward from all-out democracy development support, but proponents argue that effective outcomes count more than declaratory rhetoric. In most ways, diplomats on the ground report that human rights monitoring in Russia is more important now than a decade ago, not less.

The apparent antipathy of President Putin to any "foreign influences" in Russia has been at the basis of the recent crackdowns on international and Russian NGOs. To ascertain whether NGOs are "abiding with Russian law that bans foreign funding of political activities" (anonymous Russian spokesman), intrusive searches were conducted in March 2013, of the offices of Human Rights Watch, Transparency International and Amnesty International. Over the last year, such non-political organizations as UNICEF, the World Wildlife Federation, the International Committee of the Red Cross, the Global Fund to Fight AIDS, Tuberculosis and Malaria, the Danish Refugee Council and Médecins sans Frontières have been forced to close the doors of their Russian support operations.

Diplomats, international NGOs and Russian civil society had, for a time after the "anti-foreign influence" laws were passed, hoped that they would be there as a form of warning, but would not be acted on with great vigour. But they *were* activated — not only against international NGOs, but against a myriad of Russian organizations across the Federation, including little (non-Orthodox) church parish organizations with modest local service activities.

A high-profile prosecution against GOLOS was founded on evidence presented that it had been supported by the US National Endowment for Democracy and the European Commission, and hence was a "foreign agent." Of course, such outside support for effectively free and fair elections — and explicitly not in support of particular parties or candidates — is a widespread international institutional practice.

There is no question that Russia's relations with home authorities in Western democracies suffer politically from such prosecution. In the spring of 2013, German and French Foreign Ministry officials summoned Russia's ambassadors to reiterate the point, and EU, UK and US officials criticized Russian action in forthright terms. Chancellor Merkel of Germany made the problem of Russian crackdown explicitly and publicly an irritant in relations during meetings with President Putin. While French President Hollande indicated on his first meeting with President Putin that he was not there to "judge," asserted he nonetheless had to recognize the unpleasant facts.

Do vexed relations over these issues affect the quality of activity and overall influence of democratic diplomats on the ground in Russia? The *Handbook* records how, over the last decade, the practice of democratic diplomacy had been complementing the private state-to-state sphere with a parallel public dimension of dually representing the diplomats' "whole society to the host society, beyond traditional government-to-government communication." This has been the core of public diplomacy as practiced increasingly by Western and other ambassadors and diplomats in Moscow over the last 25 years, in the spirit of the end of the Cold War and of glasnost itself.

Perhaps the most consciously positive and effective proponent has been US Ambassador to Russia John Beyrle (in office 2008–2012), who, in fluent Russian, projected his role as "America's Ambassador," whose mission was to channel American society, in a people-to-people context. He did so with astute and effective use of social networks on which he recorded a personalized live blog, and via appearances on talk radio shows and local TV.

Ambassador Beyrle's family history had unique appeal to Russians, as his father was shot down over the USSR during World War II, and after which he apparently joined the war alongside America's Soviet allies. The ambassador was vocationally predisposed to favour public communications, having begun his government career with the US Information Service and later, the Voice of America. Two postings to Russia followed prior to his ambassadorial tenure. Beyrle was intent not just to speak to Russians, but to make sure he was "on receive" as well, in the spirit of the first of the *Handbook*'s Golden Rules, listening, respecting and understanding.

In Moscow, several Western ambassadors told the *Handbook* that it is a vital task to convince Russians that the West is not a threat and that liberal values are not hostile to what Russians consider to be traditional values of their own.

Ambassador Beyrle has explained that his purpose was to "un-demonize the US" and overcome negative stereotyping and abundant anti-American attitudes on Russian state TV. His embassy promoted educational and cultural exchanges, and, whenever possible, showcased contemporary US dance, theatre, and hip-hop and blue grass music to convey a contemporary image of America. His message that the "US is not fated to be an adversary" seemed to resonate especially with younger people, even if extremist opinion endured and pushback from the authorities was always present.

Hardline security circles vividly object to foreign diplomats or NGOs supportively engaging Russian democrats and human rights defenders, including via declaratory public diplomacy, and have adopted "dirty tricks" techniques against individual US and European diplomats they considered too forward-leaning. Ambassador Beyrle observed, at the time, an egregious doctored-video frame-up of US diplomat

Brendan Kyle Hatcher by Russian security services. In Ambassador Beyrle's words, Hatcher, who actively supported Russian civil society members pursuing greater religious freedom and political rights, was resented by "elements in Russia that did not want the two countries to develop closer ties."

US authorities gave Hatcher prominent support through professional awards for his creative service in Russia to support basic rights. The fact that Russian authorities never apologized for slandering him could be put down to their reluctance to accept responsibility for the activity of the secret services, or it could signify that it had the unofficial sanction of the leadership itself. It was not an isolated incident; the FSB has for several years been breaking into the private homes of Western diplomats as part of an antique mindset aimed at psychological destabilization.

A visible campaign of intimidation was pursued intensively against UK Ambassador Brenton (in office 2004–2008). In 2006, he attended an inaugural meeting in the margin of a G8 summit of a coalition of dissidents and democratic opposition to the Putin regime (along with Washington-based US diplomats), as part of his outreach to civil society in a supposedly pluralistic political environment. This initiative combined with the public positions he had the duty to advance on a variety of divisive issues, such as protesting the authorities' forced closing of the British Council offices in St. Petersburg, seeking the extradition of Russian citizen Andrey Lugovoy, accused of murdering Alexander Litvinenko in London, and defending UK interests in bitter high-stake commercial disputes. The Russian security services launched the campaign of intimidation against the ambassador, largely through the Nashi nationalist youth movement, which persisted to harass and threaten him and his family throughout the remainder of his posting. On the eve of his departure from Moscow, the ambassador told reporter Will Stewart (2008) that "the British Embassy in Moscow has come under a greater barrage of bugging and espionage from the Russian secret service than at any time since the end of the Cold War."

The hostility in some circles to current US Ambassador Michael McFaul's regular blogging, outreach and public profile has also been vibrant, though staying short of attempted physical intimidation of the kind inflicted on Ambassador Brenton. The material on Ambassador McFaul's blog has concerned the substance of US-Russia relations in traditional areas of cooperation and also newer topics such as innovation (where Russia lags).

On his blog, the ambassador has noted he is "struck by misunderstandings and stereotypes in commentary....Providing more accurate information to the Russian people about the United States quickly emerged as a priority for me" (McFaul, 2012).

As a former civil society democracy activist himself and a long-time associate of many Russian democrats and human rights defenders, through his time with the Carnegie Moscow Center, McFaul also persisted without hesitation of principle in legitimate outreach and contact with civil society, in the spirit of solidarity. In his blog, Ambassador McFaul noted, among many other substantive topics in the Russia-US relationship, the US "concern about a package of new Russian laws that may constrain civil society and freedoms of assembly, association, and speech" (ibid.).

Diplomats on the ground take care to phrase support for civil society in ways that cannot be construed as interference in Russia's internal political process, although contact for information's sake with the full range of political participants remains a normal activity.

Russian political actors and NGOs have adapted to the legal need to function within the prohibition in Russia against foreign funding. Russian opposition leader Boris Nemtsov made it clear that Russian democrats don't want that form of help. The US and other Western democracies indeed ceased funding political parties or movements years ago.

Outreach across Russia has become routine for democratic embassies, though in recent years it has had to acknowledge the dangers from Russian authorities requiring local organizations to register as a "foreign agent" if they engage in "political activity" with foreign support. However, hostile Russian rules keep deepening, perhaps because zealous officials compete for Kremlin favour in seeking to punish alleged offenders.

While definitions remain to be tested in Russian courts, the cloud of threat can become an inhibitor of contact. As an example of the darkening atmosphere for democratic public diplomacy, the Kostroma Center for the Defense of Public Initiatives was threatened by prosecutors with debilitating fines for participating in a February 2013 round table with a representative from the US Embassy on Russia-US relations, characterized by the embassy as "normal public diplomacy." In effect, the Russians are trying to confine public diplomacy to cultural and other affairs of no political or advocacy significance. It is an approach that EU diplomats view with distaste. EU, Canadian, Australian and other human rights diplomats continue to make field trips to Russia's regions to meet with civil society representatives who welcome the contacts.

The hostility to support for the strengthening of civil society from governments or civil society outside Russia extends increasingly even to non-political capacity-building programs that are part of foreign study. In a possibly definitive assault of free political challenge, the popular anti-corruption blogger and opposition figure Alexei Navalny has been charged/framed with fraudulent financial dealings from several years ago in an effort to remove him from the political scene. The spokesman for the federal investigative committee pursuing the charges (despite their earlier dismissal as groundless by local legal jurisdictions), Vladimir Markin, suggested "that Mr. Navalny had been trained in the West to topple Mr. Putin's government, referring acidly to the semester he spent at Yale University's World Fellows Program, a leadership training program for midcareer professionals" (Barry, 2013a). That such an anodyne exercise in positive exchange activity is now the object of official calumny is an indication of the extent of the problem going forward.

Regardless of the efforts to intimidate and constrain them, diplomats from democratic embassies continue to invoke the legitimacy of demonstrating support for Russian civil society members, social advocates and the diminishing presence of free media. They attend, when it is appropriate, the trials of human rights defenders and researchers being prosecuted or pursued in the courts, often in "show trials" produced to provide discouraging examples to dissenters.

WAYS THAT DIPLOMATS ARE MAKING A DIFFERENCE

The Golden Rules

Listening, Respecting and Understanding

There is ample evidence that outside democracies and observers got the politics and realities of Russia wrong in the early 1990s, but diplomats on the ground in those years could see the social impacts and erosion of shock therapy and made every effort to channel the information to policy makers, who had difficulty confronting a set of problems that was in many respects unprecedented in both scale and complexity.

That being said, awareness in capitals of the negative psychological impact of changes on Russians began to develop. Strobe Talbott recalls Finnish diplomat (and later President) Maati Ahtisaari advising others not to "crowd the Russians. Don't make them feel punished or on probation."

Obviously, in recent years, diplomatic reporting from Moscow has constituted essential input to home authorities preparing responses to events. Embassies have the best view on which responses are most likely to be effective and which responses are apt to be counterproductive. As the Putin administration cracks down on civil society and on freedoms generally, responses range from soft power choices to harder measures, such as targeted sanctions or visa bans on individuals. Advice from diplomats on the ground has been critical in shaping policy responses in Brussels and other capitals.

Diplomats have learned to respect the need of Russian civil society to keep a distance from outsiders. Outside support to any civil society group with an advocacy mandate is tempered by an awareness of their vulnerability to retaliation from Russian authorities, and their depiction as "foreign stooges." US Ambassador McFaul has underlined the necessity of "taking clues from those that you're seeking to help." Embassy personnel and civil society representatives from outside have learned to count on and respect the reading on risk issues of Russian partners.

There is, however, no shortage of initiatives and events to engage Russian NGOs and civil society. Advocacy groups do welcome evidence of obviously shared values with outside democracies and especially with civil society outside, though diplomats report a tendency to downplay "democracy" as a central theme of Russian advocacy NGOs.

Visiting delegations of European, US, Canadian and other Western officials and parliamentarians meet with civil society representatives on official visits as a matter of course. Annual human rights consultations between the EU and Russian authorities (which the Russians do not agree can take place in Russia) are methodically preceded by EU consultations with Russian civil society itself.

Direct contacts as a matter of routine are essential, a welcome indication of solidarity, and enable an accurate and sensitive appreciation of the circumstances in which Russian activists and advocates work, in the spirit of Carne Ross' "listen/ask/encounter" modus operandi for diplomats in the field.

The US Embassy and the EU delegation and others regularly convene conferences and round tables with the participation of Russian NGOs, to which the Ministry of Foreign Affairs is also invited. When Canadian diplomats meet in workshop formats with civil society in the field, they always invite local authorities on the grounds that there should be "nothing to hide" — in their words, "we ask the same questions if they are present or not."

Conference and workshop programming strives to reach the provinces as well as audiences in Moscow and St. Petersburg. In regular field trips to the regions to meet local NGOs and civil society representatives, EU human rights diplomats incorporate the spirit of the advice offered to the *Handbook* by a Chilean diplomat in Moscow, that outsiders should always be conscious in these contacts to practice "sharing, not showing off." Presenters from outside often find they have much in common with civil society discussants. For example:

- The Director of Programs for community immigrant integration services in Ottawa, Canada, attending an academic conference in Kazan on tolerance and accommodating diversity, found there was much common ground in his welcome additional encounters with local schoolchildren and NGOs.

- On International Defence Against Homophobia Day on May 17, 2012, the US Embassy hosted a round table that Russian civil society and Russian authorities both actively contributed to, a rare feat.

- The Moscow office of the UNHCR organized a special workshop featuring the acting Chief Commissioner of the Canadian Human Rights Commission on effective interrelationships in a federal system among federal and provincial human rights authorities and with the UN system.

Of course, EU human rights counsellors meet on a regular basis to compare notes and also to channel policy advice on how the EU and member states should react to developments in Russia, such as over the recent crackdowns on NGOs. Human rights officers of like-minded embassies exchange information and notes. Burden-sharing for the coverage of events such as Khodorkovsky's trial is coordinated among concerned embassies. There is awareness that the US and EU representations are "semi-demonized" by Russian security authorities, making it more desirable for others to step up support activity when possible.

On a country-to-country level, the history over 25 years of encouraging effective sharing of common instruments of governance within multilateral organizations has been driven by a goal of integrating Russia into commonly agreed standards, with mixed effectiveness. Such multilateral institution-sharing often comes with a requirement for human rights monitoring by embassies underscoring the importance of accurate reporting on governance conditions in Russia, which in turn enhances the value of informal sharing among democratic embassies and international NGOs of respective perceptions and experience.

Since the Charter of Paris in November 1990, the USSR (briefly), and then the Russian Federation became engaged in the OSCE, the Council of Europe (especially its Parliamentary Assembly) and the G8, built an institutionalized relationship with NATO and eventually gained membership in the WTO. However, these memberships were, from the Russian perspective, framed on the basis of shared interests and not explicitly by shared values.

The distinction took on particular significance over the deteriorating human rights situation in Russia, especially over military conduct in Chechnya. Institutional sharing was weakened in consequence: Russian voting rights in the Council of Europe Parliamentary Assembly have been suspended twice. The European Court of Justice in Strasbourg receives petitions from Russian citizens: the current backlog is over 70,000 applications for hearing.

A major activity in cooperative sharing has, of course, been the history of election observation, through the ODIHR mechanisms. Embassy personnel are on the front lines of election observation, but of course support only a transparent, "free and fair" process, not specific candidates or parties. The progressively critical findings of European institutions about the integrity of the Russian electoral process has caused hostility in Kremlin circles, which was extended to Russian election watchdog GOLOS, deepening international misgivings.

Truth in Communications

Once, of course, the USSR was a closed information bubble, but outside broadcasters such as the Voice of America and the BBC World Service reached millions of clandestine listeners. Despite the glasnost era explosion in free thought in the late 1980s, open media in Russia has become constrained and limited. Russia ranks 142 of 179 in the Press Freedom Index of Reporters Without Borders, though a few excellent independent newspaper and local radio services remain. While largely state-controlled TV is by far the dominant news provider, as elsewhere, younger people tend to stay current via the Internet.

Consequently, most embassies have built social media sites to provide factual information. Custom varies: some embassies scrupulously avoid any material beyond commercial and consular information spiced with lifestyle and literary references; others try to reflect some of the concerns at home about developments in Russia, while at the same time attempting to demystify the local notion that somehow, Western liberalism is intrinsically pitted against traditional Russian values.

Working with the Government: Ceding Priority to Working with Civil Society

Over time, sustained investment in substantive relationships with the Russian government recognizes that, on issues of international peace and security as well as in trade, economic and especially energy areas, Russian cooperation is highly desirable. The NATO-Russian Council established in 2002 prompted a number of cooperative projects in counter-terrorism, a topic that remains active again after the Boston terror bombings in April 2013 by two brothers from the North Caucasus. Extended consultations between the US and the Russian Federation are proceeding on the historically privileged bilateral topic of nuclear weapons build-down, and missile defence.

Several diplomats in Moscow confided the belief that the effectiveness of European democracy promotion in Russia fell short of possibly overoptimistic expectations because political considerations overrode candour in communication. Diplomats ventured the opinion that Russian authorities "gamed" the willingness of the EU to cooperate on the range of substantive interests and went through all the motions of process on human rights without making changes in behaviour or substance.

In recent years, state-to-state democracy development support and even cooperation in areas such as health services has pretty much ebbed. Russian authorities have proclaimed their belief that Russia is "past" such a need. This was cited as the reason for the abrupt termination of USAID program support in 2012, even though the bulk of USAID projects in Russia aimed in partnership to bolster a Russian state capacity for health services, which is manifestly inadequate. Civil society-to-civil society cooperation picks up some of the slack.

European support activities, which have been publicly financed but executed via civil society partnerships, have extended in recent years to a wide diversity of capacity-building and modernization endeavours, including:

- integration of refugees;
- the rights of children;
- the rights of the disabled;
- environmental rights;
- countering legislation against gays;
- creating an independent ombudsman for transparency in government;
- seniors' centres;
- independent journalism; and
- GOLOS and independent election observation.

A major emphasis has been on the justice system, with specific programs devoted to juvenile justice. The Moscow Helsinki Group and specifically Lyudmila Aleexnyeva have been pressing reform of the justice system for years and Europeans have lent support for the improvement in access to justice, efficiency, (free) legal aid, mediation and the appeal system.

The question is whether even such obviously non-political topics are exempt from Russian suspicions of and hostility to Western capacity-building assistance of any kind. For example, a Swedish program for training judges was terminated when the Russian State Duma passed a law forbidding the instruction or training of Russian judges by foreigners.

Dialoguing with Russian authorities on human rights issues has been an obligatory part of the agenda, though again, it is noteworthy that Russia never consented to bilateral human rights "dialogues" taking place in Russian territory or to including participants from the Interior Ministry.

The general consensus on the part of democratic partners of Russia is that dialoguing with Russian institutions should not be at the expense of connections to Russian civil society. US President Obama, for example, followed other leaders over the years from US President Clinton to UK Prime Minister Blair, who made sure their summit meetings in Russia included parallel encounters with Russian civil society, university encounters and a round table with business leaders.

Dialoguing among think tanks and Russian non-official authorities such as ex-ministers Kudrin and German Gref, or specialists in security such as Alexei Arbatov continues, with embassies in Moscow being part of the conversations. The Russian state itself has instituted several dialogue channels, such as the Valdai group which every year engages President Putin in a discussion forum with Western commentators, journalists and scholars. An unusual forum is the exclusive council formed by former Russian and American bilateral ambassadors, which has been given top access to Russian officials at its annual meetings.

Dmitri V. Trenin (2013) urges Europeans to "approach the Russians on their own terms, but they should not always expect the Russians always to conform. Unlike the EU approach toward Turkey and Ukraine (which have harbored wishes for a closer institutional relationship with the EU), the issue should not be what the Europeans want Russia to be or to become, but what they want or need from Russia." That includes emphatically the widening of democratic space in Russia.

Of course, demarching Russian authorities is part of the diplomatic routine. A typical intervention has been the Canadian ambassador's demarches to Russian authorities to take vivid exception to homophobic and anti-LGBT legislation adopted by the St. Petersburg local government. Apart from protesting the constraints imposed by Russian laws on "foreign agents," there are the usual questions of regional and international security issues.

A constant preoccupation is the extent of corruption in Russia, a phenomenon emphasized by ex-President Medvedev himself. Russia is ranked 133 out of 176 countries on Transparency International's Corrupt Perceptions Index. In consequence, Transparency International's Moscow offices have been subject to forensic and other extremely intrusive searches by Russian tax authorities and prosecutors. The question is whether Russian authorities grasp how counterproductive an image this kind of conduct radiates to foreign investors, a point the president of Transparency International is making without nuance to Russian ministers, and which Western ambassadors have been making privately to Russian leaders and ministers for 20 years. Finding the right mix of public declaratory protest and private communication to Russian officials is a constant search in Moscow — as it is in Beijing and other capitals.

Reaching Out

As outlined above, embassies and diplomats place reaching out and showcasing at the heart of public diplomacy. Not every aspect of Western society is enviable, but a multidimensional approach to diplomatic outreach platforms, which incorporates regular and non-political contacts between societies through business and educational exchanges, is proposed by several diplomats in Moscow as representing the best hope for spreading knowledge about democratic procedures and principles.

Trenin (2013) believes that in this field, the EU is especially well placed to pursue an influential relationship with Russia. He counsels the deployment by the EU of soft power to build a special relationship in such areas as trade, investment, humanitarian contacts and a "greater harmony of values, norms, and principles." He also recommends that Europe be opened even more widely to Russian citizens.

As the Russian economic recovery has proceeded, and as Russian economic circumstances have improved, embassy financing of support activities has diminished considerably — notwithstanding the polemics of accusations by Russian authorities of NGOs for being "foreign agents." At one time, democratic embassies in Moscow disposed of "post initiative funds," which were deployed with considerable local impact to ease distress and to promote transition in the aftermath of the breakdown of the economy in the 1990s.

Today, direct intervention to support distressed sectors of the society is less usual. There is awareness of the need to support Russian NGOs, which are themselves working at a grassroots level. But it has increasingly been pursued by international civil society agencies partnering Russian "umbrella" NGOs which can then relay support to grassroots NGOs too small to register officially.

Embassies tend to lend financial support rather to showcase relevant topics. For example, the UNHCR Moscow office and the Information Services of the Council of Europe join with several embassies to stage an annual international film festival on human rights.

There is a growing tendency of Russian democracy activists to focus more consciously on the functioning of local municipal councils across Russia, to develop footholds in governance and among the grassroots, in part because of the belief the national political system is a closed monopoly. Outside programs exist in support. Prague University provides a purpose-built course on improving municipal transparency. Support programs for investigative reporting in Russian independent media now often emphasize the civic value of training in "covering City Hall" forms of reporting.

Defending Democrats

Embattled NGO representatives in Russia decry the "planned destruction of the NGO sector" (cited in Elder, 2013), of a "Cold War on Russian civil society's rights to free assembly, association, and speech" and to homophobic laws and seek moral support from democrats and human rights defenders outside.

Embassies of democratic countries continue to monitor trials of Russian activists and extend virtual support whenever possible, while retaining the basic principle that Russian developments are entirely in the hands of Russians themselves. An example has been the trial of Memorial head Oleg Petrovich Orlov, whose truth-telling NGO's record has earned its officials beatings and, in the case of Natalia Estimirova, murder in Chechenya. Orlov had publicly placed responsibility for her killing in the hands of the President of the Chechen Republic, Ramzan Kadyrov, who proceeded to sue Orlov for slander. Western diplomats supported the defendant by their presence at his trial, not because he represented their interests, but because of solidarity with his fundamental rights and commitment to the truth. That the Court acquitted him in 2011 indicates that the Russian situation is not predetermined or completely settled.

The trial of anti-corruption activist and political opposition figure Alexei Navalny in Kirov has every appearance of being politically motivated, though President Putin stated he ordered that it be conducted "objectively." The US and EU diplomats' monitoring of the trial is carefully low profile, in that the defendant has been acting only according to his own beliefs, especially as Navalny has always emphasized his patriotic credentials in his political program.

The trial of GOLOS has also been observed by EU and US diplomats, again on the same principle of solidarity, along with the principle of openness that GOLOS represents and which has earned GOLOS international support in the past.

Russian authorities — unlike the Chinese — have not attempted to limit the reliance of Russians to the Internet and social media. (On average, Russian youth spend more than twice the amount of time in personal Internet sessions than their American counterparts.) But Russian security services spokesmen have expressed the belief that "Western secret services are using new technologies to create and maintain tension in societies," making the issue of continued Internet openness extremely important.

CONCLUSIONS: KUDA IDYOT RUSSIYA? ("WHITHER RUSSIA?")

Anatoly Sobchak's observation in 1991 that in Russian society, tendencies to "dictatorship and democracy are living side-by-side" is a truism about the transitions of many societies from authoritarian — and in Russia's case, totalitarian — conditions. All societies have reactionary and throwback elements that argue against liberalization using the inflammatory language of nationalists. There is rarely a straight line ahead for democratic progress.

In Russia today, the "reactionary elements" are in control of the Kremlin and are determined to crush the liberal-leaning coalitions of citizens who seek more political competition. An example is the rector of the prestigious New Economic School, Sergei Guriev, who fled Russia in May 2013 under pressure of warnings he would soon be arrested for having expressed understanding of the protest movement and Alexei Navalny's anti-corruption campaign.

Russian citizens know they are vastly better off and freer than under Stalin; yet, there is still widespread disappointment that their interrupted democratic transition was fraught with difficulty. The belief endures still that Westerners let them down. At the same time, they are trying to process the seemingly contradictory evidence that their civic norms fall well short of what is normal for European societies.

The tensions in Russian society will be resolved only when Russians resolve the issues that create them. The removal of restrictions on basic and essential rights of citizens need to be addressed as part of a package of challenges including adverse demographic trends, inadequate health services, multiple issues of corruption and a dysfunctional justice system.

It is axiomatic that democracy development in Russia needs solidarity partnerships with outside civil society. A fundamental job of democratic diplomats in Russia is to engage the Russian people in order to try to demystify the relationships between Russia and outside democratic partners. Diplomats know that the impulses for change must come from within Russian civil society, not from outsiders. This is not an argument for passivity, indifference or a false *realpolitik* aimed at pleasing those who hold power today. The *Handbook*'s overall conclusion is that the most viable long-term investment for democratic diplomacy is in the relationships among peoples themselves.

WORKS CITED

Acemoglu, Daron and James Robinson (2012). *Why Nations Fail: The Origins of Power, Prosperity, and Poverty*. New York: Crown Publishers.

Aron, Leon (2012). *Roads to the Temple: Truth, Memory, Ideas and Ideals in the making of the Russian revolution, 1987–1991*. New Haven: Yale University Press.

Barry, Ellen (2013a). "Putin's Nemesis Stays Defiant Ahead of Trial." *The New York Times*, April 16.

——— (2013b). "Polling Group in Russia Says It May Close." *The New York Times*, May 20.

Berman, Sheri (2013). "The Promise of the Arab Spring" *Foreign Affairs*, January-February.

Carrère d'Encausse, Hélène (1978). *L'empire éclaté: La revolte des nations en URSS*. Paris: Flammarion.

Dmitriev, Mikhail and Daniel Treisman (2012). "The Other Russia: Discontent Grows in the Hinterlands." *Foreign Affairs*, September/October.

The Economist (2011). "The Long Life of Homo Sovieticus." *The Economist*, December 10.

Elder, Miriam (2013). "Russia Raids Offices of Amnesty International and Other Human Rights Groups." *The Guardian*, March 27.

Friedman, Thomas L. (2012). "This Column Is Not Sponsored by Anyone." *The New York Times Sunday Review*, May 12.

Garton Ash, Timothy (2012). "The Crisis of Europe: How the Union Came Together and Why It's Falling Apart." *Foreign Affairs*, September/October.

Government of the United States (2000). *Foreign Assistance: International Efforts to Aid Russia's Transition Have Had Mixed Results*. Report to the Chairman and to the Ranking Minority Member, Committee on Banking and Financial Services, House of Representatives. US General Accounting Office Report No. GAO-01-8.

Hill, Fiona and Clifford G. Gaddy (2013). *Mr. Putin: Operative in the Kremlin*. Washington, DC: Brookings Institution Press.

Remnick, David (1994). *Lenin's Tomb: The Last Days of the Soviet Empire*. New York: Vintage Books.

McFaul, Michael (2012). "Reflections on My First Six Months as U.S. Ambassador to Russia." Michael McFaul's LiveJournal Blog, available at: http://m-mcfaul. livejournal.com.

Roxburgh, Angus (2013). *The Strongman: Vladimir Putin and the Struggle for Russia*. London: I. B. Tauris.

Saari, Sinikukka (2009).*Promoting Democracy and Human Rights in Russia*. New York: Routledge.

Sandel, Michael J. (2012). *What Money Can't Buy: The Moral Limits of Markets*. New York: Farrar, Straus and Giroux.

Shevtsova, Lilia (2012). "Implosion, Atrophy, or Revolution?" *Journal of Democracy* 23, no. 3: 19–32.

Stewart, Will (2008). "British Ambassador to Moscow: I Was Besieged by Putin Thugs." *MailOnline*, September 27.

Stoner, Kathryn and Michael McFaul (2013). *Transitions to Democracy: A Comparative Perspective*. Baltimore: Johns Hopkins University Press.

Stoner-Weiss, Kathryn (2004). "Whither the Central State? The Regional Sources of Russia's Stalled Reforms." In *After the Collapse of Communism: Comparative Lessons of Transition*, edited by Michael McFaul and Kathryn Stoner-Weiss. Pages 130–172. Cambridge: Cambridge University Press.

Talbott, Strobe (2003). *The Russia Hand: A Memoir of Presidential Diplomacy*. New York: Random House.

Treisman, Daniel (2012). *The Return: Russia's Journey from Gorbachev to Medvedev*. New York: Free Press.

Trenin, Dmitri V. (2011). *Post-Imperium: A Eurasian Story.* Washington: Carnegie Endowment for International Peace.

———— (2013). "The End of an Era in EU-Russia Relations." Carnegie Moscow Center Brief, May.

Wedel, Janine R. (1999). "U.S. Assistance for Market Reforms: Foreign Aid Failures in Russia and the Former Soviet Bloc." CATO Institute Policy Analysis No. 338.

Wilson, Paul (2012). "The Dilemma of Madeleine Albright." *The New York Review of Books*, June 7.

Yaffa, Joshua (2012). "Reading Putin: The Mind and the State of Russia's President." *Foreign Affairs*, July/August.

3 CUBAN EXCEPTIONALISM

By Jeremy Kinsman, 2010; revised 2013

INTRODUCTION

The *Handbook* presents individual country case studies in order to record the practical activity that diplomats from democratic countries have performed there in support of civil society, democracy development and human rights. Situations can, and often do, resemble each other in some recognizable respects. Our aim is to enable diplomats and civil society partners in the field to obtain insights and guidance from actions taken elsewhere, without, however, suggesting that the experiences in one country can simply be transposed directly to another, since the trajectory of each country's development is singular.

The *Handbook* inevitably tries to illuminate the prospects of democratic transition in the countries in question. The case of Cuba is extreme, and in many ways unique. Since the late nineteenth century, Cuba's history has intertwined in a singular relationship with one country, the United States. The mutual enmity between the two governments for much of the last 50 years has had a direct impact on conditions inside Cuba. Anything that diplomats of democratic countries can do in support of Cuban democracy development pales in significance to the potential effect of placing US-Cuba relations on a normal basis, possibly for the first time.

Change at Long Last?

Cuba remains the only country in the western hemisphere that does not practice some form of electoral democracy. A quarter-century after the abandonment of communism in Europe and the adoption of the market economy in China, Cuba is only now groping toward change. It has been tentative. Expectations that Cuban communism would be merely the last domino to fall failed to recognize a signal difference with Eastern Europe, where the regimes were judged to be collaborating with an outside oppressor, the USSR. The Cuban government still presents itself as the patriotic defender against an outside threat.

However, the threat is clearly diminished. The Obama administration is pursuing a policy of constructive engagement with Cuba. The US desire to see human rights prevail on the island is undiminished, but systemic hostility to the regime has been put aside. The "US economic embargo on Cuba, in place for more than half a century, continues to impose indiscriminate economic hardship on Cubans, and has failed to improve human rights in the country" (Human Rights Watch, 2012). However, the US administration is doing what it can within the constraints imposed by the Helms-Burton Act to expand people-to-people contacts and to enable Cuban-Americans to contribute to the welfare and economic prospects of Cubans by interpreting the embargo in more permissive ways.

There is no question now that for its part, Cuba is undertaking a process of economic reform. However, Alvaro Vargas Llosa (2011) reminds us that Fidel Castro has summed up the reforms as being designed "to preserve socialism." Llosa recognizes the readiness "to make concessions in many areas. But not on the definitive issue: the monopoly of power" (ibid.). Also in *The Globe and Mail*, Professor Arturo Lopez-Levy is cited as pointing out that "They are trying to let the economic genie out of the bottle while keeping the political genie in. That's not going to work" (Verma, 2011).

The economic reforms are increasingly extensive, but they are as yet unaccompanied by political reforms, apart from the announcement that President Raúl Castro will step down at the end of his five-year term in 2018. Julia Sweig and Michael J. Bustamente (2013) describe this "new moment in Cuba" arriving "not with a bang but rather on the heel of a series of cumulative measures — most prominent among them agricultural reform, the formulation of a progressive tax code, and the government's highly publicized efforts to begin shrinking the size of state payrolls by allowing for a greater number of small businesses. The beginnings of private credit, real estate, and wholesale markets promise to further Cuba's evolution. Still, Cuba does not appear poised to adopt the Chinese or Vietnamese blueprint for market liberalization anytime soon."

The process will likely quicken when Fidel Castro leaves the scene definitively. Although an orderly succession has obviously occurred as he retired from public office in July 2006, and ostensibly turned power over to his brother Raúl, the question arises whether anything really significant can change as long as he maintains his moral influence over the country, even if he is without direct control of all details as before. Having described himself in 1961 as a "Marxist-Leninist until I die," he recast himself in post-retirement writings as a "utopian socialist," adding that "one must be consistent to the end."

From the outset, the regime has been symbiotically identified with its *comandante en jefe* who led the revolution that propelled it into power on January 1, 1959. The regime he built over the decades "is not the German Democratic Republic," as one diplomat in Havana phrased it, but it is an authoritarian one-party state that has used an Orwellian security apparatus to rein in and quash democratic impulses over five decades, often citing the threat from the US as the rationale. Much of the world respects the ability of Castro's Cuba to have stared down and survived determined efforts by successive US governments to end the regime by invasion, attempted assassination, a CIA program of subversion and a punitive economic embargo. But democrats continue to rebuke the regime for its invocation of these real threats to Cuba's sovereignty to justify the continued and even tighter suffocation of human and civil rights of Cuban citizens.

This case study identifies activities by diplomats and democracies in support of Cubans' efforts to secure rights at home, including discussion of widening democratic space and simultaneously to partner Cuban economic openings in a supportive way. The study reports that until recently, these efforts tended to bounce off a tightly controlled and controlling regime that veers between self-confidence and paranoia, and discounts the pertinence of mutual leverage.

In consequence, diplomatic efforts meant to support democracy development remain especially challenged in today's Cuba. Diplomats have to manage seemingly competing professional obligations of non-interference, official engagement, a long-term developmental perspective and democratic solidarity, but signs of change are clearly present in Cuba. Coming years will engage democrats in support of efforts by the Cuban people to pursue aspirations for more significant change. However, here, as elsewhere, it will be up to Cubans themselves to accomplish.

CUBAN HISTORY

In few countries are the links between history and the present as evident on the surface as in Cuba, where the struggles and passions of the last 150 years still play out in national psychology and perspectives today. Christopher Columbus made trans-Atlantic landfall on Cuba on October 27, 1492, on his epic voyage of "discovery." By 1511, Spain had declared the island a Spanish possession and within decades, the Taino-Arawak peoples were eliminated by a combination of harsh repression, suicide, European diseases and assimilation. Except for a brief occupation of Havana by the British, Cuba remained in Spanish hands for almost 500 years, until 1898. During the nineteenth century, the island economy prospered from sugar and tobacco production that relied heavily on African slave labour until the abolition of slavery in 1886.

Influenced by European and American revolutions, a vibrant national identity emerged over time, generating a movement for independence whose moral animator was Father Félix Varela (1788–1854), one of the first great protagonists of non-violent civil resistance. Several rebellions were harshly dealt with preceding the Ten-Year War that cost tens of thousands of Cuban lives and even more on the part of the Spaniards, until a negotiated compromise, which led to the abolition of slavery in 1886.

Since adolescence, José Martí (1853–1895) was devoted to the quest for an independent and non-racial Cuba, causing his imprisonment and exile. In 1881, the nationalist writer and poet found his way to the US and began in earnest to mobilize support for an armed incursion of exiled patriots to throw the Spaniards out of Cuba.

Anxious to pre-empt the impulse toward annexation by expediting national independence as a *fait accompli*, José Martí was killed not long after he had joined the insurgents in 1895. By the following year, the rebels had succeeded in controlling most of Cuba. A growing set of frictions with Spain added to public sympathy in the US for the Cuban patriots, making the option of war against Spain popular. As future President Theodore Roosevelt wrote, "This country needs a war."

The rebellion against Spanish rule that broke out on the island in 1895 (without the exile invasion force whose ships had been impounded) suited the long-standing aversion of the US to European possessions in the western hemisphere that was codified as doctrine by US President James Monroe in 1823. The annexation of Cuba had been openly espoused by later US presidents Polk and Pierce.

In 1896, US Secretary of State James G. Blaine secretly tried to buy Cuba from a resistant Spain, but when the USS *Maine*, sent in aid of US citizens fearing for their safety, mysteriously blew up in Havana harbour in 1898, the US used it as a *casus belli*.

The latter stage of the Cuban War of Independence thereby became known in the US only as part of the larger Spanish-American War. Within the year, US intervention was decisive. Peace negotiations with Spain, from which Cubans were excluded, handed Cuba over to the US, who then occupied the country for four years. However, because the joint resolution of Congress authorizing the use of force to help the Cuban rebels had an amendment (the Teller Amendment) forbidding annexation, the US consented to Cuban independence in 1902.

As historian Alfredo José Estrada (2008) has written, it was America's "first experience of nation-building." President McKinley instructed the military expeditionary chief General Wood to "try to straighten out their courts, [and] put them on their feet as best you can. We want to do all we can for them and get out of the island as soon as we safely can" (ibid.).

But nation-building went hand-in-hand with a profitable reciprocity treaty awarding US business and trade a privileged place in the Cuban economy. Moreover, Cuban sovereignty was diluted by the "Platt Amendment" passed by US Congress in 1901 and inserted into the Cuban Constitution, which gave the US the right to intervene if its citizens or property were endangered. Indeed, US troops occupied Cuba on the occasion of various uprisings thereafter between 1906 and 1909, in 1912, and between 1917 and 1920. The amendment was abrogated in 1934.

The Twentieth Century until 1959

Cuba's enjoyment of independence was repeatedly spoiled by dictatorship and corruption. In 1925, modernizer Gerardo Machado was elected president, but soon gave in to the temptations of dictatorship. His rule was ended by violent opposition (The *Abecedarios*) and after a brief, idealistic, but chaotic socialist period, the army seized power in 1933. Authority, initially from behind the throne, was in the hands of ex-Sergeant Fulgencio Batista.

Batista initiated a democratic process and the adoption of a progressive constitution in 1940, following which he was fairly elected president, signalling the debut of Cuba's only 12 years of democracy, recalled later as the "politics of disappointment." The 1944 election was won by progressive Ramón Grau San Martin, who presided over a rising economy but also much corruption and gangsterism. His successor in 1948, Carlos Prío, brought little positive change.

Before scheduled elections in 1952, Batista seized power, suspended the constitution he had helped design and began a darker chapter of dictatorial violence and widespread corruption. Middle and upper classes prospered, but poorer people languished as disparities widened. The Batista regime's staunch anti-communism appealed to the Cold War outlook of US authorities at the expense of Cuban human rights. In 1953, a group of rebels, led by young lawyer Fidel Castro, attacked the Moncada barracks. Released from prison in 1955 for his part in these attacks, Castro organized a rebel force in Mexico that landed and launched a disciplined mountain-based guerrilla campaign, under comandantes Che Guevara, Raúl Castro and Camilo Cienfuegos in 1956. The campaign drew decisive support from peasants, sugar workers, students and their own persistence.

The Castro Victory and Its Aftermath

The hundred thousand or so refugees that followed Batista's flight from Cuba on December 31, 1958 in the inaugural wave to Miami were mostly embittered by what they had lost to the new regime.

Initially, the prevalent international reaction to the Castro victory was that despotism had been turfed out by an idealistic cause. At first, Castro tried to showcase an inclusive social-democratic coalition of a wide variety of opponents to Batista. After these attempts were shelved, disillusioned democrats began to join professionals and small businessmen to abandon what seemed to be rapidly becoming a militant ideological monolith.

As part of the process of "draining the swamp," several hundred executions took place at Havana's La Cabaña fortress, after summary trials. But as Jon Lee Anderson (1997) reports, "There was little public opposition to the wave of revolutionary justice at the time. On the contrary: Batista's thugs had committed some sickening crimes, [and] the Cuban public was in a lynching mood."

But, Anderson adds, "Whatever the 'necessity' of the revolutionary tribunals, they did much to polarize the political climate between Havana and Washington" (ibid.). The gap widened as Castro's anti-Washington rhetoric escalated and his plans to nationalize American assets in Cuba clarified. Guevara upped the ante by urging violent revolution throughout the hemisphere, which Anderson calls "a siren call to would-be revolutionaries and an implicit declaration of war against the interests of the United States" (ibid.). So began a half-century of mutual enmity.

The Castro Years, 1959–

This is not the place, however, for a detailed analysis of the dramatic history of Cuba over the last half-century. The regime was from almost the outset in a psychological and real state of siege: the failed US-financed Bay of Pigs invasion in February 1961 was the only military attack, but there were repeated attempts to assassinate Castro over the years — most notoriously as part of "Operation Mongoose," one of the biggest CIA covert operations ever undertaken. Diplomatic relations with the US were severed in 1961. Subsequent events — from the fateful Cuban Missile Crisis in 1962, which brought the world perilously close to nuclear war, through the passage by the US Congress of the Helms-Burton Act in 1996, which tightened the devastating economic embargo on Cuba — perpetuated the state of militant readiness that the Cuban leadership has invoked to justify the necessity of its strict authoritarian control.

There is no question that the revolution of 1959 had wide popular support, having overthrown what was widely held to be a tyrannical regime. Most citizens took patriotic pride in Cuba's new stature in the eyes of the world. There was also initial enthusiasm about exporting the Cuban revolution throughout Latin America but it waned and eventually died in Bolivia in 1967 with Guevara, who had become by then a revolutionary freelancer without much active Cuban government input. Cuba did take up arms in support of liberation causes, most prominently in Angola, where a Cuban expeditionary army numbering as many as 55,000 fought for years to support the leftist People's Movement for the Liberation of Angola against South African proxies. The costs to the apartheid regime were so huge that South Africans today credit Cuba with having done more to bring down white minority rule than anyone else from outside. (More than 2,000 Cubans died in the Angola fighting.)

Today, Cuba does not support armed insurrection or terrorism. At the time of the Boston Marathon bombing in April 2013, the Cuban government sent its condolences to the American people and reiterated that it "rejects and condemns unequivocally all acts of terrorism, in any place, under any circumstance, and with whatever motivation." Reflecting the unreality that still unhelpfully colours US official attitudes about Cuba, the US State Department spokesman responded that there are nonetheless "no current plans" to remove Cuba from the exclusive list of state sponsors of terrorism, which also specifies Iran, Sudan and Syria.

Over recent decades, Cuba's international "brand" became much more identified with the export of health services: 36,000 Cuban doctors are in service in over 70 countries, providing poor neighbourhoods medical facilities for the first time, such as the Barrio Adentro project in Caracas, Venezuela. South Africa pays Cuba to supply doctors to replace the many who have emigrated in the post-apartheid era. Cuba provides medical services in Venezuela in return for oil, and Cuban emergency relief teams were among the first to support relief efforts after the tsunami in Indonesia in 2004, a major earthquake in Pakistan in 2006 and were prominent closer to home more recently in earthquake-devastated Haiti. The Misión Milagros has brought hundreds of thousands of poor Latin Americans to Cuba for eye surgery and sent teams of Cuban eye doctors abroad.

In those 50-plus years, the Cuban government achieved important social goals. Diplomats in Cuba caution that whoever follows will have to accept that these achievements will need to be built upon, not dismantled. Cuban leaders, including Raúl Castro, have confided that they are struggling to find a way to enlarge the rights of individuals while conserving the sense of social solidarity they consider the hallmark of the Revolution.

Indeed, Cubans have never been as healthy, educated or more or less equal. The Cuban government states that a population that was only 60 percent literate in 1959 is 100 percent literate today, and 94 percent of Cubans finish secondary school. Today, there are 80,000 doctors compared to 6,000 at the time of the revolution (3,000 of whom emigrated). Life expectancy and infant mortality data rival those in Canada and the US, and are the best in Latin America. Latin American diplomats report that people struggling against criminal gangs in their region envy Cuba's relative absence of street violence.

The political attempt to re-engineer society along Marxist lines, however, had far-reaching social and economic consequences. Increasing ideological militancy and police control contributed to declining support, though there is no reliable way of estimating approval ratings, apart from the enduring efforts Cubans make to emigrate. The number of Cuban emigrants and families in the US today is well over a million.

Following nationalizations of private enterprise and the confiscation of US businesses, the re-engineered socialist economy became mired in centralized control and leaden bureaucracy, especially after Fidel Castro nationalized 60,000 small businesses in 1968. Social gains that also had to struggle against the effects of US sanctions were slowed. The withdrawal of Soviet "fraternal" subsidies (amounting to 21 percent of the Cuban GDP) after the collapse of the Soviet Union in 1991 essentially ended the radical Cuban social experiment. Having been overreliant on the Soviet bloc (to the extent of 80 percent of trade), Cuba faced a grave economic crisis. The government responded by suspending its economic orthodoxy to accommodate pragmatic measures under "the special period in times of peace," which introduced limited private small enterprise (self-employment or trabajo de cuenta propia) and permitted the use of foreign hard currency.

Recovery staggered, further hindered by devastating hurricanes in recent years. The collapsed sugar market has never recovered. Some reforms initiated during the "special period" authorizing the emergence of semi-autonomous enterprises and research centres were rolled back a decade later. A senior economic minister told an ambassador several years ago that the state's position as employer had dropped from 98 percent to 97 percent, but had returned to 98 percent. Diplomats report that officials who had launched new ventures and centres with government favour found themselves in sudden disfavour and relegated to a limbo of obscurity. Today, the pendulum has swung again toward liberalization of the economy more dramatically than ever. The effects, including on the rights of civil society, will be watched and, as appropriate, supported, with real and widespread interest.

CUBA TODAY: SOCIO-ECONOMIC ATROPHY

In 2004, the RAND Corporation wrote of "a vast array of dysfunctional legacies from the *fidelista* past." In general, public grievances are less related to human rights than to improving the material conditions of day-to-day living. Seventy percent of Cubans were born after 1959 and relate less to the revolutionary enthusiasm of earlier years. Cuban youth in the main wants what youth everywhere seeks, free access to popular outside cultural goods, lifestyles and freedom to travel.

Economic Reforms

The reforms announced over the last several years are an attempt to address this. Taken together, they represent the biggest shakeup of the economy since Fidel Castro expropriated small businesses in 1968, although moving in the opposite direction.

The regime under Raúl Castro appears committed to trying to improve the economy. Castro's steps to lighten the bureaucratic controls that he repeatedly criticizes, and to decentralize, have to confront ossified structures and the practical effect is diminished. About 60 percent of the economy is under the direct control of the self-financed Revolutionary Armed Forces (FAR) that constitute a powerful state-within-the-state with separate infrastructure for food, energy and transport for its members' benefit. But all in all, as Sweig and Bustamente (2013) report, "services in Cuba make up close to 75 percent of the island's GDP," limiting impact of reform on a better record of productive growth.

The reforms undertaken tentatively beginning in 2006 reflected, to some extent, a pragmatic current among political elites. Raúl Castro's own political appointees tend to be older military intimates. They are described as status quo-oriented, but not necessarily hardline ideologically. They seem mindful, however, of potential resistance from more ideological loyalists, and pay heed to the destabilizing effects of "shock therapy" in Russia and elsewhere that would in any case be anathema to a population fearful of weakening entitlement programs that at least keep everybody afloat. Nonetheless, even the most orthodox socialists were reported to see the merits of permitting the safety valves of some economic reforms, provided egalitarian principles remain paramount.

However, the differences between those who have access to the convertible currency economy and those who don't are already corrosive enough. There is a consensus among observers that the population is idle, underemployed and apathetic, worn down by the struggle to feed families from meagre personal food rations that half of the population, who lacks access to the convertible currency economy, has to rely on. Even Fidel Castro is reported to have acknowledged (to Julia E. Sweig) that the economic system no longer works, including for the regime.

In the last year, additional new reforms have taken a more definite character. Rights have been established to allow Cuban citizens to buy and sell personal property (though only second-hand cars), open businesses, hire employees and engage in self-employment in 181 categories (though still excluding professions). The government's announcement that it will reduce the number of public employees by hundreds of thousands aims at putting 35 percent of the economy in private hands by 2015. Food rationing will also be phased out. In 2009, Raúl Castro enabled small private landholdings to try to improve food production, as Cuba is now massively dependent on food imports. The US is the main supplier, as food products have been excepted from the US embargo under strict terms of cash prepayment. Finally, foreign investors can lease government land for up to 99 years.

People-to-People

As of January 14, 2013, exit controls are lifted, permitting Cubans to travel abroad. While they must still apply for a passport, early indications are that the passport regime is generally permissive. Cubans can stay or live abroad for a longer period of time before relinquishing Cuban citizenship.

The Cuban rulings need to be seen against US government relaxation of the rights of Americans to travel to Cuba for widely interpreted religious, educational and cultural travel, in addition to the lifting of limits on the rights of naturalized Cuban-Americans to visit Cuba and limits on the amounts of financial remittances they can send. In 2012, the number of Americans visiting exceeded 400,000, and Americans sent over US$1 billion of financial support and goods to Cuba.

The South Florida anti-regime Cuban contingent in Congress attempted to turn the regulations back to those applying during the Bush administration (maximum remittances of US$1,200 and only to immediate family; travel to Cuba only once every three years), but failed to gain support. The additional context is the effort to enable Cubans to enjoy electronic contact with the outside through upgrades to Internet connections and cellphone availability. Both of these technologies are expensive, but usage has increased to 1.5 million phones, up from 330,000 five years ago. The increased contact with the outside through travel and electronic access can be assumed to have the effect of increasing the appetite for political change.

Political

From the outset, the regime has maintained pervasive supervision of the population, making ample use of the Comités de Defensa de la Revolución that engage citizens as watchdogs in every block and workplace.

The question for observers is whether, despite piecemeal concessions, Cubans are likely to see any significant weakening of doctrinaire political control as long as Fidel Castro is alive. Most acknowledge thus far, it has proven to be wishful thinking to believe that pragmatic specific reforms lead inevitably to wholesale political change, as a kind of Cuban perestroika. "Elections" to local councils and state organs remain resolutely single-party.

On the eve of the regime's fortieth anniversary, Human Rights Watch (1999) wrote of the "highly effective machine of repression." Only a few years later, in March 2003, police arrested 75 democracy proponents. They have at last been released after the intervention of Cardinal Jaime Ortega. The government has pressured most of them to leave for exile — mostly to Spain, which also helped broker their release.

In 2011, the Cuban Council of Human Rights issued a list of 43 prisoners of conscience remaining in Cuban jails. A good number were prosecuted mostly as recipients of US financial aid, with internal security operatives who had infiltrated NGOs appearing as state witnesses. The propaganda machine remorselessly attacked civil society representatives as a mercenary fifth column serving Cuba's enemies.

Cubans who criticize the government are subject to criminal charges. In 2011, four Havana dissidents were sentenced to three to five years for distributing leaflets urging an end to the Castro brothers' rule. Human Rights Watch (2012) reported over 3,000 arbitrary detentions to prevent individuals from attending meetings or events. The Cuban government refuses to recognize human rights monitoring as a legitimate activity and has arrested members of human rights group attempting to visit a dissident on a hunger strike in a hospital. The question is what the impact will be of an expanding civil society.

Civil Society and the Opposition

The notion of civil society acting independently of government, that is at the core of democratic development, was, by definition, abhorrent to old-line Soviet-style Marxists. From the start, the regime appropriated Cuban patriotism as the central theme of the revolution's narrative, ultimately incarnated by the government. The external threats produced national security laws declaring the acceptance of foreign funds to support change to the Cuban system to be seditious. The views of those who advocate change are represented as being inherently anti-Cuban.

Yet, in 1992, Fidel Castro himself referred to civil society in positive terms internationally. The partial withdrawal of the state in the "special period" opened up spaces that were filled by informal arrangements among people that laid the beginnings of civil society. But a backlash in official opinion once the economy began an uneven recovery in the mid-1990s caused Cuban authorities to label notions of civil society and democracy as being part and parcel of aggressive campaigns from the US for regime change.

A pattern emerged that once an advocacy organization became prominent or effective beyond a certain point, it was shut down. An early example was the Cuban Committee for Human Rights, formed in the 1970s among imprisoned socialists and supporters of the 1959 revolution disillusioned by monolithic political control. In 1997, members of the Working Group of the Internal Dissidence were jailed, followed by more arrests in succeeding years.

The most high-profile advocacy initiative was the Varela Project, winner of the European Parliament's Sakharov Prize for Freedom of Thought and lauded publicly by Pope John Paul II and former US President Jimmy Carter on visits to Cuba. Animated by Oswaldo Payá, who had earlier founded the Christian Liberation Movement, the Varela Project took advantage of a provision of the 1992 Cuban Constitution, collecting the requisite 10,000 signatures to petition the right to a popular referendum on basic freedoms of association and the press, free elections and the right to operate a private business. It also called for an amnesty on political prisoners. The government crushed the initiative by organizing its own referendum, in which eight million Cuban citizens were herded into voting for a constitutional amendment making socialism permanent. Then, it seized 22 of the most prominent supporters of the Varela Project in its mass arrests in March 2002.

Oswaldo Payá was not among them, perhaps because of his international prominence. He continued his efforts through the Christian Liberation Movement, and by starting the Cuban Forum, which encourages discussion meetings in peoples' homes. In July 2012, Payá died in a car crash under controversial circumstances. The Cuban authorities claim the car's driver lost control and hit a tree. Paya's daughter (and the driver) claim the car was run off the road from behind by a security chase car.

While it remains subject to considerable surveillance, some observers comment that the regime has become more tolerant of civil society's efforts to organize informal discussions, showing a post-Fidel measure of acceptance that the population increasingly needs and expects a debate about the country's political future. Overall, there is public fatigue over official propaganda and intrusion into personal lives, and Raúl Castro has dialled down the propaganda volume.

But analytical opinion cautions that the discouraging material conditions mean that achieving a multi-party political system is not top in the list of Cubans' priorities. People want less economic control. They accept the social and egalitarian values that animate the Cuban revolution, but deplore inefficient and demeaning delivery of social and other services.

Despite the hard line that has persisted since 1996, civil society has continued to expand in a piecemeal fashion, including in rural areas, especially to fill the gaps created by the inadequate social delivery by the government, which itself faces an overcrowded agenda. While not presenting themselves as advocates of political change, such civil society groups obtain pertinent experience in local and personal initiative, from handling the functional issues at hand, to laying the foundations for building what the China case study refers to as the "ecology" of pluralism.

In the 1990s, the Concilio Cubano emerged as an umbrella group of 135 small organizations, including professional associations and independent journalists. It was blocked from meeting in 1996 and not revived. But over 2,000 NGOs with specific functional objectives are inscribed officially.

The Independent Library Movement addressed a gap in access to books in Spanish and built a network of over 100 libraries with over 250,000 users. Though non-political in practical purpose, its founder, human rights activist Ramon Colas, was forced into exile in 2001.

The labour movement is dominated by the official Workers' Central Union of Cuba, which is an instrument of regime control, but two more independent labour groups have emerged: the United Council of Cuban Workers and the Christian International Labour Movement.

Founded in 1996, the Federation of Latin American Rural Women has collected over 100,000 signatures for a petition protesting the inequity of a dual-currency economy, which they maintain is unfair to poorer Cubans without access to convertible pesos.

Having been identified as a supporter of Spain and then of Batista and other dictators, the Roman Catholic Church is greatly diminished institutionally in Cuba, reduced to only 300 priests, half of which are Cuban. But religious faith is by no means extinguished.

In 1992, the Cuban government dropped the country's formally atheistic character and returned the right to worship without official stigma. By the 1990s, the Catholic Church was giving thought to its social role and began a non-political program of small projects for citizens, such as daycare centres for single mothers and facilities for the elderly, which also have the effect of creating a sense of personal empowerment flowing from self-administered activities.

The Church has not become a conduit for open political challenge as in Poland in the 1980s, but it has created a space for open discussion and is supported by congregants across the country. Raúl Castro held an unprecedented four-hour meeting in May 2010 with Cardinal Jaime Ortega and the Archbishop of Santiago de Cuba, Dionisio Garcia. This has led to further discussion between Church and State, resulting in the set of concessions regarding jail sentences of prisoners of conscience, including the announced release, mostly into exile, of the remaining 52 prisoners arrested in March 2003.

A variety of congregational and religious assemblies are able to draw resources from corresponding religious communities in the US and elsewhere. For example, the traditional Afro-Cuban religious practice Santería remains part of Cuban national culture.

A plethora of associations and cooperatives have emerged for developmental purposes, working on alternative energy, agriculture and the restoration of local buildings, sometimes involving wholesale community development such as the El Condado movement aimed at remodelling the city of Santa Clara.

Artistic, intellectual and research circles have banded into informal groups. Rock music has attracted a strong following of young people, which authorities have belatedly (and without much credibility) tried to align with.

All in all, diplomats and other observers judge that the foundations of civil society, while rudimentary, are taking root, providing foreign democratic partners with a growing variety of non-state partners. Moreover, Cubans are becoming eager to take responsibility for their own lives and, for the first time, political choices.

In *The New York Review of Books*, Jose Manuel Prieto (2011) chose the image of "growing up," which Russian civil society members also chose to describe the progress of civil society in Moscow to the *Handbook* project. Prieto writes about "the reserves of people waiting to be allowed to live an adult life. The protector state, now in retreat, educated and instructed them but also immobilized them and made them dependent, confining an entire population to a prolonged childhood. The time has come to allow them to grow up" (ibid.).

Cuba's Relationships with Community of Democracies Member States

Cuba's foreign relationships have varying degrees of intensity. As described above, its relationship with the US is overwhelmingly the most important from every point of view. There is scarcely a family without relatives in the US. US policies on permissible remittances from family members, as well as on visits, are therefore of primary importance on the island. In relaxing the regulations that had been considerably hardened by its predecessor, the Obama administration has changed the whole tone of the US-Cuban relationship. In 2010, US visas were again being provided Cuban artists and performers to tour in the US, such as the emblematic poet-singer Silvio Rodríguez.

The Helms-Burton Act, however, is rooted in law, and many of the provisions of the US embargo cannot be changed by executive order. Yet, as time goes by, the ability of the harder-line exile community in South Florida to dictate terms of the relationship between the two countries diminishes. A growing number of US voters would share the consensus among non-US democratic representatives in Cuba that the US embargo and policies have been counterproductive, enabling the regime to justify strengthening its control over the population. A 2010 article by Human Rights Watch monitors Nik Steinberg and Daniel Wilkinson judged that "It is hard to think of a US policy with a longer track record of failure."

Professor Lopez-Levy has observed that the fault with US policy is that it "wants to start at the end" (cited in Verma, 2011). The Helms-Burton Act indeed rooted its embargo provisions not only in Cuba adopting a multi-party democracy, but also on the Castros being no longer in office.

Fidel Castro has always turned US policy to his advantage and has mobilized Cuban fears that the Cuban-American community aimed to restore economic and political control over the island. Cuban citizens are generally reported to be bitter about the hardline from either side: the Cuban authorities who care more about ideology than the plight of Cubans; and US authorities and lawmakers who chose to tighten sanctions and the embargo at the moment of greatest economic hardship for Cubans. By all accounts, ordinary Cubans hope the Obama administration will succeed in inducing flexibility, a relaxation of enmity and also of Cuban controls.

The Obama administration has initiated talks with Cuban authorities over immigration and overflights, as well as preliminary talks on the prospects for improving the relationship. Though Fidel Castro has never accepted the premise of "normalization" in exchange for democratization, it is implicit that both sanctions and Cuba's continuing imprisonment of prisoners of conscience must ultimately be bargaining tools in a larger picture.

The Cuban government has recognized the need to diversify relationships, having learned a harsh lesson from overdependence on the USSR. There has been something of a revival of relations with Russia, and China has become Cuba's second-largest trading partner.

Cuba's other relationships have, in some ways, been strengthened in recent years. Virtually all Latin American countries now have diplomatic representation in Cuba, especially since Cuba stopped supporting leftist uprisings in Central America in the early 1990s. Indeed, Cuba is seen by Latin Americans to have played a constructive role in mediating conflicts in the region. Generally, in line with historic Latin American neuralgia toward outside interference in domestic affairs, Latin Americans take a hands-off attitude toward Cuban governance. Cuba has been admitted to the Rio Group, devoted to economic cooperation among Latin American and Caribbean countries. Though the US has continued to resist the idea (advanced by the former Government of Canada) of inviting Cuba to Summits of the Americas, Fidel Castro was enthusiastically welcomed at the first Summit of Latin America and the Caribbean on Development hosted by Brazil, which excluded the US.

A wave of electoral victories of the left and parties long enjoying close relations with Cuban political elites, and once in office, several leaders, such as Brazilian President Luiz Inácio "Lula" da Silva, Bolivian President Evo Morales or ex-Chilean President Michelle Bachelet, also reciprocated for past Cuban support. Mexico has recently restored a productive level of political dialogue after tensions with ex-President Vicente Fox, strengthening economic relations and consulting on other issues of mutual importance such as illegal migration. President Lula da Silva, who visited Cuba several times during his tenure as president, paid a state visit to Raúl Castro in 2008. He announced a major economic assistance and development package that situates Brazil as a central partner, particularly in the energy development field.

It is unclear if Venezuela's role as a high-profile ally of the Castro regime will survive the death of President Chávez in March 2013. Venezuela has propped up the Cuban regime financially by providing most of Cuba's oil in exchange for "tens of thousands of Cuban doctors and security advisers. Nicolás Maduro, Venezuela's new president, has pledged loyalty to Cuba. But his narrow, disputed election victory [in April, 2013] and Venezuela's nosediving economy, mean that Cuba needs other options" (*The Economist*, 2013).

Dr. Julia Sweig (2009) points out that Cuba's emphases on social justice resonate in Latin American public opinion. This may explain the paradox that, while many have only recently overcome the abuse of human rights at the hands of military regimes, they nonetheless fail to criticize Cuban human rights abuses. Dr. Sweig (ibid.) assesses that "Latin American governments today generally see gradual reform under Raúl as the path most likely to bring about a more plural, open society on the island," a judgment corresponding more to the dispiriting material conditions in Cuba than to the reawakened aspirations of the people.

Canada and the European Union have always maintained relations with Cuba and have opposed Helms-Burton both for its negative impact on Cuban development and for its extraterritorial projections of US law, which foreign partners judge to be unacceptable. But "Western" democracies have also been firm about the unacceptability of Cuba's disregard for human rights and for the holding of prisoners of conscience.

After the arrests of 75 democracy activists in March 2003, the EU and its diplomatic missions in Cuba placed a severe downgrade on relations, which was only removed in 2009. There are varying degrees of warmth or lack of it among EU countries individually. Spain is the most active, including fast-track access to Spanish citizenship for Cubans with at least one Spanish grandparent, and productive partnerships in such areas as the environment, disaster preparedness and relief, and science and technology. The Czech Republic probably represents the other end of the EU scale, reflecting the priority that the former communist country places on democratic transition, and also the convictions on human rights of former President Václav Havel, who founded the International Committee for Democracy in Cuba. (The Fidel Castro government had supported the 1968 USSR invasion to crush Czechoslovak political reform). Individually, other EU countries have tried to engage the Cuban government more intensively in the last few years. The European Commission has become a Cuban development partner, but has done so in tandem with a high-level EU-Cuba dialogue on human rights.

Canada has maintained political engagement with Cuban authorities, while arguing with them "nose-to-nose" for the space to continue contacts with civil society. Although Cuba normally discounts economic leverage, the Cubans do care about their image in a country such as Canada, which sends so many tourists to Cuba and continues to be an economic partner.

There are indications that Cuba knows it needs to reach out to major democracies to balance what will likely be a wave of activity from the US if and when relations do become more normal. Cuban leaders have told European partners they would like to think that Europe's greater emphasis on social democracy will enable Cuba to cement some of the social principles of the revolution amid inevitable change.

The Cuban authorities have been cracking down on corruption in the last few years and have prosecuted several foreign businessmen in the process.

RESOURCES AND ASSETS OF DEMOCRATIC DIPLOMATS IN CUBA

The Cuban government is not isolated from the representatives of foreign democratic governments, as is Zimbabwe, nor is it indifferent to foreign views — the foreign press section of the Foreign Ministry is its biggest department.

Cuban authorities can and do turn access for foreign diplomats on and off, depending on behaviour, though the regime rarely goes so far as to request withdrawal of diplomatic representatives. Democratic diplomats exercise their **immunity** in order to meet with civil society, speak freely and even demonstrate solidarity with the victims of human rights abuse. On the other side of the coin, there have been ample reports in the past of diplomatic immunity being violated by random if systemic acts of harassment and intimidation, against mainly US diplomats, their dependents and even their pets.

Diplomats have been able to count on the **support of home authorities** for diplomatic activity corresponding to the policies of the sending government at a given time. The most protagonistic approach was assigned to US Interests Section Chief James Cason under the Bush administration from 2002 to 2005. As he took up his duties as head of the fully staffed diplomatic mission located within the Swiss Embassy, Cason recalls his political instructions: "You are not at a mission. You are on a mission…to support the democracy movement." In doing so, Cason antagonized Cuban authorities. It was an outcome that would not have been considered productive by other countries whose relationships were less officially hostile, but it was one that Washington (and Miami) at the time seemed to want. Writer Daniel P. Erikson (2008) explains that: "Castro and his top ministers despised Cason (who 'could not have cared less what Cuban officials thought' of him, his focus [being] wholly on supporting Cuba's nascent opposition movement). But they also found his overt support for Cuban dissidents to be politically useful, because it helped them to make the argument that opposition to the regime depended on overseas sponsors. Many Cubans in the system with reformist instincts found that the US Interests Section had become such a hot potato that they were forced to give it a wide berth." On the other hand, Mr. Cason's support for Cuban would-be democrats may well be remembered long after tit-for-tat antagonisms between the governments are forsaken.

The remarks of former UK Ambassador Dianna Melrose (in office 2008–2012) to a UK website on Cuban issues typify the dual track approach that most home authorities expect of their democratic diplomats — much as described elsewhere in the *Handbook* by US Ambassador McFaul about dual track diplomacy in Moscow. Ambassador Melrose spoke on the website and in an extensive interview with Patrick Pietroni (2009) of her commitment to constructive engagement with the Cuban government, but she underlined that the notion of "mutual respect" cannot be invoked to fend off criticism of the suppression of human rights in Cuba where "people are locked up for criticising the government" without "mutual respect also by the Cuban government for the European Union and the values important to us, including commitment to full civil and political rights, democratic freedoms, freedom of expression: all the rights that are fundamental to our society." On this basis, EU diplomats have continued their contacts with a range of opposition and other figures in civil society, confident they will have support at home for activities that demonstrate solidarity with those persecuted for their principles.

Former Canadian Ambassador Michael Small was always clear with Cuban authorities that his mandate was "to talk with the whole range of the country," and he was not curbed in making contacts with civil society. Bruce Levy (2009), head of the embassy's political section told a Washington conference (Cuba: An International Perspective), "we hope to see a peaceful transition to a democratic free-market system, and we use our many links to promote our values. Our two countries make it a policy to speak to each other frankly and respectfully, even on issues where the two sides disagree." The mutual respect is no doubt a function of the extent of ongoing relations.

Diplomats committed to maintaining contact with civil society and offering solidarity with human rights defenders come from the missions of several democratic countries in Cuba. The Awards to Committed Diplomacy in Cuba, offered in 2010 by Centro Para la Apertura y el Desarrollo de América Latina for "showing solidarity towards democrats in the island and for taking committed actions" on "human rights violations," honoured three diplomats from Germany, two from the US and one each from Poland, the Czech Republic and Norway. Diplomats interested in making civil society contacts on a trip also met conscientiously with Cuban official contacts. The Cuban authorities expected a certain balance. If the emphasis became tilted toward dissidents, the official contacts were cut off and diplomats were left with only dissidents to meet.

Diplomats recognize the reality that they have limited direct **influence** on any top-down regime whose political priorities are wholly internal. However, Raúl Castro has acknowledged that Cuba has to modernize, and to do this Cuba needs partners. Cuba has specific development needs and not a lot of strategic leverage over countries able to address them. This situation creates some political capital that embassies can deploy.

Financial assistance is a resource of diplomatic missions that ought to correspond to a dire shortage of resources on the part of Cuban NGOs. US agencies have very large amounts of money to disperse from funds authorized by Congress. The vast majority is spent on programs and NGOs outside Cuba, through the 1992 Cuban Democracy Act that authorized direct US funding of NGOs seeking non-violent change. Authorities have vigorously objected to embassies' direct funding of civil society groups, especially advocacy NGOs. In practice, because it was controversial, such funding often became divisive, and as mentioned, placed some Cuban recipients in a position of vulnerability. Apart from the US, diplomatic missions in Havana generally do not provide funds to support political dissidents, but they pursue the opportunity to fund developmental activities in Cuba, often preferring projects undertaken at the municipal level by local authorities or co-ops.

That some US funds were channelled to Cuban civil society via NGOs in newer democracies such as the Czech Republic and Poland is an example of **solidarity** among democracies, though most embassies of democratic countries in Cuba confide it would have been counterproductive in recent years to be closely associated with the US Interests Section on political issues which, in the words of a US diplomat, seemed "radioactive" because of the explicit US regime change agenda.

On the issues, EU countries struggled to work out a common position, but there were until recently few formal **demarches** of the EU representatives together with non-EU partners. Over the last two decades, "like-minded" embassies, including Sweden, the Netherlands, Canada, Chile, Mexico, Spain and Britain have regularly compared notes on the ground in Havana, though they do not coordinate activity in any organized way.

The election of a new US administration in 2008 made the working relationships among embassies in Havana more productive, and mutually reinforcing acts of human rights support and on development assistance issues have been more frequent.

Community of Democracies diplomats have consistently maintained the **legitimacy** of their solidarity with those seeking freedom of assembly and speech, and human rights defence. Cuba signed the Santiago Declaration in 1991, containing the "commitment to democracy, the strengthening of the rule of law, and access to effective justice and human rights." In 2008, Cuba signed the UN Covenant on Civil and Political Rights that guarantees such rights, as well as the freedom to leave the country; however, Cuba has still not ratified the covenants and there is little evidence of concrete rights becoming more available. Still, the fact that Cuba claims to be a democracy further legitimizes the right to support Cubans who seek debate about democratic norms.

APPLICATIONS

The Golden Rules

Listening, Respecting and Understanding

Understanding Cuba and its nuances is a challenge for any foreign observer; there are angles and complexities at every turn. Diplomats are reminded constantly of the need to respect the Cubans' sense of their history, both to understand the present and to grasp the fundamentals of national psychology. Many of Cuba's social organization structures are unique to that society.

Over the years, diplomats from democracies have balanced ambivalence and nuance against the need to contest the categorical denial of fundamental human rights inherent in such official acts as the harsh sentences meted out to dissidents and reformers arrested in March 2003. Though those arrested then have been released, the regime continues cynically to denigrate activists and to prosecute them. Diplomatic missions continually register their deep respect for the courage of dissidents, described by Llosa (2011) as "those who resist the dictatorship in difficult, even heroic, conditions," who continue to protest violations of human rights and who pay a high price for taking a stand, often extended to their families.

In recent years, however, the need for democratic diplomats to support those raising a voice in legitimate opposition has, in practice, had to take account of the greater vulnerability direct contact and especially direct financial support can trigger. In April 2007, Oswaldo Payá and Marta Beatriz Roque, founder of the Assembly for the Promotion of Civil Society, who had been jailed in 2003 on trumped-up charges of "acts against the independence or territorial integrity of the state," joined other democrats in stating that "achieving changes in our society is a task corresponding to Cubans and only Cubans, to define and decide freely and democratically the future of Cuba without foreign intervention." In short, supportive diplomats acknowledge they need to know when to keep their distance from those engaged in a struggle with authorities who monitor events closely, and especially contacts with foreign embassies in Cuba.

Cautious sensitivity applies to relations with Cuban officials, as well as with civil society activists. Diplomats observe that members of the political elite, even very senior figures, such as deposed former Cuban Secretary of the Council of Ministers and Vice President Carlos Lage Dávila, can abruptly back off from what had been effective mutually beneficial contacts out of a need to avoid any accusation of "dangerous associations" from security personnel. In periods of thaw, such as the mid- to late-1990s, younger officials were able to enjoy foreign contacts that, in periods of retrenchment, were held against them at a cost to their careers. The question being asked on all sides is whether the atmosphere is changing again for the better in this respect, and if so, if it will last.

Sharing

Sharing among embassies is routine practice, though some are more like-minded than others. The EU, of course, shares systematically among member-state embassies, and keeping balance and avoiding duplication in development assistance efforts. On political and human rights issues, some embassies — possibly those with fewer concrete interests at stake in Cuba — take stronger declaratory positions. There is acknowledgment of the potential for an informal division of labour and differentiation of role among democratic embassies, especially in the EU. EU diplomats have teamed up to support victims of political persecution and their families, and to demonstrate public solidarity with peaceful demonstrators.

Truth in Communications

Reporting

Analysis of the situation in Cuba has been an ongoing duty of diplomats for many years; a local form of "Kremlinology" has grown out of the need to decipher opaque relationships in the FAR and in upper reaches of the Communist Party.

As elsewhere, there have been major episodes of wishful thinking and cases of telling authorities at home what they wished to hear. In episodes of attachment to the status quo resembling *Handbook* descriptions of poor readings of countries later affected by "the Arab Spring," Morris Morley (2004) cites CIA field officers on how, prior to January 1, 1959, "Ambassadors Smith and Gardner were both absolutely convinced that Castro wasn't going to come out of the hills. They believed what Batista told them and didn't see that changes were going to come."

Contemporary diplomats do not accept, obviously, the assessments of the Cuban regime at face value. They anticipate that the current repressive system will founder once Fidel Castro disappears from the scene. But they acknowledge that there is a risk of reporting isolated reforms, gestures or contacts as already heralding the beginnings of more important structural change that has still not emerged in any fundamental rights-altering way, even if hopeful signs tempt a limited optimism.

Informing

Cuba has been a closed society as far as information is concerned. There is no access to foreign news outlets, though bureaus of foreign media are in place. There had been a short-lived tolerance and growth of autonomous media in the late 1990s, but following a crackdown on independent commentators and outlets a decade ago, none of the periodicals then published still exists, with the exception of the official *Gazeta* of the Union of Writers and Artists.

Cuban journalists have been jailed for accepting financial aid from the US. The harsh fact is that there is no independent alternative in Cuba to state-owned TV and to the propagandistic Cuban news service *Granma*. The online newspaper *Candonga* in Holguín has been blocked and its director, Yosvani Anzardo Hernández, was detained by police for two weeks and threatened with prosecution because he was acting as a correspondent for a Miami news site. Contact with foreign press is punishable in Cuba with sentences of up to 20 years. The Writers in Prison Committee of PEN International urges democratic governments to pursue the release of journalists among the prisoners of conscience in Cuban jails.

Nonetheless, the appetite of Cuban scholars and intellectuals for access to outside contacts and materials is undiminished. A semi-autonomous magazine of social commentary, *Temas*, is printed in and distributed from Colombia and has sustained a fair measure of free-wheeling debate, mirrored by its regular monthly public discussions of current social and economic issues. Some embassies help start-up magazines by providing access to newsprint.

If scholars are keen to connect with sources outside Cuba, the interest of younger Cubans in being able to connect with the outside and with each other via social media and the Internet presents Cuban authorities with almost existential challenges. Cuba has the lowest Internet user rate in the hemisphere. Until very recently, the Internet has basically not been available or affordable to citizens, though it has become possible to acquire laptops, albeit at costs prohibitive for the vast majority. An active blogging community, typified by the widely admired "Generation Y" blog of Yoani Sanchez who provides an accurate account of the daily life of the Cuban people, has operated in Cuba, but most of its readers are by definition abroad, accessed through servers off the island.

The regime seems finally to have recognized that Cuban youth access foreign websites and social networks through bootleg connections and has finally accepted the inevitability of greater openness. A submaritime communications link to Venezuela has been built, which will afford less expensive and faster communications than the present system of satellite downloads, although the prospects of it being used to transmit a wide range of free information are far from clear.

In 1983, the US, whose resident Cuban exile community argues that Cubans are brainwashed by the absence of alternative and objective views, inaugurated Radio Martí which broadcasts to the island, much as Radio Free Europe did to communist countries during the Cold War. The Cuban government eventually jammed the broadcasts, which are mostly heard on shortwave elsewhere in the hemisphere. Public distrust of the US agenda and the tone of hostility to the revolution about which Cubans are conflicted, raise questions whether Radio Martí has much concrete purpose, especially as commercial radio from Miami floods Cuba as it is.

The US Interests Section and embassies of other democratic countries have always made available news and information bulletins about world events and bilateral relations. Some welcome Cuban Internet users to embassy facilities; however, a student reported being hauled off to a police station after a free Internet session at the US Interests Section (*The Economist,* 2011).

The US Interests Section has also organized meetings and workshops, and distributed publications and information material at every opportunity, making the information program its central activity. In 2006, the Interests Section ratcheted the campaign for freer information upward by installing an electronic news ticker along the top of its Havana building, attempting to rebut Cuban government claims and views. The Cuban authorities countered with a massive protest, constructed a plaza for popular demonstrations against the US adjacent to the building, and attempted to block the electronic ticker from view by masses of black flags.

The tit-for-tat campaign spurred on by Fidel Castro and the Bush administration has since been de-escalated, and the Obama administration pulled the plug of the electronic ticker in July 2009. Here too, the question arises as to where freedom of information access in Cuba is going. The evidence seems clear that the authorities know that there is no chance of Cuba going to the next level of economic development without enabling participation in the global information revolution.

Working with the Government

Advising

The prevailing approach of diplomatically represented democracies in Cuba toward working with the Cuban government is to do so without forfeiting the need to dialogue on human rights and to demarche the Cuban authorities when the situation calls for it.

A dominant theme of foreign analysis expects that significant political reform in Cuba is more likely to emerge from circles and developments within government than from its fragmented political opponents who are not well-known to a public immersed in state propaganda, and in any case, are preoccupied by bread-and-butter issues. Few Cuban officials, however, allow themselves to be perceived by foreigners as potential agents of democratic change. Still, the functional value of developing a wide range of confidence-building contacts among government officials, including in the FAR, is undoubted. US and Cuban military authorities have cooperated on issues arising from the US presence at Guantánamo and on maritime patrolling against drug trafficking; Canadian federal police work with the Cubans on trafficking issues; and several democracies' intelligence agencies have working relationships with Cuban counterparts at the Ministry of the Interior on concrete issues where notes can usefully be compared.

The Cuban regime projects an air of supreme self-confidence that narrows opportunities for diplomats to advise the government. But confidence-building activities addressing Cuban concerns are possible. The challenges of delivering large amounts of humanitarian aid in the aftermath of devastating hurricanes, costing 20 percent of GDP, engaged the Cuban authorities for the first time in working partnerships with foreign agencies and NGOs, prominent among them, Catholic Relief Services. Several embassies work on a variety of infrastructure and social issues with municipal levels of government and local co-ops, such as projects for restoration of historic monuments, buildings and whole neighbourhoods, partnered by agencies of EU member states.

US authorities have worked effectively with their Cuban counterparts over hostage and other emergencies, even at the height of tension in relations. Under the Obama administration, there is an increase in contacts, though diplomats report disappointment among Cubans that controls persist over scholarly and cultural exchanges. Cuban authorities allowed US military overflights for emergency relief operation after the Haiti earthquake, and Cuban medical teams participated in the international effort there, which represented a change from earlier international humanitarian operations in Haiti, when the Canadian prime minister's suggestion that Cuban cooperation be engaged ran into political complications.

Dialoguing

Dialoguing with Cuban authorities takes place at the political level — with possibly increasing degrees of frankness — with ministers and senior officials from Europe, Latin America and North America. Diplomats report that senior Cuban officials take non-polemical dialogue seriously. Several ambassadors report that it is productive not to work human rights into every discussion. This may have the effect of adding force to specific demarches on human rights.

However, declarations made by Western ministers for the benefit of their domestic audiences tend to undermine the credibility of such demarches in Cuban eyes. Publicly announced exercises in passing prisoners' lists generally remained without outcome, deflected with answers like, "We'll check," or "It's on Fidel's desk." But private communications in 2008 by then Cardinal Secretary of State Tarcisio Bertone and Pope John Paul II during his own visit in 1998, did have a more productive effect, as have the discussions undertaken by Cardinal Ortega, leading to release of the 52 remaining prisoners arrested in March 2003. Carefully pre-negotiated outcomes for specific head of government visits have obtained exit permits for designated Cuban activists accepted for asylum in the country concerned. This was done without publicity.

Reaching Out

Connecting

Connecting to civil society is essential to most democratic missions, though how to do so is carefully considered. It is obvious that civil society in Cuba is underdeveloped, not well networked, and could benefit from international contacts and non-political support, but the benefits to members of civil society have to be weighed against the risks of their being accused of being subject to foreign influence.

In 2011, the Community of Democracies bestowed a Palmer Award on Dutch diplomat Caecilia Wijgers in recognition of her support for civil society opposition groups in Cuba. She personally helped to distribute their positive literature (denounced as "subversive material and enemy propaganda" by security authorities) to other members of civil society.

British Ambassador Melrose echoed the position of several ambassadors of Community of Democracies countries when she stated, "We don't accept any government can tell us who we can or can't speak to. There are British and other EU ministers who would very much like to come to Cuba. But they insist on being able to have meetings with both their Cuban government counterparts and with whoever they choose from the peaceful opposition."

US diplomats from Washington relaunched immigration talks, which had been broken off by the US in 2003, shortly after President Obama's inauguration in 2009-2010, but made a point of meeting privately with opposition figures after concluding the round of talks with officials. Cuban spokesmen initially reacted wildly to the meetings, accusing the US officials of "plotting subversion" with "dozens of their mercenaries." US Assistant Secretary Crowley responded that "meeting with representatives of civil society who simply want a voice in the future of their country is not 'subversive.'" On February 23, 2010, Ricardo Alarcón, president of the Cuban Parliament, lowered the tone of Cuban reaction, observing that such meetings with civil society are not apt to "rupture the dialogue."

Democratic embassies follow different practices for purposes of connecting to specific figures of the peaceful opposition. Many designate officers within the embassy as the primary contact, without diminishing the ambassador's political commitment. Some missions, and notably US personnel, stress the symbolic importance of the head of mission being seen personally in acts of personal solidarity and outreach.

Some ambassadors make a point of not hosting political opposition figures at their official residences, instead receiving them privately in the embassy chancery. To meet opposition figures outside, some heads of mission tend to join events that include political activists hosted by other embassy officers. As Ambassador Melrose points out, visiting ministers and senior officials of Community of Democracies countries often insist on including in their programs meetings with opposition figures, but they also generally do so privately at their embassy chancery.

Embassies play an essential role in brokering and encouraging people-to-people exchanges with groups in their own countries. Cubans are deeply committed to high performance in culture and sports, and avidly welcome connections with partners and to events abroad. The Cuban authorities are wary, and of course the hardening of US rules on exchanges has limited interchange with America in recent years, though it is now showing signs of revival.

Convening

Convening opposition or civil society members invites friction with the Cuban government, but several democratic embassies have offered embassy venues for workshops or discussions on a good offices basis without specific political goals on issues that Cubans need to resolve among themselves.

Over recent years, different democratic embassies have taken a variety of approaches to inviting civil society representatives and political activists to official receptions. As Cuban authorities object to their presence, some embassies give two distinct receptions on national holidays, while others continue to mix them together, accepting that there will, in consequence, be fewer (if any) higher level representatives from the government. Cuban authorities can be volatile when embassies alter practice in favour of greater presence of democracy activists: one year, the authorities withheld an embassy's permit to clear liquor and wine through customs until after the reception — to which dissidents had been prominently invited — had taken place.

Facilitating

The fragmentation of Cuban democratic opposition poses the question of whether democratic embassies could facilitate greater cooperation by offering their neutral good offices to groups seeking to work together more effectively, as has been done in authoritarian settings elsewhere, such as Chile or South Africa. In Cuba, that would be difficult to do, except very indirectly. Embassies also facilitate contacts between Cuban citizens and family members outside Cuba, with several making Internet access available for this purpose.

Cuba has succeeded in exporting into exile much of its opposition. Several democracies facilitate refugee status for those seeking or having to leave Cuba, especially the US, Spain, Canada, Mexico, France and Chile. These are occasionally, as mentioned above, negotiated outcomes of high-level official visits.

There has been a long tradition of the Cuban exile diaspora seeking harmony of purpose with activists inside Cuba (Jose Martí's sojourn in the US prior to the 1895 rebellion comes to mind). Democratic governments and institutions abroad frequently sponsor workshops and colloquia on Cuban human rights issues. Because of the state control of media, however, these events have minimal direct resonance within Cuba, insulated by barriers to information from outside. Cuban writer Raúl Rivero was sentenced to 20 years in prison in 2003, but released in 2004 on health grounds. He expressed appreciation for his refuge in Spain, where he acknowledged that "the community has been very welcoming…The journalistic community has embraced me" (cited in Erikson, 2008). The harshness of conditions in Cuba, however, provided him with little opportunity for reconnecting. While the direct connections between dissidents outside and civil society inside may not be robust, the knowledge inside that such mobilization of outside democrats occurs provides moral reinforcement for Cuban democrats.

Financing

Financing civil society and NGOs is controversial and subject to close official scrutiny. Direct financial support for opposition groups has resulted in accusations that they are "mercenaries," and embassies avoid those situations. But fast-disbursing small amounts of support from the mission funds of democratic embassies can be of great value to groups working on development and social issues. Embassies value the opportunities that emerge at local levels for small projects where there is less likelihood the partnerships can be misconstrued as having a political rather than developmental, or even humanitarian, agenda. Sometimes, they make contributions anonymously.

Showcasing

Showcasing experience and creative cultural performance is central to public diplomacy in Cuba. Cuban artistic and cultural life has always been vibrant. Though constrained on issues of self-expression with any political implication, graphic art, music and dance are among art forms where Cuban performance has created an audience avid for connections to performance from outside.

Cuban youth are keen to have the opportunities to consume international popular culture. The rock music scene has emerged in strength and after an extended critical attitude, the regime has bowed to the inevitable strength of popular culture.

Embassies are able to invite external experts in a range of activities where the Cuban system needs development, or where the delivery of services falls short, as well as scholars to engage with Cuban researchers and academia. For some years, Canadian cooperation was typical in lending the benefits of Canadian experience to institution building that is not overtly political, but contributes to the habits of transparency and accountability, such as the development of effective committees in Parliament, systemically greater accountability of ministers and an ombudsman's office in government — though it should be noted there is considerable criticism in Canada over neglect of these practices in recent years at home. Another notable emphasis has been on decentralized partnership activity working with Cuban unions and housing, food production or microfinancing co-ops in the provinces.

Showcasing political examples can also be effective. The Cuban ambivalence about US involvement in Cuban affairs has always had at one pole the "America of Abraham Lincoln," whose Emancipation Proclamation had enormous impact on an island where, at the time, about half the population was composed of slaves and freed slaves originally from Africa. There are differing views as to the extent to which race relations are vexed in Cuba today. Ostensibly, Cuban society is non-racial, but interest is high in others' experiences in managing pluralistic societies. This is a difficult topic for Cuba's monolithic socialist model.

Defending Democrats

Demonstrating

Demonstrating solidarity with persecuted peaceful democracy activists is part and parcel of embassy support for the rights of freedom of assembly and speech that democratic countries represent. Embassy personnel can often provide a local focus to recognition extended by their governments and parliaments to local democrats, such as successive resolutions of the European Parliament criticizing Cuban human rights violations.

In bestowing an international profile along with its annual Andrei Sakharov Award, the European Parliament may also have afforded recipient Oswaldo Payá a degree of insulation from direct persecution. But this was not the case for the Damas de Blanco ("Ladies in White"), who also received the Sakharov Award. The Damas de Blanco are wives of prisoners of conscience, arrested in March 2003 and only released in 2010. To express their silent protest, the women attended mass on Sundays in Santa Rita Church in Havana's Quinta Avenida in Miramar before proceeding on an authorized 12-block walk in public. Clearly, the dignity and moral force of their protest irked authorities to the point of retaliation. In April 2010, pro-government groups harassed the Damas de Blanco (a frequent act of organized intimidation called an acto de repudio), at one point confining them under harsh abuse for several hours. In March 2012, several were arrested for deviating from the prescribed route. Diplomats responded in support. US diplomat Lowell Dale

Lawton attended mass with the women, and German and Czech embassy officers Volker Pellet and Frantisek Fleisman accompanied them on their walks.

Verifying and Witnessing

Verifying and witnessing is an important embassy function in regard to such acts of intimidation. Chris Stimpson of the UK Embassy described his presence as a witness at the confrontation with organized counterprotestors as constituting observation "to monitor human rights and freedom of expression."

Members of Cuba's dissident group Ladies in White demonstrate during their weekly march in Havana, Cuba, Sunday, January 30, 2011. Ladies in White is an organization created by wives and mothers of political prisoners. (AP Photo/Javier Galeano)

There are also efforts to verify the health of prisoners of conscience. Cuban authorities do not grant human rights monitors access to their prisons. Recently, some prisoners of conscience have undertaken hunger strikes. One of the 75 arrested in March 2003, Orlando Zapata Tamayo, died as a result of his hunger strike on February 23, 2010. Foreign leaders, such as US Secretary of State Clinton and Spanish Prime Minister Zapatero condemned the act, which Amnesty International called "a terrible illustration of the despair facing prisoners of conscience who see no hope of being freed from their unfair and prolonged incarceration." The Mexican and Chilean parliaments adopted similar declarations. President Raúl Castro expressed unusual public regret for Zapata's death, though the authorities then arrested dozens of his supporters to prevent them from attending the funeral. It was, however, attended by diplomats from several countries. There have been concessions since, worked out in a meeting in May 2010 between Raúl Castro and Cardinal Ortega. At the meeting, measures were taken to ensure adequate hospital treatment for sick prisoners and to move prisoners to their home provinces to facilitate family contacts and in July 2010, all 52 remaining prisoners from March 2003 were released.

In August 2009, five EU diplomats from Sweden, the UK, Hungary, Poland and the Czech Republic brought food and clothing to the wife of Darsi Ferrer, imprisoned without charge in July the day before he was to lead a demonstration for human rights. The Cuban Foreign Ministry protested that "the EU is putting in danger the political dialogue begun with Cuba," but as Sven Kühn von Burgsdorff, an EU mission spokesman in Havana restated about the EU's policy on the occasion of relaunching the dialogue, "there is no reason to lack trust in our desire to do both things at the same time — improve dialogue with the government, and with civil society, including the peaceful opposition."

Such acts by diplomats, demonstrating solidarity and witnessing events, have the effect of offering some protection to activists and human rights defenders who have already courageously crossed the line of protest so that gestures of moral support for their rights do not expose them particularly to greater danger.

Direct acts of protection have also been performed by embassies in Havana over the years. Dr. Sweig (2009) records the most prominent of these:

> By March of 1980 a handful of Cuban citizens had already smuggled themselves into foreign embassies in search of asylum. The Peruvian embassy was one target, and the Peruvian government was not at the time disposed to return the intruders to Cuban authorities. Later that month, when several Cubans crashed a bus into the gate of the Peruvian complex and provoked a violent incident with Cuban soldiers, Fidel responded by removing all police protection from embassy grounds. Within 48 hours, over 10,000 citizens had taken refuge inside the gates.

Ernesto Pinto-Bazurco Rittler was the chargé d'affaires of Peru at the time and a staunch defender of non-violence, democracy and human rights in Cuba. He met with Fidel Castro and refused to hand the asylum seekers over to Cuban authorities. In 2012, Ambassador Rittler was awarded a Palmer Prize by the Community of Democracies.

The episode led to the Mariel boatlift, once US President Carter said he would open America's doors to Cubans wishing to leave. Fidel Castro took up the offer, and within months, 125,000 Cubans emigrated.

SUMMING UP/LOOKING FORWARD

Cuba represents a complex challenge for democratic diplomats today. Pressing the regime to drop its absolutist doctrines in favour of a full-blown democracy is unrewarding in practical terms, and yet, a relativist approach that concedes that the denial of essential and universal human rights can be overlooked is not one that most members of the Community of Democracies can accept.

Clearly, in Cuba, a transition is actually already underway. A successor to Raúl Castro, the Minister of Education, Miguel Díaz-Canel Bermudez, has been designated. An era will end. The outcome is unpredictable, though it is clear that the Cuban population, especially younger Cubans, want to be part of their open hemispheric world and the wider world. Diplomats in Cuba from democracies represent links to that aspiration and are its witnesses on behalf of democrats everywhere, all the while trying to engage the Cuban authorities in activity and contact that will help improve the situation of Cubans today.

There is an irreducible quid pro quo the EU and other democratic partners and their embassies keep in mind.

The US administration is also working for more normal relations. Perhaps US President Obama's words of advice for Spanish Prime Minister Zapatero in 2010 best sum up the prognosis, "Have the Foreign Minister (Miguel Angel Moratinos) tell the Cuban authorities we understand that change can't happen overnight, but down the road, when we both look at this time, it should be clear that now is when those changes began."

Ted Piccone (2013) of Brookings underlines that "the trend toward reform in Cuba is evident." He argues that the "new circumstances in Cuba offer President Obama a rare opportunity to turn the page of history from an outdated Cold War approach to a new era of constructive engagement." Undoubtedly, it will be welcomed by Cubans themselves.

In April 2013, Yoani Sanchez, who had finally been granted permission to travel abroad, addressed an audience in Miami, rejecting the false notion that Cubans had to choose between "the Cuba of Fidel" or "the Cuba of Miami." They are not, in her words, "two separate worlds, two irreconcilable worlds," but belong both "to the Cuba of Jose Martí."

> At the Community of Democracies' tenth anniversary ministerial meeting, held July 2-3, 2011 in Kraków, Poland, Father Jose Conrado of Santa Teresita de Jesus parish, Santiago de Cuba, received the Bronislaw Geremek Award for his longstanding and courageous dedication to the defense of civil and human rights in Cuba.

WORKS CITED

Anderson, Jon Lee (1997). *Che Guevara: A Revolutionary Life*. New York: Grove Press.

The Economist (2011). "The Start of a Long, Slow Goodbye." *The Economist*, April 20.

——— (2013). "A New Course: A Tale of Politics, Corruption and Golf." *The Economist*, May 25.

Erikson, Daniel P. (2008). *The Cuba Wars: Fidel Castro, the United States, and the Next Revolution*. New York: Bloombury Press.

Estrada, Alfredo José (2008). *Havana: Autobiography of a City*. New York: Palgrave Macmillan.

Human Rights Watch (1999). *Cuba's Repressive Machinery: Human Rights Forty Years After the Revolution*. Available at: www.hrw.org/reports/1999/06/01/cubas-repressive-machinery.

——— (2012). *World Report 2012*. New York: Human Rights Watch. Available at: www.hrw.org/world-report-2012.

Levy, Bruce (2009). "Cuba: An International Perspective." Remarks made at the Center for Strategic and International Studies Cuba Outlook Series Conference, July 23.

Llosa, Alvaro Vargas (2011). "Castro Brothers Still Play the 'Socialist' Card." *The Globe and Mail*, April 27.

Morley, Morris (2004). "The United States Rules Cuba, 1952–1958." In *The Cuba Reader*, edited by Aviva Chomsky, Barry Carr and Pamela Maria Smorkaloff. Pages 321–325. Durham: Duke University Press.

Piccone, Ted (2013). "Time to Bet on Cuba." Brookings blog post, March 18. Available at: www.brookings.edu/research/opinions/2013/03/18-cuba-piccone.

Pietroni, Patrick (2009). "Constructive Engagement." *The International Journal of Cuban Studies* 2, no. 1: 105–114.

Prieto, José Manuel (2011). "Havana: The State Retreats." *The New York Review of Books*, May 26.

RAND Corporation (2004). "A Legacy of Dysfunction: Cuba after Fidel." RAND Corporation Research Brief.

Sweig, Julia E. (2009). *Cuba: What Everyone Needs to Know*. New York: Oxford University Press.

Sweig, Julia E. and Michael J. Bustamente (2013). "Cuba After Communism." *Foreign Affairs*, July/August.

Verma, Sonia (2011). "Small Acts of Free Enterprise Attest to Reform Looming Large in Cuba." *The Globe and Mail*, October 18.

Wilkinson, Daniel and Nik Steinberg (2010). "Cuba — A Way Forward." *The New York Review of Books*, May 27.

4 CAN EGYPTIANS BUILD A CONSENSUS FOR FUNCTIONING DEMOCRACY?

*By Stephen McInerney, Moataz El Fegiery,
Michele Dunne, Issandr El Amrani and Kurt Bassuener,
2010; revised by Kurt Bassuener and Jeremy Kinsman,
2013*

Nota Bene: As the Handbook's *third edition goes to publication in late July 2013, the political situation is remains dire and fluid. In June and early July, widespread protests against President Morsi continued to grow. The Army threatened to intervene should no compromise be reached. On July 3, it followed through on its threat, ousting Morsi in a coup and detaining him with several other senior fellow Muslim Brotherhood figures. At time of writing, an interim government selected by Army Chief of Staff and Defence Minister Abdel Fattah al-Sisi is in control, proclaiming a "road map" back to democracy and the amendment of the controversial constitution that was adopted in a referendum in December 2012. The Muslim Brotherhood and its supporters have mounted widespread protests against the coup, calling for Morsi's reinstatement; scores have died in clashes surrounding these demonstrations. Wide restrictions on the media, especially those aligned with the Brotherhood and the ousted Morsi government, have been instituted. More than 1,000 citizens have been arrested, though a majority of them were later released (Hauslohner, 2013). The divide in Egyptian society — between those opponents of the Brotherhood and what they characterize as its insular and exclusivist decision making, and the Brotherhood, which claims electoral and democratic legitimacy — is deeper and wider than ever before. The military and security forces, which both sides attempted to enlist, maintains decisive power in determining the direction of the country.*

External actors, particularly the United States, have struggled to manage this growing divide. Widely reported attempts were made to convince President Morsi to reach out more to his secular and liberal opponents and include them in decision making and governing (Kirkpatrick and El Sheikh, 2013) — but these were fruitless. Washington now is avoiding the use of the term "coup," as, by law, it would necessitate a curtailment of foreign assistance to Egypt. The US position in Egypt now is at the lowest ebb since the Sadat era, with all actors suspicious of its motives and seeing it as having supported or lent succor to their opponents.

INTRODUCTION

Of all the case studies covered in the *Handbook*, Egypt has seen the most wrenching change since 2011 — even more than in Burma/Myanmar. It remains the centre of gravity of the Arab Spring, which began in Tunisia some weeks before its own revolutionary change began.

A proud nation with an ancient history, Egypt lies at the heart of the Arab world and is typically viewed as a bellwether for broader trends in the region. With a population of over 80 million — more than twice that of any other Arab state — and its location bridging both Africa to the Middle East and the Mediterranean to the Red Sea, Egypt has long played a pivotal role in the region. Egyptian support over time for the Middle East peace process has been crucial to US foreign policy interests.

In a region that has seen more than its share of internal political crises — military coups, civil wars and revolutions — Egypt stands out as having, until recently, experienced remarkable continuity in its domestic political scene, though the apparent stability masked significant and rising public discontent. Since the early 1920s, Egypt's political system has undergone fundamental change only twice — from a constitutional monarchy under strong British influence to an independent, authoritarian state in the 1950s, in which the military played a guiding role, and, beginning in 2011, when the authoritarian rule of Hosni Mubarak was defeated by a broad and popular revolution. The shift to popularly elected government was bewildering for all involved. Deep social and political cleavages, which the context of authoritarian rule kept in the relative background, have now come to the fore, including, prominently, the challenge of reconciling widespread religious faith and democracy. The military has proven a decisive factor, holding the balance of power between religious and secular/liberal political forces. Despite the massive changes already seen, Egypt's successful transition to functioning broad-based democracy is far from assured.

Historical Background

Since the early nineteenth century, Egypt's history has been marked by Western colonial intervention, beginning with the arrival of French troops in 1798. Throughout the first half of the 1800s, Egypt was governed by Muhammad Ali Pasha, a governor in the declining Ottoman Empire who instituted far-reaching military, economic and cultural reforms that turned Egypt into one of the most modern, developed states outside of Europe at that time. Such efforts at modernization, culminating in the Suez Canal project, drove Egypt into severe debt, facilitating the colonial penetration of Britain, which maintained control of Egypt through World War I. After the war, the British declared Egypt's nominal independence in 1922 and instituted a constitutional, parliamentary monarchy, which would remain in place until 1952. The nationalist Wafd ("delegation") Party, which had led the domestic movement for Egyptian independence, dominated parliamentary elections throughout this period. In July 1952, British-backed King Farouk was overthrown by the Free Officers Movement, a group of Egyptian Army officers led by Colonel Gamal Abdel Nasser, who became president of Egypt and would rule the country until his death in 1970.

Upon seizing power, Nasser began to gradually establish authoritarian control over the Egyptian state, banning all political parties in 1952. Two years later, he also banned the Muslim Brotherhood organization. Following an October 1954 assassination attempt by a Muslim Brotherhood member, the Nasser regime jailed thousands of Brotherhood activists.

Nasser also eventually nationalized banks, private commercial enterprises and the Suez Canal, thus consolidating the authority of the Egyptian state over both the political and economic spheres. He established a short-lived union with Syria and later Iraq, the United Arab Republic, which dissolved in 1961. In 1962, Nasser established the Arab Socialist Union as the dominant ruling political party, representing Egypt's ruling elite.

With the death of Nasser in 1970, Vice President Anwar Sadat, another one of the "free officers" of the 1952 coup, became president. Early in his rule, President Sadat oversaw the establishment of a new constitution for Egypt. This 1971 constitution legally consolidated power in the hands of the president and rendered ostensibly democratic institutions such as Parliament as weak and inconsequential. Sadat undertook dramatic steps toward shifting Egypt's external orientation, as he expelled Soviet advisers in 1972 and changed the dynamics with Israel by initiating the October War in 1973. Following the 1973 war, the US became deeply engaged in promoting dialogue between Egypt and Israel, and eventual negotiations toward a peace settlement. This culminated in Sadat's historic visit to Jerusalem in 1977, followed by the Camp David Accords of 1978 and the Israel-Egypt Peace Treaty in 1979. This solidified Egypt's standing as a uniquely powerful Arab ally to the West (particularly to the United States), while marginalizing Egypt in the Arab and Muslim world, symbolized by the Arab League expelling Egypt and moving its headquarters to Tunis. During this period, Sadat also reinstated nominal political pluralism, creating "loyal opposition" parties representing various political orientations, allowing the Wafd Party to re-emerge and allowing limited political and organizational activity by the Muslim Brotherhood.

Following the assassination of Sadat in 1981 by Islamists opposed to Camp David, his vice president and Air Force commander, Mohammed Hosni Mubarak succeeded him. Egypt experienced a short-lived period of tempered liberalization under Mubarak during the 1980s. The parliamentary elections of 1987, for example, created an assembly with 22 percent opposition representation. This trend was abruptly curtailed in the 1990s, however, as a resurgence of domestic terrorism spurred the regime to crack down on political opposition and close the narrow openings that had emerged in the political landscape.

After 2000, the ruling National Democratic Party (NDP) began to show signs of internal reform. The NDP was embarrassed by its initial showing in the 2000 parliamentary elections, in which independent candidates (most of whom later allied themselves to the NDP) won a majority of seats. This spurred the emergence of a new wave of younger-generation, Western-educated reformers within the NDP who aimed to increase Egyptian economic performance while ensuring party dominance — without opening up the political system, and by offering major economic rewards directed mainly to a cabal of party loyalists. This group was led by President Mubarak's son Gamal, who was appointed chairman of the newly instituted Policy Secretariat — the third-ranking position in the NDP — in 2002. Gamal Mubarak and his Policy Secretariat allies led an effort to transform the NDP into a modern institution modelled after Western political parties. The group around Gamal Mubarak was slick and well-schooled in marketing for Western investors and political elites, but this group had a very narrow base. They were suspected by the military of aiming to curtail their economic dominion, and by the opposition (civic and religious), which saw them as simply well-connected crony capitalists driven to ensure a dynastic succession.

Era of Hope (2004-2005)

By 2004, there were a number of signs of the potential for real political reform, owing, in part, to external pressures. In July 2004, a new cabinet was appointed, featuring Prime Minister Ahmed Nazif and 14 new ministers — most of whom were Gamal Mubarak's allies from the Policy Secretariat — who were widely perceived to be economic reformers. The Egyptian political opposition also showed signs of emerging pluralism and dynamism at this time. In late 2004 and early 2005, a new, loosely knit coalition of reformers known as Kifaya ("enough") emerged, organizing an unprecedented series of regular protests calling for political reform and openly criticizing the Mubarak regime. The licensing of the new secular, liberal Al-Ghad Party, founded by Ayman Nour, a younger generation MP who had broken ranks with the Wafd Party in 2001, also occurred in 2004.

In addition, the leading Islamist movement in Egypt, the Muslim Brotherhood, which provided extensive social services, showed signs of modernizing and embracing reform at this time, issuing a pro-democracy reform initiative in March 2004. In February 2005, President Mubarak proposed a constitutional amendment to allow for Egypt's first multi-candidate presidential election. Moreover, the Muslim Brotherhood, though it remained banned and could only run candidates for parliamentary elections as independents, was nonetheless allowed to campaign openly and given much greater access to the media. The 2005 elections also saw the first widespread election monitoring by independent NGOs. Although the elections were marred by serious irregularities, the presence of thousands of monitors in polling stations trained by Egyptian NGOs was widely viewed as an important step forward, establishing the legitimacy of independent election monitors.

Disillusionment and Regression on Reform

Despite the many signs of progress on democratic development by mid-2005, the late 2005 elections did not meet expectations. By 2006, the trends toward reform sharply reversed. Following the presidential election, Nour — the only candidate who ran a serious campaign in opposition to President Mubarak — was convicted and sentenced to five years in prison for dubious charges of forging signatures during the formation of his Al-Ghad Party. He served more than three years in jail. Following the better-than-expected performance of the Muslim Brotherhood in the first round of parliamentary elections in November 2005, the second and third rounds were marred by increasingly blatant interference, with neighbourhoods sympathetic to the Brotherhood seeing their polling stations closed down and widespread violence used to prevent voting. Since those elections, Brotherhood members were targeted in a series of campaigns with arrests and seizure of financial assets.

In April 2006, the Mubarak government extended the emergency law, despite 2005 campaign promises to eliminate it and replace it with a narrower set of anti-terrorism laws. Efforts to stifle public discourse through targeted jailing, intimidation and prosecution of dissenting voices, including bloggers and editors of independent newspapers, increased considerably beginning in 2006. In a single vote in Parliament in early 2007, the Egyptian government passed a set of constitutional amendments described by Amnesty International as the "greatest erosion of human rights [in Egypt] in 26 years." These included measures expanding the authority of military courts over civilians, weakening the authority of the Egyptian judiciary to supervise elections and legally prohibiting the formation of political parties or any political activity with "any religious frame of reference." This last amendment was clearly intended to block the main opposition group, the Muslim Brotherhood. Nearly all opposition candidates aiming to run for seats in the Shura Council (the upper house of Parliament) in 2007 and municipal councils in 2008 were denied registration by the authorities.

Intercommunal violence flared in early 2010, with a shooting outside a Coptic church and clashes with police. Later that year, more clashes between Copts and police took place in Giza over church construction. A church bombing on Orthodox New Year 2011 killed 21 in Alexandria, sparking further clashes and recriminations (BBC News, 2013). Sectarianism was rising, with the government increasingly seen as insensitive to Christian Copt concerns and allegations of discrimination and ill treatment by authorities.

Revolution and Post-revolution

With the launch of Tunisian popular demand for the end of the Ben Ali regime, Egyptians soon launched their own demonstrations against President Mubarak's nearly 30-year rule, peaceably assembling in Egypt's Tahrir ("freedom") Square and in other locations in Cairo, Alexandria, Suez and elsewhere throughout Egypt beginning on January 25, 2011. The velocity of the protest buildup, fuelled by the extensive use of social media, took citizens and the government alike by surprise; the latter showed itself to be behind the curve in response through much of the 18 days of protest prior to Mubarak stepping down. "When it erupted, the Egyptian revolution surprised civil society as much as it did the political forces," seasoned observer Mohamed Elegati noted (2012).

Attempts to shut down communications in late January had a contrary effect to what the Mubarak regime wanted: more people came to the street to demonstrate. When President Mubarak addressed an expectant nation without offering his resignation, the public reaction was indignant. Shoes were thrown at large screens projecting his address and those assembled jeered. Attempts to foment popular fears of chaos in true "après moi, le deluge" fashion followed — police disappearing, baltagiya (regime-paid thugs) staging crimes and a genuine reduction in public safety did not break the demonstrators' resolve. An attempt by security force proxies on camels and horseback to violently drive the camp out of Tahrir Square was similarly ineffectual. Broad social solidarity was also evident. In the words of one observer, looking back, "There was unity in the revolution, and not simply on getting rid of Mubarak. You could see Salafists and liberals cooperating closely."[1] The Muslim Brotherhood, long persecuted by the Mubarak regime (and his two predecessors), did not take a leading role initially in the protest movement, though it did later engage in it. The Egyptian Army was generally neutral and did not crack down on the demonstrations, despite fears it might be ordered to. The dramatic events transfixed the world, dominating television screens for weeks as the long-serving leadership was driven from power by popular will, not force. The Egyptian revolution was not without violence, however; an estimated 850 people were killed in the unrest.

The departure of Mubarak did not signal a linear path toward fully functioning democratic rule. The Supreme Council of the Armed Forces took interim control of Egypt. Suspicions among large segments of the revolutionary public grew over time that the military had abandoned an unpopular president but had no intention of abandoning its privileged and commanding role in Egyptian society. Many doubted they would abandon their privileges without a struggle and voiced fears that Mubarak's departure would be far easier than uprooting the military-industrial complex in Egypt. As preparations were made for new elections in spring and summer 2011, demonstrations continued in Tahrir Square to demand faster movement toward unfettered democratic rule and civilian control. The Muslim Brotherhood emerged as a more vocal player in street politics at this stage. The square was cleared in August 2011. The same month, former President Mubarak was put on trial for

---

1   Participant at "Pluralism and Democracy: Prospects for the Arab Middle East and North Africa," European Council on Foreign Relations and Council for a Community of Democracies round table. Canadian Cultural Centre, Paris, December 6-7, 2012.

ordering the killing of demonstrators (BBC News, 2013). Further demonstrations in Tahrir Square occurred in November 2011 against continued military control. Prime Minister Essam Sharaf resigned in response. Parliamentary elections began that month (ibid.).

In January 2012, Islamist parties, with the Muslim Brotherhood's Freedom and Justice Party as the largest single vote draw, won the parliamentary elections. In an election with low turnout, the Brotherhood's cohesion and discipline contrasted with the confusing profusion of "secular" democratic parties, which together, rivalled the Brotherhood in popular support, but split the non-Islamist vote among them. Many observers, including foreign diplomats, were surprised by the strength of religion-based parties, including the more orthodox and hardline Salafists.

In May and June 2012 presidential elections, the Brotherhood's former second in command Mohamed Morsi eked out a narrow victory over former Mubarak-era Prime Minister Ahmed Shafiq, who was seen by many as a stalking horse for the Army. However, fears of Islamist political strength led many secularists, including long-time opposition figures, to plump for Shafiq, despite his baggage. This generated discord not only between the Brotherhood and non-Islamist political actors, but among the non-Islamists themselves. So despite having lost the presidential election, the military and security state emerged with perhaps greater leverage after the election than before (ibid.).

Morsi made an effort to proclaim himself as president of all Egyptians, but many remained skeptical of the Brotherhood's intentions in power. In June 2012, the Supreme Court ruled that the parliamentary elections were invalid. While initially resisting the ruling (in a court dominated by jurists from the *ancien régime*), President Morsi adhered to it in July. In August, Prime Minister Hisham Qandil formed a government composed of Islamists and technocrats, bereft of liberals, secularists and non-Islamists in general, further generating suspicion. That same month, jihadists attacked an Army outpost in the Sinai, killing 16 soldiers — the largest number of Army casualties since the 1973 war. President Morsi took the opportunity to dismiss Defence Minister Tantawi and the chief of staff, demonstrating civilian supremacy over the military for the first time since the revolution.

In the absence of an elected Parliament, a constituent assembly composed primarily of Islamists — most secularists had earlier withdrawn — prepared to submit a draft constitution, but President Morsi stated on November 22, 2012 that there was no authority that could overturn his decrees. This generated much protest domestically — and internationally. Public protests followed and it was later rescinded, grudgingly. Nonetheless, the draft constitution was put to public referendum in December 2012 and passed. Violent street protests followed into January 2013, killing 50 people. As 2013 went on, critics of President Morsi have come up for prosecution for insulting him and offending religious Egyptians with satire. In early June 2013, the Supreme Constitutional Court ruled that the rules by which the constitution had been prepared had been illegal, placing the legitimacy of that popularly adopted foundational document into question.

Economic factors were very prominent in public disaffection from the Mubarak regime, especially on the part of the large class of underemployed professionals unable to pursue satisfactory careers in a culture of cronyism and corruption. Since the revolution, social cleavages and discontent with the lack of opportunity have deepened, especially since, as a result of the political turmoil, both tourism and investment have been hit hard, further increasing economic hardship on the Egyptian people.

International Policy Responses

Egypt's relations with its Western allies, and particularly with the United States, have long included strategic and economic partnership. The centrality of Egypt to the US agenda because of Sadat's "separate peace" with Israel deepened once the "war on terror" took over the US security agenda. Egypt became a key US partner in anti-terrorism and a favoured locale for the rendition of international terrorism suspects. The 2003 invasion of Iraq, which was vastly opposed by public opinion across the Middle East — including in Egypt, reinforced US commitment to Mubarak who was persuaded to support the US role.

There was, nonetheless, some attempt to pursue a reform agenda. Throughout the 1980s, Egypt partnered with the US on a series of economic reforms and modest steps toward political liberalization. In the 1990s, US Vice President Al Gore established a direct partnership with President Mubarak, including regular meetings between the two to address opportunities for reform. The EU's collective approach, largely subsumed under the 1995 Barcelona Process, dealt with economic prosperity, political stability and security questions such as counterterrorism and migration control.

Such partnerships, however, generally focussed more on economic reform and development than political opening. Some analysts and government officials in the US and Europe came to believe that Egypt's lack of progress on economic development owed much to its clear lack of political development, but the overarching policies did not change. The attacks of September 11, 2001 might have brought the repressive political climates across the Arab world into sharper focus, but had the effect instead of driving policy choices in the opposite direction.

US President George W. Bush's "freedom agenda" did include the use of various diplomatic techniques to spur political reform in Egypt. These appeared to contribute to some tangible steps in 2004 and 2005, such as the institution of direct popular election of the president, the organization of a large-scale electoral monitoring effort by civil society organizations, a loosening of restrictions on the media and freer campaigning by the opposition groups. EU support for these democracy promotion policies was muted; these countries had considerable business interests in Egypt. In private, European diplomats expressed skepticism that the policies would be effective. This was particularly the case with Mediterranean countries such as France and Italy, where political elites had good relations with the Mubarak regime, and where public opinion feared the risk of waves of refugees if the regimes in the region were destabilized.

The European approach was packaged alongside the promotion of trade ties and economic reform in the European Neighbourhood Policy, but the approach was heavily statist, confined mostly to cooperation with state or para-state institutions, and not with civil society. The EU's overall interest in supporting democratic development and respect for human rights was generally less pronounced in the Middle East than, for instance, in parts of Sub-Saharan Africa. In the words of German scholar Annette Jünemann (2012), "convinced that Arab autocracy [was] insuperable and misperceiving the aspirations and capabilities of modern Arab society, the EU opted for autocratic regimes." A number of factors played into this stance, including a fear of Islamist political movements becoming dominant in a more democratic environment, mass migration and senior officials' desire to have easy access to their Egyptian counterparts because of a wish to stabilize the Middle East peace process and to promote bilateral business opportunities.

Although the EU approach tended to favour a more incremental (or implied) approach to democracy promotion, compared to the more robust US approach, there was wide divergence between EU member states on this issue throughout the Middle East, and with regard to Egypt in particular. Generally speaking, southern and Mediterranean European countries, which had stronger trade and security ties with Egypt (and neuralgic fears about migration), were increasingly reluctant to focus on democracy and human rights issues in their bilateral relations. Scandinavian and other northern European countries, on the other hand, have had fewer economic interests in Egypt and manifested the strongest interest on issues of democracy and human rights. This was evident from their greater focus on these issues at the embassy level and when coordinating EU policy in Brussels, as well as a greater proportion of their aid funding being earmarked for civil society support.

By early 2006, the US administration's support for democracy in Egypt tapered off. Following the better-than-anticipated success of the Muslim Brotherhood in Egypt's parliamentary elections in late 2005, the United States became more apprehensive about the prospect of Egyptian democracy. This was then exacerbated by the Hamas victory in the January 2006 Palestinian elections (aggressively pressed for by the US), viewed by some as a warning of what could happen if Egypt were pushed to democratize. In addition, the effort to isolate the Hamas-controlled Palestinian Authority became a focus of US policy in the region, drawing energy and resources away from other priorities, including support for Egyptian reform. In the summer of 2006, the administration's focus was further diverted by the escalation of the Fatah versus Hamas conflict in Gaza and the Israeli attack on Lebanon. By January 2008, the Bush administration began to look toward the renewal of the Arab-Israeli peace process through a conference in Annapolis, the success of which would rely on Mubarak's cooperation. Around the same time, the administration also began to focus more on aligning its Arab allies against the threat of Iran's growing regional influence and nuclear program. Both of these issues contributed to a shift toward viewing Arab allies such as Egypt primarily as regimes needed for strategic purposes, further decreasing the emphasis on issues of internal reform.

President Obama attempted to reboot US relations with the Muslim world by giving an address at Cairo University on June 6, 2009. The speech was well received in much of the region, notably for its respectful approach to Islam and recognition of Palestinian suffering. President Obama raised the issue of democracy almost apologetically, recognizing that it had been tarred by association with the invasion of Iraq, adding "no system of government can or should be imposed upon one nation by any other." He reiterated the US commitment to freedom of speech, rule of law, good governance and transparency. He also added a thinly veiled reference to Islamists, echoing Bush administration concerns after Hamas' electoral victory in 2006:

> There are some who advocate for democracy only when they are out of power; once in power, they are ruthless in suppressing the rights of others. No matter where it takes hold, government of the people and by the people sets a single standard for all who hold power: you must maintain your power through consent, not coercion; you must respect the rights of minorities, and participate with a spirit of tolerance and compromise; you must place the interests of your people and the legitimate workings of the political process above your party. Without these ingredients, elections alone do not make true democracy.

This signalled a move away from a primary focus on elections in US democracy promotion, later confirmed in statements by US Secretary of State Hillary Clinton. While it is true that elections alone do not ensure democracy, within the Egyptian context this was tantamount to a pro-government position. For the three years prior to the speech, the Egyptian regime engaged in a campaign of arrests against the Muslim Brotherhood not seen since the late 1960s, blocking them from participating in elections and amending the constitution to block their ambitions to launch a political party. Overall, the speech not only contained little of substance on human rights, but was also criticized by some for having taken place in Cairo at all, since it boosted a close US ally that, between 2006 and 2009, reversed tentative moves toward democratization and continued to be a serial abuser of human rights. Indeed, primary focus of the speech (and, as a result, in US funding) was given to women's and minority rights from a US agenda, and away from the reform issues more prominent as factors in Egyptian public discontent.

Under the Obama administration, the previous administration's policy effectively continued until 2011. In part, this occurred since the relevant senior officials in the State Department were not appointed until December 2009. But concern had shifted from pressuring Egypt to reform to supporting what was seen as an increasingly weak state ahead of an uncertain presidential succession process. In 2009, then Ambassador to Egypt Margaret Scobey's chief mission was seen to be repairing the bilateral relationship that had been strained (outside of security issues) by the

Bush administration. She had considerable room to manoeuvre to achieve this in the absence of clear leadership in the State Department and US focus on other issues, most notably the global economic crisis.

With President Mubarak's three-week hospitalization in Munich for gall bladder surgery in March 2010, the question of succession became the primary interest of US civilian and military policy makers, with a first priority being ensuring minimum political turmoil during a transition period. Secretary of State Clinton downgraded the importance of reform issues in the bilateral relationship, focussing instead on strengthening Egypt's role in the Middle East peace process and assuring a smooth presidential transition.

Many European countries were relieved by the change in the US approach. From 2007 onwards, even before the launch of French President Nicolas Sarkozy's pet Mediterranean Union project in 2008, the European Commission, for all intents and purposes, downgraded the question of support for democratization and human rights to the minimum. Advocates for greater focus on political reform issues were told over this period not to expect any EU engagement. Conciliatory attitudes toward the government of Egypt were the general rule. As Jünemann (2012) assessed, "For the EU, which has extremely dense yet almost exclusively intergovernmental relations with its southern neighbors, the Arab Spring was a mortifying embarrassment because it revealed the credibility gap between the EU's normative rhetoric on democracy promotion and its 'realpolitik' on the ground, supporting autocratic regimes at the cost of domestic agents of change…The EU hesitated to change sides as long as it was unclear whether the revolutions would succeed."

Western democracies were essentially caught flat-footed by the advent of revolutionary change in the MENA region, and were particularly ill prepared for it in the case of Egypt. The mental and policy dissonance generated by the upwelling of popular demands for Mubarak's departure was perhaps best spotlighted in a US public broadcasting interview of Vice President Joe Biden in late January 2011. When questioned whether Mubarak was a dictator, Biden replied: "Mubarak has been an ally of ours in a number of things. And he's been very responsible on, relative to geopolitical interest in the region, the Middle East peace efforts; the actions Egypt has taken relative to normalizing relationship with — with Israel….I would not refer to him as a dictator" (cited in Murphy, 2011). Biden added that he didn't believe Mubarak should step down, and appeared to question the legitimacy of some of the protesters' demands (ibid.). While later pronouncements by Western leaders adapted to changing conditions, they were often far behind the curve. However, as this case study shows, Vice President Biden himself became very heavily engaged in pressing the Mubarak regime and the security apparatus (mainly through his counterpart Vice President Omar Suleiman) to refrain from cracking down violently and to respond to persistent and growing popular demands for change (BBC News, 2011).

Resources and Assets of Diplomats in Egypt

For more than three decades, Egypt has consistently received **funds** from the West on a large scale. In conjunction with the signing of the Camp David Accords in 1978 and the Israel-Egypt Peace Treaty in 1979, The US agreed to give billions in foreign assistance to each of the two countries, with overall assistance to Israel and Egypt remaining in a fixed 3:2 ratio until 2008. From 1979 to 2008, Egypt was the second-largest recipient of US foreign assistance each year, after Israel (in fiscal year 2009, Egypt was surpassed by Afghanistan in this regard, and Afghanistan and Pakistan have since each received more foreign aid than Egypt).

Egypt has received US$1.3 billion in military assistance each year since 1987. Economic assistance decreased from more than US$800 million annually in the late 1990s to around US$400 million in 2008 and roughly US$250 million in 2009 and 2010. Funding for democracy and governance programming peaked at approximately US$55 million in fiscal year 2008.

Because of restrictions within Egypt and political considerations on the donor and consumer side, funds spent often do not have significant effect. The US, in particular, has occasionally had difficulties finding competent recipients; many NGOs coming from a leftist perspective, for example, refused any dealings with the Bush administration. This may have contributed to the misspending of much of the funding available to USAID and the US-Middle East Partnership Initiative, with NGOs created for the sole purpose of drawing such funds. There is a great degree of clientelism in the local NGO market, with projects being designed to meet donor criteria, rather than being based on actual local needs.

Under the Obama administration, the US government returned to a practice that had been stopped in 2002, which was only granting USAID funding to civil society groups that were registered under the notoriously restrictive and much-criticized Egyptian NGO law. The Obama administration sharply reduced bilateral funding for democracy and governance programs in Egypt for fiscal years 2009 and 2010 to around US$20 million annually. Following Egypt's 2011 revolution, President Obama committed US$1 billion in non-military assistance (mostly economic) to Egypt, as well as the Egyptian-American Enterprise Fund, with an initial endowment of US$60 million, scheduled to rise to US$300 million (Kerry, 2013b).

Democracy support funding, however, was stymied by Egypt's crackdown on financial support from outside for NGOs. Security forces raided the offices of hundreds of foreign and Egyptian NGOs in a classic exhibition of "fear of foreign meddling."

In 2013, Egyptian courts found a wide swath of foreign NGOs guilty of illegally interfering in Egyptian affairs by providing financial support to Egyptian NGOs. US NGOs such as Freedom House, which had only opened an office after the revolution, and the arms of the National Endowment for Democracy, which had operated in Egypt for decades, were found guilty and forced to close. As Sherif Mansour, an activist forced into exile in 2006 who had returned to open Freedom House's office in 2011, reflected, "I felt that this revolution would only succeed if NGOs and the judiciary are free and independent….so far, it has been a big disappointment" (cited in Hubbard, 2013).

Egyptian civil society analyst Mohamed Elegati (2013) has described the law as having three fundamental characteristics: "the near-absolute power of the Ministry of Social Solidarity; stiffening penalties which excessively criminalize and punish the activities of [civil society organizations]; and ambiguous terminology, such as forbidding organizations from performing any 'political activities' [Article 11/3] or disturbing 'public order' [Article 11/2], which gives way to arbitrariness on behalf of the government." He added that the intelligence services were regularly consulted to vet applicants for licensing to receive foreign funds. Since requests were rarely responded to within the 45-day window stipulated by law, NGOs were left in legal limbo and accepted foreign funds at their own risk (ibid.). Although additional democracy and governance funding was available without strings through the Middle East Partnership Initiative, activists said that the funding cuts were not as important as the political message that the change in practice sent, i.e., that the US government considered the NGO law acceptable. The new Morsi government passed a new NGO law that is "even more repressive," legalizing "direct intervention of the security services on the work of civil society" and lacking transparency provisions (ibid.). The US and EU both decried the new law, with EU foreign policy chief Catherine Ashton (2013) noting that the law "still contains elements that can unnecessarily constrain the work of NGOs in Egypt and hinder our capacity as a foreign donor to support their work."

The European Union also provided large-scale funding for Egypt, including €594 million during the period from 2000 to 2006. Only a very small portion of this funding was allocated to support democracy and human rights — approximately €5 million (less than one percent), within the framework of the European Initiative for Democracy and Human Rights. Similarly, in March 2007, the Egyptian government was allocated €558 million through the European Neighbourhood Policy Instrument for the period from 2007 to 2013, of which only €13 million was allocated to democracy and good governance programs and an additional €16 million for human rights, with the Egyptian government having wide authority in supervising the implementation of such funds. However, neither the European Commission nor individual member states consider an NGO's registration status under Egyptian law when awarding grants. The EU also has the European Instrument for Democracy and Human Rights, which devoted over 25 percent of its €703 million in funding from 2007–2010 to the MENA region.[2] Since 2011, the EU has committed more funds, but roughly on the same scale — a total of €24 million that could be devoted to civil society (€17 million for the Promotion and Protection of Human Rights Program to build Egyptian institutional and civil society capacity to respect international

---

2   Participant at "Pluralism and Democracy: Prospects for the Arab Middle East and North Africa," European Council on Foreign Relations and Council for a Community of Democracies round table. Canadian Cultural Centre, Paris, December 6-7, 2012.

human rights commitments; €7 million for the Anna Lindh Euro-Mediterranean Foundation for the Dialogue between Cultures). The lion's share of funding went to various supports to government in the fields of justice, education, the environment and infrastructure. It remains to be seen what sort of civil society funding will follow in the 2014 EU budget, and whether flexibility to changing circumstances is built in. The European Endowment for Democracy, a body mirroring the US National Endowment for Democracy was just launched, with all EU member states being shareholders, and some civil society participation in the board. The endowment will split its grants 50/50 to the southern and eastern neighbourhoods.[3] While its initial endowment is very modest, it could help to compensate for the EU's relative absence in an Egyptian civic sector, which would welcome its support.

The need in the extended and troubled transitional period is great for economic support. Some regional experts believe the West is being parsimonious with its economic assistance. "I am disappointed in the US and EU — they haven't stepped up with the economic and financial support we need. I hope we won't look back wistfully at a lost chance," one noted.[4]

On issues of democratic development, diplomats in Egypt have seen fluctuating **support of home authorities** over time. On the American side, such support rose from 2002 to 2005, when reform in Egypt was a high priority of the Bush administration's freedom agenda. After 2006, while support through funding for democracy programming continued to increase, support for addressing reform issues through diplomatic engagement was largely withdrawn, although President Bush continued to raise the issue in remarks given in Egypt and elsewhere. As noted, the first Obama administration sharply reduced support for democracy and governance programming. Despite the major changes and challenges since early 2011, it seems that supporting democratic consolidation in Egypt through donor support and diplomacy is a priority for the re-elected Obama administration. Obama administration officials have claimed that concern and pressure on democracy and human rights issues is continuing in private, with public admonitions considered ineffective. There is no way to verify the impact of these pressures on Egyptian positions. In 2009, the Obama administration made no pronouncement on developments in Egypt, and has only expressed concern on two occasions in 2010 — sectarian murders of Coptic Christians in Naga Hammadi in January 2010 (which coincided with a visit to Cairo of Assistant Secretary of State for Democracy, Human Rights and Labour Michael Posner) and the renewal of the emergency law in May 2010. The hope of reviving the Israel-Palestine peace process with Egyptian involvement led to this softer approach. After the ouster of Mubarak in 2011, rhetorical support for democracy and human rights jumped, with some visible

---

3   Participant at "Pluralism and Democracy: Prospects for the Arab Middle East and North Africa," European Council on Foreign Relations and Council for a Community of Democracies round table. Canadian Cultural Centre, Paris, December 6-7, 2012.

4   Ibid.

practical effect, but it is unclear how much local room for manoeuvre US diplomats in Egypt had to drive the policy.

During the Bush administration, several members of US Congress supported reform efforts in Egypt and aimed to apply pressure on the Egyptian regime, particularly through attempts to condition US military aid to Egypt on progress on reform. The post-2008 Congress has similarly reduced its previous emphasis on reform, in part due to satisfaction with greater Egyptian efforts to stem smuggling to the Hamas-governed Gaza Strip. But the US Democratic Party, in particular, made a point of distancing itself from democracy promotion, seeing it as a Bush-era signature policy. Of course, this changed when mass protests began. But as with the Obama administration, many congressmen and -women were slow to grasp the moment and reluctant to see the end of a regime long considered crucial to US policies, particularly the Camp David peace with Israel. While some legislators embraced the revolution, many others, particularly in the Republican Party, voiced caution and criticized the Obama administration for abandoning a long-term ally.

Similarly, support from the EU and individual European governments for democratic reform in Egypt has also waxed and waned. As the tenth anniversary of the 1995 Barcelona Declaration neared, the EU issued a document in December 2003 on foreign relations with Arab countries and a March 2004 progress report on the EU partnership with southern Mediterranean and Middle East countries. Both reports emphasized issues of political, social and economic reform, and the importance of developing diplomatic dialogue with Arab countries to support democracy; yet, support for Egyptian reform from European governments declined thereafter. European diplomats in Egypt often felt that they have lacked needed support on reform issues.

Generally speaking, the EU's approach supports reform through dialogue and largely depends on the political will of the host government, with Brussels being generally reluctant to apply political pressure for the sake of democratic reform. As noted earlier, there are wide (and possibly widening) differences in the manner in which different members of the EU have approached this issue in Egypt. The period between 2007 and 2011 represented a nadir in bureaucratic and political support within the European Commission and among member states for advocating reform. By way of example, a May 2010 statement by EU High Representative Catherine Ashton on Egypt's renewal of the emergency law shocked Egyptian activists by not condemning the move. Since the EU was already on record supporting the abrogation of the law and this aim has been a component of bilateral talks, the timid language was surprising — and probably a reflection of the more indulgent attitudes of Mediterranean members of the EU. The US, in contrast, condemned the renewal.

Since the fall of the Ben Ali and Mubarak regimes, the European Union entered a phase of self-criticism and self-correction over its long-standing indulgence of the two dictators. EU Secretary-General of the External Action Service, Ambassador Pierre Vimont, acknowledged the EU's past shortcomings in a meeting in May 2011 with Egyptian and other civil society representatives. Since then, the EU and the

European Commission have made "more for more" the bywords of their linkage of financial support to demonstrable progress on reform. On June 19, 2013, Ashton pressed the need of reform on President Morsi, as well as the necessity of being able to relate to Egyptian civil society. The Egyptian president undertook to ensure that NGOs would be cleared to pursue legitimate support activity.

European support for democratic change in Egypt came most often from the European Parliament. In January 2008, it notably passed a resolution criticizing the human rights conditions in Egypt. This sparked an angry uproar from the Egyptian government, which demanded an apology, cancelled the scheduled meeting of the Egyptian-European Sub-Commission on Human Rights and temporarily withdrew the Egyptian Parliament from the Euro-Mediterranean parliamentary programs. President of the European Parliament Jerzy Buzek visited Egypt in May 2008 and delivered a speech to the Egyptian Parliament in an effort to repair relations, but he neither offered an apology nor withdrew the resolution. Following this visit, relations essentially returned to normal, and the Sub-Commission met for the first time in May 2008. The European Parliament has consistently advocated assertive EU policies to promote and support democratic change in Egypt, as well as decry abuses of power.

Aside from these two actions of the European Parliament, the period from early 2007 until early 2011 was characterized by then President Nicolas Sarkozy's tendency to focus on theatre and fellow "big men." The establishment of the Union for the Mediterranean in July 2008 was his pet project. Despite European assurances that this new initiative would be an extension of the Barcelona Process and the Euro-Mediterranean Partnership, rather than a replacement for them, it is clear that security and trade relations took precedence. The focus on political reform was abandoned altogether; the word "democracy" came up but once in the summit's final statement, as a commitment by heads of state to be pursued in 2009.[5] The co-presidency of the new Union for the Mediterranean was awarded to France and Egypt, with both governments embracing the shift away from political reform. With its founding principal, Sarkozy, defeated in France's May 2012 election and his partner, Hosni Mubarak ousted in 2011, the Union now appears moribund, yet to be invested with new content from either side of the Mediterranean Sea. In the words of one well-placed observer, "the Mediterranean Union…was a visionary idea, but it came before its time. The concept was launched without having been thought through."[6] Another was more blunt: "The Mediterranean Union got off to a lousy start — we are now recalibrating."[7]

---

5   See Final Statement, Marseilles, November, 3-4 2008, available at: http://ufmsecretariat.org/wp-content/uploads/2012/09/dec-final-Marseille-UfM.pdf.

6   Participant at "Pluralism and Democracy: Prospects for the Arab Middle East and North Africa," European Council on Foreign Relations/Council for a Community of Democracies round table, Canadian Cultural Centre, Paris, December 6-7, 2012.

7   Ibid.

The Mubarak government certainly valued its relationships with Western governments, most of all with the United States, which gave Western — and US in particular — governments **influence** with the Egyptian government. However, the historical legacy of colonialism and Western intervention in Egypt has had a limiting effect on this influence, and the government of Egypt has at times cleverly manipulated this legacy to diminish the effects of Western diplomatic pressures. The Egyptian Ministry of Foreign Affairs — particularly under the leadership of Foreign Minister Ahmed Aboul Gheit — made the rejection of "interference in Egypt's internal affairs" systematically part of the Egyptian discourse on human rights and political reform, arguing that Egypt would reform at its own pace. While this had some resonance among the Egyptian public and political elites, between 2005 and 2010, opposition groups shifted away from supporting the government's rejection of international engagement on political reform. For instance, Mohamed ElBaradei, the former International Atomic Energy Agency director who returned to Egypt in February 2010 to lead a campaign for political reform, urged Western pressure to be applied to spur political reform, also calling for the presence of international election observers in polls in 2010 and 2011. Previously, these had been rejected by most of the opposition, in part because of a widespread rejection of US efforts at democracy promotion in the context of the invasion of Iraq.

During the January and February 2011 revolutionary developments in Egypt, influence was applied from high levels, particularly from the US, to try to prevent use of force against the demonstrators in Tahrir Square and elsewhere (more in the "Defending Democrats" section below). The links to Egypt's security apparatus — and Army, in particular — were important. But the West's influence with the new forces in Egypt has been limited because of the arm's-length relationship with them, to the extent such contacts existed at all, prior to Mubarak's fall. Jünemann (2012) writes that after "having neglected civil society and having antagonized political Islam, there are no established channels of communication between the EU and the new political actors in the southern neighborhood. The EU simply does not know them."

As discussed below, US and European governments, but especially the US Congress and the European Parliament, have shown **solidarity** with some prominent Egyptian activists, most notably Saad Eddin Ibrahim and Ayman Nour. These governments later extended support to a number of younger generation bloggers targeted by the Egyptian regime. Many Egyptians viewed such solidarity, however, as having been selective, as it rarely extended to many other political activists, notably the hundreds of members of the Muslim Brotherhood who were jailed in repeated crackdowns on the organization.

A variety of regional issues — the Iraq war, the post-September 11 "war on terror," the perceived willingness of Western governments to overlook Israeli violations of international human rights law in the Palestinian territories, and the discounting of one of the Arab Middle East's two democratic elections in the Palestinian territories in 2006 — seriously undermined the **legitimacy** of Western countries in the eyes of the Egyptian public. The Mubarak government exploited this lack of legitimacy to call into question Western objections to human rights violations in Egypt. It also exploited the need for anti-terrorism measures to crack down on political opposition and excuse human rights violations under the pretense of anti-terrorism. Western countries generally had stronger relationships with Egypt's government than with its people, due to large-scale foreign assistance and valued military and trade relationships. Post-9/11 developments gave new ammunition to the Mubarak government to deflect pressure. Officials, for instance, frequently compared the emergency law to the US Patriot Act or Britain's Terrorism Act when criticized over the former's renewal — with Western diplomats rarely engaging in rebuttals to point out the vast differences between these pieces of legislation. Criticism of some of the worst aspects of Egypt's human rights practices, such as torture and prolonged administrative detention, was undermined by the rendition of terrorism suspects to Egypt by the US, often with the cooperation of European states. This legacy colours the relations with the new Morsi government, whose members were often on the receiving end of such harsh Mubarak-era policies.

There appears to be an interesting paradox when it comes to the perceived legitimacy of foreign funding in the eyes of the Egyptian public, and the civil sector in particular. European funds for civil society are viewed as being positive by 80 percent of civil society respondents in a recent survey, while American funds are viewed as suspect by about 80 percent of the respondents. Only funds from the Gulf states were viewed with more skepticism — only 10 percent of respondents approved of them (Elegati, 2013). In the general population, the same relationships held sway: European and Japanese funding were seen in a generally positive light by 70 percent and 63 percent respectively, while American and Gulf funds were seen as negative by two-thirds of respondents (ibid.). According to Elegati (2013), "Broad reservation against US government agencies are a regional feature rather than a specifically Egyptian one, which has not meaningfully changed since the fall of the Mubarak regime." NGOs often fear being tarnished by having a US donor label, though this applies more to direct US government funding than to private foundations. "European donors face less suspicion…their contribution is largely welcomed" (ibid.). The gap between the perception of US funds and their relatively greater practical sensitivity to the ground reality is noteworthy. An Egyptian civic activist noted that "France and Europe have a lot to learn from the US" in terms of relations with civil society.[8]

---

8   Participant at "Pluralism and Democracy: Prospects for the Arab Middle East and North Africa," European Council on Foreign Relations and Council for a Community of Democracies round table. Canadian Cultural Centre, Paris, December 6-7, 2012.

WAYS DIPLOMATIC ASSETS HAVE BEEN APPLIED IN EGYPT

The Golden Rules

In the past, Western diplomats described **listening** as a fundamental part of their diplomacy with Egypt. However, their listening then was generally restricted to a wide variety of actors within the Egyptian government — within the Foreign Ministry, the Ministry of Finance, the Ministry of Commerce and Energy, and the Ministry of International Cooperation, among others. During the Bush administration, there was an effort to identify genuine reformers within the government and to listen to their advice. Such listening took place through regular, formal meetings in Cairo, as well as in some private, closed-door meetings abroad. Clearly, civil society also got some face time with diplomats in Egypt, and not merely as recipients of assistance. The relationship was overwhelmingly government-to-government, however, and dominated by principals in national capitals. Now, this listening must expand to all the disparate — and often opposing — forces in Egyptian society, which should put a premium on the role of diplomats, though it is unclear whether their input will affect the overall direction of policy with their home authorities.

Diplomats met regularly with civil society activists. But some diplomats noted that they had limited **understanding** of internal reform issues, because they had not interacted with a broad enough coalition of Egyptian non-governmental actors. On the US side, such meetings increased during the Bush administration and were continued as a way of demonstrating support for Egyptian reform even after diplomatic pressure waned in 2006.

In late 2012, Middle Eastern civic activists and human rights defenders criticized a Western woodenness in response. "The West, but especially the EU, is playing an autistic role," one remarked.[9] The US and EU have both understood the profoundly negative impact of the new NGO law, which impedes their ability to assist civil society in its crucial efforts to define and ground Egyptian democracy. However, the donor approaches of Western democracies have yet to reflect such situational awareness, especially given what Mohamed Elegati (2013) calls the dominant "paranoia" of foreign influence stoked by the prior regime and held by the Morsi government and Egyptian society as a whole. Marrying greater US willingness to fund civil society to the EU's greater perceived legitimacy through some creative collaboration would be one such avenue.

Demonstrating **respect** for Egypt's government was a regular component of diplomats' engagement with Egypt, yet this was lacking for Egypt's civil society, even to the point of accepting draconian restrictions on NGO funding. However,

---

9   Participant at "Pluralism and Democracy: Prospects for the Arab Middle East and North Africa," European Council on Foreign Relations and Council for a Community of Democracies round table. Canadian Cultural Centre, Paris, December 6-7, 2012.

there were a number of occasions when the US government aimed to pressure the Mubarak regime on reform issues. The government responded by accusing the US of showing insufficient respect for Egypt's independence and sovereignty. This was the case when the US raised the issue of re-examining the foreign assistance relationship, as well as when the US offered proposals for a draft memorandum of understanding, which aimed to offer additional assistance to Egypt in exchange for the Egyptian regime fulfilling promises made during the 2005 presidential campaign. Egyptian activists often saw the Western countries as excessively deferential in their dealings with the Egyptian government, and insufficiently respectful of the rights of Egypt's citizens. Mohamed Elegati (2012) has written that "we need more involvement of civil society organizations in Euro-Egyptian relations, so they can become an effective party whose role is recognized by decision-makers. It seems that those running the state in Egypt know nothing of about civil society other than its charity role." He added that Egyptians have rejected "privatization in the economic field" and "normalization with Israel in the political field...The EU should take people's and civil society's rejection of old policies into consideration" (ibid.).

There has been some degree of **sharing** of information and tasks among Western governments on democracy and reform issues in Egypt, but seemingly less than is the case in other undemocratic countries. This is an area which needs improvement.

Such coordination varied considerably over time as the approach and priorities of Western governments have shifted and the personalities involved have changed. Such efforts included planning to jointly attend trials of political activists or to visit such activists in jail. Diplomats commented that coordinating such moves increased the impact of such gestures. Most coordination and information-sharing took place among political officers on the ground in Cairo, although at some moments, higher-level meetings of Western foreign ministers have been useful in coordinating efforts on Egypt. Western diplomats also coordinated democracy and governance assistance programs to some degree, mostly through a monthly meeting of diplomats tasked with monitoring domestic politics and human rights. Diplomats opined, however, that such efforts needed to be institutionalized. There is also a wide discrepancy in the resources that different embassies allocate to this task: in some smaller embassies, such as those of Austria or New Zealand, a political officer monitors not only several issues in the country (with the focus being on economic relations), but also issues in neighbouring countries. Embassies with dedicated staff who are well informed about the political and human rights situations and are able to attend trials, protests and other events can have much influence in informing other countries' perspectives. These include diplomats from large embassies such as those of the US, Canada, the UK and France, but also those from smaller embassies that have prioritized human rights in their relationship with Egypt, such as Sweden, the Netherlands and Ireland. Egyptian activists noted that greater awareness of the situation in Egypt can bolster their case in international platforms.

As noted previously, the level of engagement of individual countries differs widely. A division of labour seemed to emerge based on countries' policy approaches, but there was no apparent effort to coordinate strategically. The US officially committed to promoting democracy long ago through long-running programs to fund government reform efforts and NGOs, though recent restrictive laws governing outside financial support for NGOs have greatly constrained support for civil society.

The European Union delegation handled a large amount of funds, but these were mostly targeted toward economic and institutional reform efforts, with human rights and political reform playing a comparatively insignificant role in the big picture of its approach. Furthermore, reflecting disinterest in democracy promotion in Brussels and the bureaucracy of aid spending, EU delegation officials had a strong incentive to minimize any source of friction with the Egyptian government under Mubarak and to ensure that funds were disbursed quickly rather than efficiently. A failure to disburse funds, even if there is no adequate recipient, can negatively impact diplomats' careers; disbursement is seen as a criterion for success in Brussels. Reports from within the EU delegation revealed pressure on funding officers to stay away from potentially controversial programs, such as funding civil society election monitoring efforts, for fear of slowing down negotiations on trade relations should the Egyptian government take umbrage. A presentation in 2009 at a *Handbook* workshop at the College of Europe in Poland by a frequent expert consultant on financial support to Egypt made it clear that democratic governance was in no way part of the European Commission brief.

Egyptian civil society held widely varying views as to the postures and approaches of individual EU members. Generally speaking, France, Italy and Spain were seen as most likely to support the Mubarak government's position and scale down pressure. They rarely made condemnations of the government's practices, or stressed issues of human rights or political reform in public statements, and exerted pressure and influence to ensure that European Commission officials also downplayed human rights issues, including in the Commission's human rights division. Most reform-oriented funding was directed at either training programs for officials or other programs dealing with institutions.

The experiences of European countries with fewer vested strategic interests in Egypt seem to provide a better model. Sweden and the Netherlands are generally considered to be the best examples of Western engagement on human rights and democracy promotion, both in the quality of their approach and knowledge of terrain as well as the proportionally large part of their aid earmarked for those issues. The Netherlands and Denmark, for instance, focussed on the issue of torture — an urgent issue in Egypt, where it has been endemic and normalized as a tool in routine police work. They have collaborated with the International Rehabilitation Council for Torture Victims and well-regarded local NGOs, such as the Nadeem Center for the Rehabilitation of Victims of Torture, to develop an Egypt-specific program. Some medium-sized and small embassies, such as Canada and Ireland, have also chosen to use their discretionary funding to focus on issues that others ignored, such as gay rights. In general, however, funding allocation has taken place more ad hoc than as a result of consultations between embassies, leaving room for enhanced cooperation and greater visibility in overall foreign efforts in this area.

It is also important to note that some analysts observed a blind spot in the civil society engaged by external actors, particularly the EU. Jünemann (2012) writes that, prior to 2011, in European Commission usage:

> Only a very narrow spectrum of Arab society was considered "civil society." Groupings that draw their identity and their political programme from their religious beliefs were excluded. The official argument goes that religion is a primordial structure and therefore is incompatible with a European concept of "civil society." The decisive reason for not considering Islamist groupings as civil society, however, is the perception that political Islam is anti-Western, hostile, and prone to terrorism. In contrast, individuals with an explicit secular outlook became privileged partners in the EU's modest attempts to also construct a partnership on the level of civil society.

Of course, the Muslim Brotherhood's function prior to 2011 was in most respects that of civil society. Such blind spots limited not only the contacts external actors had, but their sense of the relative weight of civic actors, in the broadest sense, in Egypt.

Truth in Communications

Diplomats in Egypt regularly **report** back to their home governments on issues of concern regarding democracy and human rights, occasionally generating a high-level policy response. In addition, diplomats have been involved in **informing** not only their own governments, but also the public and the media at home and in Egypt. This has occurred not only through official annual reports on the state of human rights, but also through testimony in US congressional committee hearings, and through sporadic public statements or responses to press inquiries. This was fuelled by important openings to the media climate in Egypt — with the emergence of independent newspapers, satellite television, the Internet and new media — issues of political reform and human rights were addressed publicly in Egypt before Mubarak's ouster in ways impossible a decade before.

In addition, important foreign news outlets such as *The New York Times* and *The Washington Post* developed a keen interest in the state of democratic development in Egypt unmatched by other countries in the region. The post-September 11 interest in democracy as an antidote to extremism, along with the arrests of high-profile dissidents such as Saad Eddin Ibrahim, whose case the Western media followed closely, increased such coverage. The unfinished revolution in Egypt continues to draw popular interest and concern, with corresponding policy effects.

The emergence of social media in Egypt and its catalytic communications role in the immediate run-up to the toppling of the Mubarak regime has been a seminal feature of analysis. The murder of computer programmer Khaled Said while in custody assumed the iconic impact of the self-immolation of Mohammed Bouazizi in Tunisia when images of his battered face were posted on a Facebook group called "We are all Khaled Said," created by Wael Ghonim.

The importance of social media and the Internet during Egypt's revolution underlined the direct advocacy of freedom to communicate by the US government after the Mubarak regime attempted to limit access to social media sites such as Facebook and Twitter, and then to restrict Internet provision altogether just days after the revolution began. US President Obama stated that Egyptians had fundamental human rights to speak and assemble, calling on the Mubarak regime to "reverse the actions that they've taken to interfere with access to the Internet, to cellphone service and to social networks that do so much to connect people in the twenty-first century" (cited in Moos, 2011). Julie Moos (2011), the author of an article on Obama and Secretary Clinton's activities on this score, writes that, "in mentioning social media in the same breath as physical protests and traditional forms of dissent, Obama elevated it to a place alongside several protections offered by the First Amendment" to the US Constitution.

When a strongly anti-Muslim film, produced privately in the US, was discovered on the Internet in September 2012, it generated major protest throughout the Muslim world, including attacks on US diplomatic posts. The US Embassy in Cairo had to explain that while the film was hurtful and not backed in any way by the US government, the government could not ban it. Explaining this values balance is often difficult.

Embassies themselves now regularly use social media as part of their public outreach to inform the public in host countries. But as with all communications methods, messaging can backfire. After the announcement of the prosecution of a popular television comedian, Bassem Youssef, for poking fun at (and "insulting") President Mohamed Morsi, his US counterpart, Jon Stewart, used Morsi's archived denunciation of Jews in a segment of his program. The US Embassy retweeted a link to the Stewart program, prompting the Egyptian government to accuse the embassy of "negative propaganda" (Khalaf, 2013).

Working with the Government

The Egyptian government worked irregularly with Western governments on economic reform issues since the 1970s. At times, there was significant tension over such reforms, though the regime was generally more receptive to economic reforms and willing to cooperate on economic development issues than on political issues. The Mubarak government was receptive to external **advising** on certain economic reform issues, including financial sector reform and efforts to increase the independence of the Egyptian Central Bank. Since 2011, international efforts to advise post-Mubarak governments on economic policy have been mainly aimed at promoting policies that will allow a deal with the IMF. At the time of writing, this arrangement has yet to be concluded.

Inevitably, the political environment affects the economy. Since 2011, the impact has been decidedly negative. Cooperation with the Mubarak regime — and his successors — on political reform has generally been much more difficult. The European Union established an EU-Egypt Task Force to promote cooperation and deliver advice on a host of issues, including **institution building**.[10] There had been some success in the Mubarak era on this front as well, aimed at improving the quality of educational, judicial and legislative institutions; however, critics noted that while such programs may have improved the internal capacity and performance of institutions such as the Egyptian courts and Parliament, they did not address the fundamental need for such institutions to have increased power to act independently of the regime — nor did such programs have a benchmarked track record of having improved the situation on the ground. There was a general lack of engagement, particularly among Europeans, with the Ministry of Interior and other security institutions when it came to discussing human rights issues. Most diplomats generally raise these issues with the Ministry of Foreign Affairs, and sometimes with the Ministry of Justice. However, the Ministry of Interior was typically the chief source of such problems. Human rights activists have recommended engaging it directly on such issues rather than going through the Ministry of Foreign Affairs, which is believed to be a poor address for such messages — and had limited leverage in the domestic power hierarchy, even assuming goodwill. As the Ministry of Interior is an interlocutor on other issues, such as counterterrorism, channels often already exist, and directly addressing human rights could at least help make it more responsive and create channels to act quickly on specific cases, when possible. The US has had the best relationship with the Egyptian security services, and has on occasion intervened to get Ministry of Interior officials to meet with US rights groups such as Human Rights Watch. Europeans — especially the French, British, Dutch, Belgians, Italians and Germans — have had counterterrorism and counter-radicalization ties with the security services, but not on the same level.

For years, the excessive focus of external actors on institutions was generally welcomed by the government and civil servants. "Egypt is proud of its bureaucracy — there is very little pride on the decision making side," one regional analyst noted.[11] In general, Egypt's officialdom has proven highly resistant to advice, despite the large amount of external funding.

Most recently, the US and EU tried to **demarche** the Egyptian government of President Morsi not to adopt an even more restrictive NGO law. EU foreign policy chief Catherine Ashton noted in June 2013 that the EU "in a spirit of true

---

10   See *EU-Egypt Task Force: Supporting the Reform Process in Egypt*, available at: http://eeas. europa.eu/top_stories/2102/141112_eu-egypt-taskforce_en.htm.

11   Participant at "Pluralism and Democracy: Prospects for the Arab Middle East and North Africa," European Council on Foreign Relations and Council for a Community of Democracies round table, Canadian Cultural Centre, Paris, December 6-7, 2012.

partnership has engaged with the government and has provided technical advice to the authorities in the process of drafting a new law on associations, the NGO Law." This statement, acknowledging previously delivered advice, represented a significant switch. When 43 NGO personnel, including some Westerners, were convicted for breach of the restrictive law in June 2013, US Secretary of State John Kerry (2013a) bluntly called the trial "politically motivated" and stated that the verdict was "incompatible with the transition to democracy." He added that the "the decision to close these organizations' offices and seize their assets contradicts the Government of Egypt's commitments to support the role of civil society as a fundamental actor in a democracy and a contributor to development, especially at this critical stage in the Egyptian people's democratic transition" (ibid.). The US State Department had previously issued a strong statement of concern on Egypt's December 2012 constitutional referendum following its passage, noting that "the future of Egypt's democracy depends on forging a broader consensus behind its new democratic rules and institutions. Many Egyptians have voiced deep concerns about the substance of the constitution and the constitutional process...We hope those Egyptians disappointed by the result will seek more and deeper engagement. We look to those who welcome the result to engage in good faith. And we hope all sides will re-commit themselves to condemn and prevent violence" (Ventrell, 2012). President Morsi's November 22, 2012 decision that his decrees were beyond review infuriated Egyptian civil society and political opposition, and also elicited statements of concern from Washington. "One of the aspirations of the revolution was to ensure power was not be overly concentrated in the hands of any one person or institution," State Department spokeswoman Victoria Nuland (2012) stated.

Reaching Out

During the Bush administration, US diplomats regularly sought to foster dialogue on reform issues by **convening** a group of key Egyptian elites whom they believed shared a commitment to genuine reform. In 2002 and 2003, as support for Egyptian reform first emerged on the Bush administration's agenda, US officials convened a series of closed-door meetings outside the country with Egyptian government officials, including cabinet-level ministers, who were perceived to be reformers. The United States intended such meetings to provide a safe forum for discussion and to identify steps that the US government could take to support reform efforts, including demands that they could make of the Egyptian government as a whole (i.e., beyond the small group of reform-minded Egyptian government officials). While such meetings produced serious dialogue, US diplomats came away with the lesson that the agenda for reform should be based on interactions with a broader coalition if possible, as progress through such meetings was limited and the influence of the participating reformers within the Egyptian government waned over time.

Egyptian analyst Mohamed Elegati (2012) believes that an opportunity has been lost to date, in failing to **connect** civil servants and revolutionaries to each other, permitting the growing gulf of mutual incomprehension to continue. He — and other observers, such as the Center for Islam and Democracy's Radwan Masmoudi — believe that connecting and **facilitating** is essential to sensitizing both sides to normal interaction in a democratic framework, rather than a habitual, inherently adversarial relationship (ibid.). He noted that in 2011,

> a statement was issued by more than one-third of those who work in the Egyptian Ministry of Foreign Affairs in support of the demands for change; meanwhile, doctors of the Ministry of Health stood side by side with the revolutionaries in field hospitals but there was no communication with them or attempts to support them inside their institutions. NGOs worked in keeping old methods and customs, with state institutions regarded as part of the regime, whereas they were emerging as part of the revolution as well... its only experiences are in dealing with oppressive regimes and mainly focusing on "exposing" abuses and violations. (ibid.)

This persistent friction is likely to have helped generate the current dire situation. Egypt's NGO law impedes the forging of such needed connections. Foreign officials are still attempting to bridge these divides, though with little obvious success. In a background briefing prior to Secretary Kerry's March 2013 visit to Cairo, US State Department officials noted that it was "not only on Morsi to build consensus," and the opposition was advised to participate in the electoral process rather than boycott it.[12]

Looking forward, several civil society activists focussed on the region have advocated a far more ambitious effort to connect European and the MENA region societies in the broadest sense through emulating the European Union's Erasmus educational exchanges and other such programs.[13] "It's time to think big. Like Erasmus — we need large-scale exchange programs for teachers, others. Why not something like the Peace Corps? We need to demystify the Arab reality to the West," one speaker advocated, with general agreement on its desirability.[14] Several others, however, questioned how practical this would be in the current straitened financial circumstances of the Euro crisis.[15]

External support for political parties has generally fallen from favour among Western democracies because of its vulnerability to charges of political interference. Nonetheless, Elegati (2013) reports that the "specialized training and dialogue programs for example for political parties during elections," provided by foundations

---

12   See Senior State Department Official (2013), Background Briefing En Route to Cairo, Egypt, Special Briefing, March 2. Available at: www.state.gov/r/pa/prs/ps/2013/03/205570.htm.

13   Participants at "Pluralism and Democracy: Prospects for the Arab Middle East and North Africa," European Council on Foreign Relations/Council for a Community of Democracies round table, Canadian Cultural Centre, Paris, December 6-7, 2012.

14   Ibid.

15   Ibid.

such as the German Stiftungen, were cited by his interviewees as being among the best benefits of external financing. "Donor policies that are focused on supporting 'collective cooperation' between local organizations for the purpose of agreeing common positions," and "supporting issues and agendas that are not endorsed by the Egyptian government," were similarly cited (ibid.).

As discussed at length earlier in **funding**, diplomats have also provided support to democratic development in Egypt through **financing** for democracy and governance projects, which increased significantly after 2002. From 2004 to 2009, US$250 million was distributed by USAID in bilateral funding for democracy and governance programs in Egypt. But the impact of such programs was extremely limited, as described in an October 2009 audit by the USAID Office of the Inspector General. The audit report noted that "a major contributing factor to the limited achievements for some of these programs resulted from a lack of support from the Government of Egypt."

Legislatures have worked to ensure that their governments do not accept restrictions on what can be funded. For example, an amendment to the US appropriations bill for foreign operations, offered by then Republican Senator Sam Brownback and passed in December 2004, asserted that "with respect to the provision of assistance for Egypt for democracy and governance activities, the organizations implementing such assistance and the specific nature of that assistance shall not be subject to the prior approval by the Government of Egypt." After passage in late 2004, such language remained in each annual US appropriations act for foreign assistance through 2008. In fiscal year 2009, this language was amended to explicitly assert the authority of USAID to determine the distribution of funds in *all* countries that receive US assistance for democracy and governance, rather than specifically focussing on Egypt.

The support for indigenous civil society has been and remains perhaps the single most effective tool of the international community in Egypt, yet, restrictions on the NGO sector, carried over from the Mubarak regime, severely restrict external assistance to civil society. Established democracies are in the midst of a reassessment of how to work in this vital field after the June 2013 conviction of 43 civil society actors, Egyptian and foreign.

Defending Democrats

US and European diplomats clearly **demonstrated** their support for prominent democrats who were arrested and persecuted in Egypt. Two such cases that drew much international attention were Saad Eddin Ibrahim and Ayman Nour.

Saad Eddin Ibrahim, Egyptian-American sociology professor, author, democracy activist and head of the Ibn Khaldun Center, was arrested in June 2000 on charges of defaming Egypt's image abroad and embezzling funds received from the EU. The arrest followed a public statement and newspaper column by Ibrahim, raising concerns that President Mubarak was grooming his son Gamal to succeed him. Initially, the US Embassy made a conscious decision to respond to the case through private discussions, contacting the Egyptian Foreign Ministry, advisers to President Mubarak and even raising the issue directly in a meeting with Mubarak. Gradually, the US Embassy increased pressure on the Egyptian government in private, while at the same time steadily increasing the level of public criticism. This gradual, sequential, multi-faceted approach seems to have worked — Ibrahim was released after 45 days in prison.

Upon release, however, Ibrahim returned to his activism and questioning of the Egyptian government and was soon arrested again. This time, the US ambassador was not as directly involved in negotiations, but other officials at the US Embassy continued to engage extensively with Egyptian officials (including President Mubarak), on the case and were repeatedly reassured that if the United States would let the Egyptian justice system work, Ibrahim would ultimately be released. Ibrahim was tried and convicted of all charges in May 2001, however, and then lost an appeal in July 2002, confirming his sentence of seven years in prison with hard labour. His health deteriorated sharply due to a series of strokes in prison, leaving him partially paralyzed (he now walks with a cane). In August 2002, US President Bush informed President Mubarak in a letter that the United States would withhold US$133 million in planned supplemental economic assistance because of the case. This was the first time that the US had publicly linked foreign aid to an Arab country with that government's record on human rights issues.

This clearly angered the Egyptian government, and many in the US government were alarmed by the anger and tension and potential consequences for the US-Egypt bilateral relationship. Yet US diplomats attest that during this period, Egypt's cooperation with the US on key strategic issues — counterterrorism, Israel, military overflight privileges and Suez Canal rights — remained undiminished. On the contrary, it appears that the Egyptian government may have made more of an effort to cooperate on strategic issues in the hope of reducing pressure on the reform front. Moreover, this application of clear conditionality was apparently successful, as Ibrahim was eventually referred to a higher court, which cleared him of all charges in March 2003.

Ibrahim continued his strong criticism of the Egyptian regime, however, and in 2007, private attorneys affiliated with Egypt's ruling parties brought several suits against him while he was abroad, effectively preventing him from returning to Egypt for fear of immediate arrest. He remained outside the country, in the US and in Turkey, until 2011. The authors of the *Handbook* personally witnessed Ibrahim being verbally attacked by Egyptian diplomats who attended the Community of Democracies meeting in Lisbon in July 2009. They called for him to be handed back to face trial for his "crimes."

Foreign diplomats also defended opposition politician Ayman Nour, another high-profile figure. In January 2005, authorities arrested Nour, charging him with forging signatures filed in forming the Al-Ghad Party. Having learned the lesson from the Saad Eddin Ibrahim case, the US government responded immediately to Nour's arrest in a more assertive manner than they had done with Ibrahim. In February

2005, US Secretary of State Condoleezza Rice abruptly cancelled a visit to Cairo as a sign of protest against Nour's arrest. At around the same time, a group of members of the European Parliament, led by the British Conservative Vice President of the Parliament Edward McMillan-Scott, threatened to raise the profile of the Nour case by paying a visit to him in prison as a group. Nour was released in March 2005 and was allowed to run in Egypt's presidential election in September 2005. He finished a distant second to President Mubarak, with just under eight percent of the vote. While this was the first time Mubarak campaigned in a competitive election, the deck was stacked against opposition candidates.

Soon after the election, Nour was arrested again, convicted and sentenced to five years in prison in December 2005. On the day of Nour's conviction, the White House released a public statement calling on "the Egyptian government to act under the laws of Egypt in the spirit of its professed desire for increased political openness and dialogue within Egyptian society, and out of 'humanitarian concern,' to release Mr. Nour from detention." As in the case of Ibrahim, the White House also expressed its displeasure through a tangible act, in this case cancelling negotiations on a free trade agreement that were scheduled to begin in January 2006. Although the international community continued to raise concerns about Nour's imprisonment, he remained in jail for more than three years until his release in February 2009, when Mubarak wanted to reset his relationship with the US under the Obama administration.

Diplomats involved with both the Ibrahim and Nour cases noted that the US government, in particular, seemed to have considerably more leverage in the former case than in the latter. Ibrahim's dual US and Egyptian citizenship and his extensive ties to the United States (he has taught at numerous US universities and his wife is American) made it much more difficult for the Egyptian government to dismiss US government efforts on his behalf as illegitimate interference in Egyptian affairs. Such claims were frequently made regarding the Nour case by many actors in the Egyptian government, including several officials generally perceived to be reformers.

In addition to these two high-profile cases, Western diplomats have provided support for a number of other imprisoned political reformers and activists in Egypt. Of the dozens of bloggers in Egyptian prisons, Abdel Karim Nabil Soliman (known on his blog as Kareem Amer) was the first person imprisoned in Egypt purely for the content of his online blog. The case attracted particular attention, including in separate letters to President Mubarak and to President Bush written by numerous members of the US Congress. Incidents such as sectarian clashes or human rights abuses involving religious discrimination by the state also drew a higher profile in North America and Europe, in part due to the political weight that churches and Christian interest groups can play as lobby groups, in influencing media coverage or through elected representatives. Both focus on discrimination against Christians and politically motivated attacks on liberal reformers show the narrow base of support that exists in the West for a more thorough and approach on human rights and political freedoms. Such cases remain in the spotlight because they have a supportive and vocal constituency in Western countries. These may be émigré

Coptic groups and Christian solidarity networks, or in the case of Ibrahim and Nour, these individuals' contacts among political and media elites in Europe and the US. *The Washington Post,* for instance, campaigned continuously for both men, as well as greater US pressure on Egypt in general, in good part because its editorial page editor, Jackson Diehl, is personally committed to reform in Egypt and has good contacts with Egyptian reformists.

The arrest of hundreds of other political activists, however, did not draw this kind of assertive response from Western diplomats. This includes the numerous members of the Muslim Brotherhood in Egypt who had been jailed prior to Mubarak's ouster. While the State Department's annual Country Report on Human Rights in Egypt regularly noted the use of closed military tribunals and emergency courts to detain and convict members of the Brotherhood, they have clearly not received the same kind of support from the West as the celebrated cases described above.

The high-level statements by Western officials during the 2011 revolution to refrain from violence and for Mubarak to heed the popular will also constituted **protecting**. US Secretary of State Kerry's March 2013 high visibility meetings with civic activists and opposition figures, as well as then President Morsi, the foreign and defence ministers and the intelligence chief **demonstrated** that the US government valued their role. This came at a time when the relationship between the Morsi government, opposition and civil society was fraught. These forces are even more divided now.

The ongoing issue of restrictions on NGO funding and activity has provided perhaps the biggest post-2011 demonstration of external support for democrats and the democratic process, as broadly defined in the democratic world. UN High Commissioner for Human Rights Navi Pillay, for example, stated in 2012, as the NGO law was being discussed, that "if passed in its current form, [the law] would seriously undermine the spirit of Egypt's revolution, in which civil society played a pivotal role" (cited in Elegati, 2012). Many other such statements were cited earlier in this study.

CONCLUSION

Egypt's strategic centrality to the West, and partiçularly the United States, elevated policy decisions on the country to the highest stratum of policy making. Prior to the fall of the Mubarak regime in 2011, strategic considerations were in large part responsible for the inadequacy of understanding of the popular political forces in the country.

The Muslim Brotherhood's history as a persecuted opposition, unable to even officially compete in slanted electoral politics, clearly affected its approach to politics. Once it assumed power, civil society actors in Egypt harshly criticized its majoritarian approach to governance, noting that this undercut the potential for Egypt to develop democratically, as well as betrayed the spirit of the revolution, in which popular unity was a notable feature. The approach to constitution drafting was seen as exclusivist, both in content and participation, defying Egypt's own pre-military rule constitutionalist history. The postures of Western powers were seen as aloof or indulgent of the Brotherhood and the military, which disappointed many in the disparate civic-oriented opposition. "There are two vast segments of society which don't know how to deal with each other," according to one observer speaking in December 2012, when violent clashes accompanied President Morsi's decree that his decisions were beyond review to facilitate the Brotherhood's desired constitutional draft, which civic and secular opposition believed at the time gave the army too much sway.[16]

The relationships among the triangle of Muslim Brotherhood and its more austere Islamist political allies, the non-Islamist opposition (which covers a wide ideological spectrum), and the Mubarak-era security apparatus around the Army have defined the post-revolutionary/transitional context in Egypt to date. All three actors have manoeuvred and negotiated for political and social advantage. But the "deep state" has remained the most powerful — the swing vote/kingmaker between those operating in the political realm. The July 2013 military coup has only served to underscore its abiding power.

The Muslim Brotherhood's Freedom and Justice Party thought it had made peace with the security state in the interests of maintaining power and seeing off its political rivals. President Morsi was apparently the last to believe that the Army, commanded by a general he himself appointed, would overthrow him (Kirkpatrick and El Sheikh, 2013). There was a lack of civilian consensus on what the political rules of the road should be, giving the military much more leverage than it should ever have had in a democratic system. Civilian control of the armed forces remained a major question mark, despite high-level dismissals by Morsi in 2012, until it took over and demonstrated it answered to no authority.

Support for the secular and liberal opposition has grown in the aggregate since Mubarak's fall (and during Morsi's presidency), but the Muslim Brotherhood's early organizational advantage and social credibility was pivotal in its ability to attain power. The growth of Salafist parties to the right of the Brotherhood has surprised many observers, who see it as an ominous development.[17] The Muslim Brotherhood's performance in office, however, diminished its credibility. This appeared to increase its insularity and the polarization in Egyptian society. The perceived betrayals and compromises felt by civic political forces impeded a democratic consolidation, establishment of stability and a return to economic growth.

On July 3, 2013, a week of massive protest against Morsi by his opposition, including both those who assembled against, and who were part of, the Mubarak regime, was ended by military intervention, which suspended the new constitution and took President Morsi into custody. At time of writing, it remains unclear

---

16   Participant at "Pluralism and Democracy: Prospects for the Arab Middle East and North Africa," European Council on Foreign Relations/Council for a Community of Democracies round table, Canadian Cultural Centre, Paris, December 6-7, 2012.

17   Ibid.

whether promises of a new election will be met — or whether the Brotherhood and other Islamists will react violently to their removal from power. Ongoing protests have involved violence, but have not been "violent protests" per se; military and police reaction has usually involved violence. The Army justified its takeover by the massive protests, which they claim involved 20 million Egyptians, which immediately preceded in late June/early July 2013. Subsequently, the military called on citizens to mobilize once again in Friday demonstrations against the Brotherhood, which decried such calls as invitations to civil war. It is clear that the Mubarak-era old guard, including former NDP figures, is reasserting itself (Hauslohner, 2013). The current glidepath is far from encouraging for Egyptian democracy. This is dire for the wider Arab world.

As has long been the case, Western countries seem to lack a longer-term strategy for supporting Egyptian democracy. Due to Egypt's unique strategic importance as a critical Western ally, support for Egyptian democracy has tended to come directly from Western capitals. But in the aftermath of Morsi's election, US Ambassador Anne W. Patterson became heavily engaged as a conduit and adviser to the Morsi presidency. Patterson lobbied successfully for Secretary of State Clinton to visit Egypt. She was the most visible focal point and target for ire from opposition figures, having said in June that "I don't think the elected nature of this government is seriously in doubt," and questioning whether "street action will produce better results than elections" (cited in Landler, 2013). Such comments generated opprobrium from Morsi's opponents. But her meetings with opposition figures, also part of her mandate, earned skepticism from the Morsi camp as well. As one pro-Morsi demonstrator stated, "she should not interfere; she needs to watch from a distance" (ibid.).

Generating such widespread suspicion and condemnation is a reflection of the frequently held view that the US is dominant in Egyptian politics, but also, as commentator and former US official Vali Nasr put it, this "only represents the fact that the rest of the American administration is absent" (ibid.). At least it appeared so publicly. But the Obama administration, up to the highest level, had apparently advised Morsi to open up his government and the constitution-drafting process to a wider cross-section of Egyptian society, months before the military moved (Kirkpatrick and El Sheikh, 2013). In the final days prior to the military's ouster of Morsi, *The New York Times* reports that an Arab foreign minister acted as emissary of the US government, asking "if Mr. Morsi would accept the appointment of a new prime minister and cabinet, one that would take over all legislative powers and replace his chosen provincial governors" (ibid.). The appointment of a governor in Luxor who had been involved in an infamous attack on tourists in 1997 had generated much anger at home and abroad. The entreaty was rebuffed, with the rejection conveyed directly to Ambassador Patterson (ibid.).

Since the coup, the Obama administration has felt compelled to engage in verbal contortionism, fearing the legal necessity of curtailing US$1.3 billion in aid to Egypt if the military takeover is deemed a "coup" (Baker, 2013). "We are going to examine this and monitor this and take the time necessary in making the determination in a manner consistent with our policy objectives and our national security interests," White House spokesman Jay Carney told reporters. "But we do not believe that it is in our interests to make a precipitous decision or determination to change our assistance program right away" (cited in Baker, 2013). While Speaker of the US House of Representatives John Boehner basically applauded the military seizure of power as representing the popular will, his fellow Republican and former presidential nominee Senator John McCain was direct in his condemnation. "Morsi was a terrible president, their economy is in terrible shape thanks to their policies, but the fact is that the United States should not be supporting this coup" (ibid.). In late July, a shipment of F-16 fighter aircraft scheduled for delivery was delayed.

While much is opaque about Egypt's future, it does seem clear that strategies for supporting democratic development in Egypt cannot rely on the political will of the new Egyptian government. Neither was this possible with the troubled, democratically elected Morsi government. It was clearly and logically the hope of the established democracies that after 2011, the relationship could really begin to tackle development and cooperation in an environment of democratic accountability. Yet, as events have demonstrated, this cannot be taken for granted. There are a variety of views from within Egyptian civil society as to the posture external actors should take. But there are few in the community who wish to operate in a restricted environment, as the Morsi government seemed willing impose. The "deep state" security apparatus is bent on tightening further, with the acquiescence or outright cheerleading of much of secular and liberal Egyptian society.

Sadly, some lessons drawn from the Mubarak era may still apply to post-Mubarak Egypt — particularly if the old guard (feloul or "remnants") return to formal (as well as behind-the-scenes) power. A multi-faceted approach, in which private dialogue and selective public criticism are complemented by leveraging assets like foreign assistance, seems to show the greatest promise. Direct engagement with the beleaguered civil society actors in Egypt must continue, as must direct engagement and — where necessary — pressure upon the new Egyptian government. In applying such pressure, foreign governments should not be afraid to condition economic benefits such as trade agreements and foreign assistance — including defence assistance — on positive and meaningful steps toward instituting democratic norms.

Several Western diplomats noted the need to directly engage Egyptian government officials at the very highest levels on issues of democratic development. Willingness to apply increasing leverage in private, while accompanied by public criticisms and conditioning of benefits such as foreign aid and trade benefits, may yield results.

This case study's conclusion in the 2010 edition of the *Handbook* included the following statement: "Ultimately, it is up to the Egyptian people to bring reform and work for the transition to a genuinely democratic Egypt in the years ahead, rather than merely the transition to a new autocratic president." While the way the Mubarak regime came to an end — and may well be revived — was not envisioned by the authors, this statement remains apropos in their view. Just two years ago, a monumental paradigm shift appeared to be underway; this remains without completion. While Egyptians need to chart their own course, it is the responsibility — and in the interest — of established democracies and their representatives to support their efforts to achieve the freedom and accountable government they have so long deserved and been denied. The democratic world needs to recalibrate its diplomatic engagement to today's Egypt in recognition of how much has been irrevocably changed — and how much has stayed the same.

WORKS CITED

Ashton, Catherine (2013). "Statement by the Spokesperson of High Representative Catherine Ashton on the New NGO Law in Egypt." A 294/13 European Union, Brussels, June 2.

Baker, Peter (2013). "Assistance to Continue For Now, U.S. Says." *The New York Times*, July 9.

BBC News (2011). "Egypt Protests: US Call to Hosni Mubarak's Government." BBC News Middle East, February 9.

———— (2013). "Egypt profile — Timeline" Available at: www.bbc.co.uk/news/world-africa-13315719?print=true.

Elegati, Mohamed (2012). "Civil Society in Egypt and the Revolution of 25 January: What Role for the EU?" Euromesco/IEMed Brief no. 41, May 31.

———— (2013). *Foreign Funding in Egypt After the Revolution.* Arab Forum for Alternatives.

Hauslohner, Abigail (2013). "With Morsi Out, Egypt's Old Guard Takes the Reins." *The Washington Post*, July 20.

Hubbard, Ben (2013). "Egypt Convicts Workers at Foreign Nonprofit Groups, Including 16 Americans." *The New York Times*, June 5.

Jünemann, Annette (2012). "Civil Society, Its Role and Potential in the New Mediterranean Context: Which EU Policies?" Euromesco/IEMed Brief no. 40, May 7.

Kerry, John (2013a). "Press Statement: Egypt NGO Trial Verdicts and Sentences." June 4. Available at: www.state.gov/secretary/remarks/2013/06/210257.htm.

————. (2013b). "Remarks of U.S. Support for the Egyptian People." Washington, DC, March 3. Available at: www.state.gov/secretary/remarks/2013/03/205579.htm.

Khalaf, Roula (2013). "Egypt's Comic Twists Turning into Farce." *Financial Times*, April 8.

Kirkpatrick, David and Mayy El Sheikh (2013). "Morsi Spurned Deals, Seeing Military as Tamed." *The New York Times,* July 6. Landler, Mark (2013). "Ambassador Becomes Focus of Egyptians' Mistrust of U.S." *The New York Times*, July 3.

Moos, Julie (2011). *How Obama, Clinton Legitimized Twitter & Facebook as Tools of Democracy in Egypt.* Poynter Institute paper, February 3.

Murphy, Dan (2011). "Joe Biden Says Egypt's Mubarak No Dictator, He Shouldn't Step Down…" *Back Channels, Christian Science Monitor*, January 27.

Nuland, Victoria (2012). "Press Statement: The United States' Reaction to Egypt's November 22 Decisions." November 23. Available at: www.state.gov/r/pa/prs/ps/2012/11/200983.htm.

Ventrell, Patrick (2012). "Press Statement: Referendum on the Egyptian Constitution." December 25. Available at: www.state.gov/r/pa/prs/ps/2012/12/202381.htm.

5 DEMOCRACY AND THE "CHINESE DREAM"

By Chantal Meagher, 2010;
revised by Kurt Bassuener and Jeremy Kinsman, 2013

It would be difficult to overstate China's importance as a partner for members of the Community of Democracies. In world affairs, China's cooperation is required for the resolution of any global problem or challenge of significance. The global economy relies heavily on Chinese economic growth. Even at a "slow" 7.5 percent rate, China's continued economic growth will add more than half a trillion US dollars of global consumption and demand in 2013. Chinese economic might is accompanied by increasing military-security muscle, especially in the Asia-Pacific region, where Chinese interests run up against US military presence, and also compel China to engage with Japan and Southeast neighbours in territorial disputes.

Relations with China and the activity of diplomats in Beijing as well as in foreign ministries reflect these realities. These wide and deep state-to-state interests have not, however, subtracted from the legitimate interest of Community of Democracies members to support civil society in China, reflecting solidarity with the Chinese people, who generally agree that human rights are universal and that political rights of assembly and expression ought to be respected in their country. The Chinese government, on the other hand, is among the most resolute of countries in its hostility to real or imagined interference by foreigners in Chinese internal affairs. All in all, the rapidly evolving situation and the imperative of balancing interests against values in the management of relations with China make this case study especially complex and undoubtedly important.

INTRODUCTION

> Economic development and political development are like the two legs of a person: if one moves forward and the other one doesn't follow, then the person might lose balance and fall.
>
> — Cao Siyuan, prominent Chinese economist

China's extraordinarily rapid economic development into its superpower status dates from its "Reform and Opening," initiated by Deng Xiaoping in 1979. This development has been described as an "economic miracle," but political development has not followed.

China remains a one-party authoritarian state. The government continues to exercise strict controls on the media and freedom of expression and association, which it constantly adapts to keep abreast of technological innovations. The judiciary remains politically directed and is often required to impose sentences dictated by the Communist Party of China.

It is on these — and other — challenges that the international democratic community focusses when lamenting what it perceives to be the slow pace of political reform in China. However, China's wealth of challenges also provides the opportunities to work with its government and civil society in a spirit of cooperation and mutual benefit.

Taking a long-term view, there can be no doubt that progress has been made in the realm of political development in China. Arguably, Chinese citizens enjoy more personal freedom of a non-political nature than ever before in Chinese history. Such progress, however, does not constitute essential political reform. The path of Chinese political development has been less linear, and, in an environment sometimes described as "two steps forward, one step back," backward steps often gain greater attention than the incremental steps forward.

Ian Buruma (2013) has observed that in conditions when "normal political competition is forbidden, everything becomes political." The environment makes the political situation essentially fluid even while the Communist party leadership makes every effort to exercise control. Future developments in China are therefore very hard to predict, as economic, social and inevitably political changes continue the dramatic transformation of the country the world has known over the last 35 years in particular.

In 1978, following Mao's death two years earlier, China emerged from the "Cultural Revolution" in tatters. The preceding "Great Leap Forward," in which millions died of famine, contributed to the sense of collapse. Many of China's intellectual, political and cultural elite died during or immediately following these years of turmoil. Countless survivors had been stripped of position and possessions, and suffered from failing health and no prospects. It was from this standing start that China commenced its remarkable economic transformation.

CHINA TODAY

Now, 35 years after the end of the Cultural Revolution, China has not only reopened to the rest of the world, but it has again become the major economic and political power that it was 200 years ago. China has achieved unprecedented rates of growth in the last three decades. By spring 2013, despite a massive stimulus package,[1] foreign currency reserves were estimated at over US$3.4 trillion (Rabinovitch, 2013). China is the world's second largest economy, having surpassed Japan in 2011 and Germany as the world's largest exporter the preceding year (BBC News Asia, 2013). China is becoming the principal trading partner of every region. Its large — and growing — development and infrastructure aid to Africa and Central Asia are seen as both a boon and a challenge to the international status quo.

China today is essential to virtually any important international concert on economics, trade and transnational issues of peace and security. As a permanent member of the UN Security Council, however, China has, since its admission to the UN in 1971, consistently abstained on resolutions perceived by Beijing as interfering in a country's domestic affairs. But as China's economic and political clout grows, it is under increasing international pressure to cease playing the "sovereignty card," and to move away from its traditional non-interventionist stance. Indeed, China supported the UN Security Council's 2007 resolution on Darfur, the 2010 resolution on Iran sanctions, and did not object to resolution 1973 authorizing the March 2011 use of force to protect Libyan citizens. China has itself increasingly deployed troops in UN-mandated peacekeeping missions (*The Economist*, 2013b). However, it appears the policy choice of non-intervention remains the default position, as evidenced by Beijing's stance — together with Russia — against external direct intervention in the war in Syria.

Indeed, concerns that China is taking a less than active role with the constructs of the existing system are matched by a growing concern in some quarters that it is working steadily to develop a different paradigm that rejects the current system — which China sees as being based on traditional Western values — in favour of one based on the primacy of state sovereignty, non-interference and state-driven development. This is borne out in its increasing involvement and influence in Central Asia (and its cooperation with these countries and Russia in the Shanghai Cooperation Organization) and Africa, where its stake in trade and natural resource development has risen sharply and is now dominant in many quarters. It has also expanded its economic presence in Latin American markedly in the last decade. Its relationship with its fellow BRIC country Brazil is especially noteworthy.

Despite China's great — and increasing — clout on the world stage, it considers itself still a developing country. While it has succeeded in bringing over 300 million people out of abject poverty,[2] many still live in very basic conditions. Though China has made giant strides toward universal primary education, large regional pockets where access to schools is not universally available persist. Access to affordable

---

1   The stimulus program has been ongoing since 2009. For a sense of the scale, see Ambrose Evans-Pritchard (2012), "China launches £94 billion infrastructure stimulus package," *The Telegraph*, September 7, available at: www.telegraph.co.uk/finance/china-business/9529252/China-launches-94bn-infrastructure-stimulus-package.html.

2   The UN Development Programme estimates that in 30 years, the number of Chinese living in abject poverty has been halved. See www.undp.org.cn/modules.php?file=article&catid=10&sid=10.

medical care is similarly difficult; a serious injury or illness can bankrupt an entire extended family.

Overall, however, the standard of living for the great majority of Chinese people has increased dramatically since 1979. As of 2012, for the first time in Chinese history, urban residents now outnumber the rural (BBC News Asia, 2013). The middle class is now estimated to number 300 million; some project that this could double in a decade.[3] However, the gap between rich and poor is also more pronounced now than it has ever been in China's history. A spate of suicides in an electronics factory and the May 2010 strike in Honda's car manufacturing plants brought the low wages and poor working conditions in many of China's manufacturing sectors to the fore. China has one of the highest suicide rates in the world. Doubts have been expressed about the sustainability of China's economic progress, especially in the absence of Internet freedom, which is essential for the development of a knowledge-based economy.

China's economic model is extremely energy-intense, and at the moment, inefficient. Continuing to develop economically and feeding China's massive hunger for energy while addressing the massive resulting environmental problems will be one of the coming decade's most difficult problems. In the immediate term, keeping the economic model (which depends on spectacular growth) moving forward as the economy slows presents a major challenge.

LOOKING AT THE PAST TO UNDERSTAND THE PRESENT

Diplomats wishing to fully seize the many opportunities that exist to work with Chinese society and government to support democratic development must first recognize that peaceful political change in China will be in the context of its historical experience. It will follow its own path and will take its own form, just as is the case in other countries. Most importantly, it will be driven from within, and not as a result of external factors.

Rather than presume to summarize China's rich and complex history, this case study instead looks at key elements of China's recent history through the lens of two overwhelming preoccupations of its leadership: fear of chaos, and fear of weakness. These fears are historical and broadly shared by the Chinese Communist Party (CCP) and society alike, though the CCP, of course, sees itself as the guardian of national unity and a "harmonious society." Much of China's domestic and foreign policy can find its roots in the counterparts to these two fears: the need to preserve stability and the need to insulate itself from dependence upon unequal obligations to, or influence from, foreign nations.

---

3   See "Chinese Middle Class to Triple by 2022," available at: www.nationalww2museum.org/learn/education/for-students/ww2-history/ww2-by-the-numbers/world-wide-deaths.html.

Weakness, Foreign Influence and Unequal Treaties

At the end of the eighteenth century, China was a trading hub, with the international balance of trade in its favour. By the end of the Opium War, however, not 50 years later, it had suffered what is still seen as both a humiliating defeat at the hands of foreigners, and the first of many unequal international treaties that would steadily weaken the country over the next century.

The 1842 treaty ending the Opium War granted concessions to foreigners residing in China, forced China to cede control of its key ports to foreign powers and required the payment of crippling reparations. A similar result following the first Sino-Japanese War (1894-1895) left China further weakened at the hands of external actors.

Just a few years later, in 1900, an international force of British, French, Russian, American, German and Japanese troops crushed the so-called "Boxer Rebellion." These nations — all of whom already had concessions in China — agreed not to further partition the country. The cost of this loss, though, was still very high: payment of a huge indemnity, the amendment of commercial treaties to the advantage of the foreign powers and consent to stationing of foreign troops in Beijing. China found itself at the receiving end of "gunboat diplomacy," as foreign gunboats patrolled the Yangtze and made their presence known in China's many ports in order to preserve significant foreign interests.

Following Germany's defeat in World War I, the Chinese were exuberant, anticipating the return of Germany's concessions in return for China's contribution to the war effort. Hopes were dashed, however, when their delegation to the Versailles postwar treaty negotiations learned of the 1917 secret treaty of Great Britain, France and Italy, with Japan ensuring support of its claims in China in return for Japan's naval support during the war. News of this triggered mass protests in China. Commencing on May 4, 1919, the protests lasted for over a month. The extension of the protests to Paris prevented the Chinese delegation from signing the Versailles treaty.

What became known as the "May 4th Movement" had more popular support than events leading to the formation of the republic eight years earlier. This is also believed to be the point at which many of China's political activists and intellectuals turned from the study of Western science, democracy and schools of thought, to Marxism as the most effective road to ensure China's strength and independence.

Chaos and Dissent as Threats to Stability

Concerns of China's leadership regarding any form of organized religion, as well as the tendency to immediately quell any form of domestic unrest may well find their roots in the turbulent nineteenth century, during which time four separate uprisings were quashed. All of them started with charismatic religious leaders able to gain huge followings in relatively short periods of time drawn from rootless and disaffected groups intent on the overthrow of the current regime. The best known and most successful of these leaders was Hong Xiuquan, leader of the Taiping Rebellion. Claiming spiritual powers and advocating the creation of a Christian community, he was able to muster an army of 20,000 that took Nanjing (the southern capital) in 1853. He ruled from there for 11 years.

Sun Yat-sen's Revolutionary Alliance advocated the use of armed force for the overthrow of China's Qing leaders. His revolutionary ideas had a deep influence on the officers and soldiers of the New Army, established in 1900 as part of Qing modernization efforts. The combination of a bomb-making accident and resulting coup by revolutionaries within the New Army resulted in declaration of the Republic of China in 1912 — less than three months following the unplanned coup.

The years of 1912 to 1928 were characterized by political tension, instability and warlordism. In these years alone, Beijing saw 43 separate cabinets. In 1921, the CCP was founded. But it was soon outlawed by Nationalist leader Chiang Kai-shek, successor to Sun, who died in 1925. In 1928, Kai-shek unified China through military means. The resulting one-party rule led to corruption and economic mismanagement, plummeting China into both civil and international war (largely against the Japanese), which continued for over 20 years.

From a Chinese perspective, World War II could be said to have begun in China, beginning with Japan's seizure of Manchuria in 1931. Japan moved deeper into China beginning in 1937; the infamous "Rape of Nanking," in which well over 200,000 were estimated killed,[4] was but the most vivid example of the sort of violence visited upon the Chinese. As in Yugoslavia in the European theatre, foreign invasion combined with an ongoing Nationalist versus Communist civil war to make the war years an exceptionally bloody, wrenching and destructive conflict through most of the country. Millions were killed, sexually assaulted by Japanese occupation troops, displaced and rendered homeless.[5] The war was the culmination of decades of malign foreign involvement in China, driving the desire to see external actors expelled after the war, though both sides in the civil war received foreign support from the opposing superpowers following 1945. The echoes of World War II trauma carry into the present day, and particularly potent reference points in ongoing territorial disputes with Japan. The spectre of nationalism provides an outlet and vector for popular discontent in the eyes of China's ruling Communist Party, but it also is a force that might get beyond their control.

China has been an authoritarian state under the control of the Communist Party since 1949. In effect, the communists consolidated the authoritarian practice that had prevailed in China for centuries. Despite periods of experimentation with Western models of government in the early twentieth century, none ever took root.

---

4   See "Scarred by History: The Rape of Nanjing" (2005), BBC News, April 11, available at: http://news.bbc.co.uk/2/hi/223038.stm.

5   One estimate, from the US National World War I Museum, is that there were 3-4 million combatant and 20 million civilian deaths in China. Official Chinese estimates are higher. See www.nationalww2museum.org/learn/education/for-students/ww2-history/ww2-by-the-numbers/world-wide-deaths.html.

With the founding of the People's Republic of China, the country entered a new era of serial revolution and chaos, which at least rivalled that which had come before. These revolutions, however, differed from earlier ones in one critical respect: they were instigated by the Party, or caused by rifts within it.

Campaigns in the first few years — aimed at rural landlords, foreigners, Chinese citizens suspected of supporting the Nationalists, private business, corruption within the Party and the urban bourgeoisie — resulted in purges and thousands of executions. The use of group pressure tactics developed in these campaigns continued and became institutionalized. Some vestiges of them can still be seen today.

The Party's continuing uneasy relationship with intellectuals dates back even further than the start of Communist Party rule, and has remained constant since 1949. In the early days of the first Five-Year Plan from 1953, a recognition that intellectuals, scientists and engineers would be necessary to move China forward led to the encouragement of intellectuals expressing their views; however, it quickly became evident that such expression must stop short of criticizing the Party.

Literary critic Hu Feng's writing incurred the ire of senior Party officials and led to a brutal campaign to root out "Hu Fengism." Feng was imprisoned from 1956 to 1979, for alleged "counter-revolutionary activities." His victimization further alienated China's intellectual population and led to divisions within the Party — between those advocating cooperation with intellectuals and those maintaining that the Party was paramount and could not be criticized — a rift that exists even today.

This pattern repeated in 1957, with the short-lived and ill-fated Hundred Flowers Movement. Again encouraged to speak out against abuses, the intellectual community responded with an outpouring of criticism against the Party, and the first Democracy Wall spontaneously came into existence at Peking University.

As had been the case in the past, the new policy of openness was quickly reversed. This time, the price for five weeks of intellectual freedom was paid by over 300,000 individuals, who were labelled "rightists" and sent to jail, labour camps or to the countryside. It was not until the end of the Cultural Revolution in 1978 that China's intellectual community would again — briefly — come into the open.

Rifts within the Party further contributed to domestic instability and began to surface in the early days of Communist rule. With several purges already behind them, the genesis of the 1966 Cultural Revolution was also to be found in the intra-Party struggle for power, and can best be understood as an attempt by Mao Zedong to accrue almost absolute control in his own hands and to attack the very Party that he had been so instrumental in bringing to power. The impact on the people of China was almost unimaginable — particularly coming, as it did, on the heels of the disastrous Great Leap Forward and its forced collectivization of agriculture, which had led to the deaths of an estimated 20–35 million people.

Although Mao officially declared an end to the Cultural Revolution in 1968, the radicalism he had launched continued until his death in 1976, and the subsequent trial of the "Gang of Four" — his wife and other close officials — who were ultimately held responsible for the excesses of the Cultural Revolution.

1977 brought the "Beijing Spring" — a brief period of political liberalization during which the public was permitted to criticize the government. While, at least in the beginning, most of the criticism focussed on actions of the government during the Cultural Revolution, it also led to calls for political change and the spontaneous establishment of the Democracy Wall in 1978. Wei Jingsheng's poster calling for a "fifth modernization"[6] of freedom was the first post for individual freedoms and eventually — together with other similar actions — earned him almost two decades in prison before being exiled to the United States in 1997.

Almost 30 years following the establishment of the People's Republic of China, its people had experienced countless political campaigns and purges, collectivization and starvation. Under Communist rule, they had not only failed to develop, but had suffered extreme hardship. If the Party was to survive, it would need to regain the confidence of the people and ensure that the chaos and instability of the past would not be given a foothold in the future.

China's "New" Political Activists in the Age of Reform and Opening

Designed to make China an economic power by the early twenty-first century, the "Four Modernizations" stressed economic self-reliance. China opened up its markets, purchased more modern machinery, encouraged foreign investment and improved technologies. Thirty years on, the success of the Four Modernizations — more popularly known as "Reform and Opening" — is clear. Despite its myriad problems, China is one of the world's greatest economic powers.

But what of Wei Jingsheng's call for a Fifth Modernization — democratic freedoms? There was a time when it was believed that China's economic transformation would inevitably bring political reform in its wake. While there has certainly been political change, it would be difficult to argue that any meaningful political reform has taken place in the more than 30 years since Reform and Opening began.

Implementation of economic reforms has resulted in a huge amount of new legislation since 1979. China's accession to the WTO required it to strengthen legal institutions, particularly its system of commercial law. Efforts to combat corruption have led to even more regulations and laws. Despite, or perhaps in part because of this, China has become a country that many claim to be one of rule-by-law, rather than rule-of-law.

The People's Republic of China was made a permanent member of the UN Security Council in 1971 during the Cultural Revolution and has become

---

6   First introduced in 1963, Deng Xiaoping's proposal to modernize agriculture, national defence, industry, and science and technology did not become official policy until late 1978 — officially marking the commencement of economic reform in China.

increasingly involved on the world stage. It has signed, ratified or acceded to a number of important international human rights instruments, including the Convention Against Torture, the International Covenant of Civil and Political Rights (ICCPR; signed only), the International Covenant on Economic, Social and Cultural Rights, the Convention for the Elimination of Racial Discrimination, the Convention on the Rights of the Child, and the Convention on the Elimination of Discrimination Against Women; however, implementation of these international human rights treaties within China is imperfect, just as its implementation of its own domestic laws is imperfect.

Perhaps the most high profile call for full implementation of China's supreme law — its Constitution — came in the form of Charter 08. This call for China to become a liberal democracy in every respect was drafted by prominent activist Liu Xiaobo, together with a number of other academics and activists. The charter was issued on the sixtieth anniversary of the Universal Declaration of Human Rights and was allusive to Czechoslovakia's Charter 77, which called on that regime to live up to the commitments it made without any expectation that it would be called upon to deliver. Liu's call for change earned him the Nobel Peace Prize in 2010. From the Chinese system, however, it earned him 11 years in prison for "inciting subversion" (Moore, 2010). Following Liu's sentencing, hundreds of the original Charter signatories publicized an open letter stating, in effect, that "if Liu is guilty, then we are too." Initially signed by 303 individuals, the Charter now boasts the signatures of over 10,000 Chinese citizens.

Liu is far from alone. He is carrying on a long tradition of activism in China — one that has gained increased momentum largely thanks to modern technologies, including cellphones, Twitter and the Internet. Such activism, however, remains underground, as government efforts to quash dissent increase to keep pace. New technologies are spawning a far more nuanced and complex activism.

The mid- to late-1980s saw some loosening of restrictions, under the leadership of CCP Secretary Hu Yaobang. Optimism about the possibility of political reform spawned the Hundred Flowers Movement and the Beijing Spring. In December 1986, students in Shanghai took to the streets with demands for science and democracy — the same demands as the May 4th Movement almost 70 years earlier. The protests — sometimes involving as many as 200,000 people at one time — spread to Peking University and Nanjing University before reaching Tiananmen Square on New Year's Eve of that year. As with similar movements in the past, these protests were quashed, eventually leading to the forced resignation of Hu Yaobang, who was believed to have been sympathetic to the cause. He was replaced by Zhao Ziyang, but Deng Xiaoping still remained in ultimate control. These protests, however, were different in at least one significant respect: they were not born of a policy within the Party, but were spontaneous events with broad popular support — precisely the sort of demonstration that history had proven most dangerous to Chinese rulers.

On April 16, 1989, the day following Hu Yaobang's death, several hundred students laid a wreath for Hu at the Monument for People's Heroes in Tiananmen

Square: a spontaneous repeat of the response to Zhou Enlai's death almost exactly 13 years earlier.

The following day, thousands of students gathered, staging a vigil through the night. Groups of workers also began to gather. On April 18, the students staged a sit-in, petitioning the National People's Congress (NPC). They called for a reversal of the verdict against Hu Yaobang, the elimination of corruption and nepotism, and an end to the campaigns against "spiritual pollution" and "bourgeois liberalization." Their demands also included free press and freedom of speech, and increased democratic participation in decision making. After initially being rebuffed by the students, workers also began to gather outside the square. The numbers of protesting students and workers continued to grow steadily, though under different leadership, and with different messages, the workers being more concerned with the effects of economic mismanagement. Meanwhile, a conference of 400 young "thinkers," including several who have acceded to positions of influence in the Communist Party in 2013, deliberated the need to encourage diversity.

The novelty of events on Tiananmen Square dominated the world's news cycles for a few days, but attention soon turned to other world events. In China, however, protests spread outside Beijing, even as people began pouring into Beijing from all over the country. By May 17, the demonstration of workers and students had swollen to over a million people. Zhao Ziyang, the second Party general secretary in a row to indicate sympathy with the students and for political reform, was dismissed by the Party's "elders," who then imposed martial law.

Military efforts to enter central Beijing on May 21 were blocked by over a million protestors. On June 3, however, they successfully occupied Tiananmen Square prior to clearing it in the early morning hours of June 4 in the bloody attack known to all Chinese as "Liù-Sì" (six-four), and to the rest of the world as the Tiananmen Massacre. Over 500 people were imprisoned in the aftermath of June 4, and how many hundreds or thousands were killed remains unknown.

With the dismissal of Zhao Ziyang, leadership of the Party went to Jiang Zemin, who was then the Party secretary in Shanghai. Concerns about the impact of reform led to a period of economic retrenchment until Deng's famous 1992 Southern Tour. Deng called for intensification of reform, urging more focus on economic development and less on ideological correctness. The tour succeeded in getting the economic changes going again. From then, they advanced at a breakneck pace, the "iron rice bowl"[7] was broken, unemployment increased and the gap between rich and poor in China increased dramatically.

While the standard of living for the majority of Chinese people improved significantly as a result of these reforms, the closure of thousands of state-owned

---

7   The state's provision of subsidized housing, medical care and other benefits was referred to as the "iron rice bowl." While its beneficiaries had steadily reduced with the dismantling of state-owned enterprises, it was finally "broken" as a result of economic changes arising from China's accession to the WTO in 2001. This has had dire and unpopular effects on some segments of China's population, especially in the hinterland. It also put wind in the sails of populist neo-Maoists in the party, such as Bo Xilai, before his own fall on charges of corruption.

enterprises left millions unemployed, homeless and without any social safety net. Protests and social unrest in northeast China's "rust belt" have led to concerted efforts to rejuvenate the area. Contrary to expectations, they have not yet led to the development of an independent organized labour movement.

Political Activism and the New Media

Today, advances in communications, an exponential rise in Chinese Internet users to 564 million by late 2012 and an increasingly professional media are all contributing to faster, more and better information being available to the Chinese people (BBC News Asia, 2013). Since this case study was first written in 2010, the number of Chinese who gained Internet access jumped by an estimated 165 million. At this rate, half the Chinese population should be online within a couple years — an amazing level of penetration for a still-developing country. Social networking has taken off in a major way as well, with more than 300 million using microblogs at time of writing (ibid.).

China's media is becoming increasingly activist, with more and more investigative reporters and an increasing number of editors who are willing to push boundaries in pursuit of increased readership. Some of China's academics are increasing their calls for "democratic reforms," though most call for such reforms within the context of the one-party system. NGOs working in the area of political reform tend to operate in a far more unstable — and sometimes dangerous — environment than those focussed on environment or health-related issues. Despite a continuing difficult operating environment, however, the number and professionalism of grassroots civil society organizations is increasing.

Virtually every Chinese person has a mobile phone and a growing number of citizens use them to record and communicate violations of human rights. Blogs and tweets are flying in the millions. Efforts to restrict the Internet through the use of the "Great Firewall" (GFW) cannot keep up with the volume and ingenuity of China's next generation of technology-savvy citizens. Individuals calling for political change and reform are sharing their experiences and discovering that they are not alone, which is giving them increasing confidence and, some profess, growing optimism at the prospect of bringing about democratic change.

But they are few. In a country of over 1.3 billion people, these few thousand activists are but a tiny — if growing — voice. Despite the wonders of modern technology and communications, they remain vulnerable to arrest and imprisonment — most often for charges of "inciting subversion of state power" — an opaque and nebulous charge that may lead to up to 15 years in prison. The majority of China's population remains preoccupied with simply eking out a living or, in the case of the rapidly growing middle class, preserving their standard of living in an environment of rising costs and soaring housing prices.

However, this new middle class is discovering a sort of activism through protection of their property rights. While the Party is intent upon keeping this large group content, and therefore quiet, the activist community sees them as a potential source of future activists as they determine that the cost they are paying in personal freedoms is too high for the benefit of preserving the status quo.

The Communist Party of China, the Government of China and Inner Party Democracy: A Primer

China's government and Party structures mirror each other. The CCP now includes approximately 76 million members, and it is almost exclusively from this cohort that leaders are selected.

China is governed by a system of people's congresses, with the lowest being village (indeed, so low as to be classified as autonomous, and therefore not officially part of the formal government structure), moving up to township, county, prefecture or municipal, provincial and national. The representatives in these congresses are referred to as deputies. The NPC consists of just under 3,000 deputies, selected by people's congresses at lower levels, and is sometimes likened to a Parliament. Although it is the body that might most closely resemble Parliament, it is clearly not a democratic body. The vast majority of deputies at all levels are Communist Party members, although there are a few independents. The NPC meets once per year, for a period of 10–14 days, at which time they produce the Report on the Work of the Government (similar to a Throne Speech), ratify work reports, work plans and pass legislation. Meetings are largely held behind closed doors. Rarely does this body — often referred to as the "rubber stamp" of the Party — provide any surprises, though in recent years, it has started to become more vociferous over environmental and legal issues: it was, for instance, one of the most vocal opponents of the Three Gorges Dam project of the 1990s.

The NPC's counterpart, sometimes referred to as China's senate, though not resembling the senate of a Western democratic model, is the Chinese People's Political Consultative Congress. Retired ambassadors, members of China's eight registered minor parties (which do not pose any opposition to the Communist Party), and representatives of Macao, Hong Kong, Taiwan and others are composed within this body. The Chinese public generally refers to this body as a "flower vase," in that it is seen as purely decorative, without useful function. Its stated purpose is as a forum for political consultation, democratic supervision and participating in the administration and discussion of state affairs, but in reality, it has no decision-making clout and very little — if any — influence.

Elections

China's meaningful experience with elections is minimal. Although experimentation has been taking place for decades in the sphere of direct village-level elections (to the tune of almost one million elections), as well as several rounds of elections for village chiefs, problems with vote buying, intimidation and corruption have been rife. Despite some optimism several years ago that direct elections extend to the more significant township level, they have not done so. Experts believe that, despite experimentation in some areas, expansion is unlikely in the near future.

The level directly below elects deputies to the various levels of congresses. While Communist Party members hold the majority of these seats, non-Party members may put themselves forward upon nomination by any 10 individuals. The first successful independent candidate was Wu Qing, who became a deputy in Haidian District (part of Beijing) in 1984. These independent candidates have, in the past, experienced extreme pressure — even arrest — in the lead-up to elections. Despite this, the number of independent candidates is increasing in each election.

Every five years since 1982, China has held a Communist Party Congress. In the most recent iteration in 2012, Xi Jinping succeeded Hu Jintao as leader of the Communist Party, and then succeeded him as president in March 2013. Ten years earlier, at the 2002 Congress, Hu Jintao succeeded Jiang Zemin as head of the Communist Party, and at the 2003 annual meeting of the NPC, he succeeded him as China's president. 2002 was considered the first orderly transition of power since 1949. Prior to that, the Party was fraught with frequent purges and internecine conflict. While the internal conflict hasn't ended, it is now being handled mostly out of view and the stakes are no longer so deadly. Hints of these struggles can be found in departures by some leaders from their usual well-choreographed and closely scripted appearances, but these are rare, and do not result in the purges of the past.

Xi Jinping was long groomed to take over from President Hu Jintao, and Li Keqiang from Premier Wen Jiabao. Xi is the son of one of Mao's cadres, Xi Zhongxun, and therefore a "princeling" — a sort of communist nobility (and reputed to have the same sense of entitlement). Xi's family was reported to have amassed a fortune (Grammaticas, 2013). He has himself taken a strong stand throughout his career against corruption. He did not accede to power by being an experimenter; he is disciplined and tough on issues of control, but he also has a record of pragmatism and is personally disposed to popular outreach and communication — more candid than the Chinese have been used to.

The cast of supporting, but still very powerful, players on the Standing Committee also include many princelings. None of them was assessed by China watchers as being standout advocates of political reform, although young officials waiting in the anteroom of power, who are said to expect to be appointed to replace Hu Jintao's conservative appointees, are less reform-resistant than the preceding generation of officials. Howard Balloch, who was Canadian ambassador for six years until 2001 and who stayed on to found and run a merchant banking firm, sees the inflection point as coming in 2017, when the last politburo members representing the old conservative order will be forced in to retirement. "Then, with the appointment of a few younger leaders of Xi's choosing — some of whom were educated in the West and have already been elevated this past year to the penultimate ring of power — the inner councils will not include a single member of the Hu generation" (Kinsman, 2013). It remains to be seen what sort of policies the new leadership will adopt and how much it will differentiate itself.

Once a party of revolutionaries and ideologues, the Communist Party is now, at least at the top, a sort of meritocracy; yet, many of those rising through the ranks are sons of party officials. Factionalism remains rampant and ascension to the highest levels is not possible without powerful patrons. While necessary to improve the Party's legitimacy in the eyes of the people, tremendous skepticism about the merits of many officials remains — particularly in an environment where the people have no voice regarding who is to be appointed to leadership positions and where examples of corruption and abuse of power are rampant.

Factionalism within the Party, combined with loss of the people's confidence in it, have led to efforts for its internal revitalization. The efforts underway fall under the umbrella of "inner-Party democracy," and in theory, consist of a number of positive elements, including increased transparency, multi-candidate elections and a system of improved supervision.

But the ingrained current system rewards compliance with orders from above, rather than responding to demands of those being governed. Thus, inner-Party democracy is viewed by many as a cynical effort primarily to strengthen the Party and thus one-party rule. However, there is another camp that views inner-Party democracy as a possible interim step toward democratic reform that should not be dismissed out of hand.

Xi's disposition is still largely untested, though there are initial indicators that he appreciates the necessity of change in China while maintaining the Party's dominance and control of the process. He developed a reputation for fighting corruption in his prior posts, including Shanghai. He has articulated what he has called the "China Dream": a vision of China as a prosperous and powerful nation able to take its place among the world's great powers (ibid.). He has also tried to portray himself as a man of the people in his early months at the helm. His famous singer wife has given the role of the Chinese first lady a new profile as well. But his pragmatic, hard-edged streak was also on display early. In an early speech to Party members, he asked: "Why must we stand firm on the Party's leadership over the military? Because that's the lesson from the collapse of the Soviet Union. In the USSR, where the military was depoliticized, separated from the Party and nationalized, the Party was disarmed…a big party was gone just like that. Proportionally, the Soviet Communist Party had more members than we do, but nobody was man enough to stand up and resist" (ibid.). According to political analyst Gao Yu, "he thinks the army is the ultimate guarantee of the party's rule. The party has to control the military. It doesn't belong to the country or the people" (ibid.).

INSTITUTIONAL CHALLENGES

China faces a number of institutional challenges, presenting both difficulties and opportunities for cooperation. An understanding of these challenges is a key to the tool box for any diplomats or NGOs working with China in the area of institutional reform.

There is a tendency to think of the Communist Party of China as monolithic, but this could not be further from the truth. The Party is not unified and is more and more prey to internal debate and friction; details of such friction are not made known to the public. A common depiction is of two broad camps: the princelings, or those who come from a line of powerful parents, and the "tuanpai," those who rose to power through the ranks of the Communist Youth League. Against this depiction are substantive divisions reflecting debate over the extent of control and openness to reform.

Efforts to manage this internal friction in an orderly manner are part of the controversial reforms referred to as inner-Party democracy (as detailed above). Although not democracy, this internal competition does mean that there are an increasing number of checks on the power of the inner circle, known as the political bureau (politburo). Many in China's new power elite have risen on the basis of perceived competence, as well as loyalty. Contrary to past practice, the majority of its leadership at the central and provincial levels now possess university degrees. Younger cohorts acceding to upper-level Party positions are more apt to have studied abroad. Also in contrast to the past, where the majority of university-educated leaders were engineers, the current political elite is more diverse, including members trained in economics, politics, law, business, journalism and a variety of other areas.

There is a deep-seated belief within the power elite that the stability of the country depends upon strong leadership from within the Party and draws from the fact that the Party is the only entity that currently has influence across China's diverse society and regions. This analysis claims that low points in the country's recent history tend to coincide with — or have been caused by — divisions within the Party. Therefore, much energy is being expended upon revamping the Party from within. However, as such "reforms" take place behind closed doors, it is simply not possible to evaluate their extent or eventual impact.

Just as the Party is not monolithic, the pace of development and the degree of implementation of laws and policies differ dramatically from one province to another — even from one county to another. An old saying — "the mountains are high, and the emperor is far away" — underscores a fundamental challenge faced by the central government: many laws and policies promulgated by the centre are ignored or not even known at the local level. While over the past 30 years, China has gone from having just two laws on their books to hundreds, the resources and capacity for implementation of its laws — including the Constitution — often do not exist.

Another complicating factor exists. Local Party officials are held responsible for any failures of central government policy in their district, but there is a wide variance in how they operate. Some have instituted public consultations on such issues as budgetary expenditure. Others are apt to imprison, isolate or otherwise punish petitioners, to ensure that they cannot take their complaints to Beijing and avoid blame.

In 2011, the murder of British businessman Neil Heywood sparked a scandal that rocked the Party. Gu Kailai, the wife of powerful Chongqing regional Party boss Bo Xilai, was investigated and ultimately convicted of the murder in August 2012, just months before the Party congress. Bo Xilai was first dismissed, then expelled from the Party for abuse of office and corruption (BBC News Asia, 2013). The case opened up rifts within China, with some seeing him as being attacked for potentially challenging the planned succession.

Public resentment of endemic corruption at all levels is an increasing preoccupation of the authorities. Efforts to address this through measures such as the 2008 Open Government Information Regulations, whistleblower regulations (Basic Standard for Enterprise Internal Control) and petitioners' regulations have met with limited success — partly due to reasons cited above, and partly because where corrupt individuals are in power, they also have the power of the police at their fingertips to silence protest and the ability to ignore (or selectively implement) laws promulgated from the centre.

The case of rural, self-trained lawyer and human rights activist Chen Guengcheng is emblematic of the problems that Chinese face in dealing with corruption and general abuse of power, particularly in the provinces. Chen, blind from youth, began his public interest law career by dealing with taxes levied unfairly against him and his family, who — as with all disabled persons in China — are legally exempt from such taxes. Local authorities frequently levy them anyway, resorting to intimidation or worse to collect. Once successful with his own complaint, he became an advocate for others who faced similar difficulties in his home province of Shandong.[8]

He branched out further into advocacy against a paper mill that polluted local waters, yielding a court injunction against the factory and a British government grant for a deep well and irrigation system for residents in the area (Macleod, 2000). He later began investigating allegations that rural women who were having a second pregnancy (in violation of the 1979 one-child policy) were being forced into late-term abortions and sterilization by local authorities in Linyi County, Shandong.[9] This problem had been gaining visibility for years; in 2012, an image of an infamous

---

8   See Joseph Kahn (2006), "Advocate for China's Weak Crosses the Powerful," *The New York Times*, July 20 and Melinda Liu (2002), "Barefoot Lawyers," *Newsweek*, March 3.

9   See Philip Pan, (2005), "Who Controls the Family?" *Washington Post*, August 27.

example of the policy in Shaanxi province went "viral" in China and worldwide.[10] Chen filed a class-action suit against local authorities in 2005, alleging that this policy affected tens of thousands in that jurisdiction alone. It was the first case of its kind.[11] The case was rejected, but it attracted much domestic and external attention. Chen was later detained by local security agents who accused him of providing secret information to foreign governments (Cheung and Xio, 2005); he was later accused of supposedly instigating others to destroy police property. He was tried and sentenced in August 2006 for "damaging property and organizing a mob to disturb traffic" (BBC News, 2006). His case generated numerous expressions of concern from abroad and he was later released on appeal, but he continued to suffer regular harassment by local authorities. As we shall see later, a major diplomatic incident was generated as a result in 2012.

"Suzhe" is a Chinese concept that encompasses both the quality and capability of individuals, in both professional and personal senses. China suffers from a lack of suzhe on the part of many of its lower level people's deputies. While efforts are being undertaken to address this issue, there are millions of deputies at all levels, many of whom have little or no education, and most of whom have had little or no training with respect to how to carry out their responsibilities. Despite their title, these deputies are answerable only to the level above them in the political hierarchy. With the exception of elections that take place at only the very lowest level, the public is given no opportunity to choose their representatives. Indeed, the concept of serving the electorate is a novel one for the majority of China's people's deputies. It should be recognized, though, that while many deputies are indeed corrupt, many simply do not have the tools necessary to carry out their responsibilities, while many others do wish to improve the situation in their constituencies, but lack the financial resources or ability to do so. Maintaining stability is of paramount concern to China's leadership. Therefore, the government often short-circuits attention paid to such problems.

---

10   Feng Jianmei, who had believed that she would be exempt from the one-child policy, was taken into custody and forced to undergo a late-term abortion in June 2012. Her sister-in-law photographed Ms. Feng with her dead six-month-old fetus and posted the images online, along with a threatening and extortionate text message from local authorities, sparking a nationwide debate on the policy and general outrage. See Malcolm Moore (2012), "A Forced Abortion for a Mother who Failed to Sign a Form, *The Telegraph*, June 14 and "China Forced Abortion Photo Sparks Outrage" (2012) BBC News, June 14. In *The New Yorker*, Evan Osnos wrote that "the Feng case is emblematic of some of the most inflammatory issues on Chinese life...the case is a dramatic demonstration of exactly why the Communist Party had reason to be afraid of the Internet." See Evan Osnos (2012), "Abortion and Politics in China," June 25. The case generated international reaction, including from the European Parliament, which called for the forced abortion policy to be on the EU-China agenda. See "Joint Motion for a Resolution on the Force Abortion Scandal in China" (2012), European Parliament, July 4. Local officials were found to have acted wrongly in the case, and Ms. Feng was awarded financial compensation, though nobody was imprisoned. Ms. Feng and her family continued to report official harassment well after the event, with her husband fearing for the family's safety once the attention had shifted. See Hannah Beech, "China: Forced-Abortion Victim Promised $11,200, but Family Fears for Life."

11   See Philip Pan (2005), "Who Controls the Family?" *Washington Post*, August 27.

The issue of separatism ("splittism") in the Tibet and Xinjiang "autonomous regions" is a special concern for Beijing authorities. In the eyes of most foreign observers, they overreacted to expressions of political and cultural dissatisfaction by Uighur Muslims and Tibetan Buddhists, as well as the heavy-handed persecution of the personal empowerment movement, Falun Gong. Tibet and Xinjiang are rich in natural resources, occupy key strategic areas and account for almost a third of China's landmass. They also are now majority Han Chinese, despite being the homelands of Tibetans and Uighurs. The ethnic Tibetan area is far larger than the autonomous region.

Internally, the regime's fervent view is that the best — the only — means of maintaining stability is through the continued leadership of the Party; however, as stated earlier, the Party is not monolithic, and there are differing views from within with respect to how stability should be maintained. Some favour continued or increased controls, while others recognize the need for a "pressure valve" that can be provided through selective loosening of controls.

An estimated 80,000 to 100,000 "mass incidents" or protests, including everything from peaceful demonstrations to violent riots (based on a combination of official announcements and extrapolation), take place annually. Moreover, their numbers are increasing every year. Also apparent is that most of these incidents are protests against a breach of rights — most often, property rights.

Some experimentation by the authorities in areas such as public participation, cooperation with NGOs or selective loosening of media controls is taking place in order to address these issues, but on an ad hoc basis. In many cases, unless innovations are institutionalized, they are lost when a forward-thinking local leader is promoted away from the district. With the exception of powerful leaders, such as those of Guangdong Province, Shanghai or Chongqing, most leaders are unwilling to take on the risk of significant experimentation. Intimately familiar with their own Party's history of purges and shifting allegiances, they remain cognizant of the consequences of failed endeavours — or even successful ones that may later fall out of favour.

Also contributing to the ferment is what is seen as an impossible situation for many of China's young people. In a society where a university degree was, in the past, virtually a guarantee of a good job and everyone had work allocated to them, many graduates are now finding themselves unemployed or seriously underemployed. The economic cooling since 2012 has accentuated this problem and anxiety for central authorities, who have responded with major Keynesian infusions of spending.

China is experiencing the largest internal migration in history. The rural population is diminishing but is still approximately 700 million, or slightly more than half the total. Low wages and difficult living conditions are forcing more and more of them to migrate to the cities in search of better wages, and the state is directing a massive urban development project to accommodate another 200 million migrants to the cities over the coming decade. Many rural villages have all but disappeared, housing only the very old and the very young — all dependent on remittances from those who have moved to the cities. For these families, traditional social structure has broken down. The days of the iron rice bowl are but a distant memory; the old social safety net is gone, and the government is struggling to replace it.

Low wages also contribute to instability. An extremely low minimum wage (ranging from US$140–US$240 per month)[12] — an income not even supporting subsistence in the increasingly expensive cities — combined with rapidly escalating property prices make ownership of even a modest home an unrealistic goal for the vast majority of the population. This lies behind the spate of protests that took place in the summer of 2010.

The Chinese leadership's preoccupation with stability has made the notion of "colour revolution" a real concern: study teams sent abroad in 2005 to examine the conditions leading to the Rose, Orange and Tulip revolutions are, by many, credited with a sense of "clamping down" experienced since 2008. The Internet Manifesto, published by exiled dissident Wang Dan and others in February 2010, can only contribute to concerns of the leadership: "This is an Internet Revolution, a colour revolution with Chinese characteristics. Four hundred million Netizens are the fresh troops of China's Internet revolution. This revolution will not be won overnight, but if we persevere night and day, day in and day out, we will ultimately shake the very foundations of CCP rule."

The Party has weathered numerous crises since its inception. The past decade, in particular, has seen an increased focus on strengthening party structures. However, the huge social issues discussed above show no indications of abating; just as one problem is addressed, another raises its head. Many question whether the use of on-the-spot solutions on regional issues, combined with continuing strong-arm tactics to silence dissent can continue to keep the lid on growing discontent.

Yu Jianrong, a scholar at the prestigious Chinese Academy of Social Science, gained international stature for his work relating to social stability and the increasing frequency and violence of "mass incidents" in recent years. In a 2009 speech to the Beijing Lawyers Association, he related how discussions with current and retired senior government cadres has shifted his earlier optimism regarding China's continued stability to growing concern: these cadres have frankly expressed the view that upheaval is unavoidable.

Following an exhaustive analysis of mass incidents and the precarious nature of China's present social stability, Yu concludes that China's political power must be reformed through judicial checks and balances from the local level; to do so from a higher level is simply not feasible in the current climate. He advocates "laying ideologies aside, and just defending the Constitution." More and more scholars and activists are advocating enforcement of the constitution as a means of moving forward both protection of human rights and democratic development in China.

---

12   See www.lawtime.cn/info/laodong/zuidigongzibiaozhun/20130116137448.html and www.mohrss.gov. cn/ldgxs/LDGXqiyegongzi/LDGXzuidigongzibiaozhun/201201/t20120119_86795.htm.

CIVIL SOCIETY AND NGOs

China's regulations for NGOs are not easy to decipher or comply with: an NGO must be both sponsored by a government organization (how it can remain "non-governmental" is a reasonable question), and then registered with the Ministry of Civil Affairs. Many NGOs unable to secure a sponsor are forced, instead, to register as corporations — a very expensive and cumbersome process that also denies them access to government funding and does not permit the raising of funds from the public. Such NGOs must therefore largely rely on foreign funding for their activities.

The difficult registration process leads to a majority of NGOs eschewing this requirement and operating without official sanction. This, however, can leave them vulnerable to action by the state authorities should they run afoul of local officials in the course of their work. At the same time, legally registered organizations are by no means immune from such action; the Open Constitution Initiative was closed down in 2009 and two of its lawyers arrested. Historically, advocacy organizations, particularly those advocating political change, are far more vulnerable than those working on issues of environment, health or public participation.

China's network of NGOs includes international NGOs, government-organized NGOs (GONGOs) and various forms of grassroots civil society. In 1988, China had 4,500 officially registered NGOs (including GONGOs). By the end of 2010, according to Tsinghua University's Deng Guosheng, there were 425,000 registered NGOs.

The growth of unregistered NGOs in China is even greater: Friends of Nature, China's first activist environmental NGO was formed in 1994. Scholars now estimate that there are between one and three million unregistered NGOs operating in China.

New regulations introduced in March 2010 require legally notarized grant agreements before an NGO can receive money from foreign foundations. Although some NGOs registered with the Ministry of Civil Affairs have been able to do so, most others have been unsuccessful. As a result, the majority of NGOs are no longer able to legally receive the overseas funding which they depend upon and face the prospect of closing their doors. Experts point to this as an example of further tightening of the environment for NGOs. Others, however, stress the importance of looking at the longer-term picture, bearing in mind that NGOs, while a relatively new phenomenon in China, have nonetheless grown exponentially.

Indeed, NGOs are increasingly filling the gap — particularly with respect to social and environmental issues — that local governments are unwilling or unable to fill. Following the 2008 Sichuan earthquake, billions of renminbi (RMB, also called the yuan) flowed into the disaster zone, but the government was not equipped to disburse all the funds that were flowing in. YouChange, a Beijing-based non-profit charitable organization, partnered with the city of Mianzhu's government to integrate resources to help with earthquake relief. The initial experience of YouChange, however, is indicative of the deep government mistrust of NGOs: no government agency was willing to work with YouChange, and the project was in danger of ending before it started. This was attributed to the fear that some NGOs use aid as a pretext for anti-state and anti-government activities, and the career of any official associated with such activities would immediately end. However, a local official eventually stepped forward, stating that "one shouldn't stop eating for fear of choking."

The success of this project, which managed to directly and indirectly disseminate over 2.1 billion RMB of aid 2008–2010, has dramatically changed the attitude of local officials toward NGOs. However, there are also concerns that this same model may bring NGOs too much into the orbit of government, turning them into GONGOs and hampering their ability to play an advocacy role.

The relationship between China's NGO community and its government is conflicted. Before the Party came into power, it gained support by providing community services and teaching people how to defend their rights against the corrupt one-party government, so it recognizes the benefit of civil society organizations in theory, but also recognizes their potential threat to its dominance of the public space. Most experts agree that the services provided by the NGO community are too great to be cut off now, and that the hole that would be left by their abolition would be too large. It is probable that they will remain an element of China's development and continue to grow in response to China's needs.

DIPLOMATIC RESOURCES AND ASSETS

The diplomatic community resident in China is large. While most countries have a presence in Beijing, many also have consulates in Shanghai, Guangzhou, Hong Kong and Chongqing or Chengdu, providing resources and opportunities for research and interaction with Chinese government and civil society over a broad geographic area. Representation outside Beijing permits reporting and analysis from outside the rarified environment of the capital, as well as beneficial contact with provincial and local officials and civil society.

Hong Kong is unique in its status as part of China, but different[13] — this difference is immediately evident when alighting from Hong Kong's iconic Star Ferry, where Falun Gong protestors have a semi-permanent presence. The abundance of research facilities, NGOs and individuals studying China from Hong Kong makes it an ideal source of information and a good location for convening meetings in a more open environment.

Diplomatic immunity can also cast a protective cloak around others, foreign nationals and even Chinese. In 2005, Sharon Hom, executive director of the international NGO Human Rights in China and a US citizen, was in Beijing as part of the EU Delegation for the EU-China Human Rights Dialogue Seminar. Returning to her hotel room one evening, she was accosted by two plainclothes

---

13   Since its return to Chinese sovereignty in 1997, Hong Kong has been permitted a high degree of autonomy with its own executive and laws, currency, etc., while leaving Beijing in charge of its defence and foreign affairs.

security personnel who attempted to get her to go to a waiting car "for a chat." She refused and was able to contact the EU diplomats in her delegation. With their assistance, and that of US diplomats who were also called to the scene, she was able to resist this attempt to intimidate her. But she and her organization were pointedly not invited to future sessions of the dialogue, either in China or in Europe.

Pressure, intimidation and outright arrest of Chinese citizens by security organs occur regularly. The shield of diplomatic immunity enables diplomats to protest and this may have had a protective effect in some cases. Ultimately, Chinese activists can seek asylum in foreign embassies or claim refugee status; this case study records several such examples. But often these useful interventions are not followed by sustained support to such independent voices for fear of upsetting the Chinese government.

In an environment where individuals are not able to leave the country, it can also be difficult to transport their possessions, including writings or films, to the outside if they are not digitized. There is no formal restriction on taking personal papers out of the country, but opaque and far-reaching designations of "state secrets" can be invoked to authorize confiscation from Chinese citizens or foreigners without diplomatic immunity. When Lu Decheng left China, he left behind not only his wife and children, but also volumes of notes documenting his 10 years in prison for defacing the portrait of Mao in Tiananmen Square during the 1989 protests. These notes filled five volumes; without them it would have been near impossible to complete his memoirs. Fortunately, a diplomat heading home for summer holidays carried the material out of China. A similar action enabled delivery of a young filmmaker's feature film about corruption in China to the Montreal International Film Festival, where it won an award.

The international community spends millions of dollars every year on rule of law and governance cooperation with China. Some of this funding is carried out by international NGOs in connection with Chinese academic institutions, NGOs or the Chinese government. Some of it is government-to-government, and some of it is NGO-to-NGO. Ironically, the sheer volume of work and the geographic spread of projects taking place in China make coordination in order to avoid duplication of effort problematic. In addition, donors may find themselves returning to the same recipient time after time, as familiarity with the grant application process and reporting requirements lies with a relatively small core of NGOs and academic institutions. In an effort to expand expertise in this area, some embassies are providing training to grassroots NGOs, and at least one has hired a consultant charged with assisting applicants with the sometimes cumbersome application process.

In 1998, Canada launched the first embassy-disbursed fund, providing support for non-governmental initiatives aimed at improving democratic practices, social services, public education, legal reform and respect for human rights in China. After 10 years, the project had contributed to support for the creation of 35 new NGOs and directly helped to strengthen 160 existing NGOs. This program served as a model for other embassy-based funds and has also had significant knock-on effects, including a legal aid pilot project that spread nationwide.

The coordination of political officers focussed on human rights is, on the other hand, well developed. Some of the larger embassies have officers focussed solely on human rights, while others have officers working on human rights and domestic politics, as it is often difficult to analyze one without an understanding of the other. An informal group of about 10 missions of Community of Democracies members gathers on a regular basis to share information and analysis. The group can also serve as a catalyst for coordinating joint demarches or demonstrative action, such as the joint effort to attend the sentencing hearing of democracy activist Liu Xiaobo for inciting subversion of state power on December 25, 2009.

China is party to a number of international human rights instruments, including the Convention against Torture and the Convention on Economic, Social and Cultural Rights. China signed the ICCPR in 1998, but despite the efforts of domestic academics and the international community, ratification has not occurred.[14] Its signature, however, reinforces the legitimacy of efforts aimed at the improvement of China's performance on political rights and supports activity aimed at improving the infrastructure to pave the way for its ratification. Justice reform and amendment of China's Criminal Procedure Law, seen as necessary before China can ratify the ICCPR, are key areas of ongoing international cooperation. China's own 1982 Constitution (Article 35) is unequivocal about rights that are every day denied: "Citizens of China enjoy freedom of speech, the press, of assembly, of association, of procession, and of demonstration." The 2004 constitutional amendment stipulating that "the State respects and safeguards human rights" has not, in the absence of a constitutional court, had any visible impact.

APPLYING THE ASSETS TO MAKE A DIFFERENCE

The Golden Rules

Nota Bene: Many of the tools in the *Handbook* apply equally well to the NGO sector. Due to the sensitivity of many of the projects that are currently underway, as well as the high level of cooperation between the NGO and the diplomatic sectors, examples of the application of the tools have been drawn from both international NGO and diplomatic representatives. In addition, the sensitive nature of many of the projects involving foreign governments — even in the case of cooperation with various levels of the Chinese government — result in a reluctance to specifically name either the country or the Chinese government department involved. For this reason, many of the examples given below relating to recent or ongoing activities are — of necessity — vague and unattributed.

---

14   See www.youtube.com/watch?v=N76-OIyYyD8.

Diplomats posted to China routinely undergo extensive language training in advance of their move. While such training is, of course, pragmatic, allowing diplomats to interact directly with the Chinese people, another significant benefit is the recognition of willingness to invest the time and resources necessary to learn a language as challenging as Mandarin as a sign of respect. The lengthy and arduous language training process also doubles as an intensive course in Chinese history, culture, economics and politics, better equipping diplomats to function in China's environment upon arrival.

The UK's Strategic Engagement Policy with China, issued in early 2008, is representative of the extent to which most of China's democratic partners wish to demonstrate their understanding of China's sense of historic identity and stature, another effective demonstration of respect. By clearly setting out its foreign policy objectives in China, it has introduced greater transparency into the relationship, laying out a road map for future cooperation, and clearly flagging issues of importance. This demonstration of transparency also lends an additional layer of legitimacy to cooperation in support of China's efforts to improve transparency and accountability in its own governance.

Diplomats functioning in China must be adept at listening not only to what their Chinese interlocutors are saying, but also to the choice of words used by other representatives of their government, such as ministers and experts, and the choice of words used by interpreters in meetings. Many concepts relating to human rights and democracy do not translate well into Chinese or correspond to Chinese official thinking. Article 1 of the 1982 Constitution, for example, affirms the "people's democratic dictatorship." In order to convey the intended tone and nuance, use of the appropriate word can be critical. It is not unusual for a Chinese official — many of whom are fluent in English — to correct their interpreters in the course of meetings: their command of both languages used in meetings provides a distinct advantage.

Understanding sensitivities is critical in determining in which areas foreign governments and NGOs can be overtly involved, and where their involvement is best kept under wraps. One domestic NGO authority on democratic development is now focussed on elections, where a significant upsurge in the number of independent candidates has been recorded. In the 2006-2007 election cycle, Beijing alone put forward about 30,000 independent candidates, and the number has trebled in election cycles since. While the expert acknowledges the considerable foreign interest in this area, he advises that foreign involvement is likely to be counterproductive because of the high level of "nervousness" in the leadership.

Such nervousness is linked to concerns regarding allegations of foreign involvement in Europe's series of so-called colour revolutions, from 2000 to 2005. The phenomenon of the Arab Spring reinforced official wariness, and information about events in Egypt and Tunisia was, to the extent possible, carefully controlled. At the same time, however, this previously mentioned NGO's pilot projects in the area of public participation have come to the largely favourable attention of the highest levels in China's central government. Articles about these pilots are attracting a great deal of domestic media attention in the country's increasingly privately owned (though still strictly controlled) press. In an environment where experimentation rarely takes place in the absence of senior level approval, and where such approval is rarely — if ever — explicit, tacit government support for such pilots is often discerned by tracking commentary in the *People's Daily* (the official media organ of the Party), where favourable reports can signal an opportunity for greater openness in a field.

Similarly, many countries have experienced a greater degree of success in cooperative projects — particularly in sensitive areas — if embassies step back from direct involvement in support activity. Proposals to local governments put forward by academics, rather than a foreign government, are more apt to be accepted. In the case of one seminal conference relating to NGO development, the sponsoring government left all reference to its involvement off the conference materials and did not actively participate in the conference. Absence of the foreign presence allowed officials and NGOs to speak freely and establish contacts that some Chinese participants would not have pursued in the presence of foreigners, especially from embassies. Additionally, China's rigid system of protocol requires the presence of certain senior officials (or individuals holding a certain position) at conferences involving foreigners that can have a dampening effect on candour and outcomes.

One diplomat reported the cancellation of a poverty alleviation project in a remote province. The reason given for the cancellation of such a seemingly uncontroversial project was that the local officials did not want the fact of foreign involvement to be known. The diplomat asked not to be named, as they hoped to restart the project in the future with a different approach.

In some cases, the challenge in reaching agreement is with the language proposed, rather than the concept itself. Understanding the constraints and priorities of various government ministries has assisted in framing projects that are "win-win." The US–China Rule of Law Initiative is a classic example of this: its official title is "Cooperation in the Field of Law."

One country that wished to cooperate with China in a certain area of justice reform is having success by taking a practical approach. As an example, after listening to China's greatest concern in the area of reform, such as prison reform, the foreign partner presents a business case approach that links a human rights emphasis in international research to China's desired outcome. This approach has delivered additional dividends: an improved relationship with a generally inaccessible government ministry and improved access to prisons.

Former Canadian Ambassador Joseph Caron was never afraid to push boundaries in the course of his meetings with senior government or Party officials. He recalls lively discussions with Pan Yue, then vice minister of China's State Environment Protection Administration, arguing the necessity of freedom of the media in order to enable the government to better do its work and root out corruption. Indeed, it was one of the first areas of both increased NGO involvement and increased journalistic activism. Pan not only used the media himself to bring environmental problems to the attention of the public, but during his tenure, journalists enjoyed a greater freedom in their ability to report on environmental issues. While Ambassador Caron was unlikely to have been the only foreign diplomat stressing the economic benefits of a freer media to Pan, the recognition by diplomats of opportunities where there may be both a business case to be made, and the space to move forward (here, in the form of a forward-thinking and risk-taking leader) can support efforts to pave the path to change.

Understanding an Opaque Environment

In an environment where "tea-leaf reading"[15] is both a hobby and a professional necessity, certain developments may be assigned a significance they may not merit. Understanding the broader political environment can enable diplomats to avoid the "loosening and tightening" flavour of reporting, which can be misinterpreted in capitals and lead to an ill-supported sense of the often volatile situation on the ground.

For example, according to David Bandurski, a Hong Kong-based academic working with China's growing professional journalist community, frequent references to "another press crackdown" in China are misleading: the "crackdown" has been ongoing since 1989. While control remains constant, he maintains that the type of manipulation shifts in response to the changing reality on the ground. This changing reality is also strongly influenced by the Internet. For example, a story regarding local corruption will be picked up by the Internet, and so can't be completely silenced. Rather than banning all reporting, as would have happened several years ago, the news cycle is now used: coverage by independent media is restricted, but Xinhua (China's official news agency) is permitted to cover it. Xinhua then "exposes" the story, points the finger at local corrupt officials and gets to play the "good guy." This may be interpreted as "loosening," just as a subsequent removal of an editor for publishing an investigative analysis may be interpreted as a "crackdown." Understanding the underlying and somewhat obscure cycle of "control, change and chaos" can help better target cooperation with China's nascent domestic journalism community.

The Beijing diplomatic community focussed on human rights issues is closely knit, sharing information on a regular basis and on a variety of issues, including recent developments and new initiatives. It coordinates joint demarches, exchanges translations of key documents or articles and compares notes in analyzing the constantly changing face of China's human rights situation.

Many diplomats are also part of international, informal networks of China-watchers: academics, businesspeople, journalists and others with an ongoing interest in, or involvement with, China. Such groups are invaluable resources for the

---

15   Tea-leaf reading refers to the tendency of all China watchers — in the absence of media or government transparency and in an environment where little happens without a reason — to interpret new policies or actions by the leadership as having significance. However, the interpretation is not always correct, and there is not always an underlying agenda.

real-time exchange of information and interpretation of events in China, including detention or release of activists, updates on recent policy changes or interpretation of the actions of China's leadership. Multiple open online sources, such as *China Digital Times*, also contribute to the worldwide sharing of information about China, as well as translations of Chinese documents and articles.

Truth in Communications

Despite the existence of China's infamous GFW, information is flowing to and from China's human rights defenders, some of whom have thousands following their tweets and blogs. With more than 564 million Internet users, it is simply not possible for authorities to monitor all emails, tweets, blogs and posts that these users generate. The state incentives of the "50-cent party"[16] are having little, if any, effect on the increasingly savvy Internet population, gaining more derisory comments than converts.

Han-Han, a prominent Chinese blogger, was voted the second most influential person in the world in *Time Magazine*'s 2010 list. His acerbic, political jabs at government policy and restrictions of the media have gained him millions of followers, as well as generating controversy over authenticity of authorship. Internationally acclaimed artist Ai Weiwei and "the Butcher" are also well-known members of this growing cohort of Internet crusaders, using it as their twenty-first century Democracy Wall. The *Financial Times'* Peter Aspden (2012) wrote of Ai that "Chinese authorities know they have a problem on their hands with Ai. He is truculent, unafraid, and is just about the shrewdest user of social media around. He is up for the fight. 'No outdoor sports can be more elegant than throwing stones at autocracy; no melees can be more exciting than those in cyberspace.' His antagonists have but a feeble counter-attack. 'The government computer has but one button: delete.'"

One thing that many of these bloggers and activists have in common is the occurrence of a single event triggering their Internet activism. Although the events differ, they generally relate to the discovery of a specific injustice or cover-up, such as over the tainted milk scandal, the number of children who perished in the Sichuan earthquake or the arrest of Liu Xiaobo. The number of signatures to Charter 08 continues to grow, undeterred by Mr. Liu's sentencing.[17] Sharon Hom reports that many well-known writers who had been using pseudonyms for some of their more controversial work have ceased to do so since Xiaobo's sentencing. The Internet is encouraging a different type of activism.

---

16   Individuals who are paid a half RMB/yuan for each pro-government post they submit to chat rooms.

17   At the time of writing, one estimate of the number of signatories is 20,000. See Andreas Lorenz, "Liu Xiaobo as Role Model: Nobel Peace Prize Inspires Chinese Dissidents," *Der Spiegel Online International*, available at www.spiegel.de/international/world/liu-xiaobo-as-role-model-nobel-peace-prize-inspires-chinese-dissidents-a-723808.html.

In March 2010 following its decision to no longer comply with China's monitoring policies, Google's redirection mainland Chinese users to its Hong Kong site, google.com.hk, was hailed by many Chinese democracy activists as a great victory. While many activists are able to sidestep the GFW through a series of different and increasingly sophisticated measures, Google's move to Hong Kong is better informing the average user by now allowing them to see just how many sites are blocked — even though access to these sites remains censored.

In July 2010, the Government of China renewed Google's licence to operate its website in mainland China without changing its censorship rules. While some have criticized Google's decision, users in mainland China will have the option to click a link to switch over to the Hong Kong site. Xiao Qiang, then director of the China Internet Project at UC Berkeley, cautiously pointed out that this decision broke new ground, stating, "It is unprecedented for a private company to challenge Chinese Internet censorship…In the past, there would have been no doubt that the Chinese government would have punished Google." The government's decision, Xiao adds, is "a very calculated position that is good for China's long-term development and openness."

Many embassies make use of the Internet and blogs to reach the Chinese public. For example, one British Embassy blog, providing an account of a day spent with a migrant worker, had, after being translated into Chinese, 30,000 hits in its first five hours. This account had the effect of both informing the local population about the plight of individuals literally in their own backyard, and of providing this same population with a different view of the foreign community that they have been taught to fear.[18]

The Canadian Embassy pursues a very proactive e-diplomacy program via a webpage on the Chinese Sina Weibo platform, which specializes in 140-character bursts, much like Twitter. It has rapidly obtained a very large audience and a significant interactive following. Canadian Ambassador Mark McDowell has explained that the site aims to demystify diplomatic representation in a voice that is comparatively "young." In countering the image of diplomacy as opaque, the site showcases transparency and diversity, including of opinion, and including comment critical of Canada. One episode went viral among the Chinese audience: the preceding Canadian Ambassador David Mulroney was shown in his ambassadorial "limousine," a modest fuel-efficient Toyota Prius, which Chinese comment swiftly contrasted to the up-market limos regularly used by Chinese officials.

While the Internet revolution has shifted much focus from shortwave radio broadcasts such as Voice of America or Radio Free Asia, the important role they have played in the past — and continue to play — in providing information to populations behind the GFW should not be discounted. Lu Decheng, sentenced to 16 years (imprisoned for 10 years) after throwing ink at Mao's portrait in Tiananmen

---

18   A number of Chinese activists and academics have referred to the continuing fear and antipathy that exists toward "the West," resulting from an anti-foreign bias in the education system. They have stressed the importance of increasing people-to-people ties as a means of dissipating such perceptions.

Square, recounts how he and others relied on such broadcasts to learn about events in China, including commentaries by late astrophysicist and democracy proponent Fang Lizhi, well before the 1989 Tiananmen protests.[19] Such broadcasts are still of importance for those who either do not have access to a computer, or who have access, but are unable to scale the GFW.

Liu Xiaobo, the activist imprisoned in 2009 for 11 years for his role in drafting Charter 08, underscored the importance of international media in giving voice to those who no longer can speak in China: "I, who had been drawn into the path of dissidence by the passions of June Fourth, after leaving the Qincheng Prison in 1991, lost in the right to speak openly in my own country, and could only do so through overseas media, and hence was monitored for many years; placed under surveillance (May 1995–January 1996); educated through labour (October 1996–October 1999), and now once again am thrust into the dock by enemies in the regime."

Some diplomatic informing of the Chinese public is unequivocally popular, but correspondingly distasteful to the regime. In June 2012, Deputy Environment Minister Wu Xiaoqing warned foreign embassies to refrain from publicizing their own air pollution readings — a pointed reference to the US Embassy, which puts such data on its website for the benefit of its staff and the general public (BBC News, 2012). Wu stated that the US publishing of air pollution statistics violated the Vienna Convention on Diplomatic Relations. The figures from the embassy monitoring station were considerably higher than official statistics, sparking an outcry and forcing a reassessment of environmental monitoring in chronically polluted Beijing.

Diplomats' efforts to provide balanced reporting to capitals can be challenged by inaccurate or biased media reports in the home country media, or by inaccurate views held by individuals in capitals who still hold outdated preconceptions of Chinese society and the extent of modernization and sophistication in its cities.

A diplomat's efforts at reporting are only as useful as the willingness of the recipients to read and assess this reporting. Many diplomats based in Beijing (as elsewhere) complain about the "black hole" into which their reports often fall. However, those targeting their reports on long-term strategic issues, and who identify specific links to issues of national interest, report increased readership in capitals.

As the above makes clear, reporting has its limitations; there is no substitute for actual travel to other countries to promote understanding. Well over two million Chinese citizens have travelled abroad to study since 1979. These numbers include academics, government officials, private citizens, judges and any other imaginable category of citizen. Diplomats working on cooperative development projects have found that those officials with overseas experience are far more open to incorporation of human rights elements in the development of projects.

While informing capitals of important developments in China through reporting is an opportunity, it is also a responsibility. Activists are willing — even eager — to

---

19   See Denise Chong's memoir *Egg on Mao* (2009), an account of the events leading up to Decheng's throwing ink at the portrait of Mao during the 1989 Tiananmen demonstrations, and the resulting 16-year prison sentence.

meet with foreign diplomats and journalists. In contrast to the situation 10 years ago, they are very frank and open in their comments; yet, these same activists are still taking a risk. The diplomats with whom they meet have a corresponding responsibility to interpret and report such contacts judiciously, as well as the way they use their networks to share this information. Such information sharing can provide these risk-takers with some semblance of protection.

David Bandurski, of Hong Kong University's China Media Project, states that although the government's effort to control the media has not changed since the aftermath of Tiananmen Square, there has been a significant social change. Now, papers are market-based, so public demand is having a greater impact on what is found in the news, which is leading to watchdog journalism. He believes that a new pluralism is emerging and leading to gaps where professionals can fill the space.

But China remains a difficult environment for domestic journalists. The Committee to Protect Journalists reported that 32 journalists were imprisoned as of the end of 2012 (BBC News Asia, 2013). Reporters without Borders qualified China as an "enemy of the Internet" the same year. Sixty-nine Internet users were jailed as of early 2013 (ibid.).

Working with the Government

As the first summit meeting between US President Obama and the new President of China Xi Jinping in Palm Springs, California in May 2013 illustrated, there is a multitude of major intersecting interests between these two great powers. China's regional and increasingly global impact has central significance to the interests of other governments around the world.

Within the framework of such interests, the international community has, by now, an established history of cooperation with the Chinese government in a broad range of governance areas, from village elections to open government, accountability, human rights in prisons, procuratorate[20] reform and judges' training. This cooperation takes place with all levels of government, and may have an impact that is felt, though not yet seen. For example, a lawyer representing several well-known human rights defenders advised that he has seen a positive change in judges over the years, which he attributes to ongoing judges' training that has been undertaken by a number of nations. Some of these judges have advised, unofficially, that they agree with the arguments of the defence, despite having no flexibility regarding the verdict they must deliver. For lawyers working within this system, such recognition by judges of the illegitimacy of the process, together with a willingness to communicate such sentiments, is a small but significant step forward.

China's cooperation with other countries can, however, be held hostage to changes in policy from the centre, or at the local level. In cases where long-term programming is anticipated, making at least the principle of cooperation a part of a summit

---

20   The Supreme People's Procuratorate is responsible for prosecuting criminal cases, investigating corruption and overseeing the criminal justice system.

process, and incorporating the agreement to cooperate in a summit document, has been a means of preserving the nature of the project, and, in some cases, assuring its very existence. The US Rule of Law Initiative is an example: its inclusion in the 1997 Clinton-Jiang summit document ensured its continuing legitimacy (though it went dormant for a time due to lack of funding). Such government-to-government agreements also provide legitimacy for NGOs working in the same field. In cases where NGOs run into trouble with local authorities, it is possible to point to the high-level agreement as an indication of an area where cooperation has the blessing of the central authorities.

Sometimes the most unlikely circumstances can lead to working with the government — or at least the dissemination of central policy to local areas. In advance of the 2008 Beijing Olympics, restrictions on foreign media were relaxed, allowing reporters to interview anyone they wished, as long as that person consented. Initially, local authorities were not aware of these regulations, and would not permit journalists to enter their districts. The journalists had laminated cards printed, containing the text of the regulations, together with contact names and numbers in Beijing for further information. This relatively simple solution both informed local authorities and allowed the journalists to get on with their work.

The Human Rights Dialogues, established between a number of countries and China, have consistently come under fire from the international NGO community for their failure to achieve concrete results. Nonetheless, there is consensus among diplomats that they can serve as a springboard for a number of less visible but more effective efforts. The dialogues have been used to bring together Chinese government and NGO representatives, or high-level Chinese officials from various government departments. Some dialogues also provide an opportunity for high-level (vice-ministerial) meetings and demarches. This is particularly important in the current environment where China is increasingly resistant to accepting demarches.

The EU dialogue on the death penalty, driven by its values, has taken a practical, incremental approach. In the eight years since the dialogue started, China's attitude has gone from "the Chinese people want the death penalty" to "it will eventually be abolished." Although it has not been abolished, regulatory changes over recent years are believed to have had an effect of reducing the number of executions, although it is not possible to be certain, because these numbers remain shrouded in secrecy.

Dialogue can take many other forms, as well. The US is credited with having a positive impact on treatment of persons with hepatitis as a result of raising the issue with the Ministry of Health. In 2008, hundreds — mainly children — were poisoned (many fatally) by milk and infant formula cut with melamine as a cost-saving measure. New Zealand is credited with breaking the scandal as a result of its officials in Beijing — on the instructions of their prime minister — notifying relevant ministries in Beijing of the problem, and the failure of local authorities to institute a recall. This latter case has led to new food safety legislation, though, as with much of China's legislation, enforcement remains problematic.

When working with China on human rights issues, most countries use a combination of closed-door and public declaratory diplomacy. A number of Chinese activists, while stressing the importance of demarching, also stress the importance of determining which form of diplomacy is most likely to be effective. Says one: "Reduce the room for human rights violators to abuse the comments made, and make sure you can afford to make the statement, and are not going to be forced to back down at a later point." A 2009 case involving a foreign national, where public protest failed because of inadequate information, was Australian Prime Minister Kevin Rudd's threat of possible economic consequences in the case of Stern Hu, a Rio Tinto executive. After Hu confessed to corruption charges, he was sentenced to 10 years' imprisonment in China in 2010.

Regarding protests on apparent human rights violations on dual nationals, foreign governments need to cope with China's policy of disregarding the legitimacy of the foreign citizenship claim. Public pledges by foreign leaders to extract their citizens from their Chinese difficulties need to be carefully calibrated with the private messaging to the Chinese authorities.

When a democratic head of government has concerns over the jailing in China of a national, a dual national (a status the Chinese do not recognize) or even a Chinese citizen, the manner in which the matter is raised can influence the outcome. The Chinese recognize that the jailing of an activist as prominent as Liu Xiaobo will oblige democratic representatives to protest in public, and they generally give their side of the argument publicly. This is not apt to yield a change favouring the prisoner, but moral support and visibility is of some value to his ongoing cause. Practical outcomes are more likely to emerge from private demarches situated in the context of the bilateral relationship. Making it known in advance that such a matter will be raised is not in itself counterproductive. But if public statements imply that a summit meeting with the Chinese leadership is being sought specifically to take up a case, and especially if the statement is litigious, contentious and critical of the Chinese legal process, experience shows that the meeting is unlikely to even take place, much less help the prisoner.

There is broad agreement regarding the value of demarching in China, although tangible results have become less clear in recent years. Chinese authorities have responded positively to several private top-level demarches to permit the release of jailed activists and their travel to asylum abroad, but rarely respond positively to public campaigns, especially if these seem directed to a foreign country's domestic political constituency. As for everything in China, the best results emerge when they can be shown to have been in Chinese self-interest and not foreign pressure.

Demarches at high levels, or in advance of high-level visits, have succeeded in securing the release of a number of high visibility individuals, including Rebiya Khadeer, Jiang Weiping, Wei Jingsheng and Chen Guangcheng, and in May 2013, some of his immediate relatives, to name a few. However, this particular element of success is seen as mixed, as those who do not immediately leave China may again disappear or be arrested in very short order, as in the cases of Gao Zhisheng or Hu Jia.

Reaching Out

Former US Ambassador Winston Lord (in office 1985–1989) took advantage of a period of relative openness to meet with a wide range of academics, artists, students and others. His appearance, together with his wife Bette Bao Lord, at Beijing University's Democracy Salon in June 1988, caused a sensation — both for the hundreds of students present, but also for the Chinese leadership. Ambassador Lord was subsequently advised that he should have obtained the government's permission to speak to the students — and that this advice came directly from Deng Xiaoping. Ambassador Lord's reaction was swift and vehement, stating that no one would be expected to obtain advance clearance to meet with students at Yale or Harvard and that he had the right to do the same at Beijing University. Nothing more was heard on the matter.

Ambassador Lord first opened his residence to Chinese visitors on his arrival in 1985. He and his wife, well-known author Bette Bao Lord, opened the embassy's July 4th celebrations to Chinese civil society and worked on a daily basis to increase their people-to-people ties through a variety of means, such as a series of discussion evenings. They invited political and economic reformers to their home, together with officials, academics or other diplomats for informal discussion on a variety of topics ranging from culture to science to more overtly political topics.

Such access to the diplomatic community and to Chinese officials was rare for the academic and activist community, particularly in 1986. It not only provided the US Embassy with valuable insights into the views of some key members of the academic and cultural community in the years between the 1986 Shanghai democracy protests and the Tiananmen Square protests, but it also provided what was then a rare opportunity for different elements of China's stratified society to meet and share views with each other, representing a convening function.

Many individuals doing advocacy work in the area of human rights stress the importance of making such contacts. They advise that instances of diplomats using the embassy or their own homes as places to meet and discuss issues — be it one-on-one or as a networking opportunity — is invaluable. They stress the value of this in breaking down the antipathy and fear that many Chinese people have been taught to feel for Westerners, stating that people-to-people connections are the best means of increasing understanding and breaking down barriers, as demonstrated by the myriad exchange programs that have been instituted in recent decades, often administered or facilitated by embassy personnel.

Convening NGOs and government officials can have valuable secondary effects in a society where NGOs not only rarely have access to government officials, but are often mistrusted by them. One prominent independent people's deputy[21] and vocal women's rights advocate advised that one of her most valuable government contacts was met during a conference convened by the Canadian International Development Agency. This contact has since become instrumental in her gender equality and training work.

The Fourth World Conference on Women, held in Beijing in September 1995, has been described as a watershed for the development of China's then nascent NGO community. Although many aspects of the conference — such as confining the NGO element to a separate venue and requiring protest to take place within defined zones — came under fire from the international community, it provided a valuable and unprecedented opportunity for Chinese NGOs to witness protest, establish connections with the international NGO community and participate in an international human rights conference. One Canadian diplomat recalls racing to the protest site upon receiving information that some Canadians were preparing to unfurl a "Remember Tiananmen" banner in the designated demonstration zone. Instead of having to deal with the feared consular case, he vividly recalls watching both private citizens and local police standing by watching the Canadians demonstrate.

A three-day conference on international law in Hong Kong for a group of China's public interest lawyers was instrumental in providing them with additional tools for the protection of their clients. In particular, many of these lawyers were not aware that China is a party to the UN Convention against Torture. They were given training on the convention's provisions, and suggestions on how to use the provisions of the UN International Covenant on Economic, Social and Cultural Rights to fight for their own, and their clients' rights. These same lawyers were also provided training on how to draw up detailed and well-reasoned defence statements. Although the courts rarely permit submission of such statements, the lawyers continue to prepare them and are now posting them on the Internet as a means of publicizing their clients' arguments, and as a resource for others. When the *Handbook*'s second edition was published in 2010, none of these lawyers had been "invited to tea" by local police.[22] A British Embassy initiative relating to the implementation of the new Lawyers' Law would not have taken place without foreign involvement: they brought lawyers, judges and other officials together in one room to discuss necessary steps for implementation.

Over the past 30 years, the international community has invested considerable money and effort into a broad range of collaborative efforts with both government

---

21   While the vast majority of people's deputies are Party members, there is a slowly growing number of independent representatives, although this is only at the lowest levels. Contrary to those deputies who are Party members, and thus see themselves as answerable to the levels above them in order to advance their careers, independent representatives have no opportunity of career advancement within the system, and so work for the rights of their constituents.

22   People who have come to the attention of authorities, but who haven't broken any laws, are "invited to tea" with local police. Such invitations are often issued to activists and were offered with particular frequency to individuals who signed Charter 08. It has now become a topic of several blogs, where invitees share their experiences.

and civil society in support of China's democratic development. Justice reform, village elections, judicial training and accountability are all areas that have benefitted from direct government-to-government cooperation.

In addition to the large-scale, primarily government-to-government cooperation, there are countless examples where a relatively small amount of funding, capacity building or networking opportunities provided grassroots civil society organizations with either the push to expand their operations or the tools and encouragement necessary to continue their work.

Little Bird is a grassroots organization started by a migrant worker in Beijing, who, in the beginning, didn't even know he was starting a civil society organization — he was just connecting migrant workers with each other. In 2003, he was given the opportunity to grow through an embassy-administered civil society fund, which provided him with a small sum to set up a hotline for migrant workers. He is now partnered with local governments, has been approached to mediate labour disputes and has started similar NGOs in two other cities. Although he continues to need some foreign funding, he has also established effective partnerships with local government agencies — an occurrence that is still rare, but would have been unthinkable 15 years ago.

Until recently, all social programming in China was undertaken by the state. In recent years, NGOs have been filling in gaps where the state has been unwilling or unable to respond to increasing demand for services. Work by China's nascent civil society — particularly in the areas of environment, migrant workers and disabilities — is providing valuable experience to the Chinese public in lobbying government, organization and capacity building. A wide range of embassy-based programs and international NGO cooperation is providing support to these NGOs to develop their capacity and networks.

However, as one diplomat based in Beijing is quick to point out, the "ecology of China's civil society is still in its early stages." He cautions that until civil society is better established, the international community should not have the institutional expectations it might have of other, better developed civil societies. Until there is a critical mass of civil society organizations, they will not be able to move decisively forward with reform.

China's civil society has been developing in fits and starts, characterized by rapid expansion and sudden restrictions. Independent NGOs lead an uncertain existence in China. Recently implemented regulations relating to the foreign funding of NGOs (a global trend among authoritarian governments) have led many to conclude that the regulations are aimed at shutting down NGOs that receive foreign funding. The head of a Hong Kong-based NGO (who has personally suffered the consequences of past campaigns to silence dissent) stresses the need to first look at new policies from the perspective of a legitimate government (increasing tax revenue from funds coming into the country), rather than that of a human rights violator (stifling the environment for NGOs). He believes that this is precisely where reasonable government-to-government discussion may succeed in finding a solution. If China is immediately accused of making regulatory changes in order to further control NGOs, the door to reasonable discussion is closed, regardless of whether or not this was indeed the original intent. If, through efforts to work cooperatively, it becomes evident that measures are indeed intended to restrict the environment for NGOs, then it becomes the time to move to other means of expressing concern — through private and then perhaps more public statements.

Both he and the head of another think tank that have suffered a negative impact from these new regulations counsel creative solutions and flexibility in order to minimize the negative impact: one organization has studied the regulations and identified what must be done in order to continue receiving foreign funds. It is cumbersome, but possible. Another organization has identified a legal means to receive funds without going through the prescribed hoops — but it is an unorthodox means that many foreign governments are unwilling to follow.

Challenges

China's stature as a world power is such that fear of arousing its wrath is leading to the widespread self-censorship of businesspeople, academics and public officials outside China, as well as within its borders. It is a phenomenon described by eminent China scholar Perry Link as "the anaconda in the chandelier." It is never clear where the boundaries between allowed and illegal, or innocuous and offensive comment may be, but the anaconda remains coiled in the chandelier above your head, waiting to descend if that invisible line is crossed. So, rather than risk inciting the anaconda's wrath, it tends to be the safe road that is taken. This leads to a great deal of defensive self-censorship and conservatism.

Beijing diplomats expressed concern that groups with the loudest voices often drive priorities from capitals, possibly sending an inconsistent message to Beijing. The most obvious example was with respect to support for the situation of ethnic Tibetans or Uighurs — countries with a large or vocal ethnic Tibetan population may advocate the interests of Tibetans, or vice versa.

Defending Democrats

During the protests on Tiananmen Square between April and June 1989, representatives of the international diplomatic community could often be seen there, speaking with demonstrators and subsequently reporting back to capitals. Frequent peaceful demonstrations in Beijing also provide opportunities to both speak with petitioners and to provide these petitioners with access — albeit fleeting — to a foreign diplomat. One diplomat recalls being mobbed by petitioners who had travelled to Beijing from the countryside and were marching toward the UN offices. Thrusting copies of their petitions and supporting documents at her, they begged that their plight be made known to foreign governments. In this case, the diplomat was physically restrained by undercover police while the papers were wrenched from her grasp. This particular incident is indicative of both a concern on the part of the authorities that details of internal conflict not be made known, as well as the desperation of citizens to have their stories heard.

More recently, the diplomatic community has provided valuable support to democracy activists through their visible and high-level presence at the sentencing hearing of frequently imprisoned democracy activist Liu Xiaobo on Christmas Day, 2009. Diplomats from numerous democracies, including Australia, Canada, Great Britain, New Zealand, Sweden and the US attempted to witness Liu's trial and stood vigil outside the court, demonstrating support to Liu and his supporters (Anna, 2009). Several members of the activist community have commented on the value of this demonstration of international support to Liu's supporters — whether they were at the courthouse, under house arrest or observing events from a distance — stating that it has given many others the courage to protest. As Perry Link (2010) wrote in his blog entry from the Nobel ceremony in Oslo, "China's rulers have consistently denounced his Charter 08 as 'un-Chinese,' even while they assiduously prevent its publication inside China, apparently from a fear that ordinary people, were they to read it, might not find it so un-Chinese. The Internet is porous, and the Nobel Prize will certainly make Chinese people curious to learn more about Liu Xiaobo." Indeed, the signatures of Charter 08 increased steadily following Liu's sentencing, and many prominent authors and academics who had previously used pseudonyms came into the open with their calls for change.

Liu (2010) has made it clear that he favours evolutionary change toward democracy in China: "China's political reform…should be gradual, peaceful, orderly and controllable and should be interactive, from above to below and from below to above…orderly and controllable change is better than one which is chaotic and out of control…This is not 'inciting subversion of state power.' Opposition is not equivalent to subversion." The EU and US have called for Liu's unconditional release from imprisonment. China rebuffed such statements as attempts to interfere in its internal affairs (Grajewski, 2009; Yu, 2009).

While not a diplomatic act, awarding Liu Xiaobo the 2010 Nobel Peace Prize was seen as a valuable recognition of what has been described as the "lonely struggle" of the activist. His win sent a meaningful message to Chinese human rights defenders and activists that they remain a factor, despite all the *realpolitik* relations with the regime. It also generated massive interest: the Human Rights Watch website, which had a feature on Liu, got more hits in 24 hours from China than it typically did in a year immediately after Liu's Nobel was announced (Link, 2010).

Liu and his wife were both unable to attend the December 10, 2010 Nobel award ceremony, thus he became only the second Nobel laureate to be unrepresented. A number of countries — all authoritarian — refused to send representation, including *Handbook* cases Cuba, Egypt, Russia and Tunisia. The Chairman of the Nobel Committee, Thorbjørn Jagland, dramatically left Liu's chair empty and placed the Nobel diploma and medal upon it. Jagland noted that the award did not attack or weaken China, but only could make it stronger, much the same way that the award to Martin Luther King, Jr. pressed America to become a better country (ibid.)."We regret that the Laureate is not present here today. He is in isolation in a prison in northeast China…This fact alone shows that the award was necessary and appropriate" (ibid.). Norwegian actress Liv Ullman read Liu's court statement, titled "I have no enemies," in full in lieu of a speech: "I have no enemies, and no hatred…For hatred is corrosive of person's wisdom and conscience…I do not feel guilty for following my constitutional right to freedom of expression, for fulfilling my social responsibility as a Chinese citizen. Even if accused of it, I would have no complaints"(cited in McKey, 2010).

In the speech, "he also attacked those who have accepted the grand bargain struck by China's leaders, to provide wealth in exchange for political support, saying that the 'people immersed in the pursuit of wealth or intoxicated with the happiness of a comfortable life' are merely taking part in a 'fabricated carnival'" (cited in Moore, 2010).

Former Czech Republic President Václav Havel arrives at the Chinese Embassy to deliver a protest against imprisonment of the Chinese dissident Liu Xiaobo in Prague, Czech Republic, on January 6, 2010. Liu Xiaobo was sentenced on December 25, 2009 to 11 years in prison on subversion charges. (AP Photo / Petr David Josek)

Chinese dissidents and human rights campaigners applauded the award to Liu; three dozen attended the ceremony. Su Xiaokang, whose "River Elegy" series asserts that Communist Party rule in China was in its essence feudal and traditional, applauded Norway for giving the award. "The big democracies — America, Britain,

France, Germany — all know what democracy is but won't stand up in public to Beijing's contempt for human rights. It takes a little country to do a big thing" (cited in Link, 2010). Renée Xia of China Human Rights Defenders said the Chinese reaction to the Nobel was hardly surprising: "To us, that empty chair is not the least bit surprising. Of course Beijing treats its critics that way. This is wholly normal. If the rest of the world is startled, then good; maybe surprise can be the first step to better understanding of how things really are" (ibid.).

Fang Lizhi, also in attendance, overheard Xia and said "now the world is starting to care what happens in China. It's a sign that China is now a 'big country,' and that's what Beijing has always said it wants, right?" (ibid.). Jimmy Lai, a refugee from China who now owns media in Hong Kong and Taiwan, also attended the ceremony and opined, "now people can see that 'China' in the twenty-first century can be something much bigger and better than the Communist Party" (ibid.). Hu Ping, longtime friend of Liu Xiaobo's and editor of *Beijing Spring*, was doubtful the Communist regime would alter its formula. "As they see it, the current strategy works. The formula 'money + violence' works, and we stay on top. We know what the world means by human rights and democracy, but why should we do that? Aren't we getting stronger and richer all the time? Twenty years ago the West wasn't afraid of us, and now they have to be. Should we change what works?" (ibid.).

In 2002, after the AIDS activist organization Aizhixing drew attention to China's tainted blood banks, Wan Yanhai was arrested on suspicion of "leaking state secrets" for publishing online a government report documenting the transfusion-borne spread of AIDS. Wan, who was jailed for a month but never formally charged, credited his release to the political pressure generated by an international media campaign. Citing increasing official harassment and fears of imminent arrest, Wan moved to the US in 2010. He has, however, expressed the hope that he will be permitted to safely return to China in the future.

The case of the late astrophysicist Fang Lizhi is perhaps one of the best-known examples of a foreign embassy providing protection in China. Fang had become well known as a democracy activist as early as 1956, during the Hundred Flowers Movement. He was purged as a result of his writings at that time, but again rose to prominence in activist circles in 1985, gaining even greater prominence in the months leading up to June 4, 1989. On June 5, Fang and his wife sought refuge at the US Embassy in Beijing, where they remained for over a year before being sent by military transport to England. Fang had had frequent interaction with the previous US ambassador and his wife, and had visited their residence on several previous occasions.

More recently, the case of lawyer and human rights advocate Chen Guangfeng made international headlines. Chen was held under effective (and illegal) house arrest in Shandong province, with his family suffering harassment and visitors barred from seeing him. His plight attracted international media, diplomatic and even celebrity attention. For example, US actor Christian Bale and a CNN crew were physically assaulted and pursued by security officials when trying to meet him

(CNN, 2011). US Secretary of State Hillary Clinton expressed her "alarm" at his detention (Tandon, 2011).

Chen dramatically fled his confinement in April 2012, climbing over a wall and meeting colleagues at a pre-arranged rendezvous point, badly injuring his foot in the process (BBC News, 2013b). He was taken to the US Embassy in Beijing, where he sought asylum and was provided with medical aid and diplomatic protection. Chen demanded that Premier Wen Jiabao prosecute those local officials who persecuted his family, that their safety be guaranteed and that corruption cases be pursued under the law. He feared "insane retribution" would be visited on his family for his escape (Watts, 2012).

US Assistant Secretary of State for Asia Kurt Campbell came to Beijing to negotiate with Chinese officials on Chen's case. A deal was arrived at, under which Chen and his family would be allowed to relocate and complete his legal studies. Investigations of Shandong provincial officials would also follow (Perlez and La Franiere, 2012). Chen then voluntarily left the embassy for hospital, and had not requested asylum at that point. Soon after arriving in hospital, US diplomats were barred from meeting him. Chen began to fear that the Chinese government would not fulfill their commitments and stated that he would like to leave China with his family. His wishes and the disposition of Chinese officials were not clearly reported at the time. China requested an apology from the US for its interference in domestic affairs, questioning the motives of US Ambassador (and Chinese-American) Gary Locke, suggesting that Chen was a US stooge "for American politicians to blacken China" (Jiao, 2012; Buckley, 2012).

The situation was defused when the Chinese government stated that Chen and his family could apply to study overseas "in accordance with the law, just like any other Chinese citizen," and New York University (NYU) offered him a fellowship. US State Department spokeswoman Victoria Nuland (2012) noted that "The United States Government expects that the Chinese Government will expeditiously process his applications for (his travel documents) and make accommodations for his current medical condition. The United States Government would then give visa requests for him and his immediate family priority attention. This matter has been handled in the spirit of a cooperative US-China partnership." Chen and his family were granted visas and departed for the US some two weeks later (Quinn and Jones, 2012; Fleisher, 2012). At the time of writing, the story has returned to the news. In June 2013, Chen claimed that the Chinese government pressured NYU to end his fellowship — a claim that the university strongly denies (VOA News, 2013). NYU reports that it had always told Chen his fellowship was for one year, and he was looking into other opportunities in the US.

Less dramatic, but also effective, is the work of advocating for prisoners through letters and, where possible, prison visits. It has been established through information received from family members and interviews with prisoners, that communication from embassies or foreign governments regarding persons in prison — particularly "Re-education through Labour" facilities, also known as Laogai — can have a valuable protective result. Almost always resulting in better treatment of the prisoner, it has been, in some cases, the difference between life and death. This protection can be particularly effective in the case of lesser-known prisoners who might not have other advocates from outside China.

Conversely, extremely harsh sentences in cases such as those of Zhao Yan or Chen Guangcheng, where the international community had been actively demarching, led to concerns at the time of a possible backlash against such actions. Activists, however, are quick to stress the importance of continuing demarches, together with continued efforts to attend trials and sentencing. Although efforts to do so in an environment where even the lawyer and family of the accused are often not permitted to attend the trial have been consistently unsuccessful, the moral support to the activist community of such efforts is critical.

Autonomy/Empowerment at Post

Democratic development is an incremental process, and because it involves so many elements, determining benchmarks or evaluating progress can be problematic. Diplomats in Beijing report the temptation of home authorities to link benchmark progress to their own electoral calendars, a shallow impulse that can lead to a lack of interest in projects that may not include an imminent "deliverable." Although it can be possible to measure results in an anecdotal way, it is not always possible to pinpoint in a measurable manner concrete results of projects. It is therefore necessary to maintain a long-term view.

In order to meet with Chinese academics or think tank personnel in their offices, it is necessary to go through a sometimes cumbersome process to obtain the approval of the host institution. However, in cases where diplomats have already developed connections with their interlocutor, it is possible and preferable to meet outside the office environment, to engage in a more open discussion, skirting the official process.

Restrictions on civil society remain prevalent, but consequences of defying such restrictions can be mixed. Although often told not to meet with diplomats, journalists or foreign officials, many Chinese defy such instructions, with little or no consequence. In fact, such meetings — especially at high levels — are believed to provide some degree of protection, but can also lead to problems. For example, one week after the Swedish Foreign Minister met with a number of academics, one of them was moved to Xinjiang; however, a linkage between these events cannot be proven.

CONCLUSION

China is definitely in the midst of major socio-economic changes. The face of the country has been transformed in a historically brief period of time — just over a generation.

This updated case study provides a wide-angle snapshot on questions concerning China's democratic development. Changes are taking place at such a pace as to be impossible to track on a comprehensive level.

Not all movement has been forward. Both the Nobel Prize Award to Liu Xiaobo and the ongoing Arab Awakening have sparked considerable angst in the Party, which seeks to ensure its grip on power. President Xi's California summit with US President Obama signalled a will early in his term to try to secure a relationship with China's largest trading partner and the pre-eminent Pacific power. Xi openly proclaimed the desire to develop a "great power relationship." While the atmospherics from the June 2013 meeting were positive, the results, particularly when it comes to China's internal development, remain to be seen (BBC News, 2013a).

The Internet, reaching between one-third and one-half of all Chinese, is playing a critical role in the pluralization of opinion formation in China. Text messaging, tweets and other uses of new technologies are also critical tools for the dissemination of information and bringing people together. Demands for rights enforcement and simmering discontent in rural areas are also pushing the need for reform and to establish a dialogue on the nature of modern economies, societies and polities.

China's new leadership under Xi Jinping, though seemingly stronger and more self-assured than that of Hu Jintao, is not monolithic. Struggling with China's myriad challenges, it is also struggling with internal conflict with respect to how to best address these challenges in order to maintain — or resuscitate — its legitimacy.

China's new leaders, President Xi and Premier Li, along with the new politburo, were widely seen when selected as safe choices, not radical reformers in waiting, but the president has moved quickly to consolidate his power base (*The Economist,* 2013a). Although still in his early days at the helm, Xi thus far appears to be demonstrating a pragmatism that has been a hallmark of the Party leadership since Deng. Hu's tenure was generally very resistant to change and acquired the image of tone-deafness to popular resentment of Party entitlements. Most of those surrounding him have been sidelined.

Former leader Jiang Zemin was prominent at the Party Congress when Xi and Li were chosen to succeed Hu and Wen (BBC News Asia, 2013). It is unclear where Jiang stands on the issues of his legacy and ongoing pressure for reform. However, all in the current leadership know that they need to deliver, hence Xi's aspirational "Chinese Dream" of greater prosperity. But how to do so while maintaining the Party's control? Political reform in the sense of loosening control, according to most indications thus far, is not explicitly central to their agenda. On the other hand, such an open — and early — projection of personal command was not seen in the preceding decade under Hu.

More optimistic analysts point to the presence of reformers in the next echelon of power, ready to move up in the 2017 replenishment of top cadres, "when the last politburo members representing the old conservative order will be forced into retirement. Then, with the appointment of a few younger leaders of Xi's choosing — some of whom were educated in the West and have already been elevated in the past year to the penultimate ring of power — the inner councils will not include a single member of the Hu generation" (cited in Kinsman, 2013).

In an increasingly globalized world, China's continued stability is critical to international security. Contrary to the belief of its leadership, China's political development is not a threat to its own stability. Indeed, more and more Chinese scholars are pointing to the need for change in order to preserve stability and to allow for efficient development. Contrary to the past, when scholars were regularly purged for advocating change, there is now an uneasy truce between the leadership and scholars, with the leadership increasingly seeking the counsel of think tanks and universities. But the memory of past purges is still raw, even suggesting a move to a multi-party system remains potentially dangerous.

The pace and direction of China's development, including democratic development, will be driven by popular demand. China is more open to internal debate and external information than ever before, despite the major curbs and filters maintained by the Party to potentially destabilizing influences. Demands for public accountability are also growing as the society faces new problems. All these factors challenge the CCP's model of political dominance. Resisting popular demand for accountability may be more dangerous to the Party than trying to channel it. What remains to be seen is whether the social change unleashed will translate into political change. There is certainly no evident will at the top to accept such a shift. Aside from some very visible (and audible) figures within China, such as Ai Weiwei and Liu Xiaobo (now silenced), mass demand for a political system in which accountability could be ensured has not yet materialized. Ai remains skeptical: "I am completely disillusioned with the recent shift of power. I don't think it's even possible for this machine to produce an optimistic possibility or a language of positive change, it is so dysfunctional. [The government] knows that any sort of change will bring down the whole empire" (cited in Aspden, 2012).

China's leadership has been borrowing from a variety of international models, while steadfastly rejecting any suggestion of "Western-style" democracy. Calls are increasing from within China for enforcement of its own laws, including its constitution, as a means of moving forward with political change. The international community has a wealth of experience to share with China's ever-pragmatic leadership, and the leadership at all levels is willing to learn from the international community — on its own terms. Just one generation ago, the entire country was closed. Now, some doors are open, while others remain resolutely closed. The role of diplomats is to use the open doors in hopeful expectation that Chinese citizens will open others in their own interest.

In 2001, Gao Zhisheng was recognized by China's Ministry of Justice as one of the 10 best lawyers in the country. In 2006, after taking on a number of controversial cases relating to human rights issues, he was convicted of "inciting subversion of state power," sentenced to three years' imprisonment with a five-year suspension and one-year deprivation of political rights. His licence to practice law was also revoked. The suspension of his sentence meant that Gao was not imprisoned. He was politically outspoken and as a result, was taken from his home in 2007 and detained for two months, during which time he was tortured. He was again taken from his home in 2009, briefly reappeared in March 2010, and then disappeared again one month later. During his brief reappearance in March, he said:

> I want to emphasize that if China cannot have democracy and constitutionalism, this will be a problem not just for the Chinese themselves, but the entire world. People outside China have to understand that what happens in China and the political situation here directly impacts the situation elsewhere. I want to thank the American government and all Western people who have been concerned, and continue to show their concern, because they are our only hope. The support of the foreign media, governments and people has given us confidence and courage and made it easier for us to bear the solitude of our activism. There is one thing that I've never doubted, and that's that China will eventually have democracy and constitutionalism. Our only concern is when they will arrive. (cited in Mooney, 2010)

WORKS CITED

Anna, Cara (2009). "Diplomats Kept Away from China's Dissident Trial." *Associated Press*, December 23.

Aspden, Peter (2012). "Book of Defiance." *Financial Times*, November 24/25.

BBC News (2006). "China Abortion Activist Sentenced." *BBC News*, August 24.

—————— (2012). "China Warns Foreign Embassies not to Monitor Pollution." BBC News, June 5.

—————— (2013a) "Obama and Xi End 'Constructive Summit.'" BBC News, June 9.

—————— (2013b). "The Great Escape," BBC News, May 18.

BBC News Asia (2013). "China Profile." BBC News Asia. Available at: www.bbc.co.uk/news/world-asia-pacific-130117782?print=true.

Buckley, Chris (2012). "China Paper Calls Chen a US Pawn; Envoy is a 'Troublemaker.'" *Reuters*, May 4.

Buruma, Ian (2013). "Out Loud." *New Yorker* podcast, June 24.

Cheung, Lillian and Ding Xio (2005). "Blind Chinese Activist Describes 38-Hour Kidnapping by Shandong Officials." *Radio Free Asia*, September 8.

CNN (2011). "'Batman' Star Bale Punched, Stopped from Visiting Blind Chinese Activist." *CNN*, December 17.

The Economist (2013a) "America and China — The Summit." *The Economist*, June 8.

—————— (2013b) "Peacekeeping forces – Over There." *The Economist*, June 15.

Fleisher, Lisa (2012). "NYU Offers Position to Activist." *The Wall Street Journal*, May 4.

Grajewski, Marcin (2009). "US, EU Urge China to Release Prominent Dissident." *Reuters*, December 14.

Grammaticas, Damian (2013). "China's New President Xi Jinping: A Man with a Dream." *BBC News*, March 14. www.bbc.co.uk/news/world-asia-china-21790384?print=true.

Jiao, Priscilla (2012). "Locke Calls Daily's Bluff by Declaring His Assets." *South China Morning Post*, May 18.

Kinsman, Jeremy (2013). "US-China: It's a G2 World." *Policy Options*, July.

Link, Perry (2010). "At the Nobel Ceremony: Liu Xiaobo's Empty Chair" NYRblog, December 13. Available at: www.nybooks.com/blogs/nyrblog/2010/dec/13/nobel-peace-prize-ceremony-liu...

Liu Xiaobo (2010) "Guilty of 'Crime of Speaking.'" *South China Morning Post*, February 9.

Macleod, Calum and Lidija (2000). "Chinese Peasants Fight for Clean Water." *United Press International*, October 22.

McKey, Robert (2010). "Jailed Chinese Dissident's 'Final Statement.'" *The New York Times*, October 8.

Mooney, Paul (2010). "Lawyer Gao Zhisheng Suffers Beijing's Mafia Justice." *South China Morning Post*, June 15.

Moore, Malcolm (2010). "Nobel Peace Prize: Liu Xiaobo's Missing Speech." *The Telegraph*, December 9.

Nuland, Victoria (2012). "Chen Guangsheng — Press Statement." Statement by State Department Spokesperson Victoria Nuland, May 4.

Perlez, Jane and Sharon La Franiere (2012). "Blind Chinese Dissident Leaves US Embassy for Medical Treatment." *The New York Times*, May 2.

Quinn, Andrew and Terril Yue Jones (2012). "China Says Dissident May Apply to Study in the US." *Reuters*, May 4.

Rabinovitch, Simon (2013). "China's Forex Reserves Reach $3.4 Trillion." *Financial Times*, April 11. Available at: www.ft.com/intl/cms/s/0/d0fdafbe-a255-11e2-ad0c-00144feabdc0.html.

Tandon, Shaun (2011). "Clinton Presses China on Tibet, Blind Lawyer." *Agence France Presse*, November 10.

VOA News (2013). "Blind Dissident Says China Pressured NYU to Make Him Leave." VOA News, June 17.

Watts, Jonathan (2012). "Chinese Activist Fears 'Insane Retribution' on Family after Escape." *The Guardian*, April 27.

Yu, Jiang (2009). "Foreign Ministry Spokesperson Jiang Yu's Regular Press Conference on 24 December 2009." Ministry of Foreign Affairs, December 25.

6 UKRAINE: INDEPENDENCE, REVOLUTION, DISAPPOINTMENT AND REGRESSION

By Kurt Bassuener, 2008; revised and updated by Iryna Chupryna and Kurt Bassuener, 2010 and 2013

INTRODUCTION

Advocacy for fundamental human and civic rights, as articulated in the Helsinki Final Act, increased considerably in the 1980s in the USSR. Residents of the then Soviet republic of Ukraine were especially and deeply affected by the Chernobyl nuclear disaster in 1986 and the subsequent cover-up. The loosening of strictures on fundamental human freedoms promoted under glasnost allowed these concerns to be articulated, and a growing crop of democratic activists came to the fore. The erstwhile communist leadership of Ukraine declared its independence in 1991, realized following the final dissolution of the USSR in late December of that year. Ukraine was recognized as a new "emerging democracy," though the simultaneous transition from a totalitarian model to a newly independent democracy would be a massive challenge. Ukraine's new leadership, new political parties and civil society all requested assistance in their democratic and market transformations, and this help was forthcoming from early on from the democratic world. Ukraine also proved a willing partner in the efforts to ensure nuclear stability by giving up its nuclear weapons by 1994.

Ukraine held its first democratic presidential elections in 1994, won by rocket scientist and industrial manager Leonid Kuchma, an eastern Ukrainian, after a hard-fought campaign against incumbent — and former communist-era boss — Leonid Kravchuk. Throughout this period, Ukraine continued to receive external support for reform processes, including backing for all manner of civic engagement in public life. It also included technical support for, and observation of, democratic elections,

313

consistent with Ukraine's obligations as a member of the OSCE and the Council of Europe, to improve, ensure and promote public confidence in the process.

Yet the connection between political and economic power, with the dominance of competing regional industrial "clans," became more apparent, with attendant allegations of senior corruption. Ukraine's star began to fall with much of the democratic world, a trend accelerated by the murder of Georgiy Gongadze, a prominent journalist for the independent Internet publication *Ukrainska Pravda*, who had been investigating official corruption. Soon thereafter, opposition leaders released recordings which they said implicated Kuchma and others in his inner circle in the murder, serving to galvanize a large segment of public opinion against the government.

The 2002 parliamentary elections gave the opposition unprecedented representation. There was relative transparency due to civic efforts to track the vote through exit polls, and the results greatly boosted the democratic opposition. The polarization of the political landscape intensified, with presidential proxy attempts to amend the constitution and flawed by-elections in the western Carpathians in April 2004.

The still-unsolved dioxin poisoning of opposition presidential candidate (and later president) Viktor Yushchenko deepened the polarization of Ukrainian politics. The 2004 presidential election campaign, according to international observers of the OSCE, exhibited numerous instances of bias and abuse by the authorities. The second round, characterized by blatant and systemic fraud, galvanized public protest. Demonstrations began on election night in Kyiv and grew exponentially, drawing large numbers unforeseen by the Ukrainian activists who had anticipated malfeasance and planned the protests. These demonstrations soon snowballed into the Orange Revolution.

The democratic world recognized the importance of helping Ukrainians ensure that the 2004 presidential elections were free and fair. In full view of the Ukrainian authorities, diplomats assisted Ukrainian citizens in monitoring and upholding the democratic process. The cooperation among embassies in this effort was unprecedented. Ukraine's case involves the full array of assets that democratic diplomats have at their disposal, as well as the numerous ways that these can be applied to support civil society and the democratic process.

RESOURCES AND ASSETS OF DIPLOMATS IN UKRAINE, 2004

The G7 democracies began close cooperation to support Ukrainian civil society and the electoral process in 2001, prior to the 2002 parliamentary elections. In 2003, this was formalized in a G7 EU-Canadian-American-Japanese process through their ambassadors in Kyiv, focussed on information-sharing and coordination in support of free and fair elections, and in alerting home authorities to trends and developments.

These diplomats wielded considerable **influence** in Ukraine, due to their countries' support for Ukrainian statehood and state-building, reinforced by the expressed desire of most of the Ukrainian political spectrum — including the Kuchma administration — to shift Ukraine's orientation toward the West, to the EU and NATO, and even eventually to apply for membership status, all of which elevated the importance of the democracy and governance standards.

The ability to marshal **funds** proved an essential asset in diplomats' efforts to support a transparent and fair electoral process. This included any post funds they could disburse to Ukrainian civil society actors, and also their role in advocating programming by international NGOs and donors, adapted to the flexibility required to operate in a fast-changing environment.

Democratic embassies demonstrated **solidarity** by working together and supporting projects financially and operationally that connected democratic activists from countries that had recent civil society-driven democratic breakthroughs, including Slovakia, Serbia and Georgia, as well as an effort to bring election observers from other countries in transition.

Finally, diplomats had a strong platform of **legitimacy** from which to operate in Ukraine, given the country's obligations to observe clear human rights and democratic standards as a member of the OSCE and the Council of Europe. The OSCE's Copenhagen Criteria provided a regular talking point for democratic diplomats in Ukraine before and during the Orange Revolution. In conjunction with subsequent OSCE statements that threats to stability were not just internal affairs, these provided Western ambassadors a ready riposte to the Ukrainian Ministry of Foreign Affairs' complaints of interference.

WAYS THESE ASSETS WERE APPLIED TO MAKE A DIFFERENCE IN UKRAINE

The above assets were creatively and effectively applied in all the methods enumerated in chapter 3, the tool box chapter of this *Handbook*. Examples of each will be discussed in turn, some of which involve two or even more ways of deploying these assets.

The Golden Rules

Listening, Respecting and Understanding

Diplomats recognized the differing roles and capabilities of partners in the effort to ensure the fairness and transparency of the 2004 election, and, over time, seemed to develop a process that allowed each to play to its institutional strength.

The mechanisms developed in the working-group process (see section on Sharing below) actually seemed to be designed around these realities.

According to a seasoned civil society advocate and former funder, "People need to work together while maintaining their autonomy." One ambassador told a civil society round table when the working groups were launched in early 2004, "You do what you intend to do. Let me know if you come under pressure — I'll help."

In the disbursement of assistance, the relatively small sums managed at post allowed embassies to dispense with procedures that might impede quick reaction. Rather than simply financing training seminars and workshops, diplomats made, facilitated or encouraged grants to enable civic activists to act within their remit. This is not necessarily common.

Sharing

As mentioned above, efforts to share information and coordinate policy approaches on Ukrainian democratic development began in 2001 among G7 members. The Italian and then Dutch EU presidencies took an energetic role in bringing all the EU members into the process. Canadian Ambassador Andrew Robinson chaired the monthly meetings, with the US and EU as co-chairs. Japan remained engaged (and also had observer status at the OSCE). Members came to the process emphasizing different goals for the group: the Americans stressed more coordination, while Canadians and others were more interested in information exchange. According to Ambassador Robinson, these approaches complemented each other.

Truth in Communications

Reporting

Democratic embassies had established relationships with relevant political actors, media and civil society organizations, as well as among themselves. This broad and proactive information collection allowed them to inform and help direct their countries' policies. Canada's diplomats in Kyiv at the time felt that they were able to wield significant influence because of their reporting. Information sources later included election observers in the field, especially the European Network of Election Monitoring Organizations long-term observers, who remained in the field during the revolution when it was unclear whether there would be a continuation to the electoral process.

Informing

In this area, diplomats coordinated their activity to ensure that independent media, such as Internet daily *Ukrainska Pravda,* received sufficient funding to continue its important work of providing uncensored news, including from the embassies' own post funds. The US Embassy made one such grant to editor Yulia Mostova to finance

Dzerkalo Tyzhnia ("weekly mirror"), an Internet publication with serious analytical and investigative pieces, many of which were (and remain) translated into English for an international audience. USAID and the Open Media Fund also supported media monitoring of television content, the prime news source for most Ukrainians. The ODIHR election observation mission publicized its own independent media analysis, showing the strong slant on almost all television networks for the incumbent Prime Minister Viktor Yanukovych and against the opposition candidate Yushchenko, both in quantitative (relative air time) and qualitative (tone) terms.

Working with the Government

Advising

From the advent of Ukrainian independence and democracy, diplomats were engaged in advising both Ukrainian government institutions and civil society actors in democratic governance and economic reform. Much of this engagement was direct, both with governmental actors and with Ukraine's civil society, but it required an even greater mobilization of home authority resources to fund programs.

Dialoguing

On election and governance issues, the OSCE project coordinator office in Ukraine served as a focal point for regular discussions among the civic sector, the Ukrainian government and diplomatic actors. No embassy or government funding or assistance was undeclared; the government could in no way claim to have been uninformed about diplomatic and international donor activity prior to and during the electoral cycle.

Demarching

According to a prominent opposition figure, "The position of the diplomatic corps was taken very seriously by the authorities," and their statements influenced the authorities on numerous occasions throughout the electoral process on the need to adhere to democratic norms to which Ukraine was a party. Two examples stand out.

The first was a reaction to the widely held fear that the mobile phone network would be shut down for the election night vote count, effectively atomizing civic and opposition efforts to coordinate verification and post-election activities. Opposition figures warned the democratic embassies of the threat, and these diplomats played a key role in summoning official reaction from their capitals. EU High Representative for Common Foreign and Security Policy (CFSP) Javier Solana and senior US State Department officials called President Kuchma directly to warn against an engineered communications blackout on election night. The phone networks remained active throughout the election and post-election crisis.

In another instance, taking their cues from their embassies and the ODIHR preliminary statement on November 22, the democratic world coordinated its expression of lack of faith in the second round election results. US Secretary of State Colin Powell stated that the US "cannot accept the…result as legitimate," and called for an investigation into electoral fraud, with consequences for the Washington-Kyiv relationship if this did not occur.

Reaching Out

Connecting

Democratic ambassadors and diplomats were a crucial link between Ukrainian civil society and the full political spectrum in their home countries. Senior opposition campaign staff credited the Polish, US, French and German embassies with helping them connect with NGOs and political figures in their capitals. Such connections proved especially important during the post-election crisis that became the Orange Revolution. According to another senior opposition figure, diplomats also used "their connections with different camps to deliver messages." The embassies facilitated similar links with their home authorities and civic sectors, including with Verkhovna Rada (Parliament) speaker Volodymyr Lytvyn, who played an important role in the post-election crisis round table mediation led by Polish President Aleksander Kwasniewski, Lithuanian President Valdas Adamkus and EU CFSP High Representative Solana.

Opposition figures credit democratic embassies for facilitating an early 2004 conference in Kyiv, which drew from the full Ukrainian political spectrum and many senior external actors; later in the year former US Secretary of State Madeleine Albright adopted and promoted the idea of visa bans and asset freezes on Ukrainians responsible for impeding a fair electoral process. Indeed, prominent Kyiv oligarch and MP Hrihoriy Surkis was denied entry to the US. A long-time Yushchenko adviser summed up the significance of this message to others not yet affected: "you will lose your honestly stolen money" if you try to steal the election. This had "the most effect…even on Kuchma himself."

Convening

Most Western ambassadors hosted dinners at which political actors from across the entire political spectrum met, along with civic leaders, in "open and informal" discussions with political opponents that would not have occurred otherwise.

Facilitating

The opposition attributes the most significant facilitation by external actors in Ukraine not directly to democratic diplomats, but rather to the NDI, a foundation associated with the US Democratic Party, which is funded by the US Congress through the National Endowment for Democracy. The NDI actively helped to mediate and broker the coalition among Our Ukraine presidential candidate Viktor Yushchenko, the Bloc of Yulia Tymoshenko and Socialist Party leader Oleksandr Moroz. Moroz was the third-place finisher in the first round of the election and possessed valuable party infrastructure in northern and central Ukraine that the Yushchenko team needed for the second round.

US Ambassador Carlos Pascual encouraged NDI and IRI party assistance programs to be open to the full political spectrum. Their popularity even with "parties of power" helped ensure that they could continue activity despite post-2002 government efforts to prevent their registration.

Financing

Democratic embassies engaged in some direct financing of civil society activities related to the electoral process, but the lion's share of external funding for Ukrainian civil society came from development agencies, international NGOs and foundations. Development agencies like Sweden's International Development Agency (SIDA), CIDA and USAID had been fixtures on the donor scene since Ukraine became independent. But local civil society actors note that there appeared to be a lack of strategy and local knowledge in the international donor approach for some time. Gongadze's murder galvanized the political atmosphere. Democratic embassies feared for the integrity of the 2002 parliamentary elections, so the need for greater strategic coordination of donors and policy in support of electoral process was apparent. With training and funding to conduct exit polls for the 2002 elections, "the international community set the bar" for electoral transparency, according to a former ambassador serving at the time.

The diplomatic and donor community put together an array of programs designed to facilitate professional conduct, civic participation and verification of the 2004 presidential elections. According to a key diplomat involved, the level of coordination was "absolutely fantastic." The system functioned as a clearing house, allowing donors to know what others were doing, avoiding duplication and identifying gaps, enabling them to volunteer resources to fill those gaps. The resulting breadth of civil society programs was considerable, including funding for domestic and international election observers, voter education and mobilization, independent media (thereby informing the Ukrainian public), exit polls and parallel vote counts. Eight Western embassies and four NGOs mounted a modestly priced effort to fund exit polls in both original rounds of the election, which was "money extremely well spent," according to Ukraine specialist and historian Andrew Wilson (2005; 2006).

In light of the circumstances, donors demonstrated great flexibility in order to get the job done. Civil society actors remarked that quality project ideas could get funded without inordinate difficulty, though donors shied away from more "sensitive" activities that might be perceived as partisan. Diplomats and civil society figures interviewed stated consistently that funding was granted to support the electoral process, and not given to parties or partisan projects. A Western ambassador and a senior Ukrainian civil society figure agree that civic groups not explicitly political, such as business development and environmental groups, were as relevant as those with a political focus. The government "didn't get that this was a broad question of civic engagement in public life," according to the diplomat.

In addition, there were considerable efforts to work with the authorities to assist their capacity to conduct a proper electoral process. The Central Election Commission (CEC), lower-level electoral administrators and judiciary all received technical advisory assistance and training.

Showcasing

According to a Ukrainian think tank veteran who worked post-revolution to reform government administration, diplomats are especially well situated to impart the "lessons of democracy," such as the function of coalitions, cohabitation, conflict of interest and legal accountability. "The success of Western assistance was the sharing of knowledge and skills of how democracy works," in her view. Discussion of basic democratic and rule of law mechanics can be very instructive. Diplomats have engaged in round tables on such issues to great effect. Democratic activists from Slovakia, Serbia, Georgia and elsewhere, sponsored by grants from the diplomatic corps and foundations, reinforced a conclusion most Ukrainian democrats had drawn from their own earlier failed protests — that adopting non-violence as a strategic choice is essential to succeed in mass civic mobilization.

Defending Democrats

Demonstrating

Diplomats at all levels demonstrated their solidarity with Ukrainian citizens exercising their right to peaceably assemble by visiting the Maidan (Kyiv's Independence Square) throughout the crisis. "I could see the representatives of all diplomatic missions...this was at the ambassadorial and staff level," recalls a senior opposition logistician on the Maidan. "I saw [embassy] staff taking coffee and sandwiches to demonstrators." In a less visible way, one democratic ambassador called an opposition campaign figure multiple times daily, telling him he did so in the knowledge that his calls were monitored. He wanted the authorities to know that they were in regular contact.

Protecting

Diplomats were among the international observers monitoring the mayoral election in April 2004 in the western town of Mukachevo who witnessed serious intimidation and violence. The OSCE, Council of Europe, European Union and the US criticized these violations. The opposition credits the Czech, Slovak, Polish and

Hungarian embassies with ensuring that the family of opposition candidate Viktor Baloha could escape to safety.

On the night of November 28, 2004, US Ambassador John Herbst heard from both the opposition and from government sources that Interior Ministry troops were being sent to clear the Maidan by force. There was serious potential for violence. Herbst called Washington, and Secretary of State Colin Powell attempted to reach President Kuchma to communicate the message that he would be accountable for any violence that might ensue, while Ambassador Herbst himself passed the same message to Kuchma's son-in-law Viktor Pinchuk and Chief of Presidential Administration Viktor Medvedchuk, regarded by many as the chief advocate of a crackdown. It is impossible to know what factors, in what proportion, tipped the balance in getting the troops to stand down — there were also flurries of messages from Ukrainian Army and secret service officials warning against a crackdown, as well as opposition figure Yulia Tymoshenko meeting with the Army commander. A senior diplomat believes that "perhaps the Army was more important." But these messages no doubt made an impression. "This was a moment when the international community showed solidarity," according to one senior opposition figure.

Witnessing/Verifying

Diplomats not only engaged in their normal observation and reporting duties (including following the proceedings of Ukraine's Parliament, the Verkhovna Rada and the Supreme Court), but also travelled to observe distant campaign events and to investigate alleged abuses of state authority. They observed elections throughout the country, many as part of the International Election Observation Mission, built around the ODIHR mission, and led by a representative of the Council of Europe Parliamentary Assembly. But such witnessing was not restricted to high-profile events: Japanese Embassy personnel were among the observers in a municipal election in the central city of Poltava, and Canadian Embassy personnel observed a by-election to the Rada in Odesa prior to the 2004 presidential poll.

One adviser to former President Yushchenko recalls a bus trip he organized for a cross-section of the diplomatic community to the eastern city of Donetsk, the headquarters and base of Prime Minister and "party of power" presidential candidate Viktor Yanukovych, enabling them to learn first-hand of the difficulties the opposition had in holding events in the east.

In the tense final two weeks before the first round, the government began a new tactic: raiding civil society group offices, planting and then "discovering" explosives, and charging these groups with planning terrorist acts. Civic campaign PORA ("It's Time") offices were raided on October 15 in the first iteration of this approach. On the morning of October 23, security service officers appeared at the home of (Yellow) PORA leader Vladyslav Kaskiv, demanding to be let in to search for weapons. Two opposition MPs blocked the door and prevented a violent entry by using their parliamentary immunity. Three diplomats from the French Embassy and other international representatives from the OSCE, ODIHR and European

Commission arrived to reinforce the MPs and forestall a violent break-in by the security personnel. Their presence had the desired effect: after a number of hours (and consultation with their superiors about how to handle the observers' presence), the authorities withdrew.

EPILOGUE

After many tense moments, the 17-day Orange Revolution succeeded. Mass popular discontent changed the equation, leading state institutions to reassess their roles and responsibilities, often acting independently within their actual constitutional mandates for the first time. The Supreme Court and then Rada determined that the people would have another chance to express their will with minimal interference. Despite the deep-seated tensions in a divided society and concerted efforts to inflame them for political advantage, Ukrainian society as a whole showed remarkable restraint in avoiding violence throughout the crisis. As Andrew Wilson succinctly put it, "it takes two sides to avoid an argument."

The Orange Years

From 2005 on, Ukraine underwent another challenging period. The political infighting and inability of the "Orange forces" to deliver on the promise taxed the sense of many citizens that politics offered avenues for meaningful change. The political situation in Ukraine was often marred by political strife, confrontation and gridlock, most visibly manifest in the open confrontation between two major erstwhile allies and protagonists of the Orange Revolution, Viktor Yushchenko and Yulia Tymoshenko, leading to a succession of unstable governments during Yushchenko's term in office. Arguments between them began on economic policy, but also included the constitutional distribution of powers between the president and prime minister. While some democratic advances of the Orange Revolution were consolidated, other important reform opportunities have been progressively trimmed back or lost.

Despite the squandered opportunity to consolidate the gains of November 2004, under Yushchenko's presidency Ukraine's society enjoyed almost unrestricted freedom of speech and press, freedom of association, and respect for civil and political rights. This was for years the most durable gain for Ukraine's citizens, despite the disappointing and shambolic nature of governance, and has often been underappreciated both by external observers and Ukrainians themselves in light of the disappointment felt over the failure of the "Orange" governments to meet the high expectations set in the winter of 2004-2005. This new political and social climate stood in sharp contrast to the era under President Kuchma, which was marked by increasing censorship, media manipulation and other restrictions on civil freedoms. Yet, although a pluralistic media environment offered Ukrainians a variety of sources of information, major media outlets still remained under the influence of their private owners and efforts to create professional and non-partisan public television came to naught.

Entangled in political squabbling, Ukraine's political leaders failed to undertake fundamental economic reforms that were long overdue. Hit by a decline in demand for its industrial exports, Ukraine's economy shrank by between 14 and 15 percent in 2009, the largest drop in GDP of any country in the post-Soviet region. In 2008, Ukraine's 22.8 percent inflation rate was the highest in Europe, and the Ukrainian currency, the hryvnia, lost around 60 percent of its value against the US dollar in 2008.

The struggle against deep-seated corruption failed to gain traction — Ukraine was downgraded from 134 in 2008 to 146 in 2009 in the Transparency International Corruption Perceptions Index rankings: at roughly the level of Russia, Zimbabwe and Kenya, and even worse than Armenia, Azerbaijan, Kazakhstan and Belarus.

Ukraine intensified its cooperation with the European Union. However, a clear membership perspective was not on the table, given the EU's need to consolidate previous rounds of enlargement prior to committing to new entrants. Many disappointed Ukrainians believe that the lack of the clear potential for membership negatively affected the impetus for and pace of reforms. Negotiations on an association agreement began in September 2008 as part of the European Neighbourhood Policy, which has been described as an "everything but membership" approach. Additionally, in May 2009, Ukraine — together with Belarus, Azerbaijan, Armenia, Georgia and Moldova — also became a member of the "Eastern Partnership," a new EU initiative spearheaded by new member states. Although the partnership boosts EU-Ukraine cooperation and opens the prospects for a visa-free regime and free trade zone, it lacks the transformative potential on Ukraine's political process that a membership perspective might carry.

In May 2008, Ukraine joined the WTO, a boon to its trade-dependent economy. Membership was also an essential step to the creation of a free trade area with Ukraine's largest trading partner, the European Union. The establishment of a Deep and Comprehensive Free-Trade Area is an integral part of the future agreement. Negotiations are currently at a standstill.

The prospect of NATO membership was much more contentious, both within Ukraine and outside. The idea of NATO membership never captured a majority of the Ukrainian electorate, despite being one of the issues that the "Orange" leaders could all (at least rhetorically) agree about being in the national interest. In January 2008, President Yushchenko, Prime Minister Tymoshenko and Parliamentary Speaker Arseniy Yatseniuk sent a joint letter to then-NATO Secretary-General Jaap de Hoop Scheffer, declaring Ukraine's readiness to advance on a Membership Action Plan (MAP) with NATO. However, at the NATO Bucharest Summit in April 2008, NATO did not grant further MAPs. Following the war between Georgia and Russia in the summer of 2008, the willingness of many NATO members to allow in members from the former Soviet space cooled even more.

Three major election campaigns were held during Yushchenko's presidency. These included elections to the Verkhovna Rada, and local self-government bodies on March 26, 2006; early parliamentary elections on September 30, 2007, and presidential elections on January 17 and February 7, 2010. A historic legacy of the Orange Revolution is that the conduct of all these elections was recognized as competitive, free and fair by international observation missions.

At the first round of presidential elections on January 17, 2010, only five percent of the electorate voted for the incumbent President Yushchenko. His dismal election performance was ascribed to the failure to deliver on fundamental reforms. In the run-off on February 7, 2010, Party of Regions leader Viktor Yanukovych won by more than a four-point margin over then Prime Minister Yulia Tymoshenko.

The European Union and its members, the United States and other Western countries applauded the free and fair election, extending congratulations to Yanukovich. In addition to their senior representatives, Russian President Dmitriy Medvedev also attended the inauguration ceremony on February 25, 2010.

Post Post-Revolution

Following his election, President Yanukovych quickly consolidated his power over the legislative, executive and judicial branches. On March 11, 2010, the new government, headed by long-time Yanukovych ally Mykola Azarov, was endorsed by a parliamentary coalition. Its constitutionality, however, was initially uncertain.

Ukraine's Constitution ascribes a decisive role in the formation of a governmental coalition to parliamentary factions (parties, blocs and alliances) rather than to individual MPs. The three factions that formed the coalition — the Party of Regions, the Communist Party and the Lytvyn Bloc — were seven seats short of a majority, with only 219 of the 450 deputies.

A majority was attained by attracting (opponents allege with financial incentives) individual deputies from opposition parties, the Yulia Tymoshenko Bloc and the Our Ukraine–People's Self-Defence coalition, to the government coalition. On March 9, Ukraine's legislature amended the law on the Parliament, removing a 2008 ban on MPs leaving their factions and allowing deputies to join the coalition individually. According to local press reports, President Yanukovych consulted the ambassadors of the G8 countries (including Russia's envoy, Mikhail Zurabov) about whether their countries would accept a government elected by individual MPs. The ambassadors reportedly advised Yanukovych to obtain a Constitutional Court ruling on the constitutionality of such an arrangement, urging Party of Regions to cooperate with other political forces. President Yanukovych submitted a request concerning the legitimacy of the Azarov government to the Constitutional Court, according to Andreas Umland, political analyst and lecturer at the University of Kyiv-Mohyla Academy, specializing in Ukraine's and Russia's contemporary history.

On April 8, 2010, the Constitutional Court legitimized provisions adopted in the Rada the previous month. Yet, in September 2008, the Constitutional Court, with precisely the same membership, ruled that "only those people's deputies of Ukraine who are members of the deputies factions that form a coalition can enter the ranks of that coalition." This provision had been adopted — along with the change in the electoral system — to deter "buying" MPs, which had been a hallmark of the Kuchma era. With its 2010 reversal, opponents of Yanukovych and other observers accused the Court of having made a political decision in the interests of the government.

In the three years of his rule, Yanukovych has consolidated his power ever further. Through the Constitutional Court's ruling of September 30, 2010, constitutional amendments, which reduced presidential powers, introduced after the Orange Revolution of 2004, were annulled. This re-established a strong presidency and stripped the Parliament of some powers, such as appointing and dismissing cabinet ministers. Unlike his predecessor Yushchenko, who had to negotiate many decisions with the Parliament, Yanukovych obtained much stronger leverage.

In November 2011, Yanukovych's team adopted a new electoral law for the parliamentary elections scheduled for October 2012. This law changed the existing electoral system, which was built on proportional representation with closed party lists back to a mixed system, in which half of the deputies would be elected by closed party lists, while the other half would be elected in single-member constituencies. The electoral threshold was increased from three to five percent. This marked a return to a past system that engendered a lack of transparency and was criticized for engendering corruption. It also raised the bar for new and smaller political parties.

Accusations of "selective justice" — the arrest and prosecution of the president's political opponents and members of the opposition, have become a major theme in the current Yanukovych administration, as well as a focal point of international diplomatic engagement.

The most resonant case was the arrest and imprisonment of President Yanukovych's archrival, former Prime Minister Tymoshenko. On October 11, 2011, Tymoshenko was found guilty of abuse of office and sentenced to seven years in prison. The charges revolved around an unfavourable gas deal with Russia in 2009, when she served as prime minister. This trial was widely condemned in the West as politically motivated. Tymoshenko was banned from occupying government posts for three years after the completion of her prison term and fined 1.5 billion hryvnias in damages to the state. She appears increasingly unhealthy in prison, alleging and offering evidence of physical abuse. Former Interior Minister and another Orange Revolution leader, Yuriy Lutsenko, was detained on December 25, 2011 while walking his dog. He was arrested on charges of embezzlement and abuse of office for allegedly giving illegal bonuses to his driver. In February 2012, he was sentenced to four years in prison and many observers in Ukraine and abroad considered Lutsenko's trial to also be politically motivated. Interestingly, many of Tymoshenko's most vocal critics within the Orange camp became vociferous critics of her imprisonment.

Diplomatic engagement on this was manifest in a number of different ways. First, diplomats and their home country governments applied pressure on authorities to release Tymoshenko and Lutsenko, as well as other imprisoned members of Tymoshenko's government. Second, diplomats paid personal visits to their trials and sites of detention. Third, they published letters, articles, interviews and other appeals to Ukraine's authorities on these matters.

Democratic capitals gave the matter significant attention. Prospects of signing the EU-Ukraine Association Agreement were adversely affected: this arrangement with the European Union was linked to release of prominent political prisoners, most recently by EU Ambassador Jan Tombinski, who termed Tyomshenko's imprisonment a "stumbling block" for the deal. Lutsenko was pardoned and released on April 7, 2013, but appeals regarding Tymoshenko have thus far been rebuffed as requests for political interference in judicial matters. On March 4, 2012, five EU foreign ministers — Britain's William Hague, the Czech Republic's Karel Schwarzenberg, Germany's Guido Westerwelle, Poland's Radisław Sikorski and Sweden's Carl Bildt — published an open letter in *The New York Times* pegged to the fifth anniversary of the launch of EU-Ukraine Association Agreement negotiations. In their letter, they emphasized their assessment that processes against Tymoshenko and Lutsenko were politically motivated and were incompatible with Ukraine's aspirations to integrate with Europe.

This was also manifest in Ukraine itself. Numerous EU political figures avoided the Euro 2012 soccer competition held in Ukraine. During the game between Germany and Netherlands, held in Kharkiv on June 13, two German members of the European Parliament, Rebecca Harms and Werner Schultz, displayed banners emblazoned with "Release all political prisoners" and "Fair play in football and politics." In a similar fashion, 14 heads of state refused to participate in a summit scheduled in May 2012 in Yalta for the presidents of Central and Eastern Europe, with some of them explicitly giving the imprisonment of Yulia Tymoshenko as the reason for their unwillingness to attend. The summit was postponed indefinitely. Pat Cox, former president of the European Parliament, and former Polish President Aleksander Kwasniewski co-led a European Parliament monitoring mission to Ukraine beginning in June 2012. They made 15 visits to Ukraine and played an important role in releasing Lutsenko, in particular, by calling on Yanukovych to pardon him.

In 2009, a Ukrainian think tank, the Institute of World Policy (IWP), recognized French Ambassador to Ukraine Jacques Faure (2008–2011) as the most effective diplomat posted to the country. He harshly criticized what he saw as political trials, and was allegedly withdrawn as a result. US Ambassador John F. Tefft is among the most active Western diplomats based in Ukraine, often speaking out "selective political persecution." On October 19, 2012, Ambassador Tefft informed Deputy General Persecutor of Ukraine Renat Kuzmin, that his five-year multiple entry visa to the US had been cancelled. Kuzmin wrote an open letter to US President Obama demanding an investigation. Ambassador Tefft and EU Ambassador Jan Tombinski also called for the ability to visit Tymoshenko in prison in May 2013. Tefft was recognized by the IWP in 2011 as "the first foreign ambassador who even dared to request a visit to Tymoshenko in prison." That same year, he started a new discussion site, the US Ambassador's Forum, posting discussions on topical issues with the participation of experts from the United States.

Prosecution of Yanukovych's political opponents ahead of the October 2012 parliamentary election was generally viewed in the West as an effort to tip the scales. These elections, held on October 28, 2012, were marked by serious irregularities, especially at the stage of vote counting. The ODIHR observation mission identified cases of preliminary results being changed after they were posted on the CEC website, and there were strong indications that some results have been manipulated in favour of certain candidates. For instance, in electoral district 94, opposition candidate Viktor Romaniuk won over the candidate loyal to the current regime, Tetiana Zasuha; yet Zasuha alleged in the claims that her observers had been denied access to 28 polling stations. Following court rulings, the election results in 27 polling stations (about 30,000 votes) were invalidated by the District Electoral Commission. As a result of these invalidations, Romaniuk lost some 6,500 votes and his victory.

On November 5, the CEC unanimously adopted a decision effectively cancelling the majoritarian elections in five districts and asked Parliament to provide the legal basis for repeat elections. The following day, Parliament decided to recommend that the CEC conduct repeat elections in these constituencies, including electoral district 94.

The years of Yanukovych's regime were remarkable for increasing attacks on press freedom, hitherto one of the most robust and durable benefits of the Orange Revolution. In particular, in the run-up to parliamentary elections on October 28, 2012, one of few independent channels, TVi was removed from major cable TV networks throughout Ukraine. The television station itself suffered under a tax police raid on July 12, 2012. Journalists complained about the recurrence of the censorship of major media outlets. In 2013, the Reporters without Borders global rankings of press freedom, Ukraine slumped to 126 out of 178 countries (down from 116 in 2012). Considering all these factors, it is hardly surprising that Freedom House downgraded Ukraine from "free" to "partially free" in 2011. To date, Ukraine remains in this category.

Yanukovych made a point of making his first presidential visit to Brussels, in pursuit of eventual EU membership (which has never been offered). At the same time, the Yanukovych administration improved Ukraine's relationship with Russia. In a May 2010 visit to Ukraine, his first official visit to Ukraine since his election to the post, Russian President Medvedev signed a controversial deal with Yanukovych to extend the lease of Russian naval facilities in Sevastopol — which had been due to leave in 2017 — until 2042, in exchange for a 30 percent discount on natural gas until 2019. While delivering immediate economic benefits to a deeply depressed Ukrainian economy, including paving the way for the IMF credit, this agreement also raised political, security and constitutional concerns among many Ukrainians — particularly centred on the potential for separatism in ethnic Russian majority Crimea. The Yanukovych government also ceased to pursue NATO membership, which had been a focal point of the Yushchenko presidency. Recently, Ukrainian Foreign Minister Leonid Kozhara said "It's clear to everybody that at the moment Ukraine's non-aligned status wonderfully combines with European status."

Though Yanukovych initially refused an invitation for Ukraine to join a Customs Union composed of Russia, Belarus and Kazakhstan due to its WTO commitments, talks about possible Ukraine's accession to the Custom Union continue. The Ukrainian leadership has never ruled out potential membership.

In an interview with *Ukrainska Pravda*, EU Ambassador to Ukraine Jose Manuel Pinto Teixeira (in office 2008–2012) assessed Yanukovych's manoeuvring this way: "I think Ukraine is more interested in pretending both before the EU and Russia that it goes in one or other direction. This creates a possibility of bargaining with two parties." Diplomats on the ground have also engaged actively in defence of democratic values. The then Head of the EU Delegation in Ukraine, Teixeira openly criticized Ukrainian authorities on a number of occasions. In an interview given to *Ukrainska Pravda* shortly before he left Ukraine, he criticized Yanukovych for his arbitrary decision on the electoral legislation and selective justice towards Tymoshenko, generating the ire of the Ministry of Foreign Affairs. In its statement, the ministry said that the ambassador was soon to depart his post, and hence his opinion was unworthy of consideration by Ukrainian authorities.

The ambassador had previously engendered harsh reactions from the ministry with his statements. On February 28, 2012, Teixera claimed that Yanukovych reneged on his inaugural speech commitment to improve the business climate. In a press release, the Foreign Ministry noted that the "Ambassador's statements less and less correspond to those statements that diplomats should make." Despite the rebuffs, Teixera remained bluntly outspoken. His position was supported by the EU's External Action Service and member governments, which claimed that criticism against him was unjustified. Western ambassadors in Ukraine explicitly backed him up with a joint statement. In August 2012, the Ambassador also visited Tymoshenko in prison, following repeated denial of access by Ukrainian authorities.

CONCLUSION

Under President Yanukovych, democratic freedoms and achievements of the Orange Revolution in Ukraine have been rolled back ever further. In addition to its direct impact on citizens, it has also been detrimental for the country's European integration prospects, particularly stifling progress toward signing an association agreement and the liberalization of the visa regime with the EU. The role of the diplomatic community both outside and inside Ukraine in putting the country back on track remains vital.

WORKS CITED

Wilson, Andrew (2005). *Virtual Politics: Faking Democracy in the Post-Soviet World*. New Haven: Yale University Press.

———— (2006). *Ukraine's Orange Revolution*. New Haven: Yale University Press.

7 BELARUS: EUROPE'S LAST DICTATORSHIP

By Kurt Bassuener, 2008; revised and updated by Kurt Bassuener 2010 and 2013

INTRODUCTION

U nlike its neighbours to the west, Belarus relapsed into authoritarianism soon after its transition to democracy began and it became an independent state. While a number of post-socialist countries have had troubled transitions after the fall of the Berlin Wall in 1989 and the breakup of the USSR in 1991, Belarus remains a special case. It truly deserves the oft-heard appellation "the last dictatorship in Europe."

Belarus lies on the edge of the former Soviet Union's western frontier and is predominantly populated by Belarusians — an Eastern Slavic people (as are Russians, Ukrainians and Ruthenians). Situated in the flat "shatter belt" of Eastern Europe, the country has been dominated by stronger regional powers for much of its existence, though it was an integral, even dominant, element of the Grand Duchy of Lithuania. While Belarusians are a distinct people, national identity remains an issue.

Soviet Era

Incorporated into the Soviet Union after a brief window of independence after Soviet Russia's separate peace with Germany in 1918, Belarus was split between Poland and the Soviet Union in 1921. Heavy repression and deportations were the norm in the interwar period. In 1939, with the Molotov-Ribbentrop Non-Aggression Pact, Belarus grew to incorporate ethnically mixed areas (Belarusian/Polish) of what had been eastern Poland. World War II devastated the Byelorussian Soviet Socialist Republic (SSR): 2.2 million died, including the republic's massive Jewish population. Historian Timothy Snyder calls Belarus, along with Poland, Ukraine and the Baltic states, the "Bloodlands," in which 14 million were killed before, during and immediately after World War II for political and identity reasons alone, not as direct casualties of combat.

In the following decades as a "front line republic," the Byelorussian SSR became a centre of the Soviet military-industrial complex, as a prosperous showcase of Soviet heavy industry and high technology engineering.

The explosion of the Chernobyl nuclear reactor just over the southern border in the Ukrainian SSR in April 1986 had a devastating impact on Belarus. 70 percent of the fallout fell in the republic, particularly in the southern agricultural regions around Homel; up to 20 percent of the country remains unsuitable for residence or agriculture. The health effects on millions of Belarusians are being assessed and debated to this day.

Mikhail Gorbachev, general secretary of the Communist Party of the Soviet Union, launched into his glasnost and perestroika policies in 1986 in an attempt to reinvigorate the moribund Soviet system, increasing the space for social and political discussion. Belarus' own national reawakening was hobbled more than that of other republics by social dislocation, Sovietization and Russification. In 1998, the discovery of mass graves from the Stalin era at Kurapaty helped accelerate these stirrings.

While the electoral law favoured the communists (who won 84 percent of the seats), the March 1990 elections for the Supreme Soviet of Belarus were relatively free, and the republic declared sovereignty that July. After the failed August 1991 coup, Byelorussian SSR Supreme Chair Stanislav Shushkevich met with the Russian Federation President Boris Yeltsin and Ukrainian President Leonid Kravchuk in December 1991. At this meeting, the USSR was dissolved and Belarus became independent.

Post-Independence Democratic Window — and Its Closure

The country faced all the difficulties that a "newly independent state" might expect: institutions that now had to govern but had been facades for real party power, mis-developed economies, public distrust of government and lack of social capital. Belarus' economy took a heavy hit as producer of finished products for the now non-existent Soviet market.

At the time, the learning curve was steep for all involved — including the democratic countries and international institutions that tried to assist a democratic transition they had not expected. The international community tended to focus mainly on existing state institutions, large-scale economic assistance, Chernobyl relief and — understandably — getting the nuclear weaponry stationed in Belarus (and Ukraine and Kazakhstan) under the centralized control of Moscow.

Enter Lukashenka...

Belarus' Parliament adopted a new constitution with a presidential system in March 1994. In the elections that followed that July, relatively unknown former collective farm director Aliaksandr Lukashenka was elected by a whopping 80 percent of the vote on a populist platform. He also enjoyed the backing of numerous established and moneyed interests, who assumed he would do their bidding. He constituted a "project" for them.

The following year, independent Belarus elected its first Parliament, the Thirteenth Supreme Soviet. Lukashenka did not have a working majority, and was able to count on less than one-third of the votes. He soon began to exhibit the paranoia and bizarre behaviour for which he would later earn renown, along with a drive to centralize his control. In September 1995, his armed forces shot down a hot air balloon crossing Belarusian airspace in an international race, killing the US pilot and co-pilot. Pressure also increased against the use of the Belarusian language during this period, following the adoption of Russian as a second state language and the reversal of the state bureaucracy's post-independence transition from Russian to Belarusian.

... Exit Democracy: Lukashenka's Authoritarian Consolidation

Lukashenka moved to systematically marginalize democratic opposition to his rule. His increasingly evident authoritarian bent brought together a strange partnership of the Party of Communists of Belarus and economic liberals in Parliament. Working to head off impeachment, he developed a clone party, the Communist Party of Belarus, along with two others to siphon support from his adversaries. He held a referendum in November 1996 and then dissolved Parliament, confident that his clone parties and those he co-opted or divided from within, would allow him to govern comfortably in his new super-presidential system. Not surprisingly, he succeeded in getting it approved. "By replacing the 13th Supreme Soviet by a Parliamentary Assembly composed of the pro-Lukashenka members of the 13th Supreme Soviet, he eliminated the opposition from all state institutions (parliament, Constitutional Court, government, vertical state structure, state-controlled media) and reduced substantially the operational breathing space for the political and social opposition," noted one seasoned observer. "Lukashenka had set up a system more akin to the 'regime parties' of the old East Germany," according to German diplomat Helmut Frick. His use of "administrative resources" — the machinery of state, including the security services (the KGB retains its title to this day), enforced the consolidation of power. Public institutions merely became fronts for essentially unlimited executive power, and elections were fixed to a point that was Soviet in the method of shameless execution. According to British academic Andrew Wilson (2005), by "denying any normal space for meaningful contest…public politics since 1996 has often been little more than shadow-boxing." None of Belarus' elections since Lukashenka took office have been qualified by the ODIHR as free and fair.

Pressure on independent factors of public life — such as independent broadcasters and publications, academic freedom in educational institutions, civic associations, minority religious congregations — became increasingly acute in the late 1990s. In 1997, several activists signed Charter 97, a pro-democracy manifesto calling for respect for all internationally recognized democratic rights and civil liberties.

Opposition figures began to fear assassination or being "disappeared" — a fate that met some former regime officials, former Interior Minister Yury Zahkharanka and Vice Speaker of the Parliament Viktar Hanchar who began to develop plans to oust Lukashenka. One opposition leader, Hienadz Karpenka, died in April 1999 "when a brain hemorrhage was apparently provoked by coffee-drinking," according to the official version. Russian ORT network journalist Dzmitry Zavadsky was also "disappeared."

German Ambassador Frick, who arrived in 2001, "expected to see the agony of the old Soviet system. [He] was somewhat surprised to find how this microcosm was still working. It was quite familiar that all these systems created a façade of an 'independent press, human rights,' etc."[1] Practically speaking, information was rigidly controlled. The same Potemkin freedoms held true for civil society, according to Frick. "Some NGOs could exist, but they were unable to meet. Their contracts to rent venues were not allowed. Print houses wouldn't accept their commissions."[2] Lukashenka's was a "softer regime than the GDR or Romania, but [it was] as efficient in suppressing human rights and the opposition tendency."[3]

Beginning in 1995, Lukashenka began to pursue a union with Russia. His deluded assumption at the time was that he could assume leadership of the Russia-Belarus Union and become the vozhd ("leader") of the entire massive territory through direct elections. The succession of Yeltsin by Vladimir Putin soon robbed him of this delusion. But the union ensured continued preferential economic treatment, most importantly on oil and gas, but also in terms of markets for Belarusian goods. As the isolation of Belarus deepened, Lukashenka, in turn, deepened his relationships with other dictatorships: Slobodan Milošević's Federal Republic of Yugoslavia, Iraq and China. The union was not without its conveniences for well-connected Russian arms dealers, providing a conduit for illicit arms sales, for which Belarus soon became legendary.

Lukashenka's authoritarian grip tightened through this decade, with a series of faux elections: parliamentary in 2000 and 2004 (along with a referendum to allow a third presidential term), and presidential in 2001 and 2006. He assured his victories in each with the application of his media dominance (which, by now, is nearly total, save the Internet, which he aims to control soon), intimidation and harassment of the opposition, and the always useful organs of the state — the so-called "administrative resources."

By the presidential elections of March 19, 2006, the opposition applied lessons learned from other cases, particularly the Orange Revolution, which had occurred next door in Ukraine just over a year before, and had been witnessed in person by many in the Belarusian opposition. The lessons applied by the opposition were unity, non-violent discipline and popular concentration in visible public space while

---

1   Personal interview, February 26, 2008.

2   Ibid.

3   Ibid.

awaiting electoral results, among others. Two opposition challengers, Aliaksandr Milinkevich and Aliaksandr Kazulin, ran against Lukashenka.

The regime was closing the remaining public space by deregistering and harassing NGOs and criminalizing foreign assistance to them. Meanwhile, a crowd of opposition supporters numbering in the thousands assembled in downtown Minsk and prepared to camp out to protest the unfair election results. The square was ultimately cleared after four days, with 400 arrests on the night of camp's dispersal. Overall, about 1,000 activists were imprisoned during the presidential campaign 2006. In March 2007, thousands marched in Belarus, calling for Lukashenka to leave office; the demonstration was violently suppressed.

A later march to a prison to demand the release of political prisoners, led by Aliaksandr Kazulin, resulted in a violent assault on him and a number of others, and he was imprisoned for "hooliganism" until August 2008. Scores of peaceful demonstrators were violently assaulted and arrested by the regime at a demonstration to mark the ninetieth anniversary of the short-lived Belarusian People's Republic (which was soon invaded by Soviet Russia and subsumed into the later-formed Soviet Union). In June 2008, the Parliament passed a media law restricting online reporting. The civil society remains under tight grip of the regime, since the criminal code imposes heavy penalties for running NGOs without official registration.

Since mid-2008, Belarusian civic advocates — both in the country and outside — noted that the Lukashenka regime was applying less brute pressure than it had to date. In August 2008, former presidential candidate Kazulin and two other dissidents, Andrej Kim and Sergei Parsyukevich, were released from jail. The removal of some of the most notorious figures of the regime's repressive apparatus, such as Security Council Head Viktar Sheiman and the commander of the riot police, Dzmitry Paulichenka, a mastermind of violent crackdowns on civil protests, together with the release of political prisoners and the registration of the opposition movement "For Freedom!" signalled the softening of Lukashenka's regime and the willingness to abandon some hardline practices. In an unprecedented move, the three independent media outlets — *Narodnaya Volya*, *Nasha Niva* and *Uzgorak* — were allowed to publish in Belarus and were included in the state distribution network.

Given the built-in advantages of media, administrative and legal dominance, the September 2008 parliamentary elections unsurprisingly resulted in a sweep by government candidates. All 110 seats in the House of Representatives were occupied by pro-government candidates. The ODIHR Election Observation Mission stated that the process "ultimately fell short of OSCE commitments for democratic elections," but that "there were some minor improvements, which could indicate a step forward." Despite lack of significant improvement in the electoral process, the European Union maintained its policy of normalizing relations with Belarus. Many European officials called for continuing the dialogue with Minsk, a policy demonstrated by the visit to Minsk of then EU High Representative for CFSP Javier Solana, and his meeting with President Lukashenka in February 2009. But the thaw was not to last.

On April 25, 2010, Belarus failed another test for democratization, when voters went to the polls to elect members of local councils. Although more than 21,000 seats on local councils were contested, only roughly 360 opposition candidates competed, winning only a handful of seats. Opposition leaders claimed that elections were marred by numerous falsifications and condemned the local elections campaign as undemocratic. "As before, there are no elections in the Republic of Belarus," they said in a joint statement on April 5. International observers, except diplomats already working at foreign embassies in Minsk, were not invited, which was criticized by the Parliamentary Assembly of the Council of Europe (PACE) in a resolution at the end of April.

Overall, in the first half of 2010, the situation with human rights and democratic freedoms in Belarus again deteriorated, with a presidential campaign looming. In May, mass raids were conducted in the offices of the "Tell the Truth" civic campaign and in apartments belonging to representatives from democratic forces not only in Minsk, but across Belarus. On May 6, Vawkavysk entrepreneurs Mikalay Awtukhowich and his associate Uladzimir Asipenka were given prison sentences of several years by the Supreme Court of Belarus for the illegal handling of weapons. Since the Supreme Court is the country's court of the first instance and its verdicts take effect on their announcement, as provided by the Criminal Process Code, the accused were deprived of their right to appeal. The trial appeared politically motivated, as Awtukhowich is known for speaking publicly about alleged corruption in government bodies and promoting the rights of entrepreneurs and of Afghan war veterans (the Belarusian SSR suffered the highest number of casualties per capita of any Soviet republic). In September 2010, EU High Representative for the CFSP Baroness Catherine Ashton called for an investigation into the supposed suicide of Charter 97's webmaster, Oleg Bebenin, who was found hanged in his apartment.

In February 2010, the Union of Poles of Belarus (UPB), an ethnic Polish cultural organization unrecognized by the Belarusian authorities headed by Andzelika Borys, (ethnic Poles constitute about 4 percent or 400,000 of Belarus's 9.7 million people) came under legal assault and denied registration, while the so-called "official" UPB, led by Stanislau Syamashka, a splinter group from Borys' group, is fully backed and recognized by authorities. Since 2005, members of Borys' UPB have been subject to regular harassment and persecution. In February 2010, for example, police seized the Polish House in Ivyanets, a small city some 30 miles west of Minsk, forcibly evicting all the UPB activists from the building in favour of Syamashka's official UPB. In addition, Borys and other activists were fined, with up to 40 activists receiving brief jail sentences in the weeks following the incident. Despite its having been a champion of the Eastern Partnership initiative (see below), Poland lobbied other EU member states to review the EU's current policy of engagement toward Belarus following this attack on minority rights.

Presidential elections were held in December 2010; although Lukashenka won, the entire process (leading up to and day of) was found flawed by the ODIHR and domestic observers. In demonstrations attracting thousands in Minsk, 600 were arrested, often violently. Lukashenka was inaugurated the following month.

In April 2011, a bomb was detonated in the Minsk Metro system, killing 15 commuters. The two men accused of planting the bomb, Dmitry Konovalov and Vladislav Kovalev, were found guilty and sentenced to death in November 2011, in a trial rife with irregularities, according to local and international human rights observers. The men were reportedly subjected to torture in KGB custody. Despite international and domestic protests, Konovalov and Kovalev were executed in March 2012. Independent polling found that following the executions, capital punishment lost majority support in Belarus. According to the mother of one of the executed men, even the Russian FSB, which had been consulted in the investigation, found that the CCTV footage used as incriminating evidence had been edited. Neither man had any trace of explosives or other incriminating material on his person. Belarusian activists openly suspected that the KGB itself planted the bomb.

Belarus' economic woes also deepened. Since 2007, the country's dispute over gas payments and transit fees with Russia has recurred regularly. In January 2010, Belarus threatened to cut electricity to Russia's Baltic exclave of Kaliningrad. By June of that year, Lukashenka shut down gas transit westward, but then paid his country's outstanding debt to Russia later in the month, under considerable pressure. In the summer of 2011, the country experienced a balance of payments crisis draining its foreign currency reserves. Neither Russia nor the IMF came to the government's assistance.

The repression of political and civic opponents also continued in 2012. In March, 16 opposition leaders, independent journalists and human rights defenders, along with Andrei Sannikov's lawyer, were prevented from leaving Belarus. A presidential edict in July allowed the KGB to ban the exit of those under "preventive supervision," that is, those citizens capable of "being able to create a threat to national security." The following month, Sannikov and Zmitser Bandarenka were granted presidential pardons and released. In August, Zmitser Dashkevich, a political activist who was arrested in advance of the 2010 presidential election had one year added to his sentence for "persistent disobedience," a charge also levelled at others. Local human rights defenders classified 12 persons as Belarus' remaining political prisoners. The Council of Europe Parliamentary Assembly's Rapporteur for Belarus, Estonian Andres Herkel, noted in his October 2012 report that political prisoners were being pressured to admit guilt and seek pardons. Political prisoner Aleś Bialitski was awarded the Lech Wałęsa Prize for his work for freedom and human rights in Belarus in September 2012. He was also nominated by 83 Members of European Parliament for the Sakharov Prize for Freedom of Thought. Political prisoner Siarhei Kavalenka was released with conditions on September 26. In its 2012 press freedom rankings, Reporters without Borders rated Belarus 168 of 179 countries.

In July 2012, two Swedish activists who were also representatives of an advertising firm flew a light aircraft from Lithuania, dropping hundreds of small teddy bears with messages supporting freedom of expression in Belarus. Several high-ranking air defence officers resigned in humiliation. But even the gleefully absurd can turn nasty quickly in Lukashenko's harsh realm. The real estate agent who rented them lodging was arrested. A journalism student who published photos (which were sent anonymously to him) was also arrested. Both men are charged with complicity in an illegal crossing of the state border. If convicted, they can be sentenced to seven years imprisonment. The Swedish Ambassador also did not get his accreditation renewed as a result.

The September 2012 parliamentary elections saw not opposition members elected, but rather, only members of five pro-regime parties. The ODIHR found the poll inconsistent with international standards. Rather than opening, it appears that Lukashenka intends to keep his country locked-down tight.

INTERNATIONAL POLICY RESPONSES

The world's established democracies, particularly in Europe and the US, undertook efforts to assist Belarus' independence and democracy in the early 1990s, a period of heady optimism. Much assistance to Belarus at this time focussed on securing the nuclear weapons left by the Soviet armed forces on the country's territory and ensuring their secure transport to Russia, as well as on treating the health and environmental legacy of the Chernobyl nuclear disaster. Democracy assistance focussed heavily on state institutions, and economic assistance was channelled through the World Bank, the International Finance Corporation, and the European Bank for Reconstruction and Development. There was not much of a civil society to support, nor was there much of a track record on *how* to constructively support civil society. International organizations themselves were adapting, with the OSCE being formed and NATO constructing the North Atlantic Cooperation Council as an anteroom to enlargement.

Lukashenka's election in mid-1994 did not impede the country's January 1995 entry into NATO's Partnership for Peace program, open to all post-socialist states in Eurasia. This arrangement was not strictly security focussed: it also included political undertakings in the same vein as the OSCE's Copenhagen commitments. The policies of the international community began to shift in the mid-1990s, when the Belarusian government veered away from its commitments to democratic practice, observance of human rights and rule of law — particularly the 1996 presidential coup. The EU's institutions and the Council of Europe adopted a number of sanctions as a result: freezing contacts and suspending the ratification procedure for the EU-Belarus Partnership and Cooperation Agreement and PACE special guest status for Lukashenka's hand-picked Parliament.

In 1997, in response to the government's subversion of democracy, the OSCE dispatched, with the full approval of the Belarusian authorities, an Advisory and Monitoring Group (AMG) headed by German Ambassador Hans Georg Wieck. The mission had a very broad mandate to provide advice to both governmental and non-governmental actors in Belarus, and to endeavour to get the government to bring its practices into conformity with the international norms to which it subscribed as an OSCE member — including rule of law and freedom of the media. The AMG was a new tool allowing democratic states to work directly in a country to promote the implementation of internationally accepted democratic norms. It was reaffirmed at the Istanbul OSCE Summit in 1999 by the leaders of all OSCE members, including Belarus' Lukashenka government.

In the same period, however, the Belarusian government launched into a bizarre confrontation with the international community over diplomatic residences at Drazdy in Minsk. This neighbourhood also includes the presidential residence. Officially, the eviction of Western diplomats from their residences was for "necessary repairs." Many were physically prevented from re-entering their homes, which had their doors welded shut. There are competing theories of why Lukashenka insisted on this course. According to one later serving ambassador, it was simply because "Luka is one of those guys who wants to show you who's boss." Another noted that with his Stalinist mentality, Lukashenka didn't *need* a justification, but it was probably that he didn't want foreign diplomats so close to his home. These former residences are now part of a park around Lukashenka's residence, "guarded like the East-West frontier — with barbed wire." This crisis led to the withdrawal of these ambassadors from the country — in the case of the European countries for some months; in the case of the US, for well over a year. Eventually, a "ridiculous[ly small] sum" was paid in compensation to the German government; the US received some compensation, but no official approval for a permanent diplomatic residence.[4]

International pressure for a return to democracy and support for civil society and activist NGOs increased in the run-up to the September 9, 2001 presidential elections, as did support for civil society actions like election monitoring, get-out-the-vote campaigns and assistance to independent media. But just as the international community began to react to these highly flawed elections, the September 11 attacks in New York and Washington, DC occurred, diverting all international attention and allowing Lukashenka greater breathing space for further repression. During this period, the Belarusian, Russian and some other CIS governments succeeded in forcing the OSCE to accept that its projects had to be approved by the government. Reducing the freedom of action of this "legally installed bridgehead needed to coordinate support for the political and social opposition and…free and fair elections," meant the end of this unique policy tool.[5] The EU adopted targeted sanctions against regime figures beginning in 2002. In 2004 these "restrictive measures" (visa bans and asset freezes) were expanded and extended; the US adopted its own the same year.

Nonetheless, assistance to Belarus' growing and strengthening civil society continued. In 2004, the US Congress adopted the Belarus Democracy Act, authorizing assistance for democratic forces — in essence, augmenting resources for assistance that had already been taking place. The EU published a "non-paper"

---

4   Personal interview with Frick, 2008.

5   Personal email with Ambassador Hans Georg Wieck, March 4, 2008.

entitled "What the European Union Could Bring to Belarus" in November 2006, listing the potential benefits to the country if the government changed its policies on a host of human rights issues. Today, the Lukashenka government continues to rail against what it claims are unfair Western conditions and restrictions, while threatening to play a geopolitical card and draw closer to Russia as a result. In an unprecedented collaboration, domestic and international NGOs mobilized against Belarus' candidacy for a seat on the new UN Human Rights Council in 2007, leading the UN General Assembly to reject of its bid in favour of Bosnia and Herzegovina and Slovenia for the two European seats.

In May 2008, the Belarusian authorities expelled US Ambassador Karen Stewart and a large complement of diplomats, ostensibly in retaliation for sanctions against the Belneftekhim energy concern, but in reality, as an effort to cripple democracy support activities. Despite the diplomatic row between Minsk and Washington, the US lifted some sanctions in response to the release of political prisoners.

In May 2009, during the Czech EU Presidency, the EU launched its Eastern Partnership initiative with six former Soviet republics, including Belarus (the others being Armenia, Azerbaijan, Georgia, Moldova and Ukraine). The Partnership aims to "accelerate political association and further economic integration" between the EU and these countries. While membership is not a clear prospect, the Partnership is to "facilitate[e] approximation toward the European Union" (Council of the European Union, 2009). In June 2009, then EU External Relations Commissioner Benita Ferrero-Waldner visited Minsk, promising cooperation on "a wide range of areas of mutual interest." In a likely allusion to Russia, Lukashenka said Belarus was intent on improving relations, "no matter whom that displeases."

In its December 2009 resolution on Belarus, the European Parliament urged a new impetus to the dialogue between Belarus and the EU through interparliamentary cooperation within EURONEST, the Parliamentary Assembly of the Eastern Partnership. The resolution also called on Belarusian authorities to abolish its Criminal Code's Article 193-1, which criminalizes acting on behalf of an unregistered organization; to stop the practice of denying registration to political parties and NGOs; and to create favourable conditions for the operation of NGOs and private media outlets.

Civic activists noted in 2009 that there was "more freedom in the air" and "definitely less repression," but cautioned that only the release of the political prisoners would be concrete. The thaw in relations between Minsk and Western democracies was new, and came at a time when the divide had grown between Minsk and Moscow. Belarus needed foreign investment and loans, as the economy, long a selling point for Lukashenka, was in deep trouble. US and EU overtures to the Belarusian government in the hope of encouraging the country's transition to genuine democracy were rebuffed or ignored. In contrast to the hope generated in 2008-2009, a new wave of repression against civil society began in spring 2010 and continues to date. Flash mobs organized by mobile phone text messaging and other social media brought thousands into the streets to clap simultaneously.

The government saw this as a subversive act and arrested hundreds. The March 2012 execution of the two men for the 2011 Minsk Metro bombing was roundly condemned, and the EU withdrew its ambassador in Belarus at this time. European governments, parliamentarians and Council of Europe representatives continue to call regularly for the release of political prisoners and respect for human rights and democratic freedoms in Belarus.

The EU's efforts, driven by Belarus' neighbour Poland, to try and promote an opening in Belarus through the Eastern Partnership, have come to naught as far as Belarus is concerned. In May 2013, EU Enlargement Commissioner Štefan Füle stated before parliamentarians from five of the six member countries that 2013 is "a decisive year for the Eastern Partnership," noting that a November summit in Vilnius would succeed or fail depending on what was accomplished. Belarus had no representatives in the room because of the continued imprisonment of political prisoners disqualified it.

RESOURCES AND ASSETS OF DIPLOMATS IN BELARUS

The democratic diplomatic community in Minsk includes the following EU members: Bulgaria, the Czech Republic, Estonia, France, Germany, Hungary, Italy, Latvia, Lithuania, Romania, Slovakia, Sweden and the United Kingdom. The United States also has an embassy, as do Georgia, India, Israel, Japan, Serbia, South Korea and Turkey. Other democracies cover Belarus from their embassies in Moscow, Warsaw, Vilnius or Kyiv. The European Commission opened its representative office in Minsk in April 2008 (now the Delegation of the EU to Belarus), finally giving it a direct presence on the ground, though thus far it is seen by Belarusians as having had a limited impact. The Delegation's mandate allows it only to assist the government in promoting institution building and developing relations with civil society and to monitor the overall situation. On June 8, 2009, the Council of Europe opened its Information Point in the Belarusian capital, intended to inform Belarusians about Council of Europe activities and to convey European values and standards, particularly in the areas of human rights, democracy and the rule of law. Belarus is one of the few European states that is not a member of the Council of Europe. Diplomats on the ground in Minsk use the resources at their disposal, sometimes quite creatively, to assist civic and democratic activists. A wide cross-section of diplomats have employed their diplomatic **immunity** on behalf of dissidents, through visits to them in prisons and other detention facilities.

Minsk-based diplomats can rely on the strong **support of home authorities** — more than most diplomats can count on — made manifest in public statements by senior officials. For example, US Ambassador Stewart was able to arrange for an audience with President George W. Bush for a broad group of Belarusian civil society and opposition representatives. The French Ambassador arranged similar high-level meetings with Aliaksandr Milinkevich when he was the main opposition candidate for the 2006 presidential elections, as did the Czechs, Poles and others.

The potential **influence** of diplomatic missions in Belarus on Lukashenka's policies varies, so coordination among these missions is crucial to maximize their collective access and leverage. Most recently, missions have collaborated to attain the unconditional release of political prisoners, achieving some success — by August 2008, all political prisoners were released, including Aliaksandr Kazulin, though at least 10 activists continued to serve "restricted freedom" sentences that only permit them to leave their homes for work. Diplomats on the ground also convey personal sanctions targets such as visa bans and asset freezes to their governments, in order to build leverage on the Belarusian government. These lists have expanded over time to include figures who are involved in repression, undermining the electoral process and regime-connected business leaders.

Many embassies and other diplomatic missions also have dedicated embassy **funds** to assist civil society actors in Belarus and Belarusians outside toward promoting democratic values. Most of these funds are channelled through projects that do not require governmental approval, such as scholarships and other support for students who have left Belarus fleeing repression, or who remain in Belarus but have been expelled for political activism. The European Humanities University (EHU), founded in Minsk but now forced to operate in exile in Vilnius, is one manifestation of this support.

Solidarity with Belarusians seeking a freer political system remains a consistent point for the diplomatic community. For example, the OSCE AMG "established a fund for support to families of victims of prosecution, which included legal advice and or legal defense in court."[6] Belarusian civic and opposition activists note solidarity is best displayed by diplomatic visibility at events.

The international and domestic **legitimacy** of diplomats' efforts to assist those trying to instill democratic practice in Belarus has been a pivotal tool. The fact that Belarus is a member of the OSCE, which entails the formal and legal embrace of a whole host of democratic norms, gives the OSCE mission access to prisoners denied to other diplomats. The wide-ranging AMG mandate allowed it to facilitate negotiations between the government and opposition in the (vain) hope of ending the deadlock prior to parliamentary and presidential elections.

USING THE DIPLOMAT'S TOOL BOX IN BELARUS

Golden Rules

The democratic diplomatic corps in Belarus makes a practice of **listening** to the concerns and positions of civil society and the repressed political opposition, both in frequent meetings and by attending public events. The EU heads of mission conduct

---

6   Personal interview with Wieck, 2008.

regular collective field visits to the regions of Belarus to meet representatives of civil society and local government.

A number of diplomats, such as former US Ambassador George Krol, have made a point of learning to speak in Belarusian for public addresses and interaction with Belarusians, despite — or because of — the Lukashenka regime's efforts to squeeze Belarusian out of the public square. This conveys **respect** for Belarusians. Swedish head of mission Stefan Ericsson was "very popular in Minsk…[he] speaks Belarusian better than 70 percent of Belarusians," according to one late Belarusian civil society figure. A senior opposition adviser said that such an ability to speak Belarusian "is very important for those with national consciousness." Ericsson has also translated Belarusian literature into Swedish. Embassies have assisted in getting Belarusian literature translated into English, German and French to introduce the country to a European audience. To commemorate the ninetieth anniversary of the Belarusian National Republic, several senior diplomats took dictation in Belarusian at the Francisak Skaryna Belarusian Language Society in Minsk. In the words of one Belarusian civic activist, the supportive diplomatic role has been "tremendous," while the government has worked to identify the use of the Belarusian language with opposition political activity. In 2009, the dictation event was repeated, with 10 foreign diplomats participating. Another example of the interest that the diplomatic corps demonstrates in Belarusian culture is the rock festival held in 2006 at the US Ambassador's residence, where 16 rock bands, most of them banned from performing in Belarus, played for a predominantly Belarusian audience who could see them live nowhere else.

Coordination among diplomatic missions, including strategizing and **sharing** of information, is a stock feature of the Minsk diplomatic corps. The EU heads of missions meet regularly, every Tuesday. German Ambassador Frick remembers that the EU had "high standing" with the Belarusian population and was an "attractive brand," so there is a premium on being seen to act together on the ground. The US has a more fraught relationship with the Belarusian authorities than the EU, so has less access, making coordination all the more important. Sharing ensures that trials and events are covered, that recommendations to capitals are in sync and that regime efforts to divide the democracies — on the unconditional release of political prisoners, for example — do not succeed. There is also coordination between the US, EU and other concerned countries at the capital level and in donor meetings, which take place roughly every two months, usually in Brussels.

This was not always the case. Friction among the staff of diplomatic missions, often generated not only by personality conflicts among the opposition but also fomented by the Belarusian security services, undermined unity of effort. Prior to the 2001 presidential elections, Ambassadors Kozak and Wieck met to establish a positive working relationship.

Truth in Communications

The regular **reporting** of diplomats from Minsk has conveyed the deepening level of repression through the consolidation of the Lukashenka regime and has generated targeted policies to leverage more space for free civic activity in Belarus. The AMG, for example, with its wide mandate, reported regularly to the OSCE Permanent Council on the regime's numerous transgressions of its OSCE commitments, including the "disappearance" of regime opponents in the late 1990s and the jailing of many others.

The importance of media dominance to the Lukashenka government is hard to overstate. Most people get their news from television, which is state-controlled — and often mesmerizingly bizarre in its programming. The print realm is hardly any better. Ambassador Frick recalls that "small newspapers were allowed to appear, but they…couldn't be distributed throughout the capital — so their messages were kept marginal. The folks outside Minsk didn't even *know* that there was a different line."[7] Silitski (2008) states that "dissenting voices and media outlets (have been) silenced by repressive media laws and licensing rules, libel suits, arbitrary closure… discriminatory pricing for print and distribution, and systematic harassment of journalists."

The EU, US and others work to **inform** the Belarusian public through sponsoring or hosting broadcast efforts into Belarus from abroad, especially neighbouring countries, including the EU-funded European Radio for Belarus, Polish and Lithuanian Belsat, and US-sponsored Radio Free Europe/Radio Liberty. As these stations air primarily on shortwave frequencies, the audience of these stations is unfortunately rather low. A breakthrough effort was the launch of the first independent Belarusian TV station, Belsat, operating from Poland, on Human Rights Day, December 10, 2007. Although denied registration in Belarus and accessible only via satellite, this TV channel has a broad network of its own correspondents in Belarus providing independent and unbiased news coverage exclusively in Belarusian. The channel is funded by the Polish Ministry of Foreign Affairs, with support from the US Department of State, the British Embassy and Irish Aid. According to the channel's statistical data, it is watched by 10–20 percent of Belarusians — between one and two million people.

Diplomats also work around the media blockade to inform the public. Radio Racyja, supported by the Polish government, is broadcast from the Polish border city of Białystok. The November 2006 EU non-paper "What the European Union Could Bring to Belarus" was used by the EU diplomatic missions as a platform for presentations not only in Minsk but country-wide, working around the Lukashenka regime's control of the broadcast media and severe strictures on print journalism. With the arrival of the European Commission's own representation in Minsk, Belarusian civic activists hope that this outreach will grow. Diplomats also convey information materials in and out of Belarus — grant reports, records, magazines, newspapers and other communications.

---

7   Personal interview with Frick, 2008.

US Ambassador Stewart notes that while Belarusian TV follows all of her public appearances, if any of the footage is used, it is never to allow her to speak, but to cast her activities in a negative light. Ambassador Frick made a point of telling the Belarusian media about his visit to hunger-striking opposition figures. The existence of the external broadcasting channels, however, provides one method for diplomats to communicate unmediated to a Belarusian audience in a roundabout way.

Diplomats also avail themselves of new media to directly engage the public. British Ambassador Nigel Gould-Davies, who served in Belarus from 2007 to 2009, was an advocate of such direct people-to-people contact. He used an informal, open style of communications with citizens, kept his own Internet blog,[8] and often communicated with young activists and bloggers.

Working with the Government

Given the nature of the Lukashenka regime, working with the government is almost always difficult, and often thankless. But Belarus offers two perhaps unique diplomatic examples: the first involving the AMG under Ambassador Hans Georg Wieck; the second involving an attempt to draft a road map out of isolation by the US Ambassador, Mike Kozak.

The AMG was mandated in 1997 "to 'assist' in the establishment of democratic institutions and was duty bound to monitor the complying of Belarus with the OSCE Human Rights and Democracy standards." **Advising** the government on how to return to democratic practice after its 1996 departure, specifically on "re-introducing OSCE standards into the legislation on parliament, electoral code, media and penal code," was Ambassador Wieck's mission. He established separate working groups with the government and opposition in an effort to achieve concrete progress. The unique mandate and leverage of the mission was brought to a halt in 2002, when the Belarusian authorities denied visa renewal to its international staff. This was an effort to force the OSCE mission to clear all projects with the government, supported in the OSCE by Russia and others in the CIS. The successor mission was launched in 2003 having agreed to that stipulation.

Ambassador Kozak endeavoured to initiate a constructive **dialogue** with the Belarusian authorities soon after he arrived. Lukashenka and his officials complained about the "unfair" sanctions and restrictions that were applied to the regime, and asked how to get rid of them. Ambassador Kozak sat down with then First Deputy Foreign Minister Martynou and developed a precise road map, with actions on one side leading to corresponding reactions on the other. He began the process by asking Martynou to list what specific actions he wanted from the US government, while Kozak made a list of his own, listing the actions that the US wanted the Belarusian government to take. Kozak recalled "What he wanted was a restoration of (trade privileges) foreign assistance, etc. — all in the economic and diplomatic sectors. What I listed was the election commission, a release of political prisoners, media

---

8   The blog is available at: http://zubritanets.livejournal.com/.

freedom, and an investigation of the disappearances — all in the human rights and democracy columns. Then, we tried to sequence and link these wishes, to determine good faith. It was literally cut and pasted, with scissors and tape."[9]

Unfortunately, while there was broad approval in the Belarusian government for this approach, it was scuppered by Chairman of the Security Council Viktor Sheiman and Lukashenka himself: "he balked at investigation of some killings." But the exercise was worthwhile all the same, as "we drove some wedges within the [parts of the regime] that [were] reasonable, and only [Lukashenka] and his close cronies rejected it. It was still worth doing to prove that there was not unremitting, implacable hostility…I traded on this capital for the rest of my time there."[10] The unconditional release of all political prisoners remains linked to a lifting of certain sanctions and restrictions.

Various EU embassies hold consultations with state administrative bodies, particularly with the Foreign Ministry. In 2007, during its local presidency, Slovakia consulted with the Belarusian Ministry of Foreign Affairs' political directors, consular departments and international law departments. "The aim of all these activities is not to support the self-isolation of [the] regime, but [rather] to create basic preconditions for future full-fledged dialogue and cooperation" following liberalization, according to Slovak chargé d'affaires Ĺubomir Rehak.

Belarusian civil society figures appreciate the value of such dialogues. One notes the utility of contacts with mid-level officials, to illustrate what would be possible for "a different kind of Belarus." But he adds that "such engagement should not come at the expense of civil society, nor should it be detrimental…An increase in engagement should also come with a boost in assistance to civil society."

In addition, the broader diplomatic community regularly **demarche** the Belarusian authorities on their violation of internationally recognized human rights norms (such as the "disappearance" or imprisonment of opponents), and advise home authorities on which responsible officials, regime associates and firms should be subject to asset freezes and visa bans. Belarusian opposition figures and independent observers, as well as diplomats, make the connection between concerted diplomatic pressure from ambassadors and the release of a majority of political prisoners. There is some disagreement among Belarusian analysts on how effective the visa bans and asset freezes are. One opined that "they introduce sanctions and Luka runs with these sanctions to Moscow [to extract concessions]…So, from Luka's perspective, the US is [a] useful idiot…actually some of them…go on the UN visa (*laissez passer*)." But others are adamant that these sanctions *do* bite, citing the government's constant efforts to get them lifted and the public statements by Foreign Minister Martynou as proof.

Following the release of some high-profile political prisoners (Aliaksandr Kazulin among them) and Lukashenka's shutout of all opposition from Parliament,

---

9   Personal interview with Ambassador Kozak, January 22, 2008.

10   Ibid.

the government engaged in consultation with the OSCE on media and the election law. The EU also began engaging in an official human rights dialogue with the Belarusian government. In October 2008, the EU suspended visa sanctions against most Belarusian officials (except of the head of the country's CEC and four persons suspected of involvement in the 1999-2000 disappearances of Lukashenka's opponents) for six months and endorsed dialogue with Belarusian authorities on matters of technical cooperation. In March 2009, the suspension of the sanctions was extended another nine months to encourage the Belarusian government to carry out "further concrete measures towards democracy and respect for human rights and fundamental freedoms." Finally, in November 2009, EU foreign ministers agreed to extend the suspension until October 2010 to encourage further democratic advances of Belarus.

In June 2009, PACE voted in favour of granting the Belarusian Parliament's special guest status, suspended since 1997, with the aim of engaging in a political dialogue with the authorities while supporting the strengthening of democratic forces and civil society in the country, so long as Belarus abolished the death penalty. However, the execution of two convicts in March 2012, the government's treatment of the Polish minority, the absence of international observers during the local elections and the authorities' refusal to permit the establishment of the Council of Europe's East European School of Political Studies led to the suspension of high-level contacts with Belarusian officials amid "a lack of progress" in the country toward the Council's standards.

Reaching Out

Diplomats in Minsk help **connect** promising project ideas and potential Belarusian partners to foundations and NGOs outside. They can "act as contact points and mediators for us," said one international civil society figure. Diplomats ensure that Belarusian civil society figures meet visiting officials or get appointments with them when they are outside the country.

Diplomats also connect dissidents to external assistance, for example by facilitating efforts by the German Marshall Fund to allow opposition figures and their families to vacation in Slovakia to allow them to decompress. Lithuania has done something similar. Opposition leaders and their families — Aliaksandr Milinkevich and Iryna Kazulina, for example — have been able to receive medical care outside of Belarus, in Poland, Germany and the US. Western diplomats, as a part of their usual diplomatic business, also regularly **convened** civil society and opposition activists in Belarus in efforts not only to give them a place to meet away from government surveillance, but also to encourage this often fractious group to work together toward the common goal of re-establishing democracy. This message has been reiterated throughout the diplomatic community, which met them at their embassies, residences, dissidents' homes and outside Minsk.

Given the pressures that Belarusian civil society and democratic opposition face, **facilitating** the cooperation among this divided group is a challenge for diplomats. The basics of "retail" democratic politicking, such as direct constituency development to develop support, were often alien to the opposition, who were inclined to rely heavily on international support — and attempt to be favourites of different sponsors. This seems to have lessened since the 2001 and 2006 election debacles, with a growing recognition that opposition needs to hang together or hang separately. According to Ambassador Kozak, the joint delegation which went to meet then President Bush "got" that they needed to work together toward reinstituting democracy in Belarus before they could oppose each others' policy preferences — now was not that time.

The AMG also facilitated the domestic observation of Belarusian elections from 1999–2001. A pilot project in 1999 for local elections was successful and was followed by training thousands of observers for the subsequent parliamentary and presidential elections: 6,000 in 2000 and 15,000 in 2001. These efforts were opposed by both Belarus and Russia within the OSCE. The domestic observation effort was thwarted the day before the election, when the government rescinded accreditation for the observation coalition, Viasna ("spring").

While most **financing** is allocated at the capital level, many embassies in Minsk have funds they can disburse directly as needed to assist civil society projects. Most of these grants are small so as to work around Belarusian bureaucratic hurdles. Some are administered from outside the country, such as the Dutch Matra Programme, which aims to support "social transformation in Central and Eastern Europe," administered from the embassy in Warsaw. The US government, SIDA, Denmark's Danida, Polish Aid and Norway are enumerated in a study as being the main funders of civic activity in Belarus. Diplomats note that for Belarusian conditions, flexibility on their part, and the part of their own government aid agencies, is essential.

Education is an area in which diplomats play an important role in directing funding. The Norwegian Embassy in Kyiv is helping repressed Belarusian students continue their education through the Nordic Council and EC mechanisms. The EHU, once based in Minsk, was driven out by the Belarusian authorities who view it as subversive. The Lithuanian government invited the school to continue as a university-in-exile based in Vilnius, granting it accreditation and premises to use free of charge. The vice rector says, "Our project is academic. The authorities have a sort of interpretation of our project as a political project." The US and the EU have collaborated to fund the EHU in exile in Vilnius. At present, the school educates 1,800 students. One student notes that at EHU "you can receive a free education, where you are provoked to express your thoughts, your feelings, and where you can discuss, you can argue. And if you don't like something, your opinion will always be taken into consideration." Another noted that "the system of secondary education in Belarus brainwashes students," while yet another added "nobody [in Belarus] encouraged us to ask questions. Here it is totally different." Collectively, the Nordic Council of Ministers, the European Commission and individual governments such as Hungary and Norway, as well as the Soros Foundation, fund about 650 students. The EU is primarily giving scholarships, while the US funds their distance learning program, which is especially useful for students who have been expelled or kept out of school for their activism. The Nordic Council funds up to 100 Belarusian students studying in Ukraine, and Poland's Kalinauski program is among the largest educational efforts undertaken by the international community, with 300 Belarusian students being able to study in Polish universities. The Human Rights House in Vilnius, established by Norway, Sweden, the Czech Republic and the US, provides premises, accommodation and staff for conferences, training, research and studies outside Belarus.

Diplomatic embassies and missions also **showcase** democratic practices and norms for Belarusians, not merely through events in Minsk, as the series of press conferences and public consultations around the EU's "What the EU Could Bring to Belarus" non-paper shows. There are other notable examples, such as the Swedish Association of Local Authorities' work with its counterparts in the regions of Belarus. To showcase democratic practice, US Ambassador Stewart held a "Super Tuesday" party for Belarusians around the 28 primaries and caucuses held in the United States in February 2008, contrasting by example the array of open contests and wide fields of candidates with Belarus' simple and closed system. She also holds an annual concert at her residence with Belarusian rock bands that cannot perform publicly in the country or get radio airplay, giving them some visibility.

Defending Democrats

Demonstrating solidarity with, and support for, civic and democratic activists in Belarus is a frequent activity for diplomats posted in Minsk and helps protect dissidents from repression to a degree. EU ambassadors and others often make a point of being seen together in meeting civil society. A visit to dissidents on hunger strike by a group of ambassadors elicited an angry response from the regime, which perceived public attention of this kind as a threat. Ambassador Wieck recalls that "on the eve of the presidential elections in 2001, ambassadors of the EU countries and the Head of the OSCE mission accompanied the protest march of the opposition," along with some members of the European Parliament. More recently, diplomats have made public statements about the continued imprisonment of Aliaksandr Kazulin. Former US Ambassador Stewart used to hold Christmas parties for the families of political prisoners. Former Slovak chargé d'affaires Ĺubomir Rehak met political prisoner Zmitser Barodka upon his release from prison and escorted him home to meet his newborn twins, to ensure he did not face re-arrest. In December 2007, the US Ambassador and Slovak chargé d'affaires visited a leader of the youth opposition group Malady Front, Zmitser Fedaruk, at Minsk's Clinical Hospital No. 9 after he was beaten up at an unsanctioned opposition demonstration.

Diplomats also regularly meet with members of religious communities who often come under official pressure and harassment. Embassy personnel at all levels have also demonstrated these principles off the radar through direct engagement with the population on a whole host of topics — including utterly apolitical activities such as quilting — to forge people-to-people contacts.

Such outreach has not been a constant. Civil society figures noted that some ambassadors have been less comfortable with a forward-leaning role, so that Belarusian civil society — and younger embassy staff — have experienced a sort of "whiplash" effect of shifting sharply from strong engagement to more cautious "old school" bilateral diplomacy.

Of the frontline support activities undertaken by diplomats in Belarus, **witnessing** trials and **verifying** the whereabouts and condition of political prisoners are among the most important. This is arranged through coordination among the democratic embassies (the EU and the US, essentially) to ensure that all such trials are covered and prisoners checked on. In one case, Professor Yury Bandazheusky was targeted by the regime for publishing a study that was at variance with the government's official line that the dangers from the Chernobyl disaster were dissipating. This policy was seen as essential to restarting agriculture and industry in the region, a government priority. He was jailed for 8–10 years on trumped up charges that he took bribes from students. The EU worked successfully to get him released from jail. He was then furloughed to a collective farm, still under guard, where the German and French ambassadors came to pay an unannounced visit to check on him. Ultimately, Professor Bandazheusky was allowed to emigrate.

In undertaking such activities, diplomats can, to a certain extent, **protect** civic activists and dissidents. A host of civil society figures, Belarusian and foreign, agree that diplomatic presence at civic and opposition activity helps to insulate Belarusians from regime repression. The broad diplomatic presence at the March 2006 demonstrations against election fraud is an oft-repeated example by Belarusian activists. **Protecting** applies not only to demonstrations, or meeting over tea at the embassy or residence, but also to underground theatre events and concerts. This engagement is part of the standard operating procedure for the diplomatic corps, but especially those from Central and Eastern Europe. When former opposition presidential candidate Aliaksandr Milinkevich was detained in February 2008 with aides, the German Ambassador and American diplomats went to the detention facility where they were held, and the German Ambassador telephoned Milinkevich directly. During the March 2006 election and subsequent police crackdown, EU CFSP High Representative Javier Solana phoned Milinkevich. In the most recent cases of the imprisonment of Awtukhowich Asipenka on May 6, 2010 and of raids at the offices and flats of the Tell the Truth! activists on May 18, 2010, the British Embassy, as acting local presidency of the EU in Minsk, immediately expressed its deep concern about the events in respective official statements.

Western diplomats in Belarus have personally observed elections. For the local elections held on April 25, 2010, 50 representatives from 24 embassies were accredited by the CEC, including five US embassy officers, four diplomats representing Sweden and Lithuania each, and three representatives from the Polish, British and Slovak embassies. Interestingly, China also deployed three diplomatic election observers. Subsequent elections in December 2010 and September 2012 were also observed by diplomats posted to Belarus, along with international observers assembled by the ODIHR. Each time, those observers from Western democracies found the process deeply out of order.

CONCLUSION/LOOKING FORWARD

Belarus remains strongly in the grip of President Lukashenka and his national security state, which further consolidated its control after the 2006 elections. "Belarus is like an experimental laboratory, where 10 million people are being kept in an ideology of totalitarianism and populism," according to opposition leader Anatoly Labiedzka.

The democratic world's hopes for an opening resulting from Lukashenka's worsening relationship with Moscow and his resulting need for foreign capital were dashed very soon after they arose. Repression bit anew beginning in 2009 and continues to this day, with 12 persons still imprisoned for their political or other legitimate activities and beliefs, and still many more bearing the stain of having been convicted for such "crimes."

In August 2012, Lukashenka appointed a new foreign minister, Vladimir Makei, formerly of the presidential administration. While subject to an EU travel ban and asset freeze, he is considered "a pro-European voice in the Belarusian ruling circles." Thus far, there have been no appreciable results to warrant any hope for positive developments.

Belarusian civil society and the opposition, not often on the same page, are continuing to undertake a great deal of soul-searching on how to move forward in an effort to transform Belarus into a democratic state following the brief thaw and renewed crackdown. In this effort, the democratic diplomatic community is openly challenged to remain engaged, provide constant monitoring and reporting on the situation, tighten its coordination so each democracy can play to its strengths, and use the emerging windows of opportunity by which they can support Belarus' growing number of democrats, who will ultimately prevail.

WORKS CITED

Council of the European Union (2009). *Joint Declaration of the Prague Eastern Partnership Summit*. 8435/09. May.

Silitski, Vitali (2008). "Nations in Transit, 2008." Freedom House report. Available at: www.freedomhouse.org/report/nations-transit/nations-transit-2008.

Wilson, Andrew (2005). *Virtual Politics: Faking Democracy in the Post-Soviet World*. New Haven: Yale University Press.

8 "THE BEGINNING OF A ROAD?" BURMA/MYANMAR'S UNCERTAIN TRANSITION

By Hanna Jung and Kurt Bassuener, 2008; revised and updated by Kurt Bassuener, 2010 and 2013

INTRODUCTION

Burma/Myanmar,[1] a country of about 60 million at the crossroads of South and Southeast Asia, is a multi-ethnic nation with a long history as a state and an empire, though without a history of successful adaptation to a changing world. There has always been a strong social, cultural and even political role for the dominant religion of Buddhism.

Brought incrementally under British colonial control in the early nineteenth century, Burma/Myanmar became an independent state anew soon after the end of World War II, led by General Aung San and the Burma National Army, which turned on the occupying Japanese in 1943. He was assassinated by rivals in July 1947, but achieved his goal of ensuring Burmese independence, which was declared in January 1948. The armed forces — the Tatmadaw — had a position of central respect in independent Burma/Myanmar.

Though there were continuing insurgencies by Burma/Myanmar's numerous ethnic minorities, it was hoped that a democratic Burma/Myanmar would be able to

---

1   Both Myanmar and Burma are names that its citizens use to identify the country. After the seizure of power by the military junta, the then State Law and Order Restoration Council (SLORC) formally changed the name of the country to the more formal of the two, Myanmar, and also renamed the historic capital, Rangoon, "Yangon," building a new and remote capital, Naypyidaw. The choice of terminology is often seen to carry a political connotation: most democracy activists continue to call the country Burma and the capital Rangoon, while the use of "Myanmar" is often seen to confer legitimacy on the regime that formally adopted the name. In October 2010, the country was renamed the Republic of the Union of Myanmar, and given a new flag and national anthem.

develop a peaceful modus vivendi for all its citizens. At that point, Burma/Myanmar was seen as having excellent prospects, being the largest rice exporter in the world, rich in minerals, rubber and timber, and possessing a larger educated managerial class than most other new states. The country held democratic elections, became an important founding member in the Non-Aligned Movement in the 1950s and played an active role on the world stage. In 1960, the Burmese elected U Nu as prime minister, and the following year, Burmese diplomat U Thant succeeded Dag Hammarskjöld as UN Secretary-General.

In 1962, a military coup by General Ne Win brought Burma/Myanmar's fledgling democracy and international engagement to a halt with his "Burmese path to socialism," an isolationist policy intended to be a blend of "Marxist economics, Buddhism, and autocratic, military-dominated political rule" (Gray, 1987). All political parties, unions and associations were outlawed, protests brutally suppressed and the Burma Socialist Program Party served as a civilian front for military rule. Military intelligence services became ubiquitous, "producing a sense of fear and foreboding that permeates society" (Steinberg, 2001). Many of Burma/Myanmar's ethnic minorities — Karen, Shan, Chin, Karenni, Kachin and scores of others — had never reconciled themselves to the dominance of ethnic Burmans (the dominant and largest single group; "Burmese" usually connotes all peoples of Burma/Myanmar) post-independence and increasingly saw the Tatmadaw as an occupying and oppressive force, and increasingly rebelled against central control. As author Thant Myint-U (2008) points out, the Burmese military dictatorship is the longest-lasting military dictatorship in the world.

All aspects of governance were brought under the control of the Tatmadaw, including, most disastrously, the economy. Rice production began a long downward slide, and economic development began to increasingly lag behind neighbouring Thailand and Malaysia while physical plants decayed. An informal economy emerged to provide what the official economy could not, offering ample opportunity for military corruption. The country's professional class and academic institutions suffered greatly from the isolation and the militarization of society.

Not generally seen as a strategic interest abroad, Burma/Myanmar effectively disappeared from international consciousness for two-and-a-half decades, as the regime resisted all elements of external influence. The insurgencies that had plagued Burma/Myanmar from independence gained ground, exacerbated by the Tatmadaw's harsh tactics involving violence against civilians. These insurgent armies sometimes relied on the opium trade to finance their operations. An ambassador in Rangoon in 1987–1990 speculated that the regime allowed these insurgencies to continue on a low boil because they provided a useful justification for the necessity of military rule and prerogatives.

Burma/Myanmar's relative advantage at independence of having an educated stratum of civil servants was squandered from 1962 on, with the stifling of educational exchanges and the chilling effect of dictatorship on intellectual freedom. Well before the 1988 crackdown, Burma/Myanmar's educational establishments had fallen into sad decline, both physically and in terms of their ability to develop next generations. This deterioration only deepened, stunting Burma/Myanmar's capabilities to adapt to higher-end global economic activity.

In 1987, in an attempt to rein in the black market it had itself created, the regime declared the currency in circulation to be worthless. Naturally, this generated a public outcry, leading to demonstrations in Rangoon and elsewhere. Short-lived in themselves, the demonstrations represented a crystallization of discontent. Tension with the regime simmered in the months that followed, erupting periodically through mid-1988. Ne Win resigned after 23 years as unelected ruler, transferring power to senior officers handpicked to succeed him. But his successor, General Sein Lwin, known as the "Butcher of Burma" for his brutal suppression of student demonstrations in 1962, was not acceptable to the Burmese street, which began to mobilize in August for what became known as the 8-8-88 movement.

A massacre of students, doctors and nurses in front of Rangoon's main hospital on August 11, 1988 was a turning point. Disbelief that the army would shoot doctors and nurses caused the residual social stock of the Tatmadaw to fall precipitously. Protests broadened to include the professional classes and, importantly, Buddhist monks, and to other cities and towns, including the northern urban centre of Mandalay. After street violence driven by the regime killed 112 people in Rangoon, Sein Lwin was forced to step aside, and the first civilian leader since 1962, Attorney General Maung Maung took the helm, in title only, while the Tatmadaw remained the power in Burma/Myanmar.

In a national broadcast, Maung Maung declared the need for economic reform and patience on the part of the Burmese, and raising the possibility of — but not committing to — multi-party elections.

The opposition was fragmented. Former Prime Minister Nu pressed for the interim return of the last elected government, overthrown in 1962. Democrats around scholar and UK resident Aung San Suu Kyi, daughter of independence leader Aung San, disagreed, and asserted it was time for more thorough change. Discussions to resolve this and to announce a joint interim government were ongoing. On September 21, an announcement by Maung Maung declared that elections would be held under the supervision of the current, and not an interim government, as soon as late October. This was roundly rejected by all opposition leaders, and the situation became increasingly militant. One student group approached the US Embassy seeking weapons with which to fight, and Buddhist monks led an armed assault on an army position forcing the surrender of 100 troops. Opposition leaders issued a joint call for restraint.

The army launched a violent crackdown nationwide, killing hundreds, including monks and students. Civilians armed themselves and fought pitched street battles with whatever weapons they had at hand — mostly knives and slingshots. Troops fired into the crowd outside the US Embassy, proving wrong the expectations of many demonstrators and diplomats that the location would protect them. Students put up posters calling for "appropriate action" against the army. Aung San Suu Kyi stated that the people "are not prepared to give in, because their resentment and bitterness has reached such proportions." By September 24, the army's control over Rangoon, Mandalay and the other cities of the country appeared secure to diplomats and journalists. All opposition leaders were jailed or detained.

Estimates of the numbers killed ranged between 3,000 and 4,000. The Tatmadaw's new regime, the SLORC, renamed the country Myanmar and its capital Yangon. They mounted a campaign to forcibly resettle tens of thousands of citizens presumed to be opposition supporters outside the main cities. Many students and others sought refuge in Thailand, where most languished in a stateless status for years, with little international attention to their plight or efforts to assist on the part of democratic governments.

At the end of May 1990, the SLORC organized elections in which the opposition could participate. Western diplomats, human rights activists and journalists made the logical assumption that the elections would be neither free nor fair, given the continued imprisonment of opposition leaders like Aung San Suu Kyi, who now headed a unified opposition, the National League for Democracy (NLD). Campaigning was essentially non-existent; there was no free media. "In a free election, the [NLD] would win. Even under severe restrictions, it would do well if the votes are counted fairly," said one diplomat at the time. While voters were afraid, they turned out to cast their votes in a process that was indeed free, delivering a landslide NLD victory — 386 of the 495 seats in Parliament. The SLORC apparently had been confident that its puppet party would perform well in the countryside and overwhelm the urban vote. "It showed how positively obtuse and divorced from its own people the military was…They were pretty confident," noted then US Ambassador Burton Levin.

As soon as the gravity of its error sank in, the SLORC initiated a rearguard action to deny the election results, stating that an NLD government would not be "strong" enough. "The military…came up with one regulation and restriction after another… trash[ing] the election results," according to former Ambassador Levin. Levin noted the military self-justification was that intellectuals and businessmen could not be trusted: "we are the only ones with the requisite patriotism and selflessness to hold the country together." The regime prioritized establishing territorial control over all of Burma/Myanmar, intensifying efforts to crush ethnic minority efforts at de facto or de jure independence, even in cases where hostilities had stalled. The regime also began to expel the Muslim minority Rohingyas from western Burma/Myanmar into Thailand and Bangladesh. They were deprived of citizenship under a law passed by the Ne Win regime. Tens of thousands had been expelled in earlier waves.

In 1991, Aung San Suu Kyi was awarded the Nobel Peace Prize. The committee's chair, Francis Sejersted, called her "an outstanding example of the power of the powerless," quoting a title by former Czech dissident, by then Czechoslovak President, Václav Havel, who had become a lifelong ally of "The Lady."

The National Convention was established by the SLORC in 1993 to develop a new constitution, but failed to do so. In 1997, the SLORC changed its name to the State

Peace and Development Council (SPDC). But while there were some changes in the personnel lineup, the military's dominance and the repressive apparatus remained unchanged.

To call the Tatmadaw a state within a state is an understatement — as far as they are concerned, the generals *are* the state. A statement made on Armed Forces Day in late March 2010 — the only one in bold print on the English press release — was "the nation will be strong only when the armed forces are strong." The SPDC was theoretically a collegial body, but Senior General Than Shwe was the *primus inter pares* and demoted, sidelined or imprisoned senior officers who he considered insufficiently loyal.

The SLORC/SPDC needed foreign investment to fuel the Tatmadaw's buildup, so the regime began to open up economically — but only to the benefit of the regime and its all-controlling patronage system. There was considerable foreign investment in the 1990s, particularly in the petroleum and gas sectors, logging, mining and fishing, but also in consumer goods; however, few of the benefits have trickled down to the general population. Furthermore, the extraction of these natural resources often entails major environmental degradation.

The opposition was outlawed and heavily restricted, with Aung San Suu Kyi rarely free from house arrest from 1988 on. Freed in 2002, she was put into prison the following year. The SPDC announced a "road map to disciplined democracy" in 2003, but this was derided as a sham by the NLD, which called for international sanctions and a boycott of tourism to Burma/Myanmar. Fearing popular backlash despite the massive repressive apparatus, SPDC leader and Tatmadaw commander Senior General Than Shwe had a purpose-built capital city constructed in Burma/ Myanmar's northern highlands to further isolate the increasingly wealthy leadership from the general population and even from civilian members of the government. Reportedly, Than Shwe made the decision after consulting his court astrologer.

In September 2007, rising fuel costs sparked civil unrest anew in Rangoon and beyond. Resistance grew, drawing in thousands of Buddhist monks along with a cross-section of the broad population. The regime initially held off on cracking down, especially on the revered monks, no doubt hoping that the demonstrations would fizzle. But ultimately, in late September, the SPDC employed brute force to suppress the peaceful demonstrations and conducted invasive searches in monasteries in search of those involved. The government claimed nine were killed, but the UN Human Rights Council's Special Rapporteur for Burma/Myanmar Paulo Sérgio Pinheiro estimates the number at 31. Pinheiro also reported that protesters detained by the Burmese government were subjected to torture and cruel, inhuman and degrading treatment. He stated, "Since the crackdown there have been an increasing number of reports of deaths in custody as well as beatings, ill-treatment, lack of food, water, or medical treatment in overcrowded unsanitary detention facilities across the country." Estimates of political prisoners ranged up to 2,100, including a number of veterans of the 1988 student uprising. The brutality of the crackdown was seen by diplomats and analysts as placing a major damper on popular will to mobilize.

The junta set the date for a national referendum on the new constitution for May 10, 2008, and increased its repressive measures in advance, cracking down on those members of the opposition and civil society apt to be working to generate a "no" vote. The constitutional draft gave the Tatmadaw an automatic 25 percent of seats in both houses of the legislature, granted blanket amnesty to all soldiers for any crimes and legally disqualified Aung San Suu Kyi from political office, because she had been married to a foreigner and has children with foreign citizenship.

On the night of May 2, 2008, Tropical Cyclone Nargis hit the Irrawaddy Delta area southwest of the capital, inundating the country's most agriculturally productive land and killing tens of thousands. Storm surge inflicted most of the casualties. Over 40 warnings from Indian meteorologists were sent to the Burmese regime on the scale and likely impact area of the storm, yet these were not conveyed as proper or timely warnings to Delta residents.

External observers assessed that the flooding damage was massively exacerbated by the prior destruction of mangroves in coastal wetlands. British Ambassador Mark Canning said at the time that the scale of the required relief effort was roughly double that of the 2004 Acehnese tsunami. The health threat placed 1 to 1.5 million people in direct jeopardy. Access to disaster relief experts and those prepared to distribute aid remained severely constrained for more than a month after the cyclone. Foreign journalists reported local anger at the lack of assistance from the military. The estimated death toll was 140,000, with 2.5 million displaced. Following weeks of heavy international diplomatic engagement and pressure, the regime finally allowed some international assistance into the affected areas. Aid agencies were then permitted to operate in the disaster zone, but the initial resistance to external humanitarian involvement cast a long shadow, dissuading international assistance. One humanitarian aid worker estimated that the assistance devoted to relief for Nargis was a mere 10 percent of that dedicated to relief from the 2004 Aceh tsunami, though the scale of the suffering was comparable. A Johns Hopkins University study, conducted with Burmese volunteers, asserts that the junta sold donated aid supplies on the local market and used forced labour for reconstruction efforts and recommended that a case against the regime be brought before the International Criminal Court. Transparency International's 2008 report placed Burma/Myanmar in second-to-last place, only ahead of Somalia, in terms of corruption.

Perhaps the only positive by-product of the calamity was that ad hoc Burmese community-based organizations, many of which were organized to deliver assistance to their compatriots in the wake of Cyclone Nargis, found ways to operate with increasing confidence in a still very repressive environment. "There is still room to change at the small scale," said one AIDS activist. "People say civil society is dead. But it never dies. Sometimes it takes different forms, under the pretext of religion, under pretext of medicine." Through such tolerated activity, Burmese tried to expand the space for civic organization, with the hope of applying this organization politically at a stage when this became possible.

The regime pushed ahead with the referendum for May 10, 2008. In the wake of Cyclone Nargis, the referendum results were hardly reported in the foreign press. Journalists reporting from the disaster area without permission spoke with Delta residents who said they would vote "no" as a result of the junta's risible response. Despite some Burmese bravely (though not openly) voting against, the "overwhelming support" for the measure was never really much in doubt, given the process before the election and who counted the votes. The official figures reported 99 percent turnout and 92 percent support for the new constitution.

The violence meted out against the citizens, including monks beaten and tortured in the 2007 protests, and the callous indifference to their plight after the 2008 cyclone further diminished the regime's legitimacy in the eyes of the Burmese people. But "the memories of 2007 are still raw," according to a Rangoon-based diplomat.

In May 2009, US citizen John Yettaw swam across a lake to Aung San Suu Kyi's home uninvited; he was arrested on his swim back two days later. The incident struck many long-time Burma/Myanmar watchers as highly implausible, given the tight security around the residence. Yettaw was released after an August 2009 visit by then US Senator Jim Webb, a Virginia Democrat who chaired the Senate Foreign Relations Committee's East Asia and Pacific Affairs Subcommittee, and who has advocated greater engagement with the junta. Webb was the first member of Congress to visit the country in a decade, and the first to meet Senior General Than Shwe.

The regime accused Nobel laureate Suu Kyi of breaching the terms of her house arrest and incarcerated her in Insein Prison before her trial. With varying degrees of difficulty, diplomats were given access to the proceedings. Suu Kyi was convicted in August and her sentence, initially five years imprisonment, was commuted to 18 months additional house arrest. The British Foreign and Commonwealth Office noted that Than Shwe issued a directive to the court the day before her sentencing. Before the conviction, the NLD had stated it would participate in the election if all political prisoners (estimated in the thousands, including some arrested for distributing cyclone aid) were released, the constitution changed and international observers were admitted.

The ability to influence the inward-directed and wholly self-interested military regime remained a massive hurdle for most democracies, especially with new revenue streams coming to the military from natural gas, along with the continued destructive clear-cutting of old growth forests and trade in gemstones, and diversion of agricultural land to cultivate jatropha for biofuels. The *Financial Times* reported in July 2009 that a nouveau riche of connected urban traders was increasingly visible in Rangoon, but some questioned whether the conspicuous consumption was a sign of economic health and durable progress. "You can't put it in the bank, so you put your money in cars or a nice new house to keep the value of the money," one businessperson told the reporter.

Hopes that the elections might allow some element of open competition or result in the Tatmadaw's power being checked to some degree were dashed. In March 2010, the Burmese government annulled the results of the 1990 election, which the NLD won by a landslide, stating that the new election law that it had promulgated invalidated the prior electoral law. This new electoral law greatly expanded the pool of those who could not run for office to include those convicted of crimes (to eliminate former opposition and other political prisoners) and those belonging to religious orders (to disallow monks who participated in the attempted "Saffron Revolution" of 2007).

The new election law was roundly criticized internationally. Then Filipino Foreign Minister Alberto Romulo said in March 2010 that "unless they release Aung San Suu Kyi and allow her party to participate in elections, it's a complete farce and therefore contrary to their roadmap to democracy." UN Secretary-General Ban Ki-moon stated that any election that didn't allow Suu Kyi to participate would not be regarded as credible. US State Department spokesman P. J. Crowley stated that the laws were "a mockery of the democratic process and ensure that the upcoming election will be devoid of credibility." Suu Kyi was reported by NLD spokesperson Nyan Win to have said, "such challenges call for resolute responses and [she] calls on the people and democratic forces to take unanimous action against such unfair laws."

With so many of its leaders disqualified from participating in the elections, the NLD's leadership of roughly 100 decided against participation, after what was apparently spirited internal debate, fearing they could legitimize an inherently unfair process. Prior to the decision, long-time NLD member Win Tin described the decision to the BBC as a "matter of life and death...If we don't register, we will not have a party and we will be without legs and limbs" (Than, 2010). But Tin Oo, the NLD deputy leader recently released from prison, stated "There are many peaceful ways to continue our activities." NLD Spokesman Nyan Win told Reuters that "After a vote of the committee of members, the NLD party has decided not to register as a political party because the election laws are unjust."

The stacking of the deck for the election continued with Prime Minister Thein Sein's resignation from the military, along with about 20 other senior officers. Thein Sein, handpicked by Senior General Than Shwe to succeed him, was a longtime member of the SPDC and considered a reformist in military circles. These men then formed a political party, the Union Solidarity and Development Party (USDP) to parallel the Tatmadaw's ostensibly mass popular organization, the Union Solidarity and Development Association, which claims to have 24 million members. This move was apparently aimed at boosting the Tatmadaw's control of the elected legislature, which is composed of 25 percent of their own to begin with and requires more than 75 percent of votes to amend the constitution that now governs this "disciplined democracy." Three ministries — for defence, interior and border affairs — must be held by serving generals.

Tomás Ojea Quintana, a UN special envoy for human rights who visited the country three times, stated in a leaked report to the UN Security Council in March 2010 that the junta had engaged in "gross and systematic violation of human rights…The possibility exists that some of these human rights violations may entail categories of crimes against humanity or war crimes." These abuses were especially pronounced in the border areas and included the recruitment and use of child soldiers. The junta was estimated to be incarcerating roughly 2,100 political prisoners at the time. Quintana's report also noted that "far too many" people in Burma/Myanmar were denied basic food, shelter, health and education. Minority groups have been particularly persecuted.

The resulting desperation led to even more violence. Some, who had inked ceasefire agreements with the military years before, decided that they could no longer accept the violation of their rights and again took up arms. Khun Thurein, head of the 100-man Pao National Liberation Army operating from the eastern border region, explained to the BBC Burmese Service's Ko Ko Aung that he resumed fighting with his small force to resist persistent human rights abuses by the Tatmadaw and its effort to establish a "Burmese monoculture." "Our leaders wanted peace and democracy," he said. "They wanted to sort out the political problems by political means. We never had a chance to sort the problems politically, so I thought the Burmese government would eliminate us." When the journalist noted that a single military operation could eliminate his entire force, Khun Thurein replied that he "would rather die fighting than bowing down to the pressure of the Burmese military regime to lay down arms without a political solution." A series of coordinated bombings in a lakeside park in Rangoon in April 2010 killed nine people and wounded 75, according to state TV. Their perpetrators remain unknown. The bombing sent an ominous signal that not only Burma/Myanmar's ethnic minorities had determined that the path to political change could not be achieved peacefully.

Rumours of a Tatmadaw nuclear weapons development effort began to surface in 2009 and gained credibility in 2010 with the defection of a former officer and his allegations broadcast by the Oslo-based Democratic Voice of Burma.

One Western diplomat believed that the 2010 elections held an opportunity for Burmese civil society to mobilize ("not in a 'color revolution' way"), despite the clear determination of the generals to leave nothing to chance. This will be "the first time in 20 years for Burmese to engage in politics. Many [Burmese] think of 'politics' as a dirty word. But this is an opportunity of engaging people, and changing the regime dynamic. There will be a generational shift as well. There will be a new parliament. There will be new ways to influence policy in a positive way. It's a long shot, but the opportunities are there, both because there will be new structures and elements that are impossible to predict because of the shifting dynamics."

The new USDP claimed a resounding win in November 2010 election, which was widely condemned as fraudulent and unfair. The NLD did not participate, but a splinter fraction of the party, the National Democratic Front, did. A week later, Aung San Suu Kyi was released from house arrest and soon allowed an Internet connection. Former Prime Minister Thein Sein, now USDP leader, was sworn in as president in March 2011. The two leaders met in the new purpose-built capital, Naypyidaw, in August 2011. From this point on, developments moved rapidly.

In a move that startled many observers, President Thein Sein halted construction of the Chinese-financed Myitsone hydroelectric dam in September 2011. Once online, the dam would have delivered electricity mainly to China. The project was controversial both for environmental reasons and the level of integration it reflected with China. The halt was seen as a bow to strong public opinion on the matter.

In late 2011, a general amnesty released many prisoners, including some 200 who had been imprisoned for political activity or their beliefs. Aung San Suu Kyi said she would run for a seat in Parliament in upcoming by-elections the following spring. In December 2011, US Secretary of State Hillary Clinton met with Suu Kyi in Rangoon and then with President Their Sein in Naypyidaw. Clinton offered to upgrade relations with Burma/Myanmar should reforms continue. By the end of the year, political demonstrations were permitted and the NLD re-registered as a political party to compete in early 2012 by-elections.

Progress was also evident in regard to ongoing ethnic insurgencies — 11 major armed groups in all — throughout Burma/Myanmar. At the end of 2011, a truce was signed with the Shan State Army and military operations against the Kachin were halted. In January 2012, a ceasefire was signed with the Karen. In addition, many political prisoners were released the same month.

Prior to the awaited April 2012 by-election, Suu Kyi was philosophical. "Some are a little bit too optimistic about the situation," she said prior to the vote. "We are cautiously optimistic. We are at the beginning of a road." The NLD took 43 of the 45 seats. While this was a major victory in its first electoral test since 1990, it yielded the opposition party little actual power. It held approximately six percent of the Parliament's 664 seats. To change the constitution to allow Suu Kyi to run for the presidency, 75 percent of the members needed to vote in favour. Still, it was an auspicious beginning. Voters in the Irrawaddy Delta constituency, which Suu Kyi chose as her own, were thrilled. "I was so excited about voting I didn't sleep at all," one betel nut and bamboo farmer told a BBC correspondent. He didn't vote in 2010, since there was no candidate he liked. "Now we have Daw Suu and we all love and yearn for her." At his polling station, half the registered voters had voted by 9:30 a.m. There were voting list discrepancies, denying right to cast a ballot to many, especially those who had recently turned 18 since the 2010 vote. But the vote led some in the opposition to voice greater hope. NLD official Myo Win said at the time "The army has changed and [is] now more lenient…So there is more of a possibility that Aung San Suu Kyi can become president in 2015." The following month, Suu Kyi demonstrated her confidence that she would be allowed to return by leaving the country for the first time since her arrival in 1988.

EU foreign policy chief Catherine Ashton, British Prime Minister David Cameron, and UN Secretary-General Ban Ki-moon all visited the country in April, praising progress and pressing for deeper reform. Indian Prime Minister Manmohan Singh visited the following month, the first such visit since 1987. He signed 12 agreements, mostly to strengthen diplomatic and trade ties.

As the year went on, violence erupted between Buddhists and Rohingya Muslims in northwestern Rakhine. The violence, sparked by a reported rape and killing by a Rohingya, led to pogroms against the long-persecuted Rohingyas. Dozens were killed and thousands displaced. In August, President Thein Sein ordered a commission of inquiry.

That same month, pre-publication censorship was ended. Journalists now no longer have to have their reports vetted by censors. Hardline Information Minister Kyaw Hsan was replaced by the regime's interlocutor with Suu Kyi, Aung Kyi, a reputed moderate. The Press Scrutiny and Registration Division, the official censorship body, remained in place. In mid-2012, there were just over half a million Internet users in the country. Censorship online was assessed by the OpenNet Initiative to have declined markedly in 2012. By April 2013, four private dailies appeared for sale — 16 were granted licences for publication.

In September 2012, the government removed more than 2,000 names from a blacklist of Burmese who had hitherto been banned from return. Moe The Zun, the leader of the 8-8-88 student protests, was among those allowed to return. The same month, President Sein Thein said he would accept Suu Kyi as president, were she elected. Newly re-elected US President Obama visited Burma/Myanmar, offering the "hand of friendship" in return for continued reform. He made specific mention of the anti-Muslim violence in Rakhine state.

But early 2013 saw further worrisome developments in Burma/Myanmar. The military ended a ceasefire against the Kachin rebels near the Chinese border, launching a major offensive in January and February. The Chinese sponsored ceasefire talks in the neighbouring Chinese town of Riuli. In late May 2013, a ceasefire deal was reached, with political talks to follow. In March, a new front for Buddhist-Muslim violence had opened in Meiktila, near Mandalay, which has a 30 percent Muslim population. Several were killed and mosques and madrasas were torched; 12,000 Muslims were displaced. As in Rakhine, Buddhist monks were directly engaged in the violence, and security forces accused of complicity. This seems borne out by the available evidence. A former army captain quoted by the BBC was incredulous. "I saw eight boys killed in front of me. I tried to stop them...But they threatened me, and the police pulled me away. The police did not do anything — I don't know why. Perhaps because they lack experience, perhaps because they did not know what orders to give...On the banks thousands of people were cheering. When someone was killed, they cheered...There were women, monks, young people. I feel disgusted — and ashamed," the veteran told the BBC (BBC News Asia, 2013). Muslims, formerly prominent in the town's commerce, gathered in ersatz camps, guarded by police. One Buddhist monk openly condoned the violence, speaking of Muslim birthrates and takeover. "Now they are taking over our political parties. If this goes on, we will end up like Afghanistan or Indonesia" (ibid.). He likened the Muslims to a seed that must be uprooted before it grows big enough to do damage. President Thein Sein warned "political opportunists and religious extremists" against fomenting inter-religious strife.

Despite these developments, progress continued on other fronts in 2013. Since 2011, 750 political prisoners have been released. As of January 2013, public gatherings of more than five persons are no longer illegal. President Thein Sein launched an extensive European tour, beginning in Norway, with its considerable Burmese diaspora population, in February 2013. He later reciprocated US President Obama's visit with one of his own to Washington in May. Numerous sanctions were lifted by the EU and US, and trade ties began to proliferate.

While liberalization is an ongoing reality and Western businesses troop in to tap into a growing new market, Burma/Myanmar's direction is hardly certain. It retains some of the world's most dire human development indicators. In 2013, the country ranked 149 of 187 states on the UN Human Development Index. One quarter of its people live in poverty (measured at US$1.25 per person per day). Less than one percent of GDP is spent in public expenditure on health and education — the world's lowest proportion. There are, as yet, no indications that the Tatmadaw is willing to redirect its massive share of the national purse in that direction, as foreign donors work to pick up the pieces of its misrule. UN Secretary-General Ban Ki-moon notes that while there are fewer reports of child soldiers recruited in Burma/Myanmar, it remains a problem. Particularly troubling is the growing intercommunal violence, which is trending up just as the traditional insurgencies are being resolved in turn. There is also no clarity as of yet about whether the general elections planned for 2015 will allow full democratic competition — that is, will the country's most popular figure be allowed to run?

The case of Burma/Myanmar shows the sorts of diplomatic activities that can be pursued in a "hard case." It also may well show what can be done in a period of subsequent liberalization. It remains too early at the time of writing to know if the change is sufficiently deep and durable to produce real democracy. Given the top-down nature of the changes, the policy responses from democratic capitals have been driven from a high level. The ground-level impact on diplomatic practice is to be documented between now and 2015, in a future edition of the *Handbook*.

INTERNATIONAL POLICY POSTURES

In general, international policy responses through 2011 fell into one of two very general categories: countries that unequivocally condemned the Burmese military government and called for reinstatement of the 1990 election results and democratic transition, and those that called for engagement with the Burmese military government, rather than isolation.

Since the 1990s, Western states, including the US, EU members, Norway and Canada increasingly pursued a policy of sanctions and called unambiguously for a democratic transition. The effectiveness of sanctions in promoting positive change has long been a subject of debate. Arms embargoes are the least controversial. Australia adopted this but not other sanctions.

But partisans of economic sanctions argued that the revenues from foreign investment and purchase of Burmese exports essentially only redounded to the benefit — and repressive capacity — of the Tatmadaw by giving it foreign exchange to buy arms from China, Russia and probably North Korea. NLD leader Aung Sang Suu Kyi had long called on tourists to avoid Burma/Myanmar, but others argued that sustaining activity such as non-official tourism helped to develop Burmese civil society. The relative merits of further isolating an already insular (and hence indifferent) regime were also debated by the Burmese living outside the country. Some high-profile Burmese abroad advocated an effort to induce the regime to evolve and saw a heavily censorious Western approach as counterproductive.

By 2010, democracies observed that none of the approaches enumerated had delivered satisfactory results. "It's not a question of sides," said one Rangoon-based diplomat. "I think this sort of thinking has been a big part of the problem. We should all see what we can do together to help the people of Myanmar. There's no question that the government is underperforming and underproviding for its people — there is common agreement about that. We've got to try and find ways to change that." According to our interview with human rights activist Benedict Rogers in January 2008, "it's not a question of engagement or not — we've advocated dialogue among the regime, Aung Sang Suu Kyi and the ethnic groups…The question is what you talk about and how you do it."

The 2011 opening in Burma/Myanmar has catalyzed a convergence of policy among democracies. Without notable exception, all democracies have by now embraced President Thein Sein's actions and overtures. Detailed descriptions of policy developments follow below.

The **US government** applied economic sanctions to Burma/Myanmar immediately after the 1988 military coup and repression of the 8-8-88 pro-democracy demonstrations. Initial economic sanctions included an arms embargo and restrictions on new investments by American companies in Burma/Myanmar. The US also downgraded its relations with Burma/Myanmar, not replacing Ambassador Burton Levin, but leaving the embassy headed by a chargé d'affaires.

The 2003 Burma/Myanmar Freedom and Democracy Act banned imports from Burma/Myanmar, but allowed teak and gems processed outside the country to be imported. Subsequent legislation, the 2008 Tom Lantos Block Burmese Junta's Anti-Democratic Efforts Act closed this glaring loophole, banning importation of jadeite or rubies in any form. As a result of the government's September 2007 crackdown, the US tightened economic sanctions, enabling the Treasury Department's Office of Foreign Asset Control to deny entry to the US and to freeze the assets of individuals "responsible for human rights abuses as well as public corruption," including "those who provide material and financial backing to these individuals or to the government of Burma." However, California-based Chevron remains invested in a prior joint venture with France's oil company Total, in Burma/Myanmar's state-owned oil firm.

In February 2009, US Secretary of State Clinton announced a policy review on Burma/Myanmar. "Clearly, the path we have taken in imposing sanctions hasn't influenced the Burmese junta," she said, adding that the path taken by others, including the ASEAN, of "reaching out and trying to engage them has not influenced them, either." In March 2009, State Department official Stephen Blake met with Burmese Foreign Minister Nyan Win. US President Obama renewed the US sanctions in May 2009, and US Senator Jim Webb visited Burma/Myanmar in August 2009, meeting with both the generals in Naypyidaw and with Aung San Suu Kyi, after which American John Yettaw was released. Webb, close to Obama, has long advocated a lifting of US sanctions. But following the new election law, which impeded NLD participation, this new approach appeared to have hit a wall. The resulting policy posture was unclear. After condemning the election law and stating any results from it would lack credibility, the US State Department stated "Our engagement with Burma will have to continue until we can make clear that... the results thus far are not what we had expected and that they're going to have to do better."

Following the inauguration of President Thein Sein and the resulting thaw, Secretary Clinton visited Burma/Myanmar in November-December 2011, the first such visit since the Eisenhower administration. Visiting both the president in Naypyidaw and Aung San Suu Kyi in Rangoon, her message was that if reform continued, relations would continue to improve. In January 2012, Clinton announced that US Ambassador Derek Mitchell would be posted to Rangoon, 24 years after the last US Ambassador, Burton Levin, departed. Mitchell took his post in July, and foreign assistance is on the rise.

Secretary Clinton announced a "targeted easing" of sanctions in July 2012, allowing US companies to begin to invest at a small scale. Larger investors would be required to file regular State Department reports certifying they respected workers' rights and detailing any payments more than US$10,000 to official or government-controlled entities. However, in a move much criticized by human rights activists, investment in the state-owned oil firm was now permitted. At the same time, President Obama issued an executive order expanding the ability to apply personal sanctions to those who impede the reform process in Burma/Myanmar. Soon after his re-election in November 2012, President Obama visited Rangoon (not Naypyidaw; President Thein Sein met him in the country's commercial hub), encouraging further reform and an end to violence against Rohingya Muslims in Rakhine state. Human rights activists worried that this visit would reduce US leverage to press for further reform. Visa restrictions on many top officials were rescinded in early 2013, as was a ban on financial transactions with some Burmese banks.

President Thein Sein visited Washington six months later, in May 2013, the first such visit in 47 years. Another installment of political prisoners (about 20) were released in advance of the trip. President Obama declared his support for Thein Sein's reform effort. "We want you to know that the United States will make every effort to assist you on what I know is a long, and sometimes difficult but ultimately correct path to follow," he said. He also repeatedly called the country Myanmar, departing from common US official practice. White House spokesman Jay Carney called this a "diplomatic courtesy" offered in recognition of ongoing reform. In a background briefing, a senior administration official said that "that initial euphoria, that honeymoon period, is starting to wear off…This is a check-in meeting." During the visit, US Senator Mitch McConnell announced a bipartisan move to allow the Burmese Freedom and Democracy Act, which had been waived for a year, to lapse altogether by not renewing it when it expired. It had been renewed periodically since its adoption in 2003. "The administration has extended an olive branch to the new Burmese government and I believe it is time for Congress to do the same…I believe that renewing the sanctions would be a slap in the face to Burmese reformers and embolden those within Burma who want to slow or reverse reform," he told the Senate. Human rights campaigners again voiced concern over reducing US leverage to drive reform.

The **European Union** adopted the EU Common Position on Burma/Myanmar in 1996 and has also progressively strengthened measures since, extending EU sanctions to include an arms embargo, freezing assets and visas for government officials and their families, and prohibiting loans to Burmese state-owned enterprises. In October 2007, a ban on investment in or export of equipment for the timber, mining and gems industries was added.

In 1996, Danish consul James Leander Nichols was sentenced to three years in prison for possessing a telephone switchboard and two fax machines. He died two months later; no independent autopsy was permitted. Soon after, the EU and Canada called in the UN for pressure for a democratization process.

The EU continued, however, to provide humanitarian and development assistance to Burma/Myanmar and its sanctions regime allowed French oil giant Total to continue its exploration and drilling. Following the conviction of Aung San Suu Kyi in August 2009, the EU added members of the Burmese judiciary who were involved in her trial to a list of over 500 officials who could not enter the EU and whose assets in the EU were frozen.

While all EU members suspended bilateral aid (aside from humanitarian aid), they varied in terms of their assertiveness on democracy issues. The British in Rangoon developed a reputation as the most vocal and proactive. The Dutch and Czechs, operating from Bangkok, also have some profile. Following the conviction of Suu Kyi in August 2009 for violating the terms of her house arrest, Britain and France called for global arms and economic embargoes. The British Foreign Office also proposed EU-wide sanctions "targeting the regime's economic interests," urging the UN Security Council to adopt wider sanctions. The Foreign Office also called on Burma/Myanmar's neighbours in Asia to ratchet up the pressure. Then German Foreign Minister Frank-Walter Steinmeier called the trial a "farce" and called on the regime to free Suu Kyi immediately.

As with the US, the EU has reviewed its policy portfolio and amended it in a major way since 2011. In 2012, it suspended the majority of its sanctions against

Burma/Myanmar; only the arms embargo remained. In November that year, European Commission President Jose Manuel Barroso visited and announced €100 million in development assistance. In February-March 2013, Burmese President Thein Sein embarked on a wide European tour, visiting a number of capitals. In April 2013, despite recognizing "significant challenges" remaining, "in response to the significant changes that have taken place and in the expectation that they will continue," the EU lifted its sanctions altogether. Burmese democracy leader (and now legislator) Aung San Suu Kyi requested they be lifted. "It is time we let these sanctions go…I don't want to rely on external factors forever to bring about national reconciliation, which is the key to progress in our country." Many member state officials went on the record applauding this common move. British Foreign Secretary William Hague, for example, said the reforms to date merited such recognition, but that "the work of the EU in Burma is not remotely finished. It is important to continue working on improving human rights, on improving the humanitarian situation, in helping the Burmese to address issues of ethnic violence, particularly attacks on Muslim communities."

Thein Sein met in Brussels with EU foreign policy chief Catherine Ashton, European Council President Herman van Rompuy, and European Commission President Barroso. "You have in the European Union a committed and long-term partner for the historic journey that Myanmar and its people have started," van Rompuy told Thein Sein. The EU's move was criticized by activists as giving away leverage too soon, particularly as the government was implicated in worsening abuses against its Muslim religious minority. Human Rights Watch Asia Director Lotte Leicht called the move "premature and regrettable," adding that "gushing superlatives appear to have replaced objective assessments in EU decision-making on Burma." Leicht argued that the lifting of sanctions "imperils human rights gains made thus far." Human Rights Watch had just published a report documenting government complicity in 2012 attacks on Muslims in Rakhine state, which it called ethnic cleansing and crimes against humanity. Officials in Naypyidaw panned the report with a statement that they didn't "understand the situation on the ground." High Representative Catherine Ashton is scheduled to visit Burma/Myanmar later this year.

Norway has long backed the exiled opposition and hosts the Democratic Voice of Burma television and radio. In late February 2013, President Thein Sein launched his European tour in Oslo. "The reason I chose Norway to be my first stop is because Norway helped our people and country in terms of education, health care and support for environmental conservation," he said, thanking his hosts for forgiving US$527 million debt, thereby allowing Burma/Myanmar to receive new credits from IFIs like the IMF and the Asian Development Bank. Thein Sein also encouraged Burmese in Norway to return to help build "the Union."

Canada levied sanctions on Burma/Myanmar in 2007, barring exports to the country (except humanitarian goods), as well as imports. Regime-linked Burmese had their assets frozen, and financial and technical services were barred. Canada loosened these sanctions in April 2013, suspending the 2007 Special Economic Measures (Burma) Regulations, including on exports, imports, financial services and investment. Individually targeted sanctions remained in place. Trade Minister Ed Fast noted that Canada aimed to deepen economic ties. Ottawa also appointed its first-ever resident ambassador, Mark MacDowell, for service in Burma/Myanmar in late May 2013. Diplomatic and trade relations had previously been handled through Bangkok.

In the wake of the September 2007 crackdown, **Australia** expanded its personal sanctions of restrictions on arms sales, travel restrictions on senior figures and associates of the regime, and targeted financial sanctions to include 418 "Burmese regime figures and their supporters," but explicitly excluded "Australians with commercial dealings with regime members in the oil, gas or publishing industries." According to the Australian Department of Foreign Affairs and Trade, "Australia has never applied general trade or investment sanctions on Myanmar," aside from a ban on defence exports. Aid is now set to increase to US$100 million per year by 2015-2016. Development assistance focuses on education, health, livelihoods and rural development, peace building, and economic and democratic governance. US$20 million of this is devoted to the Myanmar-Australia Partnership for Reform to strengthen democratic institutions and promote human rights, economic governance and rule of law. Still more funds are devoted to public health, particularly malaria, HIV prevention and AIDS treatment. A defence attaché has now been sent to "encourage the development of a modern, professional defence force in Myanmar that supports democratization and reform." The arms embargo was maintained, but autonomous travel and financial sanctions were lifted in July 2012. Australia cooperates with Burma/Myanmar on counternarcotics law enforcement. Then Foreign Minister Kevin Rudd visited Burma/Myanmar in June 2011, and President Thein Sein returned the visit to Australia in March 2013.

New Zealand's minimal bilateral relationship with Burma/Myanmar is developing since the reform process began in 2011. New Zealand's representation is in Bangkok; Burma/Myanmar's representation is in Canberra. In October 2012, the Burmese foreign minister visited New Zealand. New Zealand has devoted modest support over the past decade toward humanitarian relief and development projects. It has also funded English-language training for 239 Burmese officials since 1997 at the Mekong Institute, and has also funded scholarships at New Zealand universities. "All Burmese nationals who apply for entry visas to travel to New Zealand are assessed for any risk to New Zealand's international reputation." Visa bans on military leaders and their families remain in place.

Japan has, in contrast, pursued a softer position regarding Burma/Myanmar, asserting that a policy of economic and political engagement could be more productive. During the 1988 military coup and the repression of the 8-8-88 demonstrations, Japan, along with Western states, condemned the human rights violations perpetrated by the Burmese military, but was also the first OECD country to officially recognize the new military government. It did not impose sanctions. A senior representative from the Japanese Foreign Ministry stated that Japan's position is for "pressure and dialogue. [The Japanese government tries to] keep a working relationship with the government while maintaining pressure." Consequently, Japan became Burma/Myanmar's largest official development assistance donor, contributing approximately three-quarters of Burma/Myanmar's entire foreign aid. Japan argues that its closer economic engagement gave the Japanese Foreign Ministry greater influence with the Burmese government, though the results were difficult to identify.

As a result of the September 2007 protests and the killing of Japanese photojournalist Kenji Nagai by the Burmese military, however, Japan imposed economic sanctions on the Burmese government, including halting US$4.7 million in funding for Rangoon University. Yet after being able to send observers to some polling stations in May 2009, the Japanese government declared that it had seen an "improvement in transparency." Japan also provided technical assistance to the regime for the 2010 elections.

In May 2013, Japan announced the cancellation of the Burma/Myanmar's remaining US$1.74 billion debt, which followed the write off of US$3.58 billion in January 2013. Japanese Prime Minister Shinzo Abe, in a visit to Rangoon (the first by a Japanese head of government in 36 years), announced a US$504 million loan agreement to support infrastructure, electricity generation and power generation. "It is important to continue to back up the progress of Myanmar's reforms and [Japan] will continue its support to Myanmar," he said.

China was long reputed by diplomats in Rangoon and NGO activists to have the greatest influence and potential leverage on the Burmese junta. Beijing emerged over the 1990s as Burma/Myanmar's most important regional ally, investor, trading partner, arms supplier and consumer of Burma/Myanmar's resources. It has engaged in strategic cooperation with the Burmese generals, monitoring Indian missile tests and satellite launches from Great Coco Island, as well as supplying the Burmese military with a wide variety of armament.

China has supported the Burmese status quo, and has been Burma/Myanmar's main defender in international forums such as the UN, vetoing non-punitive, multilateral UN Security Council resolutions that would have condemned the Burmese government. The Chinese position in favour of the principle of non-interference in Burmese domestic affairs has been supported by **Russia** and others, and even democracies such as **South Africa**. This support has extended to preventing humanitarian access from being placed on the agenda of the UN Security Council in the wake of Cyclone Nargis.

In the aftermath of the September 2007 protests, however, China used its influence with the Burmese government to negotiate a visit to Burma/Myanmar by UN Special Envoy Ibrahim Gambari. Though China failed to directly condemn the Burmese government's crackdown against democracy activists, Chinese officials explicitly stated that Burma/Myanmar should "push forward a democracy process that is appropriate for the country." Former Chinese Premier Wen Jiabao also urged the Burmese government to "achieve democracy and development." On October 11, 2007, China supported a UN Security Council resolution condemning the Burmese government's violence against protestors and calling for the release of political prisoners.

After Cyclone Nargis in May 2008, China continued to cover for the Burmese regime in international forums, preventing joint international sanctions from being applied. It said the international community should respect Burmese law following Aung San Suu Kyi's August 2009 conviction, but a resurgence of ethnic conflict in the northeastern Shan state, bordering China's Yunnan province, between the Tatmadaw, local allies and ethnic Chinese Kokang rebels drove tens of thousands of refugees across the border, putting Beijing in an uncomfortable position. This led to the greatest friction between the junta and Beijing in recent memory. The Chinese government called on the Burmese regime to cease its offensive and restore stability. The cessation of the Myitsene Dam project came as a shock to Beijing. It maintains close relations with Naypyidaw (though it maintains its embassy in Rangoon), working occasionally to help resolve insurgencies. The recent opening to the West signals a diversification in Burma/Myanmar's foreign policy, however, which must be unwelcome.

India, despite being the largest democracy in the world as well as the region, also maintained a policy of economic and diplomatic engagement with Burma/Myanmar for the past two decades. India is a major consumer of Burmese oil and gas, as well as a major investor in its economy; it is the country's fourth largest trade partner, after Thailand, China and Singapore. India is participating in a major trilateral road construction project with Burma/Myanmar and Thailand, scheduled for completion in 2016.

Like the ASEAN (see below), India asserted that dialogue, rather than sanctions, was the most effective way to persuade the Burmese government to improve the political and human rights situation in the country. Some observers, however, saw India's interests focussed on access to strategic resources and to countering the growing Chinese influence in Burma/Myanmar, which Indian strategists believe stole a march on India in the late 1980s and early 1990s, when it isolated the regime. It also has internal security concerns, including with rebel groups, which have shared arms with insurgents within India in the past. During the 2007 crackdown, India declared it had "no desire to interfere in the internal affairs" of Burma/Myanmar. During a visit earlier that year, Indian Foreign Minister Pranab Mukherjee said "India is a democracy and it wants democracy to flourish everywhere. But we are not interested in exporting our own ideology." In March 2008, India made a US$120 million deal with the junta to "build, operate and use" the port of Sittwe in the Bay of Bengal as part of a growing regional rivalry with China. UN Special Envoy Ibrahim Gambari called on India to employ its growing influence on the Burmese generals to gain the release of Aung San Suu Kyi and other political prisoners. India backed China and Russia in resisting broader international sanctions against the regime. India's response to the August 2009 Suu Kyi verdict was muted.

Russia has, along with China, typically vetoed efforts to apply pressure through the UN Security Council against the Burmese junta. It has also been a major arms dealer to the regime, selling it advanced fighter aircraft, and is supplying nuclear technology to build a light-water research reactor, which has generated considerable concern.

The **ASEAN**, which allowed Burma/Myanmar to join in 1997, has many member states that have maintained close relationships with the regime and are strong trading partners. Following the violent crackdown on the Saffron Revolution in 2007, ASEAN did condemn the government's violent repression. Many members seemed to lose their patience after having given the generals the benefit of the doubt for years. According to Malaysian Foreign Minister official Ahmad Shabery Cheek, "now Burma has to defend itself if it [is] bombarded at any international forum." But ASEAN still rejected calls from the US Senate to suspend Burma/Myanmar from membership. "Our approach is not to take such a confrontational, drastic action, especially when it doesn't yield good results," said ASEAN's then Secretary-General Ong Keng Yong. Following the August 2009 verdict against Aung San Suu Kyi, the ASEAN chairman released a statement expressing "deep disappointment" in the ruling, reiterating a call made at its summit the month before for "all those under detention," including the NLD leader, to be released so they could participate in the 2010 general elections. The outgoing Filipino Foreign Minister was quite incredulous about the new election law and its exclusion of Aung San Suu Kyi — but such statements remained an anomaly in the neighbourhood.

Thailand, perhaps the country most closely linked with Burma/Myanmar, took the chair of the ASEAN in July 2008. Immediately after the 1988 crackdown, Thailand helped keep the Burmese junta afloat financially by signing business deals that gave the country foreign exchange. Thailand is a major consumer of Burmese gas. Thailand's return to democratic rule led many to hope that it would become more assertive on behalf of Burma/Myanmar's democrats, as the Philippines and Indonesia have been. ASEAN parliamentarians have also been more supportive of Burmese democrats than their governments. While the site of much political turmoil over recent years, Thai policy toward Burma/Myanmar has been consistent and heavily influenced by the military, which has strong links with the junta. From the chair of the ASEAN, Thailand criticized the verdict against Aung San Suu Kyi. Thailand's former Prime Minister Abhisit Vejjajiva called for "balanced" and "complementary" international approaches toward Burma/Myanmar. Thailand's own fraught democratic practice made it less likely to carry the torch for democratic practice in Burma/Myanmar. Since the 2011 reforms began, Thailand has returned to regular democratic practice with Prime Minister Yingluck Shinawatra. Soon after Aung San Suu Kyi announced in late 2011 she would run in by-elections, the prime minister visited her in Rangoon (the first foreign leader's visit since she was released from house arrest) and gave her support for her bid. Yingluck visited Naypyidaw in September 2012, focussing on the joint project to develop the Dawei deepwater port on their border.

Bangladesh is another large, populous neighbour of Burma/Myanmar, albeit probably the poorest. The government of Prime Minister Sheikh Hasina, elected in 2008, has been vocal in its calls for democratic change. 270,000 Rohingya refugees live in southern Bangladesh; their expulsion has been a major irritant in relations between Dhaka and Naypyidaw. After the 2012 violence in Rakhine state, Bangladesh closed its frontier, much to the consternation of human rights groups and Muslims worldwide, claiming it could simply no longer absorb these Burmese citizens (which Burma/Myanmar refuses to recognize as such).

Burmese ties with the "hermit kingdom" of **North Korea** resumed after over 20 years of severed relations following a 1983 bombing in Rangoon targeted at South Korean President Chun Doo Hwan and his delegation. Seventeen South Koreans and four Burmese were killed; 46 others were injured. Since the resumption of ties, North Korea is widely suspected of selling arms, including missile and even nuclear technology, to the Burmese junta. In 2003, North Korean technicians were reportedly at Rangoon's Monkey Point naval facility. Some analysts suspect that the North Koreans, long involved in underworld transactions for hard currency, were being paid in heroin for equipment and expertise. One diplomat posted in Rangoon noted that the Naypyidaw-Pyongyang relationship is "the big question mark." Speculation on whether North Korea was involved in a suspected Burmese nuclear program gained ground in 2010. It can only be assumed that North Korea's leadership is less than thrilled with Burma/Myanmar's opening, losing a pariah ally.

The United Nations' level of engagement has varied. At the outbreak of the September 2007 protest and the government's violent reaction, then UN High Commissioner for Human Rights Louise Arbour singled out Burma/Myanmar for criticism. But in general, China and Russia have proven themselves willing to protect the junta's interests by vetoing resolutions in the Security Council. In contrast, the veto-free General Assembly has issued repeated statements on the violation of human, civil and political rights by the SLORC/SPDC. On September 26, 2007, the Security Council gave the Secretary-General unanimous support to send Special Envoy Gambari to Burma/Myanmar. In December 2008, the UN General Assembly voted to condemn Burma's human rights record: 80 voted for the resolution, with 25 against and 45 abstaining. Gambari's series of visits has achieved little from a seemingly indifferent military. Following Aung San Suu Kyi's August 2009 conviction, Gambari said that "[she] is absolutely indispensable to the resumption of a political process that can lead to national reconciliation." The UN's human rights envoy, Tomás Ojea Quintana, reported to the Security Council in 2010 on the deplorable state of human rights observance in Burma/Myanmar, at roughly the same time that the Secretary-General stated the new election law made the process non-credible. The reform process has made the UN more hospitable for Burma/Myanmar. UN Secretary-General Ban Ki-moon visited Burma in 2012 to encourage further reform. But the UN High Commissioner on Human Rights has yet to be able to open an office in Burma/Myanmar. "We are not denying the opening of the office," President Thein Sein told *The Washington Post* interviewers in May

2013, "but we are seriously considering about the pros and cons." Such an office would allow direct observation and reporting of numerous human rights concerns, such as the recently announced decision to enforce a two-child limit for the 800,000 strong Muslim Rohingya population.

RESOURCES AND ASSETS OF DIPLOMATS IN BURMA/MYANMAR

The international diplomatic community's isolation from government decision makers dating from the Ne Win regime deepened in the SLORC/SPDC era. This became even more pronounced when the capital was moved to the closed garrison city of Naypyidaw north of Rangoon, where civilian ministries are cordoned-off from those of the Tatmadaw. Diplomats posted in Rangoon bemoan their limited tool boxes, but in the absence of countervailing interests and even day-to-day contact with authorities, embassies can concentrate their local missions on supporting civil society's efforts on behalf of human rights and democracy.

Despite the regime's violation of diplomatic premises repeatedly since 1988, rarely, if ever, has the regime taken direct action against diplomatic personnel (as opposed to domestic staff). Diplomats could and did avail themselves of their **immunity** to meet with opposition and make public statements. According to an international NGO worker, "there is theoretically the risk of being expelled, but this never happens." UN Head of Mission Charles Petrie was, however, made to withdraw in late 2007 for underlining the cruel effects of the regime's destructive economic policies on the population. To date, he remains a solitary example.

Diplomats accredited to Burma/Myanmar could count on the **support of home authorities**, as most democratic national governments have been very vocal about the repression in Burma/Myanmar, with the US Secretary of State naming it an "outpost of tyranny" in 2005. EU governments represented the concern of their publics. Former US President George W. Bush and First Lady Laura Bush were widely reported to be personally engaged on Burma/Myanmar, as was former British Prime Minister Gordon Brown, who wrote on the subject and questioned his staff regularly on developments there. Former Czech President Václav Havel mobilized several fellow Nobel Peace Prize winners in favour of concerted action, including in the UN.

Without much access to SPDC officials, diplomats had limited, but occasionally significant, **influence** on the regime. Japan claimed to have somewhat more influence than either the US or the EU. A senior Japanese diplomat working on Burma/Myanmar policy stated that "Our position is for dialogue. We try to keep a working relationship with the government while maintaining pressure. This position is similar to the ASEAN approach, so I believe we can coordinate with them."

Embassies **fund** civil society development, training programs and activities to promote open and democratic discussion in Burma/Myanmar. Embassy funds are also available for international exchange programs to connect Burmese activists with politicians and activists in other countries. Most aid is now humanitarian — mainly to the health sector, delivered through embassies, development agencies and multilaterals — and therefore coordinated with the government. Due to poor government policies and transport restrictions, Burma/Myanmar began importing rice, "perversely," according to a UN World Food Program official.

The **solidarity** of the Western democratic world was clear in 1988. There was already near-total disdain for the Ne Win regime, including from the ambassadors of the USSR and China in Rangoon. During and after the 1988 crackdown, the EU ambassadors from France, Great Britain, Italy, the Netherlands and West Germany delivered a joint demarche on behalf of the EU to the regime in protest. After the 1988 crackdown, the US and West German ambassadors worked to persuade their Japanese colleague to mirror their curtailment of development aid; they ultimately succeeded. This solidarity continued in the Thein Sein era, with the US, the EU, Australia, Japan and Norway raising the need to deepen and accelerate full observance of democracy and human rights in their increasingly frequent meetings with Burmese officials. In Cyclone Nargis, the greatest adversity the Burmese people have faced since 1988, one diplomat says that democracies, and even some non-democracies, showed "extraordinary solidarity" in trying to get the door opened for humanitarian aid.

Hands reach to touch the hand of Myanmar's pro-democracy leader Aung San Suu Kyi following her release from house arrest in Yangon, Burma/Myanmar on November 13, 2010. (AP Photo)

During the SLORC/SPDC era, the democratic world's diplomats could refer back to the UN General Assembly, Security Council and other UN bodies' statements on the human rights situation in Burma/Myanmar for **legitimacy**. This, unfortunately, cut little ice with the regime. But the UN had (and has) deep reservoirs of legitimacy with the Burmese people. In addition, countries have specific resources to draw upon — Burmese demonstrators in 1988 believed that, as symbols of democracy and leaders of the "free world," the US and France would rally to their side. The increased and multiplying contact among Burmese citizens and officials with officials and citizens of democracies gave increased potential leverage.

WAYS DIPLOMATIC ASSETS WERE APPLIED IN BURMA/MYANMAR

The Golden Rules

Diplomats assigned to Burma/Myanmar long operated within an extremely constrained public and diplomatic space, but several, especially the Norwegian embassy operating from Bangkok, earned plaudits for **listening** to a wide range of groups and individuals involved in the democracy movement. Glen Hill, the former executive director of SwissAid, asserted that the Norwegians "gave the impression that they were there to learn." Seasoned Burma/Myanmar human rights activist Benedict Rogers of Christian Solidarity Worldwide said of the democratic embassies, the British and US were "by far the most robust, forward, and accessible."

While embassies tried to be approachable in the SLORC/SPDC era, all were (and surely remain) under regular surveillance by the regime, and fear of questioning or worse inhibits the civil population from coming, especially to the US Embassy. One Burmese activist noted that embassies lacked "good human intelligence" on the situation in the country, and rarely speak the language(s), limiting their **understanding**. It is hoped that the opening in Burma/Myanmar is generating more diplomats with requisite language capability to take full advantage of its opportunity.

Making an effort to recognize a country's best value added is another important element of understanding the situation. Former Czech Ambassador Jiri Šitler, operating from Bangkok, noted that the Czechs' experience of having lived under a repressive regime was something that his democratic colleagues did not have, and centred his country's approach to the Burmese around that core advantage.

The difficult situation in Burma/Myanmar was beneficial in promoting **sharing** among missions, both of information and of tasks, in a way that avoids competition and promotes comparative advantage, as detailed in chapter 3 of the *Handbook*. The US, EU, Australian and Japanese embassies in Rangoon meet regularly to coordinate strategy in pursuit of supporting and accelerating peaceful democratic change.

In the immediate aftermath of Cyclone Nargis, the differences among diplomatic approaches were set aside in light of the scale of the calamity. One Western diplomat states that "there was a common sense of urgency…we felt more common ground than previously…It was a different focus than usual; getting aid to the delta was paramount."

Since the thaw, diplomatic visits to Rangoon — including President Obama's meeting of his counterpart Sein Thein there, rather than in the military-built capital of Naypyidaw — demonstrates an understanding of the significance of this move to the NLD. The capital was never moved by popular consent — nor was the country's name changed in this way. The continued use of "Burma" and "Rangoon," widespread among most democratic countries (some others use the official and traditional names interchangeably), conveys this respect.

Truth in Communications

Reporting on the situation in Burma/Myanmar by diplomats has long been a crucial source of information, given decades of restricted international media access and independent media within Burma/Myanmar, yet freedom of movement for diplomats is restricted and the Tatmadaw's pervasive police state deters many Burmese from actively providing information.

Diplomats in embassies can be misled if their only sources of information are from within Rangoon. But even under constraints, embassies provided crucial information on the situation and their reports were read at high levels, including at 10 Downing Street and in the White House. The UNDP office in Rangoon was well situated to witness the demonstrations of the 2007 Saffron Revolution and the subsequent crackdown, and had an independent satellite communications system that also allowed for Internet access, providing an important information conduit.

In the absence of objective newsgathering — the regime has expelled most foreign journalists and blacked out websites — diplomats have a long history of informing media outlets of the internal situation. In 1988, Dutch Ambassador Peter van Walsum, based in Bangkok, gave extensive interviews to the press reporting on the nature of the crackdown and its brutality. US Ambassador Burton Levin released reports that the embassy had received "credible, first-hand reports" of beatings, torture and executions of pro-democracy activists and others, thousands of whom were arrested.

Burma/Myanmar's government long controlled public access to information and to the means of communication. Mobile phone costs were long prohibitive; this has only recently begun to change. Land lines remain primitive; Internet servers are frequently jammed. In such a closed society, rumours are rife and travel quickly. The mobile phone cameras and video uploads of protests and violence in 2007, made from outside the country, were devastating to the regime — it hadn't foreseen them. Once broadcast outside the country, such footage could boomerang back into Burma/Myanmar. An award-winning documentary by Danish filmmaker Anders Østergaard, *Burma VJ* (VJ for "video journalist") released in 2008 showed much of this footage and the documented process these reporters underwent to get their stories out.

Former British Ambassador Mark Canning was perhaps the most vocal diplomat posted to Rangoon, and was rated by one international Burma/Myanmar watcher as having been "absolutely superb…a great example of doing the right thing. He made himself accessible to human rights NGOs." He was quoted regularly in the international press and even had a regular blog where he wrote on developments in Burma/Myanmar, through the Aung San Suu Kyi trial in the grim Insein Prison. American chargé d'affaires Shari Villarosa was also a regular in the international media, particularly important in the aftermath of Cyclone Nargis. Human rights advocates sung the praises of both in their efforts to inform the world, noting that they also helped inform Burmese indirectly.

Embassies have played a key role in **informing** the Burmese public and the international community about activities and events occurring in Burma/Myanmar. Embassies have committed resources to support media and journalism trainings for young Burmese journalists. While independent media sources are now developing and more able to operate in Burma/Myanmar, the quality of reporting varies. Embassies supported training programs both in Rangoon and Thailand to help Burmese journalists learn how to write, develop, edit and market pieces for a wide range of audiences. The Czech Embassy provided a basic video and journalism course in Burma/Myanmar: how to use a camera, how to edit and how to produce a story. This was not explicitly political, but proved extremely useful in allowing Burmese to provide imagery of the 2007 crackdown.

Embassies also supported the actual dissemination of information to the Burmese public. Both the American Center and the British Council provided important access to information to Burmese citizens, such as English medium newspapers and materials published by exile groups. The information available at the centres provided Burmese users a vital link to the outside world, as well as a better understanding of what exactly is occurring in Burma/Myanmar itself. The centres also invite speakers from outside to present — and some have spoken both about the international policy toward Burma/Myanmar and the situation with the insurgencies and in refugee areas in Thailand.

The Japanese Embassy, which enjoyed greater access to the regime than other embassies, often conveyed information between the SPDC and the NLD. "I think the NLD appreciates our activities. We can give them information. Unfortunately, the NLD has no contact with the government," one diplomat explained in 2008.

In the wake of Cyclone Nargis in May 2008, diplomats were among the most quoted information sources in Burma/Myanmar on the scale of the devastation, the shocking inactivity of the Burmese military to the humanitarian need and the scale of the aid effort required. In the aftermath of both the cyclone disaster and earlier, during the protests in September 2007, then British Ambassador Canning and US chargé Villarosa were often quoted in the media, setting baselines for international response. When Aung San Suu Kyi was imprisoned and facing trial, Ambassador Canning visited her in jail and reported to the press that she was "composed" and "crackling with energy."

Despite the multiplication of independent channels since 2011, diplomats and politicians remain active today in getting information about pro-democracy events and human rights violations out to the international community. The US, UK and Australian ambassadors are present in international media, discussing Burma/Myanmar's evolving political situation and continuing abuses in the country, particularly against the Muslim minority in 2012-2013. Previously, such diplomat-sourced reports were beamed back into Burma/Myanmar by Radio Free Asia, Voice of America, the BBC, the Democratic Voice of Burma/Myanmar and exile information organs in Thailand. There are now more channels in Burma/Myanmar through which pronouncements can travel, but these external sources remain yardsticks of credibility for ordinary Burmese. They will remain important for the foreseeable future; hopefully taxpayers in democracies and other donors will continue to appreciate their utility.

Working with the Government

Given the insular nature of the regime, it was a challenge for diplomats to engage in **dialogue** with government on a regular basis, especially with the move of the capital to the purpose-built garrison city of Naypyidaw. Yet the extraordinary nature of Cyclone Nargis brought a string of international dignitaries to Burma/Myanmar to offer assistance and press the regime to allow urgent humanitarian assistance to be brought directly to the Irrawaddy Delta. UN Secretary-General Ban Ki-moon came to press for an opening to external aid. Britain alone sent two key ministers, Deputy Foreign Minister Lord Mark Malloch-Brown and Secretary of State for International Development Douglas Alexander, in as many weeks.

In the SLORC/SDPC era, officials from the US, European, Australian and Japanese embassies regularly raised issues of democracy and human rights when they had the opportunity to meet with Burmese officials. However, human rights and democracy concerns raised by Western diplomats were generally dismissed by government officials; instead, they preferred to focus on talking up their road map to democracy plan.

The increased diplomatic representation in Rangoon and far higher circulation of international and Burmese officials since 2011-2012 have multiplied the opportunities for democratic diplomats and officials to engage in dialogue with government officials, including sectoral and specialist personnel, such as military and security services.

Until very recently, diplomats on occasion tried to **advise** the Burmese government, but to no discernible effect. In 1989, US Ambassador Levin met with SLORC intelligence chief General Khin Nyunt in an attempt to see if the regime could be convinced to enter into an effort for national reconciliation and to bring in Burmese expatriate technocrats to return vibrancy to the economy. His effort elicited an earful of invective about "communists" and "traitors" straight out of the regime phrasebook. He determined such efforts were useless at that point.

Civil society in Burma/Myanmar survived suppression and has benefitted from diplomatic advice. Czech Ambassador Šitler determined early on in his tenure that his approach should be to concentrate on transferring applicable know-how to Burmese. "We discovered that our experience from transformation to democracy was exactly what they (the Burmese dissidents) needed and wanted. The old EU members who were heavily engaged (the Dutch, Danes, British and the US) could give more money, but just didn't have this experience."

Discussions between Czech diplomats and Burmese dissidents in refugee communities in Thailand included:

- the role of returned exiles in the society after democratic transition;
- how to obtain justice for crimes committed by the regime; and
- how to promote economic reforms.

There are other such examples from even further afield. In the development of this *Handbook*, the authors had the good fortune to cross paths with former human rights lawyer and later Chilean Foreign Minister (now Senator) Ignacio P. Walker at Princeton University's Woodrow Wilson School. When queried by a Western democracy promotion activist if we knew anyone who could explain the benefits of participating in a patently slanted election for the purposes of mobilization for later battles, he sprang to mind. Burmese activists were thrilled to be able to consult and discuss their concerns with someone who had also faced a brutally repressive regime, as well as a similar choice of whether to participate or not. This sort of understanding of the situation that democracy advocates face is something that can be *intellectually* appreciated by those without similar experience, but it cannot be fully appreciated except by those who have walked where they walk.

The American Center "pushed the limits" by providing journalism, human rights and democracy training. The Australian Embassy rather controversially provided human rights training to Tatmadaw officers. The Chinese and Indian embassies had and retain frequent contact with the Burmese government. Prior to the 2011 liberalization, Ichiro Maruyama stated that the Japanese Embassy, in meetings with Indian diplomats, asked the Indian and Chinese embassies to convey the Japanese Embassy's interests and concerns to the Burmese government.

Having such access does not mean it is always used to effect. Human rights activist and author Benedict Rogers cited specifically Japan, India and Thailand as potentially having a positive impact. "If they stood up to the regime more, there might be progress. They seem completely unwilling to say anything negative."

Reaching Out

Efforts to link Burmese with the outside world and with each other had to be undertaken within Burma/Myanmar even in the regime' s most repressive period. This was clearly easier to do in refugee communities outside Burma/Myanmar. Diplomatic immunity gave diplomats in Rangoon the ability to do what local and foreign NGOs would normally be doing, but could not, given the pervasive repressive apparatus of the state.

Diplomats **connect** Burmese activists to other democracy players outside of Burma/Myanmar, including Burmese activists in exile as well as activists in the diplomat's home country.

In coordination with an ongoing Dutch foreign policy training program aimed at promising young refugees, the Czech Embassy organized a three-month study segment in the Czech Republic; during the visit, participants attended three months of trainings and meetings.

The Norwegian Embassy transmitted information from exiled groups residing in Thailand to groups within Burma/Myanmar, with the objective of promoting linkages and common ground.

The American Center, located in Rangoon, helped Burmese activists to establish a peer network for those who had been imprisoned and tortured by the Burmese government. One of the goals of the peer network was to decrease the isolation of those who had experienced torture and are likely suffering from post-traumatic stress disorder, and to connect them with other survivors and activists.

Embassies and cultural centres provided essential space for Burmese activists and others to **convene** and exchange information, sometimes with government officials included, and other times without them. The Australian, Japanese, EU, US and UN missions in Rangoon all engage in this sort of activity.

Given the heavy regime surveillance of the embassies, Alliance Française, the British Council and the American Center all played critical roles in providing space for Burmese to meet and discuss a wide array of social and political issues, particularly for youth. While these were not packaged as "democracy courses," they offered young people an opportunity to explore issues of human rights, democracy and globalization in a safe space and without drawing undue attention from the Burmese government. Most of those attending, however, knowingly assume a certain amount of risk.

Cultural people-to-people contacts also came into play. In May 2009, the US State Department financed the Burmese performances of a Los Angeles-based alternative rock/hip-hop band, Ozomatli. As part of a wider Southeast Asian tour, the band visited music schools, performed with Blind Reality, a local heavy metal band composed of blind musicians and held a performance at the American Center in Rangoon. Despite the fact that the government's scrutiny board monitors Facebook — the country's only social networking site — through servers it controls, the band has garnered many Burmese "friends." Ulises Bella, the band's saxophonist, said after the trip, "I think that for me one of the things that struck me about Myanmar in particular was the strength of the people…And the hospitality and love people felt for us just being there was really eye-opening." He continued that at the American Center, "we jammed with a local rapper who came onstage and did his thing with us. He's a big deal out there. Interesting interpretations and perceptions of what hip-hop is. They're getting it from magazines and movies but also trying to incorporate their own things."

The US Embassy was among the most vocal advocates for a democratic transition, **showcasing** democracy in practice through the programs offered by the American Center. Programs include lectures covering many sensitive topics, including the situation in the ethnic minority areas, the UN Security Council, sanctions and genocide. SwissAid's Glen Hill asserted, "The American Center...didn't shy away from difficult subjects." France's Alliance Française, in collaboration with the Czech Embassy, projected films of interest that otherwise would not be seen by Burmese activists.

The American Center is also a prime example of how embassies can **facilitate** discussion among civic and opposition members. The American Center not only offered resources not readily available in Rangoon, it also provided a safe space where democracy activists could participate in training and workshops that would strengthen their ability to participate and direct the pro-democracy movement. However, it was certainly easier to facilitate dialogue among Burmese opposition and minority groups outside the restrictions in Burma/Myanmar itself, either among refugee communities or further afield, and a number of embassies in Thailand were active on this front.

During the SLORC/SPDC era, embassies financed assistance projects for Burmese civil society, though the restrictions by the regime made doing so complex. Embassy support for the democracy movement in Burma/Myanmar ranged from funding training (both short- and long-term) to financing civil society projects. Some of the funding came directly from embassy operating budgets, while funding was also available from development funding agencies, including the Japanese International Cooperation Agency and the UK Department for International Development.

When asked in 2008 what sort of diplomatic activity he would wish for, human rights activist Benedict Rogers (also the author of a recent biography of Than Shwe) said "the main thing is if embassies can provide a space for ordinary Burmese, as well as dissidents and activists, to meet, learn, develop skills, and debate." Rogers said the American and British embassies, along with the American Center and British Council, were doing this. "I would like to see more (democratic embassies) acting the same way."

One diplomat stated in mid-2009 that "we support civic activists...by trying to help them develop better knowledge, better analysis, to help them better strategize. We want to help them broaden their ways to get at democracy, good governance. We want to help break down this 'us vs. them' split between the government and the people."

Former Czech Ambassador Šitler noted that small, well-targeted grants for projects can evade regime strictures and accomplish a great deal. Some NGOs that received embassy funding managed to find ways through the bureaucratic morass by cultivating relationships with officials who helped them navigate the regulatory maze.

A variety of training and capacity-building programs were provided to democracy activists, including:

- English language and other educational courses funded by the British Council;
- English language courses, journalism and media training, human rights training, transitional justice workshops, and organizational and communication trainings funded by the American Center;
- film and media training funded by the Czech Republic (which showed its utility in documenting the 2007 protests and crackdown); and
- Foreign policy training seminar funded by the Netherlands.

Embassies also financed library resources, increasing access to books and magazines either difficult or illegal to obtain in Burma/Myanmar. The American Center and the British Council offered extensive library resources to Burmese members, including extensive offerings on democracy and Burma/Myanmar. The Czech Embassy had Czech authors' books translated to Burmese, as well as collecting and translating volumes of articles on the Czech democratic transformation. The US, UK and Czech embassies also provided direct support to local Burmese NGOs to fund environmental, social and education projects to assist community development.

Defending Democrats

Diplomats regularly **demonstrate** their support for democracy and human rights in Burma/Myanmar, and have done so for more than two decades. In 1988, US Ambassador Levin made a point of driving to observe demonstrations with his car's flag flying. British and US diplomats regularly met with NLD officials from 1990 through the 2011 thaw. When former British Ambassador Mark Canning visited the NLD office, he arrived in his official car flying the British flag. Embassies as a matter of course declare public support for Burmese demands that fundamental human rights and freedoms be respected.

Diplomats reportedly **protected** individuals who feared imprisonment or other retaliation from the Burmese government. Assistance included financial and logistical support for these individuals to reach the Thai-Burmese border. In 1989 and 1990, embassies of the democracies protested in solidarity against aggressive interrogation and other repressive measures against their local staff, including one member of the British Embassy staff who was sentenced to three years in prison by the regime. In 1988, Ambassador Levin agreed with Aung San Suu Kyi to limit their contact to reduce the potential for the regime to paint her as a US stooge.

Diplomatic protection was also given in other, less obvious, ways. By disseminating information about human and political rights violations by the Burmese government, diplomats were able to direct international scrutiny and criticism on the government. The Burmese government's reluctance to draw negative international attention constrained its actions, at least as regards the internationally known face of Burmese opposition, Aung San Suu Kyi. But the junta did not hold back when dealing with other less visible opposition figures.

It was also reported that during the September 2007 protests, the UNDP allowed demonstrators to seek refuge within its building, as well preventing the Burmese security officers from forcibly entering the premises. Even when diplomats were not able to directly protect activists, by **witnessing** and **verifying** anti-democratic activities and human rights violations committed by the Burmese government, diplomats play an integral part in collecting and disseminating information.

By publicly witnessing and verifying abuses by the government, key embassies also sent a message to the Burmese government by regularly sending officers to witness demonstrations and civil court trials, and by supportively attending prayer services, various holiday celebrations and commemorations. As noted earlier, many diplomats attended the long trial of Aung San Suu Kyi in summer 2009, among them, European, US, Russian, South Korean, Japanese, Thai and Chinese diplomats. On July 31, 2009, as the trial neared its close, a European quoted by a journalist noted that most were ambassadors. Suu Kyi thanked the diplomats for attending. She was merely the most prominent of an estimated 2,100 political prisoners in Burma/Myanmar at that time; hundreds remain, despite periodic releases by the Thein Sein government.

In an exit interview with the Burmese exile Internet publication, *The Irrawaddy*, Ambassador Mark Canning noted the counterproductive effect of the SPDC's trial of Aung San Suu Kyi. "It's ironic that a trial which is intended to marginalize her from playing a political role is having precisely the opposite effect — illustrating what a towering figure she is. If she wasn't relevant, none of this would be happening. She would be the first to recognize that many others, not least the ethnic minorities, need a voice, but there is no doubt she remains central to a meaningful process of reconciliation and that's why the international community has been united in calling for her release."

CONCLUSION: THE CHALLENGE OF AN UNCERTAIN TRANSITION

Burma/Myanmar is perhaps simultaneously the world's most hopeful and most questionable case of transition. While the impact of targeted sanctions was a factor, it remains unclear what finally drove the ruling generals in what was the SPDC to embark on this path; the only recent exogenous shock, Cyclone Nargis, infamously did not affect their constitutional referendum timetable by one day. The Tatmadaw is notoriously opaque, paranoid and convinced of its own centrality to the nation's survival. President Thein Sein told *The Washington Post* that the army "will always have a special place in government." As of now, one could say that the military's long-declared plans to introduce a "disciplined democracy" are proceeding, simply much faster than anticipated. US Ambassador Mitchell told *The Washington Post* by email that "I don't think anyone expected the speed of change we have seen in this country over the past two years, and our encouragement has sought to keep pace." In a speech on Australia Day, 2012, Australian Ambassador Bronte Moules said "the reform process is just beginning. Even where there is political will, Myanmar will need to develop greater capacity to implement the necessary changes. That is why it is so important that the international community reinforces and supports the momentum for reform."

Speaking at George Washington University in May 2013, President Thein Sein said "I know how much people want to see democracy take root," adding that Burma/Myanmar had to forge "a new and more inclusive national identity....Our goal cannot be less than sustainable peace." More ominously, he noted that "spoilers" who oppose reforms because their interests are threatened might want to derail the process. There is evidence to support the view that the president's peripatetic foreign journeys are meant to strengthen his hand against conservatives at home.

But there are also serious reasons for skepticism. Political prisoners have not been released en masse, but rather in dollops to coincide with Thein Sein's foreign charm offensive or for foreign visitors to Burma/Myanmar. To date, 850 have been released; an estimated 160–200 remain incarcerated. While some of the most protracted ethnic conflicts are being halted, no comprehensive settlements have been reached about the nature of the state. The generals are not enthusiastic about any delegation of power from the centre, while many of the insurgents advocate federalism. Several of these conflicts have been put on ice, only to be reanimated at short notice. So while signs are hopeful, this dance has gone on for decades; nothing is yet definitively resolved.

Furthermore, the increased incidence of Buddhist versus Muslim inter-religious bloodshed, with the Muslims on the losing end, is worrying. The US State Department classifies Burma/Myanmar as a country of special concern for severe violations of religious freedom, particularly against Muslims. One need not be too imaginative to wonder if there is more to military and police non-interference than unfamiliarity with such conflict. Sein Thein recently repeated the hoary line that the Rohingya minority is not "among the indigenous races" (to the extent that even matters) to Burma/Myanmar. It bears repeating that he is distinctly lukewarm toward the request of the UN High Commissioner for Human Rights to open an office in the country.

On the democracy front, there are numerous open questions. President Sein Thein's own commitment to democratic practice remains to be tested, beyond the 2012 by-elections, which brought Aung San Suu Kyi into Parliament. In a recent interview, the president repeatedly dodged a question as to whether Suu Kyi should be able to run for president. In a new and disturbing twist, he even implied that a supermajority in Parliament would be insufficient to amend the constitution; accordingly, a referendum might be required: "It needs to be discussed among the elected members of Parliament. The constitution that was adopted by the people needs the approval of the people to be amended," he told *The Washington Post* reporters. Burma specialist Andrew Selth stated that the necessary parliamentary supermajority could only be assured if the army gave the green light. He is skeptical of such a deal.

There is also the question of the NLD's ability to adapt to the new situation. Aung San Suu Kyi, who was recently recognized for her persistent advocacy for democratic change by the Community of Democracies, appears to have determined that partnership with Thein Sein is the best or only way forward. She clearly aims to run for president, a path impeded by the current constitution — by design. She favoured the removal of sanctions (as opposed to their suspension — they would now need to be legislated anew) to support the reform process. She was long reticent about months of inter-communal violence against the Rohingya in particular, only recently stating her disgust at the two-child policy announced by the government and condemning it as "illegal." Minority groups also worry that the NLD may be Burman-centric. The internal workings and membership of a party inured to decades of suppression, but without experience in actual democratic representation, require attention as well. Observers noted insularity in decision making and a wide age gap between senior members and a youthful general population. In the unlikely event that the generals decide to allow Suu Kyi to run for president in 2015, will she have a wide and deep enough supporting cast to implement her vision for a democratic Burma?

The Washington Post's Fred Hiatt (2013) explains the dilemma well:

> Western officials hope that Thein Sein, who has been in power for about two years, is bravely negotiating a treacherous path from the repressive regime he was once part of to a society in which people genuinely can choose their own leaders. Along this path, they believe, he has to battle hardliners who oppose change...If so, his circumspection may be a clever tactic to keep everyone on board as reform moves forward. Alternatively, it could be an indication that the generals remain firmly in control and that Thein Sein is not free to express a view that might offend them. Or it might be that he hopes the reform path can stop somewhere short of true democracy.

Shwe Mann, reputed architect of the reform drive, Speaker of Parliament, and number three in the SDPC, told the BBC that "[Suu Kyi] has good qualities and she loves her country. We share the same ambition — to serve the nation and people." He added in the September 2012 interview that "Our reforms are irreversible. Our goal is still to build a multi-party democratic system and market economy...It takes time to change from one system to another...I don't want to see revolution, I would rather see evolution," yet he gave no sign of being haunted by his institution's actions — or his own. "I won't say regrets (when questioned about past policies, violence and repression). But we have learned a lot. We must learn from our past so that in future we can serve our people better." It would seem axiomatic that to learn from the past, one has to agree what it was, first.

Thiha Saw, editor of the (new and independent) *Open News Weekly Journal* in Rangoon recently assessed that the reform process "hasn't reached a point of no return yet. It still needs a few more years."

There are numerous indicators that the army wants to maintain control, but could it wind this process back even if it wanted to? With each passing month, this would be harder to do.

There remain some basic indicators of whether the democratic reform process has a firm foundation. These are relatively simple to identify:

- Will all political prisoners/prisoners of conscience released?

- Will the constitution be amended to allow Aung San Suu Kyi to run for president?

- Will the tentative peace deals with the 11 major insurgencies hold and develop into durable solutions for the "inclusive national identity" that Thein Sein mooted in Washington?

- Will the violence against the Rohingya and other Muslim minorities be stopped? Will the "inclusive national identity" Thein Sein raised in Washington be extended to them as well?

- Will there be any process of accountability for crimes committed against citizens of Burma/Myanmar by their own authorities?

Even if all of these were done — and none are on the horizon at the time of writing — the achievement of durable democracy is not guaranteed. Much hard work lays ahead for those Burmese, in and out of government, who aim to develop a democratic and prosperous future for their long stunted country.

As they pursue this goal, the democratic world will have a crucial role to play. The military would not tolerate this opening if they did not see it in their interest — but there is always the risk that protection of interests will lead them to tighten the leash once more. While most democracies have, in less than two years, decided to give President Thein Sein the benefit of the doubt, reassured by Nobel laureate Suu Kyi that he is for real, there needs to be a will to constantly assess the ground reality and operate accordingly.

Not everything in the diplomatic playbook in Burma/Myanmar needs to change as a result of the evolving environment. When the *Handbook* was first drafted, a seasoned NGO activist dealing with Burma/Myanmar and its border areas said that democratic embassies and associated missions "providing space, enabling visitors to meet dissidents," was the most important value added. So additional funding for these activities is useful. One hopes that diplomats come to the country with greater language ability. Given the harsh repressive nature of the regime until recently (and to present day in large measure) and the pervasive fear of informers, citizens are more likely to trust a foreigner who speaks their language than his or her interpreter.

Insisting on full access to make these assessments throughout Burma/Myanmar is essential. Diplomats in Rangoon, Mandalay, Naypyidaw and elsewhere will be stewards of their countries' democratic values. They are now adapting to the changes at the top, trying to help the Burmese shore up reform and drive it further from below. They will need to convey to officials and ordinary Burmese of all stripes that the ability to recalibrate policy when the facts change is a central democratic tenet. If the situation warrants it, democracies will need to be able to tighten their policies, as well as loosen them.

WORKS CITED

BBC News Asia (2013). "What is Behind Burma's Wave of Religious Violence?" BBC News, April 4.

Gray, Denis D. (1987) "Letter from Rangoon." Associated Press, November 29.

Hiatt, Fred (2013). "Troubling Signs for Burma's Reforms?" *The Washington Post*, May 20.

Steinberg, David I. (2001). "Introduction." In *Burma's Armed Forces: Power without Glory* by Andrew Selth. Norwalk: East Bridge Publishing.

Than, Soe Win (2010). "Boycott Hits Burma Election Credibility." BBC News, March 30.

Thant Myint-U (2008). *The River of Lost Footsteps: A Personal History*. New York: Farrar, Straus and Giroux.

9 ZIMBABWE: AN AFRICAN TRAGEDY

*By Kurt Bassuener, 2008; revised and updated 2010
and 2013; researched by Britt Lake and Taya Weiss,
2007-2008*

Nota Bene: *At the time of publication, Zimbabwe had just completed a general election. The official results gave President Robert Mugabe and his ruling Zimbabwe African National Union-Patriotic Front (ZANU-PF) a resounding victory over the opposition MDC, led by Morgan Tsvangirai, in both presidential and parliamentary elections. The results were immediately contested by the MDC, which charged systematic electoral manipulation. Independent domestic observers pointed to irregularities which may have disenfranchised up to a million predominantly urban voters. Democratic governments in the West, but also in Africa, Botswana in particular, cited serious misgivings with the electoral process. There are signs that the country, after a few years of relative peace, might return to violence. It remains unclear what the legal contest of the results and potential unrest will mean for the economic gains and tentative print media freedom which returned under the unity government. The country is likely to remain a continuing crisis point for the world's democracies, which will need to decide how to calibrate their polices to best assist Zimbabweans back into the democratic fold.*

INTRODUCTION

Zimbabwe's precipitous decline from peaceful breadbasket to malnourished autocracy has become one of Africa's most notorious stories of post-colonial state failure. The situation was not always grim; far from it. Upon transition from white-ruled Rhodesia in 1979, the country's future appeared bright. With plentiful natural resources, a booming agricultural sector, a strong pool of educated human capital and solid government administration, Zimbabwe appeared destined for success. The government of the new Prime Minister Robert Mugabe, regarded as a liberation hero for his role in armed struggle against white supremacist rule, was racially inclusive. Mugabe also projected moderation in his language and choice of personnel. The new regime in Harare was embraced worldwide — on both sides in the Cold War, by the group of non-aligned developing states and Mugabe's wartime patron, China.

That moment of optimism was followed by an accelerating decline, blamed by many observers almost entirely on Mugabe's misrule, which has led to the crippling of a vibrant agricultural economy, repression of political dissent and violent land seizure. Others note the effect of rosy assessments early on and easy money in the 1980s, followed by the social destabilization of structural readjustments in the 1990s. As conditions in Zimbabwe began growing steadily worse in the 1990s, and as President Mugabe grew more adversarial, the European Union, the United Kingdom and the United States, among others, became ever more critical of his methods, seeking to isolate him while supporting a second track of outreach from Zimbabwe's regional neighbours.

But among Zimbabwe's neighbours in the Southern African Development Community (SADC), Mugabe's casting of Western powers as neo-colonialist meddlers carried considerable weight with politicians and a public attuned to the language of liberation struggle. For some time, President Thabo Mbeki of South Africa and other SADC leaders eschewed open criticism of Mugabe in favour of attempts at engagement and mediation. But the 2008-2009 power-sharing arrangement between President Mugabe and Prime Minister Morgan Tsvangirai was fraught from the beginning and barely functioned, despite the fact it allowed for economic stabilization and a reduction of political violence. As the violence employed by Mugabe and his party increased, criticism of his rule sharpened, even among his immediate neighbours. The Mugabe regime bequeathed Zimbabwe's people with what was the world's fastest contracting economy and one of the lowest life expectancies in the world. While a slow recovery has been in progress for Zimbabwe, the devastated economy will take years to rebuild; it has fallen far from its previous standing as one of Africa's most developed states. Political uncertainty remains a major handicap. Zimbabwean society is in dire need of reconciliation to heal the scars of political violence. Millions of Zimbabweans have left their country to survive; three to four million have emigrated to neighbouring South Africa alone. In addition, the issue of land distribution at the heart of Zimbabwean conflict for decades remains divisive, even as productivity of the land already seized has plummeted. There has also been little or no accountability for the numerous crimes committed in the past 13 years. The tasks ahead will likely require technical capacity from a government that has largely eroded and needs robust reinforcement from the donor community.

Roots of Conflict

The history of Zimbabwe's independence from British colonialism and white supremacist rule continues to play a significant role in political discourse. Southern Rhodesia, as it was formerly known, was settled by whites beginning in the late nineteenth century. In 1930, the Land Apportionment Act restricted black access to land and forced many would-be farmers into wage labour.

In 1965, Prime Minister Ian Smith, fearing that the "wind of change" sweeping over Africa in the wake of decolonization would ultimately produce majority rule in Rhodesia, unilaterally declared independence from Britain of his white-minority regime. The international community declared Rhodesia an outlaw state and imposed strict sanctions. It was recognized only by apartheid South Africa.

Liberation groups — the predominantly majority Shona and Chinese-backed Zimbabwe African National Union (ZANU) and the predominantly minority Ndebele and Soviet-backed Zimbabwe African People's Union (ZAPU) — intensified their guerilla campaign against white rule, eventually leading Smith to submit to negotiations. British-brokered talks at Lancaster House in the UK led to British-supervised elections in 1980, won by independence leader Robert Mugabe's ZANU party. Mugabe became prime minister and has remained leader of the country ever since, changing the constitution to become president in 1987.

Post-colonial Violence

In 1982, Prime Minister Mugabe feared rebellion by his political rival and cabinet member Joshua Nkomo and had him fired. Mugabe then sent the North Korean-trained Fifth Brigade, a unit subordinate directly to him and outside the military chain of command, into Matabeleland in an operation known as Gukurahundi (in Mashona, this means "the early rain that washes away the chaff before the spring rains"). Fearing for his own life, Nkomo fled to London in 1983, accusing the brigade of killing three people in his home, calling the unit a "political army" and denying that the main issue was tribal, but rather one of political control. The killings that took place over the next few years are widely referred to as a massacre, with estimates of the number killed as high as 20,000.

Diplomats in Harare conveyed the reports of massacres to their governments, but authorities at home, not eager to call into question such a recent success and fearful of further regional instability, chose not to confront Mugabe's evident intolerance for dissent. Then British Ambassador Sir Martin Ewans later wrote that "It wasn't pleasant and people were being killed but…I don't think anything was to be gained by protesting to Mugabe about it…I think the advice [from London] was to steer clear of it in the interests of doing our best positively to help Zimbabwe build itself up as a nation" (cited in Barclay, 2010). In the words of British diplomat Philip Barclay (2010), who served more than two decades later, the experience was instructive to Mugabe: "he can kill to retain power and the world will do no more than watch."

It remains a searing memory for Ndebeles and a lingering social divide in the country. A commission established to investigate the campaign drafted a report that was never publicly released. Fear of accountability or retribution for the campaign is reputed to be among the reasons Mugabe fears losing power. Mugabe eventually succeeded in bringing ZAPU to heel, signing an accord with Nkomo to merge ZAPU into ZANU in 1987, and amending the constitution to create an executive presidency. In 1987, ZAPU and ZANU formed ZANU-PF (Patriotic Front), in what was seen by some as a move toward the one-party state Mugabe had been advocating. The first decade of his rule saw a strong drive to centralize power in his own hands.

Hope and Disappointment: The 1990s

There was a glimmer of hope for anchoring multi-party democracy in 1990, when Mugabe's post-election attempt at constitutional change to establish a one-party state failed (his party and loyal security forces continued their de facto one-party rule, and Mugabe was re-elected in 1996). In 1991, hope continued to predominate among Western diplomats as Mugabe hosted the Commonwealth Summit, during which he held a garden party with Queen Elizabeth II. With his support, the Commonwealth adopted the Harare Declaration, committing member states to protect "democracy, democratic processes and institutions which reflect national circumstances, the rule of law and the independence of the judiciary, just and honest government; [and] fundamental human rights, including equal rights and opportunities for all citizens regardless of race, colour, creed or political belief." Mugabe's "constructive neutrality" was instrumental in overcoming objections from a number of autocrats: Kenya's Daniel arap Moi, Malaysia's Mahathir bin Mohamad and Uganda's still-ruling Yoweri Museveni among them.

In the early 1990s, the land distribution issue came to the fore as Mugabe seized four large white-owned farms and denied any right of appeal. He dismissed the objections of Harare-based diplomats and isolated those who protested vigorously, such as Canada's High Commissioner Charles Bassett, from government contact. The sense emanating from President Mugabe that he was embattled by foreign opponents began to dominate his public statements from this time.

Through the 1990s, Mugabe increasingly relied upon party and loyal security forces, which included the feared Central Intelligence Organization. In 1996, after being re-elected, Mugabe stated that land would be expropriated without compensation, which would be deferred until later. With infusions from IFIs drying up, both due to larger global trends and to misuse by the government, Zimbabwe sought alternative sources of income. Wealth from timber and mining concessions in the Democratic Republic of the Congo, where his armed forces participated in what became a regional war, went directly to military and party leaders. The relationships with Libya and China grew closer as the West became more estranged and less tolerant of Mugabe's authoritarian tendencies.

In Britain in 1997, John Major's Conservative government was defeated at the polls by the Labour Party under its new leader, Tony Blair. Blair's first meeting with Mugabe at the Commonwealth Summit in Edinburgh was mostly consumed by Mugabe's monologue on land compensation. The Mugabe government claimed that Britain reneged on a commitment by Blair's predecessor, John Major, to support land redistribution efforts. Britain's position was that it would support "willing seller" land purchases, along with other donors, so long as it was integrated in a wider land reform and poverty reduction policy. Earlier efforts were assessed to have benefitted ZANU-PF officials rather than the intended recipients. Mugabe never agreed to these stipulations. According to British High Commissioner Brian Donnelly, "The great Mugabe myth is that it has been lack of money that has precluded land reform. There would always have been money if he had been prepared to accept a transparent and equitable process" (cited in Kinsman, 2008). In Mugabe's worldview, this was an injustice. Perhaps more importantly, war veterans were becoming an increasingly demanding and resentful constituency that could turn against Mugabe were they not placated. A one-time payment of Z$50,000 per person was made, driving inflation, but once paid from the public purse, their demands grew. The largest repository of Zimbabwean assets rests in the commercial farming sector; this naturally became the till to which Mugabe and the ZANU-PF gravitated.

By late 1999, a government-appointed commission on drafting a new constitution recommended that Mugabe's powers be curbed and limited to two terms in office. At that point, the constitution had been amended 15 times to increase executive power. Dissenting opinions on the committee criticized the draft for leaving Mugabe too much authority. Mugabe then proposed a constitution to increase his powers, put it forward in a referendum in February 2000, and lost. A civic movement, the National Constitutional Accord met, despite official vilification, to discuss a constitution that could be accepted by a majority of Zimbabweans.

Land Seizure and Opposition Politics: Becoming a Pariah

In 2000, forcible seizures of white-owned land by ZANU-PF "war veterans" (now often party thugs too young to have fought in the wars of independence) began to seriously destabilize Zimbabwe's economy. The victims of this policy were overwhelmingly black, with over a million made homeless since 1998, 400,000 of them prematurely dead as a result. In the words of British diplomat Philip Barclay (2010), "I would fault white farmers for their Canute-like perseverance in managing their enterprises on such traditional lines. Had they educated and trained several thousand farm managers — a rural black middle class engaged in farming — it would have been much harder for ZANU-PF to argue that white agriculture had it in for the black man." Barclay notes that while donor funds were readily available in the 1980s for land redistribution and training schemes, much went unused; Mugabe seemed uninterested. "Land became a policy focus only when Mugabe began to run out of steam and saw the potential to link it to the politically explosive topics of race and colonial history. Land also became a useful, though quickly exhausted, medium for political patronage" (ibid.). It had the added benefit of hitting his political opponents while motivating his own supporters.

The 2000 Parliamentary elections saw a ZANU-PF victory over the newly formed opposition MDC, led by trade unionist Morgan Tsvangirai, but Mugabe's party lost its margin to change the constitution. MDC's first electoral showing was impressive, with the party taking nearly half — 57 of 120 — of contested seats. The election results helped drive Mugabe to ever more aggressive and violent methods to maintain power.

In 2002, Mugabe won the presidency, but the lack of freedom and fairness of the vote was condemned by Commonwealth and Western powers alike. Brussels called off a planned EU observer mission due to obstacles from the Mugabe government, despite the advice of EU ambassadors in Harare that criticism of what was already an unfair electoral process would be undermined by not having observers on the ground. Norway, however, did field an observer mission and strongly criticized the electoral process. The Commonwealth suspended Zimbabwe, citing high levels of violence in the election, which was the beginning of ongoing sanctions by the EU, US, Australia and New Zealand. South Africa, fearful of state collapse on its border, endorsed the poll, as did the rest of SADC members. The divergence between the Western democracies' views and those of most in the region widened from here. That same year, the Zimbabwean Supreme Court struck down the legislation allowing non-consensual land acquisition. Mugabe forced many judges from the bench in response.

Zimbabwe suffers from periodic droughts, and the combination of natural conditions and the chaos surrounding the country's agricultural land combined in 2002-2003 to require rapidly escalating external food assistance — received most generously from the countries most vilified by Mugabe. The economic and social ripple effect from high rates of HIV/AIDS infection also began to take their toll. Zimbabwe's agricultural productivity and economy in general began to nosedive. The government response to this popular hardship has been callous, sometimes in the extreme. As Zimbabwe depopulated, Minister of Lands Didymus Mutasa said that "We would be better off with only six million people [from 14 million in 2000]…our own people who supported the liberation struggle. We don't want all these people" (cited in Barclay, 2010).

In 2004, MDC leader Morgan Tsvangirai was tried for treason on trumped-up evidence and acquitted. Violence against MDC supporters would only escalate. The following year, the United States ramped up its anti-Mugabe rhetoric, declaring Zimbabwe one of six world "outposts of tyranny." Perhaps both threatened and emboldened by his pariah status, Mugabe authorized Operation Marambatsvina ("take out the trash"), targeting concentrations of his urban opponents. In the months leading up to another flawed election, hundreds of thousands of urban slum dwellers were forcibly displaced and their homes destroyed; hundreds of thousands of eligible citizens were unable to vote where they were registered. ZANU-PF won at the polls in the wake of this brutality. The next few years, leading up to the 2008 parliamentary and presidential elections, were marked by further sanctions, escalating rhetoric on all sides and increasing economic woes, especially for Zimbabwe's poor.

Agricultural production and distribution fell to a point where at least half of Zimbabwe's population was at risk of hunger. Inflation reached astronomical dimensions. The flow of refugees across the border to South Africa grew unabated, as Zimbabweans fled in search of jobs, food and safety from political persecution. MDC leaders and activists such as Women of Zimbabwe Arise came under increasing attack, often physical, by the government and ZANU-PF's own youth militia. At a major demonstration in March 2007, the security forces publicly beat a number of prominent opposition figures, including Tsvangirai himself. His skull was fractured in beatings while in police custody; photos of his swollen and bruised face made front pages worldwide.

The Western and African leaders' different approaches to the crisis would grow ever more divergent, with increasing isolation and condemnation by the former, contrasting to what the international press dubbed "quiet diplomacy" led by South Africa's President Thabo Mbeki — though Mbeki's passiveness following the March 29, 2008 election was increasingly contested by other SADC leaders, including Tanzanian President Jakaya Kikwete and Zambian President Levy Mwanawasa, as well as in South Africa itself. The failure of these two schools of thought to find more common policy ground on at least the shared interest in change became a subject of heated argument on both sides.

The March 2008 elections showed how deeply Mugabe and his party's popularity had fallen. Violence attended the initial campaign, but it was seen by observers to have been less than in the previous three elections. Even optimistic predictions by some foreign diplomats on the ground predicted the MDC would win only about a third of the seats, based on the simple assumption that while Mugabe might not be popular in the cities, he was in the countryside. ZANU-PF and MDC were in a race to the bottom, feeling internal resource pressures during the campaign. Locally tallied results, communicated among opposition officials and voters themselves, showed that the MDC had indeed been dominant in the cities, but also performed strongly in the rural areas. The Zimbabwe Election Commission drip-fed the parliamentary results over a course of days, delaying the (more easily tallied) presidential results for five weeks. The main, Tsvangirai-led faction of the MDC won two more seats (99) than the ZANU-PF. The smaller Mutambara MDC faction (based in Matebeleland) also won 10; had the parties remained united, there would have been 18 more seats (for a total of 117) added to a unified MDC's tally. The MDC claimed outright presidential victory early on, drawing the ire (and treason charges) of the government. Their estimate was later revised down to a bare majority, which hurt their credibility and bolstered a reputation for exaggeration. An independent network estimated the vote at 49 percent for Tsvangirai, 43 percent for Mugabe, with +/- two percent margin of error. Five weeks after the election, the Election Commission finally released the official results: 47.9 percent for Tsvangirai, 43.2 percent for Mugabe and 8.3 percent for ZANU-PF challenger Simba Makoni. Electoral rules were changed to allow the runoff to be held 90 days after the initial election, giving ZANU-PF more time to plot its response.

These results were a massive challenge to Mugabe, who reportedly considered accepting the result in early April (a month before it was made official), stung by the rebuke of a nation he believed owed him perpetual gratitude. But those in the inner circle, particularly in the security apparatus, had no intention of accepting the results, fearing prosecution for their numerous misdeeds. In April, the Joint Operations Centre (JOC), composed of hardline senior military officers, effectively took control of the situation while Mugabe was deliberating on his next move. Their conclusion was simple. According to Philip Barclay (2010), "the spirit of the people and the opposition they had shown to Mugabe on March 29 would have to be broken." The JOC also worked to wind Mugabe back up by showing him films of white resistance to farm evictions. These men saw no distinction between the ZANU-PF and the state. Mugabe's loss was unacceptable, whatever the citizens wanted.

To ensure a more favourable result in the presidential runoff, intimidation and horrific violence were unleashed on a massive scale — without regard to the long-term damage to Zimbabwe's social fabric. In the words of British diplomat Philip Barclay (2010), "ZANU's readiness when under pressure to resort to violence and target educated people shows its Maoist origins." Youths were recruited from ZANU-PF's Mashonaland redoubt (though MDC made inroads there too) for mobile teams led by security officials, briefed that the revolution was under threat by traitors, and that radical measures were required. Such measures included beatings, rape, murder (including burning perceived opponents alive) and the specific targeting of polling station officials, who frequently happened to be teachers. A teacher in the town of Zaka reported receiving a text message threatening her and her colleagues with death should the town come out in favour of Tsvangirai once again. Mass arrests of teachers were reported. The frequent use of rape as a political weapon, usually by youths plied with free beer, carried with it the potential of death, given the high incidence of AIDS in Zimbabwe. Village chiefs were also frequently recruited or press-ganged into roles as enforcers of election turnout — and results.

Mugabe won the June 27, 2008 runoff election, which Tsvangirai boycotted, stating that the election was a "violent sham" and that no free election was feasible under conditions where opposition supporters' lives were threatened. The country was devastated by the continued violence. Mugabe quickly held a defiant inaugural ceremony and then jetted off to an African Union summit. No African leaders present questioned his legitimacy openly, yet, in its election report, the SADC stated that the result did not reflect the popular will, noting state-sponsored violence, one-sided media coverage and impediments to the MDC's ability to campaign. South Africa's Thabo Mbeki continued to straddle, stating Mugabe was willing to talk to the MDC. In contrast, Botswana's Foreign Minister, Phandu Skelemani, stated baldly that "He can't pretend to act as if he won an election because he didn't," and that "SADC have failed the people of Zimbabwe...Too many in the leadership of SADC feel some kind of obligation towards Mugabe" (cited in Barclay, 2010). Efforts led by the US and UK to apply new sanctions to the Mugabe regime were rejected in the UN Security Council by China and Russia, but EU members added new sanctions on business transactions with the regime and connected individuals in August 2008.

Tsvangirai and the MDC faced a brutal choice: enter talks to share power with the regime or be condemned to irrelevance and perhaps total oblivion. The grassroots party, which had borne the brunt of government violence, was against such a deal. Provincial MDC MPs and members felt abandoned in the paroxysm of carnage that followed the runoff announcement. International opprobrium didn't lead to

Mugabe's forced ouster, as many had hoped. Tsvangirai swallowed the bitter pill. Reminiscent of the model that followed Kenya's fractious election and its bloody aftermath, Mugabe and Tsvangirai entered power-sharing talks in August 2008, which ultimately led to a deal — the Global Political Agreement in September. The implementation of the deal was stalled for months, however, over the distribution of key ministries, especially those pertaining to public security (notably the Ministry of Interior), where Mugabe's ZANU-PF insisted on a monopoly. Meanwhile, a cholera outbreak brought on by the collapse of once-enviable public health infrastructure, along with rapidly accelerating inflation (well over two million percent annualized), sent ever-greater streams of refugees to South Africa. In December, Mugabe denied there was any more cholera, a statement that shocked even his supporters, given the ugly reality. The government declared a national health emergency the same month. South Africa announced it would withhold aid until Zimbabwe had a representative government. Unpaid troops rioted in November 2008.

SADC leaders were becoming impatient with the limbo and increasingly saw Tsvangirai as the one to blame. At a meeting in late January 2009 in the exclusive Sandton district of Johannesburg, SADC leaders met with Mugabe, with Tsvangirai outside the room — yet another humiliation. Despite having planned to drive a hard bargain at the SADC meeting, Tsvangirai negotiated the right to appoint five governors and accepted the power-sharing arrangement: Mugabe would remain president, Tsvangirai would become prime minister; the next month, he was sworn in as prime minister. Foreign currencies (primarily the US dollar) were legalized to stem the hyperinflationary spiral (a Z$100 trillion note had entered circulation), allowing consumer prices to fall, but the IMF refused the new government a loan until its US$1 billion in debt was settled. China granted the country a US$950 million loan in July.

Talks between Mugabe and Tsvangirai on the shape of a new constitution resumed in July 2009, but went nowhere. In late August 2009, Mugabe railed against the West in a public rally, claiming that after opening up to the West as friends "you want to be masters."

The MDC's frustration at its separation from real levers of power grew, and attacks on its members in the capital and the hinterland continued apace. South African President Jacob Zuma came in an attempt to mediate between Mugabe and Tsvangirai to seek full implementation of the Global Political Agreement in order to "create confidence." The MDC accused hardline ZANU-PF supporters in the security forces of attempting to derail the deal. Soon after, the IMF loaned Zimbabwe US$400 million to bolster its foreign currency reserves without conditions, but placed an additional US$100 million in escrow until the country cleared its arrears. The parties differed on how the funds should be used, with ZANU-PF pushing for immediate disbursement to farmers and companies (many of which are party-linked).

The EU also sent a delegation to Zimbabwe in September 2009 to meet both Mugabe and Tsvangirai to press for progress that would allow fully normalized ties. Swedish Prime Minister (and chair of the EU Presidency at the time)

Fredrik Reinfeldt said that a curtailment of the personal sanctions was not on the agenda. "It is not the restrictions that are creating problems in Zimbabwe, it is the mismanagement [and] not respecting of human rights." The MDC wanted lifting of these sanctions to be conditional on full implementation of the Global Political Agreement, while Mugabe wanted these lifted immediately. Mugabe noted that the talks "went well...Obviously they thought the Global Political Agreement was not working well." He went on to claim that ZANU-PF had done "everything" required under the Agreement. In a speech before his meeting with the delegation, Tsvangirai said "I am not going to stand by while ZANU-PF continues to violate the law, persecutes our members, spreads the language of hate, invades our productive farms [and] ignores our international treaties. We want partners who are going to commit themselves to good governance principles. We cannot have partners of looters." Then European Commissioner for Development Karel De Gucht said "They do not have the same reading of the same document. They have a different reading on how this should be done and at what speed." Despite the positive characterization of the visit by President Mugabe, Justice Minister Patrick Chinamasa accused the EU of buying into the MDC's arguments "hook, line and sinker. They seem to want to undermine the inclusive government."

Prime Minister Tsvangirai began to boycott government meetings in October as a result of the prosecution of deputy Minister of Agriculture-designate, former coffee farmer and MDC member Roy Bennett, for terrorism, insurgency, sabotage and banditry. Bennett had been arrested earlier in February on the day government ministers were sworn in. The case drew criticism from Western capitals, including Washington and London, for having been politically motivated. Tsvangirai vowed not to go to his office until the case against Bennett was "resolved."

While shops in Harare and Bulawayo may have finally been stocked and more citizens were able to afford basic necessities, fear continued to grip the countryside. White farmers, who once had 4,000 farms and were now down to a few score nationwide, told the BBC that "anarchy and lawlessness" remained the norm well after the power-sharing deal. Former British diplomat Philip Barclay (2010) opined "I think people now realize that what the [farm evictions] policy has really been about is the transfer of land from an arrogant white elite that was at least productive to an arrogant black elite that is totally unproductive. So it's really hard to see this empowering the ordinary Zimbabweans in any way. The people who own the land now are a very small number of Mugabe's cronies." Including the Mugabes themselves, he might have added. Mugabe's wife, Grace, now owns an expropriated farm that had been selling to Nestlé, before the negative publicity compelled the corporation to end the arrangement.

Grace Mugabe also has other profit centres. In December 2010, she sued Wikileaks over allegations in leaked diplomatic cables that she was enriched by illegal diamond sales. Official diamond sales were resumed in August 2010; two of the Marenge diamond fields were approved by the Kimberley Process for sale in November 2011. This funding stream has proven a lifeline for Mugabe and ZANU-PF in general, and has led some observers to worry that "the resource curse" will allow Mugabe and company greater latitude to maintain control. Additionally, the government from March 2010 began requiring foreign-owned companies to sell majority stakes to local partners — hardly a welcome mat for foreign investment.

A teacher in West Mashonaland noted that all teachers were suspected by ZANU-PF officials, war veterans and young toughs to be MDC supporters, and were regularly harassed, intimidated or attacked. The MDC asserted that the ZANU-PF was creating militia bases in the countryside and militarizing state institutions in preparation for future elections. Military and security officials were even emplaced in the state broadcaster, the Zimbabwe Broadcasting Corporation (ZBC).

But while ZANU-PF still holds most of the high cards, the tenuous political arrangement took its toll on party unity. Mugabe himself stated at a party congress in December 2009 that "The party is eating itself up. The more intense the internal fighting is, the greater opportunity we give the opposition to thrive." Complaints about lack of pluralism in the party became more audible than before, as members looked to the inevitable post-Mugabe future. "We must win [elections] resoundingly and regain the constituents we lost," Mugabe told the 10,000 members assembled. How ZANU-PF might get out the vote might not be from the democratic retail politics playbook either.

But in March 2010, South African President Zuma mediated between President Mugabe and Prime Minister Tsvangirai to arrive at a deal to allow the government to move forward. The package of measures apparently included some senior appointments for the MDC that had long been on hold, including a new head of the Central Bank, Attorney General and provincial governors. Soon after, a Human Rights Commission and Electoral Commission were inaugurated by Mugabe and also applauded by the MDC. The former is headed by Reginald Austin, former head of the Commonwealth's legal affairs division; the latter is headed by Simpson Mutambanengwe, a former judge on the Zimbabwean Supreme Court and acting chief justice in Namibia. Of the Election Commission, Deputy Prime Minister Arthur Mutambara (from an MDC splinter party) said "The Commission will go a long way in creating conditions for free and fair elections in our country." President Zuma also made a point of meeting with Deputy Agriculture Minister designate Roy Bennett, who was still on trial. In May, Bennett was acquitted by Zimbabwe's High Court, as the judge found insufficient evidence of the charges. The government (the Justice Ministry is held by ZANU-PF) vowed to appeal the verdict. An Attorney General's office spokesman said the High Court judge had taken a "piecemeal approach. He should have considered the merits of the case and the facts which pointed to the accused." The MDC's spokesman denounced the appeal, stating "This has nothing to do with the law, but something to do with politics."

In a rare show of unity, Prime Minister Tsvangirai invited President Mugabe and Deputy Prime Minister Arthur Mutambara to join him at the World Economic Forum in Davos, where all three encouraged investment in Zimbabwe. Finance Minister and General Secretary of the MDC Tendai Biti is seen by Barclay (2010) to have "more direct power [than Tsvangirai]. At least he gets to control the budget. And given the difficulties he's faced getting public servants back to work, he's achieved a tremendous amount."

Foreign governments recognized a need to assist forward movement, however shaky. In the United States, then Senate Foreign Relations Committee Chairman John Kerry said in a press conference with Tsvangirai that the new joint government has made "real progress in stabilizing runaway inflation and trying to begin to create the conditions for democracy…I believe that we should explore our options to increase assistance for reform. Failure to act now may squander this opportunity for change, and the greatest beneficiaries will be Robert Mugabe and the other architects of Zimbabwe's destruction" (cited in Rhee, 2009).

The Zimbabwean media landscape opened more in May 2010 with the new Zimbabwe Media Commission's (ZMC) licensing of four private dailies, including the *Daily News*, which had been shut down in 2003 and whose restart was delayed since 2008. "We are here to allow Zimbabweans access to media," said the ZMC's chairman, Godfrey Majonga. A new daily, *NewsDay*, was launched. Despite these hopeful signs of some greater openness in the printed press, radio reigns supreme in Zimbabwe, and government efforts to maintain total control of broadcast media have expanded to attempts to control receivers in the hands of private citizens. Radios capable of picking up shortwave broadcasts have been seized, as well as mobile telephones. "A lot of people were taken to the police station and…warned that those…with the radios [in the future] will disappear," one villager east of Harare told the BBC in late March 2013 (Hungwe, 2013). Police said the radios, including many wind-up radios that need no batteries or external electrical power, would be used to receive "hate speech" from abroad. An MDC spokesman said that the seizure of radios was done in order to force citizens to listen to the state-run/ZANU-PF-controlled ZBC. A presidential spokesman accused foreign embassies of "smuggling" radios into Zimbabwe.

Efforts to draft a new constitution, a process begun in summer 2009, led to recriminations between Prime Minister Tsvangirai and President Mugabe, with the former alleging in September 2010 that violence was employed against MDC supporters at public consultations. Mugabe was once again nominated to run for the presidency by ZANU-PF at the end of the year.

2011 was also an indecisive year. The EU removed 35 regime officials and ZANU-PF leaders from its asset freeze list in February. The following month, Prime Minister Tsvangirai said the unity government was moribund due to ZANU-PF violence and unwillingness to hold up its end of the bargain. General Solomon Mujuru, a senior player believed to have pressured Mugabe to leave politics, died in an unexplained house fire in August. Mugabe ended the year by claiming he would indeed run again. Yet Wikileaks cables exposed speculation that he suffered from cancer, as well as exposing senior ZANU-PF figures and army officers speaking to foreign diplomats about his need to step aside. At the same time, seasoned observers of Zimbabwe noticed improvement in the material standard of infrastructure and noticed increased foreign traffic in Harare, drawn by the lure of the diamond trade. "There is a feeling that the Gods of Commerce, rather like Zimbabwe's eternal potential, and the diamonds sprouting in the east, attract more friends than critical journalists," Zimbabwean journalist and filmmaker Farai Sevenzo (2011) wrote for the BBC. He noted a widening income gap, and observed that "the MDC has seamlessly become part of the ruling class, in their official vehicles and trappings of power."

The EU lifted yet more targeted sanctions in February 2012, this time travel bans on a number of senior figures, but not Mugabe himself. In the same month, the Constitutional Select Committee tabled a draft constitution, the details of which were disputed by ZANU-PF and MDC. That spring, reports of political violence increased; the MDC claimed rallies had been cleared. By autumn 2012, human rights activists claimed to see telltale signs of the reactivation of the structures of repression and intimidation employed in the summer 2008 violence. Prime Minister Tsvangirai threatened to withdraw from the unity government in October over attacks on MDC members.

Despite all these frictions and ominous developments, 2013 began on a positive note, with Mugabe and Tsvangirai agreeing on the constitutional draft. Its provisions allow future presidents (i.e., those elected later this year) to hold office for two five-year terms — which would allow Mugabe to hold office once again. The draft constitution was overwhelmingly supported in a March 2013 referendum. In response, the EU suspended sanctions against 81 officials and eight firms. "The EU congratulates the people of Zimbabwe on a peaceful, successful and credible vote to approve a new constitution," a statement read, noting the referendum was a "significant step" toward credible general elections later in the year (Torello and Norman, 2013). Nonetheless, 10 "key decision makers," including Mugabe himself, and two firms, remain under EU sanctions (ibid.).

Following the referendum, journalists heard from ordinary citizens' accounts of life becoming more normal and hopes for the future. "Things have been difficult here for many years but we are starting to see a change. I now have hope that our country will be back to normal someday soon…I am able to plan my day now and budget for groceries. I don't worry about whether shops will still be open tomorrow or how much things will cost or even if I'll have a job to go to tomorrow," a female Harare cab driver told a BBC correspondent (BBC News Africa, 2013a). Businessmen said they could now operate — "we now have a normal business model where the price of goods and services is set by demand and supply," noted one (ibid.).

The government remains prone to ructions as elections approach in July, and there is no clear common governing agenda for the elements of the power-sharing government, short of trying to attract foreign investment to Zimbabwe. Barclay (2010) opined that the achievements of the unity government were more "results of inertia rather than of activism." There were worrying signs that the senior leadership of MDC, Tsvangiari included, enjoyed the perquisites of office — cars, good pay, expense accounts, travel — too much to rock the boat.

Nothing fundamental in the imbalance of power has changed in the years of the unity government and in advance of the July 31, 2013 election. The situation was described as a "temporary absence of violence" rather than peace (ibid.). Despite welcome signs of economic revitalization, Zimbabwe's agricultural sector — crucial for food self-sufficiency, livelihoods and export earnings — is nowhere near recovery.

The July 2013 general elections, for both the presidency and parliamentary assembly, were relatively peaceful. Official results reported Mugabe the winner of a seventh term as president by 61 percent, and his ZANU-PF won 158 seats in Parliament to the MDC's 49 — a three-quarters majority. But on the day of the poll and immediately following, fears of electoral manipulation appear to have been borne out. On August 1, Irene Petersen from the Zimbabwe Election Support Network, a domestic monitoring group, stated that the "election was seriously compromised by a systematic effort to disenfranchise urban voters — up to a million voters" (BBC News Africa, 2013b). Zimbabwe Election Commission member Mkhululi Nyathi resigned on August 3, stating "While throughout the whole process I retained some measure of hope that the integrity of the whole process could be salvaged along the way, this was not to be" (ibid.). African Union monitors, 70 in all, led by former Nigerian President Olesegun Obasanjo, found the poll "free and credible." SADC found the election "free and peaceful," but has not opined on the fairness of the process (ibid.). At issue is the inclusiveness of voter lists; many voters were reportedly turned away at the polling stations. There were also reports of "assisted voting" at some rural polling stations, where voters were intimidated into having their votes cast by others (BBC News Africa, 2013c).

The opposition MDC and Tsvangirai have decried the results, vowing to challenge them before the Constitutional Court, which Tsvangirai must do within seven days of the announcement of the results. At the time of writing, this deadline has not passed. The Court then has two weeks to rule. If it rules in Mugabe's favour, he will be sworn in within 48 hours. Already, the MDC claims its members have been attacked by ZANU-PF supporters in the capital and in Mashonaland, being told to pack and leave (BBC News Africa, 2013b). MDC Treasurer Roy Bennett told BBC Newshour that there was a "seething anger simmering across the length and breadth of Zimbabwe... for the fact that they have had their rights stolen," adding that the ZANU-PF are "a bunch of kleptocratic geriatrics who should have retired a long time ago."

International reactions have been mixed. South African President Zuma delivered his "profound congratulations." The US, UK and EU have expressed their concern with the reports of irregularities. On August 2, EU foreign policy chief Catherine Ashton issued a statement that "The EU is concerned about alleged irregularities and reports of incomplete participation, as well as identified weaknesses in the electoral process and a lack of transparency" (UPI, 2013). British Foreign Secretary William Hague expressed "grave concerns" about the process, noting that the voter rolls were not made available to all political parties as stipulated by law, which he identified as "a critical flaw." He added that large numbers of voters were turned away, especially in urban areas, that a "very high" number of extra ballots were printed and that extra polling stations were added on the day of the election. "The irregularities in the lead up to the elections and on election day itself, reported by the observer mission and in contravention of SADC's guidelines, call into serious question the credibility of the election" (BBC News Africa, 2013d). US Secretary of State John Kerry (2013) said that the elections were the "culmination of a deeply flawed process." Interestingly, both London and Washington cited the AU and SADC missions, as well as domestic monitors, as there were no Western monitors accredited. Following a long history of breaking ranks with the SADC mainstream, Botswana called for an independent audit of the electoral process. A government statement on August 5 included the following assessment: "various incidents and circumstances were revealed that call into question whether the entire electoral process, and thus its final result, can be recognized as having been fair, transparent and credible in the context of the SADC Principles and Guidelines Governing Democratic Elections within the Community. That is why the [electoral observation mission] described the elections as 'free and peaceful' as opposed to 'free and fair,' the latter being the criteria for credible elections."

Given reports of government/ZANU-PF preparation for violence as far back as 2012, reports in the immediate aftermath of attacks on MDC supporters and the MDC's own warnings that it might not be able to control its outraged supporters, the relative peace of the unity government period may be coming to an end.

DIPLOMATIC ASSETS

Diplomats have supported the quest for democratic rule in Zimbabwe since the country's early days of independence. The assets available, however, have varied largely depending on factors including historical legacy, membership in regional organizations such as the SADC and international ones such as the Commonwealth, and whether or not the diplomat's home country is in Zimbabwe's neighbourhood.

The legacy of colonialism and the power of the liberation struggle still make for strong domestic politics in Zimbabwe, and ZANU-PF has traditionally exploited its roots in the independence movement. Robert Mugabe has specifically vilified Britain, revelling in caricatured criticism of Tony Blair during his tenure as prime minister and referring to any diplomatic actions taken by British diplomats as plotting by "colonizers." After US President George W. Bush openly advocated regime change in Iraq and invaded that country in 2003, Mugabe was able to invoke the US as bogeyman, and scapegoat US sanctions for Zimbabwe's economic crisis. The dynamic created by Zimbabwe's colonial legacy has limited diplomatic assets available to many embassies. By linking diplomatic actions taken by Western countries with colonialism, the Zimbabwean government limits the **influence** that these diplomats can have. But the sense that there was a golden age of mutual understanding may be illusory. According to UK High Commissioner Brian Donnelly, "I am not sure that Mugabe ever would have been receptive to advice on democracy. Moreover, he was never very accessible to diplomats...even in the 'good' years" (cited in Kinsman, 2008). This point seems to be bolstered by the treatment meted out to outgoing Swedish Ambassador Sten Rylander in the pro-government press upon his departure in June 2010. Rylander had served throughout southern Africa, and noted Sweden's support for the liberation struggle when making criticisms over child detention, media freedoms and other matters. He was pilloried in the pro-ZANU-PF press as a simple cheerleader for the opposition and agent of "British capitalist-inspired change."

Furthermore, **immunity**, traditionally one of the greatest assets afforded to diplomats, has been called into question as Mugabe has threatened and intimidated many Western diplomats along with journalists and other critics of his government. Mugabe has grown increasingly outspoken and brazen in his actions. Security services have used violent tactics against two Canadian High Commissioners.

On March 20, 2007, President Mugabe threatened to expel Western diplomats, accusing them of meddling in Zimbabwe's domestic affairs. This warning to Western diplomats — against supporting or interacting with opposition leaders — was thought to have been aimed at scaring Zimbabweans from interaction with Western diplomats, and more specifically British Ambassador Andrew Pocock and US Ambassador Christopher Dell. Ambassador Dell walked out of the meeting in protest. In 2008, a joint team of British and Dutch diplomats was harassed and intimidated when visiting the countryside and attempting to meet an imprisoned MDC activist. "You are just not safe here, particularly when you break the rules as you have done. We just cannot guarantee that you won't be shot. You should stay in your embassy in Harare from now on," Philip Barclay (2010) was told by a Central Intelligence Organization (CIO) officer who stopped him. In his view, "the Zimbabweans considered that foreign envoys should confine themselves to attending national day functions and passing back to their capitals whatever commentary on national affairs ZANU-PF chose to provide. The UK, among other concerned nations, had a more expansive idea of what it wanted to see and do in Zimbabwe. Both sides had their own favourite clauses in the Vienna Convention" (ibid.).

Other countries, particularly those with similar historical circumstances such as South Africa, have enjoyed a larger degree of **legitimacy** in Zimbabwe — and thereby access to decision makers. Mugabe and ZANU-PF leaders perceive shared interests arising from common struggle for African self-rule in a post-independence environment. Many countries in the Southern African region directly supported Zimbabwe's independence struggle, and, once in power, Mugabe returned the favour by assisting against South African-backed insurgencies. These governments, acknowledging Zimbabwe's economic crisis, have been able to leverage these historical ties to maintain a dialogue with the ruling ZANU-PF party. In becoming an SADC member, nations agree to share values including "human rights, democracy and the rule of law," but this formal pledge has rarely been employed by SADC members to hold Zimbabwe to these commitments, in part because of questionable democratic credentials of some SADC members themselves, although Botswanan legislators operating in the SADC inter-parliamentary assembly have long been critical of Zimbabwe's anti-democratic practice; recently the Foreign Minister followed suit. Diplomats from South Africa, particularly Ambassador Jeremiah Ndou, have on occasion reminded Zimbabwe of democratic values all members have agreed to uphold. South Africa has also been leading SADC-supported negotiations between ZANU-PF and opposition parties, although MDC leader Morgan Tsvangirai publicly called for former South African President Mbeki to be replaced in this role, citing his lack of willingness to confront Mugabe.

The centrality of the British contribution to Zimbabwean independence was recognized by Mugabe until a decade ago. Other Commonwealth, EU and democratic governments such as the US and Norway also contributed a great deal to post-independence development. Western embassies have shown **solidarity** toward Zimbabwe's civil society and opposition, though often at the risk of antagonizing the government.

Finally, many diplomats have cited their ability to leverage **funds** as a useful asset to their diplomatic efforts in Zimbabwe. Funds have been used to provide support to civil society groups and democratic institutions, such as the judiciary, as part of a larger strategy to support democratic development in Zimbabwe. Zimbabwean lawyer and intellectual Alex Magaisa has emphasized the importance of these initiatives as local resources become increasingly scarce. Embassies refrained from direct support to the MDC, "since any evidence of this would be used to prosecute opposition leaders." International food aid — bilateral aid from governments (such as the UK, US and Sweden), through embassies, and multilateral aid, through programs like the World Food Program — has also been a major force by the diplomatic community in helping to stave off famine in Zimbabwe. This aid has vastly increased as Zimbabwe's food crisis has worsened in recent years as a result of land seizures, economic mismanagement, non-cancellation of debt and persistent drought. In terms of proportion, funds for democracy and civil society assistance are dwarfed by the level of humanitarian aid. The fact that most democratic governments remain skeptical that aid will be abused by the ZANU-PF dominated government has meant that food and other humanitarian assistance (particularly in the devastated education sector) has been a point of contention.

TOOL BOX APPLICATION

The Golden Rules

Many diplomats cited **listening** as an important part of their strategy for democracy support. This includes listening to all sides of the struggle for democracy in Zimbabwe. Edward Gibson Lanpher, US Ambassador to Zimbabwe from 1991–1995, said that he never turned down an invitation to speak to people throughout every region of the country. He made an effort to be very public in his conversations with a variety of stakeholders in Zimbabwe's future, including white and black farmers, rural and urban residents, and missionaries. Listening to a wide variety of perspectives helps ambassadors to better **understand** the political situation. British High Commissioner Brian Donnelly organized "road shows" rotating around the main provincial cities, including staff from all the High Commission's sections — commercial, consular, British Council and aid. This effective moving open house facilitated access for citizens. Local officials, parliamentarians, religious and civic figures were invited to evening receptions. Often the visits would be pegged to the opening of some UK-funded project in the area. The effort allowed the High Commission to counter accusations that it was acting covertly. Other embassies conducted similar efforts on a smaller scale. Swedish Ambassador Sten Rylander made a point of getting outside the capital as soon as he was accredited in 2006 to donate vehicles to a community children's rights group, and sought their views on the situation in the country. Yet the ability of diplomats to operate this freely was further curtailed soon after.

A major part of listening to stakeholders and gaining a strong understanding of the situation in Zimbabwe is showing **respect** for Zimbabweans' hopes for the country. This respect forms a major part of South Africa's diplomatic interactions with Zimbabwe, which is largely centred on listening and engaging the government and opposition, so that Zimbabweans can find a common solution to their political problems. In a personal interview, former South African Ambassador Jeremiah Ndou said "The most important thing is that Zimbabweans themselves sit down and agree on what they want," yet, the Zimbabwean opposition and civil society feel this approach is overly solicitous to Mugabe and insensitive to their democratic aspirations.

In recent years, it has become more difficult for some diplomats to engage broadly across all sectors of Zimbabwean society. This is especially true for many of the more outspoken critics of the Zimbabwean government, such as the UK, who have been unable to speak directly with government officials. Because of these limitations, information **sharing** between diplomatic missions has become an important tool for foreign offices. EU ambassadors meet regularly, Commonwealth countries have monthly lunches and constant informal bilateral exchanges among diplomats are the norm. Matthew Neuhaus, director of the Political Affairs Division of the Commonwealth, said that since Zimbabwe withdrew from the Commonwealth in 2003, it has relied largely on its relationship with the SADC for information.

Truth in Communications

Sharing information gathered from stakeholders in Zimbabwe with others through **informing** has been an equally important task of diplomats in the country. A key component of the Canadian mission's current approach is informing the public about human rights abuses and violent or undemocratic actions. Jennifer Metayer, head of Aid for the Canadian International Development Agency (CIDA), which was absorbed by the Ministry of Foreign Affairs and International Trade in 2013, says that CIDA stayed in direct contact with all of its implementing partners several times per week. If affiliated staff members disappear or experience harassment, incidents are publicly reported so as to shine a spotlight aimed at preventing further abuse.

Formal **reporting** also plays an important role in communicating the current situation in Zimbabwe to home countries and the public, especially with the government's effort to limit international media access. Eden Reid, of the South African High Commission, said in 2008 that a major role of South African diplomats inside of Zimbabwe is reporting back to the Department of Home Affairs in Pretoria. Because South African diplomats are able to talk to government officials, opposition leaders and civil society within Zimbabwe, Reid believed they were able to report an accurate picture of the situation in the country, which is useful for forming South African policy. Yet, with misgivings about South African policy, some opposition and civic figures are more apt to talk to Western diplomats. Furthermore, the humanitarian aid given by Western governments enabled insight into conditions and contacts with civil society around the country.

Some of the failure of diplomacy in Zimbabwe, however, may be attributed to a failure to heed warnings reported by diplomats. Former Canadian High Commissioner Robert MacLaren found little support at home for his alarm over reports of massacres in Matabeleland in the 1980s. A decade later, in 1995, US Ambassador Lanpher reported in his final cable to Washington DC that Zimbabwe was "increasingly corrupt" and had "the appearance of democracy, but was basically under a one-party, one-man control." In this case, it was not a failure of reporting, but a failure of capitals to follow up on these reports with action to help prevent further breakdown of democracy.

Working with Government

Though working with ZANU-PF government officials was initially the goal of most, if not all, diplomatic envoys, many diplomats soon found their efforts at democracy support severely impeded by these same officials. When Mugabe's government became increasingly authoritarian beginning in the late 1990s, many diplomats decided they could no longer stay quiet and issued public demarches condemning the actions of the ZANU-PF government. While efforts to work with the Zimbabwean government continued, illegal land seizures and violence surrounding the 2000 elections seemed to be the last straw.

Most notably, the UK and US governments attempted to pressure the Mugabe regime through public condemnation and economic sanctions, though this made their relationship with a retaliatory Zimbabwean government even more dysfunctional. UK High Commissioner Brian Donnelly was demonized in the official press and denied ministerial access, which led him to turn to public means of expressing his views on human rights, detailing the UK's large humanitarian assistance program. The Mugabe regime, seeking to undermine his local credibility, retaliated in many ways, placing Donnelly on 24-hour surveillance in 2002 and threatening to expel him in 2003, accusing him publicly of various fictitious plots ostensibly intended to overthrow the Zimbabwean government. Donnelly believes these acts were designed primarily to intimidate Zimbabwean interlocutors.

This pattern of the Zimbabwean government continuing to refuse to work with diplomats in the wake of public declarations may prompt reflection on the benefits of such proactive public diplomacy in a one-man state. While such condemnations satisfied domestic constituents' desires to have their governments speak out about human rights abuses in Zimbabwe, the ability of diplomats in the country to influence or negotiate with ZANU-PF officials via **demarches** was severely thwarted. While the softer line taken by other countries may have preserved access, their ability to influence — or will to influence — Zimbabwean policies is hardly evident.

In a personal interview, Matthew Neuhaus said that he believes that better **advising** and greater mentoring involvement with Zimbabwe's government in the early years of independence might have made a difference in the country's ultimate democratic development. Yet the first Zimbabwe cabinets included several leaders who had spent exile years in international institutions. Focussed diplomatic advising to build up more such homegrown future leaders may have forestalled the transformation to authoritarian rule that Zimbabwe later faced. Zimbabwe's government *did* avail itself of external advice in areas of concern when it was desirable. Britain, for instance, helped mould the Zimbabwean National Army, having deployed a military training mission in Zimbabwe for over 20 years. However, many in the international community were eager to overlook governance deficiencies that could have been corrected through advising earlier in exchange for having a "model" democratic African leader to point to in the once-esteemed figure of Mugabe.

The abilities of diplomats to advise the Zimbabwean government in a way that would meaningfully improve democratic development have been constrained by a frequent divergence of views with officials on what constitutes a modern democratic state in Africa. Diplomats have thus turned to civil society as a potential force to strengthen Zimbabwean governance. By advising civil society leaders and working to build their capacity, diplomats believe they are helping to create an environment conducive to better future government. It appears that the unity government, particularly Finance Minister Tendai Biti of the MDC, was more open to international advice; he was perhaps the minister most open to the international community as he pursued foreign capital for the recently stabilized economy and others are also likely receptive. The real question is who actually holds the levers of power. Of "power ministries" (defence, interior and justice) and other government bodies (such as the CIO), these remain firmly in the hands of ZANU-PF hardliners who — if they took any advice — were more likely to accept it from counterparts in Beijing, Tehran or Gadhafi's Tripoli than from the democratic world, near or far.

This advising has largely taken place through an emphasis on **dialogue** that has formed a cornerstone of many diplomats' actions in Zimbabwe. South African Ambassador Ndou emphasized the importance of dialogue, specifically citing South Africa's efforts to encourage conversations between government officials and opposition leaders using the institution of the SADC to maintain legitimacy and solidarity as an honest broker. Others tried to reel Zimbabwe back before relations with the West reached their current state. Commonwealth Secretary-General and New Zealand former Foreign Minister Don McKinnon was mandated by the Commonwealth Ministerial Advisory Group, formed as a follow-on to the 1991 Harare Declaration, to attempt to forge a creative solution, but was unsuccessful in gaining meaningful political access to Mugabe.

Following this failed attempt, the Commonwealth adopted the Abuja Process in 2001 at the request of then British Foreign Secretary Robin Cook in a bid to work with the Zimbabwean government on issues of human rights, elections and land reform. A deal was reached, but the September 11, 2001 attacks on the US diverted international attention, and Mugabe rescinded his consent to the agreement at the end of the month. According to one senior diplomat, this "led the UK (and other Western governments) to doubt the value of dialogue when the other party seemed patently insincere" (cited in Barclay, 2010).

South African President Mbeki's 2007 mediation efforts were often opaque (even to South African diplomats) and viewed with great suspicion by the MDC. His failure to condemn Tsvangirai's beating alienated the MDC further. Yet the mediation did deliver some results that were later essential in the 2008 election. One of these was that all 210 seats in the House of Representatives would be elected — none appointed by the president. In the past, appointments were a method to "stack the deck" in Parliament against the MDC, even when it had won a blocking minority that should have prevented constitutional amendments. A crucial provision quietly included by the MDC negotiators was the posting of local election results at polling stations, rather than sealing and sending them to the next level. This made it possible to tally results on election night, making fraud much harder and monitoring the statewide results for the opposition and civil society possible. Following the 2008 election, however, after which Mbeki failed to acknowledge the MDC as the first round winner, Tsvangirai said Mbeki was too partisan to mediate and called on Zambian President Mwanawasa to take on the role instead. Incoming South African President and ANC leader Jacob Zuma did criticize the poll. A spokesman for the ANC party later said "President Zuma will be more vocal in terms of what we see as deviant behaviour" (BBC News, 2009).

In 2009, the arrival of Prime Minister Morgan Tsvangirai in the unity government certainly reopened relations between Harare and much of the international community. Tsvangirai was welcomed to the White House in June 2009 by President Obama, who proclaimed his "extraordinary admiration for the courage [and] the tenacity that the prime minister has shown in navigating through some difficult political times" (cited in Lobe, 2009).

Despite the new unity government, dealing with Mugabe remains difficult. Western democracies have adopted benchmarks for granting aid to the government to ensure it is spent appropriately. These have generated predictable acrimony from Mugabe, who attacked the new US Assistant Secretary of State for African Affairs Johnnie Carson, as an "idiot" after a meeting on the sidelines of the July 2009 African Union summit in Libya. "We have the whole of SADC working with us, and you have the likes of little fellows like Carson, you see, wanting to say: 'You do this, you do that,'" the pro-government *Herald* quoted him as saying. "Who is he?...I hope he was not speaking for Obama. I told him he was a shame, a great shame, being an African-American, an Afro-American for that matter." Mugabe also refused to meet outgoing US Ambassador James McGee, who departed his post that same month. In May 2010, Carson again came under assault, this time by Zimbabwe's Ambassador to the US Machivenyika Mapuranga, who interrupted the Assistant Secretary's remarks on the state of human rights and good governance in Zimbabwe at an Africa Day dinner by shouting "You are talking like a good house slave!" He continued with "We will never be an American colony, you know that!" Carson retorted "You can sit in the audience in darkness, but the light will find you and the truth will find you...It seems that Robert Mugabe has some friends in the room tonight. Unlike in Zimbabwe, they are allowed to speak without oppression because this is a democracy. In Zimbabwe, that kind of talk would have been met with a policeman's stick. We don't do that here" (cited in Rogin, 2010). The Zimbabwean Ambassador was quietly convinced to leave by the event staff at the hotel. Another diplomat in attendance told a reporter that "In Africa, an ambassador is treated like a king. Here he can be humiliated just like anyone else" (ibid.).

Reaching Out

Former Canadian Ambassador John Schram was typical of several ambassadors over recent years who sought to encourage dialogue by **convening** a group of people who had a stake in Zimbabwe's future development and providing them with a safe place for discussion. This allowed local leaders to network with others in the country who were also working toward a more democratic Zimbabwe.

Strengthened by experience in South Africa a decade earlier, Ambassador Schram also emphasized his efforts to encourage dialogue by hosting private dinners every few weeks, attended by leaders from government, business, academia and the media, among other segments of civil society, to discuss Zimbabwe's challenges and to brainstorm solutions for the future. He and other such diplomatic hosts believe these efforts had an impact and helped to create a cadre of leaders who will be ready to help move Zimbabwe on a path toward democracy once the opportunity for change arises. The Norwegians developed a prominent profile for their outreach efforts in Zimbabwe, drawing on their experience organizing the negotiations that led to the Oslo Accords. Most embassies engaged in convening government and opposition at dinner parties and other gatherings.

Ambassador Lanpher highlighted the active participation of US diplomats in the International Visitor Program, which brings current and potential government, business and civil society leaders to the United States for 30 days to "meet and confer with their professional counterparts and to experience America firsthand." Many diplomatic missions also worked to **connect** local leaders with outside groups or individuals who might be helpful to their efforts, including in policy centres and universities outside Zimbabwe. Each year, Britain's Chevening Scholarships program sends about 20 Zimbabweans for one year of graduate training in the UK; other democracies have similar exchange programs. The British Council also organizes training programs on aspects of democratic governance inside and outside of Zimbabwe. By **showcasing** best practices through these trainings, diplomats such as those from the US Embassy attempted to build capacity of the local Zimbabwean officials, public institutions and civil society.

Much of the support that diplomats have provided to Zimbabwe has also been in the form of **financing**. Diplomats have given funds to promote dialogue, support Zimbabwe's vocal labour movement, reinforce human rights, promote gender equality and build capacity of civil society to push for democratic governance, among others. These funding mechanisms have chiefly been lauded as successful in supporting democracy development. CIDA's Jennifer Metayer points to the especially flexible and rapid-response nature of the agency's funding as critical to the impact it has had in Zimbabwe.

Beyond the direct benefit that diplomats have gained from providing funding to local groups, an additional benefit is that providing funding — especially to development or humanitarian projects — allows diplomats an opportunity to interact with people and the media in a more public way than they might otherwise be able. Canadian Ambassador Schram, for instance, cited his ability to discuss the values of human rights, democracy and rule of law enshrined in such agreements as the Harare Declaration and the New Partnership for African Development undertakings on governance, both of which Zimbabwe had signed, to the media and the public during ceremonies designed to unveil development projects funded by the Canadian government. The ability to provide funds and other forms of aid also gave diplomats some leverage over government officials who rely on these funds. US Ambassador Lanpher recalls an example from the early 1980s, when Zimbabwe was suffering from a severe food shortage due to drought. In 1982, Mugabe had imposed a food curfew on Matabeleland as part of the punishment for the perceived rebellion of Joshua Nkomo's followers. When the US sent food aid to the country, Ambassador Lanpher refused to distribute it until Mugabe's government signed an agreement stating that the food would be distributed across all areas of the country. "I had a good relationship with the government," Ambassador Lanpher stated. "But sometimes you have to be tough." This approach became increasingly difficult, and with the 2002-2003 drought and resultant food shortages, leverage was very limited, as most donor governments refused to channel aid through the Zimbabwean government for fear of it being misused or inequitably distributed.

These financing mechanisms sometimes come at a cost. The public emphasis that many Western diplomats have put on funding pro-democracy civil society groups and opposition parties has allowed Mugabe to decry that the West has been funding "regime change" and has, to some extent, delegitimized opposition groups and even some NGOs in the public eye. Methods developed in post-Cold War Europe in the 1990s were predicated on open access to all parties. Given Zimbabwe's deepening authoritarianism, support to the ruling ZANU-PF seemed perverse, but it therefore generated fierce resistance. Anecdotal evidence points to infighting that has begun to occur within NGOs and other civil society groups over access to foreign funds. . The opposition MDC party split in 2005 was reported by some sources to be driven by disagreements over spending.

Since the adoption of the power-sharing Global Political Agreement, while most democracies held off on delivering aid to the government until they see its full implementation, they have made a point of directing assistance to where it is needed most in Zimbabwe — the beleaguered public — with food aid, help for students to buy books, uniforms and other supplies, as well as to the civic sector.

Defending Democrats

Support for local leadership in the Zimbabwean struggle for democracy has also been a part of diplomatic action in the country. Diplomatic missions like the US Embassy have **demonstrated** their support by being quite vocal in defence of democrats who have been persecuted by the Mugabe regime. These diplomats have identified and called for an end to persecution through official statements, such as the following, released by the US State Department on July 26, 2007: "Yesterday's beating of over 200 Zimbabwean citizens that were peacefully demonstrating for a new constitution is an overt attempt by the Government of Zimbabwe to eliminate any criticism in advance of elections planned for next year." Following an attack on a diplomatic convoy dispatched to investigate intimidation of citizens before the June 2008 runoff election, British Foreign Secretary David Miliband said that "I think that it gives us a window into the lives of ordinary Zimbabweans, because this sort of intimidations is the sort of thing that is suffered daily, especially by those who are working with opposition groups" (cited in BBC News, 2008). South African President Jacob Zuma's visit to Deputy Agriculture Minister designate Roy Bennett, while he was still on trial for terrorism and other charges, sent a strong message to Mugabe's government, and may have stiffened the resolve of those in the judiciary to refuse to succumb to political pressure.

Jennifer Metayer of CIDA says that **verifying** the whereabouts of civil society members and reporting any disappearances or threats has formed a large part of CIDA's efforts in Zimbabwe. By verifying any persecution that civil society activists experience, CIDA let the Zimbabwean government know that the Canadian mission is watching their actions.

In May 2008, a group including the British, US, EU and Japanese ambassadors and the deputy chiefs of mission from the Netherlands and Tanzania (which chairs the African Union) and several other diplomats drove in an 11-car convoy north of the capital to investigate allegations that the government and ruling party were targeting opposition supporters in the aftermath of the first round of the presidential election, held in late March. The diplomats found a ZANU-PF detention and torture centre, and visited local hospitals to interview those injured. The diplomats pushed their way through armed guards at one hospital. On the way back to Harare, the diplomatic convoy was stopped at a roadblock, and, after hearing from a US diplomat of what they saw, a CIO officer told them "we are going to beat you thoroughly too." Diplomats prevented the agents from fleeing and photographed them. US Ambassador James McGee said afterward "We are eager to continue this type of thing, to show the world what is happening here in Zimbabwe. It is absolutely urgent that the entire world sees what is going on. The violence has to stop." A second such convoy in June 2008, including US and British diplomats, was stopped by police 80 kilometres north of Harare. After refusing to go to a police station, the convoy was chased. At another checkpoint, the cars' tires were slashed by police. The immobilized cars were then attacked by a group of "war veterans." Diplomats were threatened with being burned alive in their vehicles. A Zimbabwean driver was beaten up, and equipment was stolen. Ambassador McGee stated "Zimbabwe is now a lawless country. They are not following their own laws. They are not following international law. The government is trying to intimidate diplomats from going to the countryside to witness the violence they are perpetrating against their own citizens." The police said that the diplomats "behave like criminals and distort information" regarding the incident.

Alex Magaisa believes that the attention of the diplomatic community, including their **witnessing** trials of accused opposition supporters, has had a big impact on Zimbabwe's democratic development. "It's reassuring to know that the world is watching," Magaisa said in a personal interview. "If you get a diplomatic figure from a more powerful country, it makes news and it communicates a message to the world...I think this has been very, very useful." Visits — and attempts to visit — those imprisoned send an important message to the government that these individuals are not forgotten. This act in itself can often save lives.

Diplomats have also tried to **protect** democratic rights by identifying when these rights have been curbed or violated and publicly petitioning the Zimbabwean government to restore democratic norms, including safety for those who are working toward democratic goals. On November 26 2007, the US government released a statement: "We call on the Government of Zimbabwe to end immediately the violent attacks against democratic activists and civil society organizations, to respect the rule of law, and to allow the Zimbabwean people to exercise peacefully their political rights."

These types of public statements that defend the actions of domestic democrats have become even more important in Zimbabwe's constrained media environment. Many foreign journalists were expelled. The few who have been allowed into the country are subject to being censored and periodically arrested, as are local Zimbabwean journalists. Stories of journalists being censored, jailed or beaten have become common, as independent media within the country has withered under stifling laws. Many of the country's journalists have since taken refuge in willing host countries including Britain, the United States and South Africa, where new independent media sources covering Zimbabwe have flourished. While there are signs of liberalization in terms of print media, the broadcast media are as tightly controlled as ever.

WHAT LESSONS LEARNED?

From an early optimistic start, diplomats from both Western countries and those closest to Zimbabwe in history and geography have been able to use the assets at their disposal with diminishing success. Though colonial history has been manipulated by the Mugabe regime to exclude meaningful influence by the UK and other Western powers, the policies of entities as varied as the US government and the Commonwealth still require careful examination. In light of the diverging approaches of African and specifically SADC leaders and their diplomatic counterparts from the West, two questions are especially worth considering.

First, to what extent is public condemnation an effective diplomatic tool? The planned EU observation mission of the 2002 elections was cancelled on the grounds that the conditions of observation were unacceptably constrained, but also to defer to EU public opinion. It left EU and other missions the task of trying to monitor the elections with inadequate means (an apt example, however, of **sharing**).

Many countries and bodies have taken a hardline public stance against Mugabe and his regime. For example, then US Secretary of State Condoleezza Rice made a stern statement in 2007 which read, in part: "The world community again has been shown that the regime of Robert Mugabe is ruthless and repressive and creates only suffering for the people of Zimbabwe. We will continue to follow closely events in Zimbabwe, and we urge the Government to allow all Zimbabweans to freely express their views without being subject to violence and intimidation." In addition, "targeted" sanctions directed at regime officials and supporters have become a standard Western policy tool, which can have a strong psychological impact. While these measures are felt by their intended targets, their application — if perceived as irreversible — can also create a further obstacle to contact and influence with power brokers. Mugabe obsesses over the sanctions in most public appearances, decrying them as the reason for an economic recovery that remains unfelt by many Zimbabweans. This is not the case: investment and commerce can go forth unimpeded, except for arms sales, and Mugabe has travelled freely — even unannounced — to Davos for the World Economic Forum. But the question of the opportunity cost remains, and is difficult to answer with certainty.

Such declarations and policies probably further hampered diplomats' already reduced ability to work directly with government officials and maintain a flow of information about the situation on the ground. But democracies understandably wish to maintain what they judge is an important position of principle on human rights abuses, political violence and undemocratic action — these statements are an element of policy over which they have complete control. Inconsistencies on the part of critical democracies are exploited by autocrats and sow confusion among broad populations as well. Countries and bodies that, on the other hand, have focussed on working within official channels have been accused of silent collaboration, but they have maintained open channels of communication and information inside Zimbabwe, for what they are worth in effecting moderation and change. Both approaches have had their strengths and weaknesses, with little public acknowledgment or cooperation on either side. Neither seems to have achieved their stated aim.

The second question concerns how much open support diplomats should provide to opposition parties and democracy-promoting civil society groups. In the case of politicians especially, credibility hinges on authenticity and independence. Too much public support and funding from foreign sources opens opposition parties and civil society groups to charges that they are simply fronts for foreign governments, yet without outside support, many of these groups do not have the resources or political space to operate. It is important for diplomats to find a balance between support for a multi-party democratic process and perceived support for "regime change."

This case study does not pretend to provide an answer to these questions, but it does draw attention to the merit of creative thinking about the opening up of diplomatic space between differently positioned actors with varying strategies (an example in this case would be the SADC and the Commonwealth), to find common ground in pursuing similar goals. Rather than viewing these approaches as either-or choices, a better calibration of application might maximize the potential benefits of each: greater willingness to conduct back-channel talks on the part of Western democracies, coupled with a greater willingness by SADC members to use the access they have to influence beneficial change.

CONCLUSION

Zimbabwe requires significant outside support to put it back on track toward realizing its potential, given that its once noteworthy assets are now severely degraded through abuse or neglect. Rebuilding an effective civil service not tied to political leaders, and re-establishing an economic and fiscal climate in which trade and industry can again flourish should be priorities. Generous international support for Zimbabwe's government and civil society would hopefully help the country to enjoy at last the self-governance and prosperity by and for the people that independence and self-determination once promised. There was little movement to date on this front despite the unity government; the growing acrimony around the July 2013 general election makes such developments look highly unlikely at the time of writing.

The resilience of Zimbabwe's people after more than a decade of freefall is remarkable. Prior to the elections, in the tenuous recovery of the unity government period, Zimbabweans were understandably nervous and wary, but also hopeful — a mood summed up by a resident of the Harare suburb of Highfield, where ZANU was founded in 1963: "we might have the best constitution in the world, but if our leaders abuse it, what good is it?" (BBC News Africa, 2013a). Some of his countrymen hastened to underscore that "we don't want violence" in the upcoming election. A university student added "it is time for us as young people to rebuild this once-wonderful country and we can only do it if we stop fighting amongst each other" (ibid.). One can only hope that her advice is heeded by those in power in the aftermath of the elections.

As events in Zimbabwe unfold, diplomats will maintain a key role in helping the democratic world calibrate its approach toward the government in Harare, by identifying opportunities and threats to consolidating — or rather, rebuilding — democracy.

WORKS CITED

Barclay, Philip (2010). *Zimbabwe: Years of Hope and Despair*. New York: Bloomsbury.

BBC News (2008). "Diplomat Convoy Held in Zimbabwe." BBC News, June 5.

————— (2009). "S Africa Leader Heads to Zimbabwe." BBC News, August 27.

BBC News Africa (2013a). "Zimbabweans Hope for Democratic Rebirth." BBC News, March 20.

————— (2013b). "Supporters of Zimbabwe Opposition MDC Allege Attacks." BBC News Africa, August 5.

————— (2013c). "Harare Diary: 'Sad and Disenfranchised.'" BBC News Africa, August 2.

————— (2013d). "Zimbabwe Election: William Hague Voices 'Grave Concerns.'" BBC News Africa, August 3.

Hungwe, Brian (2013). "Why Are Zimbabwe Police Seizing Radios?" BBC News, March 25.

Kerry, John (2013). "Zimbabwe's Presidential Election," official statement. August 3. Available at: http://allafrica.com/stories/201308040030.html.

Kinsman, Jeremy (2008). "Mugabe's Zimbabwe: From Redemption to Dictatorship." *Policy Options*, September.

Lobe, Jim (2009). "Zimbabwe: Tsvangirai Gets Obama's Seal of Approval." *IPS News Agency*, June 12.

Rhee, Foon (2009). "Obama Meets with Zimbabwe Democracy Leader." *The Boston Globe* Political Intelligence blog, June 12.

Rogin, Josh (2010). "Zimbabwe Ambassador Calls US Diplomat a 'House Slave.'" *Foreign Policy*, May 26.

Sevenzo, Farai (2011). "African Viewpoint: Zimbabwe's Ghosts and Intrigues." BBC News Africa, November 1.

Torello, Alessandro and Laurence Norman (2013). "EU Suspends Sanctions on Bulk of Zimbabwe Listed Companies, People." *The Wall Street Journal*, March 25.

UPI (2013). "EU Wary of Zimbabwe Election." UPI, August 5.

10 THE FALL AND RISE OF CHILEAN DEMOCRACY: 1973–1989

By Kurt Bassuener, 2008; revised 2013

INTRODUCTION

Chile's Drift into the Abyss

Chile historically prided itself on its long democratic and constitutional practice, as well as its relative moderation in politics. Unlike many of its neighbours, it experienced military rule for only brief intervals. The armed services maintained a solid professional distance from politics, and even public life.

But Chilean politics became increasingly rancorous and polarized in the 1960s. A division into left, centre and right permeated Chile's civil society. One Chilean, looking back on the era observed that by that point "moderation was always interpreted as a sign of weakness. Anyone who was moderate was presumed to have a sort of complex."

In 1970, socialist Salvador Allende, the candidate of the left-wing Popular Unity coalition, won the presidency with a 36 percent plurality and was confirmed in Parliament. His victory raised political polarization to new heights. When the economy became rattled in 1971 by investor and market reaction to government intervention, tension between the government's supporters and its critics increased. In response, the Parliament — in which Popular Unity did not hold a majority — adopted, in 1973, a resolution accusing Allende of regularly violating the constitution and attempting to institute a totalitarian system. It was openly speculated that a coup d'état could follow.

Coup d'État and Repression

On September 11, 1973, the armed forces of Chile forcefully took over, bombing and storming La Moneda, the presidential palace in Santiago, against armed resistance, to find President Allende dead by his own hand. Army General Augusto Pinochet led the armed forces commanders' junta, declaring that Chile was in a "state of war."

The repression against Allende government supporters and anyone deemed threatening was immediate and overwhelming: roughly 7,000 people were detained, brutally interrogated and tortured at the National Stadium, and scores summarily executed. Thousands ran to foreign embassies for protection. Violent repression also struck in rural areas, where it was more difficult to find refuge. Thousands were arrested and many simply "disappeared."

The judiciary, overwhelmingly partial to the coup, did not resist the blatant illegalities being perpetrated, nor did they seek to exercise their prerogatives when civilians were being brought before military tribunals and often executed. Almost no petitions for habeas corpus were accepted.

While many Chileans welcomed the putsch, most believed that the armed forces would return to barracks and allow a return to civilian and democratic rule. They soon learned this was a false hope. Pinochet banned leftist political parties outright, suspended others, and in 1974 ordered the electoral rolls destroyed.

Church versus State: Defending Human Rights

The Catholic Church was the only institution capable of resisting the junta's repression. Chilean civil society and any political actors remaining in Chile hunkered down in the aftermath of the coup, concerned with mere survival. "The myriad institutions of civil society, including neighbourhood organizations, sports clubs and professional associations, were prohibited from meeting or tightly controlled," according to the then Ford Foundation representative in Santiago (cited in Puryear, 1994).

Fortunately, Cardinal Raúl Silva Henríquez gave support to those threatened by the junta. The ecumenical Pro-Peace Committee defended victims of human rights abuses, but was closed by Pinochet's order in 1975. The (Catholic) Vicariate of Solidarity succeeded it, helping an estimated 700,000 Chileans with legal, health, occupational and nutritional services between 1975 and 1979. International civil society was instrumental in financially sustaining these efforts.

The Church also supported the legal and evidentiary work to defend human rights, before a judiciary nearly totally sympathetic to Pinochet. According to Jaime Castillo, a pre-Allende justice minister who represented hundreds of prisoners and missing leftists, "judges almost always reacted negatively to us; they were servile and afraid, and so bitter against the Popular Unity [Allende's government]." As Ignacio Walker, later to serve as foreign minister after the return to democracy, recalled in a personal interview, "As a human rights lawyer, I lost all my cases... But winning wasn't the point. We could still protect people by making their cases publicly known. The cost was higher" for the regime to do them further harm. The World Council of Churches in Geneva played a pivotal role in publicizing such cases. While this activity was nettlesome to the regime, it was tolerated. Confronting the Church would spur social resistance in predominantly Catholic Chile. The voluminous documentation collected throughout the post-coup years on arrests and locations of detention became instrumental in establishing the truth of what happened to thousands of Chileans deemed "enemies" of the regime. What was preserved and accomplished in these especially harsh years provided the building blocks for Chile's democratic revival.

Authoritarian "Institutionalization"

While theoretically the first among equals in the junta, Pinochet proved more politically skilled at infighting than his rivals. He rapidly personalized and consolidated power, pressuring the junta to confer upon him the title "President of the Republic." Pinochet claimed it was his destiny to rule, and set out to remake Chile with a "protected" political order that would preserve his role far into the future.

Following the UN General Assembly's condemnation of the regime's human rights abuses in December 1977, Pinochet called a "consultation" at the beginning of 1978, in which citizens were called to vote on whether to "support President Pinochet in his defence of the dignity of Chile" against "international aggression" and to legitimize "the process of institutionalization." A "yes" was represented by a Chilean flag; a "no" by a black one. The process, marred by inherent fraud (there was no voter register) and intimidation, led to a 75 percent "yes" vote.

In 1980, Pinochet promulgated a constitution that retained firm military control of government. Yet Pinochet consented to holding a plebiscite in eight years' time from the adoption of the constitution and his simultaneous "election" as president — he was the sole candidate — on September 11, 1980, the seventh anniversary of the putsch. He assumed that his "re-election" in 1988 would be a foregone conclusion, but the stipulation for a plebiscite in 1988 led to Pinochet's undoing as Chile's dictator.

Part of Pinochet's "institutionalization" included radical economic reform, spearheaded by free marketeers educated abroad, dubbed the "Chicago Boys." Central to their effort to reform the Chilean economy was the privatization of state assets, often at knockdown prices. Global financial markets initially responded enthusiastically, dulling the impact of denial of credits from IFIs. The new policies spurred an economic boom in the late 1970s and early 1980s, but the growth came to an abrupt end with a set of banking failures that led to state intervention to prop them up. The downward spiral accelerated, leading to a serious economic crisis.

Fighting Brain Drain and Building Intellectual Capital for Change

Support to think tanks and policy research groups served to keep talented Chileans from joining the mass brain drain and engaged in investigating avenues to promote a return to democratic rule. Since their activities were academic in nature or packaging, more leeway was granted to them by the regime. "Some of the finest social science research in Latin America came to be associated with the Chilean informal academic sector," according to Chile expert Oxford Professor Alan Angell (1996) — and it relied almost entirely on foreign funding.

Exile's Silver Lining

Following the catastrophic failure of Chile's democratic institutions, the period in exile was one of deep soul-searching and analysis of what could have brought on the crisis and coup. A common recognition slowly crystallized among them that functioning democracy provided the only protection for human rights, and this required a will to compromise.

While all Chilean democrats subjected themselves and their ideologies to rigorous self-criticism, the socialists, the most numerous component of Allende's Popular Unity government, were affected the most profoundly. According to future President Ricardo Lagos, "Never in the history of Chile have so many Chilean women and men with varied degrees of cultural exposure — social leaders, politicians, heads of local associations, and many more — move[d] into the world...exile left its imprint, leading us to recognize the value of democracy, the higher value of human rights... abandoning the classical tools of the left in the 1960s and '70s, to be replaced by a revalorization of democracy, of human rights, of the place of the market" (cited in Sznajder and Roniger, 2007). Chilean leftists developed an appreciation for European social democracy, which they once scorned.

Christian Democrats, inflexible prior to the coup, were also affected. Some left for Venezuela where they found their sister party had a different approach, valuing the virtues of compromise.

Economic Shock and Popular Reaction:
Civil Society Stands Up

Protests and demonstrations began in 1983, sparked by a 14 percent contraction in GDP. Copper miners union leader Rodolfo Seguel organized the Workers' National Command and called for a National Day of Protest, which successfully conveyed public discontent to the regime for the first time since the coup. This popular discontent from below began opening society and revived political parties, which remained illegal.

Pinochet appointed rightist National Party leader Sergio Onofre Jarpa as interior minister and authorized him to initiate an apertura ("opening") for dialogue with right and centrist opposition parties.

Catholic Church Cardinal Francisco Fresno convened democratic opposition in the mid-1980s to forge unity. Attempts to bind the opposition together began in 1983 with the Democratic Alliance of centrist and rightist parties. This was followed by the National Accord for Transition to Full Democracy in 1985, which allied the moderate wing of the split Socialists with Christian Democrats for the first time.

The Accord demanded an immediate return to democracy with free elections, and continued to reject the 1980 constitution, with its scheduled 1988 plebiscite.

Chile's society remained divided through this period between those who saw the regime as a shield against chaos — a perception Pinochet did his best to promote, and those who saw dictatorial rule as the country's fundamental problem. According to Christian Democrat Genaro Arriagada, "There were really two worlds, two Chiles superimposed."

Demonstrations had no apparent impact. A daring 1986 attempt by leftist militants to assassinate Pinochet while leaving his country residence gave the dictator a needed pretext to violently re-impose a state of siege, and to tap into latent "middle Chilean" fears of chaos. One Chilean noted "we sank into total depression at the end of '86 because everything had failed — the communist strategy [of direct confrontation in street fights and raids] and the non-communist strategy [of demanding open elections]." There was still no strategy to end Pinochet's one-man rule.

If at First You Don't Succeed...Take Stock

In the next two years, Chile's civil society and political opposition reflected, studied and debated, and developed a consensus strategy to never again allow the radical polarization that allowed military dictatorship to take hold. Chile's research institutes and think tanks were pivotal.

Non-communist parties were legalized in 1987. Late that fall, Chilean social scientists met outside Santiago to review survey data they had collected, showing ambient fear pervasive in Chile's traumatized society. A divisive competitive electoral campaign would redound to Pinochet's advantage; he could all too easily portray it as the "chaos" he had long warned against. But a strategy of embracing the plebiscite and engaging the full democratic spectrum to generate votes for the "no" held promise: it could breach the fear barrier that kept Pinochet in power, allowing truly free elections to follow.

This was initially a hard sell with many politicians who felt this would be a capitulation to Pinochet and an acceptance of his illegal constitution. However, they were eventually convinced and devoted themselves to drumming up support for the "no."

Think Tanks, Civil Society and Opposition Work Together for the "No"

Civil society, policy think tanks and political parties aligned in a coordinated coalition to generate support for a "no" vote. This involved a massive nationwide grassroots effort to register citizens to vote, undertaken by the Crusade for Citizen Participation (Civic Crusade), which worked, in particular, to register disaffected urban youth who doubted political change could be attained without violence. The Command for the No established itself in offices around the country to generate support for a "no" vote in the plebiscite. The political opposition aligned itself for the effort in a wider spectrum than ever before — eventually 17 parties — in the Concertación. The plebiscite was promoted as a referendum on the hated dictatorship.

Getting citizens to register, encouraging them to overcome fear to vote, and building confidence and hope that victory and a brighter future were possible were all critical to success. Innovation and creativity were also in abundant supply. The Civic Crusade held free rock concerts with bands that were normally kept off the airwaves — 18–30 year olds needed only show their voter ID cards for entry. For the month before the vote, the free TV campaign spots were set at a late hour — 11:15 p.m. to 11:30 p.m. nightly — which the regime thought would limit viewership. But these creative promotional spots were built around the Command for the No's upbeat theme: "Joy is Coming!" and were viewed en masse.[1] "We managed to register seven million of eight million potential voters," reminisced Ignacio Walker in a personal interview. "We spread the 'good news' that this plebiscite was a unique chance."

The "No"s Have It!

In the plebiscite on October 5, 1988, the "no" won a decisive 55 percent victory, drawing massive turnout of over 90 percent of voters. Those within the junta who resented Pinochet's dominance welcomed the result. The air force chief acknowledged defeat with a smile on his way in to meet his colleagues, before the official media announced the result. Pinochet had to accept the "no" victory which, by the constitution, would require free presidential elections the following year.

INTERNATIONAL POLICY TOWARD THE PINOCHET REGIME

In 1973, international reaction to the coup against Allende had been swift and almost uniformly negative; Swedish Premier Olof Palme spoke for most of the democratic world when he bluntly described the junta as "despicable crooks."

Many democracies, and a number of non-democracies, acted immediately through their embassies to protect persons seeking asylum from persecution. Over the coming months and years, thousands of Chileans were resettled all over the globe. The fact that there were so many Chilean exiles elsewhere in Latin America (particularly in Venezuela, Mexico and Argentina — until its 1976 coup), in Europe and in North America (mostly Canada) gave Chilean democracy advocates a wide network in academia and civil society, as well as high visibility. The Soviet bloc took in many leftist refugees through its diplomatic missions and secondary routes. Many

---

1   A recent dramatic film on the development of the "no" campaign, directed by Chilean Pablo Larrain and starring Mexican actor Gael García Bernal, simply titled *No*, was released in 2012. The film shows the difficulties of overcoming misgivings in the opposition camp to a marketing campaign with a positive focus. The author enjoyed the film and found it a faithful representation of the effort. The trailer is available at: www.youtube.com/watch?v=lOeiw_BJPas.

Marxists gravitated to the Soviet Union, East Germany and even Romania, where Nicolae Ceaucescu had just become enamoured of Mao's Cultural Revolution. But even convinced Marxists found the atmosphere in the socialist bloc stifling and later opted to relocate.

Estimates of the number exiled vary widely, but it easily ran into the tens of thousands, and likely much higher. As of 1982, an estimated 44 percent of Chilean expatriates were in Venezuela and Mexico, with another three percent in other Latin American countries. Democratic Europe collectively was host to another nearly 40 percent, with the largest groups living in Spain, France, Italy and Sweden. Canada hosted a further nearly seven percent, and Australia nearly six percent. By this stage, less than three percent were living in the Soviet bloc. Paris and Rome were especially popular destinations, seen as cultural oases linguistically and politically close to home.

"European governments and parties felt a special affinity with Chile. The Chilean opposition had a concept of democracy that was clearly similar to that of most European political movements, based on a combination of fair elections, social justice, and the observance of basic human rights" (Angell, 1996: 192). German party foundations — Stiftungen — were very involved in Chile in the 1980s, with the Christian Democratic Konrad Adenauer Stiftung estimated to have spent about 25 million Deutschmarks in Chile from 1983–1988, and its socialist counterpart the Friedrich Ebert Stiftung spending almost 10 million Deutschmarks.

Chile's enviably strong network with foreign academia, politics and civic life was sustained with openness and generosity to political refugees. Chilean Andrés Zaldívar was leader of the Christian Democratic International in Spain. The Institute for the New Chile was founded in Rotterdam. Rome-based Chile Democratico, the collaborative effort of two Christian Democrats and two Popular Unity members, published *Chile-América* from 1974–1984. It gained a worldwide readership, with informed policy debates and analysis, along with human rights reporting from Chile. External funding from Western European governments kept these initiatives afloat.

Most democracies maintained consistent anti-Pinochet policies, decrying human rights abuses in international fora and supporting through various channels Chilean civil society, but some influential democracies' policies fluctuated considerably between 1973 and 1988. In addition, arms sales continued from a number of European countries. Britain's Labour Party governments in the 1970s curtailed arms sales and withdrew their ambassador from Santiago after abuse of a British dual national, but full representation — and an end to an embargo — returned with Margaret Thatcher's Conservative government. France's policy toward Chile took a markedly more critical turn with the arrival of Socialist President François Mitterrand in 1981, and new arms deals were not signed. As Portugal and Spain underwent democratic transitions after the coup, the favour that Marcelo Caetano and Francisco Franco had showered on Pinochet turned to hostility.

Democracies also put their money where their mouths were. "In per capita terms, amongst the most generous of the aid donors was the Netherlands," according to

Alan Angell in a personal interview. He notes that the Dutch government established and funded a number of policy institutes that were incubators for Chilean exiles and experts. The Swedish Agency for Research Cooperation with Developing Countries and Canadian International Development Research Centre were also generous.

Perhaps the most influential shifts in policy came from Washington. US President Richard Nixon and his Secretary of State Henry Kissinger did little to hide their relief at the ouster of a government that they asserted was turning Chile into "another Cuba." The brief Ford administration continued this, but reacted harshly to the 1976 car bombing assassination of Allende's Foreign Minister Orlando Letelier in downtown Washington, which killed an American citizen. The Carter administration was much harder on the Pinochet regime, co-sponsoring resolutions on human rights in the UN and applying financial levers. The Reagan administration disavowed Carter's human rights oriented policies and welcomed a positive relationship with Pinochet. US ambassador, political appointee and ideologue James Theberge even attended the eleventh anniversary of the coup, when other ambassadors stayed away. But this shifted definitively early in Reagan's second term, with Secretary of State George Shultz's decision in early 1985 to replace Theberge with career diplomat Harry Barnes, Jr. Among arguments for this policy shift was the rank inconsistency of arguing for democracy in Sandinista Nicaragua while backing a blatant military dictatorship in Chile. Congress, in contrast to the White House, was consistently vocal against Pinochet, the most active and vocal of all being Democratic Senator Edward Kennedy of Massachusetts, who initiated a cutoff of military aid to Chile in 1976 and generated congressional demands for human rights assessments on recipients of American aid.

RESOURCES AND ASSETS OF DIPLOMATS IN CHILE

In Chile, especially in the weeks after the coup, diplomats employed their **immunity** to protect human life, evidenced by Swedish Ambassador Harald Edelstam, who Pinochet expelled, and many others. Much later, US Ambassador Harry Barnes, Jr. was so assertive in his efforts to help Chileans restore their democracy that Pinochet considered declaring him *persona non grata*.

Most diplomats in Santiago were able to count on the public support of their home authorities in opposing the regime. Ambassador Barnes lined up comprehensive backing with the executive branch, but also major figures in Congress and NGOs. The visible backing of the higher reaches of government encourages NGOs and donors to take notice and devote more resources, confident that their efforts will be effective. This was the case in Chile.

Pinochet wanted to appear immune to influence by external actors, but was vulnerable to political conditionality on IFI credits. This leverage was employed repeatedly. Backed by the full US government, the assertive Ambassador Barnes may have lost a lot of his influence with Pinochet, but correspondingly gained it with the opposition and civil society, which had felt abandoned by the regime-focussed "quiet diplomacy" of the Reagan administration's early years. Many countries had strong moral and cultural influence on Chilean civil society, such as Venezuela with its two-party democracy and Germany's support through the Stiftungen. Spanish socialist Prime Minister Felipe González was highly regarded.

In most cases, funds to assist civil society and political opposition did not go through embassies, but direct channels, mostly private and quasi-public (such as the Stiftungen). Ambassadors on the ground had a role in helping these donors and programmatic organizations in their targeting and in suggesting new funding efforts — especially before the plebiscite.

The democratic states' diplomats had a rich vein of legitimacy to mine in Chile — namely the full array of international human rights treaties and guarantees to which Chile had been party, enthusiastically, in its democratic and multilateralist pre-Pinochet days. The French and Dutch ambassadors referred to Chile's obligations under the Universal Declaration on Human Rights when opposition leftists were seized in 1984. Diplomats regularly invoked them when taken to task by the regime for appearances with victims of human rights abuses, demanding information about those disappeared and demarching the government for its transgressions of international norms.

WAYS THESE ASSETS WERE APPLIED TO MAKE A DIFFERENCE IN CHILE

Golden Rules

Embassies understood the significance of Chile's democratic tradition, well-developed civic sector and intelligentsia, and assisted individuals at risk by providing asylum and economic assistance, as well as direct assistance to those attempting to keep the embers of freedom alive in the smothering first years of dictatorship, though there was too little space for progress for almost a decade after the coup. The Church was the main protector and non-state actor, through the Pro-Peace Committee and its successor, the Vicariate of Solidarity.

Chile's strong cadre of academics, professionals and intellectuals had studied abroad and had wide networks well before the coup. Many suffered persecution, including expulsion from their positions in academia and administration, and consequently left Chile for positions overseas, leaving Chilean academia decimated. The international community recognized the necessity of maintaining this human resource in Chile, and numerous donors, some public and many private, helped maintain a lifeline for them by financing academic policy research institutes. In addition, diplomats such as Ambassador Barnes respected Chilean civil society by publicly engaging them upon his arrival. Barnes met publicly with Christian

Democrat leader Gabriel Valdés soon after presenting his credentials to Pinochet, and with civil society figures in advance of introductions to Pinochet's officialdom, which riled Pinochet greatly. The optics and reality of an ambassador listening to civil society were important in rebuilding civic self-confidence and optimism. As Valdés noted at the time, "The embassy has changed completely for us."

Though there was little systematic information sharing among diplomatic missions, there were ad hoc examples of collaboration in protecting threatened Chileans, especially in the immediate aftermath of the 1973 coup. Diplomatic missions certainly interacted and compared notes regularly with the other international actors on the Chilean scene, such as political party foundations, international labour union representatives and the international press corps. Later, Ambassador Barnes created and headed the Western Hemisphere Democracy Group, including the Argentine, Brazilian and Costa Rican ambassadors. According to Barnes, "We exchanged information and discussed how we [and our governments] might be more effective in promoting greater respect for human rights and democracy" (cited in Palmer, 2003). French Ambassador Leon Bouvier was also a strong advocate for human rights and democracy.

Truth in Communications

Immediately after the coup, embassy **reporting** was vital to convey the severity of violence and repression. With access to information utterly closed at the outset and still restrictive even at the most liberal stage of the Pinochet regime, this transmission mechanism was important. Evidence of the massive human rights abuses endemic to Pinochet's regime often reached the international public — and Chileans — through this channel.

Informing the Chilean public of their solidarity and policies was nearly impossible with the self-censorship of non-government vetted media, though publications by expatriates, such as *Chile-América* out of Rome, received assistance.

The diplomatic pouch was among many tools that Chilean human rights activists could rely upon to convey details of human rights abuses to the international community. Once safely outside and reported, this information could circulate back to Chilean society at large through foreign broadcast media and expatriate publications, conveying the truth about the regime's dark practices. As space for independent media opened in the 1980s, diplomats directed assistance to independent media such as *Analisis*, *La Epoca* and CIEPLAN's popular economic review.

Working with the Government

From the beginning of his 16 years in power in 1973 to the end in 1989, Pinochet was an international pariah, rarely leaving the country. Few invitations were forthcoming. In 1980, Filipino dictator Ferdinand Marcos disinvited Pinochet from a planned state visit while Pinochet was en route to Manila. Pinochet was once again humiliated in 1983, when his government announced it was invited to the inauguration of Argentina's democratic president, Raúl Alfonsín, only to have the Argentine Foreign Ministry disavow the invitation, which Pinochet extracted from Argentina's outgoing junta. Sweden made a point of not inviting any Chilean representatives to assassinated Premier Olof Palme's funeral in 1986.

Following the coup, Italy withdrew its ambassador, maintaining a chargé in Santiago until after Pinochet was defeated in the plebiscite. Sweden never replaced its ambassador, expelled in December 1973 for his active defence of human rights. Mexico abandoned relations altogether from 1974 on, after taking in a great number of refugees, including President Allende's widow. Britain withdrew its ambassador in 1975; he was not replaced for over four years.

While relations remained open with a number of democracies represented in Santiago, there was precious little advising of the Pinochet government. Nor were there noteworthy examples of government-to-government dialoguing on human rights and democratic practices, though there were protests from democracies.

Most of the state-to-state communications in the Pinochet dictatorship period are more properly considered **demarching**, such as demands for explanations of actions, pressure to release prisoners or explain "disappearances." French Ambassador Leon Bouvier demanded explanation of the killing of a French priest by police in a poor Santiago barrio. The previous year, he was recalled for consultations by Foreign Minister Cheysson, who called Pinochet a "curse on his people," to protest human rights violations. Ambassador Barnes warned the Pinochet regime not to interfere with the 1988 plebiscite.

Reaching Out

Diplomats forged connections between Chilean civil society and opposition political figures and counterparts in their home countries as a matter of course, recognizing that creating and maintaining linkages to the outside world was essential. The web connecting Chile to the democratic world developed into an incredibly strong and resilient one. Diplomats interacted consistently with Chilean civil society and complimented the efforts of their own societies to remain engaged.

Democratic embassies — particularly those of Canada and a number of European countries — regularly invited opposition and civic figures to convene for free discussions amongst themselves and the diplomatic corps (which, of course, would tap into this resource for reporting on the situation). This circuit, together with connections which were forged among refugees abroad, developed into a network which proved very important later in planning the return to democracy.

As the repression loosened somewhat in the early and mid-1980s, the diplomatic corps worked to facilitate greater cooperation among the democratic opposition parties. In May 1985, Chilean official media reported the West German Ambassador stating that his country, along with Britain and the US, was willing to mediate between Pinochet's government and the opposition, which had become emboldened by public discontent. Soon thereafter, Ambassador Barnes arrived and pressed opposition politicians to come together behind a common approach to press for an end to dictatorship. Despite progress in building constructive relationships among parties, there was no clear strategy until late 1987 and early 1988.

Post-disbursed funds were not a major feature of international engagement, but financing by governments, quasi-governmental organizations and private foundations was indispensable for the survival and development of Chilean civil society. Embassies ensured that worthy efforts got noticed, and this lifeline gave Chilean civil society the ability to develop their winning strategy of contesting the plebiscite.

In just one example, the US government had hitherto been far less engaged in financially supporting civil society than its European counterparts, mostly operating through development agencies and quasi-governmental institutes. USAID funded the Civic Crusade, and the National Endowment for Democracy and NDI both assisted the Command for the No.

The most effective **showcasing** of democratic practices and norms was done outside Chile. Chile's tens of thousands of political and intellectual exiles experienced free democratic societies themselves, some after having had the opportunity to see firsthand the "advanced socialism" of the Soviet bloc. The honeymoon in the socialist paradise was brief for most. Socialist Party Secretary General Carlos Altamirano, who like many socialists originally fled to East Germany, later said "I jumped the wall," and was attracted to Paris by France's socialist government under President Mitterrand. Mitterrand and Italian Communist Party leader Enrico Berlinguer, progenitor of democratic "Eurocommunism," were attractive poles for the exiled Chilean left. Embassies held regular cultural events that displayed the fruits of an open, democratic society.

Defending Democrats

Democratic diplomats regularly and creatively demonstrated their support for democratic principles, fundamental freedoms and human rights in Chile throughout the Pinochet era. Initially, this was accomplished most urgently through providing humanitarian protection to those threatened with death or torture by the regime (see below). Later, diplomats like Carter-era US Ambassador George Landau made clear on his arrival in 1977 that "We can't tell a government what it can do, but we can tell it what will happen if it doesn't do certain things." Recalls of ambassadors were legion in Chile: Mexico severed relations, Sweden never replaced Ambassador Edelstam after he was expelled, Italy didn't reinstitute full ties until after Pinochet was shown the door by voters in 1988, and Britain and France recalled their ambassadors in protests during Pinochet's reign.

Other notable examples were the appearance of a host of democracies' diplomats, including those of France, Spain, Italy, Belgium and the US, at the funeral of a young man burned to death by police in 1986. The young woman who was with him was also severely burned, but survived, and was given asylum and treated in Montreal, Canada.

CASE STUDY 10 — THE FALL AND RISE OF CHILEAN DEMOCRACY: 1973–1989

Attending events by the opposition, even when it remained illegal, showed the regime that the democratic world recognized these activities as inherently legitimate, not only affording Chilean democrats some insulation from repression, but also showing that the democratic world was with them. The same principle applied to human rights events, at which democratic ambassadors and other diplomats made a point to be visible. The political use of forced exile by the regime was also publicly derided, even as Pinochet tried to earn points by incrementally allowing some exiles to return from the mid-1980s on. As one Western diplomat stated, "exile is not a question of numbers, it is a question of principle. Even one exile is too many."

Diplomats also encouraged Chilean democrats in their conviction that victory in the plebiscite was not only possible, but likely if the regime did not interfere. "I think the 'no' will win, if the process doesn't get interrupted," said Ambassador Barnes two days before the vote.

Democracies were very active in protecting Chileans (and other Latin Americans) threatened by the regime. The most vivid examples of this activity should be viewed through a primarily humanitarian lens. In the period immediately following the coup, the National Refugee Commission was set up by leading church figures to get threatened persons to foreign embassies where they could be protected. The stories are quite harrowing and vivid.

Ambassador Edelstam said at the time that "the role of the Swedish Embassy is to save the lives of people who are in danger. We know there are lists of people who supported the former regime and who are considered by the new military authorities [to be] criminals and therefore could be executed." Edelstam took the entire Cuban Embassy staff under his protection and escorted them to an Aeroflot flight out of Chile. New Zealand Ambassador John McArthur spirited a trade union leader disguised as a woman to the residence before arranging for the Swedish Embassy to arrange for his asylum. While later protecting a Uruguayan woman who had just undergone surgery, Edelstam got into a confrontation with police and was expelled. Mexican Ambassador Gonzalo Martínez Corbalá gave refuge to more than 500 at the embassy and residence. In later testimony to Spanish prosecutors who indicted Pinochet, he noted many of those he sheltered bore signs of torture inflicted at the National Stadium. Two attempted asylum seekers were shot in the back by police at the embassy door.

Immediately after the coup, roughly 50 terrorized Chileans and foreign nationals likely to be persecuted by the regime came to the door of the Canadian Embassy seeking asylum. Without instructions, the young diplomats admitted the Chileans, who remained in the chancery of the embassy until the Canadian government could evacuate them and their families two months later. Venezuela dispatched a plane to get Allende-era Foreign Minister Orlando Letelier after his release in 1974.

Diplomats continued to act throughout the dictatorship to protect Chileans. Though the massive wave of refugees naturally followed the coup and immediate repression, as late as December 1987, there were more than 500 requests for asylum per month, mostly to Sweden, with large numbers also to Canada and neighbouring (and by then democratic) Argentina.

Through holding public meetings with human rights defenders and other threatened Chileans, diplomats granted an element of protection to them. The Chilean Catholic Church, the Church-backed Vicariate of Solidarity and those operating under its protection performed the most important acts of witnessing, verifying, investigating and documenting the crimes and human rights violations of the Pinochet regime, in addition to the courageous work undertaken by many members of the clergy in protecting and defending human rights activists in danger or in prison.

Diplomats performed this role in the immediate aftermath of the coup as well, availing themselves of their immunity to find some of the missing and to protect a great number of Chileans and foreign nationals who were sought by the regime in its "state of war." Their reports not only went back to their governments, but frequently to the world at large through the media, generating international outrage.

Chileans planning the "no" campaign determined early on that election observation during the plebiscite would be essential. Many felt the regime was fully capable of killing to maintain power. According to a personal interview with Alan Angell, foreign observers "helped [Chileans] feel they could vote with impunity." Genaro Arriagada, a Christian Democrat scholar who headed the Technical Committee for the No believed that international observers were the "best guarantee" against fraud, or worse — against a move by the regime to maintain power through "disappearing" electoral workers and voters. As Arriagada said in a personal interview, "Their mere presence in the country is a guarantee…an insurance. That function is invaluable." Ambassador Barnes and his colleagues, especially from Latin America, ensured that the observers came — roughly 400 of them, officially as "tourists." High profile international observers included US senators Edward Kennedy and Richard Lugar, as well as former presidents Carter and Ford. "Had the eyes of the world not been on Chile and had there not been international observers for the plebiscite, than I think that Pinochet in any number of ways would have gotten away with it," thought US Deputy Chief of Mission George Jones. So the democratic world kept the pressure on Pinochet to ensure that the 1989 elections were held.

CONCLUSION

Diplomats joined the whole wider community of international NGOs and intergovernmental organizations — and their complex open societies back home — to support Chile's democratic revival. But the success of the "no" campaign by Chile's civil society, intellectuals and democratic opposition to Pinochet was owed to domestic initiative, strategy and pragmatism.

The latter element had been a traditional feature of Chile's democratic practice, but was effaced by doctrinaire ideologies in the 1960s. Most Chileans attribute the democratic breakdown in 1973 to domestic factors, despite foreign influence in the 1960s and 1970s, but the experience of losing democracy and its mechanisms to protect human rights and fundamental freedoms for nearly two decades has informed Chilean society. Former President Ricardo Lagos states that "there is one consensus today shared by everyone: 'never again.' Never again can Chile repeat it…that rupture in Chile's soul. Never again" (BBC Monitoring Americas, 2003).

WORKS CITED

Angell, Alan (1996). "International Support for the Chilean Opposition 1973–1989: Political Parties and the Role of Exiles." In *The International Dimensions of Democratization: Europe and the Americas*, edited by Laurence Whitehead. Pages 175–200. Oxford: Oxford University Press.

BBC Monitoring Americas (2003). "Chile's Lagos Discusses Coup Anniversary, Mexican Aid to Refugees in 1973." BBC News, September 1.

Palmer, Mark (2003). *Breaking the Real Axis of Evil: How to Oust the World's Last Dictators by 2025*. Oxford: Rowman and Littlefield.

Puryear, Jeffrey M. (1994). *Thinking Politics: Intellectuals and Democracy in Chile, 1973–1988*. Baltimore: Johns Hopkins University Press.

Sznajder, Mario and Luis Roniger (2007). "Exile Communities and Their Differential Institutional Dynamics: A Comparative Analysis of the Chilean and Uruguayan Political Diasporas." *Revista de Ciencia Politica* 27, no. 1: 54.

11 SOUTH AFRICA: "THE LONG ROAD TO FREEDOM"

By Jeremy Kinsman, 2008

INTRODUCTION

S outh Africa's struggle for democracy penetrated global consciousness as no other, engaging generations of international humanists, persons of conscience and democratic governments the world over. The uniquely pernicious racial assertions of apartheid conveyed an almost universal sense of offence. Because of its inherent immorality and what Nelson Mandela described as "the ruthlessness of the state in protecting it," the South African apartheid regime was singular in the extent to which it was regarded as illegitimate. But the struggle to overturn it was borne by South Africans themselves.

Ending apartheid peacefully and establishing democracy in a unitary state would be only part of their battle. The challenges of governance and development for a majority whose skills levels had been deliberately suppressed were formidable. Africans knew this. Mandela (1994) has written that the Freedom Charter of 1955, setting out the requirements of a free and democratic country, anticipated that "changes envisioned would not be achieved without radically altering the economic and political structure of South Africa."

That the non-white majority acceded to power 40 years later in a country with established institutions was not in itself an advantage. As Mandela (1994) wrote, "Working as a lawyer in South Africa meant operating under a debased system of justice, a code of law that did not enshrine equality, but its opposite."

A successful revolution occurred. But it is widely judged to have been a "negotiated revolution," essentially non-violent. The victory belonged to the people who had been protesting the apartheid laws since the Defiance Campaign of 1952. During the 1970s, a wide array of more or less organized groups and initiatives emerged in support of the construction of a popular civil society and in opposition to the apartheid state. By 1983, these groups had become fairly coherently allied in the UDF, a working coalition of trade unions, student and youth groups, women's groups, cultural organizations and professionals whose members, taken as a body, acquired increasing credibility and legitimacy as the civil alternative to the apartheid regime.

During those hard years, there had been many historic junctions on the "long road to freedom." Several of these are associated with cruel violence, such as the Sharpeville massacre in 1960, or the Soweto uprising in 1976. Faced with the regime's ruthlessness, in 1962, the ANC decided to desert 50 years' belief in non-violence, accepting the option of organized violence. But as Allister Sparks (1996) later wrote, Mandela "never had any illusions it could win a military victory."

He was firmly "in the negotiation camp." In eventual negotiations, beginning in the late 1980s, the government side sought to oblige the ANC to renounce having opted for organized violence. The ANC committed to a future peaceful process but would not renounce its history.

In a sense, this became the pattern for the negotiated outcome. The National Peace Accord of 1991 aimed at a vast conflict resolution. With memories inhabited by an almost unendurable history, it was necessary to exorcise the past. The Truth and Reconciliation Commission would provide amnesty for deeds committed under apartheid in exchange for truth about them. This negotiated solution did not propose that apartheid's victims forget the past, but did enable all South Africans to go forward according to a formula in which blacks had to give up the pursuit of justice for crimes against them, and whites had to give up their monopoly on power.

Violence between black Africans, and notably Inkatha and the ANC, subsided with difficulty, taking the lives of as many as 25,000 in the 1990s, and criminal violence continues in South Africa to this day at unacceptable levels. But the "South African bloodbath" so widely feared and predicted was held at bay, at least as far as violence between whites and blacks was concerned.

The 1994 elections produced majority rule in a unitary state, but without the domination of the white minority by the majority in any punitive sense. The successfully negotiated peaceful transfer of power was a mighty outcome to the struggle of South Africans over more than 50 years.

Looking back at the April 1990 Wembley Stadium concert in celebration of Nelson Mandela and his people's struggle, when he thanked the world's anti-apartheid forces for the "support and solidarity they had shown the oppressed people of South Africa," Susan Collin Marks (2000) reflected on "how easy it had been to cheer Mandela and how hard it would be to remake the nation." That struggle endures, but South Africa's gifts to the world, through its history of a successfully negotiated revolution to effect a multiracial and pluralistic democratic society, also endure as a model and a hope for many.

THE EXTERNAL ENVIRONMENT

Once South African governments adopted institutionalized apartheid in the years following World War II, it was obvious that there would be a collision with the rest of a changing world. From the time Ghana received its independence in 1957, the white regime in South Africa would find itself increasingly isolated by the "winds of change" sweeping over the continent, with reinforcement only from Rhodesia and the still-enduring Portuguese colonies.

Foreign support for the anti-apartheid struggle came from civil society — trade unions, church organizations, Parliaments and a multitude of NGOs — in many democracies, and, it should be acknowledged, support came from socialist countries allied with the Soviet Union as well. Outside South Africa, universities, research centres, NGOs and supportive citizens helped to sustain and train South African peace activists in exile, until they could return to participate freely in the process of democratic change.

International Diplomatic Activity

Diplomatic pressure over decades may have had only an uneven effect on the insulated apartheid regime's repressive laws, but it undoubtedly helped to support the credibility of the ANC as an indispensable ingredient of any South African solution by the time ANC leader Oliver Tambo met with US Secretary of State George P. Shultz in 1987.

The international diplomatic community began to pronounce on the South African situation as early as 1960, when the UN Security Council condemned the killing of 69 demonstrators at Sharpeville. South African issues were always on UN agendas thereafter.

That same year, African solidarity was extended to the ANC when Nelson Mandela visited and won the support of the great African figures of that time, including Ethiopian Emperor Haile Selassie, Tanzania's President Julius Nyerere, Zambian President Kenneth Kaunda, Tunisian President Habib Bourguiba, Algerian President Ahmed Ben Bella, Guinean President Ahmed Sékou Touré, and Senegalese President Léopold Sédar Senghor.

Such core African support was instrumental in persuading the Commonwealth of Nations to take activist positions against the apartheid regime, whose exit as a member of the Commonwealth had been steered shortly after the whites voted to declare South Africa a republic in the 1950s. By the 1985 Commonwealth Heads of Government Meeting in Nassau, the members of the Commonwealth were able to adopt a program of sanctions against South Africa, despite long-standing reservations on the part of UK Prime Minister Thatcher.

The Appeal for Sanctions and Boycotts

The ANC urged governments to ally together to introduce sanctions against South Africa. The purpose of sanctions was to induce behavioural change by imposing the psychological and economic costs of isolation on the apartheid regime. International sports and cultural groups halted South African tours and excluded South African teams. Universities disinvested South African holdings from portfolios for moral reasons, while multinational corporations relocated from South Africa for reasons of corporate strategy. Financial institutions reconsidered lending practices to the South African state and its institutions. The World Alliance of Reformed Churches suspended the Dutch Reformed Church of South Africa.

The imposition of sanctions was not without controversy. Apart from the impact on the economic interests of investors in South Africa, there was concern that sanctions would primarily hurt the economic livelihood of the black and coloured population, a warning endorsed by such a democratic activist as South African opposition MP Helen Suzman. But the fact that targeted sanctions had the full support of the ANC, which believed they were essential to the struggle, was judged to be decisive.

The South African state authorities estimated that the economic sanctions were "hurting but survivable." Taken alone, perhaps they were, though the growing isolation of South African whites from the rest of the world added a psychological toll that eroded their willingness to support the extremist state authorities to the bitter end. That there would be a certain end was overwhelmingly due to the brave perseverance of non-white South Africans and their allies among the white population who, over generations, worked to obtain the justice of a democratic outcome.

International Popular Opinion and Support

Public opinion around the world grew to be massively supportive, stimulated in part by the 1960 Nobel Peace Prize awarded to Albert Luthuli who led the ANC at the time it was first "banned." In 1984, Archbishop Desmond Tutu, who was a major force in forming the UDF, won the Nobel Peace Prize again in the name of the South African struggle for justice.

During the intervening years, tens of thousands ANC, Pan African Congress and other democracy activists had been banned and imprisoned but would not be abandoned by the world's attention. Night-long church vigils and "Free Mandela" events were frequent, often directed at fundraising for the ANC and for NGOs operating in South Africa. Funding for South African democracy activists and NGOs had begun as early as the 1960s when Danish, Norwegian and Swedish trade unions and church groups launched the first programs in support of those involved in the struggle. Before long, foundations and governments from many democracies joined them in funding NGOs and reformers, often with an emphasis on preparing for governance. External funding was important to help political organizations to finance the sorts of identity-cementing activities such as newspapers and events on which the struggle depended to sustain popular support over successive generations.

By 1983, this popular support pulled together under the loose grouping of the UDF, collecting trade unions, church and youth groups, cultural organizations and a variety of locally based civic bodies under one roof. In the circumstances when the ANC had been banned, the UDF was able to become the main instrument for organizing popular protests and boycotts meant to counter the increasingly hardline series of repressive laws and crackdowns associated with frequent states of emergency suspending rights and leading to mass arrests.

Change at Last

The position of the apartheid regime gradually unravelled as any remaining support from the international environment deteriorated. Zimbabwe had emerged in place of the racist allied regime of Rhodesia, and along with other frontline states, the newly independent Angola, Mozambique and Botswana became locales for ANC training camps, and a platform for cross-border raids. The retaliatory effectiveness of the South African Defence Force (SADF) was increasingly handicapped by re-equipment difficulties because of sanctions, and the conflict's costs began to drain South Africa's treasury and the population's support.

Once glasnost had transformed the Soviet Union under Mikhail Gorbachev, it became much more difficult for the South African regime to continue to convince the white public the ANC was part of a communist conspiracy to take over South Africa, which the authorities had been alleging since the Rivonia trials of ANC leaders in the early 1960s.

Something had to give, and by the mid-1980s, contacts encouraged by outside mediators were taking place in Mells Park in the UK. In 1987, with funding from the Friedrich Naumann Foundation, the Institute for Democracy in South Africa organized discussions in Dakar between the ANC under Thabo Mbeki and groups of white South Africans who were convinced of the need of a negotiated settlement, including the once hardline Afrikaner Broederbond.

Negotiating Democracy

By 1989, the writing on the wall was clear for most to see. The new South African government leadership under F. W. de Klerk accelerated the process and South Africa entered the phase of negotiation and preparation of majority rule.

The world's democracies played a significant role in helping the ANC and other South Africans to prepare for positions of governance through conferences, courses and other forms of training. Jurists were trained through The Aspen Institute, economists via the macroeconomic research group set up following Mandela's visit to Canada shortly after his release in 1990 and journalists via Harvard's Nieman Foundation fellowships. With the help of public broadcasters from Commonwealth countries, Australia initiated a major program for the cultural and organizational transformation of the propagandistic South African Broadcasting Corporation (SABC).

Foreign experts also converged on South Africa to provide support for the preparation and observation of the democratic elections that would bring majority rule. As conflict mediator Susan Collin Marks (2000) has observed, they and other committed international helpers "gave an increased sense of security" to democracy activists "confirming the eyes of the world were on their plight." They also "gave some real security as the police and army behaved with restraint in their presence" (ibid.).

In the end, after a successful election and peaceful handover of power, it was South Africa's turn to show the world what a negotiated revolution looked like, in the South African form of a multi-ethnic, multiracial and multicultural society which could serve as a partial model for the bridging challenges faced in the Balkans, the Middle East or elsewhere in Africa.

DIPLOMATIC RESOURCES IN SOUTH AFRICA AND THEIR APPLICATIONS IN SUPPORT OF DEMOCRACY

Assets

The diplomatic community resident in South Africa was not large, in part because the newly independent African countries did not have relations with the apartheid regime. Of the democratic countries present, those working informally and proactively together to support democratic activists and human rights defenders were relatively few in the 1960s and 1970s, but their numbers increased in the 1980s and were especially reinforced in the later 1980s when the United States became decisively committed to a democratic solution for South Africa.

South African authorities complained fairly regularly about diplomats' activities. South African Foreign Minister Pik Botha made a widely publicized speech in 1987 warning diplomats "not to meddle" in what he judged were South African internal affairs and threatening curbs on diplomats' movements. He complained specifically about foreign funding for a trip by South African anti-apartheid activists to meet ANC personnel in Dakar.

The authorities tried to intimidate diplomats, sometimes with rather brutal methods. Political Counselor of the US Embassy Robert C. Frasure (later killed on duty in Bosnia) tracked cross-border military movements of the SADF. Former UK Ambassador Robin Renwick recalled in a personal interview that the SADF retaliated by "terrorizing his wife and children during his absences from home, to such an extent Frasure had to be withdrawn."

More classically, John Schram, a senior Canadian diplomat, was shown in Foreign Ministry photos at rallies and anti-apartheid events not just observing, but actively participating, including joining in praying and marching. He was threatened with expulsion, but countered that the only result would be to reduce the numbers at the South African Embassy in Ottawa and to damage South Africa's image abroad. Schram was able to do this effectively because it was clear the embassy enjoyed the great asset of complete backing from his minister and government at home. He was also able to play to the interest South African authorities had in diminishing if possible the international shunning which was solidifying around the world.

The fact that the world community was organizing its leverage against the apartheid regime was a helpful frame of reference for diplomats on the ground in reinforcing the legitimacy of their activity. The declarations of Commonwealth Heads of Government Conferences, Summits of the European Community and the G7, or resolutions of the UN Security Council, General Assembly and its subsidiary bodies helped to cohere a common sense of purpose among affected diplomats in South Africa.

Nelson Mandela and wife Winnie, walking hand in hand, raise clenched fists upon his release from Victor prison, Cape Town, on February 11, 1990. The ANC leader had served over 27 years in detention. (AP Photo)

They often represented countries whose own histories had been propelled by democracy activists to which ANC members and others looked to for encouragement and examples: Gandhi, Martin Luther King, Jr. and later Lech Walesa, and democracy activists in the Philippines, were inspirations for the struggle, as were anti-colonialist leaders from Africa and leftist liberationists from Latin America.

Unquestionably, the funds that embassies had at their disposal for small, fast-disbursing local grants were important assets, especially as many of the beneficiaries had no funds of their own.

APPLICATIONS

The Golden Rules

Though there was worldwide dismay over the repression of the struggle for democracy in South Africa, it was most important to **respect** that it was indeed a struggle conducted often at personal risk by South Africans on behalf of their country's future, however universal the themes. As UK Ambassador Renwick phrased it, "The most that any Embassy could do was to try to help as a **facilitator** — and then let South Africans get on with a process in which too much foreign involvement was positively undesirable" (emphasis added).

Of course, some embassies leant considerably farther forward than others in such facilitation, no doubt reflecting the clear support they had at home, but it was always a problem for local diplomats when outside trainers in negotiation or mediation skills lost sight of why they were there to help. As Susan Collin Marks (2000) writes, "Suspicion grew that many [foreign trainers] were driven by personal agendas, so that they were in it for what they could get out of it, not for what they could give… training in South Africa, a conflict hot spot, gave credibility that enhanced their image elsewhere. Many of them would come into the country, give the training, and leave." It was up to embassies to try to steer outside assistance to support continuity, but in cooperation with and in deference to the international NGO community, which was closer to the ground and to the grief of the struggle.

Sharing among embassies was fundamental, especially the most like-minded such as the Australian, Dutch, Canadian and Swedish who met frequently, in part to ensure their respective funding was not at cross purposes, and that funds were distributed across a variety of needy organizations. Sharing of tasks also helped to ensure that an array of representatives was usually present at trials, funerals and demonstrations, effectively communicating the opprobrium of the wider world for the apartheid doctrine and regime, and encouragement for the non-violent struggle for justice.

Getting to the Truth

Most democratic embassies ensured that **reporting** was candid and precise, and benefitted from the contacts of what one ambassador called his "township attaches." By 1985, the South African situation had achieved a profile that meant reporting from embassies was avidly followed in capitals.

Of course, the situation was also covered by the foreign press, whose investigative reporting annoyed the authorities who, in a two-year period in the 1980s, expelled

12 correspondents from democratic countries' news outlets, including *The New York Times*, the BBC, ITN and CBS. This placed a greater onus on diplomats to play an **informing** role with their own home country news media to ensure the real story was getting out, as well as issuing information bulletins within South Africa, particularly to counter government-inspired slander. Former US Ambassador Princeton Lyman (2002) described how a predecessor, Edward Perkins, had "utilized the press to get his message across to the white population that the government of South Africa would never again have the opportunity to deal with people of the quality of Nelson Mandela, Walter Sisulu, and Thabo Mbeki."

A vital embassy service was support for independent media. A number of embassies, such as Canada, had a specific fund ("the anti-censorship fund") to help finance independent media such as the *Daily Mail*, including subsidizing subscriptions and advertising, as well as editorial and operating expenditures.

The SABC had long served as a propaganda arm of the apartheid regime by the time that the negotiation of a constitution got underway in 1992. (Over the years, the SABC helped to account for polling results such as a 1982 poll revealing that 80 percent of whites believed that communism was at the root of a struggle waged against the interests of a basically contented black population). Yet, the SABC radio audience numbered at least 15 million and the transformation of the corporation into an objective news and information service became identified as a top priority by embassies, achieved with the help of public broadcasting services from Australia, Britain and Canada. Upgrading the skills of South African journalists also became a priority through the work of the Institute for the Advancement of Journalism, founded by Allister Sparks, and the creation of many exchanges and fellowships.

Working with the Government

Prior to 1989, there was little sincere opportunity for working with the South African government on human rights issues, though some countries professed support for "constructive dialogue" and it could be argued that it did help to bring about a negotiated independence for Namibia. Embassies played an **advising** role in steering democracies to the means for helping a democratizing South Africa after 1989 to strengthen its capacities in the area of judicial training, constitutional advice, economic policy preparation, particularly via the macro-economic research group and also in supporting assistance to South Africa in disabling its emerging capability for nuclear weapons.

A particular contribution was made by Chile, which was able to advise the new South Africa on the Chilean experience in creating a Truth and Reconciliation Commission once democracy had been restored.

Several ambassadors and missions sustained **dialogues** with South African authorities. The UK and US ambassadors believed their governments' reticence about sanctions served as carrots in moderating behaviour. Ambassadors of the major democracies also claimed an "invisible mediation" role with the South African government once internal negotiations began, privately counselling the authorities as to where the "red lines" were for the international community's expectations.

But the most effective **demarches** to the South African authorities were often those that ensured that they knew their activities were being closely scrutinized internationally, especially in the anticipation of responses to demonstration and popular protest. Demarches were frequently made on behalf of democracy activists charged under the state with political and other crimes, including conveying the pleas for clemency for the lives of Nelson Mandela and fellow defendants in the "Rivonia" trials in 1964 by the leaders of the USSR and the US, among others.

Reaching Out

Connecting to civil society in South Africa and assisting its connections to NGOs and supportive institutions abroad was a critical ongoing responsibility of diplomats. Scanning for opportunities to connect African jurists to the Aspen seminars, or journalists to the Nieman fellowships, benefitted from the close contacts democratic embassies maintained with lawyers' associations and journalists. The Canadian government created an exceptionally autonomous embassy-administered fund called the "Dialogue Fund" meant to promote connections with anti-apartheid groups of all sorts inside South Africa, and funded a variety of legal and independent media defence organizations in particular.

Such connections were put to use by embassies and diplomats to **convene** activists and reformers together under a safe roof and then activists and opponents together. Jurist Richard Goldstone recalled his first meeting with representatives of the ANC at the Canadian Embassy at a critical turning point for South Africa, when he had been appointed chairperson of the Commission on Public Violence and Intimidation. Black and coloured entrepreneurs and economists were introduced to visiting businesspeople around embassy tables. Embassy personnel also made connections to South African security organizations.

Facilitating contacts was an essential service of democratic embassies, but helping with communications within South Africa and to the outside was another way they could help, as certain diplomats noted of their experience.

Targeted connections enabled embassies to pinpoint **financing** assistance such as USAID funds, which paid for the defence costs of democracy activists and human rights defenders placed on trial. The value to South African NGOs, of even small but instant embassy grants that financed the costs of publicity for demonstrations and identity-reinforcing tools such as newsletters and T-shirts, was very high.

Diplomats **showcased** applicable models of social and economic policy from home, and embassy assistance programs tried to create public events, which enabled democracy activists and representatives of civil society to participate as visible counterparts. Some aspects of governance from democracies had to be reconsidered in light of internal debate in South Africa, such as federal solutions and multiculturalism, both of which were seen as ways in which the ascent to democratic power by the black majority would be diluted.

Showcasing could also occur in an inverse direction. As long ago as 1975, Australian diplomat Diane Johnstone invited black artist Michael Muapola to her apartment to enable him to show his drawings to her guests and to help publicize and validate the strength of local culture. Within days, vengeful forces of apartheid had her evicted from her apartment, which had first been ransacked, and authorities harassed Muapola for years — but the episode was widely appreciated by the black population.

Defending Democrats

Demonstrating such solidarity with the struggle was at the core of the new public diplomacy for democratic embassies, engaging embassies in field visits and visits to the offices of human rights defenders. John Schram recounts that "the importance of putting across the message to those in the struggle that they had essential international support." As US Ambassador Lyman (2002) wrote of his predecessor Edward Perkins, the first African American ambassador to South Africa, "he stood out in the crowd attending the all too frequent funerals of activists slain during the state of emergency in the late 1980s." He was not, of course, alone. Describing the funeral for 17 activists killed in four days of rioting, Alan Cowell (1986) of *The New York Times* noted, among the 25,000 in attendance, "diplomats from the US, Britain, Australia, Canada, the Netherlands, West Germany and France."

It had its honourable risks. After Botha announced the banning of the UDF in 1988, a peaceful protest march on Parliament was broken up violently by riot police who arrested among many, many Africans, Bishop Tutu, Dutch Reformed Church cleric and activist Allan Boesak, a BBC crew and the wife of Canadian Ambassador Ron MacLean.

Verifying the trials of anti-apartheid activists had been a duty of democratic embassies from the time of the 1963 Rivonia Trial, which co-accused ANC leader Nelson Mandela said was attended by "dozens of representatives of foreign governments." Countless trials were witnessed, both as a caution to the authorities and as a form of **protection** to the defendants. Embassies made numerous demands of the government for independent investigations of the use of force against anti-apartheid protestors.

"Anti-apartheid organization members sometimes asked representatives to be present at police sites to witness and/or prevent violence" (Lyman, 2002). Protecting democrats from the ruthless power of the state was sadly not possible for the thousands who were abused, but diplomats were able in demonstrations and protests to "put themselves between the police and the protestors, and may have helped to mitigate some of the violence and prevent violence against demonstrators" (ibid.).

CONCLUSION

The words of President Mandela at his inauguration on May 10, 1994 remain an ideal for all:

"We enter into a covenant that we shall build a society in which all South Africans, both black and white, will be able to walk tall, without any fear in their hearts, assured of their inalienable right to human dignity."

That diplomats were able to support the South Africans' struggle for democracy is a record and precedent of great merit for their profession. The South African struggle continues today, for development, security and opportunity, and the need of South Africans for the support of democratic friends is undiminished.

WORKS CITED

Cowell, Alan (1986). "25,000 at Funeral in South Africa." *The New York Times,* March 6.

Lyman, Princeton N. (2002). *Partner to History: The US Role in South Africa's Transition to Democracy.* Washington, DC: United States Institute of Peace Press.

Mandela, Nelson (1994). *The Long Walk to Freedom: The Autobiography of Nelson Mandela.* Boston: Little, Brown and Company.

Marks, Susan Collin (2000). *Watching the Wind: South Africa's Transition to Democracy.* Washington, DC: United States Institute of Peace.

Sparks, Allister (1996). *Tomorrow Is Another Country: The Inside Story of South Africa's Road to Change.* Chicago: University of Chicago Press.

AUTHOR BIOGRAPHIES

Jeremy Kinsman began work on the *Diplomat's Handbook* project at Princeton University's Woodrow Wilson School, where he was Diplomat in Residence in 2007-2008 before his appointment as Regent's Lecturer at the University of California, Berkeley, where today he is Resident International Scholar at the Institute of Governmental Studies. He is concurrently Distinguished Diplomatic Visitor at Ryerson University in Toronto. For 40 years, he was a Canadian foreign service officer, and between 1992 and 2006, served as ambassador in Moscow, Rome and Brussels (EU), and as Canadian High Commissioner in London.

Kurt Bassuener is an independent policy analyst living in Sarajevo, Bosnia and Herzegovina. He began work on the *Diplomat's Handbook* in 2007. He is co-founder and senior associate of the Democratization Policy Council (www.democratizationpolicy.org), a global initiative for accountability in democracy promotion. His opinion pieces and analyses on a variety of topics have been published widely, and he has testified before the Oireachtas' (Irish Houses of Parliament) Joint Committee on European Affairs and the US Congress' joint Helsinki Commission. Previous positions include: Strategy Analyst at the Office of the High Representative (2005-2006); Political and Campaign Analyst for the OSCE ODIHR's Election Observation Mission in Ukraine (2004-2005); co-founding/co-directing the Democratization Policy Institute (2000-2002); Program Officer, US Institute of Peace Balkans Initiative (2000-2001); Associate Director of the Balkan Action Council (1998-2000); and Policy Analyst at the Balkan Institute (1997-1998).